PRE-REFERRAL INTERVENTION MANUAL

Revised and Updated Second Edition

Stephen B. McCarney
Kathy Cummins Wunderlich
Angela Marie Bauer

Printed in the
United States of America
7/99

H A W T H O R N E
Educational Services, Inc.
800 Gray Oak Drive
Columbia, MO 65201
Telephone: (573) 874-1710
FAX: (800) 442-9509

Table of Contents

I. Introduction 9

II. Using the *Pre-Referral Intervention Manual* 11

III. Interventions 12

A. Memory, Abstractions, Generalizations, and Organization

Behavior
Number
1. Is disorganized 12
2. Has limited memory skills 15
3. Has difficulty understanding abstract concepts 18
4. Fails to find locations in the building 20
5. Does not respond appropriately to environmental cues 22
6. Does not stay in assigned areas for specified time 24
7. Needs oral questions and directions frequently repeated 26
8. Demonstrates difficulty with visual memory 28
9. Demonstrates difficulty with auditory memory 30
10. Does not demonstrate an understanding of directionality 32
11. Has difficulty concentrating 33
12. Perseverates - does the same thing over and over 36
13. Fails to demonstrate logical thinking 38
14. Has difficulty retrieving, recalling, or naming objects, persons,
    places, etc. 40
15. Demonstrates visual perception problems 42
16. Has difficulty classifying 44
17. Fails to generalize knowledge from one situation to another 45
18. Demonstrates confusion 47
19. Remembers information one time but not the next 49
20. Requires slow, sequential, substantially broken-down
    presentation of concepts 51
21. Fails to remember sequences 53

B. Listening

Behavior
Number
22. Does not follow verbal directions 55
23. Does not hear word endings, does not hear key words such as
    "do not," etc. 58
24. Does not direct attention or fails to maintain attention to important
    sounds in the immediate environment 60
25. Has difficulty differentiating speech sounds heard 62
26. Is unsuccessful in activities requiring listening 63
27. Attends more successfully when close to the source of sound 65
28. Requires eye contact in order to listen successfully 67

29. Does not listen to what other students are saying 69

C. Speaking

Behavior
Number

30. Has difficulty imitating speech sounds 70
31. Omits, adds, substitutes, or rearranges sounds or words when speaking 72
32. Distorts or mispronounces words or sounds when speaking (not
    attributed to dialect or accent) 74
33. Fails to use correct subject-verb agreement when speaking 76
34. Has limited speaking vocabulary 78
35. Fails to use correct verb tenses when speaking 81
36. Speaks dysfluently 83
37. Does not complete statements or express complete thoughts
    when speaking 85

D. Reading

Behavior
Number

38. Has difficulty comprehending what he/she reads 89
39. Does not finish assignments because of reading difficulties 92
40. Fails to demonstrate word attack skills 95
41. Fails to recognize words on grade level 97
42. Loses place when reading 99
43. Has difficulty with sound-symbol relationships 100
44. Has difficulty with phonic skills when reading 101
45. Omits, adds, substitutes, or reverses letters, words, or sounds
    when reading 103
46. Fails to demonstrate word comprehension 105
47. Reads words correctly in one context but not in another 107
48. Does not read independently 109
49. Does not discriminate between similar letters and words 111
50. Does not know all the letters of the alphabet 112
51. Understands what is read to him/her but not what he/she reads
    silently 113
52. Has difficulty recalling the sequence of events in stories read 115
53. Does not demonstrate an understanding of alphabetical order 117
54. Has difficulty identifying the topic sentence and main idea
    when reading 118
55. Does not demonstrate an understanding of contractions and
    compound words 120
56. Fails to demonstrate glossary and dictionary skills 121
57. Has difficulty finding supporting details when reading 123

E. Writing

Behavior
Number

58. Performs assignments so carelessly as to be illegible 125

59. Fails to copy letters, words, sentences, and numbers from a model at a close distance 127

60. Fails to copy letters, words, sentences, and numbers from a model at a distance 129

61. Fails to use capitalization correctly when writing 131

62. Uses inappropriate spacing between words or sentences when writing 133

63. Reverses letters and numbers when writing 134

64. Fails to write within a given space 136

65. Fails to punctuate correctly when writing 137

66. Does not use appropriate subject-verb agreement when writing 139

67. Does not compose complete sentences or express complete thoughts when writing 141

68. Fails to correctly organize writing activities 143

69. Omits, adds, or substitutes words when writing 145

70. Fails to form letters correctly when printing or writing 147

71. Fails to use verb tenses correctly when writing 149

72. Uses inappropriate letter size when writing 151

F. Spelling

Behavior
Number

73. Fails to use spelling rules 153

74. Has difficulty with phonetic approaches to spelling 155

75. Omits, substitutes, adds, or rearranges letters or sound units when spelling words 157

76. Has difficulty spelling words that do not follow the spelling rules . . . 159

77. Does not use word endings correctly when spelling or omits them 161

78. Spells words correctly in one context but not in another 162

79. Requires continued drill and practice in order to learn spelling words . . 164

G. Mathematical Calculations

Behavior
Number

80. Has difficulty solving math word problems 166

81. Fails to change from one math operation to another 169

82. Does not understand abstract math concepts without concrete examples 171

83. Fails to correctly solve math problems requiring regrouping 172

84. Works math problems from left to right instead of right to left 174

85. Fails to follow necessary steps in math problems 175

86. Fails to correctly solve math problems involving fractions or decimals . . 177

87. Fails to demonstrate knowledge of place value 178

88. Confuses operational signs when working math problems 179

89. Fails to correctly solve problems involving money 180

90. Fails to correctly solve problems using measurement 182

91. Does not understand the concept of skip counting 184

92. Cannot tell time 185

93. Fails to correctly solve math problems requiring addition 186

94. Fails to correctly solve math problems requiring subtraction 188
95. Fails to correctly solve math problems requiring multiplication 190
96. Fails to correctly solve math problems requiring division 192
97. Does not remember math facts 194
98. Does not make use of columns when working math problems 196

H. Academic Performance

Behavior
Number

 99. Does not perform or complete classroom assignments during
     class time 197
100. Does not turn in homework assignments 201
101. Fails to perform assignments independently 203
102. Performs classroom tests or quizzes at a failing level 206
103. Does not prepare for assigned activities 208
104. Does not remain on task 210
105. Does not perform academically at his/her ability level 213
106. Does not follow written directions 216
107. Is reluctant to attempt new assignments or tasks 219
108. Requires repeated drill and practice to learn what other students
     master easily 222
109. Is easily distracted by auditory and visual stimuli in the classroom 223
110. Rushes through assignments with little or no regard to accuracy or
     quality of work 225
111. Fails to make appropriate use of study time 229
112. Begins assignments before receiving directions or instructions or
     does not follow directions or instructions 232
113. Changes from one activity to another without finishing the first,
     without putting things away, before it is time to move on, etc. 236
114. Does not begin assignments after receiving directions, instructions, etc. . . . 238
115. Does not complete assignments after receiving directions,
     instructions, etc. 241

I. Interpersonal Relationships

Behavior
Number

116. Makes inappropriate comments or unnecessary noises in the
     classroom 243
117. Fights with other students 246
118. Becomes physically aggressive with teachers 249
119. Makes unnecessary physical contact with others 252
120. Makes inappropriate comments to teachers 254
121. Does not respond appropriately to praise or recognition 257
122. Is easily angered, annoyed, or upset 259
123. Agitates and provokes peers to a level of verbal or physical assault 262
124. Has little or no interaction with teachers 264

125. Has little or no interaction with peers 267
126. Makes inappropriate comments to other students 269
127. Responds inappropriately to typical physical exchanges with other
     students 272
128. Responds inappropriately to friendly teasing 274
129. Is not accepted by other students 276
130. Bothers other students who are trying to work, listen, etc. 278
131. Responds inappropriately to others' attempts to be friendly,
     complimentary, sympathetic, etc. 280
132. Does not share possessions or materials 282
133. Does not allow others to take their turns, participate in activities or
     games, etc. 284
134. Does not resolve conflict situations appropriately 287
135. Does not make appropriate use of free time 289
136. Fails to work appropriately with peers in a tutoring situation 291
137. Does not share school materials with other students 294
138. Writes and passes notes 297
139. Tattles 298
140. Grabs things away from others 300
141. Interrupts the teacher 302

J. Depression/Motivation

Behavior
Number

142. Has unexcused absences 304
143. Has unexcused tardiness 306
144. Blames other persons or materials to avoid taking responsibility for
     his/her mistakes 308
145. Does not participate in classroom activities or special events that are
     interesting to other students 310
146. Blames self for situations beyond his/her control 313
147. Indicates concern regarding problems or situations in the home or in
     out-of-school situations 315
148. Is not motivated by rewards at school 317
149. Becomes upset when a suggestion or constructive criticism is given 318
150. Tries to avoid situations, assignments, responsibilities 321
151. Demonstrates self-destructive behavior 324
152. Threatens to hurt himself/herself or commit suicide 326
153. Indicates that no one likes him/her, no one cares about him/her, etc. 328
154. Ignores consequences of his/her behavior 331
155. Does not smile, laugh, or demonstrate happiness 333
156. Cheats 335
157. Throws temper tantrums 337
158. Is tired, listless, apathetic, unmotivated, not interested in school 339
159. Indicates that he/she does not care about grades, consequences
     of behavior, etc. 341
160. Is overly critical of self 343

161. Frowns, scowls, looks unhappy during typical classroom situations 345
162. Needs immediate rewards/reinforcement in order to demonstrate
    appropriate behavior 347
163. Does not care for personal appearance 349
164. Is pessimistic 351
165. Runs away to avoid problems 353
166. Whines or cries in response to personal or school experiences 355

K. Inappropriate Behavior Under Normal Circumstances

Behavior
Number

167. Behaves inappropriately when others do well or receive praise
    or attention 357
168. Behaves in a manner inappropriate for the situation 359
169. Behaves impulsively, without self-control 361
170. Exhibits extreme mood changes 363
171. Is unpredictable in behavior 365
172. Makes sexually-related comments or engages in behavior with sexual
    overtones 368
173. Moves about unnecessarily 370
174. Becomes overexcited 372
175. Lies, denies, exaggerates, distorts the truth 374
176. Speaks in an unnatural voice 376
177. Speaks incoherently 377
178. Engages in nervous habits 379
179. Destroys school or other students' property 381
180. Does not accept changes in established routine 384
181. Reacts physically in response to excitement, disappointment, surprise,
    happiness, fear, etc. 387
182. Engages in inappropriate behaviors related to bodily functions 389
183. Becomes pale, may throw up, or passes out when anxious or
    frightened 391
184. Demonstrates phobic-type reactions 393
185. Does not change behavior from one situation to another 395
186. Cannot fasten articles of clothing 397
187. Does not change clothing for physical education 398
188. Does not demonstrate appropriate mealtime behaviors 400

L. Rules and Expectations

Behavior
Number

189. Ignores consequences of his/her behavior 402
190. Does not demonstrate the ability to follow a routine 404
191. Is not responsible for appropriate care of personal property 406
192. Steals or forcibly takes things from students, teachers, the school
    building, etc. 409
193. Engages in inappropriate behaviors while seated 411
194. Does not follow directives from teachers or other school personnel 413
195. Brings inappropriate or illegal materials to school 415

196. Responds inappropriately to redirection in academic and
social situations 417
197. Does not follow school rules 419
198. Demonstrates inappropriate behavior on the school grounds before
and after school 421
199. Does not follow the rules of the classroom 423
200. Does not wait appropriately for an instructor to arrive 425
201. Does not wait appropriately for assistance or attention
from an instructor 426
202. Does not demonstrate appropriate use of school-related materials 428
203. Does not demonstrate appropriate care and handling of
others' property 431
204. Does not raise hand when appropriate 434
205. Demonstrates inappropriate behavior going to and from school 436
206. Does not take notes during class when necessary 438
207. Is under the influence of drugs or alcohol while at school 440
208. Blurts out answers without being called on 442
209. Interrupts other students 444
210. Talks to others during quiet activity periods 446
211. Leaves seat without permission 448
212. Does not come to an activity at the specified time 450

M. Group Behavior

Behavior
Number

213. Demonstrates inappropriate behavior when moving with a group 452
214. Behaves more appropriately alone or in small groups than with
the whole class or in large group activities 454
215. Demonstrates inappropriate behavior in a small academic group setting . . . 457
216. Demonstrates inappropriate behavior in the presence of a
substitute teacher 460
217. Demonstrates inappropriate behavior in a large academic group
setting 463
218. Does not work in a group situation 467
219. Does not demonstrate appropriate behavior in group games 470

IV. References 473

V. Appendix 474

VI. Index 502

I. Introduction

It has become generally accepted that educational and behavioral interventions can be implemented within regular education settings for many students who have been placed in segregated classrooms (Graden, Casey, & Christenson, 1985; Graden, Casey, & Bonstrom, 1985; Lilly & Givens-Ogle, 1981; Reynolds, Wang, and Walberg, 1987; Stainback, Stainback, Courtnage, & Jaben, 1985). As a result, pre-referral intervention has recently become a common practice in our schools designed to call early attention to student learning and behavior problems, conduct on-site adjustments in the regular classroom, and monitor student progress.

With the realization that referral, for all purposes, results in special education placement (Ysseldyke, Thurlow, Graden, Wesson, Algozzine, & Deno, 1983), pre-referral activities are being practiced to reduce the number of students referred for eligibility, evaluation and subsequent special education placement; increase skills of regular education teachers to meet academic and behavioral needs of students; and make use of available resources to benefit a broader range of student needs (Canter, 1987). The success of pre-referral intervention activities was reported by Chalfant, Pysh, and Moultrie (1979) when they indicated that of 203 students referred to Teacher Assistance Teams, 129 were helped without further testing or referral. Graden, Casey, and Bonstrom (1985) reported that testing and placement declined as a result of pre-referral intervention. The success of pre-referral activities and a trend to require pre-referral in most states has made the strategies available to them to modify and adjust instruction and behavioral interventions for students considered to be at risk. Chalfant, Pysh, and Moultrie (1979) recommended that the Teacher Assistance Team make specific recommendations to teachers for interventions to be carried out before considering formal referral. At that time no guide for pre-referral activities existed. Today it does in the form of the *Pre-Referral Intervention Manual*.

As Graden, Casey, and Christenson (1985) pointed out, current funding patterns will not allow larger numbers of students to be served in special education each year. The trend is certainly to serve students in the least restrictive environment with the least costly resource allocation. The *Pre-Referral Intervention Manual* was designed to provide school systems with the means to do just this, in the most efficient and economical way possible.

Research (Algozzine, Christenson, & Ysseldyke, 1982) indicates that 92 percent of all students referred for learning problems are tested and 73 percent receive special education services. This accounts for 5 percent of school-aged students being referred each year with the resulting dramatic increases in actual numbers of students (Algozzine, Ysseldyke, and Christenson, 1983). It is at the point of initial referral that a pre-referral intervention model (Graden, Casey, & Christenson, 1985) should provide interventions necessary to meet student needs and reduce the need for testing, identification, and placement in special education services. As Thurlow and Ysseldyke (1982) pointed out, test results are often not instructionally relevant and are not generally helpful to teachers. The historical emphasis has been on special education services for students, not on systematic attempts to implement classroom or instructional interventions prior to referral (Christenson, Ysseldyke, Wang, & Algozzine, 1983). At this time in our country there is very clearly a strong emphasis on increased regular education responsibility for students who do not respond to traditional educational approaches. Pre-referral activities and intervention strategies are one of the trends, if not the most representative trend, in the increased role of regular education in serving students with learning and behavior problems. There is no doubt that educational service delivery should be a shared responsibility of regular and special education teachers, but the responsibility for students with special needs has certainly been heavily on special education services. Pre-referral intervention will do much to create a more balanced responsibility between special and regular education and hopefully will do much to improve the skills of teachers in meeting the unique needs of all students, not just those perceived as handicapped.

The *Pre-Referral Intervention Manual* was developed in response to requests for intervention strategies for the most common learning and behavior problems encountered by regular educators in their classrooms. The intervention strategies listed for the learning and behavior problems identified in the *Pre-Referral Intervention Manual* are those that special education and regular education personnel have found most effective with students in need of more success in regular education classrooms. A wide variety of interventions are provided for each learning and behavior problem contained in the manual. The variety of interventions allows the educators involved in pre-referral to choose the interventions most likely to contribute to each individual student's success. A primary expectation is that much more consistency of behavioral and instructional intervention will be attained when the *Pre-Referral Intervention Manual* is used by those educators working with the student to find a common set of interventions to be used across classrooms and educational environments in which the student performs. This consistency of interventions on the part of all teachers working with the student is likely to enhance student success markedly.

My thanks goes to all those educators across our country who have shared their knowledge and con-

cerns for their students' success. Special thanks to Dr. Roy Moeller who helped us gather information so necessary for choosing the most common learning and behavior problems contained in the manual. Kathy Wunderlich contributed significantly to the organization and editing of the *Pre-Referral Intervention Manual* and, as always, made this project both successful and a joy to undertake. Angela Marie Bauer worked diligently on this current revision of the manual and deserves credit for making the revision possible. And once again, to Billy who now more than ever is an inspiration and source of hope for those of us working with all those children who can be so successful if we will just help them do so; God bless you, Bill. Always take care.

SBM

II. Using the *Pre-Referral Intervention Manual*

Generally, the pre-referral process begins with a regular educator calling attention to a student with learning and/or behavior problems. A team of educators, typically composed of a special educator(s), a regular educator(s), and/or a counselor(s) from that building, meets with the educator identifying a student for pre-referral attention. The team, along with input from the teacher calling attention to the student's needs, pinpoints the specific targets for improvement. Goals and objectives for the student in the regular classroom are formally or informally determined, and on-site intervention strategies are agreed upon. With consultant assistance from the pre-referral team, the classroom teacher conducts adjusted behavior and teaching approaches for the student for a specific length of time, which may be for several weeks up to a few months. The student's progress is documented and communication continues between the pre-referral team and the classroom teacher. Based on student performance in response to pre-referral intervention strategies, decisions are made as to the student's ability to succeed in the regular classroom with adjustments in instruction, materials, testing, etc. If the student is successful with these adjustments, he/she remains in the regular classroom with continued support. If the student is not successful, formal referral, assessment, and special education services are likely to follow.

The following steps are recommended for using the *Pre-Referral Intervention Manual* in the pre-referral intervention process.

Step I: The regular education teacher calls attention to the student with learning and/or behavior problems.

Step II: The pre-referral consultant team (e.g., special educator, regular educator, counselor) from that building meets with the regular education teacher to pinpoint specific learning and/or behavior problems the student exhibits.

Step III: Goals and objectives for the student are identified. Specific intervention strategies from the *Pre-Referral Intervention Manual* are selected for the student from the learning and behavior problems which were pinpointed.

Step IV: With consultant assistance from the pre-referral team, the classroom teacher conducts adjusted behavior and teaching interventions for the student.

Step V: The student's progress toward the goals and objectives identified are documented by the classroom teacher.

Step VI: The pre-referral team and the classroom teacher consult to determine the student's success.

Step VII: If the student is successful with acceptable interventions for the regular education classroom, the process is continued with consultant support for the classroom teacher and student.

Step VIII: If the student's needs cannot be met in the regular classroom, with adjusted behavior and teaching interventions, formal documentation of the student's learning and behavior performance are used to make a formal referral for assessment and consideration for special services.

(Please note: A more detailed pre-referral model is provided by J.L. Graden, A. Casey, and S.L. Christenson, (1985). Implementing a pre-referral intervention system: Part I. The model. *Exceptional Children, 51(5)*, 377-384.)

III. Interventions

1   Is disorganized

1. Have the student question any directions, explanations, and instructions he/she does not understand.

2. Assign a peer to accompany the student to specified activities in order to make certain the student has the necessary materials.

3. Provide the student with a list of necessary materials for each activity of the day.

4. Provide the student with verbal reminders of necessary materials required for each activity.

5. Provide time at the beginning of each day for the student to organize materials.

6. Provide time at various points throughout the day for the student to organize materials (e.g., before school, during recess, at lunch, at the end of the day, etc.).

7. Provide storage space for materials the student is not using at any particular time.

8. Act as a model for being organized/prepared for specified activities.

9. Make certain that work not completed because necessary materials were not brought to the specified activity is completed during recreational or break time.

10. Have the student chart the number of times he/she is organized/prepared for specified activities.

11. Remind the student at the end of the day when materials are required for specified activities for the next day (e.g., note sent home, verbal reminder, etc.).

12. Have the student establish a routine to follow before coming to class (e.g., check which activity is next, determine what materials are necessary, collect materials, etc.).

13. Have the student leave necessary materials at specified activity areas.

14. Provide the student with a container in which to carry necessary materials for specified activities (e.g., backpack, book bag, briefcase, etc.).

15. Provide adequate transition time between activities for the student to organize materials.

16. Establish a routine to be followed for organization and appropriate use of work materials. Provide the routine for the student in written form or verbally reiterate often.

17. Provide adequate time for the completion of activities.

18. Assess the quality and clarity of directions, explanations, and instructions given to the student.

19. Provide the student with structure for all academic activities (e.g., specific directions, routine format for tasks, time units, etc.).

20. Minimize materials to be kept inside the student's desk.

21. Provide an organizer for materials inside the student's desk.

22. Provide the student with an organizational checklist (e.g., routine activities, materials needed, and steps to follow).

23. Make certain that all personal property is labeled with the student's name.

24. Teach the student how to conserve rather than waste materials (e.g., amount of glue, paper, tape, etc., to use; putting lids, caps, tops on such materials as markers, pens, bottles, jars, cans, etc.).

25. Teach the student to maintain care of personal property and school materials (e.g., keep property with him/her, know where property is at all times, secure property in lockers, leave valuable property at home, etc.).

26. Provide the student with an appropriate place to store/secure personal property (e.g., desk, locker, closet, etc.) and require that the student store all property when not in use.

27. Limit the student's freedom to take school or personal property from school if the student is unable to remember to return such items.

28. Reduce the number of materials for which the student is responsible. Increase the number of materials for which the student is responsible as the student demonstrates appropriate use of materials.

29. Require that lost or damaged property be replaced by the student. If the student cannot replace the property, restitution can be made by working at school.

30. Make certain that the student is not inadvertently reinforced for losing materials. Provide the student with used materials, copies of the materials, etc., rather than new materials if the student fails to care for the materials in an appropriate manner.

31. Provide the student with more work space (e.g., a larger desk or table at which to work).

32. Reduce distracting stimuli (e.g., place the student on the front row, provide a carrel or quiet place away from distractions, etc.). This is used as a means of reducing distracting stimuli and not as a form of punishment.

33. Interact frequently with the student in order to prompt organizational skills and appropriate use of materials.

34. Assign the student organizational responsibilities in the classroom (e.g., equipment, software materials, etc.).

35. Supervise the student while he/she is performing schoolwork in order to monitor quality.

36. Act as a model for organization and appropriate use of work materials (e.g., putting materials away before getting more material out, having a place for all materials, maintaining an organized desk area, following a schedule for the day, etc.).

37. Have the student maintain an assignment notebook which indicates those materials needed for each activity.

38. Provide the student with a schedule of daily events in order that the student knows exactly what and how much there is to do in a day. (See Appendix for Schedule of Daily Events.)

39. Allow natural consequences to occur as the result of the student's inability to organize or use materials appropriately (e.g., work not done during work time must be made up during recreational time, materials not maintained must be replaced, etc.).

40. Assist the student in beginning each task in order to reduce impulsive behavior.

41. Provide the student with structure for all academic activities (e.g., specific directions, routine format for tasks, time units, etc.).

42. Provide a coded organizational system (e.g., notebook, folders, etc.).

43. Teach the student to prioritize assignments (e.g., according to importance, length, etc.).

44. Develop monthly calendars to keep track of important events, due dates, assignments, etc.

45. Give the student one task to perform at a time. Introduce the next task only when the student has successfully completed the previous task in an organized manner.

46. Assign the student shorter tasks and gradually increase the tasks over time as the student demonstrates success in organizing academic activities.

47. Require that assignments done incorrectly, for any reason, be redone.

48. Provide the student with clearly stated criteria for acceptable work (e.g., neatness, etc.).

49. Provide the student with only those materials he/she needs to complete an assignment (e.g., pencil, paper, dictionary, handwriting sample, etc.). Be certain that the student has only the necessary materials on his/her desk.

50. Identify a peer to act as a model for the student to imitate being organized/prepared for specified activities.

51. Evaluate the appropriateness of the task to determine: (a) if the task is too difficult, and (b) if the length of time scheduled to complete the task is appropriate.

52. Communicate with parents (e.g., notes home, phone calls, etc.) in order to share information concerning the student's progress and so that they can reinforce the student at home for being organized/prepared for specified activities at school.

53. Write a contract with the student specifying what behavior is expected (e.g., having necessary materials for specified activities) and what reinforcement will be made available when the terms of the contract have been met. (See Appendix for Behavioral Contract.)

54. Reinforce the student for being organized/ prepared for specified activities based on the number of times the student can be successful. Gradually increase the number of times required for reinforcement as the student demonstrates success.

55. Reinforce those students in the classroom who are organized/prepared for specified activities.

56. Establish classroom rules:
1. Have necessary materials.
2. Work on task.
3. Work quietly.
4. Remain in your seat.
5. Finish task.
6. Meet task expectations.
Reiterate rules often and reinforce students for following rules.

57. Speak to the student to explain: (a) what the student is doing wrong (e.g., failing to bring necessary materials for specified activities) and (b) what the student should be doing (e.g., having necessary materials for specified activities).

58. Reinforce the student for being organized/ prepared for specified activities: (a) give the student a tangible reward (e.g., classroom privileges, line leading, passing out materials, five minutes free time, etc.) or (b) give the student an intangible reward (e.g., praise, handshake, smile, etc.).

2 Has limited memory skills

1. Make certain the student's hearing has been recently checked.

2. Have the student question any directions, explanations, and instructions he/she does not understand.

3. Have the student act as a classroom messenger. Give the student a verbal message to deliver to another teacher, secretary, administrator, etc. Increase the length of the messages as the student demonstrates success.

4. Review the schedule of the morning and afternoon activities with the student and have him/her repeat the sequence. Increase the length of the sequence as the student is successful.

5. Have the student engage in concentration game activities with a limited number of symbols. Gradually increase the number of symbols as the student demonstrates success.

6. Reinforce the student for remembering to have such materials as pens, pencils, paper, textbooks, notebooks, etc.

7. At the end of the school day, have the student recall three activities in which he/she was engaged during the day. Gradually increase the number of activities the student is required to recall as the student demonstrates success.

8. After a field trip or special event, have the student sequence the activities which occurred.

9. After reading a short story, have the student identify the main characters, sequence the events, and report the outcome of the story.

10. Have the student deliver the schedule of daily events to other students.

11. Use multiple modalities (e.g., auditory, visual, tactile, etc.) when presenting directions, explanations, and instructional content.

12. Assign a peer tutor to engage in short-term memory activities with the student (e.g., concentration games, following directions, etc.).

13. Record a message on tape. Have the student write the message after he/she has heard it. Increase the length of the message as the student demonstrates success.

14. Involve the student in activities in order to enhance short-term memory skills (e.g., carry messages from one location to another; act as group leader, teacher assistant, etc.).

15. Have the student practice short-term memory skills by engaging in activities which are purposeful (e.g., delivering messages, being in charge of room clean-up, acting as custodian's helper, operating equipment, etc.).

16. Informally assess the student's auditory and visual short-term memory skills in order to determine which is the stronger. Utilize the results when presenting directions, explanations, and instructional content.

17. Have the student practice repetition of information in order to increase short-term memory skills (e.g., repeating names, telephone numbers, dates of events, etc.).

18. Teach the student how to organize information into smaller units (e.g., break the number sequence 132563 into units of 13, 25, 63).

19. Use sentence dictation to develop the student's short-term memory skills (e.g., begin with sentences of three words and increase the length of the sentences as the student demonstrates success).

20. Show the student an object or a picture of an object for a few seconds. Ask the student to recall specific attributes of the object (e.g., color, size, shape, etc.).

21. Deliver directions, explanations, and instructional content in a clear manner and at an appropriate pace.

22. Have the student practice taking notes for specific information the student needs to remember.

23. Teach the student to recognize key words and phrases related to information in order to increase short-term or long-term memory skills.

24. Make certain the student is attending to the source of information (e.g., eye contact is being made, hands are free of materials, student is looking at assignment, etc.).

25. Reduce distracting stimuli when information is being presented, the student is studying, etc.

26. Stop at various points during the presentation of information to check the student's comprehension.

27. Give the student one task to perform at a time. Introduce the next task only when the student has successfully completed the previous task.

28. Have the student memorize the first sentence or line of poems, songs, etc. Require more to be memorized as the student experiences success.

29. Teach the student information-gathering skills (e.g., listen carefully, write down important points, ask for clarification, wait until all information is received before beginning, etc.).

30. Have the student repeat/paraphrase directions, explanations, and instructions.

31. Reduce the emphasis on competition. Competitive activities may cause the student to hurry and begin without listening carefully.

32. Provide the student with environmental cues and prompts designed to enhance success in the classroom (e.g., posted rules, schedule of daily events, steps for performing tasks, etc.). (See Appendix for Schedule of Daily Events.)

33. Provide the student with written lists of things to do, materials needed, etc.

34. Maintain consistency in sequential activities in order to increase the likelihood of student success (e.g., the student has math every day at one o'clock, recess at two o'clock, etc.).

35. Break the sequence into units and have the student learn one unit at a time.

36. Establish a regular routine for the student to follow in performing activities, assignments, etc. (e.g., listen to the person speaking to you, wait until directions are completed, make certain you have all necessary materials, etc.).

37. Teach the student to use associative cues or mnemonic devices to remember sequences.

38. Actively involve the student in learning to remember sequences by having the student physically perform sequential activities (e.g., operating equipment, following recipes, solving math problems, etc.).

39. Have the student be responsible for helping a peer remember sequences.

40. Use concrete examples and experiences in sharing information with the student.

41. Teach the student to recognize main points, important facts, etc.

42. Teach the student to rely on resources in the environment to recall information (e.g., notes, textbooks, pictures, etc.).

43. When the student is required to recall information, provide auditory cues to help the student remember the information (e.g., key words, a brief oral description to clue the student, etc.).

44. Assess the meaningfulness of the material to the student. Remembering is more likely to occur when the material is meaningful and the student can relate to real experiences.

45. Relate the information being presented to the student's previous experiences.

46. Give the student specific categories and have the student name as many items as possible within that category (e.g., objects, persons, places, etc.).

47. Give the student a series of words or pictures and have the student name the category to which they belong (e.g., objects, persons, places, etc.).

48. Describe objects, persons, places, etc., and have the student name the items described.

49. Help the student employ memory aids in order to recall words (e.g., a name might be linked to another word; for example, "Mr. Green is a very colorful person.").

50. Give the student a series of words describing objects, persons, places, etc., and have the student identify the opposite of each word.

51. Encourage the student to play word games such as *Hangman, Scrabble,* and *Password.*

52. Have the student complete "fill-in-the-blank" sentences with appropriate words (e.g., objects, persons, places, etc.).

53. Have the student outline, highlight, underline, or summarize information which should be remembered.

54. Make certain the student has adequate opportunities for repetition of information through different experiences in order to enhance memory.

55. Label objects, persons, places, etc., in the environment in order to help the student be able to recall their names.

56. Make certain the student receives information from a variety of sources (e.g., texts, discussions, films, slide presentations, etc.) in order to enhance memory/recall.

57. Teach the student listening skills (e.g., stop working, look at the person delivering questions and directions, have necessary note-taking materials, etc.).

58. Teach the student direction-following skills (e.g., stop doing other things, listen carefully, write down important points, wait until all directions are given, question any directions not understood, etc.).

59. Have the student tape record directions, explanations, instructions, lectures, etc., in order that the student may replay the information as needed.

60. Highlight or underline important information the student reads (e.g., directions, reading assignments, math word problems, etc.).

61. Tell the student what to listen for when being given directions, receiving information, etc.

62. Have the student repeat to himself/herself information just heard in order to help remember the information.

63. Make certain the student is not required to learn more information than he/she is capable of at any one time.

64. Evaluate the appropriateness of the memory activities to determine: (a) if the task is too difficult, and (b) if the length of time scheduled to complete the task is appropriate.

65. Write a contract with the student specifying what behavior is expected (e.g., following one-step directions, two-step directions, etc.) and what reinforcement will be made available when the terms of the contract have been met. (See Appendix for Behavioral Contract.)

66. Reinforce the student for demonstrating short-term or long-term memory skills based on the length of time the student can be successful. Gradually increase the length of time required for reinforcement as the student demonstrates success.

67. Reinforce the student for demonstrating short-term or long-term memory skills: (a) give the student a tangible reward (e.g., classroom privileges, line leading, passing out materials, five minutes free time, etc.) or (b) give the student an intangible reward (e.g., praise, handshake, smile, etc.).

1. Make certain when speaking to the student to use terms which convey abstract concepts to describe tangible objects in the environment (e.g., *larger, smaller, square, triangle,* etc.).

2. Identify tangible objects in the classroom with signs that convey abstract concepts (e.g., *larger, smaller, square, triangle,* etc.).

3. Use concrete examples when teaching abstract concepts (e.g., numbers of objects to convey *more than, less than*; rulers and yardsticks to convey concepts of *height, width,* etc.).

4. Play *Simon Says* to enhance the understanding of abstract concepts (e.g., "Find the largest desk." "Touch something that is a rectangle." etc.).

5. Conduct a scavenger hunt. Have the student look for the smallest pencil, tallest boy, etc., in the classroom.

6. Teach shapes using common objects in the environment (e.g., round clocks, rectangle-shaped desks, square tiles on the floor, etc.).

7. Evaluate the appropriateness of having the student learn abstract concepts at this time.

8. Teach abstract concepts one at a time before pairing the concepts (e.g., dimensionality, size, shape, etc.).

9. Provide repeated physical demonstrations of abstract concepts (e.g., identify things far away and close to the student, identify a small box in a large room, etc.).

10. Review, on a daily basis, those abstract concepts which have been previously introduced. Introduce new abstract concepts only after the student has mastery of those previously presented.

11. Have a peer spend time each day with the student pointing out abstract concepts in the classroom (e.g., the rectangle-shaped light switch plate, the round light fixture, the tallest girl, etc.).

12. When introducing abstract concepts, rely on tangible objects (e.g., boxes for dimensionality, family members for size, distances in the classroom for space, cookie cutters for shape, etc.). Do not introduce abstract concepts by using their descriptive titles such as *square, rectangle, triangle,* etc.

13. Have the student match the names of abstract concepts with objects (e.g., *triangle, square, circle,* etc.).

14. Give the student direction-following assignments (e.g., "Go to the swing which is the farthest away." "Go to the nearest sandbox." etc.).

15. Have the student question any directions, explanations, or instructions which he/she does not understand.

16. Have the student physically perform spatial relationships (e.g., have the student stand *near* the teacher, *far* from the teacher, *over* a table, *under* a table, etc.).

17. Call attention to spatial relationships which occur naturally in the environment (e.g., call attention to a bird flying *over* a tree, a squirrel running *under* a bush, etc.).

18. For more abstract concepts such as *left* and *right; north, south, east,* and *west;* have the student follow simple map directions. Begin with a map of the building and progress to a map of the community, state, nation, etc., with more complex directions to follow.

19. To teach the student relationships of left and right, place paper bands labeled *left* and *right* around the student's wrists. Remove the paper bands when the student can successfully identify left and right.

20. Use a scale, ruler, measuring cups, etc., to teach abstract concepts using measurement.

21. Use actual change and dollar bills, clocks, etc., to teach abstract concepts of money, telling time, etc.

22. Make certain to use the terms *right* and *left* as part of the directions you are giving to the student (e.g., refer to the windows on the *left* side of the room, the chalkboard on the *right* side of the room, etc.).

23. Have the student practice following directions on paper. Instruct the student to make marks or pictures on the *right, left, middle, top* and *bottom* parts of the paper according to the directions given.

24. Avoid the problem of mirror images by standing next to the student when giving *right* and *left* directions.

25. Have the student sort *left* and *right* gloves, shoes, paper hand and foot cut-outs, etc.

26. Be certain to relate what the student has learned in one setting or situation to other situations (e.g., vocabulary words learned should be pointed out in reading selections, math problems, story writing, etc.).

27. Make certain the student is attending to the source of information (e.g., eye contact is being made, hands are free of materials, etc.) when directions are being delivered that involve abstract concepts.

28. Label abstract concepts throughout the class-room (e.g., triangle shapes on the walls, left and right sides of a desk, compass directions on the walls, etc.) to help the student understand the concepts.

29. Make certain the student is not required to learn more abstract concepts than he/she is capable of learning at any one time.

1. Have the student question any directions, explanations, and instructions he/she does not understand.

2. Have a peer accompany the student when attempting to find locations in the building.

3. Have a peer model finding locations in the building.

4. Take the student on a personal tour of various locations in the building.

5. Limit the number of locations the student is required to find on his/her own. Gradually increase the number of locations as the student demonstrates success.

6. Develop clear, concise written directions or a map for the student to use in order to find locations in the building.

7. Color code locations in the building (e.g., boys' restroom doors painted red, girls' restroom doors painted yellow, names of locations, arrows, etc.).

8. Provide universal symbols at locations throughout the building (e.g., restroom, cafeteria, library, etc.).

9. Have the student run errands to specific locations in the building for practice in finding locations in the building.

10. Inform other personnel that the student has difficulty finding locations in the building in order that assistance and supervision may be provided.

11. Make certain the behavior demands are appropriate for the student's abilities (e.g., finding locations alone, finding locations with other students around, etc.).

12. Teach the student to ask for directions when he/she has difficulty finding locations in the building.

13. Be consistent in applying consequences for behavior (e.g., appropriate behavior receives positive consequences while inappropriate behavior receives negative consequences).

14. Identify regular routes the student is required to use to find locations in the building.

15. Have the student carry a map of locations in the building.

16. Have the student develop directions for finding locations in the building.

17. Allow the student to move from one location to another in the building only at specified times (e.g., if the student has difficulty finding locations in the building when other students are in the halls, allow the student to move from one location to another when others are not present).

18. Have the student move from one location to another with a group of students until he/she develops the ability to find the locations independently.

19. Have the student identify various landmarks throughout the building which can help in finding necessary locations in the building.

20. Make certain the student is attending to the source of information (e.g., eye contact is being made, hands are free of materials, etc.) when directions are delivered concerning how to find certain locations in the school building.

21. Have the student review directions before leaving the classroom to find certain points throughout the building (e.g., have the student repeat directions back to you, have the student look at a map, etc.).

22. When giving the student directions to certain points throughout the building, use concrete clues such as the drinking fountain, restrooms, lunchroom, etc. (e.g., "Go to the room that is just past the lunchroom." "The bathroom is on the left side of the drinking fountain." etc.).

23. Teach the student direction-following skills (e.g., stop doing other things, listen carefully, write down important points, wait until all directions are given, question any directions not understood, etc.).

24. Use pictures, diagrams, the chalkboard and gestures when delivering information.

25. When delivering directions, explanations, and information, be certain to use vocabulary that is within the student's level of comprehension.

26. Evaluate the appropriateness of the task to determine: (a) if the task is too difficult and (b) if the length of time scheduled to complete the task is appropriate.

27. Communicate with parents (e.g., notes home, phone calls, etc.) in order to share information concerning the student's progress and so that they can reinforce the student at home for finding necessary locations in the school.

28. Write a contract with the student specifying what behavior is expected (e.g., going to and from the restroom in a reasonable amount of time) and what reinforcement will be available when the terms of the contract have been met. (See Appendix for Behavioral Contract.)

29. Reinforce those students in the classroom who demonstrate the ability to find necessary locations in the building.

30. Speak to the student to explain: (a) what the student is doing wrong and (b) what the student should be doing.

31. Reinforce the student for demonstrating the ability to find necessary locations in the building: (a) give the student a tangible reward (e.g., classroom privileges, line leading, passing out materials, five minutes free time, etc.) or (b) give the student an intangible reward (e.g., praise, handshake, smile, etc.).

5 Does not respond appropriately to environmental cues

1. Identify a peer to act as a model for the student to imitate appropriate responses to environmental cues.

2. Have the student question any environmental cues not understood.

3. Establish environmental cues that the student is expected to follow (e.g., bells, rules, point cards, reminders, etc.).

4. Provide supportive information to assist the student in responding appropriately to environmental cues (e.g., "When the bell rings, it is time for lunch.").

5. Provide repeated practice in responding appropriately to environmental cues.

6. Make the student responsible for identifying environmental cues for peers (e.g., bells, rules, reminders, etc.).

7. Provide the student with universal environmental cues (e.g., symbols for male and female, arrows, exit signs, danger symbols, etc.).

8. Pair environmental cues with verbal explanations and immediate reinforcement for appropriate responses.

9. Prepare the student in advance of the delivery of environmental cues in order to increase successful responding.

10. Make certain the same environmental cues are used throughout all locations in and outside of the building.

11. Match the environmental cues to the student's ability to respond (e.g., visual cues are used for students who cannot hear, symbols or auditory cues are used for students who cannot read, etc.).

12. Model appropriate responses to environmental cues for the student to imitate.

13. Have the student master appropriate responds to one environmental cue at a time, prioritizing environmental cues in order of importance for mastery, before introducing additional cues.

14. In order to increase success in learning environmental cues, have the student observe and imitate the responses of peers to environmental cues (e.g., as the student is learning to respond appropriately to doors identified as *In* and *Out*, the student can imitate the behavior of peers who use the appropriate doors to enter and leave areas of the educational environment).

15. Reinforce the student for asking the meaning of environmental cues not understood (e.g., bells, signs, etc.).

16. Provide the student with simulation activities in the classroom in order to teach successful responses to environmental cues (e.g., responses to words, symbols, directions, etc.).

17. Assign a peer to accompany the student as the student moves throughout the building, to act as a model in teaching appropriate responses to environmental cues.

18. Stop at various points throughout the day (e.g., when the lunch bell rings, when walking by restroom signs, etc.) to point out the different cues to the students.

19. Provide the student with verbal reminders or prompts when he/she misses an environmental cue.

20. Review, on a daily basis, the environmental cues that are important to the student (e.g., bells, signs, etc.).

21. When delivering directions, explanations, and information, be certain to use vocabulary that is within the student's level of comprehension.

22. Evaluate the appropriateness of the environmental cues the student is expected to follow in order to determine: (a) if the cue is too difficult and (b) if the length of time required to respond to the cue is appropriate.

23. Communicate with parents (e.g., notes home, phone calls, etc.) in order to share information concerning the student's progress and so that they can reinforce the student at home for responding appropriately to environmental cues at school.

24. Write a contract with the student specifying what behavior is expected (e.g., responding appropriately to bells, rules, point cards, reminders, etc.) and what reinforcement will be made available when the terms of the contract have been met. (See Appendix for Behavioral Contract.)

25. Reinforce the student for responding appropriately to environmental cues based on the number of environmental cues the student can successfully follow. Gradually increase the number of environmental cues required for reinforcement as the student demonstrates success.

26. Reinforce those students in the classroom who respond appropriately to environmental cues.

27. Speak to the student to explain: (a) what the student is doing wrong (e.g., failing to respond appropriately to bells, signs indicating restroom directions, etc.) and (b) what the student should be doing (e.g., responding appropriately to bells, restroom signs, etc.).

28. Reinforce the student for responding appropriately to environmental cues: (a) give the student a tangible reward (e.g., classroom privileges, line leading, passing out materials, five minutes free time, etc.) or (b) give the student an intangible reward (e.g., praise, handshake, smile, etc.).

6 Does not stay in assigned areas for specified time

1. Have the student question any directions, explanations, and instructions he/she does not understand.

2. Evaluate the appropriateness of requiring the student to stay in an assigned area for the specified time period.

3. Establish rules for the school ground (e.g. remain in assigned areas, share school equipment, use appropriate language, use school property with care, etc.).

4. Have the student question any rules he/she does not understand concerning the school grounds.

5. Separate the student from the peer(s) who stimulates inappropriate behavior in assigned areas.

6. Have the student carry a point card at all times so that he/she can be reinforced in assigned areas in the building and on the school grounds. (See Appendix for a Sample Point Card.)

7. Inform other school personnel of any behavior problems the student may have in order that supervision and assistance may be provided in assigned areas before, during, and after school.

8. Be consistent in applying consequences for behavior (i.e., appropriate behavior receives positive consequences while inappropriate behavior receives negative consequences).

9. Provide organized activities for the student to participate in before, during, and after school (e.g., board games, softball, four square, tether ball, jump rope, flash cards, etc.).

10. Identify a specified area of the school grounds to be used as a "time-out" area when the student demonstrates inappropriate behavior on the school grounds.

11. Have the student take responsibility for a younger student in assigned areas.

12. Make certain the student knows where he/she is expected to be at all times.

13. Assign a peer to remain with the student in an assigned area for the specified time period.

14. Make certain the student knows the location of all assigned areas.

15. Make certain the behavioral demands are appropriate for the student's abilities (e.g., ability to find locations of assigned areas, ability to tell time, ability to interact with peers appropriately, etc.).

16. Make certain the student is actively involved in an activity in the assigned area in order to enhance his/her ability to stay in the assigned area for the specified time period (e.g., assign the student a specific activity to perform).

17. Assign the student a responsibility to perform in an assigned area in order to keep him/ her actively involved (e.g., supervise others, be responsible for materials, act as group leader, etc.).

18. Provide the student with a timer to help him/her remain in an assigned area for the specified time period.

19. Post clocks showing the times the student should enter and leave an assigned area (i.e., one clock face indicates time to enter, another clock face indicates time to leave).

20. Have the student carry a hall pass on which teachers will indicate the time of arrival and departure at assigned areas.

21. Provide the student with predetermined signals (e.g., ring a bell, turn lights on and off, etc.) to indicate when to enter and leave assigned areas.

22. Set up physical barriers or boundary markings in order to help the student remain in an assigned area.

23. Identify areas that are off limits with signs such as "Danger," "Keep Out," etc.

24. Provide adequate supervision in assigned areas. Gradually reduce the amount of supervision as the student demonstrates success.

25. Provide the student with many opportunities for social and academic success in assigned areas.

26. Require time spent away from an assigned area to be made up during recess, lunch, free time, etc.

27. Require the student to remain in assigned areas for short periods of time. Gradually increase the length of time as the student demonstrates success.

28. Make certain the student is able to tell time in order to increase the probability that he/she will know how long to remain in an assigned area.

29. Reduce stimuli in the assigned area which would cause the student to be unable to remain in the assigned area for the specified time period.

30. Teach the student ways to deal with stimuli or problems in assigned areas which may cause him/her to leave the area (e.g., talk to a teacher, move to a quiet place in the assigned area, avoid confrontations, etc.).

31. Review, on a daily basis, where the student should be at all times (e.g., during reading the student should be at the reading table, at lunchtime the student should be at the lunch table, etc.).

32. Remind the student before the beginning of each activity where he/she should be and how long to stay in the designated area.

33. Communicate with parents (e.g., notes home, phone calls, etc.) in order to share information concerning the student's progress and so that they can reinforce the student at home for staying in an assigned area for the specified time period at school.

34. Identify a peer to act as a model for the student by staying in an assigned area for the specified time period.

35. Evaluate the appropriateness of the task to determine: (a) if the task is too difficult and (b) if the length of time scheduled to complete the task is appropriate.

36. Write a contract with the student specifying what behavior is expected (e.g., staying in an assigned area for the specified time period) and what reinforcement will be made available when the terms of the contract have been met. (See Appendix for Behavioral Contract.)

37. Reinforce the student for staying in an assigned area for the specified time period based on the length of time the student can be successful. Gradually increase the length of time required for reinforcement as the student demonstrates success.

38. Reinforce those students in the classroom who stay in an assigned area for the specified time period.

39. Establish classroom rules:
1. Work on task.
2. Work quietly.
3. Remain in assigned area.
4. Finish task.
5. Meet task expectations.
Reiterate rules often and reinforce students for following rules.

40. Speak to the student to explain: (a) what the student is doing wrong (e.g. leaving the assigned area) and (b) what the student should be doing (e.g., staying in the assigned area for the specified time period).

41. Reinforce the student for staying in an assigned area for the specified time period: (a) give the student a tangible reward (e.g., classroom privileges, line leading, passing out materials, five minutes free time, etc.) or (b) give the student an intangible reward (e.g., praise, handshake, smile, etc.).

7   Needs oral questions and directions frequently repeated

1. Make certain the student's hearing has been checked recently.

2. Present oral questions and directions in a clear and concise manner and at an appropriate pace for the student.

3. Reduce distracting stimuli (e.g., place the student on the front row, provide a carrel or "office" space away from distractions, etc.). This is used as a form of reducing distracting stimuli and not as a form of punishment.

4. Have the student take notes relative to oral questions and directions.

5. Have a peer help the student follow oral questions and directions.

6. Maintain mobility in order to provide assistance to the student.

7. Present oral questions and directions in a variety of ways in order to increase the probability of understanding (e.g., if the student fails to understand verbal directions, present them in written form).

8. Maintain consistency in the manner in which oral questions and directions are delivered.

9. Deliver oral questions that involve only one concept or step. Gradually increase the number of concepts or steps as the student demonstrates success.

10. Stand close to or directly in front of the student when delivering oral questions and directions.

11. Teach the student listening skills (e.g., stop working, look at the person delivering questions and directions, have necessary note-taking materials, etc.).

12. Deliver questions and directions in written form.

13. Identify a peer to deliver and/or repeat oral questions and directions.

14. Tell the student that oral questions and directions will be given only once.

15. Give a signal prior to delivering directions orally to the student.

16. Deliver oral directions prior to handing out materials.

17. Teach the student direction-following skills (e.g., listen carefully, write down important points, etc.).

18. Interact frequently with the student in order to help the student follow directions for an activity.

19. Have the student orally repeat or paraphrase the directions to the teacher.

20. Establish assignment rules (e.g., listen to directions, wait until all oral directions have been given, ask questions about anything you do not understand, begin the assignment when you are certain about what you are supposed to do, make certain you have all necessary materials, etc.).

21. Make certain the student is attending while you deliver oral questions and directions (e.g., making eye contact, hands free of writing materials, looking at assignment, etc.).

22. Maintain visibility to and from the student when delivering oral questions and directions. The teacher should be able to see the student and the student should be able to see the teacher, making eye contact possible at all times in order to make certain the student is attending.

23. Call the student by name prior to delivering oral questions and directions.

24. Make certain that eye contact is being made between you and the student when delivering oral questions and directions.

25. Stop at various points during the presentation of directions to check the student's comprehension.

26. Give the student one task to perform at a time. Introduce the next task only when the student has successfully completed the previous task by following directions correctly.

27. Provide visual information (e.g., written directions, instructions, etc.) to support the information the student receives auditorily.

28. Tell the student what to listen for when being given directions, receiving information, etc.

29. Use pictures, diagrams, the chalkboard, and gestures when delivering information.

30. When delivering directions, explanations, and information be certain to use vocabulary that is within the student's level of comprehension.

31. Deliver information to the student on a one-to-one basis or employ a peer tutor.

32. Make it pleasant and positive for the student to ask questions about things not understood. Reinforce the student by assisting, congratulating, praising, etc.

33. Evaluate the appropriateness of requiring the student to respond to oral questions and directions without needing repetition.

34. Have the student question any directions, explanations, and instructions he/she does not understand.

35. Identify a peer to act as a model for the student to imitate responding to oral questions and directions without requiring repetition.

36. Communicate with parents (e.g., notes home, phone calls, etc.) in order to share information concerning the student's progress and so that they can reinforce the student at home for responding to oral questions and directions without requiring repetition at school.

37. Write a contract with the student specifying what behavior is expected (e.g., following directions with one cue) and what reinforcement will be made available when the terms of the contract have been met. (See Appendix for Behavioral Contract.)

38. Reinforce the student for responding to oral questions and directions without requiring repetition based on the number of times the student can be successful. Gradually increase the number of times required for reinforcement as the student demonstrates success.

39. Reinforce those students in the classroom who respond to oral questions and directions without requiring repetition.

40. Establish classroom rules:
1. Work on task.
2. Work quietly.
3. Remain in your seat.
4. Finish task.
5. Meet task expectations.
Reiterate rules often and reinforce students for following rules.

41. Speak with the student to explain: (a) what the student is doing wrong (e.g., needing oral questions and directions repeated) and (b) what the student should be doing (e.g., responding to oral questions and directions without requiring repetition).

42. Reinforce the student for responding to oral questions and directions without requiring frequent repetition: (a) give the student a tangible reward (e.g., classroom privileges, line leading, passing out materials, five minutes free time, etc.) or (b) give the student an intangible reward (e.g., praise, handshake, smile, etc.).

1. Draw the student's attention to key aspects of visual images (e.g., highlighting, outlining, arrows, etc.).

2. Provide the student with more than one exposure to the visual information prior to requiring him/her to remember it.

3. Reduce visual distractions by isolating the information that is presented to the student (e.g., cover other information on the page, expose only a portion of a picture at a time, etc.).

4. When the student is required to recall information, provide visual cues to help the student remember the information previously presented (e.g., using key words printed on the chalkboard, exposing part or all of a picture, etc.).

5. When the student is required to recall information, provide auditory cues to help the student remember the information previously presented (e.g., say key words, give a brief oral description to clue the student, etc.).

6. When the student is required to recall information, remind him/her of the situation in which the material was originally presented (e.g., say, "Remember yesterday when we talked about . . ." "Remember when we were outside and we looked at the . . ." etc.).

7. Provide verbal information to support information the student receives visually.

8. Teach the student to learn sequences and lists of information in segments (e.g., telephone numbers are learned as 314, then 874, then 1710, etc.).

9. Cut pictures from a cartoon strip. Let the student look at the pictures in sequence, then mix them up and let him/her put them back in order.

10. Have the student play concentration games (e.g., matching numbers, words, symbols, etc., by turning them over and remembering where they were located).

11. Have the student read and follow one-, two-, and three-step directions.

12. Provide the student with written directions, rules, and lists. Reinforce the student for being able to recall the information in written form.

13. Tape record stories, directions, etc., so the student may listen to the information while reading along.

14. Require the student to recall days of the week, months of the year, birth dates, addresses, telephone numbers, etc., after seeing this information in written form.

15. Teach the student to recognize common visual symbols (e.g., a red octagon means *stop*, golden arches symbolize McDonald's fast food restaurant, a skull and crossed bones represents *poison*, etc.).

16. Use multiple modalities (e.g., auditory, visual, tactile, etc.) when presenting directions, explanations, and instructional content. Determine which modality is stronger and utilize the results.

17. Reduce the amount of information on a page if it is causing visual distractions for the student (e.g., less print to read, fewer problems, isolate information that is presented to the student).

18. Provide auditory information (e.g., verbal directions or instructions, etc.) to support information the student receives visually.

19. Identify the student's most efficient learning mode and use it consistently to increase the probability of understanding (e.g., If the student has difficulty understanding written information or directions, present it verbally.).

20. Highlight or underline important information the student reads (e.g., directions, reading assignments, math word problems, etc.).

21. Make it pleasant and positive for the student to ask questions about things not understood. Reinforce the student by assisting, congratulating, praising, etc.

22. Evaluate the appropriateness of the task to determine: (a) if the task is too difficult (e.g., too much information to remember) or (b) if the length of time required for the student to remember is inappropriate (e.g., the presentation of information was too brief, time lapse between presentation of material and request for recall was too long, etc.).

23. Reinforce the student for remembering information received visually: (a) give the student a tangible reward (e.g., classroom privileges, line leading, five minutes free time, etc.) or (b) give the student an intangible reward (e.g., praise, handshake, smile, etc.).

1. Make certain the student's hearing has been recently checked.

2. Draw the student's attention to key aspects of auditory communications as they occur (e.g., repeat important points, call the student by name, tell the student which information is particularly important, etc.).

3. Provide the student with more than one source of directions, explanations, instructions, etc., before requiring him/her to remember.

4. When the student is required to recall information, provide auditory cues to help the student remember information previously presented (e.g., say, "Remember yesterday when I said . . ." etc.).

5. Provide visual information to support information the student receives auditorily.

6. Teach the student to learn sequences and lists of information in segments (e.g., telephone numbers are learned as 314, then 874, then 1710).

7. Have the student follow verbal one-, two-, and three-step directions.

8. Provide the student with verbal directions, rules, lists, etc. Reinforce the student for being able to recall the information presented in verbal form.

9. Write stories, directions, etc., so the student may listen as he/she reads along.

10. Tell the student what to listen for before delivering auditory information.

11. Send the student on errands to deliver verbal messages to other teachers in the building.

12. Be certain that auditory information is presented slowly enough for the student to know what is being communicated.

13. Use pictures, diagrams, the chalkboard, and gestures when delivering information.

14. While reading a story to the student, stop on occasion to ask questions about the plot, main characters, events in the story, etc.

15. Have the student pretend to be a waiter/waitress. Have the student recall what a customer orders from him/her.

16. Have the student paraphrase directions, explanations, and instructions soon after hearing them.

17. Use as much visual information as possible when teaching (e.g., chalkboard, projections, pictures, etc.).

18. Have the student tape record directions, explanations, and instructions in order that he/she may replay needed information.

19. Use simple, concise sentences to convey information to the student.

20. Have the student recall names of friends, days of the week, months of the year, addresses, telephone numbers, etc.

21. After listening to a tape, story, record, etc., have the student recall characters, main events, sequence of events, etc.

22. Reduce distracting stimuli (e.g., noise and motion) around the student (e.g., place the student on the front row, provide a carrel or quiet place away from distractions, etc.). This is to be used as a means of reducing distracting stimuli and not as a form of punishment.

23. Use multiple modalities (e.g., auditory, visual, tactile, etc.) when presenting directions, explanations, and instructional content. Determine which modality is stronger and utilize the results.

24. Make certain the student is attending to the source of information (e.g., eye contact is being made, hands are free of materials, student is looking at the assignment, etc.).

25. Stop at various points during a presentation of information to check the student's comprehension.

26. Make certain the student has adequate opportunities for repetition of information through different experiences in order to enhance memory.

27. Provide visual information (e.g., written directions or instructions, etc.) to support information the student receives auditorily.

28. Make certain that all directions, questions, explanations, and instructions are delivered in the most clear and concise manner and at an appropriate pace for the student.

29. When delivering directions, explanations, and information, be certain to use vocabulary that is written at the student's level of comprehension.

30. Evaluate the appropriateness of the task to determine: (a) if the task is too difficult (e.g., too much information to remember) or (b) if the length of time required for the student to remember is inappropriate (e.g., presentation of information was too brief or time lapse between presentation of material and request for recall was too long).

31. Reinforce the student for remembering information received auditorily: (a) give the student a tangible reward (e.g., special privileges, line leading, passing out materials, five minutes free time, etc.) or (b) give the student an intangible reward (e.g., praise, handshake, smile, etc.).

10 Does not demonstrate an understanding of directionality

1. Make certain to use the terms *right* and *left* as part of the directions you are giving to the student (e.g., refer to the windows on the left side of the room, the chalkboard on the right side of the room, etc.).

2. Identify directions in the classroom with signs (e.g., on the ceiling put *up*, on the floor put *down*, etc.).

3. Have the student practice following directions on paper. Instruct the student to make a mark or picture on the right, left, middle, top and bottom parts of the paper according to the directions given.

4. Avoid the problem of mirror images by standing next to the student when giving *right* and *left* directions.

5. Design an obstacle course using materials in the room. Students can step *into* the box, crawl *over* the desk, walk *under* the coat rack, etc.

6. Use concrete examples when teaching concepts of *up-down, high-low, above-below*, etc. Use books, balls, regular classroom materials, etc., when trying to convey these concepts.

7. Hang directional signs in the room (e.g., "turn *left*," "games *under* cabinet," etc.).

8. Play *Simon Says* for directions (e.g., "Raise your *left* hand." "Walk *behind* the chair." etc.).

9. Conduct scavenger hunts. Have the student look for a pencil *in* the desk, a book *under* the table, a glass *on* the chair, etc.

10. Have the student sort *left* and *right* gloves, shoes, paper hand and foot cut-outs, etc.

11. Teach *north, south, east,* and *west* using the classroom, playground, school building, etc.

12. Label strips of paper *left* and *right* and attach them to the student's wrists.

13. Have the student practice walking *forward* and *backward*, moving toy cars and trucks *forward* and *backward*, etc.

14. Have the student identify objects which move *up* and *down* (e.g., airplanes, teeter-totter, etc.).

15. Point out doors which are labeled *push* and *pull* and activities which require *pushing* and *pulling* (e.g., opening drawers, opening doors, etc.).

16. Have the student find things that represent the concept of *in* and *out* (e.g., we pour milk *in* a glass and pour it *out*, we walk *in* a room and walk *out*; etc.).

17. Identify objects which represent *over* and *under* (e.g., a bridge is *over* water, people sleep *under* blankets, birds fly *over* our heads, rugs are *under* our feet, etc.).

18. Teach the concept of *above* and *below* with examples in the classroom (e.g., the ceiling is *above* our heads and the floor *below* our feet, etc.).

19. Teach the concept of *before* and *after* with examples from the student's daily routine (e.g., we wake up *before* we eat breakfast, we go to school *after* we eat breakfast, we eat lunch *after* we have morning recess, etc.).

20. Emphasize activities which require the action of *off* and *on* (e.g., we turn lights *on* when we need light and *off* when we do not need light, we turn the stove *on* to heat things and *off* when things are hot, we put clothes *on* to go to school, leaves fall *off* a tree in the fall, etc.).

21. Use concrete examples and experiences in teaching directionality (e.g., *east-west* signs on the wall, *left-right* armbands, etc.).

22. Review on a daily basis the concepts of directionality.

11 Has difficulty concentrating

1. Teach the student to use basic concentration and study skills (e.g., reading for the main idea, note taking, highlighting, outlining, summarizing, studying in an appropriate environment, etc.).

2. Make the subject matter meaningful to the student (e.g., explain the purpose of an assignment, relate the subject matter to the student's environment, etc.).

3. Structure the environment in such a way as to reduce distracting stimuli (e.g., place the student on the front row, provide a carrel or quiet place away from distractions, etc.). This is used as a means of reducing stimuli and not as a form of punishment.

4. Follow a less desirable task with a more desirable task, making the completion of the first necessary to perform the second.

5. Break down large tasks into smaller tasks (e.g., assign the student to write an outline for a book report, then the first rough draft, etc.).

6. Assign a peer tutor to work with the student to serve as a model for appropriate work habits.

7. Allow natural consequences to occur as a result of the student's inability to concentrate (e.g., work not done or completed inaccurately must be made up during recreational time, not concentrating while people are talking results in not knowing what to do, etc.).

8. Give directions in a variety of ways to increase the probability of understanding (e.g., if the student fails to understand verbal directions, present them in written form).

9. Provide clearly stated directions, written or verbal (i.e., make directions as simple and concrete as possible).

10. Reduce directions to steps (e.g., give the student each additional step after completion of the previous step).

11. Make certain the student knows that directions will only be given once.

12. Try various groupings in order to determine the situation in which the student can concentrate most easily.

13. Separate the student from the peers who may be encouraging or stimulating the inappropriate behavior.

14. Reinforce the student for beginning, staying on, and completing assignments.

15. Assign the student shorter tasks and gradually increase the number over time as the student demonstrates success.

16. Use a variety of high-interest means to communicate with the student (e.g., auditory, visual, manipulatives, etc.).

17. Present assignments in small amounts (e.g., assign 10 problems, use pages removed from workbooks, etc.).

18. Make certain that the student's academic tasks are on his/her ability level.

19. Teach the student note-taking skills (e.g., copy main ideas from the chalkboard, identify main ideas from lectures, condense statements into a few key words, etc.).

20. Maintain physical contact with the student while talking to him/her (e.g., touch the student's hand or shoulder).

21. Require the student to make eye contact while delivering information to him/her.

22. Deliver one-, two-, and three-step directions to the student, increasing the number of steps as the student demonstrates success in concentrating.

23. Have the student participate in games requiring varying lengths of concentration (e.g., tic-tac-toe, checkers, chess, etc.).

24. Seat the student close to the source of information.

25. Reduce distracting stimuli in and around the student's desk (e.g., materials in the desk, on the desk, etc.).

26. Highlight or underline important information the student reads (e.g., directions, reading assignments, math word problems, etc.).

27. Tell the student what to listen for when being given directions, receiving information, etc.

28. Make certain the student knows what to look for when reading (e.g., main characters, main ideas, sequence of events, etc.).

29. Provide the student with appropriate time limits for the completion of assignments.

30. Maintain visibility to and from the student at all times in order to monitor the student's concentration.

31. Provide the student with a prompt when the student is off task (e.g., move close to the student, speak to the student, etc.).

32. Use multiple modalities (e.g., auditory, visual, tactile, etc.) when presenting directions, explanations, and instructional content. By using multiple modalities, the information may hold the student's interest for a longer period of time.

33. Make certain the student is attending to the source of information (e.g., eye contact is being made, hands are free of materials, student is looking at the assignment, etc.).

34. Stop at various points during a presentation of information to check the student's comprehension.

35. Give the student one task to perform at a time. Introduce the next task only when the student has successfully completed the previous task.

36. Teach the student listening skills (e.g., stop working, look at the person delivering questions and directions, have necessary note-taking materials, etc.).

37. Reduce the amount of information on a page if it is causing visual distractions for the student (e.g., less print to read, fewer problems, isolate information that is presented to the student).

38. Use pictures, diagrams, the chalkboard, and gestures when delivering information in order to hold the student's attention.

39. Have the student repeat to himself/herself information just heard to help him/her remember the important facts.

40. Deliver information to the student on a one-to-one basis or employ a peer tutor.

41. Communicate clearly with the student the length of time he/she has to complete the assignment and when the assignment should be completed. The student may want to use a timer in order to complete the tasks within a given period of time.

42. Assess the quality and clarity of directions, explanations, and instructions given to the student.

43. Write a contract with the student specifying what behavior is expected (e.g., concentrating on a task) and what reinforcement will be made available when the terms of the contract have been met.

44. Reinforce the student for concentrating on a task for the length of time the student can be successful. Gradually increase the length of time required for reinforcement.

45. Establish classroom rules:
1. Work on task.
2. Work quietly.
3. Remain in your seat.
4. Finish task.
5. Meet task expectations.
Reiterate rules often and reinforce students for following rules.

46. Reinforce the student for concentrating: (a) give the student a tangible reward (e.g., classroom privileges, line leading, passing out materials, five minutes free time, etc.) or (b) give the student an intangible reward (e.g., praise, handshake, smile, etc.).

47. Present directions following the outline of : (1) What, (2) How, (3) Materials, and (4) When.

48. Have the student take notes when directions are being given following the "What, How, Materials, and When" format. (See Appendix for Assignment Form.)

49. While concepts are presented, have the student listen and take notes for "Who, What, Where, When, How, and Why." (See Appendix for Outline Form.)

50. Present concepts following the outline of: (1) Who, (2) What, (3) Where, (4) When, (5) How, and (6) Why.

12 Perseverates - does the same thing over and over

1. Explain that the student should be satisfied with his/her best effort rather than insisting on perfection.

2. Have the student time activities in order to monitor his/her own behavior and accept time limits.

3. Convince the student that work not completed in one sitting can be completed later. Provide the student with ample time to complete earlier assignments in order to guarantee closure.

4. Provide the student with more than enough time to finish an activity and decrease the amount of time as the student demonstrates success.

5. Structure time limits in order that the student knows exactly how long he/she has to work and when work must be finished.

6. Allow a transition period between activities in order that the student can make adjustments in his/her behavior.

7. Employ a signal technique (e.g., turning lights off and on to warn that the end of an activity is near).

8. Establish definite time limits and provide the student with this information before an activity begins.

9. Assign the student shorter activities and gradually increase the length of the activities as the student demonstrates success.

10. Maintain consistency in the daily routine.

11. Maintain consistency of expectations and keep expectations within the ability level of the student.

12. Allow the student to finish the activity unless it will be disruptive to the schedule.

13. Present instructions/directions prior to handing out necessary materials.

14. Provide the student with a list of materials needed for each activity (e.g., pencil, paper, textbook, workbook, etc.).

15. Collect the student's materials (e.g., pencil, paper, textbook, workbook, etc.) when it is time to change from one activity to another.

16. Provide the student with clearly stated expectations for all situations.

17. Provide adequate transition time for the student to finish an activity and get ready for the next activity.

18. Prevent the student from becoming so stimulated by an event or activity that the student cannot control his/her behavior.

19. Identify expectations of different environments and help the student develop the skills to be successful in those environments.

20. In conjunction with other school personnel, develop as much consistency across all school environments as possible (e.g., rules, criteria for success, behavioral expectations, consequences, etc.).

21. Have the student engage in relaxing transitional activities designed to reduce the effects of stimulating activities (e.g., put head on desk, listen to the teacher read a story, put headphones on and listen to relaxing music, etc.).

22. Provide the student with a schedule of daily events in order that the student knows exactly what is expected for the day. (See Appendix for Schedule of Daily Events.)

23. Provide the student with verbal reminders or prompts when he/she perseverates.

24. Reduce distracting stimuli (noise and motion) around the student (e.g, place the student on the front row, provide a carrel or quiet place away from distractions, etc.). This is used as a means of reducing stimuli and not as a form of punishment.

25. Provide the student with increased opportunity for help or assistance on academic tasks (e.g., peer tutoring, directions for work sent home, frequent interactions, etc.).

26. Assign a peer to provide an appropriate model for changing from one activity to another.

27. Have the student question any directions, explanations, instructions he/she does not understand.

28. Evaluate the appropriateness of the task to determine: (a) if the task is too easy, (b) if the task is too difficult, and (c) if the length of time scheduled to complete the task is appropriate.

29. Write a contract with the student specifying what behavior is expected (e.g., putting materials away and getting ready for another activity) and what reinforcement will be made available when the terms of the contract have been met.

30. Reinforce the student for demonstrating acceptable behavior based on the length of time the student can be successful. Gradually increase the length of time required for reinforcement as the student demonstrates success.

31. Reinforce those students in the classroom who change from one activity to another without difficulty.

32. Establish classroom rules:
1. Work on task.
2. Work quietly.
3. Remain in your seat.
4. Finish task.
5. Meet task expectations.
Reiterate rules often and reinforce students for following rules.

33. Speak to the student to explain: (a) what he/she is doing wrong (e.g., failing to stop one activity and begin another) and (b) what he/she should be doing (e.g., changing from one activity to another).

34. Reinforce the student for changing from one activity to another without difficulty: (a) give the student a tangible reward (e.g., classroom privileges, line leading, passing out materials, five minutes free time, etc.) or (b) give the student an intangible reward (e.g., praise, handshake, smile, etc.).

13 Fails to demonstrate logical thinking

1. Give the student responsibilities that require logical thinking (e.g., assign the student to water plants and provide a watering can and a glass, telling the student to use the most appropriate container; etc.).

2. Each day provide the student with problem-solving situations which require logical thinking (e.g., "A stranger takes you by the arm in a department store. What do you do?" "You see smoke coming out of a neighbor's house and no one is home. What do you do?" etc.).

3. Make certain the student experiences the consequences of his/her behavior (e.g., appropriate behavior results in positive consequences while inappropriate behavior results in negative consequences).

4. Provide the student with a list of questions involving logic, which he/she answers orally (e.g., "Why do we post *wet paint* signs?" "Why do we have *STOP* signs at intersections?" "Why do we wear seatbelts?" etc.).

5. When something is broken, lost, etc., have the student identify what could have been done to prevent the situation. When materials are properly organized, maintained, and serviceable, have the student discuss the value of such practices.

6. Have the student read stories involving a moral (e.g., *The Tortoise and the Hare*, *The Boy Who Cried Wolf*, etc.) and explain the reason for the outcome of the story.

7. Have the student read short stories without endings. Require the student to develop logical endings for the stories.

8. Give the student situations/pictures and have him/her explain what variables are related (e.g., "Snow is falling; the wind is blowing. Is the temperature hot or cold? What should you wear outdoors?").

9. Have the student sequence cartoon strips, after they have been cut apart and rearranged, and explain the logic of the sequence created.

10. Give the student fill-in-the-blank statements requiring an appropriate response from multiple-choice possibilities (e.g., The boy's dog was dirty so the boy decided to give his dog a ___ [dog biscuit, bath, toy]).

11. Show the student pictures of dangerous situations and have him/her explain the danger (e.g., a child running into the street between parked cars, a child riding a bicycle without using his/her hands, etc.).

12. Use cause-and-effect relationships as they apply to nature and people. Discuss what led up to a specific situation in a story or a picture, what could happen next, etc.

13. Make certain that the student can verbalize the reason for real life outcomes of behavior (e.g., why the student had to leave the class line on the way to recess, why he/she earned the privilege of being line leader, etc.).

14. Have the student make up rules. Have the student explain why each is necessary.

15. Have the student identify appropriate consequences for rules (e.g., consequences for following rules and consequences for not following rules). Have the student explain the choice of consequences he/she identified.

16. Have the student answer such questions as, "Why do we have rules?" "Why do you have to be a certain age before you can drive a car?" etc.

17. Have the student answer analogy situations (e.g., a garage is to a car as a house is to a ___).

18. Set aside time each day for a problem-solving game, analogies, decision-making activities, assigned responsibilities, etc.

19. Make certain the student is attending to the source of information (e.g., eye contact is being made, hands are free of materials, student is looking at the assignment, etc.).

20. Have the student questions any directions, explanations, and instructions he/she does not understand.

21. Reinforce those students in the classroom who demonstrate logical thinking (e.g., making appropriate decisions, solving problems, making references, etc.).

22. Reinforce the student for appropriate decision making: (a) give the student a tangible reward (e.g., classroom privileges, line leading, passing out materials, five minutes free time, etc.) or (b) give the student an intangible reward (e.g., smile, handshake, etc.).

14 Has difficulty retrieving, recalling, or naming objects, persons, places, etc.

1. Have the student act as a classroom messenger. Give the student a verbal message to deliver to another teacher, the secretary, an administrator, etc. Increase the length of the message as the student is successful.

2. Review the schedule of the morning and afternoon activities with the student and have him/her repeat the sequence. Increase the length of the sequence as the student is successful.

3. At the end of the school day, have the student recall three activities in which he/she participated during the day. Gradually increase the number of activities the student is required to recall as he/she demonstrates success.

4. After a field trip or special event, have the student recall the activities which occurred.

5. After reading a short story, have the student recall the main characters, sequence the events, and recall the outcome of the story.

6. Give the student specific categories and have him/her name as many items as possible within that category (e.g., objects, persons, places, etc.).

7. Give the student a series of words or pictures and have him/her name the category to which they belong (e.g., objects, persons, places, etc.).

8. Describe objects, persons, places, etc., and have the student name the items described.

9. Help the student employ memory aids in order to recall words (e.g., a name might be linked to another word; for example, "Mr. Green is a very colorful person.").

10. Give the student a series of words describing objects, persons, places, etc., and have him/her identify the opposite of each word.

11. Encourage the student to play word games such as *Hangman, Scrabble, Password,* etc.

12. Have the student complete "fill-in-the-blank" sentences with appropriate words (e.g., objects, persons, places, etc.).

13. Give the student a series of words (e.g., objects, persons, places, etc.) and have the student list all the words he/she can think of with similar meanings (synonyms).

14. Have the student compete against himself/herself by timing how fast a series of pictured objects can be named. Each time the student tries to increase speed.

15. Have the student take notes from classes, presentations, lectures, etc., to help facilitate recall.

16. Have the student make notes, lists, etc., of things he/she needs to be able to recall. The student carries these reminders with him/her.

17. Have the student tape record important information that should be remembered.

18. Have the student outline, highlight, underline, or summarize information that should be remembered.

19. Make certain the student has adequate opportunities for repetition of information through different experiences in order to enhance memory.

20. When the student is required to recall information, remind him/her of the situation in which the material was originally presented (e.g., "Remember yesterday when we talked about . . ." "Remember when we were outside and I told you about the . . ." etc.).

21. Have the student practice repetition of information in order to increase accurate memory skills (e.g., repeating names, telephone numbers, dates of events, etc.).

22. Call on the student when he/she is most likely to be able to respond successfully.

23. Show the student an object or a picture of an object for a few seconds. Ask the student to recall specific attributes of the object (e.g., color, size, shape, etc.).

24. Teach the student to recognize key words and phrases related to information in order to increase memory skills.

25. Label objects, persons, places, etc., in the environment in order to help the student be able to recall their names.

26. Make certain the student receives information from a variety of sources (e.g., texts, discussions, films, slide presentations, etc.) in order to enhance the student's memory/recall.

27. Reduce distracting stimuli (noise and motion) around the student (e.g., place the student on the front row, provide a carrel or quiet place away from distractions, etc.). This is used as a means of reducing distracting stimuli and not as a form of punishment.

28. Make certain the student is attending to the source of information (e.g., eye contact is being made, hands are free of materials, student is looking at the assignment, etc.).

29. Review, on a daily basis, those skills, concepts, tasks, etc., which have been previously introduced.

30. Identify the student's most efficient learning mode and use it consistently to increase the probability of understanding (e.g., If the student fails to understand information presented verbally, present it in written form. If the student has difficulty understanding written information, present it verbally.).

31. When the student has difficulty recalling information, remind the student that this can happen to everyone and not to be upset. Everyone has areas where they are weak and areas of strength as well.

32. Give the student a choice of answers on worksheets (e.g., fill-in-the-blank, multiple-choice, etc.). This increases the student's opportunity for recognizing the correct answer.

33. Reinforce the student for demonstrating accurate memory skills based on the length of time the student can be successful. Gradually increase the length of time required for reinforcement as the student demonstrates success.

34. Reinforce the student for demonstrating accurate memory skills: (a) give the student a tangible reward (e.g., classroom privileges, line leading, passing out materials, five minutes free time, etc.) or (b) give the student an intangible reward (e.g., praise, handshake, smile, etc.).

15 Demonstrates visual perception problems

1. Make certain the student has had his/her vision checked recently.

2. Give the student the opportunity to find objects which are the same or different in size, shape, color, etc.

3. Have the student sort objects according to size, shape, color, etc.

4. Have the student use play equipment such as a ladder, jungle gym, teeter-totter, or balance beam to become more aware of body position in space.

5. Have the student complete partially drawn figures, words, numbers, etc.

6. Have the student use pictures from magazines, catalogs, etc., to assemble features and body parts.

7. Have the student build an object according to a pattern (e.g., construction toys, blocks, etc.).

8. Have the student engage in sequencing activities (e.g., put numbers in order, place pictures in correct order, etc.).

9. Have the student pick out specific objects from pictures around the classroom, in the environment while on the playground, etc.

10. Have the student perform a variety of activities such as tracing, cutting, coloring, pasting, etc.

11. Have the student complete jigsaw puzzles, beginning with simple self-made puzzles and progressing to more complex puzzles.

12. Develop a variety of activities for the student using a pegboard.

13. Provide the student with a variety of classifying activities (e.g., from simple classifying of types of clothes, cars, etc., to more complex classifying of which items would be located at certain stores, etc.).

14. Have the student find specific shapes in the room (e.g., the door is a rectangle, the clock is a circle, etc.).

15. Provide the student with simple designs to be reproduced with blocks, sticks, paper, etc.

16. Have the student identify objects by looking at the outline of objects on a cardboard silhouette, etc.

17. Reduce visual stimuli on a worksheet or in a book by covering all of the page except the activity on which the student is working.

18. Have the student repeat the names of objects, shapes, numbers, or words presented to him/her for a limited time period.

19. Provide the student with a variety of exercises in which he/she must identify the missing parts, common objects, etc.

20. Provide the student with a variety of visual recall tasks (e.g., the student writes numbers, shapes, and words he/she was shown for a specific time, etc.).

21. Use a variety of colored tiles to make a pattern. Have the student duplicate the pattern while looking at the model, then complete the design from memory without using the model.

22. Place several items on a tray, such as a pencil, a flower, a penny, and a piece of gum. Allow the student to study the items, then take the items away and have the student identify what was on the tray.

23. Have the student practice tracing outlines of pictures. Worksheets with dotted lines of pictures, letters, numbers, etc., can be used to develop eye-hand coordination.

24. Play a matching game in which hidden pictures, numbers, or shapes are turned over one at a time and the student must remember where the matching picture is located.

25. Using pictures from magazines, remove an important part of the picture and ask the student to identify the missing part.

26. Read directions orally to the student before he/she is asked to begin a workbook page. Work the first problem with the student so he/she understands what is expected.

27. Reduce the amount of information on a page for the student (e.g., less print, fewer problems, etc.).

28. Provide math problems on graph paper so the numbers are in columns in the ones, tens, and hundreds places.

29. Have writing paper color-coded so the student knows where to start and stop on the page.

30. Highlight or underline important words, phrases, etc., in the student's assignments that require reading.

31. Allow the student to use a typewriter to facilitate skills and reinforce word recognition.

32. Provide the student with shorter tasks, but provide more of them. Increase the length of the tasks as the student demonstrates success.

33. Reduce distracting stimuli on or near the student's desk (e.g., materials on the desk, things inside the desk, etc.).

34. Provide the student with a quiet place to work (e.g., carrel, "office," etc.). This is used as a means of reducing distracting stimuli and not as a form of punishment.

35. Identify the student's most efficient learning mode and use it consistently to increase the probability of understanding (e.g., if the student has difficulty understanding written information or directions, present it verbally).

16 Has difficulty classifying

1. Make certain the student understands that all objects, people, ideas, actions, etc., can be grouped based on how they are alike. Provide the student with concrete examples.

2. Give the student pairs of objects and have the student name all the ways in which they are alike and then ways in which they are different. Proceed from simple things which can be seen and touched to more abstract ideas which cannot be seen or touched.

3. Name a category or group and ask the student to identify as many things as possible which belong in the group. Begin with large categories (e.g., living things) and move to more specific categories (e.g., living things which are green).

4. Explain that each new word which is learned is an example of some category. When defining a word, it should first be put into a category (e.g., a hammer is a kind of tool, anger is a kind of emotion, etc.).

5. Present a series of objects and have the student tell which one does not belong in the same category as the others.

6. Present a series of objects or words and have the student create a category into which they fit.

7. Give the student a list of words or pictures and have him/her identify the categories to which the words belong (e.g., Love and hate are both emotions. Love fits into the specific category of good feelings, and hate fits into the specific category of bad or unhappy feelings.).

8. Explain that words can be categorized according to many different attributes such as size, function, and texture.

9. Ask the student to help make lists of some categories which fit inside larger categories (e.g., flowers, trees, and bushes are all categories which can be included in the plant category).

10. Play a game such as "I'm thinking of an object" in which an object is described and the student must guess the item based on questions asked.

11. Suggest that parents ask for the student's help when grocery shopping by having him/her make a list of items needed in a particular food group (e.g., dairy products, meats, etc.).

12. Have the student cut out pictures for a notebook of favorite foods, television shows, or other categories and group them in appropriate arrangement.

13. Give the student specific categories and have him/her name as many items as possible within the category (e.g., objects, persons, places, etc.).

14. Give the student a series of words (e.g., objects, persons, places, etc.) and have him/her name as many items that he/she can think of which have similar meanings (synonyms).

15. Make the subject matter meaningful to the student (e.g., explain the purpose of an assignment, relate the subject matter to the student's environment, etc.).

16. Stop at various points during the presentation of information to check the student's comprehension.

17. Use pictures, diagrams, the chalkboard, and gestures when delivering information.

17 Fails to generalize knowledge from one situation to another

1. Make certain the student understands that all objects, people, ideas, actions, etc., can be grouped based on how they are alike. Provide the student with concrete examples (e.g., dogs, cats, cows, and horses are all mammals).

2. Give the student pairs of objects, and have the student name the ways in which they are alike and the ways they are different. Proceed from simple things which can be seen and touched to more abstract ideas which cannot be seen or touched.

3. Name a category or group and ask the student to identify as many things as possible which belong in the group. Begin with large categories (e.g., living things) and move to more specific categories (e.g., living things which are green).

4. Ask the student to help in making lists of some categories which fit inside larger categories (e.g., flowers, trees, and bushes are all categories which can be included in the plant category).

5. Identify related concepts and explain to the student how we can generalize from one to another (e.g., numbers to money, fuel to energy, words to sentences, etc.).

6. Have the student play analogy games involving multiple-choice possibilities (e.g., food is to a person as gasoline is to ___ [a skateboard, an automobile, a house]).

7. Deliver instructions by using examples of relationships (e.g., rely on what has already been learned, use examples from the student's environment, etc.).

8. Call attention to situations in the classroom which generalize to more global situations (e.g., being on time for class is the same as being on time for work; school work not done during work time has to be made up before school, after school, or during recreational time, just as responsibilities at places of employment have to be completed at night or on weekends if not completed on the job; etc.).

9. Require the student to explain outcomes, consequences, etc. (e.g., when the student earns a reward or privilege, make certain he/she can explain that the reward was the result of hard work and accomplishment; etc.).

10. Have the student respond to statements that begin with "What if" (e.g., "What if it rained for forty days and forty nights?" "What if there were no rules and laws?" etc.).

11. Be certain to relate what the student has learned in one setting or situation to other situations (e.g., vocabulary words learned should be pointed out in reading selections, math word problems, story writing, etc.).

12. Have the student write letters, fill out applications, etc., in order to see the generalization of handwriting, spelling, grammar, sentence structure, etc., to real life situations.

13. Provide the student with situations in which he/she can generalize skills learned in mathematics to simulations of the use of money (e.g., making change, financing a car, computing interest earned from savings, etc.).

14. Make certain that the student is provided with an explanation of "why" he/she is learning particular information or skills (e.g., we learn to spell, read, and write in order to be able to communicate; we learn to solve math problems in order to be able to make purchases, use a checking account, measure, and cook; etc.).

15. Have the student develop a series of responses representing his/her ability to generalize from common situations in the environment (e.g., "We should drive no more than the posted speed limit on our highways because . . ." Appropriate responses concern safety, conservation of fuel, care of vehicle, fines for speeding.).

16. As soon as the student learns a skill, make certain that he/she applies it to a real life situation (e.g., when the student learns to count by fives, have him/her practice adding nickels).

17. Use a variety of instructional approaches to help the student generalize knowledge gained to real life situations (e.g., after studying the judicial system, provide a simulated courtroom trial; etc.).

18. Use multiple-choice modalities (e.g., auditory, visual, tactile, etc.) when presenting instructional material that requires the student to generalize knowledge. Determine which modality is stronger and utilize the results.

19. Use concrete examples and experiences when teaching concepts and sharing information with the student.

20. When the student is required to generalize knowledge from one situation to another, provide him/her with visual and/or auditory cues to help in remembering the information previously presented (e.g., provide key words, expose part of a picture, etc.).

21. Use pictures, diagrams, the chalkboard, and gestures when delivering information.

22. When delivering explanations and information, be certain to use vocabulary that is within the student's level of comprehension.

23. Use daily drill activities to help the student memorize math facts, sight words, etc.

18 Demonstrates confusion

1. Make certain the student's vision has been checked recently.

2. Make certain that all directions, explanations, and instructions are delivered in a clear and concise manner.

3. Teach the student direction-following skills (e.g., stop doing other things; listen to what is being said; do not begin until all information is delivered; question any directions, explanations, and instructions you do not understand).

4. Teach the student to rely on environmental cues when moving about the school and in related areas (e.g., look for signs, room numbers, familiar surroundings, etc.).

5. Make certain the student knows how to ask questions, ask for directions, etc.

6. Teach the student a basic survival/directional word vocabulary (e.g., *ladies, gentlemen, push, pull, left, right,* etc.).

7. Have a peer accompany the student to locations in the building until the student develops familiarity with his/her surroundings.

8. Have the student practice finding various locations in the building before or after school or during classes when few students are in the halls.

9. Have the student practice finding locations in the building by following verbal directions, written directions, directions from teachers or other students, etc.

10. Have the student follow a schedule of daily events as he/she moves from place to place in the school. (See Appendix for Schedule of Daily Events.)

11. Have the student practice problem-solving skills if he/she should become lost or confused in the school environment (e.g., ask directions, return to where you started, look for familiar surroundings, read signs, etc.).

12. Make certain the student has designated instructors or peers who act as sources of information within the school.

13. Have the student learn to use a floor plan to find specific rooms, hallways, and areas while following the daily class or work schedule.

14. Pair the student with a classmate who has a similar class schedule in order to have a peer who can direct the student if he/she gets lost or confused.

15. Have the student verbally repeat/paraphrase instructions and information given so that the instructor can provide a means of clarification and redirection of the given information.

16. Make certain the student has been provided with an adequate orientation to all areas of the school environment he/she will be using.

17. Make certain the school environment is conducive to finding locations the student uses (e.g., by posting signs or directions, color-coding pods and similar areas, etc.).

18. Have the student review directions before leaving the classroom to find certain points in the building (e.g., have the student repeat directions back to you, have the student look at a map, etc.).

19. When giving the student directions to certain points in the building, use concrete clues such as the drinking fountain, restroom, or lunchroom (e.g., "Go to the room that is just past the lunchroom." "The bathroom is on the left side of the drinking fountain, around the corner.").

20. When delivering directions, explanations, and information, be certain to use vocabulary that is within the student's level of comprehension.

21. Make certain the student is attending to the source of information when directions are being given (e.g., eye contact is being made, hands are free of materials, etc.).

22. Call on the student when he/she is most likely to be able to respond successfully.

23. Reduce or remove those stimuli in the environment which are distracting to the student and interfering with the ability to listen successfully.

24. Have the student act as a peer tutor to teach another student a concept he/she has mastered. This can serve as reinforcement for the student.

25. Make certain the student has mastery of concepts at each level before introducing a new skill level.

26. Provide the student with shorter tasks, but provide more tasks throughout the day (e.g., four assignments of five problems each rather than one assignment of 20 problems).

27. Review, on a daily basis, those skills, concepts, tasks, etc., which have been previously introduced.

28. Give the student one task to perform at a time. Introduce the next task only when the student has successfully completed the previous task.

29. Stop at various points during the presentation of information to check the student's comprehension.

30. Make certain the student is attending to the source of information (e.g., eye contact is being made, hands are free of materials, student is looking at the assignment, etc.).

31. Provide the student with environmental cues and prompts designed to enhance his/her success in the classroom (e.g., posted rules, schedule of daily events, steps for performing a task, etc.).

32. Reduce the amount of information on a page if it is causing visual distractions for the student (e.g., have less print to read, give fewer problems, isolate information that is presented to the student).

33. Assign the student shorter tasks and gradually increase the number over time as the student demonstrates success.

34. Identify the student's most efficient learning mode and use it consistently to increase the probability of understanding (e.g., If the student fails to understand directions or information given verbally, present it in written form. If the student has difficulty understanding written information or directions, present it verbally.).

35. Make certain that verbal directions are delivered in a nonthreatening and supportive manner (e.g., positive voice, facial expressions, and language such as "Will you please . . ." or "You need . . ." rather than "You better . . ." or "If you don't . . .").

36. Use pictures, diagrams, the chalkboard, and gestures when delivering information.

37. Deliver information to the student on a one-to-one basis or employ a peer tutor.

19 Remembers information one time but not the next

1. Have the student take notes relative to important information that should be remembered.

2. Have the student tape record important information that should be remembered.

3. If the student has difficulty remembering information in written form, and if the student has difficulty remembering information he/she sees, present the information auditorily.

4. Have the student repeat/paraphrase important information that should be remembered.

5. Have the student outline, highlight, underline, or summarize information that should be remembered.

6. Use concrete examples and experiences in sharing information with the student.

7. Teach the student to recognize main points, important facts, etc.

8. Make certain the student has adequate opportunities for repetition of information through different experiences in order to enhance memory.

9. Make certain information is presented to the student in the most clear and concise manner possible.

10. Reduce distracting stimuli when the student is attempting to remember important information.

11. Teach the student to rely on resources in the environment to recall information (e.g., notes, textbooks, pictures, etc.).

12. When the student is required to recall information, provide auditory cues to help the student remember the information (e.g., key words, a brief oral description to clue the student, etc.).

13. When the student is required to remember information, remind him/her of the situation in which the material was originally presented (e.g., "Remember when we were outside and I told you about the . . ." "Remember yesterday when we talked about . . ." etc.).

14. Assess the meaningfulness of the material to the student. Remembering is more likely to occur when the material is meaningful and the student can relate to real experiences.

15. Relate the information being presented to the student's previous experiences.

16. Have the student make notes, lists, etc., of things that need to be remembered. The student should carry these reminders at all times.

17. Have the student follow a regular routine of daily events to establish consistency in his/her behavior pattern.

18. Have the student repeat to himself/herself information just heard to help the student remember the important facts.

19. Make certain the student is not required to learn more information than he/she is capable of at any one time.

20. Give the student a choice of answers (e.g., more than one possible answer, multiple choice on a worksheet, etc.). This increases the student's opportunity for recognizing the correct answer.

21. Call on the student when he/she is most likely to be able to respond successfully.

22. Use daily drill activities to help the student memorize math facts, vocabulary words, etc.

23. Provide reminders throughout the educational environment in order to help the student be more successful in remembering information (e.g., rules, lists, schedules, etc.).

24. Help the student employ memory aids in order to recall words (e.g., a name might be linked to another word; for example, "Mr. Green is a very colorful person.").

25. Make certain the student has adequate opportunities for repetition of information through different experiences in order to enhance his/her memory.

26. Review, on a daily basis, those skills, concepts, tasks, etc., which have been previously introduced to help the student remember information previously learned.

27. Identify the student's most efficient learning mode and use it consistently to increase the probability of understanding (e.g., If the student fails to understand directions or information given verbally, present it in written form. If the student has difficulty understanding written information or directions, present it verbally.).

28. As soon as a student learns a skill or new information, make certain that he/she applies it to other situations (e.g., When the student learns to count by fives, have him/her practice adding nickels. Vocabulary words learned should be pointed out in reading selections, etc.).

20 Requires slow, sequential, substantially broken-down presentation of concepts

1. Make certain the student's hearing has been checked recently.

2. Have the student repeat or paraphrase what is said to him/her to determine what was heard.

3. Give the student short directions, explanations, and instructions to follow. Gradually increase the length of the directions, explanations, and instructions as the student demonstrates success.

4. Maintain consistency in the delivery of verbal instructions.

5. Make certain the student is attending to the source of information (e.g., making eye contact, hands free of writing materials, looking at the assignment, etc.).

6. Provide the student with written directions and instructions to supplement verbal directions and instructions.

7. Emphasize or repeat word endings, key words, etc.

8. Speak clearly and concisely when delivering directions, explanations, and instructions.

9. Place the student near the source of information.

10. Reduce distracting stimuli (e.g., noise and motion in the classroom) in order to enhance the student's ability to listen successfully.

11. Stop at key points when delivering directions, explanations, and instructions in order to determine student comprehension.

12. Deliver directions, explanations, and instructions at an appropriate pace for the student.

13. Identify a list of word endings, key words, etc., that the student will practice listening for when someone is speaking.

14. Deliver oral questions and directions that involve only one concept or step. Gradually increase the number of concepts or steps as the student demonstrates success.

15. Move the student away from other students who may interfere with his/her ability to attend to directions, explanations, and instructions.

16. Teach the student listening skills (e.g., listen carefully, write down important points, ask for clarification, wait until all directions are received before beginning, etc.).

17. Use demonstrations along with the presentation of information.

18. Scan all materials for new words. Use simple terms when possible. Teach new vocabulary and provide practice through application.

19. Reduce abstractions by giving concrete examples and firsthand experiences. Use simple demonstrations.

20. Refer to previously presented related information when presenting a new concept.

21. Prepare or obtain simplified manuals with definitions of technical vocabulary, step-by-step instructions, and diagrams or pictures.

22. Begin with concepts that are known and then follow with skills or concepts not already mastered or integrated. Relationships will be more obvious when progressing to new skills and concepts.

23. Highlight or underline the important facts in reading material.

24. Rewrite instructions at an appropriate reading level for the student.

25. Identify the student's most efficient learning mode and use it consistently for the presentation of concepts.

26. Use multiple modalities (e.g., auditory, visual, tactile, etc.) when presenting directions, explanations, and instructional content. Determine which modality is stronger and utilize the result.

27. Use concrete examples of experiences in teaching concepts and sharing information with the student.

28. Review, on a daily basis, those skills, concepts, tasks, etc., which have been previously introduced.

29. Use pictures, diagrams, the chalkboard, and gestures when delivering information.

30. Reinforce the student for listening carefully based on the length of time the student can be successful. Gradually increase the length of time the student is required to listen as the student demonstrates success.

31. Have the student question any directions, explanations, and instructions he/she does not understand.

32. Evaluate the level of difficulty of the information to which the student is expected to listen (e.g., be sure information is communicated on the student's ability level).

33. Speak to the student to explain: (a) what the student is doing wrong (e.g., failing to listen carefully) and (b) what the student should be doing (e.g., listening carefully).

34. Reinforce the student for listening to what is said: (a) give the student a tangible reward (e.g., classroom privileges, line leading, five minutes free time, passing out materials, etc.) or (b) give the student an intangible reward (e.g., praise, handshake, smile, etc.).

21 Fails to remember sequences

1. Have the student question any directions, explanations, and instructions not understood.

2. Break the sequence into units and have the student learn one unit at a time.

3. Give the student short sequences (e.g., two components, three components, etc.) to remember. Gradually increase the length of the sequence as the student demonstrates success.

4. Provide the student with environmental cues and prompts (e.g., lists of jobs to perform, schedule of daily events, bell, timer, etc.).

5. Maintain consistency in sequential activities in order to increase the likelihood of student success (e.g, the student has math every day at one o'clock, recess at two o'clock, etc.).

6. Teach the student to use associative cues or mnemonic devices to remember sequences.

7. Have the student maintain notes, written reminders, etc., in order to remember sequences.

8. Actively involve the student in learning to remember sequences by having the student physically perform sequential activities (e.g., operating equipment, following recipes, solving math problems, etc.).

9. Have the student be responsible for helping a peer remember sequences.

10. Have the student practice remembering sequences by engaging in sequential activities which are purposeful (e.g., operating equipment, following recipes, opening a combination lock, etc.).

11. Teach the student to use environmental resources to remember sequences (e.g., calendar, dictionary, etc.).

12. Have the student maintain a notebook in which to keep notes regarding necessary sequential information (e.g., lists of things to do, schedule of events, days of the week, months of the year, etc.).

13. Provide the student with frequent opportunities to recite sequences throughout the day in order to increase memory skills.

14. Assign the student additional activities which require the use of sequences in order to enhance the ability to remember sequences.

15. Practice sequential memory activities each day for those sequences which the student needs to memorize (e.g., important telephone numbers, addresses, etc.).

16. Provide the student with a schedule of daily events for each day's activities at school. (See Appendix for Schedule of Daily Events.)

17. Teach the student to make reminders for himself/herself (e.g., notes, lists, etc.).

18. Make it pleasant and positive for the student to ask questions about things he/she does not understand. Reinforce the student by assisting the student, congratulating, praising, etc.

19. Have the student repeat to himself/herself information just heard to help him/her remember the important facts.

20. Tell the student what to listen for when being given directions, receiving information, etc.

21. Stop at various points during the presentation of information to check the student's comprehension.

22. Help the student employ memory aids.

23. Evaluate the appropriateness of the task to determine: (a) if the task is too difficult and (b) if the length of time scheduled to complete the task is appropriate.

24. Reinforce the student for remembering sequences based on the number of times the student can be successful. Gradually increase the length of the sequences required for reinforcement as the student demonstrates success.

25. Reinforce those students in the classroom who remember sequences.

26. Reinforce the student for remembering sequences: (a) give the student a tangible reward (e.g., classroom privileges, line leading, passing out materials, five minutes free time, etc.) or (b) give the student an intangible reward (e.g., praise, handshake, smile, etc.).

22 Does not follow verbal directions

1. Teach the student skills for following verbal directions (e.g., listen carefully, write down important points, use environmental cues, wait until all directions are received before beginning, etc.).

2. Give directions in a variety of ways in order to increase the probability of understanding (e.g., if the student fails to understand verbal directions, present them in written form).

3. Provide clearly stated verbal directions (e.g., make the directions as simple and concrete as possible).

4. Reduce distracting stimuli in order to increase the student's ability to follow verbal directions (e.g., place the student on the front row, provide a carrel or "office" space away from distractions, etc.). This is used as a means of reducing distracting stimuli and not as a form of punishment.

5. Interact frequently with the student in order to help him/her follow verbal directions for an activity.

6. Structure the environment in such a way as to provide the student with increased opportunity for help or assistance on academic tasks (e.g., peer tutoring, directions for work sent home, frequent interactions, etc.).

7. Provide alternatives for the traditional format of presenting verbal directions (e.g., tape record directions, summarize directions, directions given by peers, etc.).

8. Assess the quality and clarity of verbal directions, explanations, and instructions given to the student.

9. Have the student practice following verbal directions on nonacademic tasks (e.g., recipes, games, etc.).

10. Have the student repeat directions or give an interpretation after receiving verbal directions.

11. Give verbal directions before handing out materials.

12. Reduce verbal directions to steps (e.g., give the student each additional step after completion of the previous step).

13. Deliver a predetermined signal (e.g., clapping hands, turning lights off and on, etc.) before giving verbal directions.

14. Require that assignments done incorrectly, for any reason, be redone.

15. Make certain the student achieves success when following verbal directions.

16. Reduce the emphasis on competition. Competitive activities may cause the student to hurry to begin the task without verbal directions.

17. Have the student maintain a record (e.g., chart or graph) of his/her performance in following verbal directions.

18. Communicate clearly to the student when it is time to listen to verbal directions.

19. Provide the student with a predetermined signal when he/she is not following verbal directions (e.g., lights turned off and on, hand signals, etc.).

20. Follow a less desirable task with a highly desirable task, making the following of verbal directions and completion of the first task necessary to perform the second task.

21. Prevent the student from becoming overstimulated by an activity (e.g., frustrated, angry, etc.).

22. Make certain the student has all the materials needed to perform the assignment/activity.

23. Require the student to wait until the teacher gives him/her a signal to begin a task (e.g., give a hand signal, ring a bell, etc.).

24. Have a designated person be the only individual to deliver verbal directions to the student.

25. Make certain the student is attending to the teacher (e.g., making eye contact, hands free of writing materials, looking at assignment, etc.) before verbal directions are given.

26. Stand next to the student when giving verbal directions.

27. Maintain visibility to and from the student. The teacher should be able to see the student and the student should be able to see the teacher, making eye contact possible at all times when verbal directions are given.

28. Make certain that verbal directions are delivered in a nonthreatening manner (e.g., positive voice, facial expression, language, etc.).

29. Make certain that verbal directions are delivered in a supportive rather than threatening manner (e.g., "Will you please . . ." or "You need . . ." rather than "You better . . ." or "If you don't . . .").

30. Present directions in both written and verbal forms.

31. Provide the student with a written copy of verbal directions.

32. Tape record directions for the student to listen to individually and repeat as necessary.

33. Maintain consistency in the format of verbal directions.

34. Develop direction-following assignments/ activities (e.g., informal activities designed to have the student carry out verbal directions in steps, with increasing degrees of difficulty).

35. Have a peer help the student with any verbal directions he/she does not understand.

36. Seat the student close to the source of the verbal directions (e.g., teacher, aide, peer, etc.).

37. Seat the student far enough away from peers to ensure increased opportunities for attending to verbal directions.

38. Work the first problem or problems with the student in order to make certain that he/she follows the verbal directions accurately.

39. Work through the steps of the verbal directions as they are delivered in order to make certain the student follows the directions accurately.

40. Have the student carry out one step of the verbal directions at a time, checking with the teacher to make certain that each step is successfully followed before attempting the next.

41. Make certain that verbal directions are given on a level at which the student can be successful (e.g., two-step or three-step directions are not given to students who can only successfully follow one-step directions).

42. Give the student one task to perform at a time. Introduce the next task only when the student has successfully completed the previous task.

43. When delivering directions, explanations, and information, be certain to use vocabulary that is within the student's level of comprehension.

44. Assign a peer to work with the student to help him/her follow verbal directions.

45. Have the student question any verbal directions, explanations, and instructions he/she does not understand.

46. Identify a peer to act as a model for the student to imitate the appropriate following of verbal directions.

47. Evaluate the appropriateness of the task to determine: (a) if the task is too difficult and (b) if the length of time scheduled to complete the task is appropriate.

48. Communicate with parents (e.g., notes home, phone calls, etc.) in order to share information concerning the student's progress and so that they can reinforce the student at home for following verbal directions at school.

49. Reinforce those students in the classroom who follow verbal directions.

50. Write a contract with the student specifying what behavior is expected (e.g., following verbal directions) and what reinforcement will be made available when the terms of the contract have been met. (See Appendix for Behavioral Contract.)

51. Reinforce the student for following verbal directions based on the length of time the student can be successful. Gradually increase the length of time required for reinforcement as the student demonstrates success.

52. Establish classroom rules:
1. Work on task.
2. Work quietly.
3. Remain in your seat.
4. Finish task.
5. Meet task expectations.
Reiterate rules often and reinforce students for following rules.

53. Speak to the student to explain: (a) what the student is doing wrong (e.g., ignoring verbal directions) and (b) what the student should be doing (e.g., listening to and following verbal directions).

54. Reinforce the student for following verbal directions: (a) give the student a tangible reward (e.g., classroom privileges, line leading, passing out materials, five minutes free time, etc.) or (b) give the student an intangible reward (e.g., praise, handshake, smile, etc.).

23 Does not hear word endings, does not hear key words such as "do not," etc.

1. Make certain the student's hearing has been checked recently.

2. Have the student repeat or paraphrase what is said to him/her in order to determine what was heard.

3. Give the student short directions, explanations, and instructions to follow. Gradually in- crease the length of the directions, explanations, and instructions as the student demonstrates success.

4. Maintain consistency in the verbal delivery of information.

5. Make certain the student is attending to the source of information (e.g., making eye contact, hands free of writing materials, looking at assignment, etc.).

6. Provide the student with written directions and instructions to supplement verbal directions and instructions.

7. Emphasize or repeat word endings, key words, etc.

8. Speak clearly and concisely when delivering directions, explanations, and instructions.

9. Place the student near the source of information.

10. Reduce distracting stimuli (e.g., noise and motion in the classroom) in order to enhance the student's ability to listen successfully.

11. Stop at key points when delivering directions, explanations, and instructions in order to determine student comprehension.

12. Reduce the emphasis on competition in the classroom. Competition may cause the student to begin an activity before hearing all of what is said.

13. Deliver directions, explanations, and instructions at an appropriate pace.

14. Identify a list of word endings, key words, etc., that the student will practice listening for when someone is speaking.

15. Use multiple modalities (e.g., auditory, visual, tactile, etc.) when presenting directions, explanations, and instructional content. Determine which modality is stronger and utilize the results.

16. Stop at various points during the presentation of information to check the student's comprehension.

17. Teach the student listening skills (e.g., stop working, look at the person delivering questions and directions, have necessary note-taking materials, etc.).

18. Tell the student what to listen for when being given directions, receiving information, etc.

19. Make certain that all directions, questions, explanations, and instructions are delivered in the most clear and concise manner, at an appropriate pace for the student, and loudly enough to be heard.

20. Play games to teach listening skills (e.g., *Red Light-Green Light, Mother May I?, Simon Says*).

21. Have the student silently repeat information just heard to help him/her remember the important facts.

22. Have the student question any directions, explanations, and instructions he/she does not understand.

23. Evaluate the level of difficulty of information to which the student is expected to listen (e.g., be sure information is communicated on the student's ability level).

24. Reinforce the student for listening carefully based on the length of time the student can be successful. Gradually increase the length of time the student is required to listen as the student demonstrates success.

25. Speak to the student to explain: (a) what the student is doing wrong (e.g., failing to listen to word endings, key words, etc.) and (b) what the student should be doing (e.g., listening for word endings, key words, etc.).

26. Reinforce the student for listening to what is said (e.g., making eye contact, hands free of writing materials, looking at assignment, etc.): (a) give the student a tangible reward (e.g., classroom privileges, line leading, passing out materials, five minutes free time, etc.) or (b) give the student an intangible reward (e.g., praise, handshake, smile, etc.).

24 Does not direct attention or fails to maintain attention to important sounds in the immediate environment

1. Make certain the student's hearing has been recently checked.

2. Make certain the student is attending (e.g., making eye contact, hands free of materials, etc.) before delivering directions, explanations, and instructions.

3. Make certain that competing sounds (e.g., talking, movement, noises, etc.) are silenced when directions are being given, public address announcements are being made, etc.

4. Deliver a predetermined signal (e.g., hand signal, turning lights off and on, etc.) prior to bells ringing, announcements being made, directions being given, etc.

5. Give a verbal cue in order to gain the student's attention prior to bells ringing, announcements being made, etc.

6. Stand directly in front of the student when delivering information.

7. Call the student by name prior to bells ringing, announcements being made, directions being delivered, etc.

8. Seat the student next to a peer who directs and maintains attention to sounds in the immediate environment.

9. Have a peer provide the student with the information not heard.

10. Provide the student with public announcements, directions, and instructions in written form.

11. Maintain visibility to and from the student at all times in order to ensure he/she is attending.

12. Have the student verbally repeat information heard.

13. Reduce distracting stimuli in the immediate environment (e.g., place the student on the front row, provide the student with a carrel or "office" space away from distractions, etc.). This is used as a form of reducing distracting stimuli and not as a form of punishment.

14. Teach the student listening skills (e.g., listen carefully, write down important points, ask for clarification, wait until all directions are received before beginning).

15. Have the student engage in practice activities designed to develop listening skills (e.g., following one-, two-, or three-step directions; listening for the main point; etc.).

16. Make certain that directions, public announcements, etc., are delivered in a clear and concise manner (e.g., keep phrases and sentences short).

17. Give directions in a variety of ways in order to enhance the student's ability to attend.

18. Stop at various points when delivering directions, public announcements, etc., in order to ensure that the student is attending.

19. Deliver directions one step at a time. Gradually increase the number of steps as the student demonstrates the ability to direct and maintain attention.

20. Maintain consistency of the format in which auditory information is delivered (e.g., morning announcements, recess bell, delivery of directions, etc.).

21. Seat the student far enough away from peers in order to ensure the ability to successfully attend to sounds in the immediate environment.

22. Stop at various points during the presentation of information to check the student's comprehension.

23. Tell the student what to listen for when being given directions, receiving information, etc.

24. Make certain that all directions, questions, explanations, and instructions are delivered in the most clear and concise manner and at an appropriate pace for the student.

25. Use pictures, diagrams, the chalkboard, and gestures when delivering information.

26. When delivering directions, explanations, and information be certain to use vocabulary that is within the student's level of comprehension.

27. Seat the student close to the source of sound.

28. Have the student question any directions, explanations, and instructions he/she does not understand.

29. Identify a peer to act as a model for the student to imitate directing and maintaining of attention to important sounds in the immediate environment.

30. Reinforce the student for directing and maintaining his/her attention to important sounds in the immediate environment based on the length of time the student can be successful. Gradually increase the length of time required for reinforcement as the student demonstrates success.

31. Reinforce those students in the classroom who direct and maintain their attention to important sounds in the immediate environment.

32. Reinforce the student for directing and maintaining attention to important sounds in the environment: (a) give the student a tangible reward (e.g., classroom privileges, line leading, passing out materials, five minutes free time, etc.) or (b) give the student an intangible reward (e.g., praise, handshake, smile, etc.).

25 Has difficulty differentiating speech sounds heard

1. Make certain the student's hearing has been checked recently.

2. Evaluate the level of difficulty of the information to which the student is expected to listen (e.g., /ch/ and /sh/ sounds, similar consonant sounds, rhyming words, etc.).

3. Have the student repeat or paraphrase what is said to him/her in order to determine what was heard.

4. Make certain the student is attending to the source of information (e.g., making eye contact, hands free of writing materials, looking at assignments, etc.).

5. Emphasize or repeat /ch/ or /sh/ sounds, similar vowel sounds, similar consonant sounds, rhyming words, etc.

6. Speak clearly and concisely when communicating with the student.

7. Place the student in the location most appropriate for him/her to hear what is being said.

8. Reduce distracting stimuli (e.g., noise and motion in the classroom) in order to enhance the student's ability to listen successfully.

9. Stop at key points when delivering directions, explanations, and instructions in order to determine student comprehension.

10. Identify a list of /ch/ and /sh/ sounds, similar vowel sounds, similar consonant sounds, rhyming words, etc., that the student will practice listening for when someone else is speaking.

11. Stand directly in front of the student when delivering information.

12. Use pictures of similar words (e.g., if the student has trouble differentiating /ch/ and /sh/ sounds, use pictures of /ch/ and /sh/ words such as "chips" and "ship") in order to help the student recognize the difference.

13. Play a game in which the student tries to imitate the sounds made by the teacher or other students (e.g., *Simon Says*).

14. Give the student simple words and ask him/her to rhyme them orally with as many other words as possible.

15. Have the student keep a notebook with pictures of words that rhyme.

16. Use fill-in-the-blank sentences and have the student pick the correct word from a group of similar words (e.g., I _____ (wonder, wander) what's in the box.).

17. Have the student make up poems and tongue twisters using /ch/ and /sh/ sounds, similar vowel sounds, similar consonant sounds, and rhyming words.

18. Present pairs of words and have the student tell if the words rhyme.

19. Explain and demonstrate how similar sounds are made (e.g., where the tongue is placed, how the mouth is shaped, etc.).

20. Encourage the student to watch the lips of the person speaking to him/her.

21. Have the student listen to a series of directions and act out the ones that make sense (e.g., bake your head, rake your bread, shake your head).

22. Identify the speech sounds the student has difficulty differentiating. Spend time each day having the student listen to what is said and have him/her use the words.

23. Make certain the student is attending to the source of information (e.g., eye contact is being made, hands are free of +materials, the student is looking at the assignment, etc.).

24. Teach the student listening skills (e.g., stop working, look at the person delivering questions and directions, have necessary note-taking materials, etc.).

1. Make certain the student's hearing has been checked recently.

2. Seat the student close to the source of directions, explanations, and instructions.

3. Make certain the student is attending (e.g., making eye contact, hands free of writing materials, etc.) before delivering directions, explanations, and instructions.

4. Make certain that competing sounds (e.g., talking, movement, noises, etc.) are silenced when directions are being given, public address announcements are being made, etc.

5. Deliver a predetermined signal (e.g., hand signal, turning off and on lights, etc.) prior to bells ringing, announcements being made, etc.

6. Stand directly in front of the student when delivering directions, explanations, and instructions.

7. Call the student by name prior to bells ringing, announcements being made, directions being given, etc.

8. Have a peer provide the information the student does not hear.

9. Provide the student with public announcements, directions, and instructions in written form.

10. Maintain visibility to and from the student at all times to ensure he/she is attending.

11. Reduce distracting stimuli in the immediate environment (e.g., place the student on the front row, provide the student with a carrel or "office" space away from distractions, etc.). This is used as a form of reducing distracting stimuli and not as a form of punishment.

12. Have the student verbally repeat or paraphrase information heard.

13. Teach the student listening skills (e.g., listen carefully, write down important points, ask for clarification, wait until all directions are received before beginning).

14. Have the student engage in practice activities designed to develop his/her listening skills (e.g., following one-, two-, or three-step directions; listening for the main point; etc.).

15. Give directions in a variety of ways in order to enhance the student's ability to attend.

16. Stop at various points when delivering directions, public announcements, etc., in order to ensure that the student is attending.

17. Deliver directions to the student individually.

18. Demonstrate directions, explanations, and instructions as they are presented orally (e.g., use the chalkboard to work a problem for the student, begin playing a game with the student, etc.).

19. Use pictures, diagrams, and gestures when delivering information.

20. Deliver information slowly to the student.

21. Present one concept at a time. Make certain the student understands each concept before presenting the next.

22. Rephrase directions, explanations, and instructions in order to increase the likelihood of the student understanding what is being presented.

23. Present directions, explanations, and instructions as simply and clearly as possible (e.g., "Get your book. Turn to page 29. Do problems 1 through 5.").

24. When delivering directions, explanations, and instructions be certain to use vocabulary that is within the student's level of comprehension.

25. Have the student practice listening skills by taking notes when directions, explanations, and instructions are presented.

26. Play games designed to teach listening skills (e.g., *Simon Says, Red Light-Green Light, Mother May I?,* etc.).

27. Have the student practice group listening skills (e.g., "Everyone take out a piece of paper. Write your name on the paper. Number your paper from 1 to 20.").

28. Teach the student when to ask questions, how to ask questions, and what types of questions obtain what types of information.

29. Have the student silently repeat information just heard to help him/her remember the important facts.

30. Use multiple modalities (e.g., auditory, visual, tactile, etc.) when presenting directions, explanations, and instructional content. Determine which modality is stronger and utilize the results.

31. Teach the student direction-following skills (e.g., stop doing other things, listen carefully, write down important points, wait until all directions are given, question any directions not understood, etc.).

32. Interact frequently with the student. Make certain that eye contact is being made in order to ensure the student is attending.

33. Have the student tape record directions, explanations, and instructions in order that he/she may apply information as often as needed.

34. Identify the student's most efficient learning mode and use it consistently to increase the probability of understanding (e.g., if the student fails to understand directions or information presented verbally, present it in written form).

35. Have the student question any directions, explanations, and instructions he/she does not understand.

36. Identify a peer to act as a model for the student to imitate appropriate listening skills.

37. Evaluate the level of difficulty of information to which the student is expected to listen (e.g., information communicated on the student's ability level).

38. Write a contract with the student specifying what behavior is expected (e.g., listening to directions, explanations, and instructions) and what reinforcement will be made available when the terms of the contract have been met.

39. Reinforce those students in the classroom who listen to directions, explanations, and instructions.

40. Speak to the student to explain: (a) what he/she is doing wrong (e.g., not listening to directions, explanations, and instructions) and (b) what he/she should be doing (e.g., listening to directions, explanations, and instructions).

41. Reinforce the student for listening: (a) give the student a tangible reward (e.g., classroom privileges, line leading, passing out materials, five minutes free time, etc.) or (b) give the student an intangible reward (e.g., praise, handshake, smile, etc.).

27 Attends more successfully when close to the source of sound

1. Make certain the student's hearing has been checked recently.

2. Maintain mobility in order to provide assistance to the student, be frequently near the student, etc.

3. Maintain consistency in the manner in which oral questions and directions are given.

4. Deliver oral questions and directions that involve only one step. Gradually increase the number of concepts or steps as the student demonstrates success.

5. Stand close to or directly in front of the student when delivering oral questions and directions.

6. Teach the student listening skills (e.g., stop working, look at the person delivering questions and directions, have necessary note-taking materials, etc.).

7. Tell the student that oral questions and directions will only be given once.

8. Give a signal to the student before delivering directions, explanations, or instructions (e.g., clap hands, turn lights off and on, etc.)

9. Have the student repeat or paraphrase the directions orally to the teacher.

10. Teach the student direction-following skills (e.g., listen carefully, write down important points, etc.).

11. Interact frequently with the student in order to help him/her follow directions for an activity.

12. Make certain the student is attending before delivering directions, explanations, or instructions (e.g., maintaining eye contact, hands free of writing materials, looking at the assignment, etc.).

13. Establish assignment rules (e.g., listen carefully, wait until all oral directions have been given, ask questions about anything you do not understand, begin the assignment only when you are certain about what you are to do, make certain you have all necessary materials, etc.).

14. Maintain visibility to and from the student when delivering directions, explanations, or instructions (i.e., the teacher should be able to see the student and the student should be able to see the teacher, making eye contact possible at all times) in order to make certain the student is attending.

15. Call the student by name prior to delivering directions, explanations, or instructions.

16. Seat the student close to the source of information in the classroom. Gradually move the student away from the source of information as he/she demonstrates success.

17. Make certain that directions, explanations, or instructions are delivered loudly enough to be heard by the student.

18. Move the student away from other students who may interfere with his/her ability to attend to directions, explanations, or instructions.

19. Stop at key points when delivering directions, explanations, or instructions in order to determine student comprehension.

20. Present directions, explanations, or instructions as simply and clearly as possible (e.g., "Get your book. Turn to page 29. Do problems 1 through 5.").

21. Stop at various points during the presentation of information to check the student's comprehension.

22. Make certain that the student has adequate opportunities for repetition of information through different experiences.

23. Teach the student listening skills (e.g., stop working, look at the person delivering questions and directions, have necessary note-taking materials, etc.).

24. Identify the student's most efficient learning mode and use it consistently to increase the probability of understanding (e.g., if the student fails to understand information presented verbally, present it in written form).

25. Make certain that all directions, questions, explanations, and instructions are delivered in the most clear and concise manner, at an appropriate pace, and loudly enough for the student to hear.

26. Maintain mobility in order to provide assistance to the student, be frequently near the student, etc.

27. Have the student take notes relative to oral questions and directions.

28. Present oral questions and directions in a clear and concise manner.

29. Reduce distracting stimuli (e.g., make certain the classroom is quiet, reduce movement in the classroom, etc.).

30. Identify a peer to act as a model for the student to imitate responding to information from any location in the classroom.

31. Write a contract with the student specifying what behavior is expected (e.g., attending to information from any location in the classroom) and what reinforcement will be made available when the terms of the contract have been met.

32. Reinforce the student for attending to information presented from any location in the classroom: (a) give the student a tangible reward (e.g., classroom privileges, line leading, passing out materials, five minutes free time, etc.) or (b) give the student an intangible reward (e.g., praise, handshake, smile, etc.).

1. Make certain the student's hearing has been checked recently.

2. Remove the distracting stimuli in the student's immediate environment (e.g., books, writing materials, personal property, etc.).

3. Reduce visual and auditory stimuli in and around the classroom which interfere with the student's ability to listen successfully (e.g., close the classroom door and windows, draw the shades, etc.).

4. Deliver information to the student on a one-to-one basis. Gradually include more students in the group with the student as he/she demonstrates the ability to listen successfully.

5. Maintain eye contact when delivering information to the student. Gradually decrease the amount of eye contact as the student demonstrates the ability to listen successfully.

6. Reinforce the student for attending to the source of information. Continuous eye contact is not necessary for reinforcement.

7. Deliver information in a clear and concise manner.

8. Deliver information in both verbal and written form.

9. Evaluate the level of information presented to the student to determine if the information is presented at a level the student can understand.

10. Maintain visibility to and from the student at all times in order to ensure that the student is attending.

11. Make certain information is delivered loudly enough to be heard by the student.

12. Seat the student close to the source of information in the classroom. Gradually move the student away from the source of information as the student demonstrates success.

13. Make certain the student is not engaged in activities that interfere with directions, explanations, and instructions (e.g., looking at other materials, putting away materials, talking to others, etc.).

14. Require the student to repeat or paraphrase information heard in order to determine successful listening.

15. Teach the student listening skills (e.g., have hands free of writing materials, clear desk of non-essential materials, attend to the source of information, etc.) in order to enhance his/her ability to listen successfully.

16. Deliver a predetermined signal to the student (e.g., hand signal, turn lights off and on, etc.) prior to delivering information.

17. Verbally present information that is necessary for the student to have in order to perform successfully.

18. Have the student take notes when information is verbally presented.

19. Maintain consistency in the format in which information is verbally presented.

20. Call the student by name prior to delivering information.

21. Allow natural consequences to occur as a result of the student's failure to listen (e.g., the inability to respond correctly, a failing grade, etc.).

22. Make certain that the student is seated close enough to see and hear the teacher when information is being delivered.

23. Use multiple modalities (e.g., auditory, visual, tactile, etc.) when presenting directions, explanations, and instructional content. Determine which modality is stronger and utilize the results.

24. Make the subject matter meaningful to the student (e.g., explain the purpose of an assignment, relate the subject matter to the student's environment, etc.).

25. Stop at various points during the presentation of information to check the student's comprehension.

26. Tell the student what to listen for when given directions, receiving information, etc.

27. Have the student question any directions, explanations, or instructions he/she does not understand.

28. Write a contract with the student specifying what behavior is expected (e.g., listening to directions, explanations, and instructions) and what reinforcement will be made available when the terms of the contract have been met.

29. Reinforce the student for listening based on the length of time the student can be successful. Gradually increase the length of time required for reinforcement as the student demonstrates success.

30. Reinforce those students in the classroom who listen to directions, explanations, and instructions.

31. Speak to the student to explain: (a) what the student is doing wrong (e.g., failing to listen to directions, explanations, and instructions) and (b) what the student should be doing (e.g., listening to directions, explanations, and instructions).

32. Reinforce the student for listening: (a) give the student a tangible reward (e.g., classroom privileges, line leading, passing out materials, five minutes free time, etc.) or (b) give the student an intangible reward (e.g., praise, handshake, smile, etc.).

29 Does not listen to what other students are saying

1. Make certain the student's hearing has been checked recently.

2. Reinforce the student for listening to what is said to him/her by other students (e.g., making eye contact, putting aside materials, answering the students, etc.): (a) give the student a tangible reward (e.g., classroom privileges, line leading, passing out materials, five minutes free time, etc.) or (b) give the student an intangible reward (e.g., praise, handshake, smile, etc.).

3. Reinforce the students in the classroom who listen to what other students are saying.

4. Speak to the student to explain: (a) what the student is doing wrong (e.g., failing to listen to what other students are saying), and (b) what the student should be doing (e.g., listening to other students when they speak to him/her, listening to other students when they speak to a group, etc.).

5. Reinforce the student for listening to what other students are saying based on the length of time the student can be successful. Gradually increase the number of times or length of time the student is required to listen as he/she demonstrates success.

6. Have the student repeat or paraphrase what other students are saying in order to determine what was heard.

7. Make certain the student is attending to what other students are saying (e.g., making eye contact, stopping other activities, responding appropriately, etc.).

8. Make certain that other students speak clearly and concisely when speaking to the student.

9. Make certain the student is near the students who are speaking.

10. Make certain that competing sounds (e.g., talking, noises, motion in the classroom, etc.) are silenced when other students are talking, in order to enhance the student's ability to listen to what others are saying.

11. Reduce the emphasis on competition in the classroom. Competition may cause the student to be excited or distracted and fail to listen to what other students are saying.

12. Have other students stand directly in front of the student when speaking to him/her in order for the student to be more likely to listen to what others are saying.

13. Have other students call the student by name before speaking to him/her.

14. Teach the student listening skills (e.g., listen carefully, write down important points, ask for clarification, wait until all directions are received before beginning).

15. Have the student practice listening to what other students are saying (e.g., following simple instructions, sharing information, etc.).

16. Have the student silently repeat information just heard from other students in order to help in remembering important information.

17. Teach the student to respect others and what they are saying by respecting the student and what he/she says.

18. Do not force the student to interact with someone when he/she is not completely comfortable.

19. Treat the student with respect. Talk in an objective manner at all times.

20. Encourage the student to interact with others.

21. Provide the student with frequent opportunities to meet new people.

1. Make certain the student's hearing has recently been checked.

2. Be sure that the student can hear the difference between the target sound as it should be made and the way it sounds when incorrectly produced.

3. Have the student raise a hand or clap hands when he/she hears the target sound produced during a series of isolated sound productions (e.g., *ssss, shshsh, rrrr, mmmm, rrrr, t, k, rrrr, zzzz, w, nnnn, rrrr,* etc.).

4. Use a puppet to produce the target sound correctly and incorrectly. The student earns a sticker for correctly distinguishing a set number of correct/incorrect productions the puppet makes.

5. Have the student stand up each time he/she hears the target sound produced accurately as contrasted with inaccurate productions (e.g., *ssss, ththth, ssss, ssss, ththth,* etc.).

6. Have the student show "thumbs up" each time the target sound is produced accurately when pictures are labeled and "thumbs down" if the target sound is produced inaccurately.

7. Use pictures of similar-sounding words (e.g., if the student says /sh/ for /ch/, use pictures of /sh/ and /ch/ words such as "ships" and "chips"). As the teacher says the words, the student points to the appropriate picture, then the student takes a turn saying the words as the teacher points.

8. Have the student tally the number of correct productions of the targeted sound when the teacher or a peer reads a list of words.

9. Tape record a spontaneous monologue given by the student, and then have him/her listen and tally error and/or correct productions. The teacher should also listen to the tape recording, and the teacher and the student should compare their analyses of the productions.

10. Have the student read simple passages and tape record them. Then have the student listen and mark error and/or correct productions.

11. Have the student read a list of words and rate his/her production after each word.

12. Play a game such as *Simon Says* in which the student tries to imitate correct productions of targeted words.

13. Use a schematic drawing as a visual aid to show the student how the mouth looks during production of the target sound.

14. Make cards with the target sound and cards with vowels. Have the student combine a target sound card with a vowel card to make a syllable that he/she can produce (e.g., *ra, re, ro,* and *ar, er, or*).

15. Use a board game that requires the student to label pictures containing the target sound. The student needs to produce the target sound correctly before he/she can move on the game board. (This activity can be simplified or expanded based on the level of expertise of the student.)

16. Have the student cut out pictures of items depicting words containing the target sound. Display them where they can be practiced each day.

17. Provide the student with a list of words containing the target sound. Have the student practice the words daily. As the student masters the word list, add more words. (Using words from the student's everyday vocabulary, reading lists, spelling lists, etc., will facilitate transfer of correct production of the target sound into everyday speech.)

18. Have the student use phonics "fun" sheets to practice his/her sound orally. These are good for home practice also.

19. Have the student keep a list of all words he/she can think of which contain sounds he/she has difficulty producing accurately.

20. Have the student keep a notebook of difficult words encountered each day. These can be practiced by the student with teacher or peer assistance.

21. Have the student use a carrier phrase combined with a word containing the target sound (e.g., "I like ___." "I see a ___.").

22. Have the student make up sentences using words containing the target sound.

23. During oral reading, underline words containing the target sound and reinforce the student for correct productions.

24. Involve parents by asking them to rate their child's speech for a specific length of time (e.g., during dinner count "no errors," "a few errors," or "many errors").

25. Present a list of topics from which the student may select, and then have the student give a spontaneous speech for a specific length of time. Count errors and suggest ways to improve.

26. Provide the student with verbal reminders or prompts when he/she requires help imitating speech sounds.

27. Make certain the student is attending to the source of information (e.g., eye contact is being made, hands are free of materials, etc.).

28. Tell the student what to listen for when requiring him/her to imitate speech sounds.

29. Reinforce the student for correct productions of the target sound: (a) give the student a tangible reward (e.g., classroom privileges, line leading, passing out materials, five minutes free time, etc.) or (b) give the student an intangible reward (e.g., praise, handshake, smile, etc.).

30. Speak to the student to explain what he/she needs to do differently (e.g., make the sound like you do). The teacher should be careful to use the sound that is being targeted and not the letter name (e.g., *ssss* not *es*).

31. Evaluate the appropriateness of requiring the student to accurately produce certain sounds (e.g., developmentally, certain sounds may not be produced accurately until the age of 8 or 9).

31 Omits, adds, substitutes, or rearranges sounds or words when speaking

1. Make certain the student's hearing has recently been checked.

2. Be sure that the student can hear the difference between the sound as it should be made (target sound) and the way he/she is producing it incorrectly (error sound).

3. Be sure that the student can hear the difference between words as they should be made and the way the words sound when incorrectly produced (e.g., sounds inserted or omitted).

4. Have the student raise a hand or clap hands when he/she hears the target sound produced during a series of isolated sound productions (e.g., *ssss, shshsh, rrrr, mmmm, rrrr, t, k, rrrr, zzzz, w, nnnn, rrrr,* etc.).

5. Use a puppet to produce the target and error sounds. The student earns a sticker for correctly distinguishing a set number of correct/incorrect productions which the puppet makes.

6. Use a puppet to produce targeted words correctly and incorrectly. The student earns a sticker for correctly distinguishing a set number of correct/incorrect productions the puppet makes.

7. Have the student stand up each time he/she hears the target sound produced accurately in contrast to the error sound (e.g., *w, rrr, rrr, w, w, w, rrr, rrr,* etc.).

8. Have the student stand up each time he/she hears targeted words produced accurately when contrasted with inaccurate productions (e.g., *play, pay, pay, play,* etc.).

9. Have the student show "thumbs up" each time the target sound is produced accurately when a picture is labeled and "thumbs down" if the target sound is produced inaccurately.

10. Using pictures of similar-sounding words, say each word and have the student point to the appropriate picture (e.g., *run* and *one,* or *bat* and *back,* etc.).

11. Have the student tally the number of correct productions of the target sound when the teacher or a peer reads a list of words.

12. Have the student read simple passages and tape record them. Then have him/her listen and mark error and/or correct productions.

13. Tape record a spontaneous monologue given by the student, then have him/her listen and tally error and/or correct productions. The teacher should also listen to the tape recording, and the teacher and the student should compare their analyses of the productions.

14. Have the student read a list of words and rate his/her production of the target sound or words after each.

15. Identify a peer who correctly produces the target sound or word to act as a model for the student.

16. Play a game such as *Simon Says* in which the student tries to imitate the target sound or words when produced by the teacher or peers.

17. Use a schematic drawing as a visual aid to show the student how the mouth looks during production of the target sound.

18. Make cards with the target sound and cards with vowels. Have the student combine a target sound card with a vowel card to make a syllable that he/she can produce (e.g., *ra, re, ro,* and *ar, er, or*).

19. Use a board game that requires the student to label pictures containing the target sound or words. The student needs to produce the target sound or words correctly before he/she can move on the game board. (This activity can be simplified or expanded based on the level of expertise of the student.)

20. Have the student cut out pictures of items containing the target sound or words and display them where they can be practiced each day.

21. Provide the student with a list of words containing the target sound. (The student will probably be able to produce the target sound more easily at the beginning or end or a word than in the middle.) Have the student practice the words daily. As the student masters the word list, add more words. (Using words from the student's everyday vocabulary, reading lists, spelling lists, etc., will facilitate transfer of correct production of the target sound into everyday speech.)

22. Provide the student with a list of the targeted words. Have the student practice the words daily. As the student masters the word list, add more words. (Using words from the student's everyday vocabulary, reading lists, spelling lists, etc., will facilitate transfer of correct production of the target sound into everyday speech.)

23. Have the student use phonics "fun" sheets to practice his/her sound orally. These are good for home practice also.

24. Have the student keep a notebook of difficult words encountered each day. These can be practiced by the student with teacher or peer assistance.

25. Have the student use a carrier phrase combined with the target word or a word containing the target sound (e.g., "I like _____." "I see _____.").

26. Have the student keep a list of all the words he/she can think of which contain sounds that are difficult to produce accurately.

27. Have the student make up sentences using the target sound or words.

28. During oral reading, underline targeted sounds or words and reinforce the student for correct production.

29. Involve parents by asking them to rate their child's speech for a specific length of time (e.g., during dinner count "no errors," "a few errors," or "many errors").

30. Present a list of topics from which the student may select, and then have the student give a spontaneous speech for a specific length of time. Count errors and suggest ways to improve.

31. Reinforce the student for correct productions of the target sound: (a) give the student a tangible reward (e.g., classroom privileges, line leading, passing out materials, five minutes free time, etc.) or (b) give the student an intangible reward (e.g., praise, handshake, smile, etc.). Initially, each correct production may need reinforcement. As the student progresses, more random reinforcement may be adequate.

32. Speak to the student to explain what he/she needs to do differently (e.g., use the /r/ sound instead of the /w/ sound). The teacher should be careful to use the sound that is being targeted and not the letter name (e.g., *rrrr* not *ar*).

33. Evaluate the appropriateness of requiring the student to accurately produce certain sounds (e.g., developmentally, certain sounds may not be produced accurately until the age of 8 or 9).

32 Distorts or mispronounces words or sounds when speaking (not attributed to dialect or accent)

1. Make certain the student's hearing has recently been checked.

2. Be sure that the student can hear the difference between words as they should be made and the way the words sound when incorrectly produced (sounds distorted).

3. Have the student raise a hand or clap hands when he/she hears the target sound produced during a series of isolated sound productions (e.g., *ssss, shshsh, rrrr, mmmm, rrrr, t, k, rrrr, zzz, w, nnnn, rrrr*, etc.).

4. Use a puppet to produce targeted words correctly and incorrectly. The student earns a sticker for correctly distinguishing a set number of correct/incorrect productions the puppet makes.

5. Have the student stand up each time he/she hears targeted words produced accurately as contrasted with inaccurate productions (e.g., *shoup, soup, soup, shoup, soup*, etc.).

6. Have the student show "thumbs up" each time targeted words are produced accurately when pictures are labeled and "thumbs down" if targeted words are produced inaccurately.

7. Using pictures of similar-sounding words, say each word and have the student point to the appropriate picture (e.g., *run* and *one,* or *bat* and *back*, etc.).

8. Have the student tally the number of correct productions of targeted words when the teacher or a peer reads a list of words.

9. Have the student read simple passages and tape record them. Then have the student listen and mark error and/or correct productions.

10. Have the student read a list of words and rate his/her production after each word.

11. Identify a peer who correctly produces targeted words to act as a model for the student.

12. Tape record a spontaneous monologue given by the student, then have him/her listen and tally error and/or correct productions. The teacher should also listen to the tape recording, and the teacher and the student should compare their analyses of the productions.

13. Play a game such as *Simon Says* in which the student tries to imitate the targeted words when produced by the teacher or peers.

14. Using pictures of similar sounding words, have the student say each word as the teacher points to a picture (e.g., *run* and *one*, or *bat* and *back*, etc.).

15. Use a schematic drawing as a visual aid to show the student how the mouth looks during production of the target sound or words.

16. Make cards with the target sound and cards with vowels. Have the student combine a target sound card with a vowel card to make a syllable that he/she can produce (e.g., *ra, re, ro,* and *ar, er, or*).

17. Use a board game that requires the student to label pictures of the targeted words. The student needs to produce the targeted words correctly before he/she can move on the game board. (This activity can be simplified or expanded based on the level of expertise of the student.)

18. Have the student cut out pictures of items depicting the targeted words and display them where they can be practiced each day.

19. Provide the student with a list of the targeted words. Have the student practice the words daily. As the student masters the word list, add more words. (Using words from the student's everyday vocabulary, reading lists, spelling lists, etc., will facilitate transfer of correct production of the target sound into everyday speech.)

20. Have the student make up sentences using targeted words.

21. Have the student use phonics "fun" sheets to practice his/her sound orally. These are good for home practice also.

22. Have the student keep a notebook of difficult words encountered each day. These can be practiced by the student with teacher or peer assistance.

23. Have the student use a carrier phrase combined with a word containing the target sound (e.g., "I like ___." "I see a ___.").

24. Have the student keep a list of all the words he/she can think of which contain sounds that are difficult to produce accurately.

25. During oral reading, underline targeted words and reinforce the student for correct productions.

26. Involve parents by asking them to rate their child's speech for a specific length of time (e.g., during dinner count "no errors," "a few errors," or "many errors").

27. Present a list of topics from which the student may select, and then have the student give a spontaneous speech for a specific length of time. Count errors and suggest ways to improve.

28. Reinforce the student for correct production of the target sound or word: (a) give the student a tangible reward (e.g., classroom privileges, line leading, passing out materials, five minutes free time, etc.) or (b) give the student an intangible reward (e.g., praise, handshake, smile, etc.).

29. Speak to the student to explain what he/she needs to do differently (e.g., make sounds more precisely). The teacher should be careful to use the sound that is being targeted and not the letter name (e.g., *ssss* not *es*).

30. Evaluate the appropriateness of requiring the student to accurately produce certain sounds (e.g., developmentally, certain sounds may not be produced accurately until the age of 8 or 9).

33 Fails to use correct subject-verb agreement when speaking

1. Make certain the student's hearing has recently been checked.

2. Speak to the student to explain that he/she is using inappropriate subject-verb agreement and emphasize the importance of speaking in grammatically correct sentences.

3. Ascertain the type of grammatical model to which the student is exposed at home. Without placing negative connotations on his/her parent's grammatical style, explain the difference between standard and nonstandard grammar.

4. Evaluate the appropriateness of requiring the student to speak with subject-verb agreement (e.g., developmentally, a child may not utilize appropriate subject-verb agreement until the age of 6 or 7).

5. Determine if the student's errors are the result of dialectical differences (the pattern of subject-verb agreement may not be atypical within his/her social group).

6. Reinforce the student for appropriate subject-verb agreement: (a) give the student a tangible reward (e.g., classroom privileges, line leading, passing out materials, five minutes free time, etc.) or (b) give the student an intangible reward (e.g., praise, handshake, smile, etc.).

7. Increase the student's awareness of the problem by tape recording the student when speaking with another student who exhibits appropriate subject-verb agreement. Play back the tape for the student to analyze and see if he/she can identify correct/incorrect subject-verb forms.

8. Make sure the student understands the concept of "subject" and "verb" by demonstrating through the use of objects, pictures, and/or written sentences (depending on the student's abilities).

9. Identify a peer who uses appropriate subject-verb agreement to act as a model for the student.

10. Make sure the student understands that sentences express thoughts about a subject and what that subject is or does.

11. Make sure the student understands the concept of plurality (e.g., have the student "point to a picture of a cat" and "point to a picture of cats").

12. Explain that certain forms of verbs go with certain subjects and that correct subject-verb agreement requires the appropriate match of subject and verb. Be certain that the student knows the various possibilities of subject-verb agreement and how to select the correct one.

13. Provide the student with correct examples of subject-verb agreement for those combinations he/she most commonly uses incorrectly.

14. Use a private signal (e.g., touching earlobe, raising index finger, etc.) to remind the student to use correct subject-verb agreement.

15. Make a list of those verbs the student most commonly uses incorrectly. This list will become the guide for learning activities in subject-verb agreement.

16. Routinely tape record the student's speech and point out errors in subject-verb agreement. With each successive taping, reinforce the student as his/her use of grammar improves.

17. After tape recording the student's speech, have him/her identify the errors involving subject-verb agreement and make appropriate corrections.

18. Have the student complete written worksheets in which he/she must choose the correct verb forms to go with specific subjects (e.g., "I _____ (saw, seen) a new car.").

19. Have the student complete written worksheets in which he/she must choose the correct subject forms to go with specific verbs (e.g., "(I, She) ___ eats.").

20. During the day, write down specific subject-verb errors produced by the student. Read the sentences to the student and have him/her make appropriate corrections orally.

21. Write down specific subject-verb errors made by the student during the day. Give the written sentences to the student and have him/her make appropriate corrections. (At first, mark the errors for the student to correct. As the student becomes more proficient with this task, have him/her find and correct the errors independently.)

22. Have the student verbally construct sentences with specific verb forms and subjects.

23. When speaking privately with the student, restate his/her subject-verb error with a rising inflection (e.g., "He <u>done</u> it?") to see if the student recognizes errors and spontaneously makes appropriate corrections.

24. Give the student a series of sentences, both written and oral, and have him/her identify which are grammatically correct and incorrect.

25. Ask the parents to help encourage the student's correct use of grammar at home by praising him/her when correct subject-verb agreement is used.

26. Have the student identify a verb as a goal to master using correctly. As the student masters the correct use of the verb, he/she puts it on a list with a star and identifies another verb to master.

1. Make certain the student's hearing has recently been checked.

2. Have the student divide cards that label objects, persons, places, etc., in the environment into different categories (e.g., function, color, size, use, composition, etc.). Point out the similarities and differences between items as they change categories (e.g., a ball and an apple may be red, round, and smooth; but you can only eat the apple, etc.).

3. Explain to the student how to classify new words as to category, function, antonym, and synonym, etc., so the student will have a way of "filing" the words to memory.

4. In addition to labeling objects, persons, places, etc., have the student provide verbs that could be used with each (e.g., "book" - read, browse through, skim, etc.).

5. In addition to identifying objects, persons, actions, etc., have the student provide places where each could be seen (e.g., "actor" - TV, theater, stage, etc.).

6. In addition to labeling objects, have the student state the uses of each (e.g., "knife" - cut, spread, slice, etc.).

7. Use "hands-on" activities to teach vocabulary by constructing objects and/or organizing manipulatives.

8. Have the student provide as many adjectives as possible to go with a given noun. Then have the student choose one of the adjectives and produce as many nouns as possible to go with it.

9. Have the student provide as many adverbs as possible to go with a given verb. Then have the student choose one of the adverbs and produce as many verbs as possible to go with it.

10. Have the student list all the vocabulary he/she can think of that goes with a specific word (e.g., "space" - astronaut, lunar rover, rocket, shuttle, launch, etc.).

11. Give the student a picture of a specific location (e.g., grocery store) and have the student name as many objects, actions, persons, etc., as he/she can think of that can be found there.

12. Reinforce those students in the classroom who use an expanded speaking vocabulary.

13. Identify a peer who demonstrates comprehension and use of an expanded vocabulary to work with the student to improve comprehension of vocabulary and act as a model to expand the student's speaking vocabulary.

14. Teach the student to use context clues and known vocabulary to determine the meaning of unknown vocabulary.

15. Explain to the student how to use context clues to determine the meanings of words he/she hears or sees (e.g., listening to or looking at the surrounding words and determining what type of word would be appropriate).

16. Explain to the student where he/she can go to find word meanings in the classroom library (e.g., dictionary, thesaurus, encyclopedia, etc.).

17. Have the student maintain a vocabulary notebook with definitions of words whose meanings he/she does not know.

18. Prepare a list of new words which the student will encounter while reading a given assignment. Help the student (or have a peer help the student) look up each word and practice saying it and using it in a sentence before reading the given assignment.

19. Select relevant and appropriate reading material and have the student underline each unfamiliar word. Make a list of these words and review their meanings with the student until he/she can use them when speaking.

20. Use a multisensory approach to enhance retention when teaching new vocabulary (e.g., the scent of fragrant flowers or freshly baked spice cake will enhance retention of the vocabulary word *aroma*).

21. Use visual aids whenever possible when introducing new vocabulary.

22. Use a large purse, box, bag, etc., with objects inside. Have the student reach into the container and try to determine what each item is based on the way it feels before he/she is allowed to see it.

23. Take advantage of unusual or unique situations to teach new vocabulary. Typically, a student will retain information learned in a novel situation better than information learned during a regular routine. The uniqueness of the situation will also enhance the student's memory skills when you provide a reminder to help the student recall the vocabulary (e.g., "Remember yesterday during the fire drill when we talked about ___.").

24. Make up or use games to teach comprehension and expression of new vocabulary. (Research has shown that novel situations help students to learn new information.)

25. To reinforce new vocabulary, write the new word on an envelope and put pictures inside that do and do not go with it (e.g., "arctic" - polar bears, snow, parrots, palm trees, etc.). Have the student remove the inappropriate vocabulary and explain why it doesn't belong.

26. Have the student paste a picture from a magazine on one side of a piece of paper and list all of the vocabulary that could be associated with it on the other side (including verbs). Have the student dictate or write a story about the picture using the vocabulary.

27. Have the student act out verbs and label actions performed by classmates.

28. Refer to previously presented information that is related to the topic when presenting new vocabulary.

29. Teach new vocabulary within the context of known information (e.g., category, associations, etc.).

30. Have the student demonstrate and identify different verbs of the same class (e.g., walk, creep, slither, saunter, march, etc.).

31. Have the students apply new vocabulary to personal experiences in written and oral work.

32. Include new vocabulary in daily conversation as often as possible.

33. Have the student engage in role-playing to foster use of new vocabulary (e.g., set up an imaginary restaurant and have the student and peers play the various roles of customers, waiter/waitress, cook, etc., varying the time of day and the occasion).

34. Tape record the student's spontaneous speech, noting the specific words used, then have the student make a list of other words (synonyms) which could be substituted for these words.

35. Give the student a list of words and ask him/her to tell the opposite of each word.

36. Have the student make up sentences or stories using new words he/she has learned.

37. Name a category and have the student identify things within the category. Introduce new words which belong in the same group.

38. Give the student a series of words or pictures and have him/her name the category in which they belong (e.g., objects, persons, places, etc.).

39. Describe objects, persons, places, etc., and have the student name the items described.

40. Send home new vocabulary words and encourage parents to use them in activities and general conversation.

41. Discuss with parents the ways in which they can help the student develop an expanded speaking vocabulary (e.g., encouraging the student to read newspapers, novels, magazines, or other materials for enjoyment). Emphasize to parents that they can set a good example by reading with the student.

42. Give the student a "word of the day" which is to be incorporated into conversations. Reinforce the student each time he/she uses the word.

43. During conversation, repeat phrases used by the student, revising the vocabulary to include additional words (e.g., The student says, "The TV show was good." Repeat by saying, "I'm glad the TV show was so entertaining.").

44. Use new words in a sentence completion activity. Have the student explain how the use of different words changes the meaning of the sentence (e.g., I like Jerry because he is ___ [sincere, humorous, competitive]).

45. Point out words that have a variety of meanings and use them appropriately in different contexts.

46. Have the student provide associations for given words (e.g., "circus" - clown, elephant, trapeze, tent, lion tamer, etc.).

47. Review on a daily basis new vocabulary words and their meanings. Have the student use the words daily.

48. Review on a daily basis previously learned vocabulary words and meanings. Have the student incorporate previously learned vocabulary words into daily conversation and activities.

49. Have the student maintain a notebook of all new vocabulary words to refer to during daily conversation and activities.

50. Use pictures to help the student understand the meanings of new vocabulary words.

51. Make certain the student is not expected to learn more vocabulary words and meanings then he/she is capable of comprehending.

52. Make certain the student has mastery of vocabulary words at each level before introducing new words.

53. Provide the student with fewer weekly vocabulary words, and gradually increase the number of vocabulary words from week to week as the student demonstrates success.

54. Reinforce the student for using an expanded speaking vocabulary: (a) give the student a tangible reward (e.g., classroom privileges, line leading, passing out materials, five minutes free time, etc.) or (b) give the student an intangible reward (e.g., praise, handshake, smile, etc.).

55. Ascertain the type of language model the student has at home. Without placing negative connotations on the language model in his/her home, explain the difference between language which is rich in meaning and that which includes a limited repertoire of vocabulary.

56. Explain the importance of expanding one's vocabulary (i.e., comprehension and communication are based on the knowledge and use of appropriate/accurate vocabulary).

1. Make certain the student's hearing has recently been checked.

2. Explain that changes must be made in a verb to indicate when an event happened (e.g., past, present, future).

3. Ascertain the type of grammatical model to which the student is exposed at home. Without placing negative connotations on the parent's grammatical style, explain the difference between standard and nonstandard grammar.

4. Determine if the student's errors are the result of dialectical differences (i.e., the pattern of verb tense usage may not be atypical within his/her social group).

5. Reinforce the student for using verb tenses correctly: (a) give the student a tangible reward (e.g., classroom privileges, line leading, passing out materials, five minutes free time, etc.) or (b) give the student an intangible reward (e.g., praise, handshake, smile, etc.).

6. Reinforce those students in the classroom who use verb tenses correctly.

7. Tape record the student's speech to point out errors in verb tenses. With each successive taping, reinforce the student as his/her use of verb tenses improves.

8. Increase the student's awareness of the problem by tape recording the student while he/she is speaking with another student who uses verb tenses correctly. Play the tape back for the student to see if he/she can identify correct/incorrect verb tensing.

9. Identify a peer who uses verb tenses appropriately to act as a model for the student.

10. Make sure the student understands the concept of verb tenses by demonstrating what "is happening," what "already happened" and what "will happen" through the use of objects, pictures, and/or written sentences (depending on the student's abilities).

11. Determine whether the student understands the concept of time which influences comprehension of verb tensing (e.g., Can he/she answer questions using *yesterday, today, tomorrow, before, later,* etc.? Does he/she use such vocabulary when speaking even though the verb tense is incorrect?).

12. Determine whether the student has appropriate sequencing skills. The concept of sequencing influences comprehension of verb tensing (e.g., Can the student answer questions using *first, next, then,* etc.? Does he/she use such vocabulary when speaking even though verb tenses are incorrect?).

13. Use a private signal (e.g., hand over shoulder/past tense, pointing forward/future tense, etc.) to remind the student to use correct verb tense.

14. Make a list of those verb tenses the student most commonly uses incorrectly. This list will become the guide for identifying the verb tenses which the student should practice each day.

15. After tape recording the student's speech, have him/her identify the errors involving verb tenses and make appropriate corrections.

16. Have the student complete worksheets in which he/she must supply the correct verb tenses to go with the sentences (e.g., "Yesterday I ___ to school.").

17. Have the student make corrections for incorrect verb tenses on written worksheets.

18. During the day, write down specific verb tense errors produced by the student. Read the sentences to the student and have him/her make appropriate corrections orally.

19. Write down specific verb tense errors made by the student during the day. Give the written sentences to the student and have him/her make appropriate corrections. (At first, mark the errors for him/her to correct. As the student becomes more proficient with this task, have him/her find and correct the errors independently.).

20. Have the student make up sentences with given verbs in the past, present, and future tenses.

21. Give the student a sentence and have him/her change it from present to past, past to present, future to past, etc.

22. Copy a simple paragraph which is in the present tense. Highlight the verbs and have the student change all the verbs to past and/or future tense. This activity could be completed orally or in written form.

23. Have the student assist in correcting other students' written work, looking for errors in verb tenses.

24. When speaking privately with the student, restate his/her verb tense error with a rising inflection (e.g., "Yesterday he plays?") to see if the student recognizes errors and spontaneously makes appropriate corrections.

25. Give the student a series of sentences, both written and oral, and have him/her identify the ones which demonstrate appropriate verb tensing. Have him/her make appropriate modifications for those sentences which demonstrate inappropriate verb tensing.

26. Ask the parents to help encourage the student's correct use of verb tenses at home by praising him/her when appropriate verb tenses are used.

27. Have a peer practice verb tenses with the student. Each tense should be used in a sentence rather than only conjugating the verbs.

28. Make the conjugation of verbs a daily activity.

29. Have the student identify a verb as a goal to master using correctly. As the student masters the correct use of the verb, he/she puts it on a list with a star and identifies another verb to master.

30. Videotape the student and his/her classmates performing various actions. Play back the tape with the sound turned off and have the student narrate what is happening in present tense, what happened in past tense, and/or what will happen in future tense. (This activity could be modified by using a prerecorded videotape.)

31. Make headings entitled *yesterday, today,* and *tomorrow* under which the class can list activities they *were doing, are doing,* or *will do*. The following day, change the *today* heading to *yesterday* and the *tomorrow* heading to *today*. Emphasize appropriate verb tenses throughout this activity.

32. Have the student list activities he/she did when younger, activities the student can do now, and things he/she will be able to do when grown up. Emphasize appropriate verb tenses throughout this activity.

33. While the class is engaged in various activities, describe your observations using present tense. Have students do likewise. Expand this activity to include past and future tenses by asking appropriate questions (e.g., "What just happened?" "What were you doing?" "What will you do next?").

36 Speaks dysfluently

1. Make certain the student's hearing has recently been checked.

2. During conversations, calmly delay your verbal responses by one to two seconds.

3. Use a tape recorder so the student may listen to and evaluate his/her own speech.

4. Have the student identify a good speaker and give the reasons that make that person a good speaker.

5. Develop a list of the attributes which are likely to help a person become a good speaker and have the student practice each characteristic.

6. During oral reading, underline or highlight words which are difficult for the student to say and provide reinforcement when he/she says them fluently.

7. Have the student keep a list of times and/or situations in which speech is difficult (e.g., times when he/she is nervous, embarrassed, etc.). Discuss the reasons for this and seek solutions to the difficulty experienced.

8. Have the student practice techniques for relaxing (e.g., deep breathing, tensing and relaxing muscles, etc.) which can be employed when he/she starts to become dysfluent.

9. Have the student identify the specific words or phrases on which he/she becomes dysfluent and practice those particular words or phrases.

10. Encourage the student to maintain eye contact during all speaking situations. If the student is noticeably more fluent when eye contact is averted, attempt to increase eye contact on a gradual basis.

11. Have the student speak in unison with you while you are modeling slow, easy speech.

12. Reinforce the student's moments of relative fluency and emphasize that these occurred during moments when he/she was speaking slowly and easily.

13. Empathize with the student and explain that he/she is not more or less valuable as a person because of speaking dysfluently. Emphasize the student's positive attributes.

14. Empathize with feelings of anger which the student may be experiencing.

15. When the student is speaking fluently, try to extend the positive experience by allowing him/her ample opportunity to continue speaking.

16. Reinforce the student each time he/she answers a question or makes a spontaneous comment in class.

17. If the student is speaking too rapidly, remind him/her to slow down and take time. Develop a private signal (e.g., raising one finger, touching earlobe, etc.) to avoid calling too much attention to the student's speech in front of the whole class.

18. Try to give the student your undivided attention so he/she will not feel a need to hurry or compete with others for attention.

19. If the student is more dysfluent when involved in another activity at the same time he/she is talking, encourage the student to stop the other activity.

20. If the student is highly excited, wait until he/she is calmer before requiring any verbal explanations or interactions. A high level of excitement often precipitates an anxiety level that interferes with fluency.

21. During moments of nonfluency, use nonverbal activities to relax the student.

22. Do not interrupt or finish the student's sentences even if you think you can anticipate what the student is going to say. This can be extremely frustrating and may decrease the student's willingness to engage in future communicative interactions.

23. Help the student learn to identify periods of dysfluency and periods of slow, easy speech.

24. Help the student learn to identify situations in which he/she is more fluent or less fluent. Determine the aspects of the fluent situations that seem to enhance fluency, and try to transfer those features to the less fluent situations.

25. When the student is dysfluent during conversation, explain that this happens to everyone at times.

26. Have the student make a list of his/her strong points or things done well in order to improve the student's overall level of confidence.

27. Point out to the student that he/she is capable of fluent speech and is in control of speech in many situations.

28. Model slow, easy speech for the student and encourage the student to speak at a similar rate. Practice with the student for a short time each day until he/she is able to match the rate.

29. Provide the student with a list of sentences and encourage him/her to read these at a slow rate.

30. Prepare simple oral reading passages in written form in which phrases are separated by large spaces (indicating "pause"). Have the student practice reading the passages aloud.

31. Use a private cue (e.g., raise a finger, touch earlobe, etc.) to encourage the student to answer questions at a slow rate of speech.

32. Use a private cue (e.g., raise a finger, touch earlobe, etc.) to encourage the student to use a slow speaking rate during classroom activities.

33. Reduce the emphasis on competition. Competitive activities may increase the student's anxiety and cause him/her to be more dysfluent.

34. Do not require the student to speak in front of other students if he/she is uncomfortable doing so. Have the student speak to the teacher or another student privately if that would make the student more comfortable.

35. Provide the student with as many social and academic successes as possible.

36. As the student is able to speak fluently in more situations, increase those experiences as long as the student continues to be successful (e.g., delivering messages to the office, speaking with the counselor, etc.).

37. Meet with the student's parents to determine the level of dysfluency at home, parental reactions to the dysfluency, and successful strategies the parents might have employed when dealing with the dysfluent behavior.

38. Determine whether or not the student avoids certain situations because of his/her perception of increased dysfluency. Discuss with the student aspects of those situations that seem to cause increased anxiety. Examine possible modifications that could be implemented in the classroom to increase frustration tolerance (e.g., if speaking in front of the whole class causes stress, reduce the number of listeners and gradually increase the group size as the student's frustration tolerance increases).

39. Identify a peer to act as a model for appropriate speech. Pair the students to sit together, perform assignments together, etc.

40. Provide the student with an appropriate model of slow, easy speech. Lengthen the pauses between words, phrases, and sentences.

41. Evaluate the appropriateness of requiring the student to speak without dysfluency (e.g., developmentally, young children experience normal dysfluency in their speech and all persons are occasionally dysfluent).

42. Familiarize yourself and the student with the terms *fluency, dysfluency, stuttering, easy speech,* etc. Keep these words as neutral as possible, without negative connotations.

43. Reinforce the student for speaking fluently: (a) give the student a tangible reward (e.g., classroom privileges, line leading, passing out materials, five minutes free time, etc.) or (b) give the student an intangible reward (e.g., praise, handshake, smile, etc.).

37 Does not complete statements or express complete thoughts when speaking

1. Make certain the student's hearing has recently been checked.

2. Allow the student to speak without being interrupted or hurried.

3. Reduce the emphasis on competition. Competitive activities may cause the student to hurry and fail to speak in complete sentences.

4. Have the student keep a list of times and/or situations in which he/she is nervous, anxious, etc., and has more trouble than usual with speech. Help the student identify ways to feel more successful in those situations.

5. Make a list of the attributes which are likely to help a person become a good speaker (e.g., takes his/her time, thinks of what to say before starting, etc.).

6. List the qualities a good speaker possesses (e.g., rate, diction, volume, vocabulary, etc.) and have the student evaluate himself/herself on each characteristic. Set a goal for improvement in only one or two areas at a time.

7. Have the student identify a good speaker and give the reasons why that person is a good speaker.

8. Have a peer who speaks in complete sentences act as a model for the student. Assign the students to work together, perform assignments together, etc.

9. When the student has difficulty during a conversation, remind him/her that this occasionally happens to everyone.

10. Increase the student's awareness of the problem by tape recording the student while he/she is speaking with another student who uses complete sentences. Play back the tape for the student to identify incomplete sentences and nondescript terminology. Have the student make appropriate modifications.

11. Demonstrate acceptable and unacceptable speech (incomplete thoughts and nondescript terminology such as "thing," "stuff," etc.) and have the student critique each example while making suggestions for improvement.

12. Make sure the student understands the concept of a "complete" sentence by pointing out the "subject/verb/object" components through the use of objects, pictures, and/or written sentences (depending on the student's abilities).

13. Make certain the student understands that a complete sentence has to express a complete thought about a subject and what that subject is or does, and that the use of specific vs. nondescript vocabulary is important to clarify the message.

14. Teach the concept of verb and noun phrases as soon as possible so the student has a means of checking to see if a sentence is complete.

15. Use a private signal (e.g., touching earlobe, raising index finger, etc.) to remind the student to speak in complete sentences and use specific terminology.

16. Routinely tape record the student's speech and point out incomplete statements and nondescript terminology. With each successive taping, reinforce the student as his/her use of complete sentences and specific vocabulary improves.

17. Give the student a series of complete and incomplete sentences, both written and oral, and ask him/her to identify which are correct and incorrect and make appropriate modifications.

18. Have the student correct a series of phrases by making each a complete sentence.

19. Have the student give process statements to sequence an activity (e.g., how to make a peanut butter and jelly sandwich). Have the student focus on making each statement a complete thought with specific vs. nondescriptive vocabulary.

20. Have the student complete worksheets in which he/she must replace nondescriptive or in-accurate vocabulary with specific and appropriate terminology (e.g., "The thing tastes good." could be changed to "The cake (meal, soda, etc.) tastes good." or "He used the digger to make the hole." could be changed to "He used the shovel (backhoe, spade, etc.) to make the hole.").

21. Give the student a subject and have him/her make up as many complete sentences about it as possible, emphasizing the use of specific vocabulary.

22. Make groups of cards containing subjects, verbs, adjectives, etc. Have the student combine the cards in various ways to construct complete sentences.

23. Give the student several short sentences and have him/her combine them in order to produce one longer sentence (e.g., "The dog is big." "The dog is brown." "The dog is mine." becomes "The big, brown dog is mine.").

24. Give the student a list of transition words (e.g., *therefore, although, because,* etc.) and have him/her make up sentences using each word.

25. Give the student a group of related words (e.g., *baseball, fans, glove, strikeout,* etc.) and have him/her write a paragraph including each word.

26. Provide the student with sentence starters (e.g., Go ___. Run ___. Today I ___. Anyone can ___. etc.) and have him/her make up complete sentences.

27. Provide the student with a topic (e.g., rules to follow when riding your bike) and have him/her make up complete sentences about it.

28. Give the student a factual statement (e.g., Some animals are dangerous.) and have him/her provide several complete sentences relating to that topic.

29. Give the student scrambled words and have him/her put them in the correct order to form a complete sentence.

30. Choose a topic for a paragraph or story and alternate making up sentences with the student in order to provide a model of the components of a complete sentence.

31. Ask the parents to encourage the student's use of complete sentences and thoughts at home by praising him/her when these are used.

32. Have a number of students build a sentence together (e.g., The first one starts with a word such as "I." The next student adds the second word such as "like." This process continues as long as possible to create one long, complete sentence. Do not accept nondescriptive terminology.).

33. Ask questions which stimulate language. Avoid those which can be answered by yes/no or a nod of the head (e.g., "What did you do at recess?" instead of "Did you play on the slide?" or "Tell me about your vacation." instead of "Did you stay home over the holidays?").

34. Make a list of the student's most common incomplete statements and uses of nondescriptive terminology. Spend time with the student practicing how to make these statements or thoughts complete and how to make appropriate replacements for nondescriptive vocabulary.

35. Have the student role-play various situations in which good speech is important (e.g., during a job interview).

36. When speaking privately with the student, restate his/her incomplete sentences and/or non-descriptive vocabulary with a rising inflection to indicate the need for more information (e.g., "You saw the <u>stuff</u> in the sky?" or "Your brown dog . . . ?") to see if the student recognizes the problem and spontaneously makes appropriate corrections.

37. Have the student describe himself/herself and/or classmates in complete sentences with emphasis on specific vocabulary to differentiate one student from another.

38. Call on the student when he/she is most likely to be able to respond successfully.

39. Videotape the student and classmates performing various actions. Play back the tape with the sound turned off and have the student narrate observations in complete sentences with descriptive vocabulary. (This activity could be modified by using a prerecorded videotape.)

40. Using a book without words, have the student tell the story using descriptive vocabulary and complete sentences. Tape record the story and play it back for the student to listen for complete/incomplete sentences and specific/nondescriptive terminology and make appropriate corrections.

41. After a field trip or special event, have the student retell the activities which occurred with an emphasis on using descriptive vocabulary and complete sentences.

42. After reading a short story, have the student recall the main characters, sequence the events, and retell the outcome of the story.

43. Give the student a series of words or pictures and have him/her name as many items as possible within that category (e.g., objects, persons, places, things that are hot, etc.).

44. Give the student specific categories and have him/her name as many items as possible within that category (e.g., things that are cold, objects, persons, places, etc.).

45. Describe objects, persons, places, etc., and have the student name the items described.

46. Help the student employ memory aids in order to recall words (e.g., a name might be linked to another word; for example, "Mr. Green is a very colorful person.").

47. Give the student a series of words describing objects, persons, places, etc., and have him/her identify the opposite of each word.

48. Give the student a series of words (e.g., objects, persons, places, etc.) and have the student list all the words he/she can think of with similar meanings (synonyms).

49. Give the student "fill-in-the-blank" sentences to complete with appropriate words (e.g., objects, persons, places, etc.).

50. Encourage the student to use an appropriate synonym when experiencing difficulty retrieving the "exact" word he/she wants to say.

51. Have the student complete associations (e.g., knife, fork, and ___; men, women, and ___; etc.).

52. Encourage the student to use gestures when necessary to clarify his/her message. Gestures may also facilitate recall of vocabulary the student is having difficulty retrieving.

53. Have the student compete against himself/herself by timing how fast he/she can name a series of pictured objects. Each time, the student tries to increase the speed.

54. Have the student make notes, lists, etc., of vocabulary that may be needed to be recalled and carry these reminders with him/her for reference.

55. When the student is required to recall information, remind him/her of the situation in which the material was originally presented (e.g., "Remember yesterday when we talked about . . ." "Remember when we were outside and I told you about the . . ." etc.).

56. Show the student an object or a picture of an object for a few seconds. Ask the student to recall specific attributes of the object (e.g., color, size, shape, etc.).

57. Teach the student to recognize key words and phrases related to information in order to increase his/her recall.

58. Label objects, persons, places, etc., in the environment in order to help the student be able to recall names.

59. Make certain the student receives information from a variety of sources (e.g., textbooks, presentations, discussions, etc.) in order to enhance memory/recall.

60. Ask the student leading questions to facilitate the process of speaking in complete sentences and using specific vocabulary.

61. Provide the student with the first sound of a word he/she is having difficulty retrieving in order to facilitate recall.

62. Encourage verbal output. Increase the student's opportunities to communicate verbally in order to provide him/her with necessary practice.

63. Focus on completeness of the student's thought and not the grammatical accuracy of the statement. Reinforce complete thoughts that include specific vocabulary.

64. When the student uses incomplete sentences or nondescriptive terminology, provide the student with models of expansion and specific vocabulary using his/her statements as a foundation.

65. When the student is required to recall information, provide visual and/or auditory cues to help him/her remember the information (e.g., provide key words, expose part of a picture, etc.).

66. Provide frequent interactions and encouragement to support the student's confidence (e.g., make statements such as "You're doing great." "Keep up the good work." "I really am proud of you." etc.).

67. Reinforce the students in the classroom who use complete sentences or thoughts when speaking.

68. Reinforce the student for using complete sentences or thoughts when speaking: (a) give the student a tangible reward (e.g., classroom privileges, line leading, passing out materials, five minutes free time, etc.) or (b) give the student an intangible reward (e.g., praise, handshake, smile, etc.).

69. Provide the student with an appropriate model to imitate speaking in complete sentences or thoughts (e.g., speak clearly, slowly, concisely, and in complete sentences, statements, and thoughts).

70. Speak to the student to explain that he/she is using incomplete sentences or thoughts when speaking, and explain the importance of speaking in complete sentences and choosing specific words to express ideas.

38 Has difficulty comprehending what he/she reads

1. Make certain the student's hearing has recently been checked.

2. Make certain the student is reading material on his/her level. If not, modify or adjust reading material to the student's ability level.

3. Reinforce the student for demonstrating comprehension of reading material: (a) give the student a tangible reward (e.g., classroom privileges, line leading, passing out materials, five minutes free time, etc.) or (b) give the student an intangible reward (e.g., praise, handshake, smile, etc.).

4. Reduce distracting stimuli in order to increase the student's ability to concentrate on what he/she is reading (e.g., place the student on the front row, provide a carrel or "office" space away from distractions, etc.). This should be used as a means of reducing distracting stimuli and not as a form of punishment.

5. Teach the student to use context clues to identify the meanings of words and phrases not known.

6. Prerecord the student's reading material and have him/her listen to the recording while simultaneously reading the material.

7. Have the student read ahead on a subject to be discussed in class so that he/she is familiar with new vocabulary and concepts that will be used during instructional periods.

8. Outline reading material for the student using words and phrases on his/her ability level.

9. Arrange for a peer who demonstrates good comprehension skills to read with the student and help him/her with the meanings of words not understood.

10. Maintain mobility in the classroom in order to frequently be near the student to provide reading assistance.

11. Teach the student to draw from personal learning experiences to enhance comprehension of reading material. Provide a variety of learning experiences at school in order to expand the student's background of knowledge.

12. Have the student verbally paraphrase material just read in order to assess his/her comprehension.

13. Teach the student to identify main points in material in order to enhance his/her comprehension.

14. Underline or highlight important points before the student reads the material silently.

15. Have the student outline, underline, or highlight important points in reading material.

16. Have the student take notes while reading in order to increase comprehension.

17. Provide the student with written direction-following activities that target concrete experiences (e.g., following a recipe, following directions to put a model together, etc.) in order to enhance comprehension.

18. Provide the student with written one-, two-, and three-step direction-following activities (e.g., sharpen your pencil, open your text to page 121, etc.).

19. Have the student read progressively longer segments of reading material in order to build comprehension skills (e.g., begin with a single paragraph and progress to several paragraphs, chapters, short stories, etc.).

20. Have the student read high-interest signs, advertisements, notices, etc., from newspapers, magazines, movie promotions, etc., placing an emphasis on comprehension skills.

21. Reduce the emphasis on competition. Competitive activities may make it difficult for the student to comprehend what he/she reads.

22. Use a sight word vocabulary approach in order to teach the student key words and phrases when reading directions and instructions (e.g., key words such as *circle, underline, match,* etc.).

23. Have the student list new or difficult words in categories such as *people, food, animals, things that are hot,* etc.

24. Have the student maintain a vocabulary notebook with definitions of words whose meanings are not known.

25. When the student encounters a new word or one whose meaning is not understood, have the student practice making up sentences in which the word can be used in the correct context.

26. Make certain the student learns dictionary skills in order to find the meanings of words independently.

27. Have the student identify words he/she does not comprehend. Finding the definitions of these words can then become the dictionary assignment.

28. Have the student identify one word each day that is not understood and require him/her to use that word throughout the day in various situations.

29. Have the student match vocabulary words with pictures representing the words.

30. Introduce new words and their meanings to the student before reading new material.

31. Make certain the student learns the meanings of all commonly used prefixes and suffixes.

32. Write notes and letters to the student to provide reading material which he/she will want to read for comprehension. Students may be encouraged to write notes and letters to classmates at a time set aside each day, once a week, etc.

33. Give the student time to read a selection more than once, emphasizing accuracy not speed.

34. Have the student supply missing words in sentences provided by classmates and/or the teacher in order to enhance comprehension skills.

35. Cut out pictures from magazines and newspapers and have the student match captions to them. This activity could be varied by having one student write the caption while another student determines if it is appropriate.

36. Have the student read a short paragraph which contains one or more errors which make comprehension difficult. See if the student recognizes the errors. If not, encourage the student to stop frequently while reading to ask himself/herself, "Does this make sense?"

37. Determine whether or not the student can make inferences, make predictions, determine cause-effect, etc., in everyday experiences. Teach these skills in contexts that are meaningful to the student in order to enhance the ability to employ these concepts when reading.

38. Have the student read a story. Provide statements reflecting the main points of the story out of sequence. Have the student arrange the statements in the correct order to demonstrate comprehension.

39. Have the student prepare "test" questions based on information that has been read in order to enhance the ability to focus on key elements of the reading material.

40. Frequently give assignments on topics which are of interest to the student in order to reinforce the correlation between writing and reading ability.

41. Reduce the amount of material the student reads at one time (e.g., reduce reading material to single sentences on a page, a single paragraph, etc.). Gradually increase the amount of material as the student experiences success.

42. Avoid subjecting the student to uncomfortable reading situations (e.g., reading aloud in a group, reading with time limits, etc.).

43. Stop the student at various points throughout a reading selection to check for comprehension.

44. Reduce the amount of information on a page if it is causing visual distractions for the student (e.g., less print to read, fewer pictures, etc.).

45. Highlight or underline important information the student should pay close attention to when reading.

46. Make it pleasant and positive for the student to ask questions about things not understood.

47. Have the student use a highlighter pen to highlight the facts requested by the teacher.

48. Allow the student to work with a peer and teacher. The first student will dictate a short paragraph to be typed by the teacher and will also compose a comprehension question. The second student, after listening to the process, will read the story orally and point out the answer. Then student roles can be reversed.

49. Find the central word or phrase around which the story is constructed. Check for pin-point words that relate back to the central word/phrase and determine the number of times they are used and how this helps to develop the story.

39 Does not finish assignments because of reading difficulties

1. Make certain that the reading demands of the assignment are within the ability level of the student.

2. Tape record directions, explanations, and instructions in order to enhance the student's success.

3. Have a peer read directions, explanations, and instructions to the student in order to enhance success.

4. Require the student to verbally repeat directions, explanations, and instructions.

5. Read directions, explanations, and instructions to the student when necessary.

6. Use a sight word vocabulary approach in order to teach the student key words and phrases when reading directions and instructions (e.g., key words such as *circle, underline, match,* etc.).

7. Deliver all directions, explanations, and instructions orally.

8. Reduce all directions, explanations, and instructions to a minimum.

9. Shorten the length of assignments that require reading in order that the student can complete assignments in the same length of time as the other students.

10. Provide the student with additional time to complete the assignment.

11. Deliver directions, explanations, and instructions prior to handing out materials.

12. Make certain that the student's knowledge of a particular skill is being assessed rather than the student's ability to read directions, instructions, and content.

13. Maintain mobility in order to provide assistance to the student.

14. Maintain consistency in the manner in which written directions, explanations, and instructions are delivered.

15. Have the student practice timed drills consisting of reading directions, explanations, content, etc., in order to reduce reading time.

16. Plan for the student to have more than enough time to complete an assignment.

17. Assess the quality and clarity of written directions, explanations, instructions, content, etc.

18. Keep written directions as simple and concrete as possible.

19. Reduce distracting stimuli in order to increase the student's ability to follow written directions (e.g., place the student on the front row, provide a carrel or "office" space away from distractions, etc.). This is used as a means of reducing distracting stimuli and not as a form of punishment.

20. Reduce written directions to individual steps and give the student each additional step after completion of the previous step.

21. Make certain the student achieves success when following written directions.

22. Prevent the student from becoming over-stimulated by an activity (e.g., frustrated, angry, etc.).

23. Provide the student with a copy of written directions at his/her desk rather than on the chalkboard, posted in the classroom, etc.

24. Seat the student close to the source of the written information (e.g., chalkboard, projector, etc.).

25. Make certain the print is large enough to increase the likelihood of following written directions.

26. Transfer directions from texts and workbooks when pictures or other stimuli make it difficult to attend to or follow written directions.

27. Provide the student a quiet place (e.g., carrel, study booth, etc.) where he/she may go to engage in activities which require following written directions.

28. Work the first problem(s) with the student to make certain that he/she follows written directions.

29. Have the student carry out written directions one step at a time and check with you to make certain that each step is successfully followed before attempting the next.

30. Gradually increase the degree of difficulty or complexity of written directions, explanations, instructions, content, etc., as the student becomes more successful.

31. Modify or adjust the reading level of material presented to the student in order to enhance success.

32. Reduce the emphasis on competition. Competitive activities make it difficult for the student to finish assignments because of frustration with reading difficulties.

33. Introduce new words and their meanings to the student before he/she reads new materials. These may be entered in a vocabulary notebook kept by the student. If the student keeps a vocabulary book, he/she will have a reference for unknown words.

34. Avoid subjecting the student to uncomfortable reading situations (e.g., reading aloud in a group, identifying the student's reading group as the lowest level, etc.).

35. Tape record difficult reading material for the student to listen to as he/she reads along.

36. Make certain that the student's knowledge of a particular skill is being assessed rather than the student's ability to read directions, instructions, etc.

37. Give the student time to read a selection more than once, emphasizing comprehension rather than speed.

38. Use reading series material with high interest (e.g., adventures, romances, mysteries, athletics, etc.) and low vocabulary.

39. Reduce the amount of material the student reads at one time (e.g., reduce reading material to single sentences on a page, a single paragraph, etc.). Gradually increase the amount of material as the student experiences success.

40. Make the subject matter meaningful to the student (e.g., explain the purpose of an assignment, relate the subject matter to the student's environment, etc.).

41. Give the student one task to perform at a time. Introduce the next task only when the student has successfully completed the previous task.

42. Reduce the amount of information on a page if it is causing visual distractions for the student (e.g., have less print to read, have fewer pictures on the page, isolate information that is presented to the student).

43. Have the student read material orally to the teacher to determine if it is on his/her reading level.

44. Have the student use his/her finger to point to words that are being read. The teacher should observe as the student points to the words while reading. This would help to determine the causes of slow reading.

45. Reduce the student's anxiety level by not requiring the student to finish a reading assignment within a given period of time.

46. Make certain the student understands that work not done during work time must be completed at other times such as free time, recess, after school, etc.

47. Have the student question any directions, explanations, and instructions he/she does not understand.

48. Identify a peer to act as a model for the student to imitate completion of assignments.

49. Evaluate the appropriateness of the task to determine: (a) if the task is too difficult, and (b) if the length of time scheduled to complete the task is appropriate.

50. Communicate with parents (e.g., notes home, phone calls, etc.) in order to share information concerning the student's progress and so that they can reinforce the student at home for finishing assignments at school.

51. Write a contract with the student specifying what behavior is expected (e.g., finishing assignments) and what reinforcement will be made available when the terms of the contract have been met.

52. Reinforce those students in the classroom who finish assignments.

53. Reinforce the student for finishing assignments based on the number of times he/she can be successful. Gradually increase the number of times required for reinforcement as the student demonstrates success.

54. Establish classroom rules:
1. Work on task.
2. Work quietly.
3. Remain in your seat.
4. Finish task.
5. Meet task expectations.
Reiterate rules often and reinforce students for following rules.

55. Speak to the student to explain: (a) what the student is doing wrong (e.g., failing to finish assignments) and (b) what the student should be doing (e.g., finishing assignments).

56. Reinforce the student for finishing assignments: (a) give the student a tangible reward (e.g., classroom privileges, line leading, passing out materials, five minutes free time, etc.) or (b) give the student an intangible reward (e.g., praise, handshake, smile, etc.).

40 Fails to demonstrate word attack skills

1. Get a list of words and phrases which the student does not recognize from his/her reading material. Have the student practice phonic skills, context clues, picture clues, etc., using these words.

2. Have the student identify words and phrases that he/she does not recognize. Make these words the student's word list to be learned.

3. Emphasize that the student learn a root word sight vocabulary in order to be able to add various prefixes and suffixes to develop word attack skills.

4. Reinforce the student as often as an attempt is made at a word. Gradually increase the amount of time between reinforcement.

5. Use a peer tutor to review word attack skills utilizing games and activities previously learned.

6. Make certain the student uses a sight vocabulary to support weaknesses in phonic skills.

7. Make certain the student develops an awareness of hearing word sounds (e.g., say, "Listen to these words, each of them begins with a /bl/ sound: *blue, black, block, blast.*").

8. Make certain the student develops an awareness of seeing letter combinations that make the sounds (e.g., have the student circle all of the words in a reading passage that begin with the /bl/ sound).

9. Provide practice in reading /bl/ words, /pl/ words, /pr/ words, etc., by presenting a high interest paragraph or story that contains these words.

10. Demonstrate skills in decoding words (e.g., using contractions from conversation, write the abbreviated form of the word and the two complete words to show how to recognize the contraction).

11. Require the student to verbally explain context clues in sentences in order to identify words not known.

12. Encourage the student to try several sounds in order to arrive at the correct answer (e.g., omit letters from a word used in context and give several choices to be filled in).

13. Write paragraphs and short stories requiring word attack skills the student is currently learning. These passages should be of high interest to the student using his/her name, family members, friends, pets, and interesting experiences.

14. Have the student dictate stories which are then written for him/her to read. Require the student to place an emphasis on word attack skills.

15. Have the student read high-interest signs, advertisements, notices, etc., from newspapers, magazines, movie promotions, etc., placing emphasis on word attack skills.

16. Make certain the student is practicing word attack skills which are directly related to high-interest reading activities (e.g., adventures, romances, mysteries, athletics, etc.).

17. Encourage the student to scan the newspapers, magazines, etc., and underline words he/she can identify using word attack skills (e.g., phonics, context clues, picture clues, etc.).

18. Have the student use related pictures to help identify words in sentences not known.

19. Teach the student the most common prefixes and suffixes to add to root words he/she can identify.

20. When the student has difficulty with word attack skills, remind him/her that this can happen to everyone and not to be upset. Everyone has areas where they are weak and areas of strength as well, and it is important to keep trying.

21. Have the student act as a peer tutor to teach another student a concept he/she has mastered. This can serve as reinforcement for the student.

22. Tape record difficult reading material for the student to listen to as he/she reads along.

23. Avoid subjecting the student to uncomfortable reading situations (e.g., reading aloud in a group, identifying that the student's reading group is the lowest level, etc.).

24. Use reading material with pictures and predictable reading in order to help the student master word attack skills.

25. Have the student read aloud to the teacher each day in order to provide evaluative feedback.

26. Introduce new words and their meanings to the student before he/she reads new material. These may be entered in a "vocabulary" notebook kept by the student.

27. Teach the foundation for reading and writing in a sequential, systematic method with much positive reinforcement.

28. Teach the student individual consonant and vowel sounds.

29. Allow the student to use the chalkboard so that teaching and learning become active. The student hears, writes, and sees the sounds in isolation and then they "slide together" to make words.

30. The student should practice vocabulary words from required reading material by writing them while saying the sounds.

31. Teach the student pronunciation rules (e.g., vowel sounds, blends, etc.).

32. Start with simple words and sounds where the student achieves 95%-100% accuracy. Do not move on to more difficult words until practice, drill, and review of preceding lessons produces accuracy.

33. Use D'Nealian handwriting when teaching sounds by hearing, writing, and saying. This eliminates many potential reversal problems.

34. Have the student memorize meanings and practice spotting the most common prefixes and suffixes. Using a sheet of paper with a window cut in it, target the base word.

35. Play alphabet bingo with the student, using phonics instead of letter names.

41 Fails to recognize words on grade level

1. Set up a system of reinforcers which are either tangible (e.g., computer time, helper for the day, etc.) or intangible (e.g., smile, praise, handshake, etc.) to encourage the student to be more successful in reading.

2. Create a list of words and phrases from the student's reading material which he/she does not recognize (e.g., have the science teacher identify the words the student would not recognize in the following week's assignment). These words and phrases will become the student's reading word list for the following week.

3. Have the student identify words and phrases that he/she does not recognize. Make these words the student's list of words to be learned.

4. Modify or adjust reading materials to the student's ability level.

5. Outline reading material for the student using words and phrases on his/her reading level.

6. Teach the student to use context clues to identify words and phrases he/she does not know.

7. Emphasize that the student learn a root word sight vocabulary in order to be able to add various prefixes and suffixes to develop word attack skills.

8. Tape record difficult reading material for the student to listen to as he/she reads along.

9. Use a highlight marker to identify key words and phrases for the student. These words and phrases become the student's sight word vocabulary.

10. Teach the student to use related learning experiences in his/her classes (e.g., filmstrips, movies, tape recordings, demonstrations, discussions, videotapes, lectures, etc.). Encourage teachers to provide a variety of learning experiences for the student.

11. Arrange for a peer tutor to study with the student for quizzes, tests, etc.

12. Use a sight word vocabulary approach in order to teach the student key words and phrases when reading directions and instructions (e.g., key words such as *circle, underline, match,* etc.).

13. Maintain mobility in order to be frequently near the student to provide reading assistance.

14. Use lower-grade-level texts as alternative reading materials in subject areas.

15. Have lectures tape recorded in order to provide an additional source of information for the student.

16. Make a list of main points from the student's reading material, written on the student's reading level.

17. Make available for the student a learning center area where a variety of information is available in content areas (e.g., the library may have a section with films, slides, videotapes, taped lectures, etc., on such subjects as Pilgrims, the Civil War, the judicial system, etc.).

18. Encourage classroom teachers to include more alternative learning experiences in their classrooms (e.g., lectures, demonstrations, guest speakers, field trips, discussions, films, filmstrips, slides, videotapes, etc.).

19. Write paragraphs and short stories requiring skills the student is currently developing. These passages should be of high interest to the student using his/her name, family members, friends, pets, and interesting experiences.

20. Have the student dictate stories which are then written for him/her to read, placing an emphasis on reading skills.

21. Have the student read high-interest signs, advertisements, notices, etc., from newspapers, movie promotions, magazines, etc., placing an emphasis on reading skills.

22. Use reading series material with high interest (e.g., adventures, romances, mysteries, athletics, etc.) and low vocabulary.

23. Make certain the student is practicing reading skills which are directly related to high-interest reading activities (e.g., adventures, romances, mysteries, athletics, etc.).

24. When the student has difficulty with reading words on grade level, remind him/her that this can happen to everyone and not to be upset. Everyone has areas where they are weak and areas of strength as well, and it is important to keep trying.

25. Make certain that the reading demands of all subjects and assignments are within the ability level of the student. If not, modify or adjust the reading material to the student's ability level. A lower grade level text may be an alternative.

26. Make certain that the student's knowledge of a particular skill is being assessed rather than the student's ability to read directions, instructions, etc. Reading directions to the student can increase success.

27. Have the student read aloud to the teacher each day in order to provide evaluative feedback.

28. Teach the student individual consonant and vowel sounds.

29. Reduce the amount of material the student reads at one time (e.g., reduce reading material to single sentences on a page, a single paragraph, etc.). Gradually increase the amount of material as the student experiences success.

30. Provide the student with increased opportunities for help or assistance on academic tasks (e.g., peer tutoring, directions for work sent home, frequent interactions, etc.).

31. Allow students to use the chalkboard so that teaching and learning become active. The student hears, writes, and sees the sounds in isolation.

32. Have the student practice vocabulary words from required reading material by writing them while saying the sounds.

33. Start with simple words and sounds where the student achieves 95%-100% accuracy. Do not move on to more difficult words until practice, drill, and review of preceding lessons produces accuracy.

34. Use D'Nealian handwriting when teaching sounds by hearing, writing, and saying. This eliminates many potential reversal problems.

1. Make certain the student's vision has been checked recently.

2. Modify or adjust reading materials to the student's ability level.

3. Use a highlight marker to identify key syllables, words, etc., for the student. These words and phrases become the student's sight word vocabulary.

4. Have the student point to syllables, words, etc., while reading them in order to recognize omissions.

5. Tape record the student's reading in order that he/she can hear omissions.

6. Reduce the emphasis on competition. Competitive activities may cause the student to hurry and omit words.

7. Have the student read aloud to the teacher each day in order to provide evaluative feedback relative to omissions.

8. Verbally correct the student's omissions as often as possible in order that he/she hears the correct version of the reading material.

9. Make a list of those words on which the student makes omissions. Have the student practice reading these words.

10. Have the student use a paper strip to move down the page as he/she reads each line.

11. Make a reading "window" for each textbook the student uses. The student moves the reading "window" down and across the page as he/she reads.

12. Reduce the amount of material the student reads at one time (e.g., reduce reading material to single sentences on a page, a single paragraph, etc.).

13. Enlarge the print the student is reading.

14. Provide a quiet place for the student to work (e.g., "office" space, a study carrel, etc.).

15. Have the student highlight or underline the material he/she reads.

16. Have the student read aloud in order to maintain his/her place.

17. Have the student place a ruler under each line as he/she reads. The student then moves the ruler to the next line and so on.

18. Give the student time to read a selection more than once, emphasizing comprehension rather than speed.

19. Make certain that the reading demands of all subjects and assignments are within the ability level of the student. If not, modify or adjust the reading material to the student's ability level.

20. Make certain that the student's knowledge of a particular skill is being assessed rather than the student's ability to read directions, etc.

21. Reduce the amount of information on a page if it is causing visual distractions for the student (e.g., less print to read, fewer pictures, etc.).

22. Avoid subjecting the student to uncomfortable reading situations (e.g., reading aloud in a group, identifying that the student's reading group is the lowest level, etc.).

23. Have the student point to every word read in order to hold his/her place.

24. Have the student read orally, working for 95%-100% accuracy with no substitutions.

25. In a small group setting, have all students point to all words being read orally. Proceed by having each student read just one sentence, then move automatically to the next student without a break for discussion.

1. Make certain the student's hearing has been checked recently.

2. Each day have the student practice those sound-symbol relationships he/she does not know.

3. Have the student read and write friends' first names which include the sound-symbol relationships that he/she does not recognize.

4. Have the student say the sounds that consonants make as he/she points to them (e.g., *d* makes the /d/ sound, etc.).

5. Present the alphabet to the student on flash cards and have him/her make the consonant sound as each letter is flashed (e.g., *d* makes the /d/ sound, etc.). This is an appropriate activity for a peer tutor to conduct with the student each day.

6. Identify a sound the student does not know. Have the student circle all the words containing that sound in a paragraph or on a page of a book.

7. Put each letter of the alphabet on an individual card. Have the student collect all the letters for which he/she knows the sounds. The goal is to "own" all the letters of the alphabet.

8. Provide the student with sounds (e.g., /d/, /b/, /p/, etc.) and have him/her write or otherwise identify the letters that make the sounds.

9. Start by teaching the student sounds in his/her first name only. When the student has mastered the sounds in his/her first name, go on to the last name, parents' names, etc.

10. Take every opportunity throughout the day to emphasize a designated sound for that day (e.g., identify the sound when speaking, writing, reading, etc.).

11. Practice, drill, and review every day.

12. Identify a letter for the day. Have the student listen for the sound made by that letter and identify the sound-symbol relationship each time the sound is heard.

13. Assign the student a sound-symbol relationship. Have the student use a highlight marker to identify each word in a passage in which the sound-symbol relationship appears.

14. Use a Language Master to pair the sound of letters with the symbol of letters.

15. Make certain the student is not required to learn more information than he/she is capable of at any one time.

16. Have the student act as a peer tutor to teach another student a concept he/she has mastered. This can serve as reinforcement for the student.

17. Review on a daily basis those skills previously introduced.

18. Use both auditory and visual cues to help the student master sound-symbol relationships (i.e., the letter *a*, a picture of an apple, and the sound the letter *a* makes).

19. Teach intensive phonics as a foundation for reading, spelling, and handwriting.

20. Have the student say the sounds as he/she writes words (e.g., /d/ /a/ /d/).

21. Provide the student with a desktop chart of sounds. The student should be instructed to point to and say the sound the teacher says.

22. Have the student make sentences that repeatedly use the target letter sound (e.g., *t*: "Tongue twisters tease Tootsie's tonsils.").

1. Set up a system of motivators, either tangible (e.g., extra computer time, free time, etc.) or intangible (e.g., smile, handshake, praise, etc.), to encourage the student to be more successful in reading.

2. Get a list of words and phrases from the student's reading material which he/she does not recognize. Have the student practice phonic skills using these words.

3. Have the student identify words and phrases that he/she does not recognize. Make these words the student's list of words to be learned.

4. Emphasize that the student learn a root word sight vocabulary in order to be able to add various prefixes and suffixes to develop word attack skills.

5. Reinforce the student each time he/she makes an attempt to sound out a word. Gradually increase the number of attempts required for reinforcement.

6. Use a peer tutor to review phonic concepts utilizing games and activities previously learned.

7. Teach the student to use context clues to identify words and phrases he/she does not know.

8. Make certain the student uses a sight vocabulary to support weaknesses in phonic skills.

9. Make certain the student develops an awareness of hearing word sounds (e.g., say, "Listen to these words. Each of them begins with a /bl/ sound: *blue, black, block, blast.*").

10. Make certain the student develops an awareness of seeing letter combinations that produce the sounds (e.g., have the student circle all of the words in a reading passage that begin with the /bl/ sound).

11. Provide the student with verbal reminders or prompts when he/she is unsure of the sounds that letters make when blended together.

12. Provide practice in reading /bl/ words, /pl/ words, /pr/ words, etc., by presenting a high-interest paragraph story that contains these words.

13. Demonstrate skills in decoding words (e.g., using contractions from conversation, write the abbreviated form of the word and the two complete words to show how to recognize the contraction, etc.).

14. Encourage the student to try several sounds in order to arrive at the correct word (e.g., omit letters from a word used in context and give several choices to be filled in).

15. Encourage the student to scan newspapers, magazines, etc., and underline learned phonic elements.

16. Develop a list of phonic sounds the student needs to master. Remove sounds from the list as the student demonstrates mastery of phonic skills.

17. Write paragraphs and short stories requiring phonic skills the student is currently learning. These passages should be of high interest to the student using his/her name, family members, friends, pets, and interesting experiences.

18. Have the student dictate stories which are then written for him/her to read, placing emphasis on reading skills.

19. Have the student read high-interest signs, advertisements, notices, etc., from newspapers, magazines, movie promotions, etc., placing an emphasis on phonic skills.

20. Make certain the student is practicing phonic skills which are directly related to high-interest reading activities (e.g., adventures, romances, mysteries, athletics, etc.).

21. Have the student make a list of phonic skills (e.g., words he/she can identify by sounding out) that have been mastered. The student continues to add to the list as he/she identifies more and more words.

22. Make certain the student knows all beginning sounds before expecting him/her to blend sounds into words.

23. Tape record difficult reading material for the student to listen to as he/she reads along.

24. Make certain that the reading demands of all subjects and assignments are within the ability level of the student. If not, modify or adjust the reading material to the student's ability level.

25. Make certain that the student's knowledge of a particular skill is being assessed rather than the student's ability to read directions, instructions, etc. Reading directions to the student may increase success.

26. Reduce the amount of information on a page if it is causing visual distractions for the student (e.g., less print to read, fewer pictures to look at, etc.).

27. Avoid subjecting the student to uncomfortable reading situations (e.g., reading aloud in a group, identifying that the student's reading group is the lowest level, etc.).

28. Determine if the student has instant recall of all consonant and vowel sounds and combinations.

29. Practice active learning at the chalkboard by having students hear, write, and read words.

30. Practice, drill, and review every day.

31. Have students say sounds as they write them.

32. Allow students to write a story, paragraph, or sentence using phonetic shorthand. This narrowing of sounds helps the student to identify the sounds with letters used to construct words.

45 Omits, adds, substitutes, or reverses letters, words, or sounds when reading

1. Make certain the student's vision has been checked recently.

2. Set up a system of reinforcers, either tangible (e.g., extra computer time, helper for the day, etc.) or intangible (e.g., smile, handshake, praise, etc.), to encourage the student to be more successful in reading.

3. Make a list of words and phrases from the student's reading material which he/she does not recognize (e.g., have the science teacher identify the words and phrases the student would not recognize in the following week's assignment). These words and phrases will become the student's reading activities for the following week.

4. Modify or adjust reading materials to the student's ability level.

5. Have the student identify words and phrases that he/she does not recognize. Make these words the student's word list to be learned.

6. Emphasize that the student learn a root word sight vocabulary in order to be able to add various prefixes and suffixes to develop word attack skills.

7. Use a highlight marker to identify key syllables, words, etc., for the student. These words and phrases become the student's sight word vocabulary.

8. Use a sight word vocabulary approach in order to teach the student key words and phrases when reading directions and instructions (e.g., key words such as *circle, underline, match,* etc.).

9. Tape record pronunciations of words on which the student commonly makes errors in order that he/she can hear all the sounds.

10. Tape record the student's reading in order that he/she can hear omissions, additions, substitutions, or reversals.

11. Have the student point to syllables while reading them in order to help him/her recognize omissions, additions, substitutions, or reversals.

12. Make certain the student is learning basic word lists to assist in reading.

13. Reduce the emphasis on competition. Competitive activities may cause the student to omit, add, substitute, or reverse letters, words, or sounds when reading.

14. Have the student read aloud to the teacher each day in order to provide evaluative feedback relative to omissions, additions, substitutions, and reversals.

15. Verbally correct the student's omissions, additions, substitutions, and reversals as often as possible in order that he/she hears the correct version of the reading material.

16. Make a list of those words for which the student has omission, addition, substitution, or reversal errors. Have the student practice reading these words.

17. Have the student write those letters, words, or sounds in which he/she omits, adds, substitutes, or reverses in order to have a greater opportunity to see the correct version.

18. Make certain the student has an alphabet strip at his/her desk to use as a reference for the correct form of letters in order to reduce reversal-related errors when reading.

19. Teach the student to use context clues in reading. These skills will be particularly helpful when he/she is experiencing difficulty with reversals.

20. Tape record difficult reading material for the student to listen to while he/she reads along.

21. Teach reading, spelling, and handwriting simultaneously with all children at the chalkboard.

22. Make certain that the reading demands of all subjects and assignments are within the ability level of the student. If not, modify or adjust the reading material to the student's ability level.

23. Make certain that the student's knowledge of a particular skill is being assessed rather than the student's ability to read directions, instructions, etc. Reading directions, instructions, etc., to the student can increase success.

24. In a small group, require all students to point, look, and listen when other group members read orally.

25. Reduce the amount of material the student reads at one time (e.g., reduce reading material to single sentences on a page, a single paragraph, etc.). Gradually increase the amount of material as the student experiences success.

26. Reduce the amount of information on a page if it is causing visual distractions for the student (e.g., less print to read, fewer pictures on a page, etc.).

27. Use a kinesthetic approach by having the child point to every word and read orally. Stop the student for immediate correction if necessary, while continuing with ample praise for hard work and success.

28. Keep a simple picture-coded sound chart available at all times for the student to use in checking and comparing.

46 Fails to demonstrate word comprehension

1. Make certain the student is reading material on his/her level.

2. Set up a system of reinforcers, either tangible (e.g., extra computer time, helper for the day, etc.) or intangible (e.g., smile, handshake, praise, etc.), to encourage the student to be more successful in reading.

3. Modify or adjust reading materials to the student's ability level.

4. Outline reading material for the student using words and phrases on his/her reading level.

5. Use a sight word vocabulary approach to teach the student key words and phrases when reading directions and instructions (e.g., key words such as *circle, underline, match,* etc.).

6. Use a lower-grade-level text as alternative reading material in subject areas.

7. Make a list of main points from the student's reading material, written on the student's reading level.

8. Reduce distracting stimuli in order to increase the student's ability to concentrate on what he/she is reading (e.g., place the student on the front row, provide a carrel or "office" space away from distractions). This is used as a means of reducing distracting stimuli and not as a form of punishment.

9. Provide the student with a quiet place (e.g., carrel, study booth, etc.) where he/she may go to engage in reading activities.

10. Have the student verbally paraphrase material that has just been read in order to assess comprehension.

11. Have the student outline, underline, or highlight important points in reading material.

12. Have the student read high-interest signs, advertisements, notices, etc., from newspapers, magazines, movie promotions, etc., placing an emphasis on comprehension skills.

13. Have the student tape record what he/she reads in order to enhance comprehension by listening to the recording.

14. Write paragraphs and short stories requiring skills the student is currently developing. These paragraphs should be of high interest to the student using his/her name, family members, friends, pets, and interesting experiences.

15. Have the student dictate stories which are then written for him/her to read, placing an emphasis on comprehension skills.

16. Reduce the emphasis on competition. Competitive activities may make it difficult for the student to comprehend what he/she reads.

17. Have the student list new or difficult words in categories such as people, food, animals, etc.

18. Have the student match objects or pictures with sounds produced by that object (e.g., telephone, vacuum cleaner, etc.).

19. Have the student maintain a vocabulary notebook with definitions of words whose meanings he/she does not know.

20. When the student encounters a new word or one whose meaning is not known, have the student practice making up sentences in which the word can be used in the correct context.

21. Have the student identify a word each day which he/she does not understand, and require the student to use that word throughout the day in various situations.

22. Have the student identify words he/she does not comprehend. Finding the definitions of these words can then become the student's dictionary assignment.

23. Have the student match vocabulary words with pictures representing the words.

24. Make certain the student learns dictionary skills in order to be able to independently find meanings of words.

25. Have the student develop a picture dictionary of pictures representing those words which are difficult for him/her to recognize.

26. Introduce new words and their meanings to the student before he/she reads new material.

27. Make certain the student learns the meanings of all commonly used prefixes and suffixes.

28. Identify a peer the student can rely upon to help with the meanings of words not understood.

29. Provide the student with a variety of visual teaching materials to support word comprehension (e.g., filmstrips, pictures, charts, etc.).

30. Teach the student to use context clues to identify words not understood.

31. Label objects and activities in the classroom to help the student associate words with tangible aspects of the environment.

32. Have the student make a list of new words that have been learned. The student can add words to the list at his/her own pace.

33. Teach the student to read for the main point in sentences, paragraphs, etc.

34. Reinforce the student for asking the meanings of words not understood.

35. Reinforce the student for looking up the definitions of words not understood.

36. Make it pleasant and positive for the student to ask the meanings or look up words not understood. Reinforce the student by assisting, congratulating, praising, etc.

37. Make certain the student is developing a sight word vocabulary of the most commonly used words in his/her reading material.

38. Make certain the student underlines or circles words not understood. These words will become the student's vocabulary assignment for the week.

39. Before reading, tell the student what he/she should find in the story (e.g., who are the main characters, what are the main events, etc.).

40. Make certain the student is not required to learn more information than he/she is capable of at any one time.

41. Give the student time to read a selection more than once, emphasizing comprehension rather than speed.

42. Use reading series material with high interest (e.g., adventures, romances, mysteries, athletics, etc.) and low vocabulary.

43. Write notes and letters to the student to provide reading material which he/she would want to read for comprehension. Students may be encouraged to write each other notes and letters at a time set aside each day, week, etc.

44. Make certain that the reading demands of all subjects and assignments are within the ability level of the student. If not, modify or adjust the reading material to the student's ability level.

45. Make certain that the student's knowledge of a particular skill is being assessed rather than the student's ability to read directions, instructions, etc. Reading directions, instructions, etc., to the student can increase success.

46. Reduce the amount of information on a page if it is causing visual distractions for the student (e.g., less print to read, fewer pictures, etc.).

47. Avoid subjecting the student to uncomfortable reading situations (e.g., reading aloud in a group, identifying that the student's reading group is the lowest level, etc.).

48. Anticipate new vocabulary words and teach them in advance of reading a selection.

49. Prepare a written list of vocabulary words. Orally present a sentence with a "blank" and have students determine which vocabulary word should be used.

50. In daily classroom conversation, make certain to use the current vocabulary word being studied by the student.

47 Reads words correctly in one context but not in another

1. Make certain the student is reading material on his/her level.

2. Highlight or underline those words the student most frequently fails to recognize in different contexts.

3. Use a lower-grade-level text as alternative reading material in subject areas.

4. Write paragraphs and short stories using those words the student most frequently fails to recognize in different contexts. These paragraphs should be of high interest to the student using his/her name, family members, friends, pets, and interesting experiences.

5. Make a reading "window" for the student. The student moves the reading "window" down and across the page as he/she reads.

6. Have the student list those words he/she most frequently fails to recognize into categories such as people, food, animals, etc., in order to help the student recognize those words in different contexts.

7. Teach the student to use context clues to identify words not understood.

8. Identify words the student does not recognize in different contexts and put these words on flash cards. Have the student match these words to the same words in sentences, paragraphs, short stories, etc.

9. Have the student print/write those words he/she most frequently fails to recognize in different contexts.

10. Have the student maintain a list with definitions of those words he/she most frequently fails to recognize in different contexts.

11. Highlight or underline those words in reading material the student is unable to recognize. Have the student identify those words as he/she reads them.

12. Reduce distracting stimuli in order to increase the student's ability to concentrate on what he/she is reading (e.g., place the student on the front row, provide a carrel or "office" space away from distractions). This is used as a means of reducing distracting stimuli and not as a form of punishment.

13. Provide the student with a quiet place (e.g., carrel, study booth, etc.) where he/she may go to engage in reading activities.

14. Reduce the emphasis on competition. Competitive activities may cause the student to hurry and fail to recognize words in a particular context.

15. Provide the student with a dictionary, requiring him/her to find the definitions of those words not recognized.

16. Have the student read short sentences in order to make it easier to recognize words in different contexts. Longer sentences are presented as the student demonstrates success.

17. Provide the student with large-print reading material in order to increase the likelihood of the student recognizing words in different contexts.

18. Use daily drill activities to help the student memorize vocabulary words.

19. Tape record difficult reading material for the student to listen to as he/she reads along.

20. Write notes and letters to the student to provide reading material which includes words the student frequently has difficulty with.

21. Have the student read aloud to the teacher each day in order to provide evaluative feedback.

22. Reduce the amount of information on a page if it is causing visual distractions for the student (e.g., less print to read, fewer pictures to look at, etc.).

23. Avoid subjecting the student to uncomfortable reading situations (e.g., reading aloud in a group, identifying that the student's reading group is the lowest level, etc.).

24. Require the student to read a selection each day which includes the vocabulary currently being studied.

1. Make certain the student is reading material on his/her ability level.

2. Modify or adjust reading materials to the student's ability level.

3. Set up a system of reinforcers, either tangible (e.g., extra computer time, helper for the day, etc.) or intangible (e.g., smile, handshake, praise, etc.), to encourage the student to be more successful in reading.

4. Tape record reading material for the student to listen to as he/she reads along.

5. Provide the student a quiet place (e.g., carrel, study booth, "office," etc.) where he/she may go to engage in reading activities.

6. Write paragraphs and short stories for the student to read. These passages should be of high interest to the student using his/her name, family members, friends, pets, and interesting experiences.

7. Have the student dictate stories which are then written for him/her to read.

8. Have the student read high-interest signs, advertisements, notices, etc., from newspapers, magazines, movie promotions, etc.

9. Provide the student with many high-interest reading materials (e.g., comic books; magazines relating to sports, fashion, etc.).

10. Conduct a survey of the student's interests in order to provide reading material in that area.

11. Read, or have someone read, high-interest material to the student in order to promote his/her interest in reading.

12. Develop a library in the classroom that is appealing to the student (e.g., tent, bean bag chair, carpeted area, etc.).

13. Offer memberships in paperback book clubs to the student.

14. Encourage interest in reading by having students share interesting things they have read. This should be informal sharing in a group and not necessarily a "book report."

15. Have the student write to the author of material he/she reads in order to encourage an interest in reading more by the same author.

16. Make reading materials easily accessible to the student in the classroom.

17. Encourage the student to read material with many illustrations and a limited amount of print. Gradually decrease the number of pictures.

18. Encourage parents to make reading material available to the student at home and to ensure that the material is on the student's interest and reading levels.

19. Encourage parents to read to their child at home and to have their child read to them. Encourage parents to read for their own enjoyment to serve as a model for their child.

20. Have the student read lower-grade-level stories to younger children in order to enhance his/her feelings of confidence relative to reading.

21. Include predictable reading books in the class library. Predictability can make books more appealing to beginning readers and build confidence as well.

22. Avoid subjecting the student to uncomfortable reading situations (e.g., reading aloud in a group, identifying that the student's reading group is the lowest level, etc.).

23. Write periodic letters or notes to the student to encourage him/her to write back.

24. Provide assistance in helping the student find reading material according to interests and reading level. The student may not be comfortable or able to find books by himself/herself in the library.

25. Expose the student to large-print materials. Large print can appear less intimidating to the student who does not choose to read.

26. Provide the student with high-interest reading material that is also short in length in order that the student can finish reading the material without difficulty.

27. Set aside a fixed random time (e.g., a half-hour daily, an hour a week, etc.) for a "Read-In." Everyone, teacher included, chooses a book that he/she likes and reads it for pleasure.

28. To encourage reading, make certain that the student knows he/she is not reading for assessment purposes but for enjoyment.

29. Have the student act as a peer tutor to teach younger students reading or to read orally to younger students.

30. Make certain the student has mastery of reading skills before expecting him/her to read independently.

31. Incorporate listening skills/techniques as part of the daily routine in reading class (i.e., a listening center where the student reads along as a tape plays, the teacher reads to the student, students read to each other, etc.).

32. Provide reading material in various settings (e.g., art books in the art center, science books in the science center, weather books in the weather center, etc.).

33. Encourage the student to find books about different subjects being taught or discussed (e.g., when studying electricity, encourage the student to read a book about Thomas Edison).

49 Does not discriminate between similar letters and words

1. Make certain the student's hearing has been checked recently.

2. Each day have the student practice those letters and words which he/she cannot discriminate.

3. Take every opportunity throughout the day to emphasize a designated letter or word the student cannot discriminate (e.g., identify the sound when speaking, writing, reading, etc.).

4. Use highlight markers (e.g., pink and yellow) to have the student mark the letters and words in a passage he/she does not discriminate (e.g., all *m*'s marked with the pink marker, and all *n*'s marked with the yellow marker).

5. Make a list of letters and words the student cannot discriminate. Have the student and a peer work together with flash cards to develop the student's ability to recognize the differences in the letters and words.

6. Tape record stories and paragraphs the student can listen to while reading along.

7. Have the student read aloud to the teacher each day in order to provide evaluative feedback relative to his/her ability to discriminate letters and words.

8. Verbally correct the student as often as possible when he/she does not discriminate between letters and words in order that he/she hears the correct version of the reading material.

9. Have the student write those letters and words he/she has trouble discriminating in order that he/she has a greater opportunity to conceptualize the correct version.

10. Teach the student to use context clues in reading. These skills will be particularly helpful when he/she is unable to discriminate between letters and words.

11. Make certain the student looks closely at word endings as well as beginnings in order to discriminate similar words (e.g., "cap" and "cat").

12. Identify a letter or word each day which the student has difficulty discriminating. Have the student underline or highlight that letter or word each time he/she reads it that day.

13. Make certain the student has an alphabet strip at his/her desk in order to have a reference when reading or performing assignments.

14. Reduce the emphasis on competition. Competitive activities may cause the student to hurry and not discriminate between similar letters and words.

15. Make certain that the reading demands of all subjects and assignments are within the ability level of the student. If not, modify or adjust the reading material to the student's ability level.

16. Make certain that the student's knowledge of a particular skill is being assessed rather than the student's ability to read directions, instructions, etc.

17. Have the student cut out letters from magazines or newspapers and glue the letters together to make words, sentences, etc.

50 Does not know all the letters of the alphabet

1. Set up a system of reinforcers, either tangible (e.g., computer time, helper for the day, etc.) or intangible (e.g., praise, handshake, smile, etc.), to encourage the student to learn the letters of the alphabet.

2. Make certain the student has an alphabet strip at his/her desk for a reference.

3. Each day have the student print those letters of the alphabet which he/she does not know.

4. Have a peer work with the student on one letter of the alphabet each day (e.g., tracing the letter, printing the letter, recognizing the letter in words in a paragraph, etc.).

5. Have the student read and write friends' first names which include letters the student does not recognize.

6. Introduce letters to the student as partners (e.g., *Aa, Bb, Cc, Dd,* etc.).

7. Have the student say the letters of the alphabet in sequence. Repeat by rote several times a day.

8. Present the alphabet to the student on flash cards. This is an appropriate activity for a peer tutor to conduct with the student each day.

9. Identify a letter the student does not know. Have the student find the letter in all the words in a paragraph or on a page of a book.

10. Put each letter of the alphabet on an individual card. Have the student collect and keep the letters he/she knows with the goal to "own" all the letters of the alphabet.

11. Start by teaching the names of the letters in the student's first name only. When the student has mastered the letters in his/her first name, go on to the last name, parents' names, etc.

12. Give the student a word which begins with each letter of the alphabet (e.g., *apple, bad, cat,* etc.). Go over several of the words each day, stressing the alphabet letters being learned.

13. Take every opportunity throughout the day to emphasize a designated letter for that day (e.g., identify the letter when speaking, writing, reading, etc.).

14. Use daily drills to help the student memorize the alphabet.

15. Avoid subjecting the student to uncomfortable reading situations (e.g., reading aloud in a group, identifying that the student's reading group is the lowest level, etc.).

51 Understands what is read to him/her but not what he/she reads silently

1. Make certain the student is reading material on his/her level.

2. Modify or adjust reading material to the student's ability level.

3. Outline reading material the student reads silently, using words and phrases on his/her reading level.

4. Tape record difficult reading material for the student to listen to as he/she reads along.

5. Use lower-grade-level texts as alternative reading material in subject areas.

6. Make a list of main points from the student's reading material, written on the student's reading level.

7. Reduce distracting stimuli in order to increase the student's ability to concentrate on what he/she is reading (e.g., place the student on the front row, provide a carrel or "office" space away from distractions). This is used as a means of reducing distracting stimuli and not as a form of punishment.

8. Provide the student with a quiet place (e.g., carrel, study booth, etc.) where he/she may go to engage in reading activities.

9. Have the student verbally paraphrase material he/she has just read in order to assess comprehension.

10. Teach the student to identify main points in material he/she has read in order to assess comprehension.

11. Have the student outline, underline, or highlight important points in reading material.

12. Have the student take notes while reading in order to increase comprehension.

13. Have the student read progressively longer segments of reading material in order to build comprehension skills (e.g., begin with single paragraphs and progress to several paragraphs, short stories, chapters, etc.).

14. Have the student tape record what he/she reads in order to enhance comprehension by listening to the material read.

15. Teach the student to use context clues to identify words and phrases he/she does not know.

16. Write paragraphs and short stories requiring reading skills the student is currently developing. These passages should be of high interest to the student using his/her name, family members, friends, pets, and interesting experiences.

17. Have the student dictate stories which are then written for him/her to read, placing emphasis on comprehension skills.

18. Have the student read high-interest signs, advertisements, notices, etc., from newspapers, magazines, movie promotions, etc., placing emphasis on comprehension skills.

19. Make certain the student is practicing comprehension skills which are directly related to high-interest reading activities (e.g., adventures, romances, mysteries, athletics, etc.).

20. Underline or highlight important points in reading material.

21. Write notes and letters to the student to provide reading material which he/she will want to read for comprehension. Students may be encouraged to write each other notes and letters at a time set aside each day, once a week, etc.

22. Give the student time to read a selection more than once, emphasizing comprehension rather than speed.

23. Use a sight word vocabulary approach in order to teach the student key words and phrases when reading directions and instructions (e.g., key words such as *circle, underline, match,* etc.).

24. Make certain the student is not required to learn more information than he/she is capable of at any one time.

25. Use reading series materials with high interest (e.g., adventures, romances, mysteries, athletics, etc.) and low vocabulary.

26. Make certain that the reading demands of all subjects and assignments are within the ability level of the student. If not, modify or adjust the reading material to the student's ability level.

27. Have the student read aloud when reading to himself/herself.

28. Make certain that the student's knowledge of a particular skill is being assessed rather than the student's ability to read directions, instructions, etc. Reading directions, instructions, etc., to the student can increase his/her success.

29. Reduce the amount of material the student reads at one time (e.g., reduce reading material to single sentences on a page, a single paragraph, etc.). Gradually increase the amount of material as the student demonstrates success.

30. Stop at various points while the student is reading silently to check comprehension.

31. Reduce the amount of information on a page if it is causing visual distractions for the student (e.g., less print to read, fewer pictures to look at, etc.).

52 Has difficulty recalling the sequence of events in stories read

1. Check the student's understanding of first, next, and last by having the student tell what happens during daily events in first, next, and last order.

2. Provide the student with a tape of the story to listen to as he/she reads along.

3. Have the student write the main events of stories as he/she reads them.

4. Have the student read one paragraph of a new story and make notes on the events, then read the next paragraph and make notes, etc.

5. Read selections with the student and make notes of the sequence of events in order to act as a model for the student.

6. Have the student paraphrase the sequence of events in each paragraph read. The teacher can transcribe the paraphrased sequence or the student can record with a tape player.

7. Informally assess the student's auditory and visual short-term memory skills in order to determine which is the stronger. Use the student's stronger channel to facilitate retention of sequential information.

8. Give the student one task to perform at a time. Introduce the next task only when the student has successfully completed the previous task.

9. Teach the student to visualize information as if it were a movie, then play it back mentally when he/she needs to verbalize it.

10. Have the student practice repetition of information in order to increase short-term memory skills (e.g., repeating names, telephone numbers, dates of events, etc.).

11. Teach the student to identify the main idea of a story and causal relationships within the story in order to enhance recall of information in the correct order.

12. Have the student practice remembering sequences by engaging in sequential activities which are purposeful to him/her (e.g., operating equipment, following recipes, opening a combination lock, etc.).

13. Use a flannel board or *Colorforms* to practice sequencing a familiar story or a familiar action.

14. Have the student act as a peer tutor to teach another student a concept he/she has mastered. This can serve as reinforcement for the student.

15. Provide practice in sequencing using a computer software program that gives the student immediate feedback.

16. Make certain the student has mastery of reading concepts at each level before introducing a new skill level.

17. Make certain the student is not required to learn more information then he/she is capable of at any one time.

18. Reduce the emphasis on competition. Competitive activities may cause the student to hurry and commit any number of errors.

19. Reduce the amount of information on a page if it is causing visual distractions for the student (e.g., have less print to read, isolate information that is presented to the student, etc.).

20. Identify the student's most efficient learning mode and use it consistently to increase the probability of understanding (e.g., If the student fails to understand information presented verbally, present it in written form. If the student has difficulty understanding written information, present it verbally.).

21. Give the student time to read a selection more than once, emphasizing comprehension rather than speed.

22. Use reading series materials with high interest (e.g., adventures, romances, mysteries, athletics, etc.).

23. Write notes and letters to the student to provide reading material which he/she will want to read for comprehension. Students may be encouraged to write each other notes and letters at a time set aside each day, week, etc.

24. Write paragraphs and short stories requiring skills the student is currently developing. These passages should be of high interest to the student using his/her name, family members, friends, pets, and interesting experiences.

25. Make certain that the reading demands of all subjects and assignments are within the ability level of the student. If not, modify or adjust the reading material to the student's ability level. A lower-level text may be an alternative.

26. Have the student practice a new skill or assignment alone or with an aide, the teacher, or a peer before the entire group attempts the activity or before performing for a grade.

27. Speak to the student to explain: (a) what the student is doing wrong and (b) what the student should be doing.

28. Reinforce the student for sequencing: (a) give the student a tangible reward (e.g., classroom privileges, line leading, passing out materials, five minutes free time, etc.) or (b) give the student an intangible reward (e.g., praise, handshake, smile, etc.) for accurately demonstrating correct sequencing activities.

29. Communicate with parents (e.g., notes home, phone calls, etc.) in order to share information concerning the student's progress and so that they can reinforce the student at home.

30. Evaluate the appropriateness of the task to determine: (a) if the task is too difficult and (b) if the length of time scheduled to complete the task is appropriate.

31. Identify a peer to act as a model for the student to imitate and also to assist the student with directions, etc.

32. Allow the student to perform alternative versions of the assignments. Gradually introduce more components of the regular assignments until those can be performed successfully.

53 Does not demonstrate an understanding of alphabetical order

1. When lining up or dismissing the students, ask each student to tell the letter that comes next in alphabetical order. The students are dismissed as they correctly name each letter.

2. After students are proficient at telling "next" letters, try having students name "before" letters.

3. Using a small group, have one student begin saying the alphabet. When the teacher points to another student, the first student becomes quiet and the second student begins saying the alphabet at the point at which the first student stopped.

4. Provide the student with an alphabet strip to keep as a reference at his/her desk.

5. Have the student say the alphabet as he/she points to each letter in alphabetical order.

6. Have the student alphabetize 26 words, each beginning with a different letter of the alphabet.

7. After the student has mastered alphabetizing by the first letter of words, have the student alphabetize 26 words which begin with the same first letter but have each letter of the alphabet represented as the second letter (e.g., Aaron, able, acid, adapt, etc.).

8. Have the student begin alphabetizing with only two words. Add a third word and so on as the student further develops an understanding of alphabetical order.

9. Have the student act as a peer tutor to teach another student a concept he/she has mastered. This can serve as reinforcement for the student.

10. Provide practice in alphabetizing by using a computer software program that gives the student immediate feedback.

11. Make certain the student has mastery of alphabetizing concepts at each level before introducing a new skill level (e.g., alphabetizing to the first letter, second letter, third letter, etc.).

12. Make certain that the student is not required to learn more information than he/she is capable of at any one time.

13. Reduce the emphasis on competition. Competitive activities may cause the student to hurry and commit any number of errors.

14. Review, on a daily basis, those skills, concepts, tasks, etc., which have been previously introduced.

15. Reinforce the student for alphabetizing: (a) give the student a tangible reward (e.g., classroom privileges, line leading, passing out materials, five minutes free time, etc.) or (b) give the student an intangible reward (e.g., praise, handshake, smile, etc.) for demonstrating an understanding of alphabetizing.

16. Speak to the student to explain: (a) what he/she is doing wrong and (b) what he/she should be doing.

17. Evaluate the appropriateness of the task to determine: (a) if the task is too difficult and (b) if the length of time scheduled to complete the task is appropriate.

18. Identify a peer to act as a model for the student to imitate and also to assist the student with directions.

19. Have the student practice a new skill or assignment alone, with an aide, the teacher, or a peer before the entire group attempts the activity or before performing for a grade.

1. Make certain the student always considers the first sentence of a paragraph as a possible topic sentence and main idea.

2. Make certain the student understands that a topic sentence or main idea for a paragraph always will contain one or more of the following, which will be the whole idea of the paragraph: *Who, What, Where, When, How.*

3. Make certain the student understands that the topic sentence or main idea can be determined by choosing the one sentence in a paragraph that makes sense when it stands alone (e.g., in the process of elimination, isolate each sentence and decide if it tells what the whole paragraph is about).

4. Have the student write a paragraph about a favorite topic and use a triangle to determine the hierarchy of sentences:
  (1) Most important (topic),
  (2) Most important detail,
  (3) Less important detail, and
  (4) Incidental detail (e.g., could be left out without changing the paragraph meaning).

5. Have the student employ the "satellite system" to identify the main idea of a paragraph. The student should choose the one word or phrase around which the entire paragraph is built. Then the student should name the other details that describe that central figure. This allows the student to focus on the <u>subject</u> in order to spot the main idea.

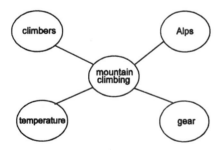

6. Reinforce the student for identifying the topic sentence and/or main idea: (a) give the student a tangible reward (e.g., classroom privileges, line leading, passing out materials, five minutes free time, etc.) or (b) give the student an intangible reward (e.g., praise, handshake, smile, etc.).

7. Speak to the student to explain: (a) what the student is doing wrong and (b) what the student should be doing.

8. Write a contract with the student specifying what behavior is expected and what reinforcement will be made available when terms of the contract have been met. (See Appendix for Behavioral Contract.)

9. Have the student question any directions, explanations, and instructions not understood.

10. Communicate with parents (e.g., notes home, phone calls, etc.) in order to share information concerning the student's progress and so that they can reinforce the student at home.

11. Evaluate the appropriateness of the task to determine: (a) if the task is too difficult and (b) if the length of time scheduled to complete the task is appropriate.

12. Identify a peer to act as a model for the student to imitate and also to assist the student with directions, etc.

13. Specify exactly what is to be done for the completion of the task (e.g., indicate definite starting and stopping points, indicate a minimum requirement, etc.).

14. Have the student act as a peer tutor to teach another student a concept he/she has mastered. This can serve as reinforcement for the student.

15. Provide practice in identifying the topic sentence and/or main idea using a computer software program that gives the student immediate feedback.

16. Make certain the student has mastery of reading concepts at each level before introducing a new skill level.

17. Make certain the student is not required to learn more information than he/she is capable of at any one time.

18. Reduce the emphasis on competition. Competitive activities may cause the student to hurry and commit any number of errors.

19. Reduce the amount of information on a page if it is causing visual distractions for the student (e.g., have less print to read, isolate information that is presented to the student).

20. Highlight or underline important information the student reads (e.g., directions, assignments, etc.).

21. Stop at various points during the presentation of information to check the student's comprehension.

22. Give the student time to read a selection more than once, emphasizing comprehension rather than speed.

23. Use reading series materials with high interest (e.g., adventures, romances, mysteries, athletics, etc.) and low vocabulary.

24. Write paragraphs and short stories requiring skills the student is currently developing. These passages should be of high interest to the student using his/her name, family members, friends, pets, and interesting experiences.

25. Make certain that the reading demands of all subjects and assignments are within the ability level of the student. If not, modify or adjust the reading material to the student's ability level. A lower-grade-level text may be an alternative.

26. Reduce the amount of material the student reads at one time (e.g., reduce reading material to single sentences on a page, a single paragraph, etc.). Gradually increase the amount of material as the student experiences success.

55 Does not demonstrate an understanding of contractions and compound words

1. Have the student identify the words which are used to make the most common contractions he/she uses (e.g., *can't, won't, wouldn't,* etc.).

2. Provide the student with a list of the most common contractions and compound words with the corresponding words from which they are created. Allow the student to keep the list at his/her desk as a reference.

3. Have the student make his/her own dictionary of contractions and compound words with the corresponding words from which they are created.

4. Include a contraction and/or compound word in each week's spelling list for the student to learn.

5. Show the student how compound words are made by writing two words on construction paper and sliding them together.

6. Have the student act as a peer tutor to teach another student a concept he/she has mastered. This can serve as reinforcement for the student.

7. Provide practice in compound words and contractions by using a computer program that gives the student immediate feedback.

8. Make certain the student is not required to learn more information than he/she is capable of at any one time.

9. Reduce the emphasis on competition. Competitive activities may cause the student to hurry and commit any number of errors.

10. Have the student question any directions, explanations, and instructions not understood.

11. Provide the student with increased opportunity for help or assistance on academic tasks (e.g., peer tutoring, directions for work sent home, frequent interactions, etc.).

12. Reinforce the student for beginning, staying on, and completing assignments.

13. Have the student practice a new skill or assignment alone or with an aide, the teacher, or a peer before the entire group attempts the activity or before performing for a grade.

14. Introduce compound words and contractions and their meanings to the student before he/she reads new material. These may be entered in a "vocabulary" notebook kept by the student.

15. Reinforce the student for demonstrating a knowledge of compound words and contractions: (a) give the student a tangible reward (e.g., classroom privileges, line leading, passing out materials, five minutes free time, etc.) or (b) give the student an intangible reward (e.g., praise, handshake, smile, etc.).

16. Communicate with parents (e.g., notes home, phone calls, etc.) in order to share information concerning the student's progress and so that they can reinforce the student at home.

17. Evaluate the appropriateness of the task to determine: (a) if the task is too difficult and (b) if the length of time scheduled to complete the task is appropriate.

18. Identify a peer to act as a model for the student to imitate and also to assist the student with directions, etc.

1. Provide the student with a dictionary. Name a word and have the student look up the word in the dictionary using the guide words at the top of each page. Time the student and see if his/her best time can be beaten.

2. Make certain the student has an understanding of how to use guide words at the tops of the dictionary pages.

3. Make certain the student knows how to alphabetize words to the first, second, third, etc., letter.

4. Make certain the student knows the reasons for using a dictionary or glossary (e.g., to look up the meanings of words, to look up how to spell words, to look up the correct pronunciation of words, etc.).

5. Make certain the student knows that the glossary is in the back of the book.

6. Make certain the student is using a dictionary that is on his/her reading level.

7. Make certain the student knows how to alphabetize.

8. Assign the student words to look up in his/her textbook glossary. Begin with easier words, and add words with more difficult spellings and definitions as the student demonstrates success.

9. Have the student find the target word of a paragraph, sentence, story, etc., and look it up in the glossary of the book.

10. Have the student select words from a spelling list and write a story using those words. Then have the student make a glossary to attach to the end of the story with word meanings shown in pictures.

11. Have the student compare a glossary from a textbook with a student-level thesaurus for building a glossary of his/her own vocabulary.

12. Have the student review the words in a textbook glossary and determine why those particular words were selected to be in the glossary and more commonly used words were not selected.

13. Reinforce the student for demonstrating knowledge of glossary and/or dictionary skills: (a) give the student a tangible reward (e.g., classroom privileges, line leading, passing out materials, five minutes free time, etc.) or (b) give the student an intangible reward (e.g., praise, handshake, smile, etc.).

14. Speak to the student to explain: (a) what the student is doing wrong and (b) what the student should be doing.

15. Reinforce the student for demonstrating the knowledge of glossary skills and/or dictionary skills based on the number of times the student can be successful. Gradually increase the number of times required for reinforcement as the student demonstrates success.

16. Communicate with parents (e.g., notes home, phone calls, etc.) in order to share information concerning the student's progress and so that they can reinforce the student at home.

17. Evaluate the appropriateness of the task to determine: (a) if the task is too difficult and (b) if the length of time scheduled to complete the task is appropriate.

18. Identify a peer to act as a model for the student to imitate and also to assist the student with directions, etc.

19. Have the student question any directions, explanations, or instructions not understood.

20. Have the student act as a peer tutor to teach another student a concept he/she has mastered. This can serve as reinforcement for the student.

21. Provide practice in glossary and/or dictionary skills by using a computer software program that gives the student immediate feedback.

22. Make certain the student has mastery of concepts at each level before introducing a new skill level.

23. Make certain the student is not required to learn more information than he/she is capable of at any one time.

24. Reduce the emphasis on competition. Competitive activities may cause the student to hurry and commit any number of errors.

25. Provide the student with increased opportunity for help or assistance on academic tasks (e.g., peer tutoring, directions for work sent home, frequent interactions, etc.).

26. Review, on a daily basis, those skills, concepts, tasks, etc., which have been previously introduced.

57 Has difficulty finding supporting details when reading

1. Have the student identify the "main idea" of each paragraph. Then have the student list all information from the paragraph which relates to the "main idea."

2. Teach the student mapping techniques to identify supporting details. (See Appendix for an example of a mapping activity.)

3. Provide the student with a diagram in which supporting details are like the legs of a bug. They can learn to make "bug notes" in this way: An oval shape is the bug's body on which the teacher writes the main idea of a paragraph. Then each supporting detail is written on a line coming out from the oval. These represent the bug's legs. The number of legs each bug note has depends on the number of supporting details there are for a given topic.

4. Have the student pretend to be a detective and play the game *Prove It*. After reading a selection, the main idea is determined and written on the chalkboard. The student must "prove it" by telling the supporting details that were discovered in the reading selection.

5. Reinforce the student for identifying supporting details: (a) give the student a tangible reward (e.g., classroom privileges, line leading, passing out materials, five minutes free time, etc.) or (b) give the student an intangible reward (e.g., praise, handshake, smile, etc.).

6. Speak to the student to explain: (a) what the student is doing wrong and (b) what the student should be doing.

7. Communicate with parents (e.g., notes home, phone calls, etc.) in order to share information concerning the student's progress and so that they can reinforce the student at home.

8. Evaluate the appropriateness of the task to determine: (a) if the task is too difficult and (b) if the length of time scheduled to complete the task is appropriate.

9. Identify a peer to act as a model for the student to imitate and also to assist the student with directions, etc.

10. Have the student question any directions, explanations, and instructions not understood.

11. Specify exactly what is to be done for the completion of the task (e.g., indicate definite starting and stopping points, indicate minimum requirements, etc.).

12. Have the student act as a peer tutor to teach another student a concept he/she has mastered. This can serve as reinforcement for the student.

13. Provide practice in identifying the supporting details by using a computer software program that gives the student immediate feedback.

14. Make certain the student has mastery of reading concepts at each level before introducing a new skill level.

15. Make certain the student is not required to learn more information than he/she is capable of at any one time.

16. Reduce the emphasis on competition. Competitive activities may cause the student to hurry and commit any number of errors.

17. Reduce the amount of information on a page if it is causing visual distractions for the student (e.g., have less print to read, isolate information that is presented to the student, etc.).

18. Highlight or underline important information the student reads (e.g., directions, assignments, etc.).

19. Stop at various points during the presentation of information to check the student's comprehension.

20. Give the student time to read a selection more than once, emphasizing comprehension rather than speed.

21. Use reading series materials with high interest (e.g., adventure, romances, mysteries, athletics, etc.) and low vocabulary.

22. Write paragraphs and short stories requiring skills the student is currently developing. These passages should be of high interest to the student using his/her name, family members, friends, pets, and interesting experiences.

23. Make certain that the reading demands of all subjects and assignments are within the ability level of the student. If not, modify or adjust the reading material to the student's ability level. A lower-grade-level text may be an alternative.

24. Reduce the amount of material the student reads at one time (e.g., reduce reading material to single sentences on a page, a single paragraph, etc.). Gradually increase the amount of material as the student experiences success.

1. Allow the student to perform schoolwork in a quiet place (e.g., study carrel, library, resource room, etc.) in order to reduce distractions.

2. Assign the student shorter tasks while increasing the quality of expectations.

3. Supervise the student while he/she is performing schoolwork in order to monitor handwriting quality.

4. Provide the student with clearly stated criteria for acceptable work.

5. Have the student read/go over schoolwork with the teacher in order that the student can become aware of the quality of his/her work.

6. Provide the student with samples of work which may serve as models for acceptable quality (e.g., the student is to match the quality of the sample before turning in the assignment).

7. Provide the student with additional time to perform schoolwork in order to achieve quality.

8. Teach the student procedures for doing quality work (e.g., listen to directions, make certain directions are understood, work at an acceptable pace, check for errors, correct for neatness, copy the work over, etc.).

9. Recognize quality (e.g., display the student's work, congratulate the student, etc.).

10. Conduct a preliminary evaluation of the work, requiring the student to make necessary corrections before final grading.

11. Establish levels of expectations for quality handwriting performance, and require the student to correct or repeat assignments until the expectations are met.

12. Provide the student with quality materials to perform assignments (e.g., pencil with eraser, paper, dictionary, handwriting sample, etc.).

13. Provide the student with ample opportunity to master handwriting skills (e.g., instruction in letter positioning, direction, spacing, etc.).

14. Provide the student with an appropriate model of handwriting (e.g., other students' work, teacher samples, commercial samples, etc.) to use at his/her desk.

15. Model appropriate handwriting at all times.

16. Provide a multitude of handwriting opportunities for the student to practice handwriting skills (e.g., writing letters to sports and entertainment figures, relatives, or friends; writing for free information on a topic in which the student is interested, etc.).

17. Have the student trace handwriting models and fade the models as the student develops the skill.

18. Gradually reduce the space between lines as the student's handwriting improves.

19. Use primary paper to assist the student in sizing upper-case and lower-case letters. Use standard-lined paper when the student's skills improve.

20. Use lined paper that is also vertically lined (e.g., | | | | |) to teach the student appropriate spacing skills (e.g., K | a | t | h | y).

21. Use adhesive material (e.g., tape, Dycem material, etc.) to keep paper positioned appropriately for handwriting.

22. Use a pencil grip (e.g., three-sided, foam rubber, etc.) in order to provide the student assistance in appropriate positioning of the pencil or pen.

23. Use handwriting models with arrows that indicate the direction in which the student should correctly form the letters.

24. Provide older students with functional handwriting opportunities (e.g., job application forms, reinforcer surveys, order forms, checks to write, etc.).

25. Make certain that all educators who work with the student maintain consistent expectations of handwriting quality.

26. Make certain the student has a number line and alphabet strip on his/her desk to use as a reference for the correct form of letters and numbers in order to reduce errors.

27. Make certain the student understands that work not done neatly must be redone until it is neat.

28. Recognize quality work (e.g., display student's work, congratulate the student, etc.).

29. Provide the student with shorter tasks, but more of them throughout the day (e.g., four assignments of five problems each rather than one assignment of 20 problems).

30. Reduce the emphasis on competition. Competitive activities may cause the student to rush through work.

31. If the student does not complete his/her work according to teacher directions and expectations, it must be completed during recreational or break time.

32. Have the student chart the number of times his/her handwriting is acceptable during a given week.

33. Use a different-sized pencil or pencil grip to assist the student with fine motor skills in order to produce acceptable handwriting.

34. Check the student's grip on the pencil to make certain that he/she is holding the pencil correctly.

35. Assign a peer to work with the student in order to provide an acceptable model for the student to imitate.

36. Evaluate the appropriateness of the task to determine: (a) if the task is too easy, (b) if the task is too difficult, and (c) if the length of time scheduled to complete the task is appropriate.

37. Communicate with parents (e.g., notes home, phone calls, etc.) in order to share information concerning the student's progress and so that they can reinforce the student at home for improving the quality of his/her handwriting at school.

38. Write a contract with the student specifying what behavior is expected (e.g., improving the quality of his/her handwriting) and what reinforcement will be made available when the terms of the contract have been met.

39. Reinforce the student for improving the quality of handwriting based on ability. Gradually increase the amount of improvement expected for reinforcement as the student demonstrates success.

40. Reinforce those students in the classroom who turn in assignments which are legible.

41. Establish classroom rules:
1. Work on task.
2. Work quietly.
3. Remain in your seat.
4. Finish task.
5. Meet task expectations.
Reiterate rules often and reinforce students for following rules.

42. Speak with the student to explain: (a) what the student is doing wrong (e.g., turning in work which has spelling errors or spacing errors, work that is illegible, etc.) and (b) what he/she should be doing (e.g., taking time to check for spelling, spacing errors, etc.).

43. Reinforce conscientiousness in improving handwriting (e.g., double-checking spelling, proper positioning of letters, correct spacing, etc.): (a) give the student a tangible reward (e.g., classroom privileges, line leading, passing out materials, five minutes free time, etc.) or (b) give the student an intangible reward (e.g., praise, handshake, smile, etc.).

59 Fails to copy letters, words, sentences, and numbers from a model at a close distance

1. Make certain the student's vision has been checked recently.

2. Enlarge the print from which the student is copying.

3. Change the format of the materials from which the student copies (e.g., have less material on a page, remove or cover pictures on pages, enlarge the print, etc.).

4. Highlight or underline the material the student is to copy.

5. Use a frame or window to cover all material except that which the student is to copy.

6. Have the student copy small amounts of material (e.g., a sentence or a line) at a time.

7. Make certain the student's desk is free of all material except that from which he/she is copying.

8. Provide the student with a private place to work (e.g., study carrel, private "office," etc.). This is used to reduce distracting stimuli and not as a form of punishment.

9. Provide a variety of ways for the student to obtain information without copying it (e.g., teacher-made material, commercially-produced material, photocopy of the material, etc.).

10. Use a projector to enlarge the material to be copied.

11. Have a peer assist the student in copying material (e.g., by reading the material aloud as the student copies it, copying the material for the student, etc.).

12. Maintain consistency in the format from which the student copies.

13. Provide more hands-on activities instead of copying materials from books.

14. Have the student practice writing letters, words, and sentences by tracing over a series of dots.

15. Make certain the student has a number line and alphabet strip on his/her desk to use as a reference for the correct form of letters and numbers in order to reduce errors.

16. Require the student to proofread all written work. Reinforce the student for each correction made.

17. Recognize quality work (e.g., display the student's work, congratulate the student, etc.).

18. Provide the student with quality materials to perform assignments (e.g., pencil with eraser, paper, dictionary, handwriting sample, etc.). Be certain that the student has only the necessary materials on his/her desk.

19. Assess the appropriateness of giving the student assignments which require copying at a close distance if the student's ability makes it impossible to complete assignments.

20. Reduce the emphasis on competition. Competitive activities may cause the student to hurry and commit any number of errors.

21. Identify any particular letters or numbers the student has difficulty copying, and have him/her practice copying those letters or numbers.

22. If a student wears glasses, encourage him/her to wear them while working.

23. Allow the student periods of rest in order to avoid eye fatigue.

24. Reduce distracting stimuli (e.g., noise and motion in the classroom, pictures in the textbook, etc.) in order to enhance the student's ability to copy letters, words, sentences, and numbers from a model at a close distance.

25. Have the student question any directions, explanations, and instructions not understood.

26. Evaluate the appropriateness of the task to determine: (a) if the task is too difficult and (b) if the length of time scheduled to complete the task is appropriate.

27. Reinforce the student for copying letters, words, sentences, and numbers from a model at a close distance: (a) give the student a tangible reward (e.g., classroom privileges, line leading, passing out materials, five minutes free time, etc.) or (b) give the student an intangible reward (e.g., praise, handshake, smile, etc.).

60 Fails to copy letters, words, sentences, and numbers from a model at a distance

1. Make certain the student's vision has been recently checked.

2. Enlarge the print from which the student is copying.

3. Change the format of the material from which the student copies (e.g., less material to be copied, enlarge the print, etc.).

4. Seat the student closer to the material being copied.

5. Highlight or underline the material the student is copying.

6. Have the student copy small amounts of material (e.g., a sentence or line) at a time.

7. Make certain that the student has only those materials necessary for copying (e.g., pencil, pen, paper, etc.) on his/her desk.

8. Provide the student with a private place to work (e.g., study carrel, "office," etc.). This is used to reduce distracting stimuli and not as a form of punishment.

9. Employ a variety of ways for the student to obtain information without copying it (e.g., teacher-made material, commercially-produced material, photocopy of the material, etc.).

10. Have a peer assist the student in copying the material (e.g., by reading the material aloud as the student copies it, copying the material for the student, etc.).

11. Make certain that the material to be copied has a clear background/foreground contrast in order to maximize visibility (e.g., black on white projections, white chalk on green chalkboard, etc.).

12. Place the material from which the student is to copy close to him/her. Gradually move the material away from the student as long as he/she can be successful.

13. Maintain consistency of the format from which the student copies.

14. Make certain that there is no glare on the material to be copied from a distance.

15. Provide the student with material to copy at his/her desk if he/she is unable to copy it from a distance.

16. Identify any particular letters or numbers the student has difficulty copying and have him/her practice copying those letters and numbers.

17. Have the student practice writing letters, words, and sentences by tracing over a series of dots.

18. Make certain the student has a number line and alphabet strip on his/her desk to use as a reference for the correct form of letters and numbers in order to reduce errors.

19. Require the student to proofread all written work. Reinforce the student for each correction made.

20. Recognize quality work (e.g., display the student's work, congratulate the student, etc.).

21. Provide the student with quality materials to perform assignments (e.g., pencil with eraser, paper, dictionary, handwriting sample, etc.). Be certain that the student has only the necessary materials on his/her desk.

22. Assess the appropriateness of giving the student assignments which require copying at a distance if the student's ability makes it impossible to complete the assignment.

23. Reduce the emphasis on competition. Competitive activities may cause the student to hurry and commit any number of errors.

24. Use the computer and monitor as an alternative writing tool.

25. If the student wears glasses, encourage him/her to wear them for board work.

26. Reduce distracting stimuli (e.g., noise and motion in the classroom) in order to enhance the student's ability to copy letters, words, sentences, and numbers from a model at a distance.

27. Have the student question any directions, explanations, and instructions not understood.

28. Evaluate the appropriateness of the task to determine: (a) if the task is too difficult and (b) if the length of time scheduled to complete the task is appropriate.

29. Reinforce the student for copying letters, words, sentences, and numbers from a model at a distance: (a) give the student a tangible reward (e.g., classroom privileges, line leading, passing out materials, five minutes free time, etc.) or (b) give the student an intangible reward (e.g., praise, handshake, smile, etc.).

61 Fails to use capitalization correctly when writing

1. Make certain the student knows how to write all the capital letters of the alphabet.

2. Highlight or underline all the capitalized letters in a passage or paragraph, and have the student explain why each is capitalized.

3. Have the student engage in writing activities which will cause him/her to do as well as possible in capitalization and other writing skills (e.g., writing letters to a friend, rock star, famous athlete, etc.).

4. Emphasize one rule of capitalization until the student masters that rule, before moving on to another rule (e.g., proper names, cities, states, streets, etc.).

5. Provide the student with lists of words and have him/her indicate which should be capitalized (e.g., *water, new york, mississippi,* etc.).

6. Have the student practice writing words which are always capitalized (e.g., countries, bodies of water, nationalities, languages, capitols, days of the week, months of the year, etc.).

7. After checking the student's work, require him/her to make all necessary corrections in capitalization.

8. Make certain the student proofreads his/her work for correct capitalization. Reinforce the student for each correction made in capitalization.

9. Give the student a series of sentences representing all the capitalization rules. Have the student identify the rules for each capitalization. Remove each sentence from the assignment when the student can explain the rules for the capitalization in the sentence.

10. Make certain the student has a list of rules for capitalization at his/her desk to use as a reference.

11. Recognize quality work (e.g., display the student's work, congratulate the student, etc.).

12. Provide the student with quality materials to perform the assignment (e.g., pencil with eraser, paper, dictionary, handwriting sample, etc.). Be certain that the student has only the necessary materials on his/her desk.

13. Make certain the student is not required to learn more information than he/she is capable of at any one time.

14. Provide practice in capitalization by using a computer software program that gives the student immediate feedback.

15. Make certain the student has mastery of capitalization at each level before introducing a new skill level.

16. Check the student's work at various points throughout an assignment to make certain the student is capitalizing where needed.

17. Make a notebook of rules for capitalization to be used to proofread work.

18. Display a capitalization rules chart in the front of the classroom.

19. Have the student find proper names, cities, states, etc., on a newspaper page and underline them.

20. Make certain the student receives instruction in the rules of capitalization (e.g., first word of a sentence; the pronoun *I*; proper names; cities; states; streets; months; days of the week; dates; holidays; titles of movies, books, newspapers and magazines; etc.).

21. Write a contract with the student specifying what behavior is expected (e.g., using capitalization correctly) and what reinforcement will be made available when the terms of the contract have been met.

22. Reduce emphasis on competition. Competitive activities may cause the student to hurry and make mistakes in capitalization.

23. Reinforce the student for capitalizing correctly: (a) give the student a tangible reward (e.g., classroom privileges, line leading, five minutes free time, etc.) or (b) give the student an intangible reward (e.g., praise, handshake, smile, etc.).

62 Uses inappropriate spacing between words or sentences when writing

1. Make certain the student's vision has been recently checked.

2. Have the student sit in an appropriate-sized chair with feet touching the floor, back pressed against the back of the chair, shoulders slightly inclined, and arms resting on the desk with elbows just off the lower edge.

3. Check the student's paper position. A right-handed person writing in cursive should tilt the paper to the left so the lower left-hand corner points toward the midsection; and as writing progresses the paper should shift, not the writing arm.

4. Make certain the student is shifting his/her paper when writing.

5. Using appropriate spacing, print or write words or sentences. Have the student trace what was written.

6. Reduce the emphasis on competition. Competitive activities may cause the student to hurry and fail to use correct spacing when writing words and sentences.

7. Provide the student with samples of hand-written words and sentences which he/she can use as a reference for correct spacing.

8. Have the student leave a finger space between each word he/she writes and dots between letters.

9. Draw vertical lines for the student to use to space letters and words (e.g., | | | |).

10. Teach the student to always look at the next word to determine if there is enough space to the margin.

11. Provide the student with graph paper, instructing him/her to write letters in each block, while skipping a block between words and sentences.

12. Recognize quality work (e.g., display the student's work, congratulate the student, etc.).

13. Provide the student with quality materials to perform the assignment (e.g., pencil with eraser, paper, dictionary, handwriting sample, etc.). Be certain that the student has only these necessary materials on his/her desk.

14. Check the student's work at various points throughout an assignment to make certain the student is using appropriate spacing.

15. Give the student one handwriting task to perform at a time. Introduce the next task only when the student has successfully completed the previous task.

16. Assign the student shorter tasks and gradually increase the number over time as the student demonstrates success.

17. Have the student practice writing letters, words, and sentences by tracing over a series of dots.

18. Have the student engage in writing activities designed to cause the student to want to be successful in writing (e.g., writing a letter to a friend, rock star, famous athlete, etc.).

19. Have the student look at correctly written material to serve as a model.

20. Have the student perform a "practice page" before turning in the actual assignment.

21. Reinforce the student for each word and/or sentence that is appropriately spaced: (a) give the student a tangible reward (e.g., classroom privileges, line leading, five minutes free time, etc.) or (b) give the student an intangible reward (e.g., praise, handshake, smile, etc.).

63 Reverses letters and numbers when writing

1. Make certain the student's vision has been checked recently.

2. Use board activities (e.g., drawing lines, circles, etc.) to teach the student proper directionality of each letter and numeral.

3. Physically guide the student's hand, providing the feeling of directionality.

4. Place letters on transparencies and project them on the chalkboard or paper. Have the student trace the letters.

5. Have the student trace letters and numbers in magazines, newspapers, etc., which he/she typically reverses when writing.

6. When correcting papers with reversed letters, use arrows to remind the student of correct directionality.

7. Identify the letters and numbers the student reverses and have him/her practice making one or more of the letters correctly each day.

8. Make certain the student recognizes the correct form of the letters and numbers when he/she sees them (e.g., *b, d, 2, 5,* etc.).

9. Make certain the student checks all work for those letters and numbers he/she typically reverses. Reinforce the student for correcting any reversed letters and numbers.

10. Provide the student with visual cues to aid in making letters and numbers (e.g., arrows indicating strokes).

11. Provide the student with large letters and numbers to trace which he/she typically reverses.

12. Given letters and numbers on separate cards, have the student match the letters and numbers that are the same.

13. Have the student keep a card with the word *bed* at his/her desk to help in remembering the correct form of *b* and *d* in a word he/she knows.

14. Have the student keep a list of the most commonly used words which contain letters he/she reverses. This list can be used as a reference when the student is writing.

15. After identifying those letters and numbers the student reverses, have him/her highlight or underline those letters and numbers found in a magazine, newspaper, etc.

16. Point out the subtle differences between letters and numbers that the student reverses. Have the student scan five typewritten lines containing only the letters or numbers that are confusing (e.g., *nnhnhhnn*). Have the student circle the "n's" and the "h's" with different colors.

17. Cursive handwriting may prevent reversals and may be used by some students as an alternative to manuscript.

18. Make certain the student has a number line and alphabet strip on his/her desk to use as a reference to make the correct form of letters and numbers.

19. Reduce the emphasis on competition. Competitive activities may cause the student to hurry and reverse numbers and letters when writing.

20. Recognize quality work (e.g., display the student's work, congratulate the student, etc.).

21. Have the student practice writing letters, words, and sentences by tracing over a series of dots.

22. Require the student to proofread all written work. Reinforce the student for each correction made.

23. Have the student engage in writing activities designed to cause the student to want to be successful in writing (e.g., writing a letter to a friend, rock star, famous athlete, etc.).

24. Make certain that the student's formation of letters is appropriate and consistently correct. In manuscript writing, all strokes progressing from top to bottom, left to right, use a forward circle (e.g., circling to the right) for letters that begin with a line (e.g., *b*), and the backward circle (e.g., circling to the left) for letters in which the circle is written before the line (e.g., *d*).

25. Reinforce the student for making letters and numbers correctly when writing: (a) give the student a tangible reward (e.g., classroom privileges, line leading, passing out materials, five minutes free time, etc.) or (b) give the student an intangible reward (e.g., praise, handshake, smile, etc.).

64 Fails to write within a given space

1. Make certain the student's vision has been checked recently.

2. Evaluate the appropriateness of the task to determine: (a) if the task is too difficult and (b) if the length of time scheduled to complete the task is appropriate.

3. Check the student's paper position. A right-handed person writing in cursive should tilt the paper to the left so the lower left-hand corner points toward the midsection; and as writing progresses the paper should shift, not the writing arm.

4. Check the student's pencil grasp. The pencil should be held between the thumb and first two fingers, holding the instrument one inch from its tip, with the top pointing toward the right shoulder (if right-handed).

5. Make certain the student is shifting his/her paper as writing progresses.

6. Draw a margin on the right side of the student's paper as a reminder for him/her to write within a given space.

7. Place a ruler or construction paper on the baseline, making certain the student touches the line for each letter.

8. Use a ruled paper with a midline, explaining to the student that minimum letters (e.g., *a, b, c, d, f, g, h,* etc.) touch the midline.

9. Highlight lines on the paper for the student to use as a prompt.

10. Reinforce the student for each word or letter correctly spaced.

11. Have the student look at correctly written material to serve as a model for him/her to imitate.

12. Provide the student with extra-large sheets of paper on which to write. Gradually reduce the size of the paper to standard size as the student demonstrates success.

13. Allow the student to draw lines on his/her paper for writing activities.

14. Provide the student with a physical prompt by guiding his/her hand as he/she writes.

15. Have the student correct his/her own writing errors.

16. Have the student perform a "practice page" before turning in the actual assignment.

17. Have the student practice writing letters, words, and sentences by tracing over a series of dots.

18. Darken the lines on the paper in order that the student can more easily use them to write within the given space.

19. Recognize quality work (e.g., display student's work, congratulate the student, etc.).

20. Provide the student with quality materials to perform the assignment (e.g., pencil with eraser, paper, dictionary, handwriting sample, etc.). Be certain that the student has only the necessary materials on his/her desk.

21. Check the student's work at various points during an assignment in order to make certain that the student is writing within a given space.

22. Give the student one handwriting task to perform at a time. Introduce the next task only when the student has successfully completed the previous task.

23. Give the student shorter writing assignments, and gradually increase the length of assignments over time as the student demonstrates success.

24. Use vertical lines or graph paper to help the student space letters correctly.

25. Have the student engage in writing activities designed to cause the student to want to be successful in writing (e.g., writing a letter to a friend, rock star, famous athlete, etc.).

65 Fails to punctuate correctly when writing

1. Give the student sentences to complete requiring specific punctuation he/she is learning to use (e.g., periods, commas, question marks, etc.).

2. Have the student practice using one form of punctuation at a time before going on to another (e.g., period, question mark, etc.).

3. Highlight or underline punctuation in passages from the student's reading assignment. Have the student explain why each form of punctuation is used.

4. Require the student to proofread all written work for correct punctuation. Reinforce the student for each correction made on punctuation.

5. Have the student keep a list of basic rules of punctuation at his/her desk to use as a reference when writing (e.g., use a period at the end of a sentence, etc.).

6. Write a contract with the student specifying what behavior is expected (e.g., using punctuation correctly) and what reinforcement will be made available when the terms of the contract have been met.

7. Make certain the student receives instruction in the rules of punctuation (e.g., a period belongs at the end of a sentence, a question mark is used when a question is asked, etc.).

8. Make certain the student knows what all punctuation marks look like and their uses.

9. Have the student engage in writing activities which will cause him/her to do as well as possible on punctuation and other writing skills (e.g., writing letters to a friend, rock star, famous athlete, etc.).

10. After checking the student's work, require him/her to make all necessary corrections in punctuation.

11. Recognize quality work (e.g., display the student's work, congratulate the student, etc.).

12. Give the student a series of sentences representing all the punctuation rules. Have the student identify the rules for each punctuation. Remove a sentence from the assignment when the student can explain the rules for punctuation in the sentence.

13. Provide the student with quality materials to perform the assignment (e.g., pencil with eraser, paper, dictionary, handwriting sample, etc.). Be certain that the student has only the necessary materials on his/her desk.

14. Make certain the student is not required to learn more information than he/she is capable of at any one time.

15. Provide practice in punctuation by using a computer program that gives the student immediate feedback.

16. Make certain the student has mastery of punctuation at each level before introducing a new skill level.

17. Check the student's work at various points throughout an assignment to make certain the student is using appropriate punctuation.

18. Give the student a set of 3 cards: one with a period, one with a question mark, and one with an exclamation point. As you read a sentence to the student have him/her hold up the appropriate punctuation card.

19. Give the student a list of sentences in which the punctuation has been omitted. Have the student supply the correct punctuation with colored pencils.

20. Make a notebook of punctuation rules to be used when the student proofreads work.

21. Use a newspaper to locate different types of punctuation. Have the student circle periods in red, commas in blue, etc.

22. Display a chart of punctuation rules in the front of the classroom.

23. Reduce the emphasis on competition. Competitive activities may cause the student to hurry and make errors in punctuation.

24. Reinforce the student for using correct punctuation when writing: (a) give the student a tangible reward (e.g., classroom privileges, line leading, five minutes free time, etc.) or (b) give the student an intangible reward (e.g., praise, handshake, smile, etc.).

66 Does not use appropriate subject-verb agreement when writing

1. Require the student to proofread his/her written work for subject-verb agreement. Reinforce the student for correcting all errors.

2. Have the student complete written worksheets on which he/she must supply the correct verb form to go with specific subjects (e.g., "He ___ the dishes.").

3. Have the student pick out the correct verb when given choices on "fill-in-the-blank" worksheets (e.g., "They ____ (have, has) a new dog.").

4. Give the student specific verb forms and have him/her supply appropriate subjects to go with each (e.g., "___ runs.").

5. Have the student make up sentences with given verbs and subjects.

6. Have the student help correct other students' written work by checking subject-verb agreement and correcting the assignment.

7. Give the student a series of sentences with both incorrect and correct usage of verbs and ask the student to identify which are correct and which are incorrect.

8. Have the student find examples of correct subject-verb agreement in his/her favorite books or magazines.

9. Identify the most common errors the student makes in subject-verb agreement. Have the student spend time each day writing one or more of these subject-verb combinations in correct form.

10. Identify and make a list of the correct forms of subject-verb combinations the student has difficulty writing and have the student keep the list at his/her desk for a reference.

11. Reduce the emphasis on competition. Competitive activities may cause the student to hurry and make errors in subject-verb agreement.

12. Make certain the student receives instruction in subject-verb agreement for those subject-verb combinations he/she commonly has difficulty writing correctly.

13. Correct the student each time he/she uses subject-verb agreement incorrectly when speaking.

14. Make certain the student knows that different forms of verbs go with subjects and that correct subject-verb agreement requires the appropriate verb form. Have the student practice matching verb forms to lists of subjects.

15. Have the student read the written work of peers in which subject-verb agreement is used correctly.

16. Highlight or underline subject-verb agreements in the student's reading in order to call attention to the appropriate combinations.

17. After checking the student's written work, make certain he/she makes all necessary corrections in subject-verb agreement.

18. Recognize quality work (e.g., display the student's work, congratulate the student, etc.).

19. Make certain the student is not required to learn more information than he/she is capable of at any one time.

20. Have the student act as a peer tutor to teach another student a concept the student has mastered. This can serve as reinforcement for the student.

21. Give the student a choice of answers on worksheets (e.g., "fill-in-the-blank"). This increases the student's opportunity for recognizing the correct answer.

22. Review, on a daily basis, those skills, concepts, tasks, etc., which have been previously introduced.

23. Provide the student with increased opportunity for help or assistance on academic tasks (e.g., peer tutoring, directions for work sent home, frequent interactions, etc.).

24. Show the student pictures of people, places, or things. Ask him/her to make a statement about each picture. Have the student identify the subject and verb of the oral sentence and tell whether or not they agree.

25. Play a game such as *Concentration* to match subject-verb agreement.

26. Speak to the student to explain that he/she is using inappropriate subject-verb agreement, and emphasize the importance of writing grammatically correct sentences.

27. Ascertain the type of grammatical model to which the student is exposed at home. Without placing negative connotations on his/her parent's grammatical style, explain the difference between standard and nonstandard grammar.

28. Make sure the student understands the concept of "subject" and "verb" by demonstrating through the use of objects, pictures, and/or written sentences (depending on the student's abilities).

29. Make sure the student understands that sentences express thoughts about a subject and what that subject is or does.

30. Make sure the student understands the concept of plurality (e.g., have the student "point to a picture of a cat" and "point to a picture of cats").

31. Explain that certain forms of verbs go with certain subjects and that correct subject-verb agreement requires the appropriate match of subject and verb. Be certain that the student knows the various possibilities of subject-verb agreement and how to select the correct one.

32. Make a list of those verbs the student most commonly uses incorrectly. This list will become the guide for learning activities in subject-verb agreement.

33. Give the student a series of sentences, both written and oral, and have him/her identify which are grammatically correct and incorrect.

34. Reinforce the student for using appropriate subject-verb agreement when writing: (a) give the student a tangible reward (e.g., classroom privileges, line leading, passing out materials, five minutes free time, etc.) or (b) give the student an intangible reward (e.g., praise, handshake, smile, etc.).

67 Does not compose complete sentences or express complete thoughts when writing

1. Require the student to proofread all written work and reinforce him/her for completing sentences or expressing complete thoughts.

2. Give the student a series of written phrases and have him/her indicate which ones express complete thoughts.

3. Have the student correct a series of phrases by making each a complete sentence.

4. After reading his/her written work, have the student explain why specific sentences do not express complete thoughts.

5. Give the student a subject and have him/her write as many complete sentences as possible.

6. Make groups of cards containing subjects, verbs, adjectives, etc. Have the student combine the cards in various ways to construct complete sentences.

7. Give the student several short sentences and have him/her combine them in order to make one longer, complete sentence (e.g., *The dog is big. The dog is brown. The dog is mine.* becomes *The big, brown dog is mine.*).

8. Give the student a list of transition words (e.g., *therefore, although, because,* etc.) and have him/her make sentences using each word.

9. Make certain the student understands that a complete sentence has to express a complete thought about a subject and what that subject is or does.

10. Have the student write a daily log, expressing his/her thoughts in complete sentences.

11. Have the student write letters to friends, relatives, etc., in order to practice writing complete sentences and thoughts.

12. Encourage the student to read written work aloud in order to identify incomplete sentences and thoughts.

13. Give the student a group of related words (e.g., *author, read, love, bestseller,* etc.) and have him/her make up a paragraph including all the words.

14. Provide the student with clearly stated criteria for acceptable work (e.g., neatness, complete sentences, etc.).

15. Recognize quality work (e.g., display the student's work, congratulate the student, etc.).

16. Check the student's written work at various points throughout the assignment to make certain the student is using complete sentences.

17. Provide the student with appropriate time limits for the completion of written assignments.

18. Play a game by providing students with a box labeled "Trash." Provide sentence strips with complete and incomplete sentences. Instruct students to "trash" incomplete sentences.

19. Provide exercises for making sentences out of nonsentence groups of words.

20. Read orally to the student to stimulate the student's thinking and writing processes.

21. Be certain to act as a model for the student to imitate writing in complete sentences or thoughts.

22. Have a peer act as a model for writing in complete sentences or thoughts. Assign the students to work together, perform assignments together, etc.

23. Have the student identify a person who he/she thinks is a good writer and tell why.

24. Identify the qualities a good writer possesses (e.g., writing in complete sentences or thoughts, using correct vocabulary, etc.), and have the student evaluate himself/herself on each characteristic. Set a goal for improvement in one or two areas at a time.

25. Reduce the emphasis on competition. Competitive activities may cause the student to hurry and fail to write in complete sentences.

26. Reinforce the students in the classroom who use complete sentences or thoughts when writing.

27. Reinforce the student for using complete sentences or thoughts when writing: (a) give the student a tangible reward (e.g., classroom privileges, line leading, passing out materials, five minutes free time, etc.) or (b) give the student an intangible reward (e.g., praise, handshake, smile, etc.).

68 Fails to correctly organize writing activities

1. Have the student practice organizational skills in writing activities by having him/her engage in writing activities designed to cause the student to want to be successful (e.g., writing a letter to a friend, rock star, famous athlete, etc.).

2. Have the student write an account of the previous week, past weekend, etc., with primary attention given to organization (e.g., sequencing events, developing a paragraph, using correct word order, etc.).

3. Require the student to proofread all written work. Reinforce all corrections in organization.

4. Have the student write a daily log, expressing his/her thoughts in complete sentences.

5. Have the student create stories about topics which are of interest. The student is more likely to try to be successful if he/she is writing about something of interest.

6. Have the student read his/her written work aloud to help identify errors in organization.

7. Make certain the student knows that paragraphs, essays, etc., need an introduction, a middle where information is contained, and a conclusion or ending.

8. Have the student arrange a series of statements on a topic in an appropriate order so that they make sense in a paragraph.

9. Teach outlining principles to the student so he/she understands the difference between main ideas and supporting details.

10. Help the student "brain storm" ideas about a topic and then show him/her how to put these ideas into outline form, combining some ideas and discarding others.

11. Give the student a group of related words (e.g., *author, read, love, bestseller*, etc.) and have him/her make up an appropriately organized paragraph including each word.

12. Provide the student with a paragraph in which one statement does not belong. Have the student find the inappropriate statement.

13. Have the student write step-by-step directions (e.g., steps in making a cake) so he/she can practice sequencing events.

14. Using a written essay that the student has not seen, cut the paragraphs apart and ask him/her to reconstruct the essay by putting the paragraphs in an appropriate order.

15. Reduce the emphasis on competition. Competitive activities may cause the student to hurry and fail to correctly organize writing activities.

16. Reduce distracting stimuli by placing the student in a study carrel or "office" when engaged in writing activities. This is used as a means of reducing distracting stimuli and not as a form of punishment.

17. Make certain the student is not interrupted or hurried when engaging in writing activities.

18. Have the student read sentences, paragraphs, stories, etc., written by peers who demonstrate good organizational skills in writing.

19. When correcting the student's organizational skills in writing, be certain to provide evaluative feedback which is designed to be instructional (e.g., help the student rewrite for better organization, rewrite passages for the student, etc.).

20. Have the student develop organizational skills in writing simple sentences. Gradually increase the required complexity of sentence structure and move on to paragraphs, short stories, etc., as the student demonstrates success.

21. Have the student develop an outline or "skeleton" of what he/she is going to write. From the outline the student can then practice organizational skills in writing.

22. Recognize quality work (e.g., display the student's work, congratulate the student, etc.).

23. Make certain the student is not required to learn more information than he/she is capable of at any one time.

24. Provide practice in organizing writing activities by using a computer software program that gives the student immediate feedback.

25. Make certain the student has mastery of writing concepts at each level before introducing a new skill level.

26. Check the student's work frequently to make certain that the student is organizing the writing activity appropriately.

27. Provide the student with appropriate time limits for the completion of assignments.

28. On a piece of paper, write five or six sentences about a story the student has read. Have the student cut the sentences apart and paste them together in the proper order.

29. Have the student write a paragraph describing the events of a daily comic strip such as *Peanuts*.

30. Reinforce the student for correctly organizing writing activities: (a) give the student a tangible reward (e.g., classroom privileges, line leading, passing out materials, etc.) or (b) give the student an intangible reward (e.g., praise, handshake, smile, etc.).

69 Omits, adds, or substitutes words when writing

1. Speak to the student to explain what he/she is doing wrong (e.g., not writing in clear and complete sentences, leaving words out, etc.) and what he/she should be doing (e.g., writing in clear and complete sentences, rereading written work, etc.).

2. Reduce the emphasis on competition. Competitive activities may cause the student to hurry and omit, add, or substitute words when writing.

3. Have the student proofread all written work for omissions, additions, or substitutions. Reinforce the student for correcting omissions, additions, or substitutions.

4. Encourage the student to read all written work aloud in order to detect omissions, additions, or substitutions.

5. Give the student several sentences and have him/her combine them to practice making a complete sentence (e.g., *The car is new. The car is red. The car is mine.* becomes *The new, red car is mine.*).

6. Give the student a list of transition words (e.g., *therefore, although, because,* etc.) and have him/her make sentences using each word.

7. Have the student write a daily log or diary expressing thoughts in complete sentences.

8. Encourage the student to create stories about topics which interest him/her in order to provide more experiences in writing.

9. Have the student complete "fill-in-the-blank" stories and sentences and then read them aloud.

10. Make certain the student is aware of the types of errors made (e.g., omits *is,* omits final *s,* etc.) in order to be more conscious of them when writing.

11. Make certain the student is not interrupted or hurried when engaged in writing activities.

12. Have the student assist in grading or proofreading other students' written work in order to become more aware of omissions, additions, and substitutions.

13. Have the student engage in writing activities designed to cause him/her to want to be successful in writing (e.g., writing a letter to a friend, rock star, famous athlete, etc.).

14. When correcting or grading the student's writing, be certain to provide evaluative feedback which is designed to be instructional (e.g., point out all omissions, additions, and substitutions; suggest more appropriate words or phrases; help the student rewrite work to make corrections in the omissions, additions, and substitutions; etc.).

15. Give the student scrambled words from a sentence and have him/her put them in the correct order to form the sentence.

16. Give the student a group of related words (e.g., *baseball, fans, glove, strikeout,* etc.) and have him/her make up a paragraph including each word.

17. Reduce distracting stimuli when the student is engaged in writing activities by placing the student in a carrel or "office" space. This is used as a means of reducing the distracting stimuli and not as a form of punishment.

18. Make a list of the student's most common omissions, additions, and substitutions and have him/her refer to the list when engaged in writing activities in order to check for errors.

19. Have the student practice writing simple sentences successfully without omissions, additions, and substitutions.

20. Make certain the student has written work proofread by someone (e.g., aide, peer, etc.) for omissions, additions, and substitutions before turning in the completed assignment.

21. Recognize quality work (e.g., display the student's work, congratulate the student, etc.).

22. Check the student's work at various points throughout a writing assignment in order to detect any omissions, additions, or substitutions.

23. Require the student to proofread all written work. Reinforce the student for each correction made.

24. Dictate sentences to the student to encourage successful writing of simple sentences.

25. Have the student read simple passages and tape record them. Then have the student underline passages that were omitted.

70 Fails to form letters correctly when printing or writing

1. Make certain the student is instructed in letter formation, giving the student oral as well as physical descriptions and demonstrations.

2. Provide the student with physical prompts by moving the student's hand, giving him/her a feeling of directionality.

3. Have the student practice tracing letters at his/her desk.

4. Have the student practice tracing letters on the chalkboard. Write the letters on the chalkboard for the student to trace.

5. Use arrows to show the student directionality when tracing or using dot-to-dot to form letters.

6. Use color cues for lines (e.g., red for the top line, yellow for the middle line, green for the bottom line) to indicate where letters are to be made.

7. Draw simple shapes and lines for the student to practice forming on lined paper.

8. Highlight the base line or top line on the paper in order to help the student stay within the given space.

9. Identify those letters the student does not form correctly. Have him/her practice the correct form of one or more of the letters each day.

10. Make certain the student sits in an appropriate-sized chair with feet touching the floor, his/her back pressed against the back of the chair, shoulders slightly inclined, and arms resting on the desk with elbows just off the lower edge.

11. Check the student's writing position. A right-handed person writing in cursive should tilt the paper to the left so the lower left-hand corner points toward the midsection. As writing progresses, the paper should shift, not the writing arm.

12. Check the student's pencil grasp. The pencil should be held between the thumb and the first two fingers, one inch from its tip, with the top pointing toward the right shoulder (if right-handed).

13. Have the student practice tracing with reduced cues. Write the complete letter and have the student trace it. Gradually provide less of the letter for the student to trace (e.g., dashes, then dots) as he/she is successful.

14. To facilitate appropriate holding of a pencil, put colored tape on parts of the pencil to correspond to finger positions. Then put colored tape on the student's fingernails and have the student match colors.

15. Reduce the emphasis on competition. Competitive activities may cause the student to hurry and fail to form letters correctly.

16. Make certain the student has an alphabet strip attached to his/her desk in either printed or written form to serve as a model for the correct form of letters.

17. Have a peer act as a model for the student while working daily on drill activities involving letter formation, ending and connecting strokes, spacing, and slant.

18. Have the student practice forming letters correctly using writing activities which are most likely to cause the student to want to be successful (e.g., writing a letter to a friend, rock star, famous athlete; filling out a job application, contest form, etc.).

19. Recognize quality work (e.g., display the student's work, congratulate the student, etc.).

20. Provide the student with quality materials to perform the assignment (e.g., pencil with eraser, paper, handwriting sample, etc.). Be certain that the student has only those necessary materials on his/her desk.

21. Make certain the student is not required to learn more information than he/she is capable of at any one time.

22. Make certain the student has mastery of handwriting concepts at each level before introducing a new skill level.

23. Check the student's handwriting work at various points throughout a handwriting activity to make certain that the student is forming letters correctly.

24. Have the student practice forming letters correctly by tracing over a series of dots.

25. Make certain the student has a number line and alphabet strip on the desk to use as a reference for the correct form of letters and numbers.

26. Require the student to proofread all written work. Reinforce the student for each correction made.

27. Use specific manipulatives (e.g., strings, toothpicks, etc.) to form letters for visual models.

28. Reinforce the student for making correct letters: (a) give the student a tangible reward (e.g., classroom privileges, line leading, passing out materials, five minutes free time, etc.) or (b) give the student an intangible reward (e.g., praise, handshake, smile, etc.).

71   Fails to use verb tenses correctly when writing

1. Provide the student with examples of verb tenses for those verbs most commonly used incorrectly, and have the student keep the examples for reference.

2. Make a list of those verbs the student most commonly uses incorrectly. This list of verb tenses will become the guide for learning activities using verb tenses.

3. Reinforce the student with praise for using verb tenses correctly when writing.

4. Write a contract with the student specifying what behavior is expected (e.g., using correct verb tenses) and what reinforcement will be made available when the terms of the contract have been met.

5. Identify a peer to act as a model for the student to imitate using correct verb tenses.

6. Make certain the student understands that changes must be made in a verb in order to indicate when an event happened (e.g., past, present, future).

7. Have the student complete written worksheets in which he/she must supply the correct verb tense to go in the sentence (e.g., "Yesterday I ___ to my house.").

8. Have the student pick out the correct verb tense on "fill-in-the-blank" worksheets (e.g., "Tomorrow she ___ (ate, eat, will eat) her supper.").

9. Give the student specific verb tenses and have him/her supply appropriate sentences to go with each (e.g., *played*: "John played at my house last night.").

10. Have the student listen to examples of incorrect verb tenses and then identify each error and correct it.

11. Give the student a series of sentences (both oral and written) and ask him/her to indicate if each is grammatically correct.

12. Have the student make up sentences with given verbs in past, present, and future tenses.

13. Present a series of sentences and ask the student to change the tense from past to present, present to future, etc.

14. Ask the parents to help encourage the student's correct use of verb tenses by praising him/her when grammar is appropriate.

15. Explain the importance of correctly written communication and what would happen if the verb tenses were used incorrectly (e.g., confusion as to when an event took place).

16. Make certain the student proofreads all written work and makes corrections in verb tenses. Reinforce the student for each correction.

17. Allow the student to assist in proofreading or grading other students' papers in order to increase awareness of correct verb tense usage.

18. Encourage the student to read written work aloud in order to find errors in verb tenses.

19. Read a series of sentences to the student and have him/her identify which ones are in the past, present, or future tense.

20. Make certain the student knows or has access to all tenses of most commonly used verbs (e.g., have the student keep a list at his/her desk of the most commonly used verbs with their tenses).

21. Have a peer practice verb tenses with the student. Each tense is used in a sentence rather than only conjugating verbs.

22. Make conjugating of verb tenses a daily activity.

23. Recognize quality work (e.g., display the student's work, congratulate the student, etc.).

24. Make certain the student is not required to learn more information than he/she is capable of at any one time.

25. Provide the student with quality materials to perform the assignment (e.g., pencil with eraser, paper, dictionary, handwriting sample, etc.). Be certain the student has only those necessary materials on his/her desk.

26. Make certain the student has mastery of writing concepts at each level before introducing a new skill level.

27. Give the student a choice of answers on worksheets (e.g., "fill-in-the-blank," etc.). This increases the student's opportunity for recognizing the correct answer.

28. Check the student's work at various points throughout the assignment to make certain the student is using appropriate verb tenses.

29. Have the student engage in writing activities designed to cause him/her to want to be successful in writing (e.g., writing a letter to a friend, rock star, famous athlete, etc.).

30. Reinforce those students in the classroom who use correct verb tenses when writing.

31. Reinforce the student for using appropriate verb tenses when writing: (a) give the student a tangible reward (e.g., classroom privileges, line leading, passing out materials, five minutes free time, etc.) or (b) give the student an intangible reward (e.g., praise, handshake, smile, etc.).

72 Uses inappropriate letter size when writing

1. Check the student's posture. Have the student sit in an appropriately-sized chair with feet touching the floor, back pressed against the back of the chair, shoulders slightly inclined, and arms resting comfortably on the desk with elbows just off the edge.

2. Check the student's paper position. A right-handed person writing in cursive should tilt the paper to the left so the lower left-hand corner points toward the midsection; and as writing progresses the paper should shift, not the writing arm.

3. Check the student's pencil grasp. The pencil should be grasped between the thumb and first two fingers, holding the instrument one inch from its tip, with the top pointing toward the right shoulder (if right-handed).

4. Use paper that has a midline and a descender space.

5. Have the student identify maximum (*b, d, f, h, k, l,*), intermediate (*t*), and minimum (*a, c, e, g, i, j, m, n, o, p, q, r, s, u, v, w, x, y, z*) letters in order to help him/her locate the correct placement of each group.

6. Make certain the student is shifting his/her paper as writing progresses.

7. Evaluate writing alignment by drawing a horizontal line across the tops of the letters that are to be of the same size.

8. Highlight lines on the paper as a reminder for the student to make the correct letter size.

9. Have a peer act as a model for the student to imitate making letters the appropriate size when writing.

10. Be certain the student has samples of letters of the appropriate size for activities requiring writing.

11. Provide the student with an alphabet strip at his/her desk with letters of the size to be used.

12. Write letters on the student's paper and have him/her trace them.

13. Write letters on the student's paper in broken lines and have the student connect the lines.

14. Darken the lines on the student's paper which should be used for correct letter size.

15. Have the student correct his/her mistakes in letter size.

16. Draw boxes to indicate the size of specific letters in relationship to the lines.

17. Using examples written on grid paper, have the student copy the examples beneath them.

18. Using tracing paper, have the student trace over specific letters or words.

19. Using a series of dots, have the student trace words or sentences.

20. Using an original story written by the student, prepare a transparency to use on an overhead projector. Project the story onto a paper on the wall for the student to trace. This is particularly appropriate for those students who want to write too small.

21. Provide the student with clearly stated criteria for acceptable work (e.g., neatness, etc.).

22. Recognize quality work (e.g., display the student's work, congratulate the student, etc.).

23. Provide the student with quality materials to perform the assignment (e.g., pencil with eraser, paper, dictionary, handwriting sample, etc.). Be certain that the student has only those necessary materials on his/her desk.

24. Make certain the student has mastery of handwriting concepts at each level before introducing a new skill level.

25. Check the student's work at various points throughout the assignment to make certain that the student is making letters the appropriate size.

26. Use vertical lines or graph paper to help the student space letters correctly.

27. Provide the student with a different-sized pencil or pencil grip.

28. Evaluate the appropriateness of the task to determine: (a) if the task is too difficult and (b) if the length of time scheduled to complete the task is appropriate.

29. Reinforce the student for using appropriate letter size when writing: (a) give the student a tangible reward (e.g., classroom privileges, line leading, passing out materials, five minutes free time, etc.) or (b) give the student an intangible reward (e.g., praise, handshake, smile, etc.).

30. Make certain the student's vision has been recently checked.

73 Fails to use spelling rules

1. Have the student write current spelling words in different locations throughout the classroom as he/she is learning them (e.g., on the chalkboard, transparencies, a posted list at his/her desk, etc.).

2. Teach spelling rules integrated with the total language arts program (e.g., activities, methods, and materials related to the teaching of spelling, reading, and language as a whole rather than in parts).

3. Require the student to use a dictionary to find the correct spelling of any word he/she cannot spell correctly. The emphasis in this situation becomes spelling accurately rather than memorizing spelling words.

4. Have the student practice spelling rules in a meaningful manner which will cause him/her to want to be successful (e.g., writing a letter to a friend, rock star, famous athlete, etc.).

5. Make certain the student knows why he/she is learning spelling rules (e.g., provide the student with a concrete example of how each word can be used in his/her life).

6. Have the student identify a list of spelling words (e.g., 5, 10, or 15) each week which he/she wants to learn to spell. Have the student learn to spell these words using the spelling rules.

7. Make certain the student has had adequate practice using the spelling rules in writing words, sentences, etc.

8. Make certain the student has adequate time to perform written assignments in order to increase the likelihood of using spelling rules.

9. Reduce distracting stimuli in the classroom when the student is working on spelling and related activities (e.g., place the student in a carrel or "office" space).

10. Make certain the student is not being required to learn too many spelling words at one time.

11. Make certain the student learns to use spelling rules to spell words correctly rather than simply memorizing the spelling of words for testing purposes (e.g., *I* before *e* except after *c*, etc.).

12. Have the student keep a dictionary of "most often misspelled words" at his/her desk, and require the student to check the spelling of all words he/she is not certain are spelled correctly.

13. Have the student practice one spelling rule consistently until that rule is mastered (e.g., *I* before *e* except after *c*, etc.). When one rule is mastered, a new one is introduced.

14. Require the student to proofread written assignments using spelling rules. Reinforce the student for each correction made when using spelling rules.

15. Develop a list of spelling rules. Have the student keep the list of spelling rules at his/her desk, and require the student to refer to the rules when writing words, sentences, etc.

16. Require the student to verbally explain how he/she spells words using spelling rules (e.g., *I* before *e* except after *c*, etc.).

17. Require the student to practice those basic spelling rules which he/she uses on a daily basis.

18. Recognize quality work (e.g., display the student's work, congratulate the student, etc.).

19. Make certain the student is not required to learn more information than he/she is capable of at any one time.

20. Have the student act as a peer tutor to teach another student a spelling concept he/she has mastered. This can serve as reinforcement for the student.

21. Provide practice in spelling by using a computer software program that gives the student immediate feedback.

22. Make certain the student has mastery of spelling concepts at each level before introducing a new skill level.

23. Use daily drill activities to help the student memorize spelling rules.

24. Provide the student with self-checking materials, requiring correction before turning in assignments.

25. Have the student practice a new spelling skill with an aide, the teacher, a peer, etc., before the entire group attempts the activity or before performing for a grade.

26. Make certain the student has adequate opportunities for repetition of information through different experiences in order to enhance his/her memory.

27. Review, on a daily basis, those spelling skills which have been previously introduced.

28. Deliver information to the student on a one-to-one basis or employ a peer tutor.

29. Make up a rap using the spelling rule.

30. Print a spelling word and cut it apart letter-by-letter to make a puzzle word. Have the student scramble the letters and then arrange them in the correct order to spell the word.

31. Have the student type a list of spelling words.

32. Keep a salt box (or a sandbox) for the student to trace spelling words in.

33. Give the student a magazine or newspaper. Have him/her highlight words which follow spelling rules being studied.

34. Every day have the student practice using spelling rules in written words, sentences, etc.

35. Have a peer spend time each day with the student to practice the use of spelling rules when writing words, sentences, etc.

36. Reduce the emphasis on competition. Competitive activities may cause the student to hurry and make mistakes.

37. Reinforce the student for using spelling rules: (a) give the student a tangible reward (e.g., classroom privileges, line leading, passing out materials, five minutes free time, etc.) or (b) give the student an intangible reward (e.g., praise, handshake, smile, etc.).

1. Give the student fewer words to learn to spell at any one time, spending more time on each word until the student can spell it correctly.

2. Have a peer spend time with the student each day engaged in drill activities on spelling words phonetically.

3. Have the student use a phonetic approach to spelling words in sentences written each day.

4. Teach spelling integrated with the total language arts program (e.g., activities, methods, and materials are related to the teaching of reading and language as a whole rather than in parts).

5. Have the student identify a list of words each week which he/she wants to learn to use in writing activities. Teach the student phonetic approaches to spelling these words.

6. Try various activities to help strengthen and reinforce the phonetic spelling of words (e.g., writing his/her own story, sentences, etc.).

7. Make certain the student knows the sounds that letters make. Have the student practice making the letter sounds as he/she sees the letters on flash cards.

8. Have the student practice spelling phonetically the words most commonly used in everyday speech and writing.

9. Have a peer act as a model for spelling words phonetically. Have the student read the material the peer writes phonetically.

10. Give the student short drill activities in spelling each day which require selected phonetic sounds. Increase the phonetic sounds as the student masters each new one.

11. Reduce distracting stimuli in the classroom when the student is working on spelling and related activities (e.g., place the student in a carrel or "office" space).

12. Have the student keep a dictionary of "most often misspelled words," and require the student to check the spelling of all words he/she is not certain are spelled correctly.

13. Make certain the student is not required to learn too many spelling words at one time.

14. Have the student write sentences, paragraphs, or a story each day about a favorite subject. Encourage the student to use a phonetic approach to spelling the words he/she uses.

15. Require the student to use a phonetic approach to spelling any word he/she does not know how to spell.

16. Be certain to provide the student with an example of phonetic spelling for those words he/she fails to attempt to spell phonetically.

17. Provide the student with a list of words he/she is required to spell phonetically. Provide the student with evaluative feedback indicating how the words can be spelled phonetically.

18. Make certain the student hears correctly the sounds in the words he/she misspells. Have the student say the words aloud to determine if he/she is aware of the letters or sound units in the words.

19. Recognize quality work (e.g., display the student's work, congratulate the student, etc.).

20. Make certain the student is not required to learn more information than he/she is capable of at any one time.

21. Have the student act as a peer tutor to teach another student a spelling concept he/she has mastered. This can serve as reinforcement for the student.

22. Provide practice in spelling by using a computer software program that gives the student immediate feedback.

23. Make certain the student has mastery of spelling concepts at each level before introducing a new skill level.

24. Have the student practice a new spelling lesson or assignment alone or with an aide, the teacher, or a peer before the entire group attempts the spelling lesson or before performing for a grade.

25. Help the student separate his/her spelling list into those which are spelled phonetically and those which are not.

26. Dictate one sound at a time for the student to spell.

27. Let the student dictate sounds for you to spell.

28. Use flash cards to teach the words. Have students look at the word, say the word, then spell the word aloud as they are looking at the word.

29. Print a spelling word and cut it apart letter-by-letter to make a puzzle word. Have the student scramble the letters and then arrange them in the correct order to spell the word.

30. Reinforce the student for spelling words phonetically: (a) give the student a tangible reward (e.g., classroom privileges, line leading, passing out materials, five minutes free time, etc.) or (b) give the student an intangible reward (e.g., praise, handshake, smile, etc.).

75 Omits, substitutes, adds, or rearranges letters or sound units when spelling words

1. Give the student fewer words to learn to spell at any one time, spending more time on each word until the student can spell it correctly.

2. Have a peer spend time each day engaged in drill activities with the student on his/her spelling words.

3. Identify those words the student misspells by omitting, substituting, adding, or rearranging letters or sound units. Have the student practice spelling the words correctly in written sentences each day.

4. Require the student to use the dictionary to find the correct spelling of any word he/she does not spell correctly. The emphasis in this situation becomes spelling accurately rather than memorizing spelling words.

5. Have the student use current spelling words in a meaningful manner which will cause him/her to want to be successful (e.g., writing a letter to a friend, rock star, famous athlete, etc.).

6. Make certain the student knows why words need to be spelled correctly (e.g., provide the student with a concrete example of how each word can be used in his/her life).

7. Have the student identify a list of words (e.g., 5, 10, or 15) each week which he/she wants to learn to spell. If the student is interested in cars, identify words from automotive magazines, advertisements, etc.

8. Have the student keep a dictionary of "most often misspelled words," and require the student to check the spelling of all words he/she is not certain are spelled correctly.

9. Make certain the student is not being required to learn too many words at one time.

10. Make certain that the student's spelling words are those which he/she sees on a routine basis, rather than infrequently, in order to assure correct spelling and use of the words.

11. Make a list of words with letters or sound units the student omits, substitutes, adds, or rearranges. Have the student practice spelling these words using the letters or sound units correctly.

12. Make a list of the words the student misspells by omitting, substituting, adding, or rearranging letters or sound units. Have the student practice spelling the words correctly, removing each word from the list as the student demonstrates mastery.

13. Highlight or underline in the student's reading assignments, those letters or sound units the student omits, substitutes, adds, or rearranges in order to direct the student's attention to the correct spelling of words.

14. Have the student proofread all written work for omissions, substitutions, additions, or rearranged letters or sound units. Reinforce the student for each correction made.

15. Make certain the student "hears" correctly those letters or sound units omitted, substituted, added, or rearranged when spelling words. Have the student say the words aloud to determine if the student is aware of the letters or sound units in the words.

16. Have the student act as a peer tutor to teach another student a spelling concept he/she has mastered. This can serve as reinforcement for the student.

17. Provide practice in spelling by using a computer software program that gives the student immediate feedback.

18. Make certain the student has mastery of spelling concepts at each level before introducing a new skill level.

19. Use daily drill activities to help the student memorize spelling words.

20. Recognize quality work (e.g., display the student's work, congratulate the student, etc.)

21. Provide magnetic or felt letters for the student to sequence. Supply the list of words, spelled correctly, and allow the student to correct his/her words.

22. Have the student type the list of spelling words.

23. Print a spelling word and cut it apart letter-by-letter to make a puzzle word. Have the student scramble the letters and then arrange them in the correct order to spell the word. Do this with each word.

24. Reduce the emphasis on competition. Competitive activities may cause the student to hurry and misspell words.

25. Reinforce the student for spelling words correctly: (a) give the student a tangible reward (e.g., classroom privileges, line leading, five minutes free time, etc.) or (b) give the student an intangible reward (e.g., praise, handshake, smile, etc.).

76 Has difficulty spelling words that do not follow the spelling rules

1. Require the student to use a dictionary to find the spelling of any words he/she cannot spell correctly. The emphasis in this situation becomes spelling correctly rather than memorizing spelling words.

2. Have the student identify a list of spelling words (e.g., 5, 10, or 15) each week which he/she wants to learn to spell. These words become the student's spelling words for the week.

3. Make certain the student has had adequate time to perform written assignments in order that he/she will be more likely to spell words correctly.

4. Reduce distracting stimuli in the classroom when the student is working on spelling and related activities (e.g., place the student in a carrel or "office" space).

5. Have the student keep a dictionary of "most often misspelled words," and require the student to check the spelling of all words he/she is not certain are spelled correctly.

6. Require the student to proofread written assignments for spelling errors. Reinforce the student for each correction made.

7. Identify the most common words the student uses which do not follow spelling rules. Have the student learn to spell these words as a sight word vocabulary.

8. Develop a spelling list of words the student uses which do not follow the spelling rules. Add new words to the list as the student demonstrates mastery of any of the words.

9. Make certain the student does not have too many words to learn to spell at one time.

10. Make a list of the words the student most commonly misspells. Keep a copy of the list of correctly spelled words at his/her desk to use as a reference when writing.

11. Have the student use current spelling words in a meaningful manner which will cause him/her to want to be successful (e.g., writing a letter to a friend, rock star, famous athlete, etc.).

12. Make certain the student "hears" the sounds in the words misspelled. Have the student say the words aloud to determine if the student is aware of the letters or sound units in the words.

13. Recognize quality work (e.g., display the student's work, congratulate the student, etc.).

14. Make certain the student is not required to learn more information than he/she is capable of at any one time.

15. Have the student act as a peer tutor to teach another student a spelling concept the student has mastered. This can serve as reinforcement for the student.

16. Provide practice in spelling by using a computer software program that gives the student immediate feedback.

17. Make certain the student has mastery of spelling concepts at each level before introducing a new skill level.

18. Use daily drill activities to help the student memorize spelling words (e.g., flash cards, writing the spelling words three times, etc.).

19. Have the student practice a new skill or assignment alone, with an aide, the teacher, or a peer tutor before the entire group attempts the activity or before performing for a grade.

20. Review, on a daily basis, those spelling words which have been previously introduced.

21. Print a spelling word and cut it apart letter-by-letter to make a puzzle word. Have the student scramble the letters and then arrange them in the correct order to spell the word.

22. Have the student type the list of spelling words.

23. Have the student make a song or chant of spelling words (e.g., L-A-UGH, L-A-UGH).

24. Have the student write current spelling words in different locations throughout the classroom as he/she is learning them (e.g., on the chalkboard, transparencies, a posted list on his/her desk, etc.).

25. Have a peer spend time each day with the student to practice spelling words which do not use spelling rules.

26. Give the student fewer words to learn to spell at any one time, spending more time on each word until the student can spell it correctly.

27. Reinforce the student for spelling words that do not follow spelling rules: (a) give the student a tangible reward (e.g., classroom privileges, line leading, passing out materials, five minutes free time, etc.) or (b) give the student an intangible reward (e.g., praise, handshake, smile, etc.).

77 Does not use word endings correctly when spelling or omits them

1. Have a list of word endings (e.g., *-ed, -ing, -ly, -er,* etc.) and sample words attached to the student's desk for use as a reference when writing.

2. Use wall charts showing word endings (e.g., *-ed, -ing, -ly, -er,* etc.) and sample words for the student to use as a reference when writing.

3. Require the student to use the dictionary to find the spelling of any words he/she cannot spell correctly. The emphasis in this situation becomes spelling accurately rather than memorizing spelling words.

4. Have the student use current spelling words in a meaningful manner which will cause him/her to want to be successful (e.g., writing a letter to a friend, rock star, famous athlete, etc.).

5. Require the student to proofread all written work for spelling errors. Reinforce the student for correcting each spelling error.

6. Have the student keep a dictionary of "most often misspelled words," and require the student to check the spelling of all words he/she is not certain are spelled correctly.

7. Have the student spend time daily practicing the use of one word ending (e.g., *-ing*). When the student demonstrates mastery of that word ending, he/she begins practicing a new one.

8. Highlight or underline word endings (e.g., *-ed, -ing, -ly, -er,* etc.) in the student's reading assignments in order to call attention to the appropriate use of word endings.

9. Identify a list of words the student has difficulty spelling correctly with word endings. Use this list as ongoing spelling words.

10. Make certain the student has received instruction in using word endings (e.g., *-ed, -ing, -ly, -er,* etc.).

11. Have the student keep a copy of the rules for word endings at his/her desk.

12. Make certain the student hears correctly the sounds misspelled. Have the student say the words aloud to determine if the student is aware of the letters or sound units in the words.

13. Recognize quality work (e.g., display the student's work, congratulate the student, etc.).

14. Make certain the student is not required to learn more information than he/she is capable of at any one time.

15. Have the student act as a peer tutor to teach a peer a spelling concept the student has mastered. This can serve as reinforcement for the student.

16. Provide practice in word endings by using a computer software program that gives the student immediate feedback.

17. Make certain the student has mastery of spelling concepts at each level before introducing a new skill level.

18. Have the student practice a new skill or assignment alone, with an aide, a teacher, or a peer before the entire group attempts the activity or before performing for a grade.

19. Have a peer spend time each day engaged in drill activities with the student on word endings.

20. Give the student fewer words to learn to spell at any one time, spending more time on each word until the student can spell it correctly.

21. Reduce the emphasis on competition. Competitive activities may cause the student to hurry and make mistakes in using word endings.

22. Reinforce the student for using word endings correctly when spelling: (a) give the student a tangible reward (e.g., classroom privileges, line leading, five minutes free time, etc.) or (b) give the student an intangible reward (e.g., praise, handshake, smile, etc.).

78 Spells words correctly in one context but not in another

1. Have the student use current spelling words in sentences written each day.

2. Write sentences, paragraphs, etc., for the student to read which repeat the student's spelling words throughout the material.

3. Have the student write his/her spelling words in different locations throughout the classroom as he/she is learning them (e.g., on the chalkboard, transparencies, a posted list, etc.).

4. Have a list of the student's current spelling words taped on his/her desk with the requirement that they be practiced whenever the student has time. Reinforce the student for practicing the writing of the spelling words.

5. Teach spelling integrated with the total language arts program (e.g., activities, methods, and materials are related to the teaching of reading and language as a whole rather than in parts).

6. Require the student to use the dictionary to find the spelling of any word he/she cannot spell correctly. The emphasis in this situation becomes spelling accurately rather than memorizing spelling words.

7. Have the student use current spelling words in a meaningful manner which will cause him/her to want to be successful (e.g., writing a letter to a friend, rock star, famous athlete, etc.).

8. Make certain the student knows why he/she is learning each spelling word (e.g., provide the student with a concrete example of how each word can be used in his/her life).

9. Have the student identify a list of words (e.g., 5, 10, 15) each week which he/she wants to learn to spell. If the student is interested in cars, identify words from automotive magazines, advertisements, etc.

10. Have a peer spend time each day engaged in drill activities with the student on spelling words.

11. Try various activities to help strengthen and reinforce the visual memory of the spelling words (e.g., flash cards, word lists on the chalkboard, a list on the student's desk, etc.).

12. Make certain the student has had adequate practice in writing the spelling words (e.g., drill activities, sentence activities, etc.).

13. Make certain the student has adequate time to perform written assignments.

14. Reduce distracting stimuli in the classroom when the student is working on spelling and related activities (e.g., place the student in a carrel or "office" space).

15. Have the student maintain a folder of all spelling words. Require the student to refer to the list when he/she is engaged in writing activities in order to check spelling.

16. Make certain the student learns to "use" spelling words rather than simply memorizing the spelling of the words for testing purposes (e.g., have the student use the words in writing activities each day).

17. Require the student to proofread all written work for spelling errors. Reinforce the student for correcting each spelling error.

18. Have the student keep a dictionary of "most often misspelled words," and require the student to check the spelling of all words he/she is not certain are spelled correctly.

19. Require the student to write spelling words frequently in order to increase the student's visual memory of the spelling words.

20. Make certain the student is not being required to learn too many spelling words at one time.

21. Recognize quality work (e.g., display the student's work, congratulate the student, etc.).

22. Make certain that the student's spelling words are those which he/she sees on a routine basis rather than infrequently, in order to assure correct spelling and use of the words.

23. Make certain the student is not required to learn more information than he/she is capable of at any one time.

24. Only give tests and quizzes when the student is certain to succeed (e.g., after you are sure the student has learned and retained the information).

25. Provide the student with self-checking materials, requiring correction before turning in assignments.

26. Give the student fewer words to learn to spell at any one time, spending more time on each word until the student can spell it correctly.

27. Reduce the emphasis on competition. Competitive activities may cause the student to hurry and make mistakes in spelling.

28. Reinforce the student for spelling words correctly in all contexts: (a) give the student a tangible reward (e.g., classroom privileges, line leading, passing out materials, five minutes free time, etc.) or (b) give the student an intangible reward (e.g., praise, handshake, smile, etc.).

1. Have the student highlight or underline spelling words in passages from reading assignments, newspapers, magazines, etc.

2. Develop crossword puzzles which contain only the student's spelling words and have him/her complete them.

3. Write sentences, passages, paragraphs, etc., for the student to read which repeat the student's spelling words throughout the material.

4. Have the student act as a peer tutor to teach spelling words to another student.

5. Have the student write spelling words in different locations throughout the classroom as he/she is learning them (e.g., on the chalkboard, transparencies, a posted list, the desk, etc.).

6. Have the student indicate when he/she has learned one of the spelling words. As the student demonstrates he/she can spell the word, it is removed from the current spelling list.

7. Have a list of the student's current spelling words taped on his/her desk with the requirement that they be practiced whenever the student has time. Reinforce the student for practicing the writing of the spelling words.

8. Have the student review spelling words each day for a short period of time rather than two or three times per week for longer periods of time.

9. Teach spelling integrated with the total language arts program (e.g., activities, methods, and materials are related to the teaching of reading and language as a whole rather than in parts).

10. Require the student to use a dictionary to find the spelling of any word he/she cannot spell correctly. The emphasis in this situation becomes spelling accurately rather than memorizing spelling words.

11. Have the student quiz others over spelling words (e.g., teacher, aide, peers, etc.).

12. Make certain that the student's spelling instruction is on a level where success can be met. Gradually increase the degree of difficulty as the student demonstrates success.

13. Initiate a "Learn to Spell a Word a Day" program with the student.

14. Use words for the student's spelling list which are commonly found in his/her daily surroundings (e.g., commercials, hazard signs, directions, lunch menu, etc.).

15. Evaluate the appropriateness of the task to determine: (a) if the task is too difficult and (b) if the length of time scheduled to complete the task is appropriate.

16. Have the student's current spelling words listed on the chalkboard at all times.

17. Have the student use current spelling words in a meaningful manner which will cause him/her to want to be successful (e.g., writing a letter to a friend, rock star, famous athlete, etc.).

18. Require the student to proofread all written work for spelling errors. Reinforce the student for correcting each spelling error.

19. Make certain the student knows why he/she is learning each spelling word (e.g., provide the student with a concrete example of how each word can be used in his/her life).

20. Have the student identify a list of spelling words (e.g., 5, 10, 15) each week which he/she wants to learn to spell. If the student is interested in cars, identify words from automotive magazines, advertisements, etc.

21. Recognize quality work (e.g., display the student's work, congratulate the student, etc.).

22. Make certain the student is not required to learn more information than he/she is capable of at any one time.

23. Provide practice in spelling by using computer software programs that give the student immediate feedback.

24. Have the student practice a new list of spelling words alone, with an aide, the teacher, or a peer before the entire group attempts the activity or before performing for a grade.

25. Have the student use current spelling words by writing sentences each day.

26. Have a peer spend time each day engaged in drill activities with the student on his/her spelling words.

27. Give the student fewer words to learn to spell at any one time, spending more time on each word until the student can spell it correctly.

28. Reduce the emphasis on competition. Competitive activities may cause the student to hurry and make mistakes in spelling.

29. Reinforce the student for learning to spell words correctly: (a) give the student a tangible reward (e.g., classroom privileges, line leading, passing out materials, five minutes free time, etc.) or (b) give the student an intangible reward (e.g., praise, handshake, smile, etc.).

80 Has difficulty solving math word problems

1. Make certain that the student's inability to read is not the cause of his/her difficulty in solving math word problems.

2. Have the student read the math word problem first silently and then aloud and identify the mathematical operation required.

3. Provide word problems that require a one-step process, making certain that the sentences are short and concise.

4. Teach the student to look for "clue" or "key" words in word problems that indicate the mathematical operations.

5. Have the student orally analyze the steps that are required to solve word problems (e.g., "What is given?" "What is asked?" "What operation(s) is used?" etc.).

6. Represent the numerical amounts, in concrete forms, that are presented in the word problems (e.g., problems involving money can be represented by providing the student with the appropriate amount of real or play money).

7. Have the student write a number sentence after reading a math word problem. (This process will help the student see the numerical relationship prior to finding the answer.)

8. Have the student create word problems for number sentences. Place the number sentences on the chalkboard and have the student tell or write word problems that could be solved by the number sentence.

9. Have the student restate math word problems in his/her own words.

10. Ask the student to identify the primary question that must be answered to solve a given word problem. Continue this activity using more difficult word problems containing two or more questions. Make sure the student understands that questions are often implied rather than directly asked.

11. Have the student make up word problems. Direct the student to write problems involving specific operations. Other students in the classroom should be required to solve these problems. The student can also provide answers to his/her own problems.

12. Supplement textbook problems with teacher-made problems. These problems can deal with classroom experiences. Include students' names in the word problems to make them more realistic and meaningful to the student.

13. Use word problems that are of interest to the student and related to his/her experiences.

14. Make certain the student reads through the entire word problem before attempting to solve it.

15. Teach the student to break down each math word problem into specific steps.

16. Have the student make notes to "set the problem up" in written form as he/she reads the math word problem.

17. Have the student simulate situations which relate to math word problems (e.g., trading, selling, buying, etc.).

18. Have the student solve math word problems by manipulating objects and by stating the process(es) used.

19. Help the student recognize common patterns in math word problems (e.g., how many, add or subtract, etc.).

20. Discuss and provide the student with a list of words/phrases which usually indicate an addition operation (e.g., *together, altogether, sum, in all, both, gained, received, total, won, saved,* etc.).

21. Discuss words/phrases which usually indicate a subtraction operation (e.g., *difference between, from, left, how many (more, less), how much (taller, farther, heavier), withdrawal, spend, lost, remain, more,* etc.).

22. Discuss words/phrases which usually indicate a multiplication operation (e.g., *area, each, times, product, double, triple, twice,* etc.).

23. Discuss words/phrases which usually indicate a division operation (e.g., *into, share, each, average, monthly, daily, weekly, yearly, quotient, half as many,* etc.).

24. Teach the student to convert words into their numerical equivalents to solve word problems (e.g., two weeks = 14 days, one-third = ⅓, one year = 12 months, one quarter = 25 cents, one yard = 36 inches, etc.).

25. Teach the student relevant vocabulary often found in math word problems (e.g., dozen, amount, triple, twice, etc.).

26. Allow the student to use a calculator when solving word problems.

27. Require the student to read math word problems at least twice before beginning to solve the problem.

28. Have the student begin solving basic word problems which combine math problems and word problems such as:

> 7 apples
> and 3 apples
> equals 10 apples

Gradually change the problems to word problems as the student demonstrates success.

29. Before introducing complete word problems, present the student with phrases to be translated into numbers (e.g., six less than ten equals 10 - 6).

30. Assign a peer to act as a model for the student and to demonstrate for the student how to solve math word problems.

31. Reduce the number of problems assigned to the student at one time (e.g., five problems instead of ten).

32. Demonstrate for the student how to solve math word problems by reading the problem and solving the problem on paper step-by-step.

33. Speak with the student to explain: (a) what the student is doing wrong (e.g., using the wrong operation, failing to read the problem carefully, etc.) and (b) what the student should be doing (e.g., using the appropriate operation, reading the problem carefully, etc.).

34. Evaluate the appropriateness of the task to determine: (a) if the task is too difficult and (b) if the length of time scheduled to complete the task is appropriate.

35. Correlate word problems with computation procedures just learned in the classroom (e.g., multiplication, operations with multiplication word problems, etc.).

36. Teach the student the meaning of mathematical terms (e.g., *sum, dividend,* etc.). Frequently review terms and their meanings.

37. Highlight or underline key words in math problems (e.g., the reference to the operation involved, etc.).

38. Provide the student with a checklist to follow in solving math word problems (e.g., what information is given, what question is asked, what operation(s) is used).

39. Make certain the student has a number line on his/her desk to use as a reference.

40. Make certain the student knows why he/she is learning to solve math word problems. Provide the student with concrete examples and opportunities to apply these concepts in real-life situations.

41. Have the student talk through math word problems as he/she is solving them in order to identify errors the student is making.

42. Develop a math reference sheet for the student to keep at his/her desk (e.g., steps used in doing subtraction, multiplication, addition, and division problems).

43. Have the student check his/her word problems using a calculator. The calculator can also be used to reinforce the learning of math facts.

44. Make certain the student knows the concepts of *more than, less than, equal to*, and *zero*. The use of tangible objects will facilitate the learning process.

45. Recognize quality work (e.g., display the student's work, congratulate the student, etc.).

46. Make certain the student is not required to learn more information than he/she is capable of at any one time.

47. Have the student act as a peer tutor to teach a peer a math concept the student has mastered. This can serve as reinforcement for the student.

48. Provide practice in solving math word problems by using a computer software program that gives the student immediate feedback.

49. Provide the student with a quiet place to work (e.g., "office" or study carrel, etc.). This is used as a means of reducing distracting stimuli and not as a form of punishment.

50. Make certain the student has mastery of math concepts at each level before introducing a new skill level.

51. Have the student manipulate objects (e.g., apples, oranges, toy cars, toy airplanes, etc.) as the teacher describes the operation.

52. Reduce the emphasis on competition. Competitive activities may cause the student to hurry and do math word problems incorrectly.

53. Have the student question any directions, explanations, or instructions he/she does not understand.

54. Reinforce the student for solving math word problems: (a) give the student a tangible reward (e.g., classroom privileges, line leading, passing out materials, five minutes free time, etc.) or (b) give the student an intangible reward (e.g., praise, handshake, smile, etc.).

81 Fails to change from one math operation to another

1. Use visual cues (e.g., *Stop* signs or red dots) on the paper when the student must change operations. Have the student raise his/her hand when reaching *Stop* signs, and provide instructions for the next problem.

2. Use color coding (e.g., make addition signs green, subtraction signs red, etc.). Gradually reduce the use of colors as the student demonstrates success.

3. Reduce the number of problems on a page (e.g., five problems to a page with the student being required to do four pages of work throughout the day).

4. Make certain the student recognizes all math operation symbols (e.g., $+, -, \div, \times$).

5. Have the student practice recognizing series of math symbols (e.g., $+, -, \div, \times$).

6. Use a written reminder beside each math problem to indicate which math operation is to be used (e.g., division, addition, subtraction, etc.). Gradually reduce the use of reminders as the student demonstrates success.

7. Make the math operation symbols, next to the problems, extra large in order that the student will be more likely to observe the symbols.

8. Require the student to go through math assignments highlighting or otherwise marking the operation of each problem before beginning to solve the math problems.

9. Work the first problem or two of a math assignment for the student in order that he/she knows which operation to use.

10. Use a separate piece of paper for each type of math problem. Gradually introduce different types of problems on the same page.

11. Recognize quality work (e.g., display the student's work, congratulate the student, etc.).

12. Teach the student direction-following skills: (a) listen carefully, (b) ask questions, (c) use environmental cues, (d) rely on examples provided, (e) wait until all directions have been given before beginning.

13. Assess the quality and clarity of directions, explanations, and instructions given to the student.

14. Make certain the student knows why he/she is learning a math concept. Provide the student with concrete examples and opportunities for the student to apply those concepts in real-life situations.

15. Have the student talk through math problems as the student is solving them in order to identify errors he/she is making.

16. Develop a math reference sheet for the student to keep at his/her desk (e.g., steps used in doing subtraction, multiplication, addition, and division problems).

17. Have the student check his/her math assignments using a calculator. The calculator can also be used to reinforce the learning of math facts.

18. Make certain the student is not required to learn more information than he/she is capable of at any one time.

19. Provide practice in math by using a computer software program that gives the student immediate feedback.

20. Reduce the amount of information on a page if it is causing visual distractions for the student (e.g., fewer problems, less print, etc.).

21. Evaluate the appropriateness of a task to determine: (a) if the task is too difficult and (b) if the length of time scheduled for the task is appropriate.

22. Speak to the student to explain: (a) what the student is doing wrong (e.g., adding instead of subtracting) and (b) what the student should be doing (e.g., adding addition problems, subtracting subtraction problems, etc.).

23. Reinforce the student for correctly changing from one math operation to another: (a) give the student a tangible reward (e.g., classroom privileges, line leading, passing out materials, five minutes free time, etc.) or (b) give the student an intangible reward (e.g., praise, handshake, smile, etc.).

82 Does not understand abstract math concepts without concrete examples

1. Have the student practice the concept of re-grouping by "borrowing" and "carrying" from objects in columns set up like math problems.

2. Have the student use "sets" of objects from the environment to practice addition, subtraction, multiplication, and division problems.

3. Use actual change and dollar bills, clocks, etc., to teach concepts of money, telling time, etc.

4. Make certain all of the student's math problems have concrete examples associated with each one (e.g., 9 minus 7 becomes 9 apples minus 7 apples, etc.).

5. Work the first problem or two with the student, explaining how to associate concrete examples with each problem (e.g., 9 minus 7 becomes 9 apples minus 7 apples).

6. Have a peer tutor assist the student in solving math problems by providing concrete examples associated with each problem (e.g., 9 minus 7 becomes 9 apples minus 7 apples).

7. Use a scale, ruler, measuring cups, etc., to teach math concepts using measurement.

8. Make certain to use terms when speaking to the student which convey abstract concepts to describe tangible objects in the environment (e.g., larger, smaller, square, triangle, etc.).

9. Use concrete examples when teaching abstract concepts (e.g., numbers of objects to convey "more than," "less than"; rulers and yardsticks to convey concepts of height, width, etc.).

10. Teach shapes using common objects in the environment (e.g., round clocks, rectangle desks, square tiles on the floor, etc.).

11. Evaluate the appropriateness of having the student learn abstract concepts at this time (i.e., Is it too difficult for the student?).

12. Teach the student concepts one at a time before pairing the concepts (e.g., dimensionality, size, space, shape, etc.).

13. Provide repeated physical demonstrations of abstract concepts (e.g., identify things far away and close to the student, a small box in a large room, etc.).

14. Review, on a daily basis, those abstract concepts which have been previously introduced. Introduce new abstract concepts only after the student has mastery of those previously presented.

15. Make certain the student knows why he/she is learning a math concept. Provide the student with concrete examples and opportunities for the student to apply those concepts in real-life situations.

16. Make it pleasant and positive for the student to ask questions about things he/she does not understand. Reinforce the student by assisting, congratulating, praising, etc.

17. Make certain the student is not required to learn more information than he/she is capable of at any one time.

18. Have the student act as a peer tutor to teach a peer a concept the student has mastered. This can serve as reinforcement for the student.

19. Make certain the student has mastery of math concepts at each level before introducing a new skill level.

20. Using measuring cups, teaspoons, etc., have the student follow a recipe to make a treat for the class.

83 Fails to correctly solve math problems requiring regrouping

1. Evaluate the appropriateness of the task to determine if the student has mastered the skills needed for regrouping.

2. Provide the student with many concrete experiences to help learn and remember regrouping skills. Use popsicle sticks, tongue depressors, paper clips, buttons, base ten blocks, etc., to form groupings to teach regrouping.

3. Provide practice in regrouping facts by using a computer software program that gives immediate feedback to the student.

4. Use daily drill activities to help the student with regrouping (e.g., written problems, flash cards, etc.).

5. Have the student perform timed drills to reinforce regrouping. The student competes against his/her own best time and score.

6. Find opportunities for the student to apply regrouping to real-life situations (e.g., getting change in the cafeteria, figuring how much items cost when added together while shopping, etc.).

7. Develop a regrouping reference for the student to use at his/her desk when solving math problems which require regrouping.

8. Have the student solve half of the math problems each day and use the calculator as reinforcement to complete the other half of the math assignment.

9. Reinforce the student for attempting and completing work. Emphasize the number correct, then encourage the student to see how many more he/she can correct without help. Have the student maintain a "private" chart of math performance.

10. Make certain the student understands number concepts and the relationship of number symbols to numbers of objects before requiring him/her to solve math problems requiring regrouping.

11. Make certain the student knows the concepts of *more than, less than, equal,* and *zero.* The use of tangible objects will facilitate the learning process.

12. Have the student practice the concept of regrouping by *borrowing* and *carrying* from objects in columns set up like math problems.

13. Provide the student with opportunities for tutoring from peers or a teacher. Allow the student to tutor others when he/she has mastered a concept.

14. Make certain that the language used to communicate with the student about regrouping is consistent (e.g., *borrow, carry,* etc.).

15. Provide the student with shorter math assignments, but more of them throughout the day (e.g., four assignments of five problems each rather than one assignment of twenty problems).

16. Work the first problem or two of the math assignment with the student in order to make certain that he/she understands the directions and the operation necessary to solve the problems.

17. Have the student talk through math problems as he/she solves them in order to identify errors the student is making.

18. Require the student to check subtraction problems by adding (i.e., the difference plus the subtrahend equals the minuend). Reinforce the student for each error corrected.

19. Make certain the student has a number line on his/her desk to use as a reference.

20. Develop a math reference sheet for the student to keep at his/her desk (e.g., steps used in doing subtraction problems, addition problems, etc.).

21. Have the student check his/her math assignments using a calculator. The calculator can also be used to reinforce the learning of math facts.

22. Use manipulative objects (e.g., base ten blocks) to teach the student regrouping.

23. Make certain the student understands the concept of place value and that place values move from right to left beginning with the ones column.

24. Make certain the student is not required to learn more than he/she is capable of at any one time.

25. Make certain the student has mastery of math concepts at each level before introducing a new skill level.

26. Have the student solve math problems by manipulating objects to experience regrouping.

27. Reduce the emphasis on competition. Competitive activities may cause the student to hurry and make mistakes in regrouping.

28. Reinforce the student for solving math problems that require regrouping: (a) give the student a tangible reward (e.g., classroom privileges, line leading, five minutes free time, etc.) or (b) give the student an intangible reward (e.g., praise, handshake, smile, etc.).

84 Works math problems from left to right instead of right to left

1. Use large colored arrows to indicate where the student begins to work math problems (e.g., right to left).

2. Work the first problems for the student as he/she watches in order to provide a demonstration and an example.

3. Put the student's math problems on graph paper or vertically lined paper to emphasize columns, with directions to begin each problem at the right.

4. Make certain the student has mastered place value concepts and understands that columns to the left have higher values than those to the right.

5. Require the student to solve math problems by place value (e.g., begin with ones column, then the tens column, hundreds column, etc.).

6. Speak to the student to explain: (a) what the student is doing wrong (e.g., working math problems from left to right) and (b) what the student should be doing (e.g., working math problems from right to left).

7. Write the place value above each math problem in order to remind the student to begin with the ones column to solve the problems.

8. Have the student use a calculator to solve math problems.

9. Display a large posterboard sign or use the chalkboard to display a message that indicates reading begins to the left and math problems begin to the right (e.g., **READING BEGINS ON THE LEFT. MATH BEGINS ON THE RIGHT.**).

10. Make certain the student has a number line on his/her desk to use as a reference.

11. Have the student talk through math problems as he/she is solving them in order to identify errors the student is making.

12. Make certain the student knows why he/she is learning a math concept. Provide the student with concrete examples and opportunities for the student to apply those concepts in real-life situations.

13. Recognize quality work (e.g., display the student's work, congratulate the student, etc.).

14. Provide the student with practice in math by using a computer software program that gives immediate feedback.

15. Make certain the student has mastery of math concepts at each level before introducing a new skill level.

16. Reduce the amount of information on a page if it is causing visual distractions for the student (e.g., fewer math problems, less print, etc.).

17. Have the student check math assignments using a calculator.

18. Develop a math reference sheet for the student to keep at his/her desk (e.g., steps used in doing addition problems, subtraction problems, multiplication problems, division problems).

19. Have a peer tutor work with the student each day on solving math problems from right to left.

20. Reduce the emphasis on competition. Competitive activities may cause the student to hurry and make mistakes in math problems.

21. Reinforce the student for working math problems from right to left: (a) give the student a tangible reward (e.g., classroom privileges, line leading, passing out materials, five minutes free time, etc.) or (b) give the student an intangible reward (e.g., praise, handshake, smile, etc.).

85   Fails to follow necessary steps in math problems

1. Make certain the student recognizes all math operation symbols (e.g., ×, -, +, ÷).

2. Use written reminders by math problems to indicate which step is to be done. Gradually reduce the use of reminders as the student demonstrates success.

3. Put all math problems involving the same steps in a single line, on a separate sheet of paper, etc.

4. Make the math operation symbols next to the problems extra large in order that the student will be more likely to observe the symbol.

5. Color-code math steps next to math problems in order that the student will be more likely to follow the steps (e.g., the adding step in multiplication problems, etc.).

6. Work the first problem or two of a math assignment for the student in order that he/she knows what steps to use.

7. Use a separate piece of paper for each type of math problem, gradually introducing different types of problems on the same page.

8. Provide the student with a list of steps necessary for the problems assigned. Have the student keep the list at his/her desk for a reference while solving math problems.

9. List the steps in solving math problems on the chalkboard, bulletin board, etc.

10. Have a peer tutor work with the student while he/she learns to follow the steps in math problems.

11. Have the student check answers to math problems on a calculator.

12. Have the student act as a peer tutor for another student who is learning new math concepts. Explaining steps in basic math problems will help the student cement his/her own skills.

13. Have the student equate math problems to real-life situations in order that he/she will better understand the steps involved in solving the problems (e.g., 4 x 25 is the same as 4 baskets of apples with 25 apples in each basket. How many apples do you have?).

14. Be certain to assign the student math problems requiring the same operation to make it easier for the student to follow steps in solving the problems. More than one operation may be required in an assignment as the student demonstrates success.

15. Make certain the student has a number line on his/her desk to use as a reference.

16. Have the student talk through math problems as he/she is solving them in order to identify errors the student is making.

17. Develop a math reference sheet for the student to keep at his/her desk (e.g., steps used in doing subtraction, multiplication, addition, and division problems).

18. Have the student check his/her math assignments using a calculator. The calculator can also be used to reinforce the learning of math facts.

19. Use vertical lines or graph paper in math to help the student keep math problems in correct order.

20. Make certain the student is not required to learn more information than he/she is capable of at any one time.

21. Provide practice in math by using a computer software program that gives the student immediate feedback.

22. Make certain the student has mastery of math concepts at each level before introducing a new skill level.

23. Have the student work math problems at the board so the teacher can see the steps being performed.

24. Reduce the emphasis on competition. Competitive activities may cause the student to hurry and fail to follow necessary steps in math problems.

25. Evaluate the appropriateness of a task to determine: (a) if the task is too difficult and (b) if the length of time scheduled for the task is appropriate.

26. Reinforce the student for following necessary steps in math problems: (a) give the student a tangible reward (e.g., classroom privileges, line leading, passing out materials, five minutes free time, etc.) or (b) give the student an intangible reward (e.g., handshake, praise, smile, etc.).

86 Fails to correctly solve math problems involving fractions or decimals

1. Make certain the student understands that 8/8 equals a whole, 10/10 equals a whole, etc.

2. Make certain the student understands the concept of regrouping.

3. Identify a peer to work with the student on problems involving fractions or decimals.

4. Have the student solve math problems involving fractions and decimals by using tangible objects (e.g., pennies which are one-tenth of a dime, inch cubes which are one-twelfth of a foot, etc.).

5. Provide the student with many concrete experiences to help him/her learn to use fractions and decimals (e.g., using money, cutting pie-shaped pieces, measuring, weighing, telling time, etc).

6. Have the student use a calculator in learning to solve problems involving decimals.

7. Make certain the student understands number concepts and the relationship of number symbols to numbers of objects before requiring him/her to solve math problems involving fractions and decimals.

8. Provide the student with enjoyable math activities involving fractions and decimals which he/she can perform for drill and practice either alone or with a peer (e.g., computer games, math games, manipulatives).

9. Work the first few problems of the math assignment with the student in order to make certain that he/she understands the directions and the operation necessary to solve the problems.

10. Cut pieces of paper into equal numbers (e.g., fourths, sixths, tenths, etc.); have the student add fractions together, subtract fractions, etc.

11. Have the student do skip counting by fractions (e.g., 2/8, 4/8, 6/8, etc.).

12. Have the student do skip counting by decimals (e.g., .2, .4, .6, .8, etc.).

13. For math problems involving fractions with unlike denominators, have the student use a tangible object such as a yardstick to help him/ her solve the problem.

14. Make certain the student knows why he/she is learning a math concept. Provide the student with concrete examples and opportunities to apply these concepts in real life situations.

15. Develop a reference sheet of fractions and decimals for the student to keep at his/her desk.

16. Make certain the student is not required to learn more information than he/she is capable of at any one time.

17. Provide practice in fractions and decimals by using a computer software program that gives the student immediate feedback.

18. Reinforce the student for correctly solving problems involving fractions or decimals: (a) give the student a tangible reward (e.g., classroom privileges, line leading, passing out materials, five minutes free time, etc.) or (b) give the student an intangible reward (e.g., praise, handshake, smile, etc.).

87 Fails to demonstrate knowledge of place value

1. Reduce the emphasis on competition. Competitive activities may cause the student to hurry and make mistakes in math problems.

2. Provide the student with concrete experiences to help him/her learn and remember math facts. Use popsicle sticks, tongue depressors, paper clips, buttons, etc., to form groupings to teach math facts.

3. Have the student use a calculator to reinforce learning math facts. Have the student solve several problems each day using a calculator.

4. Provide practice of place value by using a computer with software programs that give immediate feedback for the student.

5. Have a peer tutor work with the student each day on place value activities (e.g., flash cards).

6. Use manipulative objects (e.g., base ten blocks, connecting links, etc.) to teach the student place value and to provide a visual image.

7. Make certain the student has the prerequisite skills to learn place value (e.g., counting, writing numbers to 100, etc.).

8. Make certain the student knows the concepts and terminology necessary to learn place value (e.g., *set, column, middle, left, digit,* etc.).

9. Make certain the student understands that the collective value of ten "ones" is equal to one ten and that ten "tens" is equal to one hundred.

10. Provide the student with learning experiences in grouping tangible objects into groups of tens, hundreds, etc.

11. Have the student practice labeling columns to represent ones, tens, hundreds, etc.

12. Have the student practice regrouping a number in different positions and determining its value (e.g., 372, 627, 721).

13. Make certain the student understands the zero concept in place value (e.g., there are no tens in the number 207, so a zero is put in the tens column).

14. Money concepts will help the student learn place value association (e.g., $1.26 is the same as six pennies or six ones; two dimes or two tens; one dollar or one hundred).

15. Use vertical lines or graph paper to help the student visualize columns and put a single digit in a column.

16. Make certain the student understands that math problems of addition, subtraction, and multiplication move from right to left beginning with the ones column.

17. Make certain the student knows why he/she is learning a math concept. Provide the student with concrete examples and opportunities to apply those concepts in real-life situations.

18. Have the student talk through math problems as he/she is solving them in order to identify errors in place value the student is making.

19. Develop a math reference sheet for the student to keep at his/her desk (e.g., steps used in doing subtraction, multiplication, addition, and division problems).

20. Have the student check his/her math assignments using a calculator. The calculator can also be used to reinforce the learning of math facts.

21. Make certain the student is not required to learn more information than the student is capable of at any one time.

22. Make certain the student has mastery of math concepts at each level before introducing a new skill level.

88 Confuses operational signs when working math problems

1. Evaluate the appropriateness of the task to determine: (a) if the task is too difficult and (b) if the length of time scheduled for the task is appropriate.

2. Have the student practice recognizing operational symbols (e.g., flash cards of $\div$, +, -, $\times$).

3. Use a written reminder beside math problems to indicate which math operation is to be used (e.g., addition, subtraction, multiplication, division). Gradually reduce the use of reminders as the student demonstrates success.

4. Make the math operation symbols next to the problems extra large in order that the student will be more likely to observe the symbols.

5. Color-code math operation symbols next to math problems in order that the student will be more likely to observe the symbols.

6. Require the student to go through the math problems on each daily assignment, highlighting or otherwise marking the operation of each problem before he/she begins to solve them.

7. Work the first problem or two of the math assignment for the student in order that he/she knows which operation to use.

8. Use a separate piece of paper for each type of math problem. Gradually introduce different types of math problems on the same page.

9. Place the math operation symbols randomly around the room and have the student practice identifying the operation as he/she points to the symbol.

10. Provide the student with a math operation symbol reference sheet to keep and use at his/her desk (e.g., + means add, - means subtract, $\times$ means multiply, $\div$ means divide).

11. At the top of each sheet of math problems, provide a math operational symbol reminder for the student (e.g., + means add, - means subtract, $\times$ means multiply, $\div$ means divide).

12. Have the student practice matching math operation symbols to the word identifying the operation by using flash cards (e.g., +, -, $\times$, $\div$; add, subtract, multiply, divide).

13. Have the student solve his/her math problems using a calculator.

14. Have a peer work with the student to act as a model and provide reminders as the student solves his/her math problems.

15. Make certain the student knows why he/she is learning a math concept. Provide the student with concrete examples and opportunities for the student to apply those concepts in real-life situations.

16. Have the student check his/her math assignments using a calculator. The calculator can also be used to reinforce the learning of math facts.

17. Make certain the student is not required to learn more information then he/she is capable of at any one time.

18. Provide practice in operational signs by using a computer software program that gives the student immediate feedback.

19. Make certain the student has mastery of math concepts at each level before introducing a new skill level.

20. Highlight operational signs so that the student is sure to notice the signs before beginning the operation.

89 Fails to correctly solve problems involving money

1. Beginning with the addition and subtraction facts, separate the basic facts into "sets," each to be memorized successively by the student.

2. Use the tracking technique to help the student learn math facts. Present a few facts at a time. Gradually increase the number of facts the student must remember as he/she demonstrates success.

3. Have the student use a calculator to reinforce learning to solve problems involving money. Have the student solve several money problems each day using the calculator.

4. Provide practice in solving money problems by using a computer software program that gives the student immediate feedback.

5. Use real-life situations for the student to practice money problems (e.g., paying for lunch in the cafeteria line, making purchases from book order clubs, purchasing a soft drink, etc.).

6. Use actual coins in teaching the student coin value (e.g., counting by ones, fives, tens, etc.; matching combinations of coins; etc.).

7. Make certain the student recognizes all coins (e.g., penny, nickel, dime, quarter).

8. Make certain the student recognizes common denominations of paper money (e.g., one dollar bill, five dollar bill, ten dollar bill, twenty dollar bill, etc.).

9. Have a peer work with the student every day practicing coin values, paper money values, combinations, etc.

10. Have the student match equal values of coins (e.g., two nickels to a dime, two dimes and a nickel to a quarter, five nickels to a quarter, etc.).

11. Make certain the student understands all math operation concepts involved in using money (e.g., addition, subtraction, multiplication, division, decimals, etc.).

12. Make certain the student can solve the necessary math problems involved in the use of money (i.e., the student can solve math problems of the same difficulty as those involving money).

13. Make certain the student can count by pennies, nickels, dimes, quarters, and half-dollars.

14. Have the student use actual money to simulate transactions in the classroom (e.g., purchasing lunch, groceries, snacks, clothing, etc.). Have the student practice acting as both a customer and a clerk.

15. Provide the student with math word problems involving the use of money, making certain the appropriate operation is clearly stated.

16. Provide the student with a daily shopping list of items and a corresponding list of the cost of each item. Have the student determine the cost of his/her purchase.

17. Bring a selection of menus to the classroom to have the student select items for a meal and compute the cost of the items.

18. Have the student use a newspaper or a catalog to make a list of things advertised which he/she would like to purchase. Have the student determine the total cost of the items selected.

19. Have the student earn a hypothetical income and engage in money-related math problems. The degree of difficulty of the problems is matched to the student's ability level (e.g., taxes, social security, savings, rent, food, clothing, auto payments, recreation, etc.).

20. Have the student talk through money math problems while solving them in order to identify his/her errors.

21. Using money stamps, make individual work sheets for the student with only a few problems on each page.

22. Make certain the student is not required to learn more information than the student is capable of at any one time.

23. Make certain the student knows why he/she is learning the concept of money. Provide the student with concrete examples and opportunities to apply those concepts in real-life situations.

24. Review, on a daily basis, those skills, concepts, tasks, etc., which have been previously introduced.

25. Reduce the emphasis on competition. Competitive activities may cause the student to hurry and make mistakes in solving problems involving money.

26. Reinforce the student for correctly solving problems involving money: (a) give the student a tangible reward (e.g., classroom privileges, line leading, passing out materials, five minutes free time, etc.) or (b) give the student an intangible reward (e.g., praise, handshake, smile, etc.).

90 Fails to correctly solve problems using measurement

1. Find opportunities for the student to apply measurement facts to real-life situations (e.g., cooking, measuring the lengths of objects, etc.).

2. Develop a measurement reference sheet for the student to use at his/her desk when solving math problems.

3. Call on the student when he/she is most likely to be able to respond successfully.

4. Provide the student with enjoyable activities during free time in the classroom (e.g., computer games, math games, etc.).

5. Make certain that the language used to communicate with the student about measurement is consistent (e.g., meters, grams, etc.).

6. Make certain the student has mastery of math concepts at each level before introducing a new skill.

7. Work the first problem or two of the math assignment with the student in order to make certain that he/she understands the directions and the operation necessary to solve the problems.

8. Have the student practice basic measurement concepts (e.g., pound, ounce, inch, foot, etc.) using everyday measurement devices in the environment (e.g., rulers, measuring cups, etc.).

9. Have the student practice measuring items in the environment to find their length, weight, etc.

10. Make certain the student knows the basic concepts of fractions before requiring him/her to solve problems involving measurement (e.g., 1/4 inch, 1 ½ feet, etc.).

11. Have the student practice using smaller units of measurement to create larger units of measurement (e.g., twelve inches to make one foot, three feet to make one yard, eight ounces to make one cup, four cups to make one quart, etc.).

12. Assign the student measurement problems that he/she will want to be able to perform successfully (e.g., following a recipe, building a model, etc.).

13. Have the student begin solving measurement problems which require same and whole units (e.g., 10 pounds minus 8 pounds, 24 inches plus 12 inches, etc.). Introduce fractions and mixed units (e.g., pounds and ounces, etc.) only after the student has demonstrated success with same and whole units.

14. Have the student use a calculator to solve measurement problems, check the accuracy of problems worked, etc.

15. Have the student use software programs to practice measurement skills on the computer.

16. Have the student begin to solve measurement problems by using measurement devices before solving the problems on paper (e.g., 5 inches plus 4 inches using a ruler; 3 liquid ounces plus 5 liquid ounces using a measuring cup; etc.).

17. Let students use dry ingredients such as macaroni, beans, rice, etc., to measure cup fractions.

18. Make certain the student knows why he/she is learning measuring concepts. Provide the student with concrete examples and opportunities to apply those concepts in real-life situations.

19. Make certain the student is not required to learn more information than the he/she is capable of at any one time.

20. Provide practice in solving measurement problems by using a computer software program that gives the student immediate feedback.

21. Review, on a daily basis, those skills, concepts, tasks, etc., which have been previously introduced.

22. Have the student participate in an actual "hands-on" experience by following simple recipes (e.g., making gelatin, cookies, etc.).

23. Evaluate the appropriateness of the task to determine: (a) if the task is too difficult and (b) if the length of time scheduled for the task is appropriate.

24. Assign a peer to act as a model for the student to demonstrate how to solve measurement problems.

25. Discuss and provide the student with a list of words/phrases which usually indicate measurement problems (e.g., pound, inches, millimeter, kilogram, etc.).

26. Reduce the emphasis on competition. Competitive activities may cause the student to hurry and solve measurement problems.

27. Reinforce the student for correctly solving problems involving measurement: (a) give the student a tangible reward (e.g., classroom privileges, line leading, passing out materials, five minutes free time, etc.) or (b) give the student an intangible reward (e.g., praise, handshake, smile, etc.).

91 Does not understand the concept of skip counting

1. Have the student count nickels, dimes, quarters, etc.

2. Have a peer work with the student to help him/her understand the concept of skip counting.

3. Have the student use a number line when counting by 2's, 5's, 10's, etc., in order that he/she can see that the increments are being added.

4. Have the student count by 2's, 5's, 10's, etc.; and have the student write the numbers as he/she counts. The student can then go back to the numbers he/she has written and see that the increment of 2, 5, 10, etc., is added to each number.

5. Have the student use tangible objects (pennies, paper clips, etc.) when counting by 2's, 5's, 10's, etc., in order to see that the total number is increasing in successive increments.

6. Have the student use a calculator to do skip counting, adding 2, 5, 10, etc., to each successive number in order to see that skip counting increases by the increment used in counting.

7. Have the student use a clock in the classroom to count by 2's, 3's, 5's, etc.

8. Make certain the student understands number concepts and the relationships of symbols to numbers of objects before requiring him/her to solve math problems requiring addition.

9. Make certain the student has a number line on his/her desk to use as a reference.

10. Make certain the student knows why he/she is learning a math concept. Provide the student with concrete examples and opportunities to apply those concepts in real-life situations.

11. Use manipulative objects (e.g., abacus, base ten blocks, etc.) to teach the student the concept of skip counting.

12. Make certain the student is not required to learn more information than he/she is capable of at any one time.

13. Have the student practice a new skill or assignment alone, with an aide, the teacher, or a peer before the entire group attempts the activity or before performing for a grade.

14. Have the student act as a peer tutor to teach another student a concept he/she has mastered. This can serve as reinforcement for the student.

15. Provide practice in skip counting by using a computer software program that gives the student immediate feedback.

16. Make certain the student has mastery of math concepts at each level before introducing a new skill level.

1. Make certain the student understands all concepts involved in telling time (e.g., counting by 15's, 10's, 5's; the big hand and the little hand; etc.).

2. Make certain the student understands the concepts of morning, afternoon, evening, and night.

3. Make certain the student understands which seasons come before and after other seasons.

4. Make certain the student understands the concept of length of a minute, five minutes, ten minutes, fifteen minutes, one hour, ninety minutes, twenty-four hours, etc.

5. Make certain the student has a standard clock in the classroom to use as a visual reference.

6. Make certain the student knows the number of hours in a day, days in a week, weeks in a year, etc.

7. Make certain the student understands the terms used in telling time (e.g., "a quarter 'til," "half past," "ten 'til," "a quarter after," etc.).

8. Make certain the student can count by common divisors of time (e.g., one minute, five minutes, ten minutes, thirty minutes, an hour, etc.).

9. Have the student recognize when events occur in the daily routine (e.g., recess at 10:15, lunch at 11:45, dismissal at 3:20, etc.).

10. Have the student indicate when the clock in the classroom is on the hour.

11. Have the student indicate when the clock in the classroom is on the half hour.

12. Have the student indicate when the clock in the classroom is on the quarter hour.

13. Have the student set the hands on a clock as the teacher/tutor indicates times of the day.

14. Give the student time word problems involving math concepts on his/her ability level (e.g., "At 10 minutes after 9 o'clock you will begin walking to school. It takes 10 minutes to walk to school. What time will it be when you arrive?").

15. Make certain the student has a clock face with hands to manipulate when learning to tell time.

16. Using a large clock face, set the hands and have the student indicate the time. Begin with the hours, the half hours, the quarter hours, etc.

17. Make certain the student can read a digital clock or watch.

18. Have watches in the classroom which the student can "borrow" to wear during the school day while he/she is learning to tell time.

19. Make certain the student knows why he/she is learning to tell time. Provide the student with concrete examples and opportunities to apply those concepts in real-life situations.

20. Make certain the student is not required to learn more information than the student is capable of at any one time.

21. Have the student learn to recognize one specific "important" time and let the teacher know when the clock has reached that specific time.

22. Have the student work with a peer each day practicing skills required for telling time.

23. Provide practice in telling time by using computer software programs that give immediate feedback to the student.

24. Reinforce the student for telling time correctly: (a) give the student a tangible reward (e.g., classroom privileges, line leading, five minutes free time, passing out materials, etc.) or (b) give the student an intangible reward (e.g., praise, handshake, smile, etc.).

93 Fails to correctly solve math problems requiring addition

1. Have the student solve addition problems by manipulating objects and stating the process(es) used.

2. Discuss and provide the student with a list of words/phrases which indicate an addition operation in word problems (e.g., *together, altogether, sum, in all, both, gained, received, total, saved,* etc.).

3. Assign a peer to act as a model for the student and to demonstrate how to solve addition problems.

4. Evaluate the appropriateness of the task to determine: (a) if the task is too difficult and (b) if the length of time scheduled for the task is appropriate.

5. Provide the student with many concrete experiences to help him/her learn and remember math facts. Use popsicle sticks, tongue depressors, paper clips, buttons, fingers, etc., to form groupings to teach addition facts.

6. Have the student use a calculator to reinforce solving of addition problems. Have the student solve several problems each day using a calculator.

7. Provide practice of addition facts by using a computer with software programs that give immediate feedback to the student.

8. Use daily drill activities to help the student memorize addition facts (e.g., written problems, flash cards, etc.).

9. Have the student use a number line attached to his/her desk to solve addition problems.

10. Have the student use a calculator for drill activities of basic addition facts.

11. Find opportunities for the student to apply addition facts to real-life situations (e.g., buying lunch in the cafeteria, measuring the lengths of objects in industrial arts, etc.).

12. Have the student perform timed drills in addition to reinforce basic math facts. The student "competes" against his/her own best time.

13. Develop a math facts reference sheet for addition for the student to use at his/her desk when solving math problems.

14. Have the student solve half of the math problems each day and use the calculator as reinforcement to complete the other half of the assignment.

15. Make certain the student understands number concepts and the relationships of number symbols to numbers of objects before requiring the student to solve math problems requiring addition.

16. Make certain the student knows the concepts of *more than, less than, equal,* and *zero.* The use of tangible objects will facilitate the learning process.

17. Have the student make sets of objects and add the sets together to obtain a sum total.

18. Provide the student with opportunities for tutoring from peers or a teacher. Allow the student to tutor others when he/she has mastered a concept.

19. Reinforce the student for attempting and completing work. Emphasize the number correct, then encourage the student to see how many more he/she can correct without help. Have the student maintain a "private" chart of math performance.

20. Call on the student when he/she is most likely to be able to respond successfully.

21. Provide the student with enjoyable math activities during free time in the classroom (e.g., computer games, math games, manipulatives, etc.).

22. Allow the student to perform alternative assignments. Gradually introduce more components of the regular assignments until those assignments can be performed successfully by the student.

23. Make certain that the language used to communicate with the student about addition is consistent (e.g., "Add the numbers. What is the total?" or "Find the sum.").

24. Have the student check all math work. Reinforce the student for each error corrected.

25. Make certain the student has mastery of math concepts at each level before introducing a new skill level.

26. Provide the student with shorter math tasks, but more of them throughout the day (e.g., four assignments of five problems each rather than one assignment of twenty problems).

27. Work the first problem or two of the math assignment with the student in order to make certain that he/she understands the directions and the operation necessary to solve the problems.

28. Teach the student to use resources in the environment to help solve math problems (e.g., counting figures, counting numbers of objects, using a calculator, etc.).

29. Have the student talk through the math problems as he/she solves them in order to identify errors the student is making.

30. Have the student add numbers of objects. Have the student then pair number symbols with the numbers of objects while he/she solves simple addition problems. Gradually remove the objects as the student demonstrates success in solving simple addition problems.

31. Require the student to use graph paper to make certain the numbers are lined up correctly.

32. Make certain the student is not required to learn more information than the student is capable of at any one time.

33. Make certain the student knows why he/she is learning a math concept. Provide the student with concrete examples and opportunities to apply those concepts in real-life situations.

34. Have the student act as a peer tutor to teach another student a concept the student has mastered. This can serve as reinforcement for the student.

35. Provide the student with self-checking materials, requiring correction before turning in assignments.

36. Make certain that all directions, questions, explanations, and instructions are delivered in the most clear and concise manner and at an appropriate pace for the student.

37. Provide the student with increased opportunities for help or assistance on academic tasks (e.g., peer tutoring, directions for assignments sent home, frequent interactions, etc.).

38. Deliver information to the student on a one-to-one basis or employ a peer tutor.

39. Reduce the emphasis on competition. Competitive activities may cause the student to hurry and solve addition problems incorrectly.

40. Provide the student with a quiet place to work (e.g., "office," study carrel, etc.). This is used as a means of reducing distracting stimuli and not as a form of punishment.

41. Reinforce the student for correctly solving addition problems: (a) give the student a tangible reward (e.g., classroom privileges, line leading, passing out materials, five minutes free time, etc.) or (b) give the student an intangible reward (e.g., praise, handshake, smile, etc.).

94 Fails to correctly solve math problems requiring subtraction

1. Discuss words and phrases which usually indicate subtraction operations (e.g., *difference between, from, left, how many more or less, how much taller, how much farther*, etc.).

2. Assign a peer to act as a model for the student and to demonstrate how to solve subtraction problems.

3. Evaluate the appropriateness of the task to determine: (a) if the task is too difficult and (b) if the length of time scheduled for the task is appropriate.

4. Provide the student with many concrete experiences to help learn and remember math facts. Use popsicle sticks, paper clips, fingers, etc., to form groupings to teach subtraction facts.

5. Have the student use a calculator to reinforce the solving of math problems requiring subtraction. Have the student solve several problems each day using a calculator.

6. Provide practice of subtraction facts by using a computer with software programs that give immediate feedback for the student.

7. Use daily drill activities to help the student memorize subtraction facts (e.g., written problems, flash cards, etc.).

8. Have the student perform timed drills in subtraction to reinforce basic math facts. The student "competes" against his/her own best times.

9. Have the student use a number line attached to his/her desk to solve subtraction problems.

10. Have the student use a calculator for drill activities of basic subtraction facts.

11. Find opportunities for the student to apply subtraction facts to real-life situations (e.g., getting change in the cafeteria, measuring the lengths of objects in industrial arts, etc.).

12. Develop a reference sheet of subtraction math facts for the student to use at his/her desk when solving math problems.

13. Have the student independently solve half the assigned subtraction problems each day and use a calculator as reinforcement to solve the rest of the problems.

14. Make certain the student understands number concepts and the relationships of number symbols to numbers of objects before requiring him/her to solve math problems requiring subtraction.

15. Make certain the student knows the concepts of *more than, less than, equal,* and *zero.* The use of tangible objects will facilitate the learning process.

16. Provide the student with opportunities for tutoring from peers or a teacher. Allow the student to tutor others when he/she has mastered a concept.

17. Reinforce the student for attempting and completing work. Emphasize the number correct, then encourage the student to see how many more can be corrected without help. Have the student maintain his/her own "private" chart of math performance.

18. Call on the student when he/she is most likely to be able to respond successfully.

19. Provide the student with enjoyable math activities during free time in the classroom (e.g., computer games, math games, manipulatives, etc.).

20. Allow the student to perform alternative assignments. Gradually introduce more components of the regular assignments until those assignments can be performed successfully by the student.

21. Have the student check all math work. Reinforce the student for each error corrected.

22. Make certain that the language used to communicate with the student about subtraction is consistent (e.g., "Subtract the numbers. What is the difference?" etc.).

23. Make certain the student has mastery of math concepts at each level before introducing a new skill level.

24. Provide the student with shorter math tasks, but more of them throughout the day (e.g., four assignments of five problems rather than one assignment of twenty problems).

25. Work the first problem or two of the math assignment with the student in order to make certain that he/she understands the directions and the operation necessary to do the problems.

26. Teach the student to use resources in the environment to help solve math problems (e.g., counting figures, counting numbers of objects, using a calculator, etc.).

27. Have the student learn to subtract numbers of objects. Then have the student pair symbols with numbers of objects while solving the subtraction problems. In the last step, the student subtracts the number symbols without using objects.

28. Have the student talk through math problems while solving them in order to identify errors he/she is making.

29. Require the student to check subtraction problems by adding (i.e. the difference plus the subtrahend equals the minuend). Reinforce the student for each error corrected.

30. Make certain the student learns the concept of take away (e.g., "You have 3 toys and I take away 2 of them. How many do you have left?").

31. Require the student to use graph paper to make certain that columns are lined up appropriately.

32. Make certain the student knows why he/she is learning a math concept. Provide the student with concrete examples and opportunities to apply those concepts in real-life situations.

33. Make certain the student is not required to learn more information than the student is capable of at any one time.

34. Have the student act as a peer tutor to teach another student a concept he/she has mastered. This can serve as reinforcement for the student.

35. Provide the student with self-checking materials, requiring correction before turning in assignments.

36. Make certain that all directions, questions, explanations, and instructions are delivered in the most clear and concise manner and at an appropriate pace for the student.

37. Provide the student with increased opportunities for help or assistance on academic tasks (e.g., peer tutoring, directions for assignments sent home, frequent interactions, etc.).

38. Deliver information to the student on a one-to-one basis or use a peer tutor.

39. Have the student solve math problems by manipulating objects and stating the process(es) used.

40. Reduce the emphasis on competition. Competitive activities may cause the student to hurry and do subtraction problems incorrectly.

41. Provide the student with a quiet place to work (e.g., "office," carrel, etc.). This is used as a means of reducing distracting stimuli and not as a form of punishment.

42. Reinforce the student for correctly solving subtraction problems: (a) give the student a tangible reward (e.g., class privileges, line leading, passing out materials, five minutes free time, etc.) or (b) give the student an intangible reward (e.g., praise, handshake, smile, etc.).

95 Fails to correctly solve math problems requiring multiplication

1. Have the student solve math problems by manipulating objects and stating the process(es) involved.

2. Discuss words/phrases which usually indicate a multiplication operation (e.g., *area, each, times, product, double, triple, twice,* etc.).

3. Assign a peer to act as a model for the student and to demonstrate how to solve multiplication problems.

4. Evaluate the appropriateness of the task to determine: (a) if the task is too difficult and (b) if the length of time scheduled for the task is appropriate.

5. Provide the student with many concrete experiences to help the student learn and remember math facts. Use popsicle sticks, tongue depressors, paper clips, buttons, fingers, etc., to form groupings to teach multiplication facts.

6. Have the student use a calculator to reinforce learning multiplication facts. Have the student solve several multiplication problems each day using a calculator.

7. Provide practice of multiplication facts by using a computer with software programs that give immediate feedback to the student.

8. Use daily drill activities to help the student memorize multiplication facts (e.g., written problems, flash cards, etc.).

9. Have the student perform timed drills in multiplication to reinforce basic math facts. The student "competes" against his/her own best time.

10. Have the student use a calculator for drill activities of basic multiplication facts.

11. Develop a math facts reference sheet for multiplication for the student to use at his/her desk when solving math problems.

12. Have the student independently solve half of the assigned multiplication problems each day and use the calculator as reinforcement to complete the other half of the assignment.

13. Make certain the student understands number concepts and the relationship of number symbols to numbers of objects before requiring him/her to solve math problems requiring multiplication.

14. Provide the student with opportunities for tutoring from peers or a teacher. Allow the student to tutor others when he/she has mastered a concept.

15. Reinforce the student for attempting and completing work. Emphasize the number correct, then encourage the student to see how many more can be performed correctly without help. Have the student maintain a "private" chart of math performance.

16. Call on the student when he/she is most likely to be successful.

17. Provide the student with enjoyable math activities during free time in the classroom (e.g., computer games, math games, manipulatives, etc.).

18. Allow the student to perform alternative math assignments. Gradually introduce more components of the regular assignments until those assignments can be performed.

19. Have the student check all math work. Reinforce the student for each error corrected.

20. Provide the student with shorter tasks, but more of them throughout the day (e.g., four assignments of five problems each rather than one assignment of twenty problems).

21. Work the first problem or two of the math assignment with the student in order to make certain that he/she understands directions and the operation necessary to solve the problems.

22. Make certain the student has mastery of math concepts at each level before introducing a new skill level.

23. Teach the student to use resources in the environment to help solve math problems (e.g., counting figures, counting numbers of objects, using a calculator, etc.).

24. Have the student talk through the math problems as he/she solves them in order to identify errors made.

25. Make certain the student understands that multiplication is a short way of adding by giving examples of how much longer it takes to add than to multiply.

26. Practice skip counting with 2's, 3's, and 5's.

27. Teach the student the identity element of one. Any number times one is always that number.

28. Have the student count by equal distances on a number line. Demonstrate that the equal distances represent skip counting or equal addition, which is the concept of multiplication.

29. Teach the student the zero element. Any number times zero will be zero.

30. Have the student practice the multiplication tables each day with a peer using flash cards.

31. Identify specific multiplication problems the student fails to correctly solve and target these problems for additional instruction and time to be spent in tutoring and drill activities.

32. Require the student to use graph paper to make certain columns are lined up appropriately.

33. Make certain the student knows why he/she is learning a math concept. Provide the student with concrete examples and opportunities to apply those concepts in real-life situations.

34. Make certain the student is not required to learn more information than the student is capable of at any one time.

35. Have the student act as a peer tutor to teach another student a concept the student has mastered. This can serve as reinforcement for the student.

36. Make certain the student has mastery of math concepts at each level before introducing a new skill level.

37. Provide the student with self-checking materials, requiring correction before turning in assignments.

38. Make certain that all directions, questions, explanations, and instructions are delivered in the most clear and concise manner and at an appropriate pace for the student.

39. Provide the student with increased opportunities for help or assistance on academic tasks (e.g., peer tutoring, directions for assignments sent home, frequent interactions, etc.).

40. Deliver information to the student on a one-to-one basis or employ a peer tutor.

41. Reduce the emphasis on competition. Competitive activities may cause the student to hurry and do multiplication problems incorrectly.

42. Provide the student with a quiet place to work (e.g., "office," study carrel, etc.). This is used as a means of reducing distracting stimuli and not as a form of punishment.

43. Reinforce the student for correctly solving multiplication problems: (a) give the student a tangible reward (e.g., classroom privileges, line leading, passing out materials, five minutes free time, etc.) or (b) give the student an intangible reward (e.g., praise, handshake, smile, etc.).

96 Fails to correctly solve math problems requiring division

1. Have the student solve math problems by manipulating objects and stating the process(es) used.

2. Discuss words and phrases which usually indicate a division operation (e.g., *into, share, each, average, quotient, half as many,* etc.).

3. Assign a peer to act as a model for the student and to demonstrate how to solve division problems.

4. Evaluate the appropriateness of the task to determine: (a) if the task is too difficult and (b) if the length of time scheduled for the task is appropriate.

5. Provide the student with many concrete experiences to help him/her learn and remember math facts. Use popsicle sticks, tongue depressors, paper clips, buttons, fingers, etc., to form groupings to teach division facts.

6. Have the student use a calculator to reinforce learning division. Have the student solve several problems each day using a calculator.

7. Provide practice of division facts by using a computer with software programs that give immediate feedback to the student.

8. Use daily drill activities to help the student memorize division facts (e.g., written problems, flash cards, etc.).

9. Have the student perform timed drill activities to reinforce basic math facts. The student "competes" against his/her own best time.

10. Have the student use a calculator for drill activities of basic division facts.

11. Find opportunities for the student to apply division facts to real-life situations (e.g., money, average length of time it takes to do a job, etc.).

12. Call on the student when he/she is most likely to be able to respond successfully.

13. Develop a math fact reference sheet for division for the student to use at his/her desk when solving math problems.

14. Have the student independently solve half of the assigned division problems each day and use a calculator as reinforcement to complete the other half of the problems.

15. Make certain the student understands number concepts and the relationship of number symbols to numbers of objects before requiring him/her to solve division problems.

16. Make certain the student knows the concepts of *more than, less than, equal,* and *zero.* The use of tangible objects will facilitate the learning process.

17. Give the student several objects (e.g., one inch cubes, connecting links, etc.) and have him/her divide them into groups.

18. Provide the student with opportunities for tutoring from peers or a teacher. Allow the student to tutor others when he/she has mastered a concept.

19. Reinforce the student for attempting and completing work. Emphasize the number correct, then encourage the student to see how many more he/she can correct without help. Have the student maintain a "private" chart of math performance.

20. Provide the student with enjoyable math activities during free time in the classroom (e.g., computer games, math games, manipulatives).

21. Allow the student to perform alternative versions of the assignments. Gradually introduce more components of the regular assignments until those assignments can be performed successfully.

22. Make certain that the language used to communicate with the student about division is consistent (e.g., "Divide the numbers." "What is the divisor?" "What is the dividend?" etc.).

23. Have the student check all math work. Reinforce the student for each error corrected.

24. Make certain the student has mastery of math concepts at each level before introducing a new skill level.

25. Provide the student with shorter math tasks, but more of them throughout the day (e.g., four assignments of five problems each rather than one assignment of twenty problems).

26. Work the first problem or two of the assignment with the student in order to make certain that he/she understands directions and the operation necessary to solve the problems.

27. Teach the student to use resources in the environment to help solve math problems (e.g., counting figures, counting numbers of objects, using a calculator, etc.).

28. Have the student learn to divide numbers of objects. Then the student pairs number symbols with numbers of objects while solving the division problem. In the last step, the student divides without using objects.

29. Have the student talk through the math problem as he/she solves it in order to identify errors the student is making.

30. Teach the student the identity element of one. Any number divided by one is always the number.

31. Have the student practice the division tables each day by using flash cards with a peer.

32. Identify specific division problems the student fails to correctly solve, and target problems for additional instruction and time to be spent in tutoring and drill activities.

33. Have the student list all the skills necessary to work a division problem (e.g., subtraction, multiplication, etc.).

34. Make certain that all directions, questions, explanations, and instructions are delivered in the most clear and concise manner and at an appropriate pace for the student.

35. Use practical applications of division. Have each student bring something that must be divided among the whole class.

36. Use task analysis on each problem to determine where the student is breaking down.

37. Make certain the student knows why he/she is learning a math concept. Provide the student with concrete examples and opportunities to apply those concepts in real-life situations.

38. Make certain the student is not required to learn more information than he/she is capable of at any one time.

39. Have the student act as a peer tutor to teach another student a concept he/she has mastered. This can serve as reinforcement for the student.

40. Have the student check all math work. Reinforce the student for each error corrected.

41. Provide the student with increased opportunities for help or assistance on academic tasks (e.g., peer tutoring, directions for assignments sent home, frequent interactions, etc.).

42. Deliver information to the student on a one-to-one basis or employ a peer tutor.

43. Reduce the emphasis on competition. Competitive activities may cause the student to hurry and do division problems incorrectly.

44. Provide the student with a quiet place to work (e.g., "office," study carrel, etc.). This is used as a means of reducing distracting stimuli and not as a form of punishment.

45. Reinforce the student for solving division problems: (a) give the student a tangible reward (e.g., classroom privileges, line leading, passing out materials, five minutes free time, etc.) or (b) give the student an intangible reward (e.g., praise, handshake, smile, etc.).

97 Does not remember math facts

1. Beginning with the addition and subtraction facts, separate the basic facts into "sets," each to be memorized successively by the student.

2. Using the tracking technique to help the student learn math facts, present a few facts at a time. Gradually increase the number of facts the student must remember as he/she demonstrates success.

3. Provide the student with many concrete experiences to help learn and remember math facts. Use popsicle sticks, tongue depressors, paper clips, buttons, etc., to form groupings to teach math facts.

4. Use fingers to teach the student to form addition and subtraction combinations. Have the student hold up fingers and add or subtract other fingers to find the correct answer.

5. Have the student use a calculator to reinforce learning of the math facts. Have the student solve several problems each day using a calculator.

6. Provide practice of math facts by using a computer with software programs that provide immediate feedback for the student.

7. Use daily drill activities to help the student memorize math facts (e.g., written problems, flash cards, etc.).

8. Develop and post basic addition, subtraction, multiplication, and division charts which the student can use in solving math problems.

9. Build upon math facts the student already knows, reinforcing facts the student has mastered. Add one new fact at a time as the student demonstrates success.

10. Have the student perform timed drills to reinforce basic math facts. The student "competes" against his/her own best time.

11. Have the student use a number line attached to his/her desk to add and subtract.

12. Choose one fact with which the student is unsuccessful and review it several times a day. Make that fact the student's "fact of the day."

13. Have the student complete a math facts worksheet and use a calculator to check and correct the problems.

14. Have a peer tutor work with the student each day on drill activities (e.g., flash cards).

15. Avoid going on to multiplication and division facts until addition and subtraction facts have been mastered.

16. Have the student use math fact records and tapes for math fact drill activities.

17. Use manipulative objects (e.g., peg board, abacus, base ten blocks, etc.) to teach the student basic math facts while providing a visual image.

18. Have the student use a calculator for drill activities of basic math facts.

19. Find opportunities for the student to apply math facts to real-life situations (e.g., getting change in the cafeteria, measuring the lengths of objects in industrial arts, etc.).

20. Develop a math facts reference sheet for addition, subtraction, multiplication, or division for the student to use at his/her desk when solving math problems.

21. Have the student solve half of his/her math problems each day and use the calculator as reinforcement to complete the other half of the assignment.

22. Make certain the student is not required to learn more information than he/she is capable of at any one time.

23. Review, on a daily basis, those skills, concepts, tasks, etc., which have been previously introduced.

24. Reduce the emphasis on competition. Competitive activities may cause the student to hurry and make mistakes in math problems.

25. Reinforce the student for improving retention of math facts: (a) give the student a tangible reward (e.g., classroom privileges, line leading, passing out materials, five minutes free time, etc.) or (b) give the student an intangible reward (e.g., praise, handshake, smile, etc.).

98 Does not make use of columns when working math problems

1. Use manipulative objects (e.g., base ten blocks, connecting links, etc.) to teach the student place value by providing a visual image.

2. Make certain the student has the prerequisite skills to learn place value (e.g., counting orally, writing numbers to 100, etc.).

3. Make certain the student knows the concepts of terminology necessary to learn place value (e.g., *set, column, middle, left, digit,* etc.).

4. Make certain the student understands that the collective value of ten "ones" is equal to one ten and that ten "tens" is equal to one hundred.

5. Provide the student with learning experiences in grouping tangible objects into groups of tens, hundreds, etc.

6. Have the student practice labeling columns to represent ones, tens, hundreds, etc.

7. Have the student practice regrouping a number in different positions and determining its value (e.g., 372, 647, 751).

8. Make certain the student understands the zero concept in place value (e.g., there are no tens in the number "207," so a zero is put in the tens column).

9. Money concepts will help the student learn place value by association (e.g., $1.26 is the same as six pennies or six ones; two dimes or two tens; one dollar or one hundred).

10. Use vertical lines on graph paper to help the student visualize columns and put a single digit in a column.

11. Make certain the student understands that math problems of addition, subtraction, and multiplication are worked from right to left beginning with the ones column.

12. Provide the student with many opportunities to indicate the value of columns in multiple-digit numbers (e.g., 56 = _tens and _ones; 329 = _ hundreds, _tens, and _ones; etc.).

13. Teach the student the concept of filling each column and moving on to the next column from ones to tens, hundreds, thousands, etc.

14. Develop a marked column format (e.g., | thousands | hundreds | tens | ones |) on a master which can be copied for the student to use in solving all math problems assigned.

15. Require the student to check all math assignments for accuracy. Reinforce the student for each correction made in the use of columns.

16. Have the student use a calculator to solve math problems involving the use of columns.

17. Make certain the student knows why he/she is learning a math concept. Provide the student with concrete examples and opportunities to apply those concepts in real-life situations.

18. Have the student talk through math problems as he/she is solving them in order to identify errors the student is making.

19. Provide practice of using columns in math by using a computer with software programs that give immediate feedback for the student.

20. Identify a peer to act as a model for the student to demonstrate the use of columns when working math problems.

21. Reinforce the student for making use of columns when working math problems: (a) give the student a tangible reward (e.g., classroom privileges, line leading, passing out materials, five minutes free time, etc.) or (b) give the student an intangible reward (e.g., praise, handshake, smile, etc.).

99 Does not perform or complete classroom assignments during class time

1. Reinforce the student for attempting and completing classroom assignments during class time: (a) give the student a tangible reward (e.g., classroom privileges, line leading, passing out materials, five minutes free time, etc.) or (b) give the student an intangible reward (e.g., praise, handshake, smile, etc.).

2. Speak with the student to explain: (a) what the student is doing wrong (e.g., not completing assignments) and (b) what the student should be doing (e.g., completing assignments during class).

3. Establish classroom rules:
1. Work on task.
2. Work quietly.
3. Remain in your seat.
4. Finish task.
5. Meet task requirements.

Reiterate rules often and reinforce students for following rules.

4. Reinforce the student for attempting and completing assignments based on the amount of work he/she can successfully complete. Gradually increase the amount of work required for reinforcement as the student demonstrates success.

5. Write a contract with the student specifying what behavior is expected (e.g., attempting and completing class assignments) and what reinforcement will be made available when the terms of the contract have been met. (See Appendix for Behavioral Contract.)

6. Have the student keep a chart or graph representing the number of class assignments completed.

7. Evaluate the appropriateness of the task to determine: (a) if the task is too difficult, and (b) if the length of time scheduled for the task is appropriate.

8. Assign a peer to help the student with class assignments.

9. Assess the degree of task difficulty in comparison with the student's ability to perform the task.

10. Assign the student shorter tasks (e.g., modify a 20-problem math activity to 4 activities of 5 problems each, to be done at various times during the day). Gradually increase the number of problems over time.

11. Present tasks in the most attractive and interesting manner possible.

12. Reduce distracting stimuli (e.g., place the student in the front row, provide a carrel or quiet place away from distractions). This is used as a means of reducing stimuli and not as a form of punishment.

13. Interact frequently with the student in order to maintain involvement with class assignments (e.g., ask the student questions, ask the student's opinion, stand close to the student, seat the student near the teacher's desk, etc.).

14. Allow the student additional time to complete class assignments.

15. Supervise the student during class assignments in order to maintain on-task behavior.

16. Deliver directions orally in order to increase the probability of the student's understanding of class assignments.

17. Repeat directions in order to increase the probability of the student's understanding.

18. Encourage the student to ask for clarification of directions for classroom assignments.

19. Follow a less desirable task with a highly desirable task, making the completion of the first necessary to perform the second.

20. Give directions in a variety of ways to increase the probability of understanding (e.g., if the student fails to understand verbal directions, present them in written form).

21. Provide the student with step-by-step written directions for doing class assignments.

22. Make certain the student understands the natural consequences of failing to complete assignments (e.g., students who do not finish their work are not allowed to do more desirable activities).

23. Allow the student to perform alternative assignments. Gradually introduce more components of the regular assignments until those assignments are routinely performed.

24. Explain to the student that work not done during work time will have to be done during other times (e.g., break time, recreational time, after school, etc.).

25. Take steps to deal with student refusal to perform an assignment in order that the rest of the group will not be exposed to contagion (e.g., refrain from arguing with the student, place the student at a carrel or other quiet place to work, remove the student from the group or classroom, etc.).

26. Maintain consistency of expectations while keeping expectations within the ability level of the student.

27. Allow the student the option of performing the assignment at another time (e.g., earlier in the day, later, on another day, or at home).

28. Provide the student with a selection of assignments and require him/her to choose a minimum number from the total (e.g., present the student with ten academic tasks from which six must be finished that day.).

29. Maintain consistency in daily routine.

30. Work a few problems with the student on an assignment in order to serve as a model and help the student begin a task.

31. Reinforce the student for beginning, staying on, and completing assignments.

32. Communicate with parents (e.g., notes home, phone calls, etc.) in order to share information concerning the student's progress and so that they can reinforce the student at home for completing assignments at school.

33. Identify a peer to act as a model for the student to imitate appropriate completion of assignments.

34. Have the student question any directions, explanations, and instructions not understood.

35. Assess the quality and clarity of directions, explanations, and instructions given to the student.

36. Structure the environment in such a way as to provide the student with increased opportunity for help or assistance.

37. Communicate clearly to the student the length of time he/she has to complete the assignment.

38. Communicate clearly to the student when the assignment should be completed.

39. Have the student time assignments in order to monitor his/her own behavior and accept time limits.

40. Structure time units in order that the student knows exactly how long he/she has to work and when to be finished.

41. Provide the student with more than enough time to finish an activity, and decrease the amount of time as the student demonstrates success.

42. Have the student repeat the directions orally to the teacher.

43. Rewrite directions at a lower reading level.

44. Provide the student with shorter tasks given more frequently.

45. Provide the student with a schedule of daily events in order that he/she knows exactly what and how much there is to do in a day. (See Appendix for Schedule of Daily Events.)

46. Prevent the student from becoming over-stimulated by an activity (e.g., frustrated, angry, etc.).

47. Specify exactly what is to be done for the completion of the task (e.g., indicate definite starting and stopping points, indicate a minimum requirement, etc.).

48. Require the student to begin each assignment within a specified period of time (e.g., three minutes, five minutes, etc.).

49. Provide clearly stated directions in written or verbal form (i.e., make the directions as simple and concrete as possible).

50. Interact frequently with the student in order to help him/her follow directions for the assignments.

51. Provide alternatives for the traditional format of directions (e.g., tape record directions, summarize directions, directions given by peers, etc.).

52. Practice direction-following skills on nonacademic tasks (e.g., recipes, games, etc.).

53. Reduce directions to steps (e.g., give the student each additional step after completion of the previous step).

54. Make certain the student achieves success when following directions.

55. Reduce the emphasis on early completion. Hurrying to complete assignments may cause the student to fail to follow directions.

56. Have the student use a timer in order to complete tasks within a given period of time.

57. Present one assignment at a time. As each assignment is completed, deliver reinforcement along with the presentation of the next assignment.

58. Establish assignment rules:
1. Listen to directions.
2. Wait until all directions have been given.
3. Ask questions about anything not understood.
4. Make certain you have all necessary materials.
5. Begin assignment when you are certain about what to do.

Reiterate rules often and reinforce students for following rules.

59. Allow the student access to pencils, pens, etc., only after directions have been given.

60. Make certain that the student is attending to the teacher when directions are given (e.g., making eye contact, hands free of writing materials, looking at assignment, etc.).

61. Maintain visibility to and from the student in order to make certain the student is attending. The teacher should be able to see the student and the student should be able to see the teacher, making eye contact possible at all times.

62. Along with the student, chart those assignments that have been completed in a given period of time.

63. Reduce the emphasis on academic and social competition. Fear of failure may cause the student to not want to complete the required number of assignments in a given period of time.

64. Have the student complete assignments in a private place (e.g., carrel, "office," quiet study area, etc.) in order to reduce the anxiety of public failure.

65. Provide the student with the opportunity to perform assignments in a variety of ways (e.g., on tape, with a calculator, orally, etc.).

66. Have the student explain to the teacher what should be done in order to perform the assignments.

67. Make it pleasant and positive for the student to ask questions about things he/she does not understand. Reinforce the student by assisting, congratulating, praising, etc.

68. Provide the student with quality material to perform the assignment (e.g., pencil with eraser, paper, dictionary, handwriting sample, etc.). Be certain that the student has only the necessary material on his/her desk.

69. Make certain the student is not required to learn more information than he/she is capable of at any one time.

70. Provide the student with increased opportunities for help or assistance on academic tasks (e.g., peer tutoring, directions for work sent home, frequent interactions, etc.).

71. Reduce the amount of information on a page if it is causing visual distractions for the student (e.g., less print to read, fewer problems, isolate information that is presented to the student).

1. Reinforce the student for turning in homework. Gradually increase the number of times required for reinforcement as the student demonstrates success.

2. Write a contract with the student specifying what behavior is expected (e.g., turning in homework) and what reinforcement will be made available when the terms of the contract have been met. (See Appendix for Behavioral Contract.)

3. Communicate with the parents (e.g., notes home, phone calls, etc.) in order to share information concerning the student's progress and so that they can reinforce the student at home for turning in homework at school.

4. Evaluate the appropriateness of the homework assignment to determine: (a) if the task is too difficult, and (b) if the length of time scheduled to complete the task is appropriate.

5. Identify a peer to act as a model for the student to imitate turning in homework assignments.

6. Have the student keep a chart or graph of the number of homework assignments turned in to the teacher.

7. Have the student question any directions, explanations, and instructions not understood.

8. Assess the appropriateness of assigning the student homework if his/her ability or circumstances at home make it impossible to complete and return the assignments.

9. Meet with parents to instruct them in appropriate ways to help the student with homework.

10. Assign a peer to help the student with homework.

11. Present the tasks in the most attractive and interesting manner possible.

12. Allow the student additional time to turn in homework assignments.

13. Deliver directions orally in order to increase the probability of the student's understanding of homework assignments.

14. Chart homework assignments completed.

15. Repeat directions in order to increase the student's probability of understanding.

16. Allow the student to perform a highly desirable task when homework has been turned in.

17. Give directions in a variety of ways in order to increase the probability of understanding (e.g., if the student fails to understand verbal directions, present them in written form).

18. Provide the student with written directions for doing homework assignments.

19. Allow natural consequences to occur for failure to turn in homework assignments (e.g., students who do not finish their homework do not get to engage in more desirable activities).

20. Encourage the parents to provide the student with a quiet, comfortable place and adequate time to do homework.

21. Introduce the student to other resource persons who may be of help in doing homework (e.g., other teachers, the librarian, etc.).

22. Allow the student to perform alternative homework assignments. Gradually introduce more components of the regular homework assignment until the assignments are routinely performed and returned to school.

23. Take proactive steps to deal with student refusal to perform a homework assignment in order that the rest of the group will not be exposed to contagion (e.g., refrain from arguing with the student, place the student in a carrel or other quiet place to work, remove the student from the group or classroom, etc.).

24. Reinforce those students who complete their assignments at school during the time provided.

25. Maintain consistency of expectations and keep the expectations within the ability level of the student.

26. Work a few problems with the student on homework assignments in order to serve as a model and start the student on a task.

27. Make certain that homework is designed to provide drill activities rather than introduce new information.

28. Develop a contract with the student and his/her parents requiring that homework be done before more desirable activities take place at home (e.g., playing, watching television, going out for the evening, etc.).

29. Should the student fail to take necessary materials home, provide a set of these materials to be kept at home and send directions for homework with the student.

30. Assign small amounts of homework initially, gradually increasing the amount as the student demonstrates success (e.g., one or two problems may be sufficient to begin the homework process).

31. Find a tutor (e.g., peer, volunteer, etc.) to work with the student at home.

32. Maintain consistency in assigning homework (i.e., assign the same amount of homework each day).

33. Provide time at school for homework completion when the student cannot be successful in performing assignments at home.

34. Provide the student with a book bag, backpack, etc., to take homework assignments and materials to and from home.

35. Send homework assignments and materials directly to the home with someone other than the student (e.g., brother or sister, neighbor, bus driver, etc.).

36. Schedule the student's time at school in order that homework will not be absolutely necessary if he/she takes advantage of the school time provided to complete assignments.

37. Create a learning center at school, open the last hour of each school day, where professional educators are available to help with homework.

38. Do not use homework as a punishment (i.e., homework should not be assigned as a consequence for inappropriate behavior at school).

39. Arrange with the student's parents to pick up homework each day if the student has difficulty "remembering" to take it home.

40. Set up a homework system for the student (e.g., 2 days a week work with drill flash cards, 3 days a week work on book work sent home, etc.). This will add some variety to homework.

41. Specify exactly what is to be done for the completion of the homework task (e.g., indicate definite starting and stopping points, indicate the minimum requirements, etc.).

42. Make certain the student has mastered the concepts presented at school. All homework should be a form of practice for what has been learned at school.

43. Reinforce those students in the classroom who turn in their homework assignments.

44. Establish homework assignment rules:
1. Work on task.
2. Finish task.
3. Meet task expectations.
4. Turn in task.
Reiterate rules often and reinforce students for following rules.

45. Speak to the student to explain: (a) what the student is doing wrong (e.g., not turning in homework assignments) and (b) what the student should be doing (e.g., completing homework assignments and returning them to school).

46. Reinforce the student for turning in homework assignments: (a) give the student a tangible reward (e.g., classroom privileges, line leading, passing out materials, five minutes free time, etc.) or (b) give the student an intangible reward (e.g., praise, handshake, smile, etc.).

1. Establish classroom rules:
1. Work on task.
2. Work quietly.
3. Request assistance when needed.
4. Remain in your seat.
5. Finish task.
6. Meet task expectations.

Reiterate rules often and reinforce students for following rules.

2. Reinforce those students in the classroom who communicate needs to others when necessary.

3. Reinforce the student for communicating needs to others based on the number of times he/she can be successful. Gradually increase the number of times required for reinforcement as the student demonstrates success.

4. Write a contract with the student specifying what behavior is expected (e.g., asking for teacher assistance when necessary) and what reinforcement will be made available when the terms of the contract have been met. (See Appendix for Behavioral Contract.)

5. Communicate with parents (e.g., notes home, phone calls, etc.) in order to share information concerning the student's progress and so that they can reinforce the student at home for communicating needs to others when necessary at school.

6. Identify a peer to act as a model for the student to imitate communication of needs to others.

7. Encourage the student to question any directions, explanations, and instructions not understood.

8. Evaluate the appropriateness of expecting the student to communicate needs to others when necessary.

9. Maintain mobility throughout the classroom in order to determine the student's needs.

10. Offer the student assistance frequently throughout the day.

11. Make certain that directions, explanations, and instructions are delivered on the student's ability level.

12. Structure the environment in order that the student is not required to communicate all needs to others (i.e., make certain the student's tasks are on his/her ability level, be sure that instructions are clear, and maintain frequent interactions with the student in order to ensure success).

13. In order to detect the student's needs, communicate with the student as often as opportunities permit.

14. Demonstrate accepting behavior (e.g., willingness to help others, making criticisms constructive and positive, demonstrating confidentiality in personal matters, etc.).

15. Communicate to the student an interest in his/her needs.

16. Communicate to the student that he/she is a worthwhile individual.

17. Call on the student often in order to encourage communication.

18. Teach the student communication skills (e.g., hand raising, expressing needs in written and/or verbal forms, etc.).

19. Encourage communication skills in the classroom.

20. Communicate your own personal needs and feelings to the student.

21. Encourage the student to communicate needs to other personnel in the educational environment (e.g., school counselor, school psychologist, principal, etc.).

22. Communicate with parents, agencies, or appropriate parties in order to inform them of the problem, determine the cause of the problem, and find solutions to the problem.

23. Teach the student to communicate needs in an appropriate manner (e.g., raise hand, use a normal tone of voice when speaking, verbally express problems, etc.).

24. Recognize the student's attempts to communicate needs (e.g., facial expressions, gestures, inactivity, self-depreciating comments, etc.).

25. Have the student interact with a peer in order to encourage him/her to communicate needs to others. Gradually increase the number of peers the student interacts with as he/she demonstrates success in communicating needs to others.

26. Pair the student with a nonthreatening peer, a peer with similar interests and ability level, etc.

27. Give the student responsibilities in the classroom in order to increase the probability of communication (e.g., passing out materials, collecting lunch money, collecting schoolwork, etc.).

28. Give the student responsibilities in the classroom that require communication (e.g., peer tutor, group leader, teacher assistant, etc.).

29. Have the student keep a chart or graph representing the number of assignments performed independently.

30. Assess the degree of task difficulty in comparison with the student's ability to perform the task.

31. Assign the student shorter tasks (e.g., modifying a 20-problem math activity to 4 activities of 5 problems each, to be done at various times during the day). Gradually increase the number of problems as the student demonstrates success.

32. Present the task in the most interesting manner possible.

33. Reduce distracting stimuli (e.g., place the student in the front row, provide a carrel or quiet place away from distractions, etc.). This is to be used as a means of reducing stimuli and not as a form of punishment.

34. Allow the student additional time to complete assignments when working independently.

35. Encourage the student to ask for clarification of directions for assignments.

36. Provide the student with step-by-step written directions for assignments.

37. Allow the student to perform alternative assignments. Gradually introduce more components of the regular assignments until those assignments are routinely performed.

38. Explain to the student that work not done during work time will have to be done during other times (e.g., break time, recreational time, after school, etc.).

39. Maintain consistency of expectations while keeping expectations within the ability level of the student.

40. Maintain consistency in daily routine.

41. Work a few problems with the student on an assignment in order to serve as a model and help the student begin a task.

42. Reinforce the student for beginning, working on, and completing assignments.

43. Provide the student with a selection of assignments and require him/her to choose a minimum number of assignments to perform independently (e.g., present the student with 10 academic tasks from which six must be finished that day).

44. Communicate clearly with the student the length of time he/she has to complete the assignment and when the assignment should be completed. The student may want to use a timer in order to complete tasks within a given period of time.

45. Specify exactly what is to be done for the completion of the task (e.g., indicate definite starting and stopping points, indicate the minimum requirements, etc.).

46. Reinforce the student for performing assignments independently.

47. Speak to the student to explain: (a) what the student is doing wrong (e.g., asking for teacher assistance when not necessary) and (b) what the student should be doing (e.g., asking for teacher assistance when necessary).

48. Reinforce the student for communicating needs to others when necessary: (a) give the student a tangible reward (e.g., classroom privileges, line leading, passing out materials, five minutes free time, etc.) or (b) give the student an intangible reward (e.g., praise, handshake, smile, etc.).

102 Performs classroom tests or quizzes at a failing level

1. Have the student question anything he/she does not understand while taking tests or quizzes.

2. Make certain that the tests or quizzes measure knowledge of content and not related skills, such as reading or writing.

3. Teach the student test-taking strategies (e.g., answer questions you are sure of first, learn to summarize, check each answer, etc.). (See Appendix for Test-Taking Strategies.)

4. Give shorter tests or quizzes, but give them more frequently. Increase the length of tests or quizzes over time as the student demonstrates success.

5. Have tests or quizzes read to the student.

6. Have the student answer tests or quizzes orally.

7. Have the tests or quizzes tape recorded and allow the student to listen to questions as often as necessary.

8. Allow the student to take tests or quizzes in a quiet place in order to reduce distractions (e.g., study carrel, library, etc.).

9. Have the student take tests or quizzes in the resource room where the resource teacher can clarify questions, offer explanations, etc.

10. Provide the student with opportunities for review before taking tests or quizzes.

11. Teach and encourage the student to practice basic study skills (e.g., reading for the main point, note taking, summarizing, highlighting, studying in an appropriate environment, using time wisely, etc.) before taking tests or quizzes. (See Appendix for study skill areas.)

12. Assess student performance in a variety of ways (e.g., have the student give verbal explanations, simulations, physical demonstrations of a skill, etc.).

13. Have the student maintain a performance record for each subject in which he/she is experiencing difficulty.

14. Arrange a time for the student to study with a peer tutor before taking tests or quizzes.

15. Provide a variety of opportunities for the student to learn the information covered by tests or quizzes (e.g., films, visitors, community resources, etc.).

16. Allow the student to respond to alternative test or quiz questions (e.g., more generalized questions which represent global understanding).

17. Provide the opportunity for the student to study daily assignments with a peer.

18. Have the student take a sample test or quiz before the actual test.

19. Remove the threat of public knowledge of failure (e.g., test or quiz results are not read aloud or posted, test ranges are not made public, etc.).

20. Reduce the emphasis on formal testing by grading the student on daily performance.

21. Provide parents with information on test or quiz content (e.g., which material will be covered by the test or quiz, format, types of questions, etc.).

22. Modify instructions to include more concrete examples in order to enhance student learning.

23. Monitor student performance in order to detect errors and determine where learning problems exist.

24. Reduce the emphasis on competition. Students who compete academically and fail may cease to try to succeed and do far less than they are capable of achieving.

25. Only give tests and quizzes to the student when he/she is certain to succeed (e.g., after determining that the student has learned the information).

26. Make certain the student has mastery of skills at each level before testing a concept.

27. Make certain that all directions, questions, explanations, and instructions are delivered in the most clear and concise manner and at an appropriate pace for the student.

28. Provide the student with increased opportunities for help or assistance on academic tasks (e.g., peer tutoring, directions for work sent home, frequent interactions, etc.).

29. Identify the student's most efficient learning mode and use it when giving tests or quizzes in order to increase the probability of understanding.

30. Evaluate the appropriateness of the task to determine: (a) if the task is too difficult, and (b) if the length of time scheduled for the task is appropriate.

31. Communicate with the parents (e.g., notes home, phone calls, etc.) in order to share information concerning the student's progress and so that they can reinforce the student at home for improved test or quiz scores.

32. Write a contract with the student specifying what behavior is expected (e.g., improved test or quiz scores) and what reinforcement will be made available when the terms of the contract have been met. (See Appendix for Behavioral Contract.)

33. Reinforce those students who demonstrate improved test or quiz scores. (It may be best to reinforce privately rather than publicly.)

34. Establish classroom rules:
   1. Work on task.
   2. Work quietly.
   3. Remain in your seat.
   4. Finish task.
   5. Meet task expectations.
Reiterate rules often and reinforce students for following rules.

35. Speak with the student to explain: (a) what the student is doing wrong (e.g., not attending during class, not using study time, etc.) and (b) what the student should be doing (e.g., attending during class, asking questions, using study time, etc.).

36. Reinforce improved test or quiz scores: (a) give the student a tangible reward (e.g., classroom privileges, line leading, passing out materials, five minutes free time, etc.) or (b) give the student an intangible reward (e.g., praise, handshake, smile, etc.).

1. Assign a peer to accompany the student to specified activities in order to make certain the student has the necessary materials.

2. Provide the student with a list of necessary materials for each activity of the day.

3. Provide the student with verbal reminders of materials required for each activity.

4. Provide time at the beginning of each day for the student to organize his/her materials (e.g., before school, during recess, at lunch, at the end of the day, etc.).

5. Act as a model for being prepared for assigned activities.

6. At the end of the day, remind the student when materials are required for specified activities for the next day (e.g., send a note home, give a verbal reminder, etc.).

7. Have the student establish a routine to follow before coming to class (e.g., check which activity is next, determine what materials are necessary, collect materials, etc.).

8. Have the student leave necessary materials at specified activity areas.

9. Provide the student with a container in which to carry necessary materials for specified activities (e.g., backpack, book bag, briefcase, etc.).

10. Assess the quality and clarity of directions, explanations, and instructions given to the student.

11. Provide the student with structure for all academic activities (e.g., specific directions, routine format for tasks, time units, etc.).

12. Minimize materials needed.

13. Provide the student with adequate time at school to prepare for assigned activities (e.g., supervised study time).

14. Make certain that failure to be prepared for assigned activities results in loss of the opportunity to participate in activities or a failing grade for that day's activity.

15. Assign a peer tutor to work with the student in order to prepare for assigned activities.

16. Reduce the number/length of assignments. Gradually increase the number/length of assignments as the student demonstrates success.

17. Specify exactly what is to be done for the completion of assignments (e.g., make definite starting and stopping points, determine a minimum requirement, etc.).

18. Allow natural consequences to occur when the student is unprepared for assigned activities (e.g., the student fails a test or quiz, work not done during work time must be completed during recreational time, etc.).

19. Ask the student why he/she is unprepared for assigned activities. The student may have the most accurate perception of the problem.

20. Communicate with parents or guardians in order to inform them of the student's homework assignments and what they can do to help him/her prepare for assigned activities.

21. Provide the student with written directions to follow in preparing for all assigned activities.

22. Provide the student with a written list of assignments to be performed each day and have him/her check each assignment as it is completed.

23. Provide individual assistance in order to help prepare for assigned activities (e.g., time set aside during the day, during study hall, after school, etc.).

24. Identify other personnel in the school who can assist the student in preparing for assigned activities (e.g., aide, librarian, other teachers, etc.).

25. Meet with parents to instruct them in appropriate ways to help the student with homework.

26. Make certain the student is not required to learn more information than he/she is capable of at any one time.

27. Review, on a daily basis, those skills, concepts, tasks, etc., which have been previously introduced.

28. Have the student question any directions, explanations, and instructions not understood.

29. Identify a peer to act as a model for the student to imitate being prepared for assigned activities.

30. Evaluate the appropriateness of the task to determine: (a) if the task is too difficult, and (b) if the length of time scheduled to complete the task is appropriate.

31. Communicate with parents (e.g., notes home, phone calls, etc.) in order to share information concerning the student's progress and so that they can reinforce the student at home for being prepared for assigned activities at school.

32. Write a contract with the student specifying what behavior is expected (e.g., studying for tests or quizzes) and what reinforcement will be made available when the terms of the contract have been met. (See Appendix for Behavioral Contract.)

33. Reinforce the student for being prepared for assigned activities based on the number of times he/she can be successful. Gradually increase the number of times required for reinforcement as the student demonstrates success.

34. Reinforce those students in the classroom who are prepared for assigned activities.

35. Establish classroom rules:
1. Work on task.
2. Work quietly.
3. Remain in your seat.
4. Finish task.
5. Meet task expectations.
Reiterate rules often and reinforce students for following rules.

36. Speak to the student to explain: (a) what he/she is doing wrong (e.g., failing to study, complete assignments, bring materials to class, etc.) and (b) what the student should be doing (e.g., studying, completing assignments, bringing materials to class, etc.).

37. Reinforce the student for being prepared for assigned activities: (a) give the student a tangible reward (e.g., classroom privileges, line leading, passing out materials, five minutes free time, etc.) or (b) give the student an intangible reward (e.g., praise, handshake, smile, etc.).

1. Evaluate the auditory and visual stimuli in the classroom in order to determine the level of stimuli to which the student can respond in an appropriate manner.

2. Reduce auditory and visual stimuli to a level at which the student can successfully function. Gradually allow auditory and visual stimuli to increase as the student demonstrates that he/she can successfully tolerate the increased levels.

3. Seat the student so that he/she experiences the least amount of auditory and visual stimuli.

4. Provide the student with a quiet place in which to work where auditory and visual stimuli are reduced. This is used to reduce distracting stimuli and not as a form of punishment.

5. Seat the student away from those peers who create the most auditory and visual stimulation in the classroom.

6. Provide the student with a carrel or divider at his/her desk to reduce auditory and visual stimuli.

7. Make certain that all auditory and visual stimuli in the classroom are reduced as much as possible for all learners.

8. Provide the student with the opportunity to move to a quiet place in the classroom any time that auditory and visual stimuli interfere with the ability to function successfully.

9. Provide the student with earphones to wear if auditory stimuli interfere with the ability to function. Gradually remove the earphones as the student can more successfully function in the presence of auditory stimuli.

10. Allow the student to close the door or windows in order to reduce auditory and visual stimuli from outside of the classroom.

11. Remove the student from an activity until he/she can demonstrate appropriate on-task behavior.

12. Require the student to be productive in the presence of auditory and visual stimuli for short periods of time. Gradually increase the length of time the student is required to be productive as he/she becomes successful.

13. Provide the student with shorter tasks which do not require extended attention in order to be successful. Gradually increase the length of the tasks as the student demonstrates success.

14. Have the student engage in small group activities (e.g., free time, math, reading, etc.) in order to reduce the level of auditory and visual stimuli in the group. Gradually increase group size as the student can function successfully.

15. Model for the student appropriate behavior in the presence of auditory and visual stimuli in the classroom (e.g., continuing to work, asking for quiet, moving to a quieter part of the classroom, etc.).

16. Assign the student shorter tasks but more of them (e.g., modify a 20-problem math activity to 4 activities of 5 problems each, to be performed at various times during the day). Gradually increase the number of problems for each activity as the student demonstrates success.

17. Present tasks in the most attractive and interesting manner possible.

18. Assess the degree of task difficulty in relation to the student's ability to successfully perform the task.

19. Interact frequently with the student in order to maintain involvement in the activity (e.g., ask the student questions, ask the student's opinion, stand close to the student, seat the student near the teacher's desk, etc.).

20. Provide the student with a timer to be used to increase the amount of time during which he/she maintains attention (e.g., have the student work on the activity until the timer goes off).

21. Provide the student with a predetermined signal (e.g., hand signal, verbal cue, etc.) when he/she begins to display off-task behaviors.

22. Structure the environment to reduce the opportunity for off-task behavior. Reduce lag time by providing the student with enough activities to maintain productivity.

23. Have the student work with a peer tutor in order to maintain attention to task.

24. Make certain the student has all necessary materials to perform assignments.

25. Make certain the student knows what to do when he/she cannot successfully perform assignments (e.g., raise hand, ask for assistance, go to the teacher, etc.).

26. Maintain visibility to and from the student. The teacher should be able to see the student and the student should be able to see the teacher, making eye contact possible at all times.

27. Make certain to recognize the student when his/her hand is raised in order to convey that assistance will be provided as soon as possible.

28. Teach the student how to manage time until the teacher can provide assistance (e.g., try the problem again, go on to the next problem, wait quietly, etc.).

29. Communicate clearly with the student the length of time he/she has to complete the assignment and when the assignment should be completed. The student may want to use a timer in order to complete tasks within a given period of time.

30. Specify exactly what is to be done for the completion of the task (e.g., indicate definite starting and stopping points, indicate the minimum requirements, etc.).

31. Make certain the student understands that work not done during work time must be completed at other times such as recess, free time, after school, etc.

32. Provide the student with increased opportunities for help or assistance on academic tasks (e.g., peer tutoring, directions for work, frequent interactions, etc.).

33. Identify the student's most efficient learning mode and use it consistently to increase the probability of understanding and remaining on task for longer periods of time.

34. Give the student one task to perform at a time. Introduce the next task only when the student has successfully completed the previous task.

35. Have the student question any directions, explanations, and instructions not understood.

36. Identify a peer to act as a model for the student to imitate on-task behavior.

37. Communicate with parents (e.g., notes home, phone calls, etc.) in order to share information concerning the student's progress and so that they can reinforce the student at home for staying on task in the classroom.

38. Write a contract with the student specifying what behavior is expected (e.g., establish a reasonable length of time to stay on task) and what reinforcement will be made available when the terms of the contract have been met. (See Appendix for Behavioral Contract.)

39. Reinforce the student for attending to task based on the length of time he/she can be successful. Gradually increase the length of time required for reinforcement as the student demonstrates success.

40. Reinforce those students in the classroom who demonstrate on-task behavior.

41. Establish classroom rules:
1. Work on task.
2. Work quietly.
3. Remain in your seat.
4. Finish task.
5. Meet task expectations.
Reiterate rules often and reinforce students for following rules.

42. Speak to the student to explain: (a) what the student is doing wrong (e.g., failing to attend to tasks) and (b) what the student should be doing (e.g., attending to tasks).

43. Reinforce the student for staying on task in the classroom: (a) give the student a tangible reward (e.g., classroom privileges, line leading, passing out materials, five minutes free time, etc.) or (b) give the student an intangible reward (e.g., praise, handshake, smile, etc.).

105 Does not perform academically at his/her ability level

NOTE: Make certain that the academic programming is appropriate for the student's ability level.

1. Assess student performance in a variety of ways (e.g., have the student give verbal explanations, simulations, physical demonstrations, etc.).

2. Give shorter assignments, but give them more frequently. Increase the length of the assignments as the student demonstrates success.

3. Structure the environment in such a way as to provide the student with increased opportunity for help or assistance on academic or homework tasks (e.g., provide peer tutors, seat the student near the teacher or aide, etc.).

4. Provide the student with clearly stated written directions for homework in order that someone at home may be able to provide assistance.

5. Teach the student study skills.

6. Reduce distracting stimuli (e.g., place the student in the front row, provide a carrel or "office" space away from distractions, etc.). This is used as a means of reducing distracting stimuli and not as a form of punishment.

7. Interact frequently with the student to monitor task performance.

8. Have the student maintain a chart representing the number of tasks completed and the accuracy rate of each task.

9. Provide time at school for the completion of homework if homework assigned has not been completed or has resulted in failure. (The student's failure to complete homework assignments may be the result of variables in the home over which he/she has no control.)

10. Assess the quality and clarity of directions, explanations, and instructions given to the student.

11. Teach the student note-taking skills.

12. Assess the appropriateness of assigning homework to the student.

13. Teach the student direction-following skills: (a) listen carefully, (b) ask questions, (c) use environmental cues, (d) rely on examples provided, etc.

14. Identify resource personnel from whom the student may receive additional assistance (e.g., librarian, special education teacher, other personnel with expertise or time to help, etc.).

15. Establish a level of minimum accuracy which will be accepted as a level of mastery.

16. Deliver reinforcement for any and all measures of improvement.

17. Mastery should not be expected too soon after introducing new information, skills, etc.

18. Provide the student with self-checking materials, requiring correction before turning in assignments.

19. Should the student consistently fail to complete assignments with minimal accuracy, evaluate the appropriateness of tasks assigned.

20. Provide instruction and task format in a variety of ways (e.g., verbal instructions, written instructions, demonstrations, simulations, manipulatives, drill activities with peers, etc.).

21. If the student has difficulty completing homework assignments with minimal accuracy, provide a time during the day when he/she can receive assistance at school.

22. Make certain the assignments measure knowledge of content and not related skills such as reading or writing.

23. Have assignments read to the student.

24. Have the student respond to tasks orally.

25. Have the assignments tape recorded, allowing the student to listen to questions as often as necessary.

26. Provide the student with opportunities for review prior to grading assignments.

27. Teach the student to practice basic study skills (e.g., reading for the main idea, note taking, summarizing, highlighting, studying in a good environment, using time wisely, etc.). (See Appendix for various study skill areas.)

28. Arrange a time for the student to study with a peer tutor before completing a graded assignment.

29. Provide multiple opportunities for the student to learn the information covered by assignments (e.g., films, visitors, community resources, etc.).

30. Allow the student to respond to alternative assignment questions (e.g., more generalized questions that represent global understanding).

31. Provide parents with information regarding appropriate ways in which to help their child with homework (e.g., read directions with the student, work a few problems together, answer questions, check the completed assignment, etc.).

32. Modify instruction to include more concrete examples in order to enhance student learning.

33. Monitor student performance in order to detect errors and determine where learning problems exist.

34. Reduce the emphasis on competition. Students who compete academically and fail to succeed may cease to try to do well and do far less than they are able.

35. Allow/require the student to make corrections after assignments have been checked the first time.

36. Maintain consistency in assignment format and expectations so as not to confuse the student.

37. Provide the student with evaluative feedback for assignments completed (i.e., identify what the student did successfully, what errors were made, and what should be done to correct the errors).

38. Provide adequate repetition and drill to assure minimal accuracy of assignments presented (i.e., require mastery/minimal accuracy before moving to the next skill level).

39. It is not necessary to grade every assignment performed by the student. Assignments may be used to evaluate student ability or knowledge and provide feedback. Grades may not need to be assigned until mastery/minimal accuracy has been attained.

40. Provide the student with a selection of assignments and require him/her to choose a minimum number from the total amount (e.g., present the student with ten academic tasks from which six must be finished that day).

41. Allow the student to put an assignment away and return to it at a later time if he/she could be more successful.

42. Have the student practice an assignment with the teacher, aide, or peer before performing the assignment for a grade.

43. Monitor the student's performance of the first problem or part of the assignment in order to make certain the student knows what is expected.

44. Provide frequent interactions and encouragement to support the student's confidence and optimism for success (e.g., make statements such as "You're doing great." "Keep up the good work." "I'm really proud of you." etc.).

45. Build varying degrees of difficulty into assignments in order to insure the student's self-confidence and at the same time provide a challenge (e.g., easier problems are intermingled with problems designed to measure knowledge gained).

46. Work the first few problems of an assignment with the student in order to make certain that he/she knows what to do, how to perform the assignment, etc.

47. Modify academic tasks (e.g., format, requirements, length, etc.).

48. Provide the student with clearly stated step-by-step directions for homework in order that someone at home may be able to provide assistance.

49. Make certain that homework relates to concepts already taught rather than introducing a new concept.

50. Allow the student to perform alternative versions of the assignments. Gradually introduce more components of the regular assignments until those can be performed successfully.

51. Communicate clearly with the student the length of time he/she has to complete the assignment and when the assignment should be completed. The student may want to use a timer in order to complete tasks within a given period of time.

52. Have the student act as a peer tutor to teach another student a concept he/she has mastered. This can serve as reinforcement for the student.

53. Make certain the student has mastery of concepts at each level before introducing a new skill level.

54. Make certain the student is not required to learn more information than he/she is capable of at any one time.

55. Identify the student's most efficient learning mode and use it consistently to increase the probability of understanding.

56. Have the student question any directions, explanations, and instructions not understood.

57. Evaluate the appropriateness of the task to determine: (a) if the task is too difficult, and (b) if the length of time scheduled to complete the task is appropriate.

58. Communicate with parents (e.g., notes home, phone calls, etc.) in order to share information concerning the student's progress and so that they can reinforce the student at home for improving his/her academic task and homework performance.

59. Write a contract with the student specifying what behavior is expected (e.g., completing an assignment with __% accuracy) and what reinforcement will be made available when the terms of the contract have been met.

60. Reinforce those students in the classroom who show improvement on academic task and homework performance.

61. Establish classroom rules:
1. Work on task.
2. Work quietly.
3. Remain in your seat.
4. Finish task.
5. Meet task expectations.
Reiterate rules often and reinforce students for following rules.

62. Speak to the student to explain: (a) what the student is doing wrong (e.g., performing below his/her ability level, failing assignments, etc.) and (b) what the student should be doing (e.g., improving his/her academic task and homework performance).

63. Reinforce the student for improving academic task and homework performance: (a) give the student a tangible reward (e.g., classroom privileges, line leading, passing out materials, five minutes free time, etc.) or (b) give the student an intangible reward (e.g., praise, handshake, smile, etc.).

Please note: If the student continues to fail in spite of the above interventions and is not being served by special education personnel, he/she should be referred for consideration for special education services.

1. Have the student question any written directions, explanations, and instructions he/she does not understand.

2. Assign a peer to work with the student to help him/her follow written directions.

3. Teach the student skills for following written directions (e.g., read carefully, write down important points, ask for clarification, wait until all directions are received before beginning, etc.).

4. Give directions in a variety of ways to increase the probability of understanding (e.g., if the student fails to understand written directions, present them in verbal form).

5. Provide clearly stated written directions (e.g., make the directions as simple and concrete as possible).

6. Reduce distracting stimuli in order to increase the student's ability to follow written directions (e.g., place the student on the front row, provide a carrel or "office" space away from distractions, etc.). This is used as a means of reducing distracting stimuli and not as a form of punishment.

7. Interact frequently with the student in order to help him/her follow written directions.

8. Structure the environment in such a way as to provide the student with increased opportunities for help or assistance on academic tasks (e.g., peer tutoring, directions for work sent home, frequent interactions, etc.).

9. Provide alternatives for the traditional format of presenting written directions (e.g., tape record directions, summarize directions, directions given by peers, etc.).

10. Assess the quality and clarity of written directions, explanations, and instructions given to the student.

11. Practice the following of written directions on nonacademic tasks (e.g., recipes, games, etc.).

12. Have the student repeat written directions orally to the teacher.

13. Reduce written directions to individual steps (e.g., give the student each additional step after completion of the previous step).

14. Deliver a predetermined signal (e.g., clapping hands, turning lights off and on, etc.) before giving written directions.

15. Deliver written directions before handing out materials.

16. Require that assignments done incorrectly, for any reason, be redone.

17. Make certain the student achieves success when following written directions.

18. Reduce the emphasis on competition. Competitive activities may cause the student to hurry to begin the task without following written directions.

19. Have the student maintain a record (e.g., chart or graph) of his/her performance in following written directions.

20. Follow a less desirable task with a highly desirable task, making the completion of the first necessary to perform the second.

21. Prevent the student from becoming overstimulated by an activity (e.g., frustrated, angry, etc.).

22. Require the student to wait until the teacher gives him/her a signal to begin an activity after receiving written directions (e.g., hand signal, bell ringing, etc.).

23. Make certain that the student is attending to the teacher (e.g., making eye contact, hands free of writing materials, looking at assignment, etc.) before giving written directions.

24. Make certain that written directions are presented on the student's reading level.

25. Maintain visibility to and from the student. The teacher should be able to see the student and the student should be able to see the teacher, making eye contact possible at all times in order to make certain the student is attending to written directions.

26. Present directions in both written and verbal form.

27. Provide the student with a copy of written directions at his/her desk rather than on the chalkboard, posted in the classroom, etc.

28. Tape record directions for the student to listen to individually and repeat as necessary.

29. Develop assignments/activities for following written directions (e.g., informal activities designed to have the student carry out directions in steps, increasing the degree of difficulty).

30. Maintain consistency in the format of written directions.

31. Have a peer help the student with any written directions not understood.

32. Seat the student close to the source of the written directions (e.g., chalkboard, projector, etc.).

33. Make certain that the print is large enough to increase the likelihood of following written directions.

34. Transfer directions from texts and workbooks when pictures or other stimuli make it difficult to attend to or follow written directions.

35. Work through the steps of written directions as they are delivered in order to make certain the student follows the directions accurately.

36. Work the first problem or problems with the student to make certain that he/she follows the written directions accurately.

37. Have the student repeat to himself/herself information just read to help in remembering the important facts.

38. Have the student carry out written directions one step at a time, checking with the teacher to make certain that each step is successfully followed before attempting the next.

39. Make certain that directions are given at the level at which the student can be successful (e.g., two-step or three-step directions should not be given to students who can only successfully follow one-step directions).

40. Use visual cues such as *green dot* to start, *red dot* to stop, arrows, etc., in written directions.

41. Highlight, circle, or underline key words in written directions (e.g., key words such as *match, circle, underline*).

42. Make certain that all directions, questions, explanations, and instructions are delivered in a clear and concise manner and at an appropriate pace for the student.

43. Identify a peer to act as a model for the student to imitate appropriate following of written directions.

44. Evaluate the appropriateness of the task to determine: (a) if the task is too easy, (b) if the task is too difficult, and (c) if the length of time scheduled to complete the task is appropriate.

45. Communicate with parents (e.g., notes home, phone calls, etc.) in order to share information concerning the student's progress and so that they can reinforce the student at home for following written directions at school.

46. Write a contract with the student specifying what behavior is expected (e.g., following written directions) and what reinforcement will be made available when the terms of the contract have been met.

47. Reinforce the student for following written directions based on the length of time he/she can be successful. Gradually increase the length of time required for reinforcement as the student demonstrates success.

48. Reinforce those students in the classroom who follow written directions.

49. Establish classroom rules:
1. Work on task.
2. Work quietly.
3. Remain in your seat.
4. Finish task.
5. Meet task expectations.

Reiterate rules often and reinforce students for following rules.

50. Speak to the student to explain: (a) what the student is doing wrong (e.g., ignoring written directions) and (b) what the student should be doing (e.g., following written directions).

51. Reinforce the student for following written directions: (a) give the student a tangible reward (e.g., classroom privileges, line leading, passing out materials, five minutes free time, etc.) or (b) give the student an intangible reward (e.g., praise, handshake, smile, etc.).

1. Present the task in the most interesting and attractive manner possible.

2. Maintain mobility in order to provide assistance to the student.

3. Structure time units in order that the student knows exactly how long he/she has to work and when the work must be finished.

4. Provide the student with more than enough time to finish an activity, and decrease the amount of time as the student demonstrates success.

5. Give directions in a variety of ways in order to increase the probability of understanding (e.g., if the student fails to understand verbal directions, present them in written form).

6. Have the student repeat the directions orally to the teacher.

7. Give a signal (e.g., clapping hands, turning lights off and on, etc.) before giving verbal directions.

8. Provide the student with a predetermined signal when he/she is not beginning a task (e.g., verbal cue, hand signal, etc.).

9. Tell the student that directions will only be given once.

10. Rewrite directions at a lower reading level.

11. Deliver verbal directions in a more basic way.

12. Help the student with the first few items on a task and gradually reduce the amount of help over time.

13. Follow a less desirable task with a highly desirable task, making the completion of the first necessary to perform the second.

14. Provide the student with shorter tasks given more frequently.

15. Provide the student with a schedule of daily events in order that he/she knows exactly what and how much there is to do in a day. (See Appendix for Schedule of Daily Events.)

16. Prevent the student from becoming over-stimulated by an activity (e.g., frustrated, angry, etc.).

17. Specify exactly what is to be done for the completion of a task (e.g., definite starting and stopping points, a minimum requirement, etc.).

18. Require the student to begin each assignment within a specified period of time (e.g., three minutes, five minutes, etc.).

19. Provide the student with a selection of assignments, requiring him/her to choose a minimum number from the total (e.g., present the student with ten academic tasks from which six must be finished that day).

20. Start with a single problem and add more problems to the task over time.

21. Reduce the emphasis on competition (e.g., academic or social). Fear of failure may cause the student to refuse to attempt new assignments/ tasks.

22. Provide the student with self-checking materials in order that he/she may check work privately, thus reducing the fear of public failure.

23. Have the student attempt the new assignment/task in a private place (e.g., carrel, "office," quiet study area, etc.).

24. Have the student practice a new skill (e.g., jumping rope, dribbling a basketball, etc.) alone, with a peer or the teacher before the entire group attempts the activity.

25. Provide the student with the opportunity to perform the assignment/task in a variety of ways (e.g., on tape, with a calculator, orally, etc.).

26. Allow the student to perform a new assignment/task in a variety of places in the building (e.g., resource room, library, learning center, etc.).

27. Provide the student with a sample of the assignment/task which has been partially completed by a peer or teacher (e.g., book report, project, etc.).

28. Do not require the student to complete the assignment/task in one sitting.

29. Allow the student the option of performing the assignment/task at another time (e.g., earlier in the day, later, on another day, etc.).

30. Deliver directions/instructions before handing out materials.

31. Make certain that the student has all the materials needed in order to perform the assignment/task.

32. Have the student paraphrase to the teacher what should be done in order to perform the assignment/task.

33. Explain to the student that work not done during work time will have to be made up at other times (e.g., at recess, before school, after school, during lunch time, etc.).

34. Teach the student direction-following skills: (a) listen carefully, (b) ask questions, (c) use environment cues, (d) rely on examples provided, and (e) wait until directions are given before beginning.

35. Provide the student with optional courses of action to prevent total refusal to obey teacher directives.

36. Allow the student to perform alternative versions of a new assignment. Gradually introduce more components of the regular assignments until those can be performed successfully.

37. Have the student act as a peer tutor to teach another student a concept he/she has mastered. This can serve as reinforcement for the student.

38. Provide practice in new assignments or tasks by using a computer software program that gives the student immediate feedback.

39. Make certain the student has mastery of concepts at each level before introducing a new skill level.

40. Have the student time activities in order to monitor his/her own behavior and accept time limits.

41. Communicate clearly to the student when it is time to begin.

42. Have the student maintain a record (e.g., chart or graph) of his/her performance in attempting new assignments/tasks.

43. Reduce distracting stimuli (e.g., place the student on the front row, provide a carrel or "office" space away from distractions, etc.). This is used as a means of reducing distracting stimuli and not as a form of punishment.

44. Structure the environment in such a way as to provide the student with increased opportunities for help or assistance.

45. Assign a peer or volunteer to help the student begin a task.

46. Assess the quality and clarity of directions, explanations, and instructions given to the student.

47. Have the student question any directions, explanations, and instructions not understood.

48. Evaluate the appropriateness of the task to determine: (a) if the task is too difficult, and (b) if the length of time scheduled to complete the task is appropriate.

49. Communicate with parents (e.g., notes home, phone calls, etc.) in order to share information concerning the student's progress and so that they can reinforce the student at home for attempting a new assignment/task at school.

50. Write a contract with the student specifying what behavior is expected (e.g., attempting a new assignment/task) and what reinforcement will be made available when the terms of the contract have been met. (See Appendix for Behavioral Contract.)

51. Reinforce the student for attempting a new assignment/task within the length of time he/she can be successful. Gradually decrease the amount of time to begin the task in order to be reinforced as the student demonstrates success.

52. Reinforce those students in the classroom who attempt a new assignment/task.

53. Speak with the student to explain: (a) what the student is doing wrong (e.g., not attempting a new task) and (b) what the student should be doing (e.g., asking for assistance or clarification, following directions, starting on time, etc.).

54. Reinforce the student for attempting a new assignment/task: (a) give the student a tangible reward (e.g., classroom privileges, line leading, passing out materials, five minutes free time, etc.) or (b) give the student an intangible reward (e.g., praise, handshake, smile, etc.).

1. Reduce the emphasis on competition. Competitive activities may cause the student to hurry and make mistakes.

2. Give the student fewer concepts to learn at any one time, spending more time on each concept until the student can learn it correctly.

3. Have a peer spend time each day engaged in drill activities with the student.

4. Have the student use new concepts frequently throughout the day.

5. Have the student highlight or underline key words, phrases, and sentences from reading assignments, newspapers, magazines, etc.

6. Develop crossword puzzles which contain only the student's spelling words and have him/her complete them.

7. Write sentences, passages, paragraphs, etc., for the student to read which reinforce new concepts.

8. Have the student act as a peer tutor to teach concepts just learned to another student.

9. Have the student review new concepts each day for a short period of time rather than two or three times per week for longer periods of time.

10. Use wall charts to introduce new concepts, with visual images such as pictures for the student to associate with previously learned concepts.

11. Initiate a "learn a concept a day" program with the student and incorporate the concept into the assigned activities for the day.

12. Require the student to use resources (e.g., encyclopedia, dictionary, etc.) to provide information to help him/her be successful when performing tasks.

13. Tape record important information for the student to listen to as often as necessary.

14. Allow the student to use devices to help him/her successfully perform tasks (e.g., calculator, multiplication tables, abacus, dictionary, etc.).

15. Provide the student with various times throughout the day when he/she can engage in drill activities with the teacher, an aide, a peer, etc.

16. Provide the student with opportunities for drill activities in the most interesting manner possible (e.g., working with a computer, using a calculator, playing educational games, watching a film, listening to a tape, etc.).

17. Give the student a list of key words, phrases, or main points to learn for each new concept introduced.

18. Underline, circle, or highlight important information from any material the student is to learn (e.g., science, math, geography, etc.).

19. Provide the student with the information he/she needs to learn in the most direct manner possible (e.g., a list of facts, a summary of important points, an outline of important events, etc.).

20. Have the student practice a new skill or assignment alone, with an aide, the teacher, or a peer before the entire group attempts the activity or before performing for a grade.

21. Allow the student to perform alternative versions of the assignments. Gradually introduce more components of the regular assignments until those can be performed successfully.

22. Provide practice in new concepts by using a computer software program that gives the student immediate feedback.

23. Make certain the student has mastery of concepts at each level before introducing a new skill.

109   Is easily distracted by auditory and visual stimuli in the classroom

1.   Reduce visual and auditory stimuli to a level at which the student can successfully function. Gradually allow visual and auditory stimuli to increase as the student demonstrates that he/she can successfully tolerate the increased levels.

2.   Seat the student so that he/she experiences the least possible amount of visual and auditory stimuli.

3.   Provide the student with a quiet place in which to work where visual and auditory stimuli are reduced. This is used to reduce distracting stimuli rather than as a form of punishment.

4.   Place the student away from those peers who create the most visual and auditory stimulation in the classroom.

5.   Provide the student with a carrel or divider at his/her desk in order to reduce visual and auditory stimuli.

6.   Make certain that all visual and auditory stimuli in the classroom are reduced as much as possible for all learners.

7.   Provide the student with the opportunity to move to a quiet place in the classroom any time that visual and auditory stimuli interfere with the ability to function successfully.

8.   Provide the student with earphones to wear if auditory stimuli interfere with the ability to function successfully. Gradually remove the earphones as the student can more successfully function in the presence of auditory stimuli.

9.   Allow the student to close the door or windows in order to reduce visual and auditory stimuli outside of the classroom.

10.   Require the student to be productive in the presence of visual and auditory stimuli for short periods of time. Gradually increase the length of the tasks as the student demonstrates he/she can be successful in the presence of visual and auditory stimuli.

11.   Provide the student with shorter tasks which do not require extended attention in order to be successful. Gradually increase the length of the tasks as the student demonstrates he/she can be successful in the presence of visual and auditory stimuli.

12.   Have the student engage in small group activities (e.g., free time, math, reading, etc.) in order to reduce the level of visual and auditory stimuli in the group. Gradually increase group size as the student can function successfully in the presence of visual and auditory stimuli.

13.   Teach the student appropriate ways to respond to visual and auditory stimuli in the classroom (e.g., moving to another part of the room, asking others to be quiet, leaving the group, etc.).

14.   Model for the student appropriate behavior in the presence of visual and auditory stimuli in the classroom (e.g., continuing to work, asking for quiet, moving to a quieter part of the classroom, etc.).

15.   Remove the student from an activity in the classroom if he/she is unable to function appropriately in the presence of visual and auditory stimuli involved in the activity.

16.   Have the student practice a new skill or assignment alone, with an aide, the teacher or a peer before the entire group attempts the activity or before performing for a grade.

17.   Evaluate the visual and auditory stimuli in the classroom in order to determine what level of stimuli the student can respond to appropriately.

18.   Have the student question any directions, explanations, and instructions not understood.

19.   Identify a peer to act as a model for the student to imitate functioning appropriately in the presence of visual and auditory stimuli in the classroom.

20. Communicate with parents (e.g., notes home, phone calls, etc.) in order to share information concerning the student's progress and so that they can reinforce the student at home for functioning appropriately in the presence of visual and auditory stimuli in the classroom.

21. Write a contract with the student specifying what behavior is expected (e.g., maintaining self-control in the presence of visual and auditory stimuli in the classroom) and what reinforcement will be made available when the terms of the contract have been met. (See Appendix for Behavioral Contract.)

22. Reinforce the student for functioning appropriately in the presence of visual and auditory stimuli in the classroom based on the length of time the student can be successful. Gradually increase the length of time required for reinforcement as the student demonstrates success.

23. Reinforce those students in the classroom who function appropriately in the presence of visual and auditory stimuli in the classroom.

24. Establish classroom rules:
1. Work on task.
2. Work quietly.
3. Remain in your seat.
4. Finish task.
5. Meet task expectations.

Reiterate rules often and reinforce students for following rules.

25. Speak to the student to explain: (a) what the student is doing wrong (e.g., failing to attend, getting out of seat, fighting with a peer, talking, etc.) and (b) what the student should be doing (e.g., maintaining self-control in the presence of visual and auditory stimuli in the classroom).

26. Reinforce the student for functioning appropriately in the presence of visual and auditory stimuli in the classroom: (a) give the student a tangible reward (e.g., classroom privileges, line leading, passing out materials, five minutes free time, etc.) or (b) give the student an intangible reward (e.g., praise, handshake, smile, etc.).

110 Rushes through assignments with little or no regard to accuracy or quality of work

1. Allow the student to perform schoolwork in a quiet place (e.g., study carrel, library, resource room, etc.) in order to reduce distractions.

2. Assign the student shorter tasks while increasing accuracy and quality expectations.

3. Supervise the student while he/she is performing schoolwork in order to monitor accuracy and quality.

4. Provide the student with clearly stated criteria for acceptable work.

5. Have the student read/go over schoolwork with the teacher in order that the student can become more aware of the accuracy and quality of his/her work.

6. Provide the student with samples of work which may serve as models for acceptable levels of accuracy and quality (e.g., the student is to match the quality of the sample before turning in the assignment).

7. Provide the student with additional time to perform schoolwork in order to achieve increased accuracy and quality.

8. Teach the student procedures for improving accuracy and quality of work (e.g., listen to directions, make certain directions are understood, work at an acceptable pace, check for errors, correct for neatness, copy the work over, etc.).

9. Recognize accuracy and quality (e.g., display student's work, congratulate the student, etc.).

10. Conduct a preliminary evaluation of the work, requiring the student to make necessary corrections before final grading.

11. Establish levels of expectations for accuracy and quality of performance and require the student to correct or repeat assignments until the expectations are met.

12. Provide the student with quality materials to perform the assignment (e.g., pencil with eraser, paper, dictionary, handwriting sample, etc.).

13. Make certain that all educators who work with the student maintain consistent expectations of accuracy and quality.

14. Have the student question any directions, explanations, and instructions not understood.

15. Assess student performance in a variety of ways (e.g., have the student give verbal explanations, simulations, physical demonstrations, etc.).

16. Give shorter assignments, but give them more frequently. Increase the length of assignments as the student demonstrates success.

17. Structure the environment in such a way as to provide the student with increased opportunities for help or assistance on academic or homework tasks (e.g., peer tutors, seat the student near the teacher or aide, etc.).

18. Provide the student with clearly stated written directions for homework in order that someone at home may be able to provide assistance.

19. Teach the student study skills.

20. Reduce distracting stimuli (e.g., place the student in the front row, provide a carrel or "office" space away from distractions, etc.). This is to be used as a means of reducing distracting stimuli and not as a form of punishment.

21. Interact frequently with the student to monitor task performance.

22. Have the student maintain a chart representing the number of tasks completed and the accuracy rate of each task.

23. Assess quality and clarity of directions, explanations, and instructions given to the student.

24. Provide time at school for the completion of homework if homework assigned has not been completed or has resulted in failure. (The student's failure to complete homework assignments may be the result of variables in the home over which he/she has no control.)

25. Teach the student note-taking skills.

26. Assess the appropriateness of assigning homework to the student.

27. Teach the student direction-following skills: (a) listen carefully, (b) ask questions, (c) use environmental cues, (d) rely on examples provided, etc.

28. Identify resource personnel from whom the student may receive additional assistance (e.g., librarian, special education teacher, other personnel with expertise or time to help, etc.).

29. Deliver reinforcement for any and all measures of improvement.

30. Mastery should not be expected too soon after introducing new information, skills, etc.

31. Provide the student with self-checking materials, requiring correction before turning in assignments.

32. Should the student consistently fail to complete assignments with minimal accuracy, evaluate the appropriateness of tasks assigned.

33. Provide instruction and task format in a variety of ways (e.g., verbal instructions, written instructions, demonstrations, simulations, manipulatives, drill activities with peers, etc.).

34. If the student has difficulty completing homework assignments with minimal accuracy, provide a time during the day when assistance can be given at school.

35. Make certain the assignments measure knowledge of content and not related skills such as reading or writing.

36. Have the student respond to tasks orally.

37. Have the assignments tape recorded, allowing the student to listen to questions as often as necessary.

38. Provide the student with opportunities for review prior to grading assignments.

39. Teach the student to practice basic study skills (e.g., reading for the main idea, note taking, summarizing, highlighting, studying in a good environment, using time wisely, etc.).

40. Arrange a time for the student to study with a peer tutor before completing a graded assignment.

41. Provide multiple opportunities for the student to learn information covered by assignments (e.g., films, visitors, community resources, etc.).

42. Allow the student to respond to alternative assignment questions (e.g., more generalized questions that represent global understanding).

43. Provide parents with information regarding appropriate ways in which to help their child with homework (e.g., read directions with the student, work a few problems together, answer questions, check the completed assignment, etc.).

44. Modify instructions to include more concrete examples in order to enhance student learning.

45. Monitor student performance in order to detect errors and determine where learning problems exist.

46. Reduce the emphasis on competition. Students who compete academically and fail to succeed may cease to try to do well and do far less than they are able.

47. Allow/require the student to make corrections after assignments have been checked the first time.

48. Provide the student with evaluative feedback for assignments completed (i.e., identify what the student did successfully, what errors were made, and what should be done to correct the errors).

49. Maintain consistency in assignment format and expectations so as not to confuse the student.

50. Provide adequate repetition and drill to assure minimal accuracy of assignments presented (i.e., require mastery/minimal accuracy before moving to the next skill level).

51. It is not necessary to grade every assignment performed by the student. Assignments may be used to evaluate student ability or knowledge and provide feedback. Grades may not need to be assigned until mastery/minimal accuracy has been attained.

52. Provide the student with a selection of assignments and require him/her to choose a minimum number from the total amount (e.g., present the student with ten academic tasks from which six must be finished that day).

53. Allow the student to put an assignment away and return to it at a later time if this helps the student be more successful.

54. Have the student practice an assignment with the teacher, an aide, or a peer before performing the assignment for a grade.

55. Monitor the first problem or part of the assignment in order to make certain the student knows what is expected.

56. Provide frequent interactions and encouragement to support the student's confidence and optimism for success (e.g., make statements such as, "You're doing great." "Keep up the good work." "I'm really proud of you." etc.).

57. Build varying degrees of difficulty into assignments in order to insure the student's self-confidence and at the same time provide a challenge (e.g., easier problems are intermingled with problems designed to measure knowledge gained).

58. Communicate with parents (e.g., notes home, phone calls, etc.) in order to share information concerning the student's progress and so that they can reinforce the student at home for improving the accuracy and quality of assignments at school.

59. Modify academic tasks (e.g., format, requirements, length, etc.).

60. Provide the student with clearly stated step-by-step directions for homework in order that someone at home may be able to provide assistance.

61. Make certain that homework relates to concepts already taught rather than introducing a new concept.

62. Ask parents to set aside an established length of time each evening (e.g., 45 minutes, one hour, etc.) for homework rather than allowing the student to watch TV or play "as soon as the homework is finished."

63. Make certain that your comments take the form of constructive criticism rather than criticism that can be perceived as personal, threatening, etc. (e.g., instead of saying, "You always make the same mistake." say, "A better way to do that might be . . .").

64. Along with a directive, provide an incentive statement (e.g., "When you finish your work neatly, you may have free time." etc.).

65. Assign a peer to work with the student in order to provide an acceptable model for the student to imitate.

66. Evaluate the appropriateness of the task to determine: (a) if the task is too difficult and (b) if the length of time scheduled for the task is appropriate.

67. Work the first few problems of an assignment with the student in order to make certain that he/she knows what to do, how to perform the assignment, etc.

68. Write a contract with the student specifying what behavior is expected (e.g., improving the accuracy and quality of assignments) and what reinforcement will be made available when the terms of the contract have been met. (See Appendix for Behavioral Contract.)

69. Reinforce those students in the classroom who turn in assignments which are accurate and of high quality.

70. Reinforce the student for improving the accuracy and quality of his/her work based on ability. Gradually increase the amount of improvement expected for reinforcement as the student demonstrates success.

71. Establish classroom rules:
1. Work on task.
2. Work quietly.
3. Remain in your seat.
4. Finish task.
5. Meet task requirements.

Reiterate rules often and reinforce the student for following rules.

72. Speak with the student to explain: (a) what the student is doing wrong (e.g., turning in work which has spelling errors, work which has spacing errors, work that is illegible, etc.) and (b) what the student should be doing (e.g., taking time to check for spelling, spacing errors, etc.).

73. Reinforce conscientiousness in improving accuracy and quality of assignments (e.g., double checking spelling, proper positioning of letters, adequate spacing, etc.): (a) give the student a tangible reward (e.g., classroom privileges, line leading, passing out materials, five minutes free time, etc.) or (b) give the student an intangible reward (e.g., praise, handshake, smile, etc.).

111   Fails to make appropriate use of study time

1. Assess the degree of task difficulty in comparison with the student's ability to perform the task.

2. Assign the student shorter tasks (e.g., modify a 20-problem math activity to 4 activities of 5 problems each, to be done at various times during the day). Gradually increase the number of problems over time.

3. Present tasks in the most attractive and interesting manner possible.

4. Reduce distracting stimuli (e.g., place the student in the front row, provide a carrel or quiet place away from distractions). This is used as a means of reducing stimuli and not as a form of punishment.

5. Interact frequently with the student in order to maintain involvement with class assignments (e.g., ask the student questions, ask the student's opinion, stand close to the student, seat the student near the teacher's desk, etc.).

6. Allow the student additional time to complete class assignments.

7. Supervise the student during study time in order to maintain on-task behavior.

8. Deliver directions orally in order to increase the probability of the student's understanding of class assignments.

9. Repeat directions in order to increase the probability of understanding.

10. Encourage the student to ask for clarification of directions for classroom assignments.

11. Follow a less desirable task with a highly desirable task, making the completion of the first necessary to perform the second.

12. Give directions in a variety of ways to increase the probability of understanding (e.g., if the student fails to understand verbal directions, present them in written form).

13. Provide the student with step-by-step written directions for doing class assignments.

14. Make certain the student understands the natural consequences of failing to complete assignments (e.g., students who do not finish their work will not be allowed to do more desirable activities).

15. Allow the student to perform alternative assignments during study time. Gradually introduce more components of the regular assignments until those assignments are routinely performed.

16. Explain to the student that work not done during work time (study time) will have to be done during other times (e.g., break time, recreational time, after school, etc.).

17. Take steps to deal with student refusal to perform assignments during study time in order that the rest of the group will not be exposed to contagion (e.g., refrain from arguing with the student, place the student at a carrel or other quiet place to work, remove the student from the group or classroom, etc.).

18. Maintain consistency of expectations while keeping expectations within the ability level of the student.

19. Allow the student the option of performing assignments during another study time (e.g., earlier in the day, later, on another day, or at home).

20. Provide the student with a selection of assignments and require him/her to choose a minimum number from the total amount (e.g., present the student with ten academic tasks from which six must be finished that day).

21. Maintain consistency in daily routine.

22. Work a few problems with the student on an assignment in order to serve as a model and help the student begin a task.

23. Practice direction-following skills on nonacademic tasks.

24. Reinforce the student for beginning, staying on, and completing assignments during study time.

25. Communicate with parents (e.g., notes home, phone calls, etc.) in order to share information concerning the student's progress and so that they can reinforce the student at home for completing assignments at school.

26. Identify a peer to act as a model for the student to imitate appropriate completion of assignments.

27. Have the student question any directions, explanations, and instructions not understood.

28. Assess the quality and clarity of directions, explanations, and instructions given to the student.

29. Structure the environment in such a way as to provide the student with increased opportunities for help or assistance.

30. Communicate clearly to the student the length of time available to complete the assignment.

31. Communicate clearly to the student when the assignment should be completed.

32. Have the student time his/her assignments in order to monitor personal behavior and accept time limits.

33. Structure time units in order that the student knows exactly how much time is available to work and when work should be finished.

34. Provide the student with more than enough time to finish an activity and decrease the amount of time as the student demonstrates success.

35. Have the student repeat the directions orally to the teacher.

36. Rewrite directions at a lower reading level.

37. Provide the student with shorter tasks given more frequently.

38. Provide the student with a schedule of daily events in order that he/she knows exactly what and how much there is to do in a day. (See Appendix for Schedule of Daily Events.)

39. Prevent the student from becoming overstimulated by an activity (e.g., frustrated, angry, etc.).

40. Specify exactly what is to be done for the completion of the task (e.g., indicate definite starting and stopping points, indicate a minimum requirement, etc.).

41. Require the student to begin each assignment within a specified period of time (e.g., three minutes, five minutes, etc.).

42. Provide clearly stated directions in written or verbal form (i.e., make the directions as simple and concrete as possible).

43. Interact frequently with the student in order to help him/her follow directions for the assignments.

44. Provide alternatives for the traditional format of directions (e.g., tape record directions, summarize directions, directions given by peers, etc.).

45. Reduce directions to steps (e.g., give the student each additional step after completion of the previous step).

46. Make certain the student achieves success when following directions.

47. Reduce the emphasis on early completion. Hurrying to complete assignments may cause the student to fail to follow directions.

48. Establish assignment rules (e.g., listen to directions, wait until all directions have been given, ask questions about anything you do not understand, make certain you have all necessary materials, begin assignments only when you are certain about what you are supposed to do, etc.).

49. Allow the student access to pencils, pens, etc., only after directions have been given.

50. Make certain that the student is attending to the teacher when directions are given (e.g., making eye contact, hands free of writing materials, looking at assignment, etc.).

51. Maintain visibility to and from the student in order to make certain the student is attending. The teacher should be able to see the student and the student should be able to see the teacher, making eye contact possible at all times.

52. With the student, chart those assignments that have been completed in a given period of time.

53. Present one assignment at a time. As each assignment is completed, deliver reinforcement along with the presentation of the next assignment.

54. Have the student use a timer in order to complete the tasks within a given period of time.

55. Reduce emphasis on academic and social competition. Fear of failure may cause the student to not want to complete assignments in a given period of time.

56. Have the student complete assignments in a private place (e.g., carrel, "office," quiet study area, etc.) in order to reduce the anxiety of public failure.

57. Provide the student with the opportunity to perform assignments/activities in a variety of ways (e.g., on tape, with a calculator, orally, etc.).

58. Have the student explain to the teacher what should be done in order to perform the assignments.

59. Along with a directive, provide an incentive statement (e.g., "If you make appropriate use of study time, you may have free time." etc.).

60. Use a timer to help the student know how much time he/she has to study.

61. Make certain the student has assignments to work on during study time.

62. Assign a peer to help the student with class assignments during study time.

63. Evaluate the appropriateness of the task to determine: (a) if the task is too difficult and (b) if the length of time scheduled to complete the task is appropriate.

64. Have the student keep a chart or graph representing the number of class assignments completed during study time.

65. Write a contract with the student specifying what behavior is expected (e.g., working on class assignments during study time) and what reinforcement will be made available when the terms of the contract have been met. (See Appendix for Behavioral Contract.)

66. Reinforce the student for attempting and completing assignments based on the amount of work the student successfully completes. Gradually increase the amount of work required for reinforcement as the student demonstrates success.

67. Reinforce those students in the classroom who attempt and complete assignments during study time.

68. Establish classroom rules:
1. Work on task.
2. Work quietly.
3. Remain in your seat.
4. Finish task.
5. Meet task requirements.
Reiterate rules often and reinforce students for following rules.

69. Speak with the student to explain: (a) what the student is doing wrong (e.g., not working during study time) and (b) what the student should be doing (e.g., completing assignments during study time, studying, etc.).

70. Reinforce the student for attempting and completing class assignments during study time: (a) give the student a tangible reward (e.g., classroom privileges, line leading, passing out materials, five minutes free time, etc.) or (b) give the student an intangible reward (e.g., praise, handshake, smile, etc.).

112 Begins assignments before receiving directions or instructions or does not follow directions or instructions

1. Evaluate the appropriateness of the task to determine: (a) if the task is too difficult and (b) if the length of time scheduled to complete the task is appropriate.

2. Have the student question any directions, explanations, and instructions not understood.

3. Assess the quality and clarity of directions, explanations, and instructions given to the student.

4. Assign a peer or volunteer to help the student begin a task.

5. Structure the environment in such a way as to provide the student with increased opportunities for help or assistance.

6. Reduce distracting stimuli (e.g., place the student in the front row, provide a carrel or "office" space away from distractions, etc.). This is used as a means of reducing distracting stimuli and not as a form of punishment.

7. Have the student maintain a record (e.g., chart or graph) of performance in attempting new assignments/activities.

8. Communicate clearly to the student when it is time to begin.

9. Have the student time his/her activities in order to monitor personal behavior and accept time limits.

10. Present the task in the most interesting and attractive manner possible.

11. Maintain mobility in order to provide assistance to the student.

12. Structure time units in order that the student knows exactly how long to work and when to be finished.

13. Provide the student with more than enough time to finish an activity, and decrease the amount of time as the student demonstrates success.

14. Give directions in a variety of ways to increase the probability of understanding (i.e., if the student fails to understand verbal directions, present them in written form).

15. Have the student repeat the directions orally to the teacher.

16. Give a signal (e.g., clapping hands, turning lights off and on, etc.) before giving verbal directions.

17. Provide the student with a predetermined signal when he/she is not beginning a task (e.g., turning lights off and on, hand signals, etc.).

18. Tell the student that directions will be given only once.

19. Rewrite directions at a lower reading level.

20. Deliver verbal directions in a more basic way.

21. Help the student with the first few items on a task and gradually reduce the amount of help over time.

22. Follow a less desirable task with a highly desirable task, making the completion of the first necessary to perform the second.

23. Provide the student with a schedule of activities in order to know exactly what and how much there is to do in a day.

24. Specify exactly what is to be done for the completion of the task (e.g., make definite starting and stopping points, identify a minimum requirement, etc.).

25. Prevent the student from becoming over-stimulated by an activity (e.g., frustrated, angry, etc.).

26. Require the student to begin each assignment within a specified period of time (e.g., three minutes, five minutes, etc.).

27. Provide the student with shorter tasks given more frequently.

28. Provide the student with a selection of assignments, requiring him/her to choose a minimum number from the total (e.g., present the student with ten academic tasks from which six must be finished that day).

29. Provide the student with a certain number of problems to do for the assignment, requiring him/her to choose a minimum number from the total (e.g., present the student with ten math problems from which seven must be completed).

30. Start with a single problem and add more problems to the task over time.

31. Reduce emphasis on competition (e.g., academic or social). Fear of failure may cause the student to refuse to attempt new assignments/activities.

32. Provide the student with self-checking materials in order to check work privately, reducing the fear of public failure.

33. Have the student attempt the new assignment/activity in a private place (e.g., carrel, "office," quiet study area, etc.) in order to reduce the fear of public failure.

34. Have the student practice a new skill (e.g., jumping rope, dribbling a basketball) alone, with a peer, or with the teacher before the entire group attempts the activity.

35. Provide the student the opportunity to perform the assignment/activity in a variety of ways (e.g., on tape, with a calculator, orally, etc.).

36. Deliver directions/instructions before handing out materials.

37. Allow the student to perform new assignments/activities in a variety of places in the building (e.g., resource room, library, learning center, etc.).

38. Provide the student with a sample of the assignment/activity which has been partially completed by a peer or teacher (e.g., book reports, projects).

39. Do not require the student to complete the assignment/activity in one sitting.

40. Allow the student the option of performing the assignment at another time (e.g., earlier in the day, later, on another day).

41. Make certain that the student has all materials needed in order to perform the assignment/activity.

42. Have the student explain to the teacher what is to be done in order to perform the assignment.

43. Explain to the student that work not done during work time will have to be made up at other times (e.g., during recess, before school, after school, during lunch time).

44. Teach the student direction-following skills (e.g., listen carefully, write down important points, ask for clarification, wait until all directions are received before beginning).

45. Provide clearly stated directions, written or verbal (e.g., make the directions as simple and concrete as possible).

46. Interact frequently with the student in order to help him/her follow directions for the activity.

47. Provide alternatives to the traditional format for directions (e.g., tape record directions, summarize directions, directions given by peers, etc.).

48. Practice direction-following skills on nonacademic tasks.

49. Deliver directions and instructions before handing out materials.

50. Structure the environment in such a way as to provide the student with increased opportunities for help or assistance on academic tasks (e.g., peer tutoring, directions for work sent home, frequent interactions, etc.).

51. Reduce the number of directions given at one time (i.e., give the student each additional step after completion of the previous step).

52. Require that assignments done incorrectly, for any reason, be redone.

53. Make certain the student achieves success when following directions.

54. Reduce the emphasis on competition. Competitive activities may cause the student to hurry into the assignment without following the directions.

55. Establish assignment rules (e.g., listen to directions, wait until all directions have been given, ask questions about anything you do not understand, begin assignments only when you are certain about what is required, make certain you have all necessary materials, etc.).

56. Reinforce those students who receive directions before beginning a new task.

57. Require the student to wait until the teacher gives a signal to begin (e.g., hand signal, ringing of bell, etc.).

58. Require the student to wait until other students begin the task.

59. Require the student to have all necessary materials before beginning the task.

60. Allow the student access to pencils, pens, etc., only after directions have been given.

61. Make certain that the student is attending to the teacher (e.g., making eye contact, hands free of writing materials, looking at assignment, etc.) before directions are given.

62. Stand next to the student when giving directions.

63. Require the student to ask permission from the teacher to begin.

64. Maintain visibility to and from the student (i.e., the teacher should be able to see the student and the student should be able to see the teacher, making eye contact possible at all times) in order to make certain the student is attending.

65. Along with a directive, provide an incentive statement (e.g., "If you wait to begin your work, I will come around to help you with the first problem." etc.).

66. Communicate with parents (e.g., notes home, phone calls, etc.) in order to share information concerning the student's progress and so that they can reinforce the student at home for beginning assignments after receiving directions at school.

67. Write a contract with the student specifying what behavior is expected (e.g., beginning assignments after listening to directions) and what reinforcement will be made available when the terms of the contract have been met. (See Appendix for Behavioral Contract.)

68. Reinforce the student for beginning assignments after receiving directions, instructions, etc., based on the length of time the student can be successful. Gradually decrease the amount of time to begin the task in order for the student to be reinforced.

69. Establish classroom rules:
1. Work on task.
2. Work quietly.
3. Remain in your seat.
4. Finish task.
5. Meet task expectations.

Reiterate rules often and reinforce students for following rules.

70. Speak with the student to explain: (a) what the student is doing wrong (e.g., not following directions when performing academic tasks) and (b) what he/she should be doing (e.g., listening to directions, asking for clarification if not understood, taking notes, following one step at a time, etc.).

71. Reinforce the student for beginning assignments after receiving directions or instructions; (a) give the student a tangible reward (e.g., classroom privileges, line leading, passing out materials, five minutes free time, etc.) or (b) give the student an intangible reward (e.g., praise, handshake, smile, etc.).

113 Changes from one activity to another without finishing the first, without putting things away before it is time to move on, etc.

1. Evaluate the appropriateness of the task to determine: (a) if the task is too difficult and (b) if the length of time scheduled to complete the task is appropriate.

2. Have the student question any directions, explanations, and instructions not understood.

3. Assign a peer to work with the student to provide an appropriate model.

4. Explain to the student that satisfaction with his/her best effort is far better than insisting on perfection.

5. Prevent the student from becoming over-stimulated by an activity. Supervise student behavior in order to limit overexcitement in physical activities, games, parties, etc.

6. Have the student time activities in order to monitor his/her own behavior and accept time limits.

7. Convince the student that work not completed in one sitting can be completed later. Provide the student with ample time to complete earlier assignments in order to guarantee closure.

8. Provide the student with more than enough time to finish an activity. Decrease the amount of time provided as the student demonstrates success.

9. Structure time limits in order that the student knows exactly how long he/she has to work and when to be finished.

10. Allow a transition period between activities in order that the student can make adjustments in behavior.

11. Employ a signal technique (e.g., turning lights off and on) to warn that the end of an activity is near.

12. Establish definite time limits and provide the student with this information before the activity begins.

13. Assign the student shorter activities and gradually increase the length of the activities as the student demonstrates success.

14. Maintain consistency in daily routine.

15. Maintain consistency of expectations and keep expectations within the ability level of the student.

16. Allow the student to finish an activity unless it will be disruptive to the schedule.

17. Schedule activities so the student has more than enough time to finish an activity if working consistently.

18. Provide the student with a list of materials needed for each activity (e.g., pencil, paper, textbook, workbook, etc.).

19. Present instructions/directions prior to handing out necessary materials.

20. Collect the student's materials (e.g., pencil, paper, textbook, workbook, etc.) when it is time to change from one activity to another.

21. Provide the student with clearly stated expectations for all situations.

22. Provide adequate transition time for the student to finish an activity and get ready for the next activity.

23. Prevent the student from becoming so stimulated by an event or activity that he/she cannot control behavior.

24. Identify the expectations of different environments and help the student develop the skills to be successful in those environments.

25. Establish rules that are to be followed in various parts of the school building (e.g., lunchroom, music room, art room, gymnasium, library, playground, etc.).

26. In conjunction with other school personnel, develop as much consistency across the various environments as possible (e.g., rules, criteria for success, behavioral expectations, consequences, etc.).

27. Reduce the student's involvement in activities which prove too stimulating.

28. Have the student engage in relaxing transitional activities designed to reduce the effects of stimulating activities (e.g., put head on desk, listen to the teacher read a story, put headphones on and listen to relaxing music, etc.).

29. Use a timer to help the student know when it is time to change to a new activity.

30. Communicate with parents (e.g., notes home, phone calls, etc.) in order to share information concerning the student's progress and so that they can reinforce the student at home for demonstrating acceptable behavior at school.

31. Write a contract with the student specifying what behavior is expected (e.g., putting materials away and getting ready for another activity) and what reinforcement will be made available when the terms of the contract have been met. (See Appendix for Behavioral Contract.)

32. Reinforce the student for demonstrating acceptable behavior based on the length of time the student can be successful. Gradually increase the length of time required for reinforcement as the student demonstrates success.

33. Reinforce those students in the classroom who change from one activity to another without difficulty.

34. Establish classroom rules:
1. Work on task.
2. Work quietly.
3. Remain in your seat.
4. Finish task.
5. Meet task expectations.
Reiterate rules often and reinforce students for following rules.

35. Speak to the student to explain: (a) what the student is doing wrong (e.g., failing to stop one activity and begin another) and (b) what the student should be doing (e.g., changing from one activity to another).

36. Reinforce the student for changing from one activity to another without difficulty: (a) give the student a tangible reward (e.g., classroom privileges, line leading, passing out materials, five minutes free time, etc.) or (b) give the student an intangible reward (e.g., praise, handshake, smile, etc.).

114   Does not begin assignments after receiving directions, instructions, etc.

1.   Structure the environment in such a way as to provide the student with increased opportunities for help or assistance.

2.   Reduce distracting stimuli (e.g., place the student on the front row, provide a carrel or "office" space away from distractions, etc.). This is used as a means of reducing distracting stimuli and not as a form of punishment.

3.   Have the student maintain a record (e.g., chart or graph) of his/her performance in attempting new assignments/activities.

4.   Communicate clearly to the student when it is time to begin.

5.   Have the student time activities in order to monitor personal behavior and accept time limits.

6.   Present the task in the most interesting and attractive manner possible.

7.   Maintain mobility in order to provide assistance to the student.

8.   Structure time units in order that the student knows exactly how long he/she has to work and when the work must be finished.

9.   Provide the student with more than enough time to finish an activity, and decrease the amount of time as the student demonstrates success.

10.   Give directions in a variety of ways to increase the probability of understanding (i.e., if the student fails to understand verbal directions, present them in written form in order to ensure understanding).

11.   Have the student repeat the directions orally to the teacher.

12.   Give a signal (e.g., clapping hands, turning lights off and on, etc.) before giving verbal directions.

13.   Provide the student with a predetermined signal when he/she is not beginning a task (e.g., turning lights off and on, hand signals, etc.).

14.   Tell the student that directions will only be given once.

15.   Rewrite directions at a lower reading level.

16.   Deliver verbal directions in a more basic way.

17.   Help the student with the first few items on a task and gradually reduce the amount of help over time.

18.   Follow a less desirable task with a highly desirable task, making the completion of the first necessary to perform the second.

19.   Provide the student with a schedule of activities in order that he/she knows exactly what and how much there is to do in a day.

20.   Prevent the student from becoming overstimulated by an activity (e.g., frustrated, angry, etc.).

21.   Specify exactly what is to be done for the completion of the task (e.g., make definite starting and stopping points, identify a minimum requirement, etc.).

22.   Require the student to begin each assignment within a specified period of time (e.g., three minutes, five minutes, etc.).

23.   Provide the student with shorter tasks given more frequently.

24.   Provide the student with a selection of assignments, requiring the student to choose a minimum number from the total (e.g., present the student with ten academic tasks from which six must be finished).

25.   Start with a single problem and add more problems to the task over time.

26. Reduce emphasis on competition (e.g., academic or social). Fear of failure may cause the student to refuse to attempt new assignments/activities.

27. Provide the student with self-checking materials in order that he/she may check work privately, reducing the fear of public failure.

28. Have the student attempt a new assignment/activity in a private place (e.g., carrel, "office," quiet study area, etc.) in order to reduce the fear of public failure.

29. Have the student practice a new skill (e.g., jumping rope, dribbling a basketball, etc.) alone, with a peer, or with the teacher before the entire group attempts the activity.

30. Provide the student with the opportunity to perform the assignment/activity in a variety of ways (e.g., on tape, with a calculator, orally, etc.).

31. Allow the student to perform new assignments/activities in a variety of places in the building (e.g., resource room, library, learning center, etc.).

32. Provide the student with a sample of the assignment/activity which has been partially completed by a peer or teacher (e.g., book reports, projects, etc.).

33. Do not require the student to complete the assignment/activity in one sitting.

34. Allow the student the option of performing the assignment at another time (e.g., earlier in the day, later, on another day, etc.).

35. Deliver directions/instructions before handing out materials.

36. Make certain the student achieves success when following directions.

37. Have the student explain to the teacher what he/she thinks should be done in order to perform the assignment/activity.

38. Explain to the student that work not done during work time will have to be made up at other times (e.g., at recess, before school, after school, during lunch time, etc.).

39. Teach the student direction-following skills (e.g., listen carefully, write down important points, ask for clarification, and wait until all directions are received before beginning).

40. Provide clearly stated directions, written or verbal (e.g., make the directions as simple and concrete as possible).

41. Interact frequently with the student in order to help him/her follow directions for the activity.

42. Structure the environment in such a way as to provide the student with increased opportunity for help or assistance on academic tasks (e.g., peer tutoring, directions for work sent home, frequent interactions, etc.).

43. Provide alternatives to the traditional format for directions (e.g., tape record directions, summarize directions, directions given by peers, etc.).

44. Practice direction-following skills on nonacademic tasks.

45. Reduce the number of directions given at one time (i.e., give the student each additional step after completion of the previous step).

46. Deliver directions and instructions before handing out materials.

47. Require that assignments done incorrectly, for any reason, be redone.

48. Make certain that the student has all the materials needed in order to perform the assignment/activity.

49. Reduce the emphasis on competition. Competitive academic activities may cause the student to hurry into the assignment without following the directions.

50. Establish assignment rules (e.g., listen to directions, wait until all directions have been given, ask questions about anything you do not understand, begin assignments only when you are certain about what is required, make certain you have all necessary materials, etc.).

51. Make certain that the student is attending to the teacher (e.g., making eye contact, hands free of writing materials, looking at assignments, etc.) before directions are given.

52. Stand next to the student when giving directions.

53. Require the student to ask permission from the teacher to begin.

54. Maintain visibility to and from the student. The teacher should be able to see the student and the student should be able to see the teacher, making eye contact possible at all times in order to make certain the student is attending.

55. Along with a directive, provide an incentive statement (e.g., "When you begin your work, I will come around to see if you have questions." etc.).

56. Use a timer to help the student know how much time he/she has to follow through with directions.

57. Assign a peer or volunteer to help the student begin a task.

58. Assess the quality and clarity of directions, explanations, and instructions given to the student.

59. Have the student question any directions, explanations, and instructions not understood.

60. Evaluate the appropriateness of the task to determine: (a) if the task is too difficult and (b) if the length of time scheduled to complete the task is appropriate.

61. Communicate with parents (e.g., notes home, phone calls, etc.) in order to share information concerning the student's progress and so that they can reinforce the student at home for beginning assignments after receiving directions, instructions, etc., at school.

62. Write a contract with the student specifying what behavior is expected (e.g., begin assignments after listening to directions) and what reinforcement will be made available when the terms of the contract have been met. (See Appendix for Behavioral Contract.)

63. Reinforce the student for beginning assignments after receiving directions, instructions, etc., based on the length of time the student can be successful. Gradually decrease the amount of time to begin the task in order to be reinforced.

64. Establish classroom rules:
1. Work on task.
2. Remain in your seat.
3. Finish task.
4. Meet task expectations.
5. Raise your hand.

Reiterate rules often and reinforce students for following rules.

65. Speak to the student to explain: (a) what the student is doing wrong (e.g., not beginning assignments after receiving directions, instructions, etc.) and (b) what the student should be doing (e.g., listening to directions, asking for clarification if directions are not understood, taking notes, following one step at a time, etc.).

66. Reinforce the student for beginning assignments after receiving directions, instructions, etc.: (a) give the student a tangible reward (e.g., classroom privileges, line leading, passing out materials, five minutes free time, etc.) or (b) give the student an intangible reward (e.g., praise, handshake, smile, etc.).

115 Does not complete assignments after receiving directions, instructions, etc.

1. Structure the environment in such a way as to provide the student with increased opportunities for help or assistance.

2. Reduce distracting stimuli (e.g., place the student on the front row, provide a carrel or "office" space away from distractions, etc.). This is used as a means of reducing distracting stimuli and not as a form of punishment.

3. Have the student maintain a record (e.g., chart or graph) of his/her performance in completing assignments.

4. Communicate clearly to the student the length of time he/she has to complete an assignment.

5. Have the student time assignments in order to monitor personal behavior and accept time limits.

6. Present the task in the most interesting and attractive manner possible.

7. Maintain mobility in order to provide assistance to the student.

8. Structure time units in order that the student knows exactly how long he/she has to work and when the work must be finished.

9. Provide the student with more than enough time to finish an activity and decrease the amount of time as the student demonstrates success.

10. Give directions in a variety of ways to increase the probability of understanding (e.g., if the student fails to understand verbal directions, present them in written form).

11. Have the student repeat the directions orally to the teacher.

12. Rewrite directions at a lower reading level.

13. Deliver verbal directions in a more basic way.

14. Provide the student with shorter tasks given more frequently.

15. Provide the student with a schedule of activities in order that he/she knows exactly what and how much there is to do in a day.

16. Prevent the student from becoming over-stimulated by an activity (e.g., frustrated, angry, etc.).

17. Specify exactly what is to be done for the completion of the task (e.g., indicate definite starting and stopping points, indicate a minimum requirement, etc.).

18. Require the student to begin each assignment within a specified period of time (e.g., three minutes, five minutes, etc.).

19. Follow a less desirable task with a highly desirable task, making the completion of the first necessary to perform the second.

20. Provide the student with a selection of assignments, requiring the student to choose a minimum number from the total (e.g., present the student with ten academic tasks from which six must be finished that day).

21. Provide the student with a certain number of problems to do on an assignment, requiring the student to choose a minimum number from the total (e.g., present the student with ten math problems from which six must be completed).

22. Along with a directive, provide an incentive statement (e.g., "After your work is finished, you may play a game." etc.).

23. Use a timer to help the student know how much time he/she has to finish an assignment.

24. Reinforce those students in the classroom who complete assignments after receiving directions, instructions, etc.

25. Assess the quality and clarity of directions, explanations, and instructions the student does not understand.

26. Have the student question any directions, explanations, and instructions not understood.

27. Identify a peer to act as a model for the student to imitate appropriate completion of assignments after receiving directions, instructions, etc.

28. Evaluate the appropriateness of the task to determine: (a) if the task is too difficult and (b) if the length of time scheduled to complete the task is appropriate.

29. Communicate with parents (e.g., notes home, phone calls, etc.) in order to share information concerning the student's progress and so that they can reinforce the student at home for completing assignments after receiving directions, instructions, etc., at school.

30. Write a contract with the student specifying what behavior is expected (e.g., following directions, meeting task expectations, completing assignments, etc.) and what reinforcement will be made available when the terms of the contract have been met. (See Appendix for Behavioral Contract.)

31. Reinforce the student for completing assignments after receiving directions, instructions, etc., based on the length of time the student can be successful. Gradually decrease the length of time required for reinforcement as the student demonstrates success.

32. Assign a peer to work with the student and aid him/her in completing an assignment.

33. Establish classroom rules:
1. Work on task.
2. Remain in your seat.
3. Finish task.
4. Meet task expectations.
5. Raise your hand.
Reiterate rules often and reinforce students for following rules.

34. Speak to the student to explain: (a) what the student is doing wrong (e.g., not following directions when performing academic tasks) and (b) what the student should be doing (e.g., listening to directions, asking for clarification, taking notes, following one step at a time, etc.).

35. Reinforce the student for completing assignments after receiving directions, instructions, etc: (a) give the student a tangible reward (e.g., classroom privileges, line leading, passing out materials, five minutes free time, etc.) or (b) give the student an intangible reward (e.g., praise, handshake, smile, etc.).

116 Makes inappropriate comments or unnecessary noises in the classroom

1. Remove the student from the group or activity until he/she can demonstrate appropriate behavior and self-control.

2. Write a contract with the student specifying what behavior is expected (e.g., making appropriate comments) and what reinforcement will be made available when the terms of the contract have been met. (See Appendix for Behavioral Contract.)

3. Communicate with the parents (e.g., notes home, phone calls, etc.) in order to share information concerning the student's progress and so that they can reinforce the student at home for making appropriate comments at school.

4. Evaluate the appropriateness of the task to determine: (a) if the task is too long, and (b) if the length of time scheduled for the task is appropriate.

5. Make certain that reinforcement is not inadvertently given for inappropriate behavior (e.g., making inappropriate comments or unnecessary noises).

6. Give adequate opportunities to respond (i.e., enthusiastic students need many opportunities to contribute).

7. Have the student be the leader of a small group activity if he/she possesses mastery of skills or an interest in that area.

8. Provide the student with a predetermined signal if he/she begins to make inappropriate comments or unnecessary noises.

9. Explain to the student that he/she may be trying too hard to fit in and that he/she should relax and make more appropriate comments.

10. Structure the environment in such a way as to limit opportunities for inappropriate behaviors (e.g., keep the student engaged in activities, have the student seated near the teacher, etc.).

11. Give the student responsibilities in the classroom (e.g., running errands, opportunities to help the teacher, etc.).

12. Reduce activities which might threaten the student (e.g., announcing test score ranges or test scores aloud, making students read aloud in class, emphasizing the success of a particular student or students, etc.).

13. Provide the student with many social and academic successes.

14. Make the necessary adjustments in the environment to prevent the student from experiencing stress, frustration or anger (e.g., reduce peer pressure, academic failure, teasing, etc.).

15. Maintain visibility to and from the student. The teacher should be able to see the student and the student should be able to see the teacher, making eye contact possible at all times.

16. Interact frequently with the student to reduce his/her need to make inappropriate comments or unnecessary noises.

17. Assess the appropriateness of the social situation in relation to the student's ability to function successfully.

18. Try various groupings in order to determine the situation in which the student is most comfortable.

19. Reinforce the student for raising his/her hand in order to be recognized.

20. Call on the student when he/she is most likely to be able to respond correctly.

21. Teach the student to recognize and make appropriate comments (e.g., comments within the context of the situation, comments that are a follow-up to what has just been said, etc.).

22. Encourage the student to model the behavior of peers who are successful.

23. Have the student work in small groups in which he/she will have frequent opportunities to speak. Gradually increase the size of the group as the student learns to wait longer for a turn to speak.

24. Make certain that the student's feelings are considered when it is necessary to deal with his/her inappropriate comments (i.e., handle comments in such a way as to not diminish the student's enthusiasm for participation).

25. Help the student improve concentration skills (e.g., listening to the speaker, taking notes, preparing comments in advance, making comments in the appropriate context, etc.).

26. Have the student question any directions, explanations, and instructions not understood.

27. Deliver directions, explanations, and instructions in a clear and concise manner in order to reduce the student's need to ask questions.

28. Have the student practice waiting for a turn to speak for short periods of time. Gradually increase the length of time required for reinforcement as the student demonstrates success.

29. Explain to the student the reasons why making inappropriate comments and unnecessary noise is not acceptable (e.g., is impolite, might hurt others' feelings, etc.).

30. Attempt to provide equal attention to all students in the classroom.

31. Make the student aware of the number of times he/she makes inappropriate comments and unnecessary noises.

32. Allow natural consequences to occur due to the student making inappropriate comments or unnecessary noises in the classroom (e.g., making noises and inappropriate comments during class time will cause the student to have to make up the work during recreational time).

33. Do not inadvertently reinforce the student's inappropriate behavior by laughing when the student is silly, rude, etc.

34. Make certain the student sees the relationship between his/her behavior and the consequences which may follow (e.g., failing to listen to directions and making distracting noises will cause the student to not understand what to do).

35. Remove the student from the situation until he/she can demonstrate appropriate behavior.

36. Provide the student with a predetermined signal when he/she begins to display inappropriate behavior.

37. Make certain the student knows when it is acceptable to interrupt others (e.g., an emergency).

38. Teach the student acceptable ways to communicate displeasure, anger, frustration, etc.

39. Have the student put himself/herself in someone else's place (e.g., "How would you feel if someone called you dumb or stupid?").

40. Do not force the student to interact with others.

41. Reinforce the student for making appropriate comments based on the length of time the student can be successful. Gradually increase the length of time required for reinforcement as the student demonstrates success.

42. Reinforce those students in the classroom who make appropriate comments.

43. Establish classroom rules:
   1. Work on task.
   2. Work quietly.
   3. Remain in your seat.
   4. Finish task.
   5. Meet task expectations.
Reiterate rules often and reinforce students for following rules.

44. Speak with the student to explain: (a) what the student is doing wrong (e.g., making inappropriate comments or unnecessary noises) and (b) what the student should be doing (e.g., waiting until it is appropriate to speak, thinking of comments which relate to the situation, etc.).

45. Reinforce the student for making appropriate comments in the classroom: (a) give the student a tangible reward (e.g., classroom privileges, line leading, passing out materials, five minutes free time, etc.) or (b) give the student an intangible reward (e.g., praise, handshake, smile, etc.).

1. Teach the student problem-solving skills: (a) identify the problem, (b) identify goals and objectives, (c) develop strategies, (d) develop a plan of action, and (e) carry out the plan.

2. Provide the student with positive feedback which indicates he/she is successful, important, respected, etc.

3. Structure the environment to reduce opportunities for the student to become physically aggressive toward other students (e.g., seating arrangement, supervision, etc.).

4. Maintain visibility to and from the student. The teacher should be able to see the student and the student should be able to see the teacher, making eye contact possible at all times.

5. Be mobile in order to be frequently near the student.

6. Reduce activities which might be threatening to the student (e.g., announcing test score ranges or test scores aloud, making students read aloud in class, emphasizing the success of a particular student(s), etc.).

7. Try various groupings in order to determine the situation in which the student is most likely to succeed socially.

8. Make the necessary adjustments in the environment that will prevent the student from becoming overstimulated by peers.

9. Reduce the emphasis on competition and perfection. Repeated failure and frustration may cause outbursts of physical aggression.

10. Teach the student alternative ways to deal with situations which make him/her feel frustrated or angry (e.g., withdrawing, talking, etc.).

11. Facilitate on-task behavior by providing a full schedule of activities. Prevent lag time from occurring when the student would be free to engage in inappropriate behavior.

12. Maintain supervision in order that the student is not left alone with other students.

13. Provide the student with as many high- interest activities as possible to keep him/her from becoming physically aggressive toward other students.

14. Provide the student with opportunities for social and academic success.

15. Make certain that all school personnel are aware of the student's tendency to become physically aggressive in order that they will monitor the student's behavior.

16. Limit the student's independent movement in the school environment.

17. Provide a quiet place for the student to work independently, away from peer interactions. This is not to be used as a form of punishment but rather as an opportunity to increase the student's success in his/her environment.

18. Place reinforcement emphasis on academic productivity and accuracy in order to reduce the likelihood of the student becoming physically aggressive (i.e., increased productivity and accuracy will reduce the likelihood of inappropriate behavior).

19. Reduce or remove any stimulus in the environment which leads to the student's physically aggressive behavior (e.g., possessions, competition, teasing, etc.).

20. Make certain the student understands the natural consequences of hurting other students (e.g., less freedom, more restrictive environment, assault charges, etc.).

21. Prevent the student from receiving too much stimulation (e.g., monitor or supervise student behavior to limit overexcitement in physical activities, games, parties, etc.).

22. Limit the student's opportunity to enter areas of the school environment where he/she is more likely to be physically aggressive.

23. Separate the student from the peer(s) who may be encouraging or stimulating the student's inappropriate behavior.

24. Do not force the student to interact or remain in a group when he/she is physically aggressive (e.g., daily reading group, physical education group, etc.).

25. Maintain maximum supervision of the student and gradually decrease supervision over time as the student demonstrates appropriate behavior.

26. Intervene early when there is a problem with fighting in order to prevent more serious problems from occurring.

27. Encourage the student to tell you about problems that occur with other students at school.

28. Make certain there will always be adult supervision where the student will be.

29. Do not force the student to play with other students with whom he/she is not completely comfortable.

30. Make certain the student does not become involved in overstimulating activities.

31. Talk with the student about individual differences, and discuss strengths and weaknesses of individuals the student knows. Stress that the student does not have to do the same things everyone else does.

32. Find a peer to play with the student who will be a good influence (e.g., someone younger, older, of the same sex, of the opposite sex, etc.).

33. Have the student put himself/herself in someone else's place (e.g., "How would you feel if someone called you dumb or stupid?").

34. Make certain the student is not allowed time alone with other students when he/she is upset or angry.

35. Do not force the student to interact with others.

36. Before beginning an activity or game, make certain the student knows the rules, is familiar with the activity or game, and will be compatible with the other individuals who will be playing.

37. Teach the student to ask for things in a positive manner. Teach key words and phrases (e.g., "May I borrow your pencil?" "Do you mind if I play the game with you?" etc.).

38. Do not leave a lot of unstructured time for the student.

39. Teach the student to "think" before acting (e.g., ask himself/herself: "What is happening?" "What am I doing?" "What should I do?" "What will be best for me?").

40. Have the student practice appropriate verbal exchanges which should be made when typical physical exchanges take place (e.g., "Excuse me." "I'm sorry." etc.).

41. Make certain the student is allowed to voice an opinion in situations in order to avoid becoming angry or upset.

42. Talk to the student about ways of handling conflict situations successfully (e.g., walk away from a situation, change to another activity, ask for help, etc.).

43. Prevent frustrating or anxiety-producing situations from occurring (e.g., give the student tasks only on his/her ability level, give the student only the number of tasks that he/she can tolerate in one sitting, reduce social interactions which stimulate the student to become physically aggressive, etc.).

44. Evaluate the appropriateness of the task to determine: (a) if the task is too difficult and (b) if the length of time scheduled to complete the task is appropriate.

45. Communicate with parents (e.g., notes home, phone calls, etc.) in order to share information concerning the student's progress and so that they can reinforce the student at home for respecting the norms of physical proximity at school.

46. Write a contract with the student specifying what behavior is expected (e.g., respecting the norms of physical proximity) and what reinforcement will be made available when the terms of the contract have been met. (See Appendix for Behavioral Contract.)

47. Remove the student from the group or activity until he/she can demonstrate appropriate behavior and self-control.

48. Reinforce the student for demonstrating appropriate behavior based on the length of time the student can be successful. Gradually increase the length of time required for reinforcement as the student demonstrates success.

49. Reinforce those students in the classroom who demonstrate appropriate behavior when interacting with other students.

50. Establish classroom rules:
  1. Work on task.
  2. Work quietly.
  3. Remain in your seat.
  4. Finish task.
  5. Meet task expectations.
Reiterate rules often and reinforce students for following rules.

51. Speak with the student to explain: (a) what the student is doing wrong (e.g., scratching, hitting, pulling hair, etc.) and (b) what the student should be doing (e.g., following rules, interacting in appropriate ways, dealing with anger and frustration in appropriate ways, etc.).

52. Reinforce the student for demonstrating appropriate behavior: (a) give the student a tangible reward (e.g., classroom privileges, line leading, passing out materials, five minutes free time, etc.) or (b) give the student an intangible reward (e.g., praise, handshake, smile, etc.).

1. Prevent frustrating or anxiety-producing situations from occurring (e.g., give the student tasks only on his/her ability level, give the student only the number of tasks that can be tolerated in one sitting, reduce social interactions which stimulate the student to become physically aggressive, etc.).

2. Teach the student problem-solving skills: (a) identify the problem, (b) identify goals and objectives, (c) develop strategies, (d) develop a plan of action, and (e) carry out the plan.

3. Provide the student with positive feedback which indicates he/she is successful, important, respected, etc.

4. Structure the environment to prevent opportunities for the student to become physically aggressive toward teachers (e.g., interact frequently with the student to prevent him/her from becoming frustrated).

5. Maintain maximum supervision of the student and gradually decrease supervision over time as the student demonstrates appropriate behavior.

6. Maintain visibility to and from the student. The teacher should be able to see the student and the student should be able to see the teacher, making eye contact possible at all times.

7. Be mobile in order to be frequently near the student.

8. Reduce activities which might be threatening to the student (e.g., announcing test score ranges or test scores aloud, making students read aloud in class, emphasizing the success of a particular student, etc.).

9. Try various groupings in order to determine the situation in which the student is most successful.

10. Reduce the emphasis on competition and perfection. Repeated failure and frustration may cause outbursts of physical aggression.

11. Make the necessary adjustments in the environment to prevent the student from becoming overstimulated by peers, which in turn would make it necessary for the teacher to intervene.

12. Teach the student alternative ways to deal with situations which make him/her frustrated or angry (e.g., withdrawing, talking, etc.).

13. Facilitate on-task behavior by providing a full schedule of activities. Prevent lag time from occurring when the student would be free to engage in inappropriate behavior.

14. Provide the student with as many high-interest activities as possible to keep him/her from becoming physically aggressive toward teachers.

15. Provide the student with opportunities for social and academic success.

16. Make certain that all school personnel are aware of the student's tendency to become physically aggressive in order that they will monitor his/her behavior.

17. Limit the student's independent movement in the school environment.

18. Provide a quiet place for the student to work independently, away from peer interactions. This is not to be used as a form of punishment but as an opportunity to increase the student's success in his/her environment.

19. Place reinforcement emphasis on academic productivity and accuracy in order to reduce the likelihood of the student becoming physically aggressive toward teachers (i.e., increased productivity and accuracy will reduce the likelihood of inappropriate behavior).

20. Reduce or remove any stimulus in the environment which leads to the student's physically aggressive behavior (e.g., possessions, competition, teasing, etc.).

21. Make certain the student understands the natural consequences of becoming physically aggressive toward a teacher (e.g., less freedom, more restrictive environment, assault charges, etc.).

22. Prevent the student from receiving too much stimulation (e.g., monitor or supervise student behavior to limit overexcitement in physical activities, games, parties, etc.).

23. Limit the student's opportunity to enter areas of the school environment in which he/she is more likely to be physically aggressive.

24. Do not force the student to interact or remain in a group when he/she is physically aggressive (e.g., daily reading group, physical education group, etc.).

25. Always provide the student with behavioral options (e.g., sitting out of an activity, going to a quiet place in the room, performing another activity, etc.).

26. Avoid arguing with the student (e.g., calmly deliver consequences without reacting to the student's remarks).

27. Maintain consistency in behavioral expectations and consequences in order to reduce the likelihood of the student becoming upset by what he/she considers unfair treatment.

28. Avoid physical contact with the student who is likely to become physically aggressive.

29. Maintain an appropriate physical distance from the student when interacting with him/her in order to avoid stimulation of aggressive behavior.

30. Use language that is pleasant and calming when speaking with the student in order to avoid stimulation of aggressive behavior.

31. Deliver directions in a supportive rather than a threatening manner (e.g., "Please finish your math assignment before going to recess." rather than "You had better turn in your math or else!").

32. Do not criticize when correcting the student; be honest yet supportive. Never cause the student to feel badly about himself/herself.

33. Intervene early when there is a problem in order to prevent more serious problems from occurring.

34. Be careful to avoid embarrassing the student by giving him/her orders, demands, etc., in front of others.

35. Teach the student acceptable ways to communicate displeasure, anger, frustration, etc.

36. Have the student put himself/herself in someone else's place (e.g., "How would you feel if someone called you dumb or stupid?").

37. Do not force the student to interact with others.

38. Teach the student to "think" before acting (e.g., ask himself/herself: "What is happening?" "What am I doing?" "What should I do?" "What will be best for me?").

39. Have the student practice appropriate verbal exchanges which should be made when typical physical exchanges take place (e.g., "Excuse me." "I'm sorry." etc.).

40. Make certain the student is allowed to voice an opinion in a situation in order to avoid becoming angry or upset.

41. Evaluate the appropriateness of the task to determine: (a) if the task is too difficult and (b) if the length of time scheduled for the task is appropriate.

42. Communicate with parents (e.g., notes home, phone calls, etc.) in order to share information concerning the student's progress and so that they can reinforce the student at home for respecting the norms of physical proximity at school.

43. Remove the student from the group or activity until he/she can demonstrate appropriate behavior and self-control.

44. Write a contract with the student specifying what behavior is expected (e.g., respecting the norms of physical proximity) and what reinforcement will be made available when the terms of the contract have been met. (See Appendix for Behavioral Contract.)

45. Reinforce the student for demonstrating appropriate behavior based on the length of time the student can be successful. Gradually increase the length of time required for reinforcement as the student demonstrates success.

46. Establish classroom rules:
1. Work on task.
2. Work quietly.
3. Remain in your seat.
4. Finish task.
5. Meet task expectations.

Reiterate rules often and reinforce students for following rules.

47. Reinforce those students in the classroom who demonstrate appropriate behavior when interacting with teachers.

48. Speak to the student to explain: (a) what the student is doing wrong (e.g., pushing, pulling away, grabbing, etc.) and (b) what the student should be doing (e.g., following rules, interacting in appropriate ways, dealing with anger and frustration in appropriate ways, etc.).

49. Reinforce the student for demonstrating appropriate behavior: (a) give the student a tangible reward (e.g., classroom privileges, line leading, passing out materials, five minutes free time, etc.) or (b) give the student an intangible reward (e.g., praise, handshake, smile, etc.).

1. Reinforce the student for respecting the norms of physical proximity based on the length of time the student can be successful. Gradually increase the length of time required for reinforcement as the student demonstrates success.

2. Remove the student from the group or activity until the student can demonstrate appropriate behavior and self-control.

3. Write a contract with the student specifying what behavior is expected (e.g., shaking hands rather than hugging) and what reinforcement will be made available when the terms of the contract have been met. (See Appendix for Behavioral Contract.)

4. Communicate with parents (e.g., notes home, phone calls, etc.) in order to share information concerning the student's progress and so that they can reinforce the student at home for respecting the norms of physical proximity at school.

5. Separate the student from the person who is the primary focus of the student's attempts to make frequent physical contact.

6. Reduce the opportunity for the student to engage in inappropriate physical contact (e.g., stand an appropriate distance from the student when interacting).

7. Model socially acceptable physical contact for the student (e.g., handshake, pat on the back, etc.).

8. Provide the student with many social and academic successes.

9. Indicate to the student that public displays of frequent physical contact are inappropriate.

10. When working directly with the student, always be in the presence of others.

11. Provide the student with verbal recognition and reinforcement for social and academic successes.

12. Give the student your full attention when communicating with him/her in order to prevent the student's need for physical contact.

13. Provide the student with social interaction in place of physical interaction (e.g., call the student by name, speak to the student, praise, congratulate, etc.).

14. Provide the student with high-interest activities (e.g., academic activities which are inherently interesting, activities during free time, etc.).

15. Try various groupings to find a situation in which the student's need for physical attention can be satisfied by socially acceptable interactions (e.g., holding hands while dancing in an extracurricular activity, a hug for an accomplishment, handshake or "high five" in sports, etc.).

16. Acknowledge the student when he/she seeks attention verbally instead of making it necessary for the student to gain attention through physical contact.

17. Allow natural consequences to occur as a result of the student's inappropriate behavior (e.g., excessive physical contact may cause people to stay away from the student or may result in pushing, shoving, etc.).

18. Make certain that reinforcement is not inadvertently given for inappropriate behavior (e.g., attending to the student only when he/she makes unnecessary physical contact).

19. Prevent the student from becoming overstimulated by an activity (e.g., monitor or supervise student behavior to limit overexcitement in physical activities, games, parties. etc.).

20. Teach the student appropriate ways to interact with others (e.g., verbal and physical introductions, interactions, etc.).

21. Avoid inadvertently stimulating the student's unnecessary physical contact (e.g., attire, language used, physical proximity, etc.).

22. Make certain the student sees the relationship between his/her behavior and the consequences which may follow (e.g., touching and hugging people all of the time may result in others not wanting to be around him/her).

23. Find a peer to play with the student who would be a good influence (e.g., someone younger, older, of the same sex, of the opposite sex, etc.).

24. Reinforce those students in the classroom who interact appropriately with other students or teachers.

25. Establish classroom rules:
    1. Work on task.
    2. Work quietly.
    3. Remain in your seat.
    4. Finish task.
    5. Meet task expectations.
Reiterate rules often and reinforce students for following rules.

26. Speak with the student to explain: (a) what the student is doing wrong (e.g., touching, hugging, etc.) and (b) what the student should be doing (e.g., talking, exchanging greetings, etc.). Discuss appropriate ways to seek attention.

27. Reinforce the student for respecting the norms of physical proximity: (a) give the student a tangible reward (e.g., classroom privileges, line leading, passing out materials, five minutes free time, etc.) or (b) give the student an intangible reward (e.g., praise, handshake, smile, etc.).

1.   Teach the student appropriate ways to communicate displeasure, anger, etc.

2.   Reduce stimuli which contribute to the student's derogatory comments or inappropriate gestures.

3.   Provide the student with a quiet place to work. This is to be used as a means of reducing distracting stimuli and not as a form of punishment.

4.   Provide the student with the opportunity to work with a peer who will be a model for communicating in an appropriate manner.

5.   Make certain the student understands the natural consequences of inappropriate behavior (e.g., teachers choose not to interact with him/her, exclusion from activities, etc.).

6.   Require that the student identify alternative appropriate behaviors following an instance of derogatory comments or inappropriate gestures.

7.   Facilitate on-task behavior by providing a full schedule of activities. Prevent lag time from occurring when the student would be free to engage in inappropriate behavior.

8.   Reduce the emphasis on competition. Repeated failure may result in anger and frustration which may take the form of derogatory comments or inappropriate behavior.

9.   Emphasize individual success or progress rather than winning or "beating" other students.

10. Modify or adjust situations which contribute to the student's use of obscene or profane language (e.g., if an assignment causes the student to become upset, modify the assignment to a level at which the student can be successful).

11. Interact frequently with the student in order to monitor language used.

12. Try various groupings in order to determine the situation in which the student is most successful.

13. Maintain visibility to and from the student. The teacher should be able to see the student and the student should be able to see the teacher, making eye contact possible at all times.

14. Prevent frustrating or anxiety-producing situations from occurring (e.g., give the student tasks only on his/her ability level, give the student only the number of tasks that can be successfully managed in one sitting, reduce social interactions which stimulate the student's use of obscene language, etc.).

15. Reduce activities which might threaten the student (e.g., announcing test score ranges or test scores aloud, making students read aloud in class, emphasizing the success of a particular student, etc.).

16. Discuss with the student ways to deal with unpleasant experiences which would typically cause him/her to use obscene language (e.g., talk to the teacher, go to a quiet area in the room, visit a counselor, etc.).

17. Make certain that positive reinforcement is not inadvertently given for inappropriate language (e.g., attending to the student only when he/she is using profane or obscene language).

18. Provide the student with a predetermined signal when he/she begins to use inappropriate language.

19. Deal with the student in a calm and deliberate manner rather than in a manner that would show evidence of shock and surprise.

20. Act as an appropriate role model by using appropriate language at all times (e.g., use appropriate language to convey disappointment, unhappiness, surprise, etc.).

21. Teach the student appropriate words or phrases to use in situations of anger, stress, frustration, etc.

22. Have the student question any directions, explanations, and instructions not understood.

23. Intervene early when inappropriate behavior occurs in order to prevent the behavior from becoming more serious. Deliberate interventions may prevent future problems.

24. Avoid arguing with the student.

25. Be consistent in expectations and consequences of behavior.

26. Treat the student with respect. Talk to the student in an objective and professional manner at all times.

27. Avoid ignoring the student's inappropriate behavior. Ignored behavior may increase in frequency and may lead to contagion on the part of other students.

28. Avoid confrontations with the student which lead to inappropriate behavior on the part of the student (e.g., give the student options for alternative tasks, other times to perform assignments, assistance in performing assignments, etc.).

29. Develop a routine schedule of activities and tasks for the student in order that he/she knows what to expect at all times.

30. Evaluate the appropriateness of the task in relation to the student's ability to perform the task.

31. Avoid physical contact with the student who is likely to become verbally abusive (e.g., a pat on the back may cause the student to argue, threaten, call names, curse, etc.).

32. Maintain an appropriate physical distance from the student when interacting with him/her in order to avoid stimulating the student to make inappropriate comments.

33. Use language that is pleasant and calming when speaking with the student in order to avoid stimulating the student to make inappropriate comments.

34. Do not criticize. When correcting the student, be honest yet supportive. Never cause the student to feel badly about himself/herself.

35. Deliver directions in a supportive rather than a threatening manner (e.g., "Please finish your math paper before going to recess." rather than "You had better finish your math paper or else!").

36. Treat the student with respect. Talk in an objective manner at all times.

37. Be careful to avoid embarrassing the student by giving him/her orders, demands, etc., in front of others.

38. Teach the student acceptable ways to communicate displeasure, anger, frustration, etc.

39. Have the student put himself/herself in someone else's place (e.g., "How would you feel if someone called you dumb or stupid?").

40. Make certain that your comments to the student take the form of constructive criticism rather than criticism that can be perceived as personal, threatening, etc. (e.g., instead of saying, "You always make the same mistake." say, "A better way to do that might be . . .").

41. Make sure you express your feelings in a socially acceptable manner.

42. Teach the student to "think" before acting (e.g., ask himself/herself: "What is happening?" "What am I doing?" "What should I do?" "What will be best for me?").

43. Make certain the student is allowed to voice an opinion in a situation in order to avoid becoming angry or upset.

44. Evaluate the appropriateness of the task to determine: (a) if the task is too difficult and (b) if the length of time scheduled for the task is appropriate.

45. Communicate with parents (e.g., notes home, phone calls, etc.) in order to share information concerning the student's progress and so that they can reinforce the student at home for communicating in an appropriate manner at school.

46. Remove the student from the group or activity until he/she can demonstrate appropriate behavior.

47. Write a contract with the student specifying what behavior is expected (e.g., using appropriate language) and what reinforcement will be made available when the terms of the contract have been met. (See Appendix for Behavioral Contract.)

48. Reinforce the student for communicating in an appropriate manner based on the length of time the student can be successful. Gradually increase the length of time required for reinforcement as the student demonstrates success.

49. Reinforce those students in the classroom who communicate in an appropriate manner with teachers.

50. Establish classroom rules:
1. Work on task.
2. Work quietly.
3. Remain in your seat.
4. Finish task.
5. Meet task expectations.
Reiterate rules often and reinforce students for following rules.

51. Speak with the student to explain: (a) what the student is doing wrong (e.g., arguing, threatening, calling names, etc.) and (b) what the student should be doing (e.g., following rules, staying on task, attending to his/her responsibilities, etc.).

52. Reinforce the student for communicating in an appropriate manner with teachers: (a) give the student a tangible reward (e.g., classroom privileges, line leading, passing out materials, five minutes free time, etc.) or (b) give the student an intangible reward (e.g., praise, handshake, smile, etc.).

121 Does not respond appropriately to praise or recognition

1. Model appropriate ways to respond to interactions with other students or teachers.

2. Try various groupings in order to determine the situation in which the student is most comfortable.

3. Praise or recognize the student in private. The public aspect of praise or recognition is often the cause of the inappropriate response.

4. Provide the student with many social and academic successes in order that he/she may learn how to respond appropriately.

5. Assess the appropriateness of the social situation in relation to the student's ability to function successfully.

6. Distribute praise and recognition equally to all members of the class.

7. Provide praise or recognition for smaller increments of success so that the student may gradually become accustomed to the recognition.

8. Provide praise and recognition as a natural consequence for appropriate behavior.

9. Praise or recognize the student when he/she will most likely be able to demonstrate an appropriate response (e.g., when the student is not being singled out in a group).

10. Make certain that reinforcement is not inadvertently given for inappropriate behavior (e.g., attending to the student only when he/she responds inappropriately to praise or recognition).

11. Use alternative forms of praise or recognition which are not threatening to the student (e.g., written notes, telephone calls to parents, display of work done well, etc.).

12. Present praise with a matter-of-fact delivery and avoid exaggerated exclamations of success.

13. Use feedback related to performance (e.g., test scores, grades, etc.) in place of praise or recognition. Gradually deliver verbal praise and recognition as the student becomes more capable of accepting praise and recognition.

14. Rather than emphasizing winning or "beating" other students in competition, encourage individual success or progress which may be enjoyed privately rather than publicly.

15. Treat the student with respect. Talk in an objective manner at all times.

16. Maintain trust and confidentiality with the student at all times.

17. Make certain that other teachers and school personnel who work with the student know that the student does not respond appropriately to praise and recognition.

18. Teach the student acceptable ways to communicate displeasure, anger, frustration, etc.

19. Make sure you express your feelings in a socially acceptable way.

20. Communicate with parents (e.g., notes home, phone calls, etc.) in order to share information concerning the student's progress and so that they can reinforce the student at home for responding appropriately to praise or recognition at school.

21. Write a contract with the student specifying what behavior is expected (e.g., saying "thank you" when given praise or recognition) and what reinforcement will be made available when the terms of the contract have been met. (See Appendix for Behavioral Contract.)

22. Reinforce the student for responding appropriately to praise or recognition based on the number of times the student can be successful. Gradually increase the number of times required for reinforcement as the student demonstrates success.

23. Reinforce those students in the classroom who respond appropriately to praise or recognition.

24. Speak with the student to explain: (a) what the student is doing wrong (e.g., behaving inappropriately when recognized by others) and (b) what the student should be doing (e.g., saying "thank you," smiling, etc.).

25. Reinforce the student for responding appropriately to praise or recognition: (a) give the student a tangible reward (e.g., classroom privileges, line leading, passing out materials, five minutes free time, etc.) or (b) give the student an intangible reward (e.g., praise, handshake, smile, etc.).

A Reminder: Do not punish a student for his/her inability to respond appropriately to praise or recognition.

1. Prevent frustrating or anxiety-producing situations from occurring (e.g., give the student tasks only on his/her ability level, give the student only the number of tasks that can be tolerated in one sitting, reduce social interactions which stimulate the student to become physically abusive, etc.).

2. Teach the student problem-solving skills: (a) identify the problem, (b) identify goals and objectives, (c) develop strategies, (d) develop a plan of action, and (e) carry out the plan.

3. Provide the student with positive feedback which indicates he/she is successful, important, respected, etc.

4. Maintain maximum supervision of the student. Gradually decrease supervision over time as the student demonstrates self-control.

5. Maintain visibility to and from the student. The teacher should be able to see the student and the student should be able to see the teacher, making eye contact possible at all times.

6. Be mobile in order to be frequently near the student.

7. Reduce activities which might threaten the student (e.g., announcing test score ranges or test scores aloud, making students read aloud in class, emphasizing the success of a particular student or students, etc.).

8. Try various groupings in order to determine the situation in which the student is most successful.

9. Make the necessary adjustments in the environment to prevent the student from experiencing stress, frustration, and anger.

10. Reduce the emphasis on competition and perfection. Repeated failure and frustration may cause the student to become angered, annoyed, or upset.

11. Teach the student alternative ways to deal with situations which make him/her frustrated, angry, etc. (e.g., withdrawing, talking, etc.).

12. Facilitate on-task behavior by providing a full schedule of daily events. Prevent lag time from occurring when the student would be likely to become involved in activities which would cause him/her to be angered, annoyed, or upset. (See Appendix for Schedule of Daily Events.)

13. Maintain supervision in order that the student is not left alone or allowed to be unsupervised with other students.

14. Provide the student with as many high-interest activities as possible.

15. Provide the student with opportunities for social and academic success.

16. Make other personnel aware of the student's tendency to become easily angered, annoyed, or upset.

17. Provide a quiet place for the student to work independently, away from peer interactions. This is not to be used as a form of punishment but as an opportunity to increase the student's success in his/her environment.

18. Place reinforcement emphasis on academic productivity and accuracy to divert the student's attention away from others who cause him/her to become angered, annoyed, or upset.

19. Make the student aware of the natural consequences for becoming easily angered, annoyed, or upset (e.g., loss of friendships, injury, more restrictive environment, legal action, etc.).

20. Separate the student from the peer(s) who may be encouraging or stimulating the student to become angered, annoyed, or upset.

21. Do not force the student to interact or remain in a group if he/she is likely to become angered, annoyed, or upset.

22. Provide the student with a selection of optional activities to be performed if he/she becomes angered, annoyed, or upset.

23. Maintain consistency in expectations.

24. Maintain consistency in daily routine.

25. Remove the student from the group or activity until he/she can demonstrate self-control.

26. Maintain a positive/calm environment (e.g., positive comments, acknowledgment of successes, quiet communications, etc.).

27. Allow flexibility in meeting academic demands when the student becomes angered, annoyed, or upset (e.g., allow more time, modify assignments, provide help with assignments, etc.).

28. Present tasks in the most attractive and interesting manner possible.

29. Make certain to ask the student why he/she becomes easily angered, annoyed, or upset. The student may have the most accurate perception as to why he/she becomes easily angered, annoyed, or upset.

30. Teach the student decision-making steps: (a) think about how others may be influenced, (b) think about consequences, (c) carefully consider the unique situation, (d) think of different courses of action which are possible, (e) think about what is ultimately best, etc.

31. Avoid topics, situations, etc., that may cause the student to become easily angered, annoyed, or upset (e.g., divorce, death, unemployment, alcoholism, etc.).

32. Discourage the student from engaging in those activities that cause him/her to become easily angered, annoyed, or upset.

33. Teach the student to verbalize his/her feelings before losing self-control (e.g., "The work is hard." "Please leave me alone; you're making me angry." etc.).

34. Deliver directions in a supportive rather than a threatening manner (e.g., "Please finish your math assignment before going to recess." rather than "You had better finish your math or else!").

35. Do not criticize. When correcting the student, be honest yet supportive. Never cause the student to feel badly about himself/herself.

36. Intervene early when the student becomes angered, annoyed, or upset in order to prevent more serious problems from occurring.

37. Make certain the student does not become involved in overstimulating activities which cause him/her to become angered, annoyed, or upset.

38. Treat the student with respect. Talk in an objective manner at all times.

39. Be careful to avoid embarrassing the student by giving him/her orders, demands, etc., in front of others.

40. Find a peer to work with the student who would be a good influence (e.g., someone younger, older, of the same sex, of the opposite sex, etc.).

41. Allow the student to attempt something new in private before doing so in front of others.

42. Teach the student acceptable ways to communicate displeasure, anger, frustration, etc.

43. Do not force the student to interact with others.

44. Encourage the student to use problem-solving skills: (a) identify the problem, (b) identify goals and objectives, (c) develop strategies, (d) develop a plan of action, and (c) carry out the plan.

45. Make sure you express your feelings in a socially acceptable way.

46. Make certain the student is allowed to voice an opinion in a situation in order to avoid becoming angry or upset.

47. Teach the student to "think" before acting (e.g., ask himself/herself: "What is happening?" "What am I doing?" "What should I do?" "What will be best for me?").

48. Talk to the student about ways of handling situations successfully without conflict (e.g., walk away from a situation, change to another activity, ask for help, etc.).

49. Have the student question any directions, explanations, and instructions not understood.

50. Identify a peer to act as a model for the student to imitate self-control.

51. Evaluate the appropriateness of the academic task to determine: (a) if the task is too difficult and (b) if the length of time scheduled to complete the task is appropriate.

52. Communicate with parents, agencies, or appropriate parties in order to inform them of the problem, determine the cause of the problem, and find solutions to the problem.

53. Communicate with parents (e.g., notes home, phone calls, etc.) in order to share information concerning the student's progress and so that they will reinforce the student at home for demonstrating self-control at school.

54. Write a contract with the student specifying what behavior is expected (e.g., problem solving, moving away from the situation, asking for assistance from the teacher, etc.) and what reinforcement will be made available when the terms of the contract have been met. (See Appendix for Behavioral Contract.)

55. Reinforce the student for demonstrating self-control based on the length of time the student can be successful. Gradually increase the length of time required for reinforcement as the student demonstrates success.

56. Reinforce those students in the classroom who demonstrate self-control.

57. Establish classroom rules:
1. Work on task.
2. Work quietly.
3. Remain in your seat.
4. Finish task.
5. Meet task expectations.
Reiterate rules often and reinforce students for following rules.

58. Speak to the student to explain: (a) what the student is doing wrong (e.g., hitting, arguing, throwing things, etc.) and (b) what the student should be doing (e.g., moving away from the situation, asking for assistance from the teacher, etc.).

59. Reinforce the student for demonstrating self-control in those situations in which he/she is likely to become angry, annoyed, or upset: (a) give the student a tangible reward (e.g., classroom privileges, line leading, passing out materials, five minutes free time, etc.) or (b) give the student an intangible reward (e.g., praise, handshake, smile, etc.).

123 Agitates and provokes peers to a level of verbal or physical assault

1. Teach the student acceptable ways to communicate displeasure, anger, etc.

2. Reduce the stimuli that contribute to the student's derogatory comments or inappropriate gestures.

3. Provide the student with a quiet place to work (e.g., study carrel, "private office," etc.). This is used as a means of reducing distracting stimuli and not as a form of punishment.

4. Provide the student with the opportunity to work with a peer who will be an appropriate model.

5. Separate the student from the peer(s) who is the primary stimulus or focus of the derogatory comments or inappropriate gestures.

6. Make certain the student understands the natural consequences of inappropriate behavior (e.g., peers choosing not to interact with him/her, exclusion from activities, etc.).

7. Require that the student identify alternative appropriate behaviors following an instance of derogatory comments or inappropriate gestures.

8. Facilitate on-task behavior by providing a full schedule of daily events. Prevent lag time from occurring when the student would be free to engage in inappropriate behavior. (See Appendix for Schedule of Daily Events.)

9. Reduce the emphasis on competition. Repeated failure may result in anger and frustration that may take the form of derogatory comments or inappropriate gestures.

10. Emphasize individual success or progress rather than winning or "beating" other students.

11. Intervene early when the student begins to agitate or provoke peers.

12. Treat the student with respect. Talk in an objective manner at all times.

13. Remove the student from the classroom if he/she is unable to demonstrate self-control. The student should not be allowed to remain in the classroom and be abusive to peers.

14. Maintain visibility to and from the student. The teacher should be able to see the student and the student should be able to see the teacher, making eye contact possible at all times.

15. Inform others (e.g., teachers, school personnel, etc.) of the behavior expected of the student in order that they will encourage appropriate behavior from the student.

16. Make certain there will always be adult supervision where the student will be (e.g., lunch, recess, P.E., etc.).

17. Be careful to avoid embarrassing the student by giving him/her orders, demands, etc., in front of others.

18. Have the student put himself/herself in someone else's place (e.g., "How would you feel if someone called you dumb or stupid?")

19. Do not force the student to interact with others.

20. Encourage the student to use problem-solving skills: (a) identify the problem, (b) identify goals and objectives, (c) develop strategies, (d) develop a plan of action, and (e) carry out the plan.

21. Do not leave a lot of unstructured time for the student.

22. Teach the student to "think" before acting (e.g., ask himself/herself: "What is happening?" "What am I doing?" "What should I do?" "What will be best for me?").

23. Make certain the student is allowed to voice an opinion in a situation in order to avoid becoming angry or upset.

24. Evaluate the appropriateness of the task to determine: (a) if the task is too difficult and (b) if the length of time scheduled for the task is appropriate.

25. Communicate with parents (e.g., notes home, phone calls, etc.) in order to share information concerning the student's progress and so that they can reinforce the student at home for demonstrating appropriate behavior at school.

26. Write a contract with the student specifying what behavior is expected (e.g., communicating with peers in a positive manner) and what reinforcement will be made available when the terms of the contract have been met. (See Appendix for Behavioral Contract.)

27. Remove the student from the group or activity until he/she can demonstrate appropriate behavior.

28. Reinforce the student for communicating in an appropriate manner based on the length of time the student can be successful. Gradually increase the length of time required for reinforcement as the student demonstrates success.

29. Reinforce those students in the classroom who communicate in an appropriate manner.

30. Establish classroom rules:
1. Work on task.
2. Work quietly.
3. Remain in your seat.
4. Finish task.
5. Meet task expectations.
Reiterate rules often and reinforce students for following rules.

31. Speak with the student to explain: (a) what the student is doing wrong (e.g., calling names, making inappropriate gestures, etc.) and (b) what the student should be doing (e.g., following rules, staying on task, attending to his/her responsibilities, etc.).

32. Reinforce the student for communicating in an appropriate manner with peers: (a) give the student a tangible reward (e.g., classroom privileges, line leading, passing out materials, five minutes free time, etc.) or (b) give the student an intangible reward (e.g., praise, handshake, smile, etc.).

1. Give the student the responsibility of acting as a teacher's assistant for an activity (e.g., holding up flash cards, demonstrating the use of equipment, etc.).

2. Give the student the responsibility of tutoring another student.

3. Be certain to greet or recognize the student as often as possible (e.g., greet in the hallways or cafeteria, welcome to class, acknowledge a job well done, call the student by name, etc.).

4. Request that the student be the leader of a small group activity if he/she possesses mastery of skills or an interest in that area.

5. Have the student run errands which will require interactions with teachers (e.g., delivering attendance reports, taking messages to other teachers, etc.).

6. Interact with the student from a distance, gradually decreasing the distance until a close proximity is achieved.

7. Arrange for one-to-one, teacher/student interactions.

8. Use an alternative form of communication (e.g., puppet).

9. Provide the student with many social and academic successes.

10. Create situations in which the student must interact (e.g., handing completed assignments to the teacher, delivering a message to a teacher, etc.).

11. Identify a peer to act as a model for the student to imitate appropriate interaction with teachers.

12. Encourage the student to question any directions, explanations, and instructions not understood.

13. Evaluate the appropriateness of expecting the student to communicate needs to teachers.

14. Maintain mobility throughout the classroom in order to determine the student's needs.

15. Offer the student assistance frequently throughout the day.

16. Make certain that directions, explanations, and instructions are delivered on the student's ability level.

17. Structure the environment in order that the student is not required to communicate all needs to teachers (e.g., make certain the student's tasks are on his/her ability level, be sure instructions are clear, and maintain frequent interactions with the student in order to ensure success).

18. In order to detect the student's needs, communicate with the student as often as opportunities permit.

19. Demonstrate accepting behavior and interest in the student's needs (e.g., willingness to help others, making criticisms constructive and positive, demonstrating confidentiality in personal matters, etc.).

20. Communicate to the student that he/she is a worthwhile individual.

21. Call on the student often in order to encourage communication.

22. Teach the student communication skills (e.g., hand raising, expressing needs in written and/or verbal form, etc.).

23. Encourage the student to communicate needs to other personnel in the educational environment (e.g., school counselor, school psychologist, principal, etc.).

24. Communicate with parents, agencies, or appropriate parties in order to inform them of the problem, determine the cause of the problem, and find solutions to the problem.

25. Recognize the student's attempts to communicate needs (e.g., facial expressions, gestures, inactivity, self-depreciating comments, etc.).

26. Teach the student appropriate positive verbal greetings (e.g., "Hi." "How are you doing?" "Good to see you." "Haven't seen you in a long time." etc.).

27. Teach the student appropriate positive verbal requests (e.g., "Please pass the paper." "May I be excused?" "Will you please help me?" etc.).

28. Teach the student appropriate positive ways to verbally indicate disagreement (e.g., "Excuse me." "I'm sorry, but I don't think that's correct." etc.).

29. Model for the student appropriate positive verbal greetings, requests, and indications of disagreement.

30. Teach the student appropriate verbalization for problem resolution as an alternative (e.g., "Let's talk about it." "Let's compromise." "Let's see what would be fair for both of us." etc.).

31. Require the student to practice positive verbal communications with an identified number of teachers throughout the school day.

32. Make certain that all teachers interact with the student on a regular basis and use positive verbal communications when speaking to him/ her.

33. Require the student to interact with several adults (e.g., run errands, request materials, etc.) in order to increase the opportunities for communication with adults.

34. Teach the student appropriate ways to communicate to teachers that a problem exists (e.g., "I don't understand the directions." "I couldn't complete my assignment." "I can't find all of my materials." etc.).

35. Identify teachers with whom the student most often interacts in order to make certain that they model appropriate verbal communications for the student.

36. Spend some time each day talking with the student on an individual basis about his/her interests.

37. Teach the student skills in maintaining positive conversations with teachers (e.g., asking questions, listening while the other person speaks, making eye contact, head nodding, making comments which relate to what the other person has said, etc.).

38. Help the student become aware of his/her tone of voice when greeting, requesting, and/or disagreeing by calling attention to inappropriate voice inflections for the situation.

39. Determine an individual(s) in the school environment with whom the student would most want to converse (e.g., custodian, librarian, resource teacher, principal, older student, etc.). Allow the student to spend time with the individual(s) each day.

40. Pair the student with an outgoing student who engages in conversation with teachers on a frequent basis.

41. Deliver directions in a supportive rather than a threatening manner (e.g., "Please finish your math paper before going to recess." rather than "You had better finish your math paper or else!").

42. Do not criticize. When correcting the student, be honest yet supportive. Never cause the student to feel badly about himself/herself.

43. Treat the student with respect. Talk in an objective manner at all times.

44. Be careful to avoid embarrassing the student by giving him/her orders, demands, etc., in front of others.

45. Maintain trust and confidentiality with the student at all times.

46. Spend individual time with the student. Do not give more attention to students who are more outgoing.

47. Communicate with parents (e.g., notes home, phone calls, etc.) in order to share information concerning the student's progress and so that they may reinforce the student at home for interacting with teachers at school.

48. Do not force the student to interact.

49. Write a contract with the student specifying what behavior is expected (e.g., sitting near the teacher, talking to the teacher, etc.) and what reinforcement will be made available when the terms of the contract have been met.

50. Reinforce the student for interacting with teachers based on the length of time the student can be successful. Gradually increase the length of time required for reinforcement as the student demonstrates success.

51. Reinforce those students in the classroom who interact appropriately with teachers.

52. Establish classroom rules:
   1. Work on task.
   2. Work quietly.
   3. Remain in your seat.
   4. Finish task.
   5. Meet task expectations.
Reiterate rules often and reinforce students for following rules.

53. Speak with the student to explain: (a) what the student is doing wrong (e.g., not talking, not making eye contact, etc.) and (b) what the student should be doing (e.g., talking, looking at the teacher, etc.).

54. Reinforce the student for interacting with teachers: (a) give the student a tangible reward (e.g., classroom privileges, line leading, passing out materials, five minutes free time, etc.) or (b) give the student an intangible reward (e.g., praise, handshake, smile, etc.).

A Reminder: Do not "force" the student to interact with teachers.

1. Assign a peer to sit/work directly with the student (e.g., in different settings or activities such as art, music, P.E., on the bus, tutoring, group projects, running errands in the building, recess, etc.). Gradually increase group size when the student has become comfortable working with another student.

2. Encourage or reward others for interacting with the student.

3. Give the student the responsibility of acting as a teacher's aide for an activity (e.g., holding up flash cards, demonstrating the use of equipment, etc.).

4. Give the student the responsibility of tutoring a peer.

5. Ask the student to choose a peer to work with on a specific assignment. If the student has difficulty choosing someone, determine the student's preference by other means such as a class survey.

6. Request that the student be the leader of a small group activity if he/she possesses mastery of skills or an interest in that area.

7. Try various groupings to determine the situation in which the student is most comfortable.

8. Assess the appropriateness of the social setting in relation to the student's ability to interact with peers.

9. Provide the student with many social and academic successes.

10. Assign the student to work with one or two peers on a long-term project (e.g., mural, bulletin board, report, etc.).

11. Create situations in which the student must interact (e.g., returning completed assignments to students, proofreading other students' work, etc.).

12. Have the student work with a peer who is younger or smaller (e.g., choose a peer who would be the least threatening).

13. Establish social rules:
1. Share materials.
2. Use a quiet voice in the building.
3. Walk indoors.
4. Use care in handling materials.
Reiterate rules often and reinforce students for following rules.

14. Identify a peer to act as a model for the student to imitate appropriate interactions with peers.

15. Determine the peer(s) the student would most prefer to interact with and attempt to facilitate this interaction.

16. Assign an outgoing, nonthreatening peer to help the student interact more appropriately with peers.

17. Structure the environment so that the student has many opportunities to interact with peers.

18. Have the student run errands with a peer in order to facilitate interaction.

19. Conduct a sociometric activity with the class in order to determine the peer who would most prefer to interact with the student.

20. Make certain the student understands that interacting with a peer is contingent upon appropriate interactions.

21. Teach the student appropriate ways to interact with another student (e.g., how to greet another student, suggest activities, share materials, problem solve, take turns, converse, etc.).

22. Supervise interaction closely in order that the peer with whom the student interacts does not stimulate the student's inappropriate behavior.

23. Make certain that the interaction is not so stimulating as to make successful interaction with another student difficult.

24. Involve the student in extracurricular activities in order to encourage interactions with peers.

25. Assign an older peer with desirable social skills to interact with the student (e.g., in the play area, cafeteria, hallways, etc.).

26. Reduce the emphasis on competition. Failure may cause the student to be reluctant to interact with peers.

27. Teach the student problem-solving skills in order that he/she may better deal with problems that occur in interactions with another peer (e.g., talking, walking away, calling upon an arbitrator, compromising, etc.).

28. Find a peer with whom the student is most likely to be able to interact successfully (e.g., a student with similar interests, background, classes, behavior patterns, nonacademic schedule, etc.).

29. Structure the interaction according to the needs/abilities of the student (e.g., establish rules, limit the stimulation of the activity, limit the length of the activity, consider time of day, etc.).

30. Limit opportunities for interaction on those occasions when the student is not likely to be successful (e.g., when the student has experienced academic or social failure prior to the scheduled nonacademic activity).

31. Select nonacademic activities designed to enhance appropriate interaction of the student and a peer (e.g., board games, model building, coloring, etc.).

32. Through interviews with other students and observations, determine those characteristics of the student which interfere with successful interactions in order to determine skills or behaviors the student needs to develop.

33. Have the student practice appropriate interactions with the teacher(s).

34. Make certain the student understands that failing to interact appropriately with a peer may result in removal from the activity and/or loss of participation in future activities.

35. Encourage the student to interact with others.

36. Have the student interact with a peer for short periods of time in order to enhance success. Gradually increase the length of time as the student experiences success.

37. Do not force the student to interact with someone with whom he/she is not completely comfortable.

38. Communicate with parents (e.g., notes home, phone calls, etc.) in order to share information concerning the student's progress and so that they can reinforce the student at home for interacting with peers at school.

39. Write a contract with the student specifying what behavior is expected (e.g., sitting near another student, talking to another student, etc.) and what reinforcement will be made available when the terms of the contract have been met.

40. Reinforce the student for interacting with peers based on the length of time he/she can be successful. Gradually increase the length of time required for reinforcement as the student demonstrates success.

41. Reinforce those students in the classroom who interact appropriately with peers.

42. Establish classroom rules:
   1. Work on task.
   2. Work quietly.
   3. Remain in your seat.
   4. Finish task.
   5. Meet task expectations.
Reiterate rules often and reinforce students for following rules.

43. Speak with the student to explain: (a) what he/she is doing wrong (e.g., not talking, sharing, etc.) and (b) what he/she should be doing (e.g., talking, sharing, etc.).

44. Reinforce the student for interacting with peers: (a) give the student a tangible reward (e.g., classroom privileges, line leading, passing out materials, five minutes free time, etc.) or (b) give the student an intangible reward (e.g., praise, handshake, smile, etc.).

A Reminder: Do not "force" the student to interact with peers.

126 Makes inappropriate comments to other students

1. Teach the student appropriate ways to communicate displeasure, anger, etc.

2. Reduce the stimuli which contribute to the student's arguing, calling names, cursing, etc.

3. Provide the student with a quiet place to work. This is used as a means of reducing distracting stimuli and not as a form of punishment.

4. Provide the student with the opportunity to work with a peer who will be an appropriate model for interacting with other students.

5. Separate the student from the student(s) who is the primary stimulus or focus of the inappropriate comments.

6. Make certain the student understands the natural consequences of inappropriate behavior (e.g., peers will choose not to interact with him/her, exclusion from activities, etc.).

7. Require that the student identify alternative appropriate behaviors following an instance of inappropriate comments (e.g., walking away from the peer, seeking teacher intervention, etc.).

8. Facilitate on-task behavior by providing a full schedule of daily events. Prevent lag time from occurring when the student would be free to engage in inappropriate behavior. (See Appendix for Schedule of Daily Events.)

9. Reduce the emphasis on competition. Repeated failure may result in anger and frustration which may take the form of inappropriate comments.

10. Emphasize individual success or progress rather than winning or "beating" other students.

11. Teach the student problem-solving skills: (a) identify the problem, (b) identify goals and objectives, (c) develop strategies, (d) develop a plan for action, and (e) carry out the plan.

12. Teach the student positive ways to interact with other students.

13. Make certain the student recognizes inappropriate comments (e.g., call attention to the comments when they occur, record each instance, terminate the activity when the comment occurs, etc.).

14. Interact frequently with the student in order to monitor language used.

15. Maintain visibility to and from the student. The teacher should be able to see the student and the student should be able to see the teacher, making eye contact possible at all times.

16. Prevent the student from becoming overstimulated by an activity (e.g., monitor or supervise student behavior to limit overexcitement).

17. Prevent frustrating or anxiety-producing situations from occurring (e.g., give the student tasks only on his/her ability level, give the student only the number of tasks that can be successfully managed in one sitting, reduce social interactions which stimulate the student's use of obscene language, etc.).

18. Reduce activities which might threaten the student (e.g., announcing test score ranges or test scores aloud, making students read aloud in class, emphasizing success of a particular student or students, etc.).

19. Assess the appropriateness of the social situation in relation to the student's ability to function successfully.

20. Discuss with the student ways he/she could deal with unpleasant experiences which would typically cause him/her to use obscene language (e.g., talk to the teacher, go to a quiet area in the school, talk with a counselor, etc.).

21. Provide the student with a predetermined signal when he/she begins to use inappropriate language.

22. Make certain that positive reinforcement is not inadvertently given for inappropriate language (e.g., attending to the student only when he/she is using profane or obscene language).

23. Deal with the student in a calm and deliberate manner rather than in a manner that would show evidence of shock and surprise.

24. Act as an appropriate role model by using appropriate language at all times (e.g., use appropriate language to convey disappointment, unhappiness, surprise, etc.).

25. Teach the student appropriate words or phrases to use in situations of anger, stress, frustration, etc.

26. Intervene early when the student begins to make inappropriate comments to other students in order to help prevent the student from losing control.

27. Make certain the student knows which comments will not be tolerated at school.

28. Avoid discussion of topics that are sensitive to the student (e.g., divorce, unemployment, alcoholism, etc.).

29. Intervene early when there is a problem in order to prevent more serious problems from occurring.

30. Teach the student to respect others and their belongings by respecting the student and his/her belongings.

31. Make certain there will be adult supervision where the student will be (e.g., at P.E., lunch, recess, etc.).

32. Do not force the student to interact with other students with whom he/she is not completely comfortable.

33. Treat the student with respect. Talk in an objective manner at all times.

34. Have the student put himself/herself in the other student's place (e.g., "How would you feel if someone called you dumb or stupid?").

35. Encourage the student to interact with others.

36. Provide frequent opportunities for the student to meet new people.

37. Do not force the student to interact with others.

38. Make sure you express your feelings in a socially acceptable manner.

39. Teach the student to "think" before acting (e.g., ask himself/herself: "What is happening?" "What am I doing?" "What should I do?" "What will be best for me?").

40. Have the student practice appropriate verbal exchanges which should be made (e.g., "Excuse me." "I'm sorry." etc.).

41. Make certain the student is allowed to voice an opinion in a situation in order to avoid becoming angry or upset.

42. Evaluate the appropriateness of the task to determine: (a) if the task is too difficult and (b) if the length of time scheduled for the task is appropriate.

43. Communicate with parents (e.g., notes home, phone calls, etc.) in order to share information concerning the student's progress and so that they can reinforce the student at home for communicating in an appropriate manner with other students at school.

44. Write a contract with the student specifying what behavior is expected (e.g., communicating with other students in an appropriate manner) and what reinforcement will be made available when the terms of the contract have been met. (See Appendix for Behavioral Contract.)

45. Remove the student from the group or activity until he/she can demonstrate appropriate behavior.

46. Reinforce those students in the classroom who communicate in an appropriate manner with other students.

47. Reinforce the student for communicating in an appropriate manner based on the length of time the student can be successful. Gradually increase the length of time required for reinforcement as the student demonstrates success.

48. Establish classroom rules:
1. Work on task.
2. Work quietly.
3. Remain in your seat.
4. Finish task.
5. Meet task expectations.

Reiterate rules often and reinforce students for following rules.

49. Speak with the student to explain: (a) what the student is doing wrong (e.g., calling names, arguing, cursing, etc.) and (b) what the student should be doing (e.g., following rules, staying on task, attending to responsibilities, etc.).

50. Reinforce the student for communicating in an appropriate manner with other students: (a) give the student a tangible reward (e.g., classroom privileges, line leading, passing out materials, five minutes free time, etc.) or (b) give the student an intangible reward (e.g., praise, handshake, smile, etc.).

127 Responds inappropriately to typical physical exchanges with other students

1. Make certain that peers are, in fact, accidently bumping, touching, or brushing against the student.

2. Have the student walk on the right-hand side of the hallways, stairways, etc.

3. Have the student lead the line, walk beside the line, walk at the end of the line, etc., in order to avoid or reduce typical physical exchanges with other students.

4. Have the student avoid crowded areas. Gradually allow the student access to crowded areas as he/she develops the ability to deal with typical physical exchanges with other students in an appropriate manner.

5. Have the student practice dealing with typical physical exchanges in the classroom (e.g., peers bumping against his/her desk, bumping into peers when forming a line, etc.).

6. Seat the student away from classroom movements in order to reduce typical physical exchanges with other students.

7. Call attention to those times when the student bumps, touches, or brushes against other students. Help the student realize that those physical exchanges were typical and accidental.

8. Have the student practice appropriate verbal exchanges which should be made when typical physical exchanges take place (e.g., "Excuse me." "I'm sorry." etc.).

9. Teach the student to avoid typical physical exchanges by giving peers room to pass, taking turns, watching the movement of others around him/her, etc.

10. Point out the natural consequences of failing to respond appropriately to typical physical exchanges with other students (e.g., other students will avoid him/her, loss of friendships, loss of opportunity to interact with peers, etc.).

11. Have a peer accompany the student in congested areas of the school in order to reduce typical physical exchanges and/or intercede should problems occur.

12. Practice role-playing which involves typical physical exchanges (e.g., being bumped, touched, brushed against, etc.).

13. Intervene early when there is a problem in order to prevent more serious problems from occurring.

14. Make certain there will be adult supervision where the student will be (e.g., at P.E., lunch, recess, etc.).

15. Avoid subjecting the student to crowded situations where he/she might feel uncomfortable.

16. Teach the student acceptable ways to communicate displeasure, anger, frustration, etc.

17. Do not force the student to interact with others.

18. Teach the student to "think" before acting (e.g., ask himself/herself: "What is happening?" "What am I doing?" "What should I do?" "What will be best for me?").

19. Identify a peer to act as a model for the student to imitate the appropriate manner in which to respond to typical physical exchanges with other students.

20. Establish classroom rules:
   1. Work on task.
   2. Work quietly.
   3. Remain in your seat.
   4. Finish task.
   5. Meet task expectations.
Reiterate rules often and reinforce students for following rules.

21. Communicate with parents (e.g., notes home, phone calls, etc.) in order to share information concerning the student's progress and so that they may reinforce the student at home for responding appropriately to typical physical exchanges with other students at school.

22. Write a contract with the student specifying what behavior is expected (e.g., responding appropriately to typical physical exchanges with other students) and what reinforcement will be made available when the terms of the contract have been met. (See Appendix for Behavioral Contract.)

23. Reinforce the student for responding appropriately to typical physical exchanges with other students based on the length of time the student can be successful. Gradually increase the length of time required for reinforcement as the student demonstrates success.

24. Reinforce those students in the classroom who respond appropriately to typical physical exchanges with other students.

25. Speak to the student to explain: (a) what the student is doing wrong (e.g., hitting other students) and (b) what the student should be doing (e.g., accepting typical physical exchanges in an appropriate manner).

26. Reinforce the student for responding appropriately to typical physical exchanges with other students: (a) give the student a tangible reward (e.g., classroom privileges, line leading, passing out materials, five minutes free time, etc.) or (b) give the student an intangible reward (e.g., praise, handshake, smile, etc.).

1. Point out to the student, when he/she is teasing others, that no harm is meant and that the same holds true when others do the teasing.

2. Explain to the student that friendly teasing is a positive means by which people demonstrate that they like other people and enjoy their company.

3. Act as a model for friendly teasing by joking with the students and laughing when they tease you.

4. Help the student recognize the difference between friendly teasing and unkind, rude remarks in order that the student can accept and appreciate friendly teasing.

5. Help the student learn to deal with teasing which upsets him/her by having the student avoid the teasing, walk away from the situation, move to another location, etc.

6. Teach the student appropriate ways in which to respond to friendly teasing (e.g., laugh, joke in return, etc.).

7. Talk with the student about choosing friends who are friendly and sincere.

8. Help the student understand that if he/she cannot accept friendly teasing, it will be best to avoid those situations where teasing may occur.

9. Discuss with the student's peers his/her sensitivity and difficulty in dealing with friendly teasing in order that they can adjust their behavior accordingly.

10. Discuss with the students those topics which are not appropriate for friendly teasing (e.g., death, disease, handicaps, poverty, etc.).

11. Intervene early when there is a problem in order to prevent more serious problems from occurring.

12. Do not force the student to interact with others with whom the student is not completely comfortable.

13. Treat the student with respect. Talk in an objective manner at all times.

14. Allow the student to attempt something new in private before doing so in front of others.

15. Teach the student acceptable ways to communicate displeasure, anger, frustration, etc.

16. Encourage others to compliment the student.

17. Make sure you express your feelings in a socially acceptable way.

18. Make certain the student is allowed to voice an opinion in a situation in order to avoid becoming angry or upset.

19. Identify a peer to act as a model to imitate appropriate response to friendly teasing.

20. Evaluate the appropriateness of the interaction to determine: (a) if the interaction is appropriate, (b) if the timing of the interaction is appropriate, and (c) if the student will be able to handle the interaction successfully.

21. Communicate with parents (e.g., notes home, phone calls, etc.) in order to share information concerning the student's progress and so that they can reinforce the student at home for responding appropriately to friendly teasing at school.

22. Write a contract with the student specifying what behavior is expected (e.g., laughing, joking in return, etc.) and what reinforcement will be made available when the terms of the contract have been met. (See Appendix for Behavioral Contract.)

23. Reinforce the student for responding appropriately to friendly teasing based on the number of times the student can be successful. Gradually increase the number of times required for reinforcement as the student demonstrates success.

24. Reinforce those students in the classroom who respond appropriately to friendly teasing.

25. Speak to the student to explain: (a) what the student is doing wrong (e.g., becoming upset, fighting, etc.) and (b) what the student should be doing (e.g., laughing, joking in return, etc.).

26. Reinforce the student for responding appropriately to friendly teasing: (a) give the student a tangible reward (e.g., classroom privileges, line leading, passing out materials, five minutes free time, etc.) or (b) give the student an intangible reward (e.g., praise, handshake, smile, etc.).

1. Have the student be the leader of a small group activity if he/she possesses the skills or has an interest in that area.

2. Give the student the responsibility of tutoring a peer if he/she possesses the necessary skills.

3. Provide the student with a predetermined signal (e.g., hand signal, verbal cue, etc.) when he/she begins to exhibit an inappropriate behavior(s).

4. Maintain maximum supervision of the student's interaction and gradually decrease the amount of supervision over time.

5. Try various groupings in order to determine the situation in which the student is most comfortable.

6. Modify or adjust situations that cause the student to demonstrate behaviors that are different or extreme.

7. Give the student responsibilities in group situations in order that peers may view the student in a more positive way.

8. Assess the social situation in relation to the student's ability to function successfully (e.g., number of students in the group, behavior of students in the group, etc.).

9. Provide the student with as many academic and social successes as possible in order that peers may view the student in a more positive way.

10. Encourage the student to further develop any ability or skill he/she may have in order that peers may view the student in a more positive way.

11. Model appropriate social behavior for the student at all times.

12. Help the student to identify inappropriate behaviors and teach him/her ways to change those behaviors.

13. Reduce the emphasis on competition. Social interactions may be inhibited if the student's abilities are constantly made public and compared to others.

14. Teach the student to be satisfied with personal best effort and not to insist on perfection.

15. Encourage and assist the student in joining extracurricular activities, clubs, etc.

16. Help the student develop friendships by pairing him/her with another student for activities. Gradually increase the number of students in the group as the student is socially successful.

17. Make certain the student is allowed to voice an opinion in a situation in order to avoid becoming upset or angry.

18. Do not criticize. When correcting the student, be honest yet supportive. Never cause the student to feel badly about himself/herself.

19. Intervene early when there is a problem in order to prevent more serious problems from occurring.

20. Encourage the student to tell you about problems that occur with peers (e.g., being "bullied," teased by others, etc.).

21. Do not force the student to interact with others with whom he/she is not completely comfortable.

22. Treat the student with respect. Talk in an objective manner at all times.

23. Maintain trust and confidentiality with the student at all times.

24. Allow the student to attempt something new in private before doing it in front of others.

25. Speak with the student to explain that he/she may be trying too hard to fit in and should relax and allow friendships to develop naturally.

26. Do not force the student to interact with others.

27. Communicate with parents (e.g., notes home, phone calls, etc.) in order to share information concerning the student's progress and so that they can reinforce the student at home for appropriately interacting with other students at school.

28. Write a contract with the student specifying what behavior is expected (e.g., sitting near a student, talking to a student, etc.) and what reinforcement will be made available when the terms of the contract have been met. (See Appendix for Behavioral Contract.)

29. Reinforce those students in the classroom who appropriately interact with the student.

30. Remove the student from the group or activity until he/she can demonstrate appropriate behavior and self-control.

31. Reinforce the student for demonstrating appropriate behavior based on the length of time the student can be successful. Gradually increase the length of time required for reinforcement as the student demonstrates success.

32. Establish classroom rules:
1. Work on task.
2. Work quietly.
3. Remain in your seat.
4. Finish task.
5. Meet task expectations.
Reiterate rules often and reinforce students for following rules.

33. Reinforce the student for appropriately interacting with other students: (a) give the student a tangible reward (e.g., classroom privileges, line leading, passing out materials, five minutes free time, etc.) or (b) give the student an intangible reward (e.g., praise, handshake, smile, etc.).

130 Bothers other students who are trying to work, listen, etc.

1. Reduce distracting stimuli (e.g., place the student on the front row, provide a carrel or "office" away from distractions, etc.). This is used as a means of reducing distracting stimuli and not as a form of punishment.

2. Interact frequently with the student in order to maintain his/her involvement in the activity (e.g., ask the student questions, ask the student's opinion, stand close to the student, seat the student near the teacher's desk, etc.).

3. Maintain visibility to and from the student. The teacher should be able to see the student and the student should be able to see the teacher, making eye contact possible at all times.

4. Assess the degree of task difficulty in relation to the student's ability to perform the task successfully.

5. Provide a full schedule of activities. Prevent lag time from occurring when the student can bother other students.

6. Remove the student from the group or activity until he/she can demonstrate appropriate behavior and self-control.

7. Teach the student appropriate ways to communicate needs to others (e.g., waiting a turn, raising his/her hand, etc.).

8. Provide the student with enjoyable activities to perform when he/she completes a task early.

9. Seat the student near the teacher.

10. Provide the student with frequent opportunities to participate, share, etc.

11. Provide students with frequent opportunities to interact with one another (e.g., before and after school, between activities, etc.).

12. Seat the student away from those students he/she is most likely to bother.

13. Intervene early when there is a problem in order to prevent a more serious problem from occurring.

14. Teach the student to respect others and their belongings by respecting the student and his/her belongings.

15. Identify a peer who would be a good influence to interact with the student (e.g., someone younger, older, of the same sex, of the opposite sex, etc.).

16. Make certain the student knows when it is acceptable to interrupt others (e.g., an emergency).

17. Do not leave a lot of unstructured time for the student.

18. Reinforce those students in the classroom who demonstrate on-task behavior.

19. Have the student question any directions, explanations, and instructions not understood.

20. Identify a peer to act as a model for the student to imitate appropriate behavior.

21. Evaluate the appropriateness of the task to determine: (a) if the task is too difficult and (b) if the length of time scheduled to complete the task is appropriate.

22. Communicate with parents (e.g., notes home, phone calls, etc.) in order to share information concerning the student's progress and so that they can reinforce the student at home for demonstrating appropriate behavior at school.

23. Write a contract with the student specifying what behavior is expected (e.g., demonstrating appropriate behavior) and what reinforcement will be made available when the terms of the contract have been met. (See Appendix for Behavioral Contract.)

24. Reinforce the student for demonstrating appropriate behavior based on the length of time the student can be successful. Gradually increase the length of time required for reinforcement as the student demonstrates success.

25. Reinforce those students in the classroom who demonstrate appropriate behavior.

26. Establish classroom rules:
1. Work on task.
2. Work quietly.
3. Remain in your seat.
4. Finish task.
5. Meet task expectations.
Reiterate rules often and reinforce students for following rules.

27. Speak to the student to explain: (a) what the student is doing wrong (e.g., bothering other students who are trying to work, listen, etc.) and (b) what the student should be doing (e.g., demonstrating appropriate behavior).

28. Reinforce the student for demonstrating appropriate behavior: (a) give the student a tangible reward (e.g., classroom privileges, line leading, passing out materials, five minutes free time, etc.) or (b) give the student an intangible reward (e.g., praise, handshake, smile, etc.).

131 Responds inappropriately to others' attempts to be friendly, complimentary, sympathetic, etc.

1. Try various groupings in order to determine the situation in which the student is most comfortable.

2. Assign a peer to sit/work directly with the student (e.g., in different settings or activities such as art, music, P.E., tutoring, group projects, recess, etc.). Gradually increase group size when the student has become comfortable working with one other student.

3. Provide the student with positive feedback which indicates he/she is important.

4. Provide the student with many social and academic successes.

5. Provide opportunities for appropriate interactions within the classroom (e.g., peer models engaged in appropriate interactions).

6. Assess the appropriateness of the social situation in relation to the student's ability to be successful.

7. Reduce stimuli which contribute to the student's inappropriate responses to others' attempts to interact.

8. Intervene early to prevent the student from losing self-control.

9. Limit interactions with the peer(s) who is the primary focus of the student's inappropriate responses.

10. Respect the student's right to a reasonable amount of privacy.

11. Allow the student to be a member of a group without requiring active participation.

12. Teach the student social interaction skills (e.g., ways in which to appropriately respond to others' attempts to be friendly, complimentary, sympathetic, etc.).

13. Help the student develop social awareness (e.g., people may be embarrassed by what you say, feelings can be hurt by comments, tact is the best policy, remember interactions which have made you feel good and treat others in the same manner, etc.).

14. Be a model by demonstrating appropriate ways to respond to others who are friendly, complimentary, sympathetic, etc.

15. Treat the student with respect. Talk in an objective manner at all times.

16. Provide the student with frequent opportunities to meet new people.

17. Encourage the student to interact with others.

18. Encourage others to compliment the student.

19. Make certain you express your feelings in a socially acceptable way.

20. Speak to the student to explain: (a) what the student is doing wrong (e.g., using inappropriate language, responding negatively, calling names, making inappropriate gestures, etc.) and (b) what the student should be doing (e.g., being positive in response to others).

21. Communicate with parents (e.g., notes home, phone calls, etc.) in order to share information concerning the student's progress and so that they can reinforce the student at home for responding appropriately to others' attempts to be friendly, complimentary, sympathetic, etc., at school.

22. Write a contract stating appropriate ways to respond to others and identify what reinforcement will be made available when the terms of the contract have been met. (See Appendix for Behavioral Contract.)

23. Reinforce other students for responding appropriately to interactions with students or teachers.

24. Reinforce the student for responding appropriately to others' attempts to be friendly, complimentary, sympathetic, etc.: (a) give the student a tangible reward (e.g., classroom privileges, line leading, passing out materials, five minutes free time, etc.) or (b) give the student an intangible reward (e.g., praise, handshake, smile, etc.).

1. Assess the appropriateness of the task or social situation in relation to the student's ability to perform successfully.

2. Encourage sharing by giving assignments which require sharing in order to complete the activity (e.g., making murals, bulletin boards, maps, art projects, etc.).

3. Encourage peers to share with the student.

4. Teach the student the concept of sharing by having the student borrow from others or loan things to others.

5. Have the student work directly with a peer in order to model sharing. Gradually increase the group size as the student demonstrates success.

6. Reduce competitiveness in the school environment (e.g., avoid situations where refusing to share contributes to winning; situations where winning or "beating" someone else becomes the primary objective of a game, activity, or academic exercise; etc.).

7. Create and reinforce activities (e.g., school bulletin board, class project, bake sale, etc.) in which students work together for a common goal rather than individual success or recognition. Point out that larger accomplishments are realized through group effort than by individual effort.

8. Put the student in charge of communal school items (e.g., rulers, pencils, crayons, etc.) in order to experience sharing.

9. Allow the student to have many turns and enough materials to satisfy his/her immediate needs. Gradually require sharing and taking turns as the student demonstrates success.

10. Provide special activities for the entire class at the end of the day which are contingent upon sharing throughout the day.

11. Provide enough materials, activities, etc., in order that sharing will not always be necessary.

12. Structure the classroom environment in such a way as to take advantage of natural sharing opportunities (e.g., allowing more group activities, pointing out natural consequences when a student shares, etc.).

13. Capitalize on opportunities to share and help (e.g., when there is a spill, assign students different responsibilities for cleaning it up; when a new student enters the classroom, assign students responsibilities for his/her orientation, etc.).

14. Discourage students from bringing personal possessions to school which others might desire. Encourage the use of communal school property.

15. Model sharing behavior by allowing students to use your materials contingent upon return of the items.

16. Provide the student with many opportunities to both borrow and lend in order to help the student learn the concept of sharing.

17. Make certain that every student gets to use materials, take a turn, etc., and that there is no opportunity for selfishness.

18. Point out to the student the natural rewards of sharing (e.g., personal satisfaction, friendships, having people share in return, etc.).

19. Make certain that those students who are willing to share are not taken advantage of by their peers.

20. Make certain that other students are sharing with the student in order that a reciprocal relationship can be achieved.

21. Maintain a realistic level of expectation for sharing.

22. Practice sharing by having each student work with a particular school material for an established length of time. At the end of the time period (e.g., ten minutes) have each student pass his/her material to another student.

23. Provide students with adequate time to complete activities requiring sharing, in order that the selfish use of school materials is not necessary for success. Students are less likely to share if sharing reduces the likelihood of finishing on time, being successful, etc.

24. Reduce the demands for the student to make verbal exchanges when sharing (e.g., shyness may inhibit sharing if the student is required to verbally communicate with others). Materials should be placed in a central location when not in use so that they can be obtained by the students. This will enhance the aspect of sharing which makes materials available to others when not in use.

25. Establish rules for sharing school materials:
  1. Ask for materials you wish to use.
  2. Exchange materials carefully.
  3. Return materials when not in use.
  4. Offer to share materials with others.
  5. Take care of shared materials.
  6. Call attention to materials that need repair.
Reiterate rules often and reinforce students for following rules.

26. Intervene early when there is a problem in order to prevent more serious problems from occurring.

27. Teach the student to respect others' belongings by respecting the student's belongings.

28. Do not force the student to interact with other students with whom he/she is not completely comfortable.

29. Be a model for sharing (e.g., by loaning pencils, paper, etc.).

30. Teach the student to "take turns" sharing materials (e.g., each student may use the colored pencils for 15 minutes, one student cuts while the other student uses the glue, etc.).

31. Provide the student and others with enough "things" that sharing will not be necessary. Gradually reduce the number of things as the student learns to share.

32. Do not allow the student to bring those things to school that he/she is not willing to share (e.g., games, toys, etc.).

33. Make certain the student is not expected to share everything (e.g., do not punish the student for not sharing a hat, gloves, personal items, etc.). Everyone has things they would prefer to not share with others.

34. Communicate with parents (e.g., notes home, phone calls, etc.) in order to share information concerning the student's progress and so that they can reinforce the student at home for sharing at school.

35. Write a contract with the student specifying what behavior is expected (e.g., sharing) and what reinforcement will be made available when the terms of the contract have been met. (See Appendix for Behavioral Contract.)

36. Reinforce those students in the classroom who share.

37. Speak with the student to explain: (a) what the student is doing wrong (e.g., failing to give others opportunities to use things) and (b) what the student should be doing (e.g., sharing materials).

38. Reinforce the student for sharing: (a) give the student a tangible reward (e.g., classroom privileges, line leading, passing out materials, five minutes free time, etc.) or (b) give the student an intangible reward (e.g., praise, handshake, smile, etc.).

133 Does not allow others to take their turns, participate in activities or games, etc.

1. Assess the appropriateness of the task or social situation in relation to the student's ability to perform successfully.

2. Encourage group participation by giving students assignments which require working together in order to complete the activity (e.g., making murals, bulletin boards, maps, art projects, etc.).

3. Encourage peers to take turns with the student.

4. Have the student work directly with a peer in order to model taking turns. Gradually increase group size over time.

5. Reduce competitiveness in the school environment (e.g., avoid situations where refusing to take turns contributes to winning; situations where winning or "beating" someone else becomes the primary objective of a game, activity, or academic exercise; etc.).

6. Create and reinforce activities in which students work together for a common goal rather than individual success or recognition (e.g., school bulletin board, class project, bake sale, etc.). Point out that larger accomplishments are realized through group effort than by individual effort.

7. Allow the student to have many turns and enough materials to satisfy immediate needs, and gradually require sharing and taking turns.

8. Provide special activities for the entire class at the end of the day which are contingent upon taking turns throughout the day.

9. Structure the classroom environment in such a way as to take advantage of natural opportunities to take turns (e.g., allow more group activities, point out natural consequences when a student takes turns, etc.).

10. Discourage students from bringing personal possessions to school which others might desire. Encourage the use of communal school property.

11. Capitalize on opportunities to work together (e.g., when there is a spill, assign students different responsibilities for cleaning it up; when a new student enters the classroom, assign different students responsibilities for his/her orientation; etc.).

12. Require the student to practice taking turns if he/she is unable to willingly do so.

13. Provide enough materials, activities, etc., in order that taking turns will not always be necessary.

14. Provide the student with many opportunities to take turns in order to help the student learn the concept of taking turns.

15. Make certain that every student gets to use materials, take a turn, etc., and that there is no opportunity for selfishness.

16. Point out to the student the natural rewards of taking turns (e.g., personal satisfaction, friendships, companionship, etc.).

17. Make certain that those students who are willing to take turns are not taken advantage of by their peers.

18. Make certain that other students are taking turns with the student in order that a reciprocal relationship can be achieved.

19. Maintain a realistic level of expectation for taking turns.

20. Have the student engage in an activity with one peer, and gradually increase the size of the group as the student demonstrates success.

21. Determine the peers with whom the student would most prefer to interact and attempt to facilitate the interaction.

22. Assign an outgoing, nonthreatening peer to interact with the student.

23. Assign the student to interact with younger peers.

24. Assign the student to engage in activities in which he/she is likely to interact successfully with peers.

25. Make certain the student understands that interacting with peers is contingent upon appropriate behavior.

26. Teach the student appropriate ways to interact with peers in group games (e.g., suggest activities, share materials, problem solve, take turns, follow game rules, etc.).

27. Supervise activities closely in order that the peer(s) with whom the student interacts does not stimulate inappropriate behavior.

28. Make certain that activities are not so stimulating as to make successful interactions with peers difficult.

29. Involve the student in extracurricular activities in order to encourage appropriate interaction with peers.

30. Find the peer with whom the student is most likely to be able to successfully interact (e.g., a student with similar interests, background, classes, behavior patterns, nonacademic schedule, etc.).

31. Make certain, beforehand, that the student is able to successfully engage in the activity (e.g., the student understands the rules, the student is familiar with the game, the student will be compatible with the other students playing the game, etc.).

32. Make certain the student understands that failing to interact appropriately with peers during activities may result in termination of the game and/or loss of future opportunities to engage in activities.

33. Design activities in which each student takes short turns. Increase the length of each student's turn as the student demonstrates success at taking turns.

34. Establish a set of standard behavior rules for group games:
1. Follow rules of the game.
2. Take turns.
3. Make positive comments.
4. Work as a team member.
5. Be a good sport.

Reiterate rules often and reinforce students for following rules.

35. Allow natural consequences to occur when the student fails to take turns (e.g., other students will not want to interact with him/her, other students will not be willing to take turns, etc.).

36. Talk to the student before playing a game and remind the student of the importance of taking turns.

37. Intervene early when there is a problem in order to prevent more serious problems from occurring.

38. Make certain there is adult supervision when the student is playing games with others.

39. Do not force the student to interact with someone with whom he/she is not completely comfortable.

40. Make certain the student does not become involved in overstimulating activities in which he/she gets excited and cannot settle down.

41. Treat the student with respect. Talk in an objective manner at all times.

42. Provide the student with a predetermined signal when he/she begins to display inappropriate manners.

43. Teach the student to "take turns" (e.g., each student may use the colored pencils for 15 minutes, each student may have three turns, etc.).

44. Communicate with the parents (e.g., notes home, phone calls, etc.) in order to share information concerning the student's progress and so that they can reinforce the student at home for taking turns at school.

45. Write a contract with the student specifying what behavior is expected (e.g., taking turns) and what reinforcement will be made available when the terms of the contract have been met. (See Appendix for Behavioral Contract.)

46. Reinforce those students in the classroom who take turns.

47. Speak with the student to explain: (a) what the student is doing wrong (e.g., failing to give others opportunities to have a turn) and (b) what the student should be doing (e.g., allowing others to have a turn).

48. Reinforce the student for taking turns: (a) give the student a tangible reward (e.g., classroom privileges, line leading, passing out materials, five minutes free time, etc.) or (b) give the student an intangible reward (e.g., praise, handshake, smile, etc.).

1. Evaluate the student's problem-solving ability and limit his/her exposure to conflict situations to a level the student can deal with appropriately.

2. Teach the student a variety of ways to solve problems in conflict situations (e.g., withdrawing, reasoning, calling upon an arbitrator, apologizing, compromising, allowing others the benefit of the doubt, etc.).

3. Model for the student a variety of ways to solve problems in conflict situations (e.g., withdrawing, reasoning, apologizing, compromising, etc.).

4. Provide the student with hypothetical conflict situations and require him/her to suggest appropriate solutions to the situation.

5. Have the student role-play ways to solve problems in conflict situations with peers and adults (e.g., withdrawing, reasoning, calling upon an arbitrator, apologizing, compromising, allowing others the benefit of the doubt, etc.).

6. Make certain the student understands that natural consequences will occur if he/she reacts inappropriately in conflict situations (e.g., peers will not want to interact, teachers will have to intervene, etc.).

7. Teach the student to solve problems in conflict situations before the situations become too difficult for him/her to solve.

8. Teach the student to avoid becoming involved in conflict situations (e.g., move away from the situation, change his/her behavior, etc.).

9. Explain to the student that it is natural for conflict situations to occur. What is important is how he/she reacts to the situations.

10. Identify typical conflict situations for the student, and discuss appropriate solutions to specific situations (e.g., peers taking things from him/her, peers hitting or grabbing, peers not following rules, etc.).

11. When the student has responded inappropriately to a conflict situation, take time to explore with him/her appropriate solutions which could have been used in dealing with the problem.

12. Maintain mobility throughout the classroom in order to supervise student interactions and intervene in conflict situations in which the student(s) is unable to successfully resolve the problem.

13. Intervene early when there is a problem in order to prevent more serious problems from occurring.

14. Do not force the student to interact with someone with whom he/she is not completely comfortable.

15. Make certain the student does not become involved in overstimulating activities which may cause a conflict situation.

16. Treat the student with respect. Talk in an objective manner at all times.

17. Teach the student acceptable ways to communicate displeasure, anger, frustration, etc.

18. Have the student put himself/herself in someone else's place (e.g., "How would you feel if someone called you dumb or stupid?").

19. Do not assume that the student is being treated nicely by others. Peers may be stimulating the inappropriate behavior of the student.

20. Encourage the student to interact with others.

21. Do not force the student to interact with others.

22. Make sure you express your feelings in a socially acceptable way.

23. Teach the student to "think" before acting (e.g., ask himself/herself: "What is happening?" "What am I doing?" "What should I do?" "What will be best for me?").

24. Make certain the student is allowed to voice an opinion in a situation in order to avoid becoming angry or upset.

25. Have the student question any directions, explanations, and instructions not understood.

26. Identify a peer to act as a model for the student to imitate the ability to appropriately solve problems in conflict situations.

27. Communicate with parents (e.g., notes home, phone calls, etc.) in order to share information concerning the student's progress and so that they can reinforce the student at home for demonstrating the ability to appropriately solve problems in conflict situations at school.

28. Write a contract with the student specifying what behavior is expected (e.g., withdrawing from conflict situations) and what reinforcement will be made available when the terms of the contract have been met. (See Appendix for Behavioral Contract.)

29. Reinforce the student for demonstrating the ability to appropriately solve problems in conflict situations based on the number of times the student can be successful. Gradually increase the number of times required for reinforcement as the student demonstrates success.

30. Reinforce those students in the classroom who demonstrate the ability to appropriately solve problems in conflict situations.

31. Speak to the student to explain: (a) what the student is doing wrong (e.g., fighting, name calling, etc.) and (b) what the student should be doing (e.g., withdrawing from conflict situations, compromising, etc.).

32. Reinforce the student for demonstrating the ability to appropriately solve problems in conflict situations: (a) give the student a tangible reward (e.g., classroom privileges, line leading, passing out materials, five minutes free time, etc.) or (b) give the student an intangible reward (e.g., praise, handshake, smile, etc.).

135 Does not make appropriate use of free time

1. Evaluate the appropriateness of free time activities in order to determine whether or not the student can be successful with the activity and the length of time scheduled.

2. Encourage the student's peers to include him/her in free-time activities.

3. Encourage the student to assist younger peers in free-time activities.

4. Develop, with the student, a list of high-interest, free-time activities that require various amounts of time to perform.

5. Place free-time materials (e.g., paper, pencil, glue, crayons, games, etc.) in a location where the student can obtain them on his/her own.

6. Establish centers of high-interest activities at appropriate levels of difficulty for the student's use during free time.

7. Provide a quiet, reasonably private area where the student can do nothing during free time.

8. Separate the student from the peer(s) who stimulates his/her inappropriate use of free time.

9. Encourage the student to plan the use of free time in advance.

10. Provide sign-up sheets for free-time activities.

11. Give the student an individual schedule to follow so that when an activity is finished he/she knows what to do next.

12. Assign a peer for the student to interact with during free time.

13. Identify a specified activity for the student to engage in during free time.

14. Have the student act as a peer tutor during free time.

15. Have the student act as a teacher assistant during free time.

16. Allow the student to go to other classrooms for specified activities during free time (e.g., typing, home economics, industrial arts, etc.).

17. Have the student begin an ongoing project to work on during free time which will in turn become a regular free-time activity.

18. Make certain that free time is contingent upon academic productivity and accuracy (e.g., the student must finish three activities with 80% accuracy before having free time).

19. Provide high-interest, free-time activities for completion of assignments (e.g., listening to music, reading, socializing, going to another part of the building, etc.).

20. Provide the student with a list of quiet activities to engage in when he/she finishes assignments early.

21. Find educationally-related, free-time activities for the student to perform (e.g., flash card activities with peers; math, reading, or spelling board games; etc.).

22. Engage in free-time activities with the student in order to model appropriate use of free time.

23. Make certain that the free-time activity is not so overstimulating as to cause the student to demonstrate inappropriate behavior.

24. Make certain the student is able to successfully engage in the free-time activity (e.g., the student understands the rules, the student is familiar with the activity, the student will be compatible with other students engaged in the activity, etc.).

25. Provide supervision of free-time activities in order to monitor the student's appropriate use of free time.

26. Make certain the student is aware of the length of free time available when beginning the free-time activity.

27. Make certain the student understands that failing to make appropriate use of free time may result in termination of free time and/or loss of future free time.

28. Make certain the student understands that failure to conclude free-time activities and return to assignments may result in loss of opportunity to earn free time.

29. Provide the student with frequent short-term, free-time activities in order that he/she can learn to finish free-time projects at another time and be willing to go back to assignments.

30. Give the student a special responsibility during free time (e.g., grading papers, straightening books, feeding pets, etc.).

31. Provide things that entertain the student during free time (e.g., headphones, coloring books, reading material, etc.).

32. Intervene early when there is a problem in order to prevent more serious problems from occurring.

33. Make certain the student does not become involved in overstimulating activities.

34. Do not leave a lot of unstructured time for the student.

35. Have the student question any directions, explanations, or instructions not understood.

36. Identify a peer to act as a model for the student to imitate appropriate use of free time.

37. Communicate with parents (e.g., notes home, phone calls, etc.) in order to share information concerning the student's progress and so that they can reinforce the student at home for making appropriate use of free time at school.

38. Write a contract with the student specifying what behavior is expected (e.g., talking quietly, sitting quietly, studying, etc.) and what reinforcement will be made available when the terms of the contract have been met. (See Appendix for Behavioral Contract.)

39. Reinforce the student for making appropriate use of free time based on the length of time the student can be successful. Gradually increase the length of time required for reinforcement as the student demonstrates success.

40. Reinforce those students in the classroom who make appropriate use of free time.

41. Establish free-time rules:
1. Find an activity.
2. Spend time quietly.
3. Remain in assigned areas.
4. Put materials away when free time is over.

Reiterate rules often and reinforce students for following rules.

42. Speak to the student to explain: (a) what the student is doing wrong (e.g., talking loudly, getting out of seat, etc.) and (b) what he/she should be doing (e.g., talking quietly, sitting quietly, etc.).

43. Reinforce the student for making appropriate use of free time: (a) give the student a tangible reward (e.g., classroom privileges, line leading, passing out materials, five minutes free time, etc.) or (b) give the student an intangible reward (e.g., praise, handshake, smile, etc.).

136 Fails to work appropriately with peers in a tutoring situation

1. Reinforce the student for working appropriately with peers in a tutoring situation: (a) give the student a tangible reward (e.g., classroom privileges, line leading, passing out materials, five minutes free time, etc.) or (b) give the student an intangible reward (e.g., praise, handshake, smile, etc.).

2. Speak to the student to explain: (a) what he/she is doing wrong (e.g., not attending to the tutor, arguing with peers, etc.) and (b) what he/she should be doing (e.g., attending to the tutor, doing his/her own work, etc.).

3. Establish tutoring rules:
   1. Work on task.
   2. Work quietly.
   3. Remain in your seat.
   4. Finish task.
   5. Meet task expectations.

Reiterate rules often and reinforce students for following rules.

4. Reinforce those student in the classroom who work appropriately with peers in a tutoring situation.

5. Reinforce the student for working appropriately with peers in a tutoring situation based on the length of time he/she can be successful. Gradually increase the length of time required for reinforcement as the student demonstrates success.

6. Write a contract with the student specifying what behavior is expected (e.g., attending to the tutor, taking turns, sharing materials, etc.) and what reinforcement will be made available when the terms of the contract have been met.

7. Communicate with parents (e.g., notes home, phone calls, etc.) in order to share information concerning the student's progress and so that they can reinforce the student at home for working appropriately with peers in a tutoring situation at school.

8. Evaluate the appropriateness of the tutoring situation in order to determine: (a) if the task is too easy, (b) if the task is too difficult, and (c) if the length of time scheduled to complete the task is appropriate.

9. Identify a peer to act as a model for the student to imitate working appropriately with peers in a tutoring situation.

10. Have the student question any directions, explanations, and instructions he/she does not understand.

11. Make certain that the student and peer tutor are compatible (e.g., the student accepts his/her role in the tutoring situation, the student and peer tutor are accepting of one another, the peer tutor has skills and knowledge to share, etc.).

12. Be certain that the opportunity to work with a peer tutor is contingent upon appropriate behavior prior to and during the tutoring situation.

13. Make certain that the students being tutored together are on the same ability level.

14. Teach the student appropriate behavior for peer tutoring situations (e.g., follow directions, work quietly, etc.).

15. Supervise tutoring situations closely in order to make certain that the student's behavior is appropriate, the task is appropriate, he/she is learning from the situation, etc.

16. Make certain the tutoring activity involves practice, drill, or repetition of information or skills previously presented.

17. Determine the peer(s) the student would most prefer to interact with in tutoring situations and attempt to group these students together for peer tutoring.

18. Assign an outgoing, nonthreatening peer to act as a peer tutor.

19. Structure the environment so that the student has many opportunities for success in the tutoring situation.

20. Assign the student to tutoring situations in which he/she is likely to interact successfully with peers being tutored.

21. Conduct a sociometric activity with the class in order to determine the peer(s) who would most prefer to interact with the student in tutoring situations.

22. Make certain that the student demonstrates appropriate behavior in tutoring situations prior to pairing him/her with a peer.

23. Make certain the student understands that interacting with a peer(s) in tutoring situations is contingent upon appropriate behavior.

24. Supervise tutoring situations closely in order that the peer(s) with whom the student works does not stimulate inappropriate behavior.

25. Make certain that the tutoring situation is not so overstimulating as to make successful interactions with another peer difficult.

26. Reduce the emphasis on competition. Fear of failure may stimulate inappropriate behavior in tutoring situations.

27. Teach the student problem-solving skills in order that he/she may better deal with problems that occur in interactions with another peer(s) in tutoring situations (e.g., talking, walking away, calling upon an arbitrator, compromising, etc.).

28. Find a peer with whom the student is most likely to be able to successfully interact in tutoring situations (e.g., a student with similar interests, background, ability, behavior patterns, etc.).

29. Through interviews with other students and observation, determine those characteristics of the student which interfere with successful interactions during tutoring situations in order to determine skills or behaviors the student needs to develop for successful interactions.

30. Structure the activities of the tutoring situation according to the needs/abilities of the student (e.g., establish rules, limit the stimulation of the activity, limit the length of the activity, consider the time of day, etc.).

31. Limit opportunities for interaction in tutoring situations on those occasions when the student is not likely to be successful (e.g., the student has experienced academic or social failure prior to the scheduled tutoring activity).

32. Select nonacademic activities designed to enhance appropriate interaction of the student and a peer(s) (e.g., board games, model building, coloring, etc.).

33. Have the student work with the teacher to practice appropriate interactions in tutoring situations.

34. Make certain the student is able to successfully engage in the tutoring activity (e.g., the student understands the rules, the student is familiar with the activity, the student will be compatible with the other students engaged in the free-time activity, etc.).

35. Make certain the student understands that failing to interact appropriately with a peer(s) during tutoring activities may result in removal from the activity and/or loss or participation in future activities.

36. Have the student engage in the tutoring situation with peers for short periods of time and gradually increase the length of time as the student demonstrates success.

37. Provide an appropriate location for the tutoring situation (e.g., quiet corner of the classroom, near the teacher's desk, etc.).

38. Intervene early when there is a problem in order to prevent a more serious problem from occurring.

39. Do not force the student to work in a tutoring situation with a peer with whom he/she is not completely comfortable.

40. Provide the student with a predetermined signal when he/she begins to display inappropriate behaviors in a tutoring situation with peers.

41. Allow the student to attempt something new in private before doing so in a tutoring situation with peers.

137   Does not share school materials with other students

1. Teach sharing by giving students an assignment which requires sharing to complete the activity (e.g., materials for making murals, bulletin boards, maps, art projects, etc.).

2. Encourage peers to share with the student.

3. Teach the student the concept of sharing by having the student borrow from others and loan things to others.

4. Have the student work directly with one peer in order to model sharing and taking turns. Gradually increase group size as the student demonstrates success.

5. Reduce competitiveness in the school environment (e.g., avoid situations where refusing to share contributes to winning; where winning or beating someone else becomes the primary objective of a game, activity, or academic exercise; etc.)

6. Create and reinforce activities in which students work together for a common goal rather than individual success or recognition. Point out that larger accomplishments are realized through group effort than by individual effort.

7. Put the student in charge of communal school items such as rulers, pencils, crayons, etc., in order to experience sharing.

8. Provide the student with enough materials to satisfy immediate needs (e.g., one of everything). Gradually reduce the number of materials over time, requiring the student to share the available materials as he/she becomes more successful at doing so.

9. Provide special activities for the entire class to engage in at the end of the day which are contingent upon sharing school materials throughout the day.

10. Discourage students from bringing personal possessions to school which others would desire. Encourage the use of communal school property.

11. Structure the classroom environment in such a way as to take advantage of natural sharing opportunities (e.g., have more group activities, allow for natural consequences when a student refuses to share, etc.).

12. Provide enough materials, activities, etc., in order that sharing or taking turns will not always be necessary.

13. Model sharing behavior by allowing students to use your materials contingent upon the return of the items.

14. Provide the student with many opportunities to both borrow and lend materials in order to help the student learn the concept of sharing.

15. Make certain that every student gets to use materials in order that selfishness can be reduced.

16. Point out to the student the natural rewards of sharing school materials (e.g., personal satisfaction, friendships, having people share in return, etc.).

17. Make certain that those students who are willing to share are not taken advantage of by other students.

18. Make certain that other students are sharing with the student in order that a reciprocal relationship can be expected.

19. Maintain a realistic level of expectation for sharing school materials based on the student's age level and ability to share.

20. Practice sharing by having each student work with a particular school material for an established length of time. At the end of each time period (e.g., ten minutes) have each student pass his/her material to another student.

21. Do not expect the student to share all materials. Students need to "own" some materials (e.g., jewelry, clothing, etc.).

22. Provide students with adequate time to complete activities requiring sharing, in order that the selfish use of school materials is not necessary for success. Students are less likely to share if sharing reduces the likelihood of finishing on time, being successful, etc.

23. Reduce the demands for the student to make verbal exchanges when sharing (i.e., shyness may inhibit sharing if the student is required to verbally communicate with others). Materials may be placed in a central location when not in use so that they may be obtained by the students.

24. Establish rules for sharing school materials:
1. Ask for materials you wish to use.
2. Exchange materials carefully.
3. Return materials when not in use.
4. Offer to share materials with others.
5. Take care of shared materials.
6. Call attention to materials that need repair.

Reiterate rules often and reinforce students for following rules.

25. In group situations provide the student with necessary materials for the activity in order that sharing problems do not disrupt the learning experience.

26. Point out to the student the natural consequences of refusing to share (e.g., students will not share in return, students will not want him/her in their group, loss of friendships, inability to successfully complete activities that require sharing, etc.).

27. Make certain that shared materials are returned to the student in order that he/she will develop a positive concept of sharing.

28. Provide the student with many experiences to share with others and have materials returned. When the student learns that shared materials will be returned, the student will be more likely to share in the future.

29. Make certain the student understands that if shared materials are used up, worn out, broken under normal use, etc., they will be replaced.

30. Do not force the student to interact with others.

31. Do not make sharing mandatory until the student develops the ability to share. Sharing should not be a "must" until the student develops some degree of tolerance for sharing with others.

32. Students who cannot share with one another because of their personal dislike for each other should not be placed in the same group when sharing is required. If a student prefers not to share with one other person, it does not mean that he/she does not have the ability to share.

33. Make certain the student understands that students do not own school materials and that he/she should not feel threatened to share school materials since there is nothing personal to lose.

34. Intervene early when there is a problem in order to prevent more serious problems from occurring.

35. Teach the student to respect others' belongings by respecting the student's belongings.

36. Do not force the student to interact with other students with whom he/she is not completely comfortable.

37. Be a model for sharing (e.g., by loaning pencils, paper, etc.).

38. Teach the student to "take turns" sharing possessions (e.g., each student may use the colored pencils for 15 minutes, one student cuts while the other student uses the glue, etc.).

39. Provide the student and others with enough "things" that sharing will not be necessary. Gradually reduce the number of things as the student learns to share.

40. Do not allow the student to bring those things to school which he/she is not willing to share.

41. Make certain the student is not expected to share all of his/her personal items (e.g., crayons, magic markers, etc.).

42. Assess the appropriateness of the task or social situation.

43. Communicate with parents (e.g., notes home, phone calls, etc.) in order to share information concerning the student's progress and so that they can reinforce the student at home for sharing school materials at school.

44. Write a contract with the student specifying what behavior is expected (e.g., sharing) and what reinforcement will be made available when the terms of the contract have been met. (See Appendix for Behavioral Contract.)

45. Reinforce those students who share school materials with other students.

46. Speak with the student to explain: (a) what the student is doing wrong (e.g., failing to give others the opportunity to use school materials) and (b) what the student should be doing (e.g., sharing school materials).

47. Reinforce the student for sharing school materials: (a) give the student a tangible reward (e.g., classroom privileges, line leading, passing out materials, five minutes free time, etc.) or (b) give the student an intangible reward (e.g., praise, handshake, smile, etc.).

1. Provide a full schedule of daily events. Prevent lag time from occurring when the student can engage in writing and passing notes. (See Appendix for Schedule of Daily Events.)

2. Seat the student near the teacher.

3. Maintain visibility to and from the student. The teacher should be able to see the student and the student should be able to see the teacher, making eye contact possible at all times.

4. Interact frequently with the student in order to monitor his/her behavior.

5. Remove the student from the peer(s) with whom he/she is writing and passing notes.

6. Provide students with frequent opportunities to interact with one another (e.g., before and after school, between activities, etc.).

7. Use "note writing" as a language arts activity each day.

8. Make certain the student understands the consequences of writing and passing notes.

9. Be consistent when delivering consequences to those students who write and pass notes.

10. Set aside time each day when the student is permitted to write notes to other students.

11. Make certain the student understands that passing notes when someone else is talking or giving directions is rude.

12. Do not leave a lot of unstructured time for the student.

13. Identify a peer to act as a model for the student to imitate appropriate behavior.

14. Communicate with parents (e.g., notes home, phone calls, etc.) in order to share information concerning the student's progress and so that they can reinforce the student at home for demonstrating appropriate behavior at school.

15. Write a contract with the student specifying what behavior is expected (e.g., demonstrating appropriate behavior) and what reinforcement will be made available when the terms of the contract have been met. (See Appendix for Behavioral Contract.)

16. Reinforce the student for demonstrating appropriate behavior based on the length of time the student can be successful. Gradually increase the length of time required for reinforcement as the student demonstrates success.

17. Reinforce those students in the classroom who demonstrate appropriate behavior.

18. Establish classroom rules:
    1. Work on task.
    2. Work quietly.
    3. Remain in your seat.
    4. Finish task.
    5. Meet task expectations.
Reiterate rules often and reinforce students for following rules.

19. Speak to the student to explain: (a) what the student is doing wrong (e.g., writing and passing notes) and (b) what the student should be doing (e.g., working quietly).

20. Reinforce the student for demonstrating appropriate behavior: (a) give the student a tangible reward (e.g., classroom privileges, line leading, passing out materials, five minutes free time, etc.) or (b) give the student an intangible reward (e.g., praise, handshake, smile, etc.).

1. Make certain the student knows what information is appropriate to report (e.g., peers' emergencies, injuries, fighting, etc.).

2. Make certain the student knows what information is not appropriate to report (e.g., peers whispering, not working, copying, wasting time, etc.).

3. Maintain mobility in order to prevent the student's need to tattle. If you see behavior occur, it will not be necessary for the students to call attention to it.

4. Do not inadvertently reinforce tattling by overreacting.

5. In order to maintain objectivity, make decisions based on what you observe rather than what is reported to you.

6. Be a model for appropriate student behavior. Publicly praise and privately redirect student behavior.

7. Reduce the emphasis on competition. A highly competitive environment may increase the likelihood of tattling.

8. Explain the natural consequences of tattling to the student (e.g., peers will not want to interact with him/her, peers will retaliate, etc.).

9. Teach the student appropriate ways to communicate displeasure, anger, frustration, etc.

10. When the student comes to you to tattle, stop and ask the student, "Is this something that is so important that you need to come to me?" "Is someone hurt?" "Is this something you can solve without me?" etc.

11. Encourage the student to use problem-solving skills: (a) identify the problem, (b) identify goals and objectives, (c) develop strategies, (d) develop a plan for action, and (e) carry out the plan.

12. Refuse to listen to the student by immediately stopping the student when tattling begins.

13. Make certain the student does not go to another adult when you won't respond to his/her tattling.

14. Reduce the opportunity for the student to be in competitive activities that may cause tattling.

15. Immediately remove the student from interacting with others when tattling begins.

16. Be consistent in dealing with tattling. Do not allow tattling one time and expect appropriate behavior the next time.

17. Make a list of the number of times each day the student tattles. Make the student aware of the number of times each day he/she comes to you to tattle.

18. If the student has difficulty playing nicely with others, do not allow playtime.

19. Make sure that others are friendly and cooperative when interacting with the student.

20. Encourage the student to play with peers who do not tattle.

21. Remind the student before interacting with others of which situations are important enough to involve an adult and which situations are considered tattling.

22. Do not make the student play with a certain child or group of children. Allow the student to pick his/her own friends.

23. Determine the thing about which the student most frequently tattles (e.g., not playing a certain game fairly, someone calling names, someone playing with a certain toy, etc.), and remove whatever it is from the student's situation (e.g., take the game away, do not have the student interact with someone who calls him/her names, remove the toy that always causes problems, etc.).

24. Determine if there is legitimate reason for the student to report the behavior of others (another student may be playing too roughly, breaking toys, etc.).

25. Talk to the student about ways of handling situations successfully without tattling (e.g., walk away from the situation, change to another activity, ask for help, etc.).

26. Make certain there are enough materials for all students so that sharing is not a problem.

27. Identify a peer to act as a model for the student to imitate appropriate behavior.

28. Communicate with parents (e.g., notes home, phone calls, etc.) in order to share information concerning the student's progress and so that they can reinforce the student at home for demonstrating appropriate behavior at school.

29. Write a contract with the student specifying what behavior is expected (e.g., demonstrating appropriate behavior) and what reinforcement will be made available when the terms of the contract have been met. (See Appendix for Behavioral Contract.)

30. Reinforce the student for demonstrating appropriate behavior based on the length of time the student can be successful. Gradually increase the length of time required for reinforcement as the student demonstrates success.

31. Reinforce those students in the classroom who demonstrate appropriate behavior.

32. Establish classroom rules:
1. Work on task.
2. Work quietly.
3. Remain in your seat.
4. Finish task.
5. Meet task expectations.

Reiterate rules often and reinforce students for following rules.

33. Speak to the student to explain: (a) what the student is doing wrong (e.g., tattling) and (b) what the student should be doing (e.g., attending to his/her own activities).

34. Reinforce the student for demonstrating appropriate behavior: (a) give the student a tangible reward (e.g., classroom privileges, line leading, passing out materials, five minutes free time, etc.) or (b) give the student an intangible reward (e.g., praise, handshake, smile, etc.).

140   Grabs things away from others

1. Structure the environment so that time does not permit inappropriate behavior.

2. Teach the student the concept of borrowing by loaning and requiring the return of those things the student has been taking from others.

3. Identify those things the student has been grabbing from others and provide the student with those items as reinforcers for appropriate behavior.

4. Reduce the opportunity to take things from other students by restricting students from bringing unnecessary items to school.

5. Maintain visibility to and from the student. The teacher should be able to see the student and the student should be able to see the teacher, making eye contact possible at all times.

6. Supervise the student in order to monitor behavior.

7. Encourage all students to monitor their own belongings.

8. Make certain the student has his/her own necessary school-related items (e.g., pencil, ruler, paper, etc.).

9. Use a permanent marker to label all property brought to school by students and teachers.

10. Secure all school items of value (e.g., cassette tapes, lab materials, industrial arts and home economics supplies, etc.).

11. Make certain the student understands the natural consequences of inappropriate behavior (e.g., the student must make restitution for taking things which belong to others).

12. Communicate with the student's family to establish procedures whereby the student may earn those things he/she would otherwise take from other students.

13. Teach the student to share (e.g., schedule activities daily which require sharing).

14. Help the student build or create a prized possession to satisfy the need for ownership (e.g., this can be done in art, home economics, industrial arts, etc.).

15. Deal with the grabbing of belongings privately rather than publicly.

16. Provide multiples of the items which are being taken in order to have enough for all or most students to use (e.g., pencils, erasers, rulers, etc.).

17. Intervene early when there is a problem in order to prevent more serious problems from occurring.

18. Teach the student to respect others and their belongings by respecting the student's belongings.

19. Make certain the student does not become involved in overstimulating activities when playing with others.

20. Find a peer to play with the student who will be a good influence (e.g., someone younger, older, of the same sex, of the opposite sex, etc.).

21. Teach the student acceptable ways to communicate displeasure, anger, frustration, etc.

22. Do not assume the student is being treated nicely by others. Peers may be stimulating inappropriate behavior.

23. Teach the student to ask for things in a positive manner. Teach key words and phrases (e.g., "May I borrow your pencil?" "Do you mind if I play with your ball?" etc.).

24. Teach the student the concept of borrowing by allowing the student to borrow things from you and requiring him/her to ask permission before doing so.

25. Teach the student to "take turns" sharing possessions (e.g., each child may use the markers for 15 minutes, one child bats while the other throws the ball, players change places after three hits, etc.).

26. Provide the student with enough "things" that sharing will not be necessary. Gradually reduce the number of things as the student learns to share.

27. Teach the student to "think" before acting (e.g., ask himself/herself: "What is happening?" "What am I doing?" "What should I do?" "What will be best for me?" etc.).

28. Communicate with the parents (e.g., notes home, phone calls, etc.) in order to share information concerning the student's appropriate behavior and so that they can reinforce the student at home for appropriate use or consideration of others' belongings at school.

29. Write a contract with the student specifying what behavior is expected (e.g., not grabbing things away from others) and what reinforcement will be made available when the terms of the contract have been met. (See Appendix for Behavioral Contract.)

30. Remove the student from the group or activity until he/she can demonstrate appropriate behavior and self-control.

31. Reinforce the student for demonstrating appropriate behavior based on the length of time the student can be successful. Gradually increase the length of time required for reinforcement as the student demonstrates success.

32. Reinforce those students in the classroom who demonstrate appropriate behavior in reference to others' belongings.

33. Establish classroom rules:
1. Work on task.
2. Remain in your seat.
3. Finish task.
4. Meet task expectations.
Reiterate rules often and reinforce students for following rules.

34. Speak with the student to explain: (a) what the student is doing wrong (e.g., grabbing things from others) and (b) what the student should be doing (e.g., asking to use things, borrowing, sharing, returning, etc.).

35. Reinforce the student for demonstrating appropriate behavior: (a) give the student a tangible reward (e.g., classroom privileges, line leading, passing out materials, five minutes free time, etc.) or (b) give the student an intangible reward (e.g., praise, handshake, smile, etc.).

1.　Make certain that reinforcement is not inadvertently given for inappropriate behavior (e.g., interrupting the teacher).

2.　Give adequate opportunities to respond (i.e., enthusiastic students need many opportunities to contribute).

3.　Provide the student with a predetermined signal if he/she begins to interrupt.

4.　Structure the environment in such a way as to limit opportunities for interrupting the teacher (e.g., keep the student engaged in activities, have the student seated near the teacher, etc.).

5.　Reduce activities which might cause the student to interrupt or talk out (e.g., announcing test score ranges or test scores aloud, emphasizing the success of a particular student or students, etc.).

6.　Provide the student with many social and academic successes.

7.　Make the necessary adjustments in the environment to prevent the student from experiencing stress, frustration, or anger (e.g., reduce peer pressure, academic failure, teasing, etc.).

8.　Maintain visibility to and from the student. The teacher should be able to see the student and the student should be able to see the teacher, making eye contact possible at all times.

9.　Interact frequently with the student to reduce the need to interrupt the teacher.

10.　Reinforce the student for raising his/her hand in order to be recognized.

11.　Call on the student when he/she is most likely to be able to respond correctly.

12.　Teach the student to recognize the appropriate time to speak (e.g., when the teacher has finished speaking, after raising his/her hand, to make comments within the context of the situation, to make comments that are a follow-up to what has just been said, etc.).

13.　Have the student work in small groups in which there are frequent opportunities to speak. Gradually increase the size of the group as the student learns to wait longer for a turn to speak.

14.　Make certain that the student's feelings are considered when it is necessary to deal with his/her interruptions (i.e., handle comments in such a way as to not diminish the student's enthusiasm for participation).

15.　Encourage the student to model the behavior of peers who are successful.

16.　Help the student improve concentration skills (e.g., listening to the speaker, taking notes, preparing comments in advance, making comments in the appropriate context, etc.).

17.　Have the student question any directions, explanations, and instructions not understood.

18.　Deliver directions, explanations, and instructions in a clear and concise manner in order to reduce the student's need to ask questions.

19.　Have the student practice waiting for short periods of time for a turn to speak. Gradually increase the length of time required for reinforcement as the student demonstrates success.

20.　Explain to the student why it is inappropriate to interrupt the teacher (e.g., is impolite, is unfair to other students, others cannot hear what the teacher is saying, etc.).

21.　Attempt to provide equal attention to all students in the classroom.

22.　Make the student aware of the number of times he/she interrupts the teacher.

23.　Do not criticize when correcting the student, be honest yet supportive. Never cause the student to feel badly about himself/herself.

24.　Talk to the student before beginning an activity and remind him/her of the importance of listening and not interrupting.

25. Treat the student with respect. Talk in an objective manner at all times.

26. Provide the student with a predetermined signal when he/she begins to display inappropriate manners.

27. Make certain the student knows when it is acceptable to interrupt others (e.g., in an emergency).

28. Acknowledge the student's presence and/or need to talk with you (e.g., by saying, "Just a minute"; putting your arm around the student; smiling and nodding your head; etc.).

29. Evaluate the appropriateness of the task to determine: (a) if the task is too difficult and (b) if the length of time scheduled to complete the task is appropriate.

30. Communicate with parents (e.g., notes home, phone calls, etc.) in order to share information concerning the student's appropriate behavior and so that they can reinforce the student at home for waiting his/her turn to speak at school.

31. Write a contract with the student specifying what behavior is expected (e.g., waiting for a turn to speak) and what reinforcement will be made available when the terms of the contract have been met. (See Appendix for Behavioral Contract.)

32. Remove the student from the group or activity until he/she can demonstrate appropriate behavior and self-control.

33. Reinforce the student for waiting for a turn to speak based on the length of time the student can be successful. Gradually increase the length of time required for reinforcement as the student demonstrates success.

34. Reinforce those students in the classroom who wait their turn to speak.

35. Establish classroom rules:
1. Work on task.
2. Remain in your seat.
3. Finish task.
4. Meet task expectations.
5. Raise your hand.
Reiterate rules often and reinforce students for following rules.

36. Speak with the student to explain: (a) what the student is doing wrong (e.g., interrupting the teacher) and (b) what the student should be doing (e.g., waiting until it is appropriate to speak, waiting to be called on, etc.).

37. Reinforce the student for waiting for a turn to speak: (a) give the student a tangible reward (e.g., classroom privileges, line leading, passing out materials, five minutes free time, etc.) or (b) give the student an intangible reward (e.g., praise, handshake, smile, etc.).

1. Communicate with parents, agencies, or appropriate parties in order to inform them of the problem, determine the cause of the problem, and consider possible solutions to the problem.

2. Record or chart attendance with the student.

3. Begin the day or class with a success-oriented activity which is likely to be enjoyable for the student.

4. Give the student a preferred responsibility to be performed at the beginning of each day or each class (e.g., feeding the classroom pet, helping to get the classroom ready for the day, etc.).

5. Reinforce the student for getting on the bus or leaving home on time.

6. Assess the degree of task difficulty in comparison with the student's ability to perform the task.

7. Provide the student with as many high-interest activities as possible.

8. Involve the student in extracurricular activities.

9. Provide the student with many social and academic successes.

10. Provide the student with academic activities presented in the most attractive and interesting manner possible.

11. Require the student's attendance to be documented by his/her teachers (e.g., have teachers sign an attendance card).

12. Interact with the student in a positive manner frequently throughout the day.

13. Collect anecdotal information on the student's absent behavior. If a trend can be determined, remove the student from the situation, modify the situation, or help the student develop the skills to be more successful in the situation.

14. Have the parent bring the student to school.

15. Have a responsible peer walk to school/class with the student.

16. Establish a time for the student to leave his/her home in the morning.

17. Require that time spent away from class/school be made up at recess, during lunch, or after school.

18. Have the student document personal attendance at the end of each school day (e.g., have the student maintain a record of attendance in the library, office, etc., and fill in the data at the end of each day).

19. Make certain the student is appropriately placed in those classes in which he/she is enrolled (e.g., the class is not too difficult).

20. Reduce the emphasis on competition. Repeated failure may cause the student to remove himself/herself from the competition by not attending school or class.

21. Help the student develop friendships which may encourage his/her attendance in school/class.

22. Maintain open communication with the student's family in order to make certain that the student is leaving for school at the designated time.

23. Do not force the student to interact with others or do things that make him/her uncomfortable and would cause the student to not want to come to school.

24. Make certain the student and parents are aware of the laws involving attendance in school.

25. Evaluate the appropriateness of the task to determine: (a) if the task is too difficult and (b) if the length of time scheduled to complete the task is appropriate.

26. Communicate with the parents (e.g., notes home, phone calls, etc.) in order to share information concerning the student's progress and so that they can reinforce the student at home for coming to school and class.

27. Write a contract with the student specifying what behavior is expected (e.g., being in attendance) and what reinforcement will be made available when the terms of the contract have been met. (See Appendix for Behavioral Contract.)

28. Reinforce those students who come to school/class.

29. Establish classroom rules:
1. Work on task.
2. Work quietly.
3. Remain in your seat.
4. Finish task.
5. Meet task expectations.

Reiterate rules often and reinforce students for following rules.

30. Speak with the student to explain: (a) what the student is doing wrong (e.g., being absent from school/class) and (b) what the student should be doing (e.g., being in attendance).

31. Reinforce the student for coming to school/class: (a) give the student a tangible reward (e.g., classroom privileges, line leading, passing out materials, five minutes free time, etc.) or (b) give the student an intangible reward (e.g., praise, handshake, smile, etc.).

1. Provide the student with a schedule of daily events in order that he/she will know which activities to attend and at what times. (See Appendix for Schedule of Daily Events.)

2. Make certain that the student's daily schedule follows an established routine.

3. Limit the number of interruptions in the student's schedule.

4. Make certain the student has adequate time to get to an activity.

5. Make certain that the student knows how to get from one activity to another.

6. Use a timer to help the student get to activities at specified times.

7. Give the student a specific responsibility to be performed at the beginning of each activity or class in order to encourage the student to be on time.

8. Provide the student with verbal cues when it is time to change activities (e.g., "It is time for the red group to have reading." "Now it is time for the red group to put away materials and move to the next activity." etc.).

9. Determine why the student is not arriving at activities at the specified times.

10. Ask the student the reason for not arriving at activities at the specified times. The student may have the most accurate perception as to why he/she is not arriving at activities at the specified times.

11. Help the student understand that it is permissible to leave work unfinished and return to it at a later time.

12. Determine if there are aspects of activities that the student dislikes. Remove, reduce, or modify the unpleasant aspects of activities in order to encourage the student to be on time for and participate in activities.

13. Make the student responsible for time missed (i.e., if the student misses five minutes of an activity, the time must be made up during recess, lunch, or other desired activities).

14. Have a peer accompany the student to activities.

15. Make certain that the student is successful in school-related activities. The student will be more likely to be on time for activities in which he/she experiences success.

16. Make the student a leader of the activity or group.

17. Make certain that other students do not make it unpleasant for the student to attend activities.

18. Make certain the student has all necessary materials for activities.

19. Record or chart promptness with the student.

20. Begin activities with a task that is highly reinforcing to the student.

21. Give the student a preferred responsibility to be performed at the beginning of each activity.

22. Assess the appropriateness of the degree of difficulty of the task in comparison with the student's ability to perform the task successfully.

23. Provide the student with as many high-interest activities as possible.

24. Provide the student with many social and academic successes.

25. Provide the student with academic activities presented in the most attractive manner possible.

26. Give the student a schedule of daily events to be signed by each teacher in order to document promptness. (See Appendix for Schedule of Daily Events.)

27. Collect anecdotal information on the student's behavior. If a trend can be determined, remove the student from the situation and/or help the student to be prompt.

28. Have the student document personal attendance at the end of each activity.

29. Make certain the student is appropriately placed according to ability level in those classes in which he/she is enrolled.

30. Reduce the emphasis on competition. Repeated failure may cause the student to avoid being on time for activities which are competitive.

31. Involve the student in extracurricular activities.

32. Interact with the student in a positive manner throughout the day.

33. Give the student a special responsibility for each morning (e.g., feeding the student classroom pet, helping to get the classroom ready for the day, etc.).

34. Maintain open communication with the student's family in order to make certain that the student is leaving for school at the designated time.

35. Do not force the student to interact with others or do things that make him/her uncomfortable and would cause the student to want to be late.

36. Begin each day with a fun activity which will cause the student to want to be on time for class.

37. Identify a peer to act as a model for the student to imitate arriving at an activity at the specified time.

38. Evaluate the appropriateness of the task to determine: (a) if the task is too difficult and (b) if the length of time scheduled to complete the task is appropriate.

39. Communicate with parents (e.g., notes home, phone calls, etc.) in order to share information concerning the student's progress and so that they can reinforce the student at home for coming to activities at the specified times at school.

40. Write a contract with the student specifying what behavior is expected (e.g., coming to school on time) and what reinforcement will be made available when the terms of the contract have been met. (See Appendix for Behavioral Contract.)

41. Reinforce the student for coming to an activity within a given period of time. Gradually reduce the length of time the student has to come to an activity as the student becomes more successful at being punctual.

42. Reinforce those students in the classroom who come to an activity at the specified time.

43. Establish classroom rules:
1. Come to class on time.
2. Work on task.
3. Work quietly.
4. Remain in your seat.
5. Finish task.
6. Meet task expectations.
Reiterate rules often and reinforce students for following rules.

44. Speak to the student to explain: (a) what the student is doing wrong (e.g., coming late to an activity) and (b) what the student should be doing (e.g., coming to an activity at the specified time).

45. Reinforce the student for coming to an activity at the specified time: (a) give the student a tangible reward (e.g., classroom privileges, line leading, passing out materials, five minutes free time, etc.) or (b) give the student an intangible reward (e.g., praise, handshake, smile, etc.).

144   Blames other persons or materials to avoid taking responsibility for his/her mistakes

1. Structure the environment for the student in order to reduce interference from peers (e.g., remove the opportunity to blame others).

2. Teach the student problem-solving skills: (a) identify the problem, (b) identify goals and objectives, (c) develop strategies, (d) develop a plan of action, and (e) carry out the plan.

3. Provide the student with as many social and academic successes as possible.

4. Make the necessary adjustments in the environment to prevent the student from experiencing stress, frustration, anger, etc.

5. Provide the student with positive feedback which indicates he/she is successful, competent, important, valuable, etc.

6. Make certain that excuses are not accepted in place of meeting responsibility.

7. Make certain that all materials are appropriate and in good working order.

8. Be certain to recognize the student when he/she indicates a need for help.

9. Provide the student with all necessary information prior to an activity in order to increase the likelihood of success.

10. Reduce stimuli in the environment which may contribute to the student's failures or difficulties.

11. Provide the student with a quiet place to work. This is used as a form of reducing distracting stimuli and not as a form of punishment.

12. Program assignments which will ensure initial success. Gradually increase the degree of difficulty of assignments as the student's ability and responsibility increases.

13. Make certain that instructions and expectations are clearly stated.

14. Reduce the emphasis on competition. Repeated failure may result in the student blaming someone or something for his/her own failure.

15. Encourage the student to begin assignments early in order to have time to deal with problems which may arise.

16. Provide the student with a schedule of daily events in order to plan his/her time accordingly. (See Appendix for Schedule of Daily Events.)

17. When the student blames others for his/her behavior, calmly confront the student with the facts. Encourage an open and honest line of communication. Do not make the student fearful of telling the truth even though you may not be happy about the behavior.

18. Help the student to feel comfortable coming to you for assistance with a problem by listening and helping with a solution to the problem.

19. Be consistent with the student. Do not discipline for misbehavior one time and ignore misbehavior the next time.

20. The student must understand that, regardless of the reason, it is necessary to take responsibility for not turning in math papers, losing pencils, etc.

21. Do not put the student in a situation where the student feels that he/she must blame others for his/her mistakes.

22. Attempt to have an open, honest relationship with the student. Encourage the student to tell the truth, and do not use threats to make him/her tell the truth (e.g., "You had better tell the truth or else!").

23. Avoid arguing with the student concerning whether or not he/she is making excuses; simply explain that he/she is not being completely honest about a situation.

24. Make certain that consequences delivered for inappropriate behavior are not extreme and are directly related to the inappropriate behavior (e.g., things that are destroyed must be replaced, work not done during work time has to be made up during recreational time, etc.).

25. Avoid arguing with the student concerning whether or not he/she is telling the truth. If you do not have proof, it is better to avoid blaming someone who might be innocent.

26. Always determine the accuracy of the student's claim that someone or something caused him/her to have a problem or to fail. In some cases someone or something may legitimately be causing the student to experience problems or failure.

27. Make certain the student understands that not being honest when confronted will result in more negative consequences than telling the truth. Be certain to be very consistent in this approach.

28. Explain to the student that he/she should be satisfied with personal best effort rather than perfection.

29. Evaluate the appropriateness of the task to determine: (a) if the task is too difficult and (b) if the length of time scheduled to complete the task is appropriate.

30. Communicate with parents (e.g., notes home, phone calls, etc.) in order to share information concerning the student's progress and so that they can reinforce the student at home for accepting the responsibility for his/her behavior at school.

31. Remove the student from the group or activity until the student can accept responsibility for his/her behavior.

32. Write a contract with the student specifying what behavior is expected (e.g., accepting responsibility for his/her own mistakes) and what reinforcement will be made available when the terms of the contract have been met. (See Appendix for Behavioral Contract.)

33. Reinforce the student for accepting responsibility for his/her own behavior based on the length of time the student can be successful. Gradually increase the length of time required for reinforcement as the student demonstrates success.

34. Reinforce those students in the classroom who accept responsibility for their own behavior.

35. Establish classroom rules:
1. Work on task.
2. Work quietly.
3. Remain in your seat.
4. Finish task.
5. Meet task expectations.
Reiterate rules often and reinforce students for following rules.

36. Speak with the student to explain: (a) what the student is doing wrong (e.g., failing to take responsibility for his/her behavior, blaming other persons or materials, etc.) and (b) what the student should be doing (e.g., accepting responsibility for his/her own behavior, accepting outcomes, etc.).

37. Reinforce the student for accepting responsibility for his/her own behavior: (a) give the student a tangible reward (e.g., classroom privileges, line leading, passing out materials, five minutes free time, etc.) or (b) give the student an intangible reward (e.g., praise, handshake, smile, etc.).

145 Does not participate in classroom activities or special events that are interesting to other students

1. Encourage or reward others for participation in group or special activities.

2. Give the student the responsibility of helping another student in the group.

3. Give the student responsibilities in a group in order that others might view him/her in a positive light.

4. Ask the student questions that cannot be answered "yes" or "no."

5. Call on the student when he/she is most likely to be able to respond successfully (e.g., when discussing something in which the student is interested, when the teacher is certain the student knows the answer, etc.).

6. Try various groupings in order to determine the situation in which the student is most successful.

7. Have peers invite the student to participate in school or extracurricular activities.

8. Request that the student be the leader of a small group activity if he/she possesses mastery or an interest in the activity.

9. Allow the student to be present during group activities without requiring active participation.

10. Reduce the emphasis on competition. Frequent or continuous failure is likely to result in embarrassment which will cause reluctance to participate.

11. Demonstrate respect for the student's opinions, responses, suggestions, etc.

12. Provide the student with many social and academic successes.

13. Provide the student with positive feedback which indicates he/she is successful.

14. Present tasks in the most attractive and interesting manner possible.

15. Determine the student's interests in order that activities which require participation might be presented through his/her interests.

16. Allow the student to choose a special event or interesting activity for the class.

17. Provide the student with success-oriented special events or activities in order that he/she may develop an interest in them.

18. Modify or adjust situations that cause the student to be reluctant to participate (e.g., degree of difficulty, competition, fear of failure, threat of embarrassment, etc.).

19. Emphasize individual success or progress rather than winning or "beating" other students.

20. Provide the student with opportunities for small group participation as opposed to large group participation.

21. Encourage the student to participate in small groups. Gradually increase group size as the student demonstrates success.

22. Encourage the student to share things of special interest with other members of the class.

23. Identify a peer to act as a model for the student to imitate appropriate interactions in classroom activities.

24. Have the student question any directions, explanations, and instructions not understood.

25. Allow the student to choose a group of peers with whom he/she feels comfortable.

26. Determine the peers the student would most prefer to interact with in classroom activities and attempt to facilitate the interaction.

27. Assign outgoing, nonthreatening peers to help the student participate in classroom activities.

28. Structure the environment so that the student has many opportunities to interact with other peers in classroom activities.

29. Assign the student to classroom activities in which he/she is likely to interact successfully with peers.

30. Conduct a sociometric activity with the class in order to determine those peers who would most prefer to interact with the student in classroom activities.

31. Teach the student appropriate ways to interact with peers in classroom activities (e.g., share materials, problem solve, take turns, converse, etc.).

32. Supervise classroom activities closely in order that peers with whom the student interacts do not stimulate inappropriate behavior.

33. Make certain that the classroom activity is not so stimulating as to make successful interactions with peers difficult.

34. Teach the student problem-solving skills in order to better deal with problems that may occur in interactions with peers in classroom activities (e.g., talking, walking away, calling upon an arbitrator, compromising, etc.).

35. Limit opportunities for interaction in classroom activities on those occasions when the student is not likely to be successful (e.g., when the student has experienced academic or social failure prior to the scheduled classroom activity).

36. Select nonacademic activities designed to enhance appropriate social interaction of the student and peers during classroom activities (e.g., board games, model building, coloring, etc.).

37. Treat the student with respect. Talk in an objective manner at all times.

38. Through interviews with other students and observations, determine those characteristics of the student which interfere with successful interactions during classroom activities. Use information gained to determine skills or behaviors the student needs to develop for successful interactions.

39. Have the student practice appropriate interactions with the teacher(s) in classroom activities (e.g., stimulations, role-playing, etc.).

40. Make certain, beforehand, that the student is able to successfully engage in the classroom activity (e.g., the student understands the rules, is familiar with the activity, will be compatible with peers engaged in the activity, etc.).

41. Make certain the student has the necessary materials for the classroom activity.

42. Assign the student responsibilities to perform during classroom activities in order to enhance peer interaction (e.g., being a leader, passing out materials, acting as a peer tutor, etc.).

43. Make certain the student knows how to use all materials for the classroom activity.

44. Do not punish the student for not participating in classroom activities or special events.

45. Do not force the student to interact with someone with whom he/she is not completely comfortable.

46. Be careful to avoid embarrassing the student by giving him/her orders, demands, etc., in front of others.

47. Make positive comments about participating in school and special events.

48. Do not force the student to interact with others.

49. Go with the student or have someone else accompany the student to those things he/she may not want to participate in. Gradually decrease the length of time you or someone else stays with the student.

50. Carefully consider those things the student does not want to participate in. If something unpleasant is causing the student to not participate, do all you can to change the situation.

51. Assign a peer to sit/work directly with the student (e.g., in different settings or activities such as art, music, P.E., tutoring, group projects, recess, etc.). Gradually increase group size when the student has become comfortable working with one other student.

52. Evaluate the appropriateness of the task to determine: (a) if the task is too difficult and (b) if the length of time scheduled to complete the task is appropriate.

53. Communicate with parents (e.g., notes home, phone calls, etc.) in order to share information concerning the student's progress and so that they can reinforce the student at home for participating in group activities or special events at school.

54. Write a contract with the student specifying what behavior is expected (e.g., taking part in group activities) and what reinforcement will be made available when the terms of the contract have been met. (See Appendix for Behavioral Contract.)

55. Reinforce other students in the classroom for participating in group activities or special events.

56. Establish classroom rules:
1. Work on task.
2. Work quietly.
3. Remain in your seat.
4. Finish task.
5. Meet task expectations.
Reiterate rules often and reinforce students for following rules.

57. Speak with the student to explain: (a) what the student is doing wrong (e.g., failing to take part) and (b) what the student should be doing (e.g., talking, taking turns, playing, sharing, etc.).

58. Reinforce the student for participating in group activities or special events: (a) give the student a tangible reward (e.g., classroom privileges, line leading, passing out materials, five minutes free time, etc.) or (b) give the student an intangible reward (e.g., praise, handshake, smile, etc.).

A Reminder: Do not "force" the student to take part in any activity or special event.

146 Blames self for situations beyond his/her control

1. Reinforce the student for improvement rather than expecting excellence.

2. Recognize the student often and in various settings (e.g., hallways, cafeteria, etc.).

3. Provide the student with positive feedback which indicates he/she is successful, competent, important, valuable, etc.

4. Provide the student with success-oriented tasks (i.e., the expectation is that success will result in more positive attitudes and perceptions toward self and environment).

5. Provide the student with as many social and academic successes as possible.

6. Make the necessary adjustments in the environment to prevent the student from experiencing stress, frustration, etc.

7. Assign a peer to help the student with class assignments, homework, etc.

8. Emphasize individual differences and the fact that everyone has strengths and weaknesses.

9. Reduce emphasis on competition and perfection. Repeated failure may result in unwarranted self-blame or self-criticism.

10. Encourage the student to refrain from comparing his/her performance to other students' performances, and emphasize personal improvement (e.g., maintain records of own progress rather than comparing work to others).

11. Provide the student with evidence of his/her ability in order that the student might better understand that self-blame/self-criticism is unwarranted.

12. Have the student regularly record his/her own progress in order to have tangible evidence of success.

13. Deliver praise and constructive criticism consistently to all students.

14. When accidents occur, make "cleanup" a group responsibility in order to convey the idea that we all make mistakes and accidents are common to all of us.

15. Call on the student when he/she will most likely be able to answer correctly.

16. Encourage the student to act as a peer tutor in order that the student may recognize his/her own strengths and abilities.

17. Reduce activities which might threaten the student (e.g., announcing test score ranges or test scores aloud, making students read aloud in class, emphasizing the success of a particular student(s), etc.).

18. Intervene early when there is a problem in order to prevent more serious problems from occurring.

19. Reduce or remove punishment for accidents or situations with inadequate evidence. Placing too much emphasis on uncontrollable situations may cause the student to feel guilty.

20. Encourage the student to use problem-solving skills: (a) identify the problem, (b) identify goals and objectives, (c) develop strategies, (d) develop a plan of action, and (e) carry out the plan.

21. Evaluate the appropriateness of the task to determine: (a) if the task is too difficult and (b) if the length of time scheduled to complete the task is appropriate.

22. Write a contract with the student specifying what behavior is expected (e.g., accepting his/her own best effort) and what reinforcement will be made available when the terms of the contract have been met. (See Appendix for Behavioral Contract.)

23. Reward others for accepting errors they make.

24. Speak with the student to explain: (a) what the student is doing wrong (e.g., being overly critical of himself/herself) and (b) what the student should be doing (e.g., being more constructive in self-criticism when evaluating himself/herself).

25. Reinforce the student for accepting errors that he/she makes.

26. Explain to the student that he/she should be happy with personal best effort rather than expecting perfection.

A Reminder: Make certain that the self-blame or self-criticism is in fact unwarranted.

147 Indicates concern regarding problems or situations in the home or in out-of-school situations

1. Discuss concerns with other professionals to determine if further investigation is warranted (e.g., abuse, neglect).

2. Record or chart the number of times the student expresses concerns or worries about school or home in order to make the student aware of the frequency of his/her behavior.

3. Evaluate the appropriateness of the task to determine: (a) if the task is too difficult and (b) if the length of time scheduled to complete the task is appropriate.

4. Take the time to listen so the student realizes that your concern is genuine.

5. Explain that concerns or worries, while legitimate, are not unusual for students (e.g., everyone worries about tests, grades, etc.).

6. Identify persons the student may contact with worries or concerns (e.g., guidance counselor, school nurse, social worker, school psychologist, etc.).

7. Discuss ways in which to practice self-improvement.

8. Provide the student with opportunities for social and academic success.

9. Separate the student from a peer who may be encouraging or stimulating inappropriate behavior.

10. Provide praise and recognition as often as possible.

11. Encourage participation in school and extra-curricular activities.

12. Provide opportunities for tutoring from peers or a teacher.

13. Reduce the emphasis on competition. Repeated failure may heighten anxiety about performance.

14. Provide parents with necessary information to help the student with homework and study activities at home.

15. Try various groupings in order to determine the situation in which the student is most successful.

16. Make the necessary adjustments in the environment to prevent the student from experiencing stress, frustration, anxiety, etc.

17. Structure the environment in such a way that time does not permit opportunities for the student to dwell on concerns or worries.

18. Have peers invite the student to participate in extracurricular activities.

19. Demonstrate respect for the student's opinions, responses, suggestions, etc.

20. Provide the student with alternative approaches to testing (e.g., test the student orally, make tests shorter, allow the student to respond orally, allow the student to take the test in the resource room, etc.).

21. Assign a peer to sit/work directly with the student.

22. Call attention to the student's accomplishments (e.g., publicly or privately depending on which is more appropriate).

23. Avoid discussion of topics sensitive to the student (e.g., divorce, death, unemployment, alcoholism, etc.).

24. Provide the student with opportunities for special project responsibilities, leadership, etc.

25. Provide as many enjoyable and interesting activities as possible.

26. Seek assistance from the school counselors, the principal, other teachers, etc., to help the student learn to deal with personal problems so he/she can concentrate at school.

27. Treat the student with respect. Talk in an objective manner at all times.

28. Maintain trust and confidentiality with the student at all times.

29. Encourage the student to use problem-solving skills: (a) identify the problem, (b) identify goals and objectives, (c) develop strategies, (d) develop a plan of action, and (e) carry out the plan.

A Reminder: Do not "force" the student to participate in any activity.

1. Conduct a reinforcer survey with the student in order to determine his/her reinforcer preferences. (See Appendix for Reinforcer Survey.)

2. Communicate with parents in order to determine what the student finds reinforcing at home.

3. Make an agreement with the parents in order that enjoyable activities at home (e.g., watching television, riding a bike, visiting with friends, etc.) are contingent upon appropriate behavior at school.

4. Write a contract with the student in order that he/she can earn reinforcement at home for appropriate behavior at school. (See Appendix for Behavioral Contract.)

5. Make certain that the student can be successful at school in order to earn reinforcement.

6. Provide a wide variety of reinforcers for the student at school (e.g., eating lunch with the teacher, one-to-one time with the teacher, principal's assistant, assistant to the custodian, extra time in a favorite class, etc.).

7. Present tasks in the most attractive and interesting manner possible.

8. Communicate with parents, agencies, or appropriate parties in order to inform them of the problem, determine the cause of the problem, and consider solutions to the problem.

9. Provide reinforcers that are social in nature (e.g., extracurricular activities; clubs; community organizations such as 4-H, scouting, YMCA; etc.).

10. Help the student develop an interest in a hobby which can be used as a reinforcer at school (e.g., stamp collecting, rock collecting, model building, photography, art, reading, sewing, cooking, etc.).

11. Reinforce or praise the student in private. Public reinforcement might embarrass the student.

12. Have the student make a list of reinforcements which he/she is willing to work for.

149 Becomes upset when a suggestion or constructive criticism is given

1. Reinforce the student for responding in an appropriate manner to constructive criticism based on the number of times the student can be successful. Gradually increase the number of times required for reinforcement as the student demonstrates success.

2. Remove the student from the group or activity until he/she can demonstrate appropriate behavior or self-control.

3. Write a contract with the student specifying what behavior is expected (e.g., responding appropriately to constructive criticism) and what reinforcement will be made available when the terms of the contract have been met. (See Appendix for Behavioral Contract.)

4. Communicate with the parents (e.g., notes home, phone calls, etc.) in order to share information concerning the student's progress and so that they can reinforce the student at home for responding in an appropriate manner to constructive criticism at school.

5. Evaluate the appropriateness of the task to determine: (a) if the task is too difficult and (b) if the length of time scheduled for the task is appropriate.

6. Demonstrate appropriate ways to respond to constructive criticism.

7. Try various groupings in order to determine the situation in which the student is most comfortable.

8. Provide the student with positive feedback which indicates he/she is successful, competent, important, valuable, etc.

9. Provide the student with many social and academic successes.

10. Assess the appropriateness of the social situation in relation to the student's ability to function successfully.

11. Structure the environment in such a way that the teacher is the only one providing constructive criticism. As the student learns to accept constructive criticism from the teacher, allow input from others.

12. Provide constructive criticism in private.

13. Provide constructive criticism equally to all members of the class.

14. Provide constructive criticism when the student is most likely to demonstrate an appropriate response.

15. Make certain that positive reinforcement is not inadvertently given for inappropriate behavior (e.g., lowering expectations because the student becomes upset when criticism is delivered).

16. Make certain the student receives adequate, positive reinforcement whenever he/she is behaving in an appropriate manner.

17. Assess criticism to make certain it is constructive and positive.

18. Have the student question anything he/she does not understand while performing assignments.

19. Encourage the student to check and correct his/her own work.

20. Explain to the student that constructive criticism is meant to be helpful, not threatening.

21. Reduce the emphasis on competition and perfection. A highly competitive atmosphere or repeated failure may cause the student to react in inappropriate ways to constructive criticism from others.

22. Make the necessary adjustments in the environment to prevent the student from experiencing stress, frustration, anger, etc.

23. Provide the student with academic tasks which can be self-checked.

24. Supervise the student while he/she is performing tasks in order to monitor quality.

25. Provide the student with clearly stated criteria for acceptable work.

26. Make certain that constructive criticism is tactfully conveyed.

27. Make certain that an offer of assistance is made at the same time constructive criticism is delivered.

28. Require a demonstration of ability rather than having the student perform the entire assignment or activity again (e.g., work a few problems correctly rather than repeating the entire assignment).

29. Identify a peer to act as a model for the student to imitate appropriate responses to constructive criticism.

30. Have the student question any directions, explanations, and instructions not understood.

31. Allow natural consequences to occur when the student fails to respond appropriately to constructive criticism (e.g., make highly reinforcing activities contingent upon responding appropriately to redirection in academic and social situations).

32. Make certain that attention is not inadvertently given to the student for failing to respond appropriately to constructive criticism (i.e., remove attention from the student when he/she fails to respond appropriately to redirection in academic and social situations in those instances when attention is reinforcing inappropriate behavior).

33. Provide adequate time for the student to respond appropriately to constructive criticism.

34. Deliver instructions in a clear and concise manner.

35. Assist the student in responding appropriately to constructive criticism (e.g., help the student correct one or two items in order to get him/her started).

36. Develop subsequent tasks to be performed the next day based on errors the student makes rather than requiring immediate correction of work done incorrectly.

37. Do not criticize when correcting the student; be honest yet supportive. Never cause the student to feel badly about himself/herself.

38. Intervene early when there is a problem in order to prevent more serious problems from occurring.

39. Treat the student with respect. Talk in an objective manner at all times.

40. Be careful to avoid embarrassing the student by giving him/her orders, demands, etc., in front of others.

41. Allow the student to attempt something new in private before doing so in front of others.

42. Provide constructive criticism in a private setting rather than in front of others.

43. Make certain that your comments take the form of constructive criticism rather than criticism that can be perceived as personal, threatening, etc. (e.g., instead of saying, "You always make the same mistakes." say, "A better way to do that might be . . .").

44. Reinforce those students in the classroom who respond appropriately to constructive criticism.

45. Establish classroom rules:
1. Work on task.
2. Work quietly.
3. Remain in your seat.
4. Finish task.
5. Meet task expectations.
Reiterate rules often and reinforce students for following rules.

46. Speak with the student to explain: (a) what the student is doing wrong (e.g., yelling, cursing, making derogatory comments, crying, etc.) and (b) what the student should be doing (e.g., asking for directions, help, clarification, etc.).

47. Reinforce the student for responding in an appropriate manner to constructive criticism: (a) give the student a tangible reward (e.g., classroom privileges, line leading, passing out materials, five minutes free time, etc.) or (b) give the student an intangible reward (e.g., praise, handshake, smile, etc.).

150 Tries to avoid situations, assignments, responsibilities

1. Identify a peer to act as a model for the student to imitate appropriate participation, performance of assignments, or acceptance of responsibilities.

2. Have the student question any directions, explanations, and instructions not understood.

3. Give the student assignments and responsibilities he/she will enjoy performing (e.g., teacher assistant, line leading, chores in the classroom, etc.). Gradually introduce less desirable assignments and responsibilities as the student demonstrates success.

4. Follow a less desirable activity with a more desirable activity, requiring the student to complete the first in order to perform the second.

5. Make certain the student understands that leaving the classroom may only be done at regularly scheduled intervals (e.g., during recess, break time, lunch, class changes, etc.).

6. Provide the student with many academic and social successes.

7. Assess the appropriateness of the social setting in relation to the student's ability to function successfully (i.e., do not place the student with peers who are threatening to him/her).

8. Program alternative activities for the student to perform or engage in if he/she has difficulty performing assigned activities. Gradually remove the alternative activities as the student demonstrates success.

9. Allow the student to leave the classroom to get materials from his/her locker, use the restroom, go to the nurse's office, go to the counselor's office, etc., after assignments are completed or responsibilities are fulfilled.

10. Provide the student with positive feedback that indicates he/she is successful, competent, important, valuable, etc.

11. Have the student record and chart his/her own appropriate behavior (e.g., participating in classroom activities, performing assignments, taking care of responsibilities, etc.).

12. Make certain that reinforcement is not inadvertently given for complaints of physical discomfort (e.g., allowing the student to leave the room, avoid assignments, leave school, etc.).

13. Seek student input in planning the curriculum, extracurricular activities, etc.

14. Reduce the emphasis on competition. Repeated failure may cause the student to avoid situations, assignments, or responsibilities.

15. Provide the student with a selection of assignments and require the student to choose a minimum number from the total amount (e.g., present the student with ten academic tasks from which six must be finished each day).

16. Explain to the student that work not done during work time must be done during other times (e.g., recreational time, break time, after school, etc.).

17. Give the student a preferred responsibility to be performed at various times throughout the day.

18. Present assignments and responsibilities in the most attractive and interesting manner possible.

19. Interact frequently with the student in order to maintain his/her involvement in assignments, responsibilities, etc.

20. Make the necessary adjustments in the environment to prevent the student from experiencing stress, frustration, anger, etc., as much as possible.

21. Allow the student to attempt something new in private before doing so in front of others.

22. Identify variables in the environment which cause the student to avoid situations, assignments, or responsibilities; and reduce or remove these variables from the environment.

23. Vary the student's assignments and responsibilities in order that the student does not get tired of doing the same things.

24. Limit the number of assignments and responsibilities for which the student is responsible and gradually increase the number as the student demonstrates the ability to get things done on time.

25. Make certain the student has all the necessary materials in order to get assignments and responsibilities done on time.

26. Do not accept excuses. The student must understand that, regardless of the reasons, it is necessary that he/she takes responsibility for not turning in a math assignment, losing pencils, etc.

27. Carefully consider those things the student may be trying to avoid. If something unpleasant is causing the student to pretend to be sick, do all you can to change the situation.

28. Give the student a special job to do after completing his/her work (e.g., collecting math papers, passing out materials, sharpening pencils, etc.).

29. Deliver directions in a supportive rather than threatening manner (e.g., "Please turn in your math paper." rather than "You had better turn in your math paper or else!").

30. Sit down with the student and discuss a list of assignments, responsibilities, etc., that he/she needs to do.

31. Assist the student in performing responsibilities. Gradually require the student to independently assume more responsibility as he/she demonstrates success.

32. Schedule the student's work and responsibilities around highly enjoyable activities (e.g., the student may go to recess after the math assignment is finished).

33. Go with the student or have someone else accompany the student to those things he/she may be trying to avoid. Gradually decrease the length of time you or someone else stays with the student.

34. Make positive comments about school and the importance of school.

35. Set aside time each day for everyone in the classroom to care for belongings.

36. Evaluate the appropriateness of the task to determine: (a) if the task is too difficult and (b) if the length of time scheduled to complete the task is appropriate.

37. Communicate with parents, agencies, or appropriate parties in order to inform them of the problem, determine the cause of the problem, and consider possible solutions to the problem.

38. Communicate with parents (e.g., notes home, phone calls, etc.) in order to share information concerning the student's progress and so that they can reinforce the student at home for appropriate behavior at school.

39. Write a contract with the student specifying what behavior is expected (e.g., participating, performing assignments, or taking responsibilities) and what reinforcement will be made available when the terms of the contract have been met. (See Appendix for Behavioral Contract.)

40. Reinforce the student for participating, performing assignments, or taking responsibilities based on the length of time the student can be successful. Gradually increase the length of time required for reinforcement as the student demonstrates success.

41. Reinforce those students in the classroom who are participating, performing assignments, or taking responsibilities.

42. Speak to the student to explain: (a) what he/she is doing wrong (e.g., complaining, asking to leave the room, etc.) and (b) what he/she should be doing (e.g., reporting legitimate discomfort or needs).

43. Establish classroom rules:
1. Work on task.
2. Work quietly.
3. Remain in your seat.
4. Finish task.
5. Meet task expectations.

Reiterate rules often and reinforce students for following rules.

44. Determine if physical discomfort is being used as an excuse to escape situations and that it is not the result of a medical problem, neglect, or abuse.

45. Reinforce the student for participating, performing assignments, or taking responsibilities: (a) give the student a tangible reward (e.g., classroom privileges, line leading, passing out materials, five minutes free time, etc.) or (b) give the student an intangible reward (e.g., praise, handshake, smile, etc.).

A Reminder: Do not "force" the student to participate in any activity.

151 Demonstrates self-destructive behavior

1. Remove the student from the group or activity until he/she can demonstrate appropriate behavior and self-control.

2. Write a contract with the student specifying what behavior is expected (e.g., not engaging in self-destructive behavior) and what reinforcement will be made available when the terms of the contract have been met. (See Appendix for Behavioral Contract.)

3. Communicate with parents (e.g., notes home, phone calls, etc.) in order to share information concerning the student's progress and so that they can reinforce the student at home for appropriate behavior at school.

4. Evaluate the appropriateness of the task to determine: (a) if the task is too difficult and (b) if the length of time scheduled to complete the task is appropriate.

5. Prevent frustrating or anxiety-producing situations from occurring (e.g., give the student tasks on his/her ability level, give the student only the number of tasks that can be tolerated in one sitting, stop social situations which stimulate the student to become self-destructive, etc.).

6. Interact frequently with the student to prevent self-destructive behavior by meeting the student's needs as they occur.

7. Maintain visibility to and from the student. The teacher should be able to see the student and the student should be able to see the teacher, making eye contact possible at all times.

8. Facilitate on-task behavior by providing a full schedule of daily events. Prevent lag time from occurring when the student will be free to engage in self-destructive behavior. (See Appendix for Schedule of Daily Events.)

9. Remove from the environment any object which the student may use to hurt himself/herself.

10. Provide the student with a quiet place to work (e.g., carrel, study area).

11. Provide the student with positive feedback which indicates he/she is successful, important, respected, etc.

12. Maintain a positive/calm environment (e.g., deliver positive comments, acknowledgment of successes, quiet communications, etc.).

13. Reduce the emphasis on competition. Repeated failure may result in anger and frustration which may cause the student to try to hurt himself/herself.

14. Maintain consistency in expectations in order to reduce the likelihood of the student hurting himself/herself.

15. Allow the student to have an input relative to making decisions (e.g., changing activities, choosing activities, deciding length of activities, etc.).

16. Provide the student with a selection of optional activities to be performed (e.g., if an activity results in self-destructive behaviors, an optional activity can be substituted).

17. Teach the student appropriate ways to deal with anxiety, frustration, and anger (e.g., move away from the stimulus, verbalize unhappiness, choose another activity, etc.).

18. Teach the student problem-solving skills: (a) identify the problem, (b) identify goals and objectives, (c) develop strategies, (d) develop a plan of action, and (e) carry out the plan.

19. Maintain consistency in daily routine.

20. Avoid discussions or prevent stimuli in the environment which remind the student of unpleasant experiences/sensitive topics (e.g., divorce, death, unemployment, alcoholism, etc.).

21. Do not criticize. When correcting the student, be honest yet supportive. Never cause the student to feel badly about himself/herself.

22. Intervene early when there is a problem in order to prevent more serious problems from occurring.

23. Make certain the student does not become involved in overstimulating activities.

24. Treat the student with respect. Talk in an objective manner at all times.

25. Teach the student acceptable ways to communicate displeasure, anger, frustrations, etc.

26. Make sure you express your feelings in a socially acceptable way.

27. Teach the student to think before acting (e.g., ask himself/herself: "What is happening?" "What am I doing?" "What should I do?" "What will be best for me?").

28. Make certain the student is allowed to voice an opinion in a situation in order to avoid becoming angry or upset.

29. Talk to the student about ways of handling situations successfully without conflict (e.g., walk away from a situation, change to another activity, ask for help, etc.).

30. Reinforce the student for demonstrating appropriate behavior based on the length of time the student can be successful. Gradually increase the amount of time required for reinforcement as the student demonstrates success.

31. Reinforce those students in the classroom who engage in appropriate behaviors.

32. Establish classroom rules:
1. Work on task.
2. Work quietly.
3. Remain in your seat.
4. Finish task.
5. Meet task expectations.

Reiterate rules often and reinforce students for following rules.

33. Speak with the student to explain: (a) what the student is doing wrong (e.g., hurting self) and (b) what the student should be doing (e.g., talking about the situation, demonstrating self-control, problem solving, etc.).

34. Reinforce the student for engaging in appropriate behavior: (a) give the student a tangible reward (e.g., classroom privileges, line leading, passing out materials, five minutes free time, etc.) or (b) give the student an intangible reward (e.g., praise, handshake, smile, etc.).

NOTE: Help the student accept the fact that self-improvement is more important than getting the highest grade in the class, making all A's, being the first one finished with an assignment, etc., by reinforcing and grading on the basis of self-improvement.

1. Remove the student from the group or activity until he/she can demonstrate appropriate behavior and self-control.

2. Communicate with parents (e.g., notes home, phone calls, etc.) in order to share information concerning the student's progress and so that they can reinforce the student at home for appropriate behavior at school.

3. Evaluate the appropriateness of the task to determine: (a) if the task is too difficult and (b) if the length of time scheduled to complete the task is appropriate.

4. Prevent frustrating or anxiety-producing situations from occurring (e.g., give the student tasks on his/her ability level, give the student only the number of tasks that can be tolerated in one sitting, stop social interactions that stimulate the student to threaten self-harm, etc.).

5. Interact frequently with the student to prevent self-abusive behavior by meeting the student's needs as they occur.

6. Maintain visibility to and from the student. The teacher should be able to see the student and the student should be able to see the teacher, making eye contact possible at all times.

7. Facilitate on-task behavior by providing a full schedule of daily events. Prevent lag time from occurring when the student will be free to engage in self-abusive behavior. (See Appendix for Schedule of Daily Events.)

8. Remove from the environment any object that the student may use to hurt himself/herself.

9. Provide the student with positive feedback that indicates he/she is successful, important, respected, etc.

10. Maintain a positive/calm environment (e.g., positive comments, acknowledgment of successes, quiet communications, etc.).

11. Provide the student with a quiet place to work (e.g., carrel, study area).

12. Reduce the emphasis on competition. Repeated failure may result in anger and frustration that may cause the student to try to hurt himself/herself.

13. Maintain consistency in expectations.

14. Allow the student to have input relative to making decisions (e.g., changing activities, choosing activities, deciding length of activities, etc.).

15. Provide the student with a selection of optional activities to be performed (e.g., if an activity results in harmful behaviors, an optional activity can be substituted).

16. Teach the student appropriate ways to deal with anxiety, frustration, and anger (e.g., move away from the stimulus, verbalize unhappiness, choose another activity, etc.).

17. Teach the student problem-solving skills: (a) identify the problem, (b) identify goals and objectives, (c) develop strategies, (d) develop a plan of action, and (e) carry out the plan.

18. Maintain consistency in the daily routine.

19. Do not allow the student to be unsupervised anywhere in the school environment.

20. Avoid discussions or prevent stimuli in the environment that remind the student of unpleasant experiences/sensitive topics (e.g., divorce, death, unemployment, alcoholism, etc.).

21. Do not criticize. When correcting the student, be honest yet supportive. Never cause the student to feel badly about himself/herself.

22. Intervene early when there is a problem in order to prevent more serious problems from occurring.

23. Treat the student with respect. Talk in an objective manner at all times.

24. Maintain trust and confidentiality with the student at all times.

25. Make certain the student is allowed to voice an opinion in a situation in order to avoid becoming angry or upset.

26. Talk to the student about ways of handling situations successfully without conflict (e.g., walk away from a situation, change to another activity, ask for help, etc.).

27. Reinforce the student for demonstrating appropriate behavior based on the length of time the student can be successful. Gradually increase the amount of time required for reinforcement as the student demonstrates success.

28. Reinforce those students in the classroom who engage in appropriate behavior.

29. Establish classroom rules:
1. Work on task.
2. Work quietly.
3. Remain in your seat.
4. Finish task.
5. Meet task expectations.
Reiterate rules often and reinforce students for following rules.

30. Speak with the student to explain: (a) what the student is doing wrong (e.g., threatening to hurt self) and (b) what the student should be doing (e.g., talking about the situation, demonstrating self-control, problem solving, etc.)

31. Reinforce the student for engaging in appropriate behavior: (a) give the student a tangible reward (e.g., classroom privileges, line leading, passing out materials, five minutes free time, etc.) or (b) give the student an intangible reward (e.g., praise, handshake, smile, etc.).

NOTE: All references to suicide should be considered serious, and steps should be taken to respond to the situation.

1. Provide the student with as many academic and social successes as possible in order that peers may view him/her in a more positive way.

2. Make the necessary adjustments in the environment to prevent the student from experiencing stress, frustration, anger, etc.

3. Assign additional responsibilities to the student (e.g., chores, errands, etc.) to give him/ her a feeling of success or accomplishment.

4. Structure the environment so that the student does not have time to dwell on real or imagined problems.

5. Take the time to listen in order for the student to realize your concern and interest.

6. Identify for the student more appropriate ways to express his/her feelings.

7. Reduce stimuli that contribute to the student's verbal expression of unhappiness (e.g., seek input from the student as to what upsets him/her).

8. Separate the student from the peer(s) who stimulates the verbal expression of unhappiness.

9. Try various groupings in order to determine the situation in which the student is most comfortable.

10. Encourage the student to participate in extracurricular activities that will help develop those skills necessary to interact appropriately with others at school.

11. Make certain that reinforcement (e.g., getting attention, getting his/her way, etc.) is not inadvertently given for verbal expressions of unhappiness.

12. Provide the student with alternative activities to perform in case some activities prove upsetting.

13. Reduce the emphasis on competition. Repeated failure may cause the student to feel that others do not like or care about him/her.

14. Reinforce those students in the classroom who deal with unhappiness in an appropriate manner.

15. Encourage and help the student to make friends (e.g., pair the student with a peer; when that relationship is successful, introduce other students).

16. When natural consequences occur as a result of the student's displays of unhappiness, point them out to him/her (e.g., peers prefer not to interact with the student).

17. Provide the student with as many positive interactions as possible (e.g., recognize the student, greet the student, compliment attire, etc.).

18. Discourage the student from engaging in those activities that cause him/her unhappiness.

19. Help the student identify things he/she wishes were in the environment, and work with the student toward those goals.

20. Teach the student alternative ways to deal with unpleasant social interactions during the school-age experience (e.g., deal with problems when they arise, practice self-control at all times, share problems or concerns with others, etc.).

21. Teach the student alternative ways to communicate unhappiness (e.g., in writing, by talking, etc.).

22. Speak with the student to explain that he/she may be trying too hard to fit in and that he/she should relax and allow friendships to develop naturally.

23. Reinforce those students in the classroom who appropriately interact with other students.

24. Have the student be the leader of a small-group activity if he/she possesses mastery of skills or an interest in that area.

25. Give the student the responsibility of tutoring a peer if he/she possesses the skills to be shared.

26. Provide the student with a predetermined signal (e.g., verbal cue, hand signal, etc.) when he/she begins to demonstrate inappropriate behaviors when interacting with others (e.g., whining, fighting, throwing objects, refusing to share, etc.).

27. Maintain maximum supervision of the student's interactions and gradually decrease the amount of supervision over time.

28. Give the student responsibilities in group situations in order that peers may view the student in a more positive way.

29. Encourage the student to further develop any ability or skill he/she may have in order that peers may view the student in a more positive way.

30. Help the student to identify his/her inappropriate behaviors and teach the student ways to change those behaviors.

31. Ask the student to choose a peer to work with on a specific assignment. Encourage the student and peer to interact with each other in nonacademic areas (e.g., recess, lunch, break time, etc.).

32. Do not criticize. When correcting the student, be honest yet supportive. Never cause the student to feel badly about himself/herself.

33. Do not force the student to interact with students with whom he/she is not completely comfortable.

34. Treat the student with respect. Talk in an objective manner at all times.

35. Allow the student to attempt something new in private before doing so in front of others.

36. Do not assume that the student is being treated nicely by other students. Others may be stimulating inappropriate behavior on the part of the student.

37. Encourage the student to interact with others.

38. Provide the student with frequent opportunities to meet new people.

39. Do not force the student to interact with others.

40. Make certain the student is not demonstrating a lack of confidence to get the attention of others.

41. Teach the student problem-solving skills: (a) identify the problem, (b) identify goals and objectives, (c) develop strategies, (d) develop a plan of action, and (e) carry out the plan.

42. Record or chart the number of times the student verbally expresses that others do not like or care about him/her in order to make the student aware of the frequency.

43. Communicate with parents (e.g., notes home, phone calls, etc.) in order to share information concerning the student's progress and so that they can reinforce the student at home for interacting appropriately with others at school.

44. Write a contract with the student specifying what behavior is expected (e.g., interacting appropriately with others) and what reinforcement will be made available when the terms of the contract have been met. (See Appendix for Behavioral Contract.)

45. Remove the student from the group until he/she can interact appropriately with others.

46. Reinforce the student for interacting with others based on the length of time the student can be successful. Gradually increase the length of time required for reinforcement as the student demonstrates success.

47. Reinforce those students in the classroom who make positive, supportive comments to the student.

48. Establish classroom rules:
  1. Work on task.
  2. Work quietly.
  3. Remain in your seat.
  4. Finish task.
  5. Meet task expectations.
Reiterate rules often and reinforce students for following rules.

49. Reinforce the student for interacting with others: (a) give the student a tangible reward (e.g., classroom privileges, line leading, passing out materials, five minutes free time, etc.) or (b) give the student an intangible reward (e.g., praise, handshake, smile, etc.).

A Reminder: Do not "force" the student to interact with others with whom he/she is uncomfortable.

1. Make certain that consequences are delivered consistently for behavior demonstrated (e.g., appropriate behavior results in positive consequences and inappropriate behavior results in negative consequences).

2. Provide the student with many social and academic successes.

3. Structure the environment in such a way as to limit opportunities for inappropriate behavior (e.g., keep the student engaged in activities, have the student seated near the teacher, maintain visibility to and from the student, etc.).

4. Prevent the student from becoming overstimulated by an activity (e.g., monitor or supervise student behavior to limit overexcitement in physical activities, games, parties, etc.).

5. Provide the student with natural consequences for inappropriate behavior (e.g., for disturbing others during group activities, the student should have to leave the activity).

6. Provide the student with a clearly identified list of consequences for inappropriate behavior.

7. Teach the student problem-solving skills: (a) identify the problem, (b) identify goals and objectives, (c) develop strategies, (d) develop a plan of action, and (e) carry out the plan.

8. Clarify for the student that it is his/her behavior which determines consequences (e.g., positive or negative).

9. Provide a learning experience which emphasizes the cause-and-effect relationship between behavior and the inevitability of some form of consequence (e.g., both negative and positive behaviors and consequences).

10. Point out the consequences of other students' behavior as they occur (e.g., take the opportunity to point out that consequences occur for all behavior and for all persons).

11. Call on the student when he/she can answer successfully.

12. Supervise the student closely in situations in which he/she is likely to act impulsively (e.g., maintain close physical proximity, maintain eye contact, communicate frequently with the student, etc.).

13. Prevent peers from engaging in those behaviors which would cause the student to fail to consider or regard the consequences of his/her behavior (e.g., keep other students from upsetting the student).

14. Make the consequence of a behavior obvious by identifying the consequence as it occurs and discussing alternative behavior which would have prevented the particular consequence.

15. Avoid competition. Failure may cause the student to ignore consequences of his/her behavior.

16. Allow the student more decision-making opportunities relative to class activities and assignments.

17. Present tasks in the most attractive and interesting manner possible.

18. Give the student responsibilities in the classroom (e.g., teacher assistant, peer tutor, group leader, etc.).

19. Evaluate the appropriateness of the task in relation to the student's ability to perform the task successfully.

20. Show an interest in the student (e.g., acknowledge the student, ask the student's opinion, spend time working one-on-one with the student, etc.).

21. Intervene early when there is a problem in order to prevent more serious problems from occurring.

22. Inform others who will be working with the student (e.g., teachers, the principal, clerks, etc.) about the student's tendency to ignore consequences of his/her behaviors.

23. Make certain the student does not become involved in overstimulating activities.

24. Teach the student to "think" before acting (e.g., ask himself/herself: "What is happening?" "What am I doing?" "What should I do?" "What will be best for me?").

25. Evaluate the appropriateness of the task to determine: (a) if the task is too difficult and (b) if the length of time scheduled to complete the task is appropriate.

26. Communicate with parents (e.g., notes home, phone calls, etc.) in order to share information concerning the student's progress and so that they can reinforce the student at home for engaging in appropriate behaviors at school.

27. Write a contract with the student specifying what behavior is expected (e.g., acting in a deliberate and responsible manner) and what reinforcement will be made available when the terms of the contract have been met. (See Appendix for Behavioral Contract.)

28. Remove the student from the group or activity until he/she can demonstrate appropriate behavior and self-control.

29. Reinforce the student for demonstrating appropriate behavior based on the length of time the student can be successful. Gradually increase the length of time required for reinforcement as the student demonstrates success.

30. Reinforce those students in the classroom who engage in appropriate behavior.

31. Establish classroom rules:
1. Work on task.
2. Work quietly.
3. Remain in your seat.
4. Finish task.
5. Meet task expectations.

Reiterate rules often and reinforce students for following rules.

32. Speak with the student to explain: (a) what the student is doing wrong (e.g., taking action before thinking about what he/she is doing) and (b) what the student should be doing (e.g., considering consequences, thinking about the correct response, considering other persons, etc.).

33. Reinforce the student for engaging in appropriate behavior: (a) give the student a tangible reward (e.g., classroom privileges, line leading, passing out materials, five minutes free time, etc.) or (b) give the student an intangible reward (e.g., praise, handshake, smile, etc.).

155 Does not smile, laugh, or demonstrate happiness

1. Present tasks in the most attractive and interesting manner possible.

2. Determine those activities the student prefers and provide them often.

3. Reduce or discontinue competitive activities. Repeated failure reduces enjoyment of the activity.

4. Make every attempt to create a positive atmosphere in the classroom (e.g., cooperative group activities, positive motivation strategies, positive communications, etc.).

5. Provide the student with as many social and academic successes as possible.

6. Include the student in classroom/group activities (e.g., invite the student to join a group, assign the student a part or responsibility in an activity, etc.).

7. Indicate a need for the student's involvement in an activity (e.g., the student is a part of the class/activities, is valued and needed, etc.).

8. Include fun and enjoyable activities as a part of the daily curriculum.

9. Have peers invite the student to participate in school and extracurricular activities.

10. Avoid discussions of topics sensitive to the student (e.g., divorce, death, unemployment, alcoholism, etc.).

11. Be certain to greet or recognize the student as often as possible (e.g., greet in hallways or in the cafeteria, welcome to class, acknowledge a job well done, etc.).

12. Call attention to the student's accomplishments (e.g., publicly or privately, depending on which is most appropriate).

13. Interact frequently with the student.

14. Try various groupings in order to determine the situation in which the student is most comfortable.

15. Make certain that interactions with the student are natural and not contrived.

16. Help the student develop a friendship by assigning him/her to work with a peer on an activity, project, etc.

17. Have the student complete a reinforcer survey in order to determine his/her interests, his/her favorite activities, what is rewarding to the student, etc.; and use the information obtained to create a pleasant atmosphere at school for the student. (See Appendix for Reinforcer Survey.)

18. Speak to the student to explain: (a) that you recognize he/she is unhappy and (b) appropriate ways to deal with unhappiness.

19. Reinforce those students in the classroom who deal with unhappiness in an appropriate manner.

20. Take time to talk with the student in order for the student to realize that the teacher's interest in him/her is genuine.

21. Make certain that reinforcement is not inadvertently given when the student does not smile, laugh, or demonstrate happiness (e.g., attending to the student only when he/she demonstrates unhappiness).

22. Discourage the student from engaging in those activities which cause him/her unhappiness.

23. Give the student additional responsibilities (e.g., chores, errands, etc.) in order to give him/her a feeling of success or accomplishment.

24. Help the student identify things he/she wishes were in the environment and work with the student toward these goals.

25. Treat the student with respect. Talk in an objective manner at all times.

26. Allow the student to attempt something new in private before doing so in front of others.

27. Encourage the student to interact with others.

28. Provide the student with frequent opportunities to meet new people.

29. Do not force the student to interact with others.

30. Make sure you express your feelings in a socially acceptable way.

31. Evaluate the appropriateness of the task to determine: (a) if the task is too difficult and (b) if the length of time scheduled to complete the task is appropriate.

32. Communicate with parents, agencies, or appropriate parties in order to inform them of the problem, determine the cause of the problem, and consider possible solutions to the problem.

33. Reinforce those students in the classroom who engage in classroom activities or special events.

34. Encourage the student to engage in classroom activities or special events.

35. Reinforce the student for demonstrating happiness when appropriate: (a) give the student a tangible reward (e.g., classroom privileges, line leading, passing out materials, five minutes free time, etc.) or (b) give the student an intangible reward (e.g., praise, handshake, smile, etc.).

1. Have the student question any directions, explanations, and instructions not understood.

2. Review prior to administering tests and quizzes in order to better prepare the student.

3. Reduce the emphasis on test and quiz scores by grading the student's daily performances.

4. Maintain mobility in order to be frequently near the student when he/she takes tests or quizzes or performs daily assignments.

5. Reduce the emphasis on competition. Fear of failure may cause the student to resort to cheating or copying others' work in order to be successful.

6. Seat the student away from others if he/she is prone to cheating and/or copying others' work.

7. Seat the student near the teacher when taking tests or quizzes.

8. Make certain that other students do not allow the student to look at their work during tests and quizzes or while performing assignments.

9. Make certain the student is aware of the consequences for cheating and/or copying others' work (e.g., assignments will be taken away, failing grades will be recorded, etc.).

10. Arrange to have a peer help the student study for tests and quizzes and perform daily assignments.

11. Evaluate the level of difficulty in relation to the student's ability to perform the task.

12. Make certain the student understands all directions, explanations, and instructions prior to taking tests or quizzes and performing assignments.

13. Make certain the student knows that questions can be asked when taking tests and quizzes or performing assigned activities.

14. Communicate with parents or guardians in order that they can help the student study for tests and quizzes (e.g., send home directions, explanations, and instructions relating to content covered on tests, quizzes, material to review, etc.).

15. Have the student take tests and quizzes elsewhere in the building under the individual supervision of an instructor (e.g., in the library, resource room, counselor's office, etc.).

16. Check the student for obvious attempts to cheat prior to taking a test or quiz (e.g., "cheat sheet," answers written on hands or cuffs, etc.).

17. Help the student accept the fact that self-improvement is more important than getting the highest grade in the class, making all A's, being the first one done with an assignment, etc., by reinforcing and grading on the basis of self-improvement.

18. Teach the student to ask for help, stop playing, etc., when he/she feels like cheating.

19. Help the student improve skills in activities in which he/she has cheated in order to reduce the need to cheat.

20. Do not put an emphasis on perfection or winning. If the student feels that perfection or winning is the most important thing, he/she may resort to cheating in order to reach perfection or to win.

21. Limit the student's participation in competitive activities.

22. Teach the student appropriate ways in which to deal with anger, frustration, etc., so the student does not feel the need to cheat.

23. Help the student accept the fact that self-improvement is more important than being the best, "winning," "beating" someone else, etc. (e.g., improving his/her own best time in swimming is better than always trying to "beat" someone else, etc.).

24. Before beginning a game or assignment, make sure the student knows the rules, is familiar with the game, understands directions, etc.

25. Encourage the student to engage in less competitive activities (e.g., reading, clubs, scouts, student council, etc.).

26. Help the student to develop self-confidence and satisfaction in personal self-worth and successes by pointing out strengths, emphasizing positive aspects, etc.

27. Deal with the student's behavior consistently each time there is a problem with cheating (e.g., when the student cheats, remove him/her from the situation and do not allow him/her to return, etc.).

28. Deal with the student's cheating privately rather than in public.

29. Do not take action unless you know for certain that the student is cheating.

30. Identify a peer to act as a model for the student to imitate performing his/her own work.

31. Evaluate the appropriateness of the task to determine: (a) if the task is too difficult and (b) if the length of time scheduled to complete the task is appropriate.

32. Communicate with parents (e.g., notes home, phone calls, etc.) in order to share information concerning the student's progress and so that they can reinforce the student at home for doing his/her own work at school.

33. Write a contract with the student specifying what behavior is expected (e.g., doing his/her own work) and what reinforcement will be made available when the terms of the contract have been met. (See Appendix for Behavioral Contract.)

34. Reinforce the student for doing his/her own work based on the length of time the student can be successful. Gradually increase the length of time required for reinforcement as the student demonstrates success.

35. Reinforce those students in the classroom who do their own work.

36. Establish classroom rules:
1. Work on task.
2. Work quietly.
3. Remain in your seat.
4. Finish task.
5. Meet task expectations.
Reiterate rules often and reinforce students for following rules.

37. Speak to the student to explain: (a) what the student is doing wrong (e.g., cheating, copying, etc.) and (b) what the student should be doing (e.g., his/her own work).

38. Reinforce the student for doing his/her own work: (a) give the student a tangible reward (e.g., classroom privileges, line leading, passing out materials, five minutes free time, etc.) or (b) give the student an intangible reward (e.g., praise, handshake, smile, etc.).

1.　Assess the situations in which the student throws temper tantrums. Based on these observations, determine ways to prevent situations which stimulate the student to throw temper tantrums.

2.　Try various groupings in order to determine the situation in which the student is most comfortable.

3.　Provide the student with many social and academic successes.

4.　Take the time to talk with the student in order for the student to realize that your interest in him/her is genuine.

5.　Teach/demonstrate methods for dealing with problems early in order to prevent problems from becoming overwhelming.

6.　Encourage and help the student to make friends (e.g., pair the student with a peer and when that relationship is successful, introduce other peers).

7.　Explain to the student that feelings of unhappiness are natural, but there is an appropriate length of time for public display of that emotion.

8.　When natural consequences occur as a result of the student's throwing temper tantrums, point them out to the student (e.g., peers prefer not to interact with him/her; property is damaged or destroyed, resulting in loss of use or costly replacement; etc.).

9.　Provide the student with as many positive interactions as possible (e.g., recognize the student, greet the student, compliment his/her attire, etc.).

10.　Provide the student with preferred responsibilities throughout the school environment.

11.　Encourage the student to use problem-solving skills: (a) identify the problem, (b) identify goals and objectives, (c) develop strategies, (d) develop a plan of action, and (e) carry out the plan.

12.　Make certain that reinforcement is not inadvertently given for inappropriate behavior (e.g., attending to the student only when he/she throws a temper tantrum).

13.　Make certain that consequences for both appropriate and inappropriate behavior are consistent.

14.　Encourage and assist the student in joining extracurricular activities, clubs, etc.

15.　Move the student away from the peer(s) who may be causing his/her unhappiness.

16.　Discourage the student from engaging in those activities which cause him/her unhappiness.

17.　Provide the student with positive feedback which indicates he/she is successful, competent, important, respected, etc.

18.　Identify individuals the student may contact concerning his/her unhappiness (e.g., guidance counselor, school nurse, social worker, school psychologist, etc.).

19.　Assign additional responsibilities to the student (e.g., chores, errands, etc.) to give him/ her a feeling of success or accomplishment.

20.　Structure the environment so that the student does not have time to dwell on real or imagined problems.

21.　Help the student identify how he/she would like things in the environment and work with the student toward those goals.

22.　Teach the student alternative ways to deal with demands, challenges, and pressures of the school-age experience (e.g., deal with problems when they arise, practice self-control at all times, share problems or concerns with others, etc.).

23.　Help the student identify when he/she is getting upset so something can be done to help him/her calm down (e.g., walk away, talk about feelings in a socially acceptable way, seek help from an adult, etc.).

24. Teach the student alternative ways to communicate unhappiness (e.g., communicate in writing, verbally, etc.).

25. Avoid topics, situations, etc., which remind the student of unpleasant experiences or problems (e.g., divorce, death, unemployment, alcoholism, etc.).

26. Follow less desirable activities with more desirable activities.

27. Provide the student with alternative activities to perform in case some activities prove upsetting.

28. Give the student some decision-making power (e.g., seating assignment, order of tasks, daily schedule, etc.).

29. Reduce the emphasis on competition. Repeated failure may cause the student to throw a temper tantrum.

30. Help the student choose activities that do not cause anger, frustration, anxiety, etc.

31. Ignore the student's temper tantrums. Do not let the student have his/her way when crying.

32. Show the student how to control angry feelings when things do not go his/her way (e.g., count to ten, say the alphabet, etc.).

33. Make certain you do not give in to the student's temper tantrums because others are present. Maintain consistency at all times.

34. Write a contract with the student specifying what behavior is expected (e.g., dealing with unhappiness in an appropriate manner) and what reinforcement will be made available when the terms of the contract have been met. (See Appendix for Behavioral Contract.)

35. Provide the student with alternative activities, games, etc., in case some activities prove upsetting.

36. Communicate with parents, agencies, or appropriate parties in order to inform them of the problem, determine the cause of the problem, and consider possible solutions to the problem.

37. Evaluate the appropriateness of the task to determine: (a) if the task is too difficult and (b) if the length of time scheduled to complete the task is appropriate.

38. Communicate with parents (e.g., notes home, phone calls, etc.) in order to share information concerning the student's progress and so that they can reinforce the student at home for dealing with unhappiness in an appropriate manner at school.

39. After telling the student that he/she cannot do or have something, explain the reason.

40. Remove the student from the group or activity until he/she can demonstrate appropriate behavior and self-control.

41. Reinforce the student for dealing with unhappiness in an appropriate manner based on the number of times he/she can be successful. Gradually increase the number of times required for reinforcement as the student demonstrates success.

42. Reinforce those students in the classroom who deal with unhappiness in an appropriate manner.

43. Establish classroom rules:
1. Work on task.
2. Remain in your seat.
3. Finish task.
4. Meet task expectations.
5. Raise your hand.
Reiterate rules often and reinforce students for following rules.

44. Speak with the student to explain: (a) that you recognize that he/she is unhappy and (b) appropriate ways to deal with unhappiness.

45. Reinforce the student for dealing with unhappiness in an appropriate manner (e.g., verbally stating his/her unhappiness, problem solving, etc.): (a) give the student a tangible reward (e.g., classroom privileges, line leading, passing out materials, five minutes free time, etc.) or (b) give the student an intangible reward (e.g., praise, handshake, smile, etc.).

158 Is tired, listless, apathetic, unmotivated, not interested in school

1. Call on the student when he/she can answer successfully.

2. Avoid competition. Failure may cause the student to lose interest or not participate in school activities.

3. Allow the student more decision-making opportunities relative to class activities and assignments.

4. Present tasks in the most attractive and interesting manner possible.

5. Give the student responsibilities in the classroom (e.g., teacher assistant, peer tutor, group leader, etc.).

6. Provide a full schedule of daily events to keep the student actively involved. (See Appendix for Schedule of Daily Events.)

7. Provide the student with as many academic and social successes as possible.

8. Evaluate the appropriateness of the task in relation to the student's ability to perform the task successfully.

9. Determine the student's preferred activities, interests, etc., and incorporate them into the daily schedule, program, etc., at various points throughout the day.

10. Provide the student with "real-life" experiences from the environment. Have individuals from the work force (e.g., mechanic, draftsman, secretary, etc.) visit the class to relate the importance of school to work experiences that involve math, reading, writing, etc.

11. Show an interest in the student (e.g., acknowledge the student, ask the student's opinion, spend time working one-on-one with the student, etc.).

12. Investigate the possibility of the student being involved in the use of drugs or alcohol.

13. Do not criticize when correcting the student; be honest yet supportive. Never cause the student to feel badly about himself/herself.

14. Be careful to avoid embarrassing the student by giving the student orders.

15. Treat the student with respect. Talk in an objective manner at all times.

16. Make positive comments about school and the importance of school.

17. Allow the student to attempt something new in private before doing it in front of others.

18. Provide the student with frequent opportunities to meet new people.

19. Evaluate the appropriateness of the task to determine: (a) if the task is too difficult and (b) if the length of time scheduled to complete the task is appropriate.

20. Communicate with parents, agencies, or appropriate parties in order to inform them of the problem, determine the cause of the problem, and consider possible solutions to the problem.

21. Communicate with parents (e.g., notes home, phone calls, etc.) in order to share information concerning the student's progress and so that they can reinforce the student at home for showing an interest in participating in school activities.

22. Write a contract with the student specifying what behavior is expected (e.g., showing an interest and participating in school activities) and what reinforcement will be made available when the terms of the contract have been met. (See Appendix for Behavioral Contract.)

23. Reinforce the student for showing an interest and participating in school activities based on the length of time he/she can be successful. Gradually increase the length of time required for reinforcement as the student demonstrates success.

24. Reinforce those students in the classroom who show an interest and participate in school activities.

25. Establish classroom rules:
1. Work on task.
2. Remain in your seat.
3. Finish task.
4. Meet task expectations.
5. Raise your hand.

Reiterate rules often and reinforce students for following rules.

26. Speak with the student to explain: (a) what the student is doing wrong (e.g., failing to show an interest and participate in school activities) and (b) what the student should be doing (e.g., showing an interest and participating in school activities).

27. Reinforce the student for showing an interest and participating in school activities: (a) give the student a tangible reward (e.g., classroom privileges, line leading, passing out materials, five minutes free time, etc.) or (b) give the student an intangible reward (e.g., praise, handshake, smile, etc.).

28. Investigate the student's eating habits and the amount of rest he/she is getting outside of school.

159 Indicates that he/she does not care about grades, consequences of behavior, etc.

1. Call on the student when he/she can answer successfully.

2. Avoid competition. Failure may cause the student to lose interest or not participate in school activities.

3. Allow the student more decision-making opportunities relative to class activities and assignments.

4. Present tasks in the most attractive and interesting manner possible.

5. Give the student responsibilities in the classroom (e.g., teacher assistant, peer tutor, group leader, etc.).

6. Provide a full schedule of daily events to keep the student actively involved. (See Appendix for Schedule of Daily Events.)

7. Provide the student with as many academic and social successes as possible.

8. Evaluate the appropriateness of the task in relation to the student's ability to perform the task successfully.

9. Determine the student's preferred activities, interests, etc., and incorporate them into the daily schedule, program, etc., at various points throughout the day.

10. Provide the student with "real-life" experiences from the environment. Have individuals from the work force (e.g., mechanic, draftsman, secretary, etc.) visit the class to relate the importance of schoolwork to work experiences that involve, math, reading, writing, etc.

11. Show an interest in the student (e.g., acknowledge the student, ask the student's opinion, spend time working one-on-one with the student, etc.).

12. Make certain the student does not become involved in overstimulating activities.

13. Intervene early when there is a problem in order to prevent more serious problems from occurring.

14. Inform others who will be working with the student (e.g., teachers, principals, clerks, etc.) about the student's tendency to ignore consequences of his/her behavior.

15. Teach the student to "think" before acting (e.g., ask himself/herself, "What is happening?" "What am I doing?" "What should I do?" "What will be best for me?").

16. Evaluate the appropriateness of the task to determine: (a) if the task is too difficult and (b) if the length of time scheduled to complete the task is appropriate.

17. Communicate with parents, agencies, or appropriate parties in order to inform them of the problem, determine the cause of the problem, and consider possible solutions to the problem.

18. Communicate with the parents (e.g., notes home, phone calls, etc.) in order to share information concerning the student's progress and so that they can reinforce the student at home for showing an interest and participating in school activities.

19. Write a contract with the student specifying what behavior is expected (e.g., showing an interest and participating in school activities) and what reinforcement will be made available when the terms of the contract have been met. (See Appendix for Behavioral Contract.)

20. Reinforce the student for showing an interest and participating in school activities based on the length of time he/she can be successful. Gradually increase the length of time required for reinforcement as the student demonstrates success.

21. Reinforce those students in the classroom who show an interest and participate in school activities.

22. Establish classroom rules:
1. Work on task.
2. Remain in your seat.
3. Finish task.
4. Meet task expectations.
5. Raise your hand.

Reiterate rules often and reinforce students for following rules.

23. Speak with the student to explain: (a) what the student is doing wrong (e.g., failing to show an interest and participate in school activities) and (b) what the student should be doing (e.g., showing an interest and participating in school activities).

24. Reinforce the student for showing an interest and participating in school activities: (a) give the student a tangible reward (e.g., classroom privileges, line leading, passing out materials, five minutes free time, etc.) or (b) give the student an intangible reward (e.g., praise, handshake, smile, etc.).

1. Explain to the student that he/she should be happy with personal best effort rather than expecting perfection.

2. Reinforce the student for accepting errors that he/she makes.

3. Speak with the student to explain: (a) what the student is doing wrong (e.g., being overly critical of himself/herself) and (b) what the student should be doing (e.g., being more constructive in self-criticism when evaluating himself/herself).

4. Reward others for accepting errors they make.

5. Write a contract with the student specifying what behavior is expected (e.g., accepting personal best effort) and what reinforcement will be made available when the terms of the contract have been met. (See Appendix for Behavioral Contract.)

6. Evaluate the appropriateness of the task to determine: (a) if the task is too difficult and (b) if the length of time scheduled to complete the task is appropriate.

7. Reinforce the student for improvement rather than expecting excellence.

8. Recognize the student often and in various settings (e.g., hallways, cafeteria, etc.).

9. Provide the student with positive feedback which indicates he/she is successful, competent, important, valuable, etc.

10. Provide the student with success-oriented tasks. The expectation is that success will result in more positive attitudes and perceptions toward self and environment.

11. Provide the student with as many social and academic successes as possible.

12. Make the necessary adjustments in the environment to prevent the student from experiencing stress, frustration, etc.

13. Assign a peer to help the student with class assignments, homework, etc.

14. Emphasize individual differences and that everyone has strengths and weaknesses.

15. Reduce emphasis on competition and perfection. Repeated failure may result in unwarranted self-blame or self-criticism.

16. Encourage the student to refrain from comparing personal performance to other students' performances, and emphasize giving attention to personal improvement (e.g., maintain records of own progress rather than comparing work to others).

17. Provide the student with evidence of his/her ability in order that he/she might better understand that self-blame/self-criticism is unwarranted.

18. Have the student regularly record his/her own progress in order to have tangible evidence of success.

19. Deliver praise and constructive criticism consistently to all students.

20. Make cleaning up accidents a group responsibility in order to convey the idea that we all make mistakes and accidents are common to all of us.

21. Call on the student when he/she will most likely be able to answer correctly.

22. Encourage the student to act as a peer tutor in order to recognize his/her own strengths and abilities.

23. Reduce activities which might threaten the student (e.g., announcing test score ranges or test scores aloud, making students read aloud in class, emphasizing the success of a particular student or students, etc.).

24. Help the student learn those skills necessary to improve his/her personal appearance and hygiene.

25. Make certain that your comments take the form of constructive criticism rather than criticism that can be perceived as personal, threatening, etc. (e.g., instead of saying, "You always make that same mistake." say, "A better way to do that might be . . .").

26. Deliver a predetermined signal when the student begins to be overly critical of self.

27. Assess the appropriateness of the social situation and place the student in the group in which he/she will be most successful.

28. Pair the student with a younger or less capable peer in order to enhance his/her feelings of success or accomplishment.

29. Deliver praise and recognition privately in order that the student is not aware of the performance of others.

30. Encourage all students to be complimentary of others' performances.

31. Do not criticize when correcting the student; be honest yet supportive. Never cause the student to feel badly about himself/herself.

32. Talk with the student about individual differences and discuss strengths and weaknesses of individuals the student knows. Stress that the student does not have to do the same things everyone else does.

33. Encourage the student to refrain from comparing himself/herself to others.

A Reminder: Make certain that the self-blame or self-criticism is in fact unwarranted.

161 Frowns, scowls, looks unhappy during typical classroom situations

1. Share concerns with administration and seek referral to an agency for investigation of abuse or neglect.

2. Communicate your concern to the student.

3. Reinforce the student for engaging in appropriate behavior: (a) give the student a tangible reward (e.g., classroom privileges, line leading, passing out materials, five minutes free time, etc.) or (b) give the student an intangible reward (e.g., praise, handshake, smile, etc.).

4. Provide the student with success-oriented tasks (i.e., the expectation is that success will result in more positive attitudes and perceptions toward self and environment).

5. Assign a peer to engage in recreational activities with the student in order to develop a friendship.

6. Provide the student with positive feedback that indicates he/she is successful, competent, important, valuable, etc.

7. Give the student additional responsibilities (e.g., chores, errands, etc.) to give the student a feeling of success or accomplishment.

8. Identify individuals the student may contact with concerns or problems (e.g., guidance counselor, school nurse, social worker, school psychologist, etc.).

9. Create the most positive environment possible.

10. Seek the student's input in planning the curriculum and extracurricular activities, classes, etc. (i.e., attempt to include student preferences and favored activities).

11. Follow less desirable activities with more desirable activities throughout the day in order to maintain interest and variety.

12. Facilitate the development of friendships with peers (e.g., assign activities for the student involving peers, give the student and a peer joint responsibilities, etc.).

13. Reduce emphasis on competition. Repeated failure will most likely contribute to the student's unhappiness.

14. Teach the student to be satisfied with personal best effort rather than insisting on perfection (e.g., reduce the emphasis on competition, help the student realize that success is individually defined).

15. De-emphasize arbitrary levels of success (i.e., rather than absolute excellence, progress of any amount should be considered a measure of success).

16. Respect the student's right to privacy when appropriate.

17. Take the time to listen so the student realizes that your concern/interest is genuine.

18. Maintain consistency in interactions (e.g., do not provide extra attention when the student is demonstrating facial expressions of displeasure).

19. Ask the student why he/she frowns, scowls, or looks unhappy during typical classroom situations. The student may have the most accurate perception.

20. Communicate with parents, agencies, or appropriate parties in order to inform them of the problem, determine the cause of the problem, and consider possible solutions to the problem.

21. Do not punish the student for not participating in classroom activities.

22. Do not force the student to interact with individuals with whom he/she is not completely comfortable.

23. Treat the student with respect. Talk in an objective manner at all times.

24. Be careful to avoid embarrassing the student by giving him/her orders, demands, etc., in front of others.

25. Make positive comments about participating in school and special activities.

26. Go with the student or have someone else accompany the student to those activities in which he/she may not want to participate. Gradually decrease the length of time you or someone else stays with the student.

27. Carefully consider those things the student does not want to participate in. If something unpleasant is causing the student to not participate, do all you can to change the situation.

28. Do not force the student to interact with others.

162 Needs immediate rewards/reinforcement in order to demonstrate appropriate behavior

1. Have the student maintain a chart representing his/her own appropriate behavior in order that success is recognized.

2. Provide the student with positive feedback which indicates he/she is successful, competent, important, valuable, etc. (e.g., provide social reinforcement in place of tangible reinforcement).

3. Make certain that natural consequences follow appropriate behavior (e.g., recognition from the group for success, compliments, congratulations, etc.).

4. Reduce the emphasis on material rewards and increase the emphasis on intrinsic rewards (e.g., emphasize a job well done, improvement, personal success, etc.).

5. Provide the student with an abundance of tangible reinforcement in order that it may satisfy his/her need for gratification.

6. Present the task in an attractive and interesting manner with as much success built in as possible (e.g., the task should be inherently reinforcing).

7. Be certain to greet and acknowledge the student as often as possible rather than providing recognition only as a reinforcer.

8. Encourage the student to save tokens, points, etc., over time for delayed reinforcement (e.g., make tangible reinforcement a goal rather than an immediate need).

9. Make certain that reinforcement is not inadvertently given for inappropriate behavior (e.g., responding to the student only when he/she makes errors, responding to the student when he/she misrepresents a need for help, etc.).

10. Interact frequently with the student in order to replace tangible reinforcement with social reinforcement.

11. Reinforce with tangibles less often as the student experiences more satisfaction with a job well done (i.e., intrinsic satisfaction begins to replace tangibles as reinforcement).

12. Make certain that reinforcement is used as a natural consequence for a job well done or for appropriate behavior.

13. Provide reinforcement at routine intervals in order that the student learns that reinforcement is delayed but forthcoming (e.g., free time, end of the day, Friday afternoon, etc.).

14. Do not criticize. When correcting the student, be honest yet supportive. Never cause the student to feel badly about himself/herself.

15. Evaluate the appropriateness of the task to determine: (a) if the task is too difficult or (b) if the length of time scheduled to complete the task is appropriate.

16. Communicate with parents (e.g., notes home, phone calls, etc.) in order to share information concerning the student's progress and so that they can reinforce the student at home for tolerating extended time periods between reinforcement at school.

17. Write a contract with the student specifying what behavior is expected (e.g., working 5 minutes without asking for reinforcement) and what reinforcement will be available when the terms of the contract have been met. (See Appendix for Behavioral Contract.)

18. Reinforce those students who can accept extended time periods between reinforcement.

19. Establish classroom rules:
1. Work on task.
2. Remain in your seat.
3. Finish task.
4. Meet task expectations.
5. Raise your hand.

Reiterate rules often and reinforce students for following rules.

20. Speak with the student to explain: (a) what the student is doing wrong (e.g., asking for reinforcement as soon as a task is completed) and (b) what the student should be doing (e.g., waiting for reinforcement until the end of the activity or until an established time, saving tokens or points for reinforcement at a later time, etc.).

21. Reinforce the student as often as necessary while gradually increasing the amount of time between reinforcement: (a) give the student a tangible reward (e.g., classroom privileges, line leading, passing out materials, five minutes free time, etc.) or (b) give the student an intangible reward (e.g., praise, handshake, smile, etc.).

163   Does not care for personal appearance

* Evidence of inappropriate care for personal appearance would include such things as dirt on body and under fingernails, dirty hair, body odor, unbrushed teeth, offensive breath, failure to use a handkerchief appropriately, and toileting accidents.

1.   Identify a peer to act as a model for the student to imitate appropriate hygiene (e.g., wearing clean clothing, washing hair, cleaning fingernails, etc.).

2.   Have the student question any hygiene expectations not understood.

3.   Establish hygiene rules:
    1. Bathe regularly.
    2. Brush teeth.
    3. Wash hair.
    4. Launder clothing after wearing.
    5. Clean and trim nails.
    6. Maintain personal cleanliness after using restroom.
    7. Use a handkerchief.
Reiterate rules often and reinforce students for following rules.

4.   Evaluate the demands of the responsibility on the student for personal hygiene in order to determine if the expectations are too high. If expectations are too difficult for the student, assistance should be provided.

5.   Designate one adult in the educational environment to work directly with the student to help him/her care for personal appearance.

6.   Provide the student with training in the use of personal grooming and related materials (e.g., washcloth, soap, shampoo, toothbrush, toothpaste, hairbrush, comb, nail clippers, toilet paper, handkerchief, etc.).

7.   Allow the student to attend to personal hygiene needs at school if the opportunity is not available elsewhere (e.g., launder clothing, bathe, wash hair, etc.).

8.   Maintain personal hygiene materials at school for the student's use.

9.   Provide a comprehensive unit of information and instruction on personal hygiene. The unit should include health and appearance aspects. Classroom visitors can include a dentist, nurse, doctor, cosmetologist, etc.

10.   Communicate with parents, agencies, or appropriate parties in order to inform them of the problem, determine the cause of the problem, and consider possible solutions to the problem.

11.   Require the student to maintain a daily routine of grooming and attending to personal hygiene at school.

12.   Have the student keep a change of clean clothing at school.

13.   As part of instruction on interviewing and job placement, emphasize the importance of personal hygiene and grooming (e.g., have a representative of business or industry visit the class to make a presentation on the importance of personal appearance).

14.   Provide the student with a checklist of personal hygiene activities and have the student complete the checklist daily.

15.   Provide visual reminders of personal hygiene in appropriate locations (e.g., picture of washing hands and brushing teeth at sink, picture of deodorant in restroom, etc.).

16.   Teach the student to launder clothing.

17.   Reinforce the student for gradually improving personal hygiene over time rather than expecting total mastery of personal hygiene skills immediately.

18.   Make certain that all communications with the student concerning personal hygiene are conducted in a private manner.

19.   Provide the student with scheduled times during the day to attend to personal hygiene needs.

20. Allow the student to arrive early at school in order to care for his/her personal appearance.

21. Do not criticize when correcting the student; be honest yet supportive. Never cause the student to feel badly about himself/herself.

22. Communicate with parents (e.g., notes home, phone calls, etc.) in order to share information concerning the student's progress and so that they can reinforce the student at home for caring for personal appearance.

23. Write a contract with the student specifying what behavior is expected (e.g., wearing clean clothing, washing hair, cleaning fingernails, etc.) and what reinforcement will be made available when the terms of the contract have been met. (See Appendix for Behavioral Contract.)

24. Reinforce the student for caring for personal appearance based on the length of time the student can be successful. Gradually increase the length of time required for reinforcement as the student demonstrates success.

25. Reinforce those students in the classroom who care for their personal appearance.

26. Speak to the student to explain: (a) what the student is doing wrong (e.g., wearing dirty clothing, failing to wash hair or clean fingernails, etc.) and (b) what the student should be doing (e.g., wearing clean clothing, washing hair, cleaning fingernails, etc.).

27. Reinforce the student for caring for personal appearance: (a) give the student a tangible reward (e.g., classroom privileges, line leading, passing out materials, five minutes free time, etc.) or (b) give the student an intangible reward (e.g., praise, handshake, smile, etc.).

28. Carefully consider the student's age and experience before expecting him/her to care for personal hygiene independently.

29. Make certain that the student sees the relationship between his/her behavior and the consequences which follow (e.g., offending others, being avoided by others, not being able to participate in special activities, etc.).

30. Set an example for the student by caring about your personal appearance (e.g., combing your hair, bathing daily, etc.).

31. Encourage the student to take a home economics class, a health class, etc., to learn the importance of personal hygiene.

32. Make certain that the student understands that others might "make fun" if the student does not comb hair, zip pants, tie shoes, etc.

33. Compliment the student for being neat, clean, etc.

34. Set aside time to practice hair combing, putting on makeup, shaving, using deodorant, etc.

35. Stress to the student the social importance of brushing teeth, washing hair, bathing, etc. Not only is inadequate hygiene offensive, but other children can be cruel.

164 Is pessimistic

1. Communicate with parents, agencies, or appropriate parties in order to inform them of the problem, determine the cause of the problem, and consider possible solutions to the problem.

2. Evaluate the appropriateness of the task to determine: (a) if the task is too difficult or (b) if the length of time scheduled to complete the task is appropriate.

3. Identify a peer to act as a model for the student to imitate positive reactions to situations.

4. Have the student question any directions, explanations, and instructions not understood.

5. Remove the student from the group or activity until he/she can be more positive.

6. Provide the student with positive feedback which indicates he/she is successful, competent, important, respected, etc.

7. Modify the environment to reduce situations which cause the student to be pessimistic (e.g., determine those activities the student dislikes, and avoid forcing the student to engage in those activities).

8. Encourage the student to participate in those activities in which he/she is successful.

9. Provide the student with many social and academic successes.

10. Identify individuals the student may contact concerning his/her unhappiness (e.g., guidance counselor, school nurse, social worker, school psychologist, etc.).

11. Encourage and help the student to make friends (e.g., pair the student with a peer; when that relationship is successful, introduce other peers).

12. Explain to the student that feelings of pessimism are natural, but public display of that emotion should be limited.

13. Make the student aware of natural consequences that occur due to the student's displays of pessimism (e.g., others prefer not to interact with the student, he/she will not be chosen by peers to join in activities, etc.).

14. Provide the student with as many positive interactions as possible (e.g., recognize the student, greet the student, compliment his/her attire, etc.).

15. Require the student to make at least one positive comment about himself/herself daily. Gradually increase the number of positive comments required as the student demonstrates success.

16. Encourage and assist the student in joining extracurricular activities, clubs, etc.

17. Assign the student additional responsibilities (e.g., chores, errands, etc.) to give him/her a feeling of success or accomplishment.

18. Help the student identify how he/she would like things in the environment and work with the student toward those goals.

19. Take time to talk with the student in order that the student will realize your interest in him/her is genuine.

20. Conduct a reinforcer survey with the student in order to determine his/her reinforcer preferences. (See Appendix for Reinforcer Survey.)

21. Communicate with parents in order to determine what the student finds reinforcing at home.

22. Help the student to be satisfied with personal best effort rather than insisting on perfection.

23. Identify the words or phrases the student uses to indicate his/her pessimism. Help the student recognize and in turn limit the statements.

24. Give the student a predetermined signal when he/she begins to be pessimistic.

25. Along with a directive, provide an incentive statement (e.g., "When you finish your math, you may have free time." "You may play a game when your desk is cleaned up." etc.).

26. Do not criticize when correcting the student; be honest yet supportive. Never cause the student to feel badly about himself/herself.

27. Teach the student to respect others by respecting the student.

28. Treat the student with respect. Talk in an objective manner at all times.

29. Make positive comments about school and the student.

30. Teach the student acceptable ways to communicate displeasure, anger, frustration, etc.

31. Teach the student to "think" before acting (e.g., ask himself/herself: "What is happening?" "What am I doing?" "What should I do?" "What will be best for me?").

32. Make certain the student is allowed to voice an opinion in a situation in order to avoid becoming angry or upset.

33. Communicate with parents (e.g., notes home, phone calls, etc.) in order to share information concerning the student's progress and so that they can reinforce the student at home for being more positive at school.

34. Write a contract with the student specifying what behavior is expected (e.g., making positive comments) and what reinforcement will be made available when the terms of the contract have been met. (See Appendix for Behavioral Contract.)

35. Reinforce the student for being more positive based on the length of time the student can be successful. Gradually increase the length of time required for reinforcement as the student demonstrates success.

36. Reinforce those students in the classroom who are positive when reacting to situations.

37. Establish classroom rules:
1. Work on task.
2. Remain in your seat.
3. Finish task.
4. Meet task expectations.
5. Raise your hand.
Reiterate rules often and reinforce students for following rules.

38. Speak to the student to explain: (a) what the student is doing wrong (e.g., complaining, not taking part, reacting negatively, etc.) and (b) what the student should be doing (e.g., taking part, being enthusiastic, etc.).

39. Reinforce the student for being more positive in reacting to situations (e.g., attempting a task, making a positive comment about an activity, etc.): (a) give the student a tangible reward (e.g., classroom privileges, line leading, passing out materials, five minutes free time, etc.) or (b) give the student an intangible reward (e.g., praise, handshake, smile, etc.).

1. Structure the environment in order to reduce opportunities to run away from the school/ classroom (e.g., change seating, increase supervision, reduce stimuli which contribute to running away, etc.).

2. Maintain supervision of the student at all times and in all parts of the school.

3. Maintain visibility to and from the student. The teacher should be able to see the student and the student should be able to see the teacher, making eye contact possible at all times.

4. Provide the student with as many academic and social successes as possible.

5. Record or chart attendance with the student.

6. Give the student a preferred responsibility to be performed at various times throughout the day.

7. Present tasks in the most attractive and interesting manner possible.

8. Interact frequently with the student in order to maintain involvement in the activity (e.g., ask the student questions, ask the student's opinion, stand close to the student, seat the student near your desk, etc.).

9. Make the necessary adjustments in the environment to prevent the student from experiencing stress, frustration, anger, etc., as much as possible.

10. Make certain all school personnel are aware of the student's tendency to run away.

11. Limit the student's independent movement in the school environment.

12. Discuss with the student ways to deal with unpleasant experiences which would typically cause him/her to run away (e.g., talk to a teacher, visit with a counselor, go to a quiet area in the school, etc.).

13. Identify variables in the environment which cause the student to become upset, and reduce or remove those variables.

14. Do not provide the student with additional opportunities to run away by seating the student in the hallway, sending him from class, etc.

15. Consider alternative forms of negative consequences if current consequences cause the student to run away. Do not use negative consequences which contribute to a worsening of the situation.

16. Intervene early to prevent the student from becoming upset enough to run away.

17. Provide the student with a quiet place as an alternative to running away. This can be a place where the student elects to go as a form of self-control in place of running away.

18. Identify the student's favorite activities and provide as many of these as possible throughout the day.

19. Do not criticize when correcting the student; be honest yet supportive. Never cause the student to feel badly about himself/herself.

20. Inform others (e.g., teachers, aides, lunchroom clerks, etc.) of the student's tendency to run away to avoid problems.

21. Intervene early when there is a problem in order to prevent more serious problems from occurring.

22. Make certain there will be adult supervision at all times for the student (e.g., during P.E., recess, lunch, etc.).

23. Treat the student with respect. Talk in an objective manner at all times.

24. Be careful to avoid embarrassing the student by giving him/her orders, demands, etc., in front of others.

25. Teach the student acceptable ways to communicate displeasure, anger, frustration, etc.

26. Encourage the student to use problem-solving skills: (a) identify the problem, (b) identify goals and objectives, (c) develop strategies, (d) develop a plan of action, and (e) carry out the plan.

27. Teach the student to "think" before acting (e.g., ask himself/herself: "What is happening?" "What am I doing?" "What should I do?" "What will be best for me?").

28. Make certain the student is allowed to voice an opinion in a situation in order to avoid becoming angry or upset.

29. Talk to the student about ways of handling situations successfully without conflict (e.g., walk away from a situation, change to another activity, ask for help, etc.).

30. Evaluate the appropriateness of the task to determine: (a) if the task is too difficult, or (b) if the length of time scheduled to complete the task is appropriate.

31. Communicate with parents (e.g., notes home, phone calls, etc.) in order to share information concerning the student's progress and so that they can reinforce the student at home for dealing with problems in appropriate ways at school.

32. Write a contract with the student specifying what behavior is expected (e.g., asking for help) and what reinforcement will be made available when the terms of the contract have been met. (See Appendix for Behavioral Contract.)

33. Remove the student from the group or activity until he/she can demonstrate appropriate behavior and self-control.

34. Reinforce the student for dealing with problems in appropriate ways based on the length of time the student can be successful. Gradually increase the length of time required for reinforcement as the student demonstrates success.

35. Reinforce those students in the classroom who deal with problems in appropriate ways.

36. Establish classroom rules:
1. Work on task.
2. Remain in your seat.
3. Finish task.
4. Meet task expectations.
5. Raise your hand.
Reiterate rules often and reinforce students for following rules.

37. Speak with the student to explain: (a) what the student is doing wrong (e.g., running away from situations, running out of the room, running away from school, etc.) and (b) what the student should be doing (e.g., asking for help, calling attention to the problem, practicing problem-solving skills, using self-control, etc.).

38. Reinforce the student for dealing with problems in appropriate ways: (a) give the student a tangible reward (e.g., classroom privileges, line leading, passing out materials, five minutes free time, etc.) or (b) give the student an intangible reward (e.g., praise, handshake, smile, etc.).

166 Whines or cries in response to personal or school experiences

1. Modify the environment in order to reduce situations which cause the student to be unhappy (e.g., if the student is upset by losing in competitive activities, reduce the number of competitive activities).

2. Share concerns with the administration and seek referral to an agency for investigation of possible abuse or neglect.

3. Try various groupings in order to determine the situation in which the student is most comfortable.

4. Provide the student with many social and academic successes.

5. Take time to talk with the student in order that the student realizes your interest in him/her is genuine.

6. Teach/demonstrate methods for dealing with problems early in order to prevent problems from becoming overwhelming.

7. Explain to the student that feelings of unhappiness are natural, but that there is an appropriate length of time for public displays of that emotion.

8. When natural consequences occur as the result of the student's display of unhappiness, point them out to the student (e.g., peers prefer not to interact with him/her).

9. Provide the student with as many positive interactions as possible (e.g., recognize the student, call the student by name, compliment his/her attire, etc.).

10. Make certain that positive reinforcement is not inadvertently given for inappropriate behavior.

11. Make certain that consequences for inappropriate behavior are consistent.

12. Encourage and assist the student in joining extracurricular activities, clubs, etc.

13. Remove the student from the peer(s) who is causing his/her unhappiness.

14. Discourage the student from engaging in those activities which cause his/her unhappiness.

15. Encourage the student to use problem-solving skills: (a) identify the problem, (b) identify goals and objectives, (c) develop strategies, (d) develop a plan of action, and (e) carry out the plan.

16. Identify individuals the student may contact concerning his/her unhappiness (e.g., guidance counselor, school nurse, social worker, school psychologist, etc.).

17. Give the student additional responsibilities (e.g., chores, errands, etc.) to give him/her a feeling of success or accomplishment.

18. Structure the environment so that the student does not have time to dwell on real or imagined problems.

19. Teach the student to be satisfied with his/her own best effort rather than perfection.

20. Maintain anecdotal records of the student's behavior to check for patterns or changes in behavior.

21. Teach the student alternative ways to express his/her unhappiness (e.g., talking, writing, creating, etc.).

22. Provide the student with a quiet place to relax when becoming upset. This is not to be used as a form of punishment but as an opportunity to function more successfully in the environment.

23. Do not criticize. When correcting the student, be honest yet supportive. Never cause the student to feel badly about himself/herself.

24. Treat the student with respect. Talk in an objective manner at all times.

25. Be careful to avoid embarrassing the student by giving orders, demands, etc., in front of other students.

26. Make positive comments about school and the student.

27. Teach the student acceptable ways to communicate displeasure, anger, frustration, etc.

28. Make certain you express your feelings in a socially acceptable way.

29. Make certain the student is allowed to voice an opinion in a situation in order to avoid becoming angry or upset.

30. Communicate with parents, agencies, or appropriate parties in order to inform them of the problem, determine the cause of the problem, and consider solutions to the problem.

31. Evaluate the appropriateness of the task to determine: (a) if the task is too difficult and (b) if the length of time scheduled to complete the task is appropriate.

32. Communicate with parents (e.g., notes home, phone calls, etc.) in order to share information concerning the student's progress and so that they can reinforce the student at home for dealing with unhappiness in an appropriate manner at school.

33. Write a contract with the student specifying what behavior is expected (e.g., dealing with unhappiness in an appropriate manner) and what reinforcement will be made available when the terms of the contract have been met. (See Appendix for Behavioral Contract.)

34. Remove the student from the group or activity until he/she can demonstrate appropriate behavior and self-control.

35. Reinforce the student for dealing with unhappiness in an appropriate manner based on the length of time the student can be successful. Gradually increase the amount of time required for reinforcement as the student demonstrates success.

36. Reinforce those students in the classroom who deal with unhappiness in an appropriate manner.

37. Establish classroom rules:
1. Work on task.
2. Remain in your seat.
3. Finish task.
4. Meet task expectations.
5. Raise your hand.
Reiterate rules often and reinforce students for following rules.

38. Speak with the student to explain: (a) that you recognize he/she is unhappy and (b) appropriate ways for dealing with his/her unhappiness (e.g., by talking, problem solving, etc.).

39. Reinforce the student for demonstrating appropriate behavior in response to unpleasant situations (e.g., failure, peer pressure, disappointment, losing in competition, etc.): (a) give the student a tangible reward (e.g., classroom privileges, line leading, passing out materials, five minutes free time, etc.) or (b) give the student an intangible reward (e.g., praise, handshake, smile, etc.).

167 Behaves inappropriately when others do well or receive praise or attention

1. Make certain to help the student achieve a level of success in an activity in order that he/she will do well and receive praise or attention.

2. Make certain that the student is assigned a role in an activity in which he/she can be successful in order to be a participant and enjoy the activity (e.g., banker in *Monopoly*, scorekeeper in a game, teacher assistant, note taker in discussions, etc.).

3. Make certain that some attention is given to the student when others do well or receive praise or attention. Gradually reduce the attention given to the student as he/she demonstrates appropriate behavior when others do well or receive praise or attention.

4. Deliver praise or attention as privately as possible in order to reduce the likelihood of upsetting any students in the classroom.

5. Reduce the emphasis on competition. Encourage and reinforce participation, team work, good sportsmanship, personal improvement, etc.

6. Gradually increase the degree of difficulty of the task or activity as the student demonstrates success.

7. Make certain that the student succeeds or receives attention often enough to create a balance with those times when other students succeed or receive praise or attention.

8. Make certain that the teacher is a good role model by participating in games, demonstrating good sportsmanship, complimenting others, etc.

9. Establish rules and go over them at the beginning of an activity in order to reduce the likelihood of misunderstanding.

10. Encourage the student to leave situations which may cause him/her to become upset, angry, embarrassed, etc.

11. Encourage an atmosphere of students helping one another, congratulating each other, finding something about each other to compliment, etc.

12. Have the student take part in activities with students who are appropriate models for behavior when others do well or receive praise or attention.

13. If the student becomes frustrated or upset by the task or activity, remove him/her from the situation, stop the activity, or provide an alternative activity.

14. Make certain that the student understands that an inability to behave appropriately during a game or activity will result in the termination of the activity.

15. Be certain to provide close supervision of the student in tasks and activities in order to intervene early and provide problem-solving alternatives should inappropriate behaviors occur.

16. Help the student find activities (e.g., reading, creating, peer tutoring, etc.) in which he/she can achieve personal satisfaction and success.

17. Do not require the student to participate in games and activities which may be threatening or cause him/her to demonstrate inappropriate behavior.

18. Make certain the student does not participate in activities with another student(s) who is likely to stimulate inappropriate behavior.

19. Provide the student with several activities throughout the day in which he/she can do well and receive praise and attention.

20. Be aware of the student's strengths and limitations in order to have the student participate in activities in which he/she will succeed rather than fail.

21. Have the student engage in games or activities with a younger student with whom he/she will not have a competitive relationship. Gradually have the student participate in games or activities with older, more skilled peers as the student demonstrates appropriate behavior.

22. Call on the student when he/she is most likely to be able to respond correctly (e.g., when discussing something in which the student is interested, when the teacher is certain he/she knows the answer, etc.).

23. Carefully consider the student's age and experience before expecting him/her to behave appropriately when others do well or receive praise or attention.

24. Teach the student to respect others by respecting the student.

25. Encourage the student to refrain from comparing himself/herself to others.

26. Make sure you express your feelings in a socially acceptable way.

27. Do not allow the student to participate if the task or situation is too stimulating.

28. Have the student question any directions, explanations, or instructions not understood.

29. Identify a peer to act as a model for the student to imitate behaving appropriately when others do well or receive praise or attention.

30. Evaluate the appropriateness of the task or situation to determine: (a) if the task is too difficult and (b) if the length of time scheduled to complete the task is appropriate.

31. Communicate with parents (e.g., notes home, phone calls, etc.) in order to share information concerning the student's progress and so that they can reinforce the student at home for behaving appropriately at school.

32. Write a contract with the student specifying what behavior is expected (e.g., making a positive comment) and what reinforcement will be made available when the terms of the contract have been met. (See Appendix for Behavioral Contract.)

33. Reinforce the student for behaving appropriately based on the length of time the student can be successful. Gradually increase the length of time required for reinforcement as the student demonstrates success.

34. Reinforce those students in the classroom who behave appropriately when others do well or receive praise or attention.

35. Speak to the student to explain: (a) what the student is doing wrong (e.g., getting angry, tantruming, etc.) and (b) what the student should be doing (e.g., making positive comments, continuing to participate appropriately, etc.).

36. Reinforce the student for behaving appropriately when others do well or receive praise or attention: (a) give the student a tangible reward (e.g., classroom privileges, line leading, passing out materials, five minutes free time, etc.) or (b) give the student an intangible reward (e.g., praise, handshake, smile, etc.).

168 Behaves in a manner inappropriate for the situation

1. Reduce stimuli which would contribute to unrelated or inappropriate behavior (e.g., testing situations, peers, physical activities, etc.).

2. Interact frequently with the student to maintain involvement.

3. Structure the environment so that time does not permit unrelated or inappropriate behavior from occurring.

4. Give the student responsibilities to keep him/her actively involved in the activity.

5. Modify or adjust situations which cause the student to demonstrate unrelated or inappropriate behavior (e.g., keep the student from becoming overstimulated in activities).

6. Make the necessary adjustments in the environment to prevent the student from experiencing stress, frustration, anger, etc., as much as possible.

7. Reduce distracting stimuli (e.g., place the student in the front row, provide a carrel or quiet place away from distractions, etc.). This is used as a means of reducing distracting stimuli and not as a form of punishment.

8. Try various groupings in order to determine the situations in which the student demonstrates appropriate behavior.

9. Interact frequently with the student in order to maintain his/her attention to the activity (e.g., ask the student questions, ask the student's opinions, stand close to the student, seat the student near the teacher's desk, etc.).

10. Model socially acceptable behavior for the student (e.g., pat on the back, handshake, etc.).

11. Talk to the student about ways of handling situations successfully without conflict (e.g., walk away from the situation, change to another activity, ask for help, etc.).

12. Maintain a consistent routine.

13. Make certain that reinforcement is not inadvertently given for the student's inappropriate comments or behaviors (e.g., attending to the student only when he/she demonstrates behaviors which are inappropriate to the situation).

14. Prevent the student from becoming overstimulated by an activity (e.g., monitor or supervise student behavior to limit overstimulation in physical activities, games, parties, etc.).

15. Help the student develop attention-maintaining behaviors (e.g., maintain eye contact, take notes on the subject, ask questions related to the subject, etc.).

16. Assign a peer to work with the student in order to model on-task behavior.

17. Reduce the emphasis on competition. Repeated failure may result in behaviors which are inappropriate for the situation.

18. Make the student aware of activities or events well in advance in order that he/she may prepare for them.

19. Deliver a predetermined signal (e.g., hand signal, verbal cue, etc.) when the student begins to display behaviors which are inappropriate for the situation.

20. Do not criticize. When correcting the student, be honest yet supportive. Never cause the student to feel badly about himself/herself.

21. Intervene early when there is a problem in order to prevent a more serious problem from occurring.

22. Make certain the student does not become involved in overstimulating activities.

23. Provide the student with a predetermined signal when he/she begins to display inappropriate behaviors.

24. Teach the student to "think" before acting (e.g., ask himself/herself: "What is happening?" "What am I doing?" "What should I do?" "What will be best for me?" etc.).

25. Evaluate the appropriateness of the task to determine: (a) if the task is too difficult, and (b) if the length of time scheduled for the task is appropriate.

26. Communicate with parents (e.g., notes home, phone calls, etc.) in order to share information concerning the student's progress and so that they can reinforce the student at home for demonstrating appropriate behaviors related to situations at school.

27. Write a contract with the student specifying what behavior is expected (e.g., demonstrating appropriate behavior related to the situation) and what reinforcement will be made available when the terms of the contract have been met. (See Appendix for Behavioral Contract.)

28. Remove the student from the group or activity until he/she can demonstrate appropriate behavior and self-control.

29. Reinforce the student for demonstrating appropriate behaviors related to the situation based on the length of time the student can be successful. Gradually increase the length of time required for reinforcement as the student demonstrates success.

30. Reinforce those students in the classroom who demonstrate appropriate behaviors related to the situation.

31. Establish classroom rules:
  1. Work on task.
  2. Work quietly.
  3. Remain in your seat.
  4. Finish task.
  5. Meet task expectations.
Reiterate rules often and reinforce students for following rules.

32. Speak with the student to explain: (a) what the student is doing wrong (e.g., laughing when a peer gets hurt) and (b) what the student should be doing (e.g., helping the peer).

33. Reinforce the student for demonstrating appropriate behaviors related to the situation: (a) give the student a tangible reward (e.g., classroom privileges, line leading, passing out materials, five minutes free time, etc.) or (b) give the student an intangible reward (e.g., praise, handshake, smile, etc.).

A Reminder: Do not "force" the student to participate in any activity he/she finds unpleasant, embarrassing, etc.

1. Reduce the opportunity to act impulsively by limiting decision making. Gradually increase opportunities for decision making as the student demonstrates success.

2. Maintain supervision at all times and in all areas of the school environment.

3. Maintain visibility to and from the student. The teacher should be able to see the student and the student should be able to see the teacher, making eye contact possible at all times.

4. Be mobile in order to be frequently near the student.

5. Assign additional responsibilities to the student (e.g., chores, errands, etc.) to give him/her a feeling of success or accomplishment.

6. Prevent the student from becoming overstimulated by an activity (e.g., monitor or supervise student behavior to limit overexcitement in physical activities, games, parties, etc.).

7. Provide the student with adequate time to perform activities in order to reduce his/her impulsive behavior.

8. Provide the student with a routine to be followed when making decisions (e.g., place a list of decision-making strategies on the student's desk).

9. Explain to the student that he/she should be satisfied with personal best effort rather than expecting perfection.

10. Provide the student with clear, simply stated explanations, instructions, and directions so that he/she knows exactly what is expected.

11. Assist the student in beginning each task in order to reduce impulsive responses.

12. Have a peer work with the student in order to model deliberate and responsible behavior in academic and social settings.

13. Reduce distracting stimuli (e.g., place the student on the front row, provide a carrel or quiet place away from distractions, etc.). This is used as a means of reducing distracting stimuli and not as a form of punishment.

14. Teach the student decision-making steps: (a) think about how other persons may be influenced, (b) think about consequences, (c) carefully consider the unique situation, (d) think of different courses of action which are possible, and (e) think about what is ultimately best for him/her.

15. Make the student aware of the reasons we all must practice responsibility (e.g., others' rights are not infringed upon, others are not hurt, order is not lost, property is not damaged or destroyed, etc.).

16. Reduce the emphasis on competition. Competition may result in impulsive behavior in order to win or be first.

17. Emphasize individual success or progress rather than winning or "beating" other students.

18. Make certain that all students get equal opportunities to participate in activities (e.g., students take turns, everyone has an equal opportunity to be first, etc.).

19. Allow natural consequences to occur in order that the student can learn that persons who take turns and act in a deliberate fashion are more successful than those who act impulsively (e.g., if you begin an activity before understanding the directions, you will finish early; but you may perform the assignment incorrectly and receive a failing grade, you may have to repeat the assignment, etc.).

20. Deliver a predetermined signal (e.g., hand signal, verbal cue, etc.) when the student begins to demonstrate impulsive behaviors.

21. Make certain the student does not become involved in overstimulating activities on the playground, during P.E., during lunch, etc.

22. Make certain the student has an adequate amount or number of activities scheduled in order to prevent the likelihood of impulsively engaging in unplanned activities. (See Appendix for Schedule of Daily Events.)

23. Assign the student to an area of the classroom where he/she is to remain at any one time.

24. Maintain consistency in the daily routine of activities.

25. Make certain the student knows which areas in the classroom are "off limits" to him/her.

26. In order to determine if the student heard a direction, have the student repeat it.

27. Do not criticize the student. When correcting the student, be honest yet supportive. Never cause the student to feel badly about himself/herself.

28. Intervene early when there is a problem in order to prevent a more serious problem from occurring.

29. Do not leave a lot of unstructured time for the student.

30. Teach the student to "think" before acting (e.g., ask himself/herself: "What is happening?" "What am I doing?" "What should I do?" "What is best for me?").

31. Evaluate the appropriateness of the task to determine: (a) if the task is too difficult and (b) if the length of time scheduled to complete the task is appropriate.

32. Communicate with parents (e.g., notes home, phone calls, etc.) in order to share information concerning the student's progress and so that they can reinforce the student at home for acting in a deliberate and responsible manner at school.

33. Write a contract with the student specifying what behavior is expected (e.g., acting in a deliberate and responsible manner) and what reinforcement will be made available when the terms of the contract have been met. (See Appendix for Behavioral Contract.)

34. Remove the student from the group or activity until he/she can demonstrate appropriate behavior and self-control.

35. Reinforce the student for demonstrating appropriate behavior based on the length of time the student can be successful. Gradually increase the length of time required for reinforcement as the student demonstrates success.

36. Reinforce those students in the classroom who act in a deliberate and responsible manner.

37. Establish classroom rules:
1. Work on task.
2. Work quietly.
3. Remain in your seat.
4. Finish task.
5. Meet task expectations.
Reiterate rules often and reinforce students for following rules.

38. Speak with the student to explain: (a) what the student is doing wrong (e.g., taking action before thinking about what he/she is doing) and (b) what the student should be doing (e.g., considering consequences, thinking about the correct response, considering others, etc.).

39. Reinforce the student for acting in a deliberate and responsible manner: (a) give the student a tangible reward (e.g., classroom privileges, line leading, passing out materials, five minutes free time, etc.) or (b) give the student an intangible reward (e.g., praise, handshake, smile, etc.).

A Reminder: Do not confuse impulsive behavior with enthusiasm. Impulsive behavior should be controlled while enthusiasm should be encouraged.

1. Provide the student with as many social and academic successes as possible.

2. Make the necessary adjustments in the environment to prevent the student from experiencing stress, frustration, anger, etc.

3. Provide a consistent routine for the student in order to enhance stability.

4. Try various groupings in order to determine the situation in which the student is most comfortable.

5. Allow flexibility in meeting academic demands when the student demonstrates sudden or dramatic mood changes (e.g., allow more time, modify assignments, provide help with assignments, etc.).

6. Separate the student from the peer who stimulates the sudden or dramatic mood changes.

7. Teach the student problem-solving skills: (a) identify the problem, (b) identify goals and objectives, (c) develop strategies, (d) develop a plan of action, and (e) carry out the plan.

8. Teach the student to recognize a mood change in order that he/she may deal with it appropriately.

9. Provide a pleasant/calm atmosphere which will lessen the possibility of sudden or dramatic mood changes.

10. Inform the student in advance when a change at school is going to occur (e.g., change in routine, special events, end of one activity and beginning of another, etc.).

11. Give the student adequate time to make adjustments to activity changes, new situations, etc. (e.g., provide the student with several minutes to move from one activity to another).

12. Do not criticize. When correcting the student, be honest yet supportive. Never cause the student to feel badly about himself/herself.

13. Prevent the occurrence of specific stimuli that cause the student to demonstrate sudden or dramatic mood changes (e.g., demanding situations, interruptions, competition, announcing test scores, abrupt changes, etc.).

14. Avoid discussions or prevent stimuli in the environment that remind the student of unpleasant experiences/sensitive topics (e.g., divorce, death, unemployment, alcoholism, etc.).

15. Intervene early when there is a problem in order to prevent a more serious problem from occurring.

16. Make certain the student does not become involved in overstimulating activities that would cause him/her to have mood changes.

17. Be careful to avoid embarrassing the student by giving him/her orders, demands, etc., in front of others.

18. Teach the student acceptable ways to communicate displeasure, anger, frustration, etc.

19. Make sure you express your feelings in a socially acceptable way.

20. Teach the student to "think" before acting (e.g., ask himself/herself: "What is happening?" "What am I doing?" "What should I do?" "What will be best for me?").

21. Talk to the student about ways of handling situations successfully without conflict (e.g., walk away from a situation, change to another activity, ask for help, etc.).

22. Communicate with parents, agencies, or appropriate parties in order to inform them of the problem, determine the cause of the problem, and consider possible solutions to the problem.

23. Evaluate the appropriateness of the task to determine: (a) if the task is too difficult and (b) if the time scheduled to complete the task is appropriate.

24. Reinforce the student for demonstrating appropriate behavior (academic or social) based on the length of time he/she can be successful. Gradually increase the length of time required for reinforcement as the student demonstrates success.

25. Communicate with parents (e.g., notes home, phone calls, etc.) in order to share information concerning the student's progress and so that they can reinforce the student at home for demonstrating consistent and appropriate behavior at school.

26. Write a contract with the student specifying what behavior is expected (e.g., consistent and appropriate behavior) and what reinforcement will be made available when the terms of the contract have been met. (See Appendix for Behavioral Contract.)

27. Establish classroom rules:
1. Work on task.
2. Remain in your seat.
3. Finish task.
4. Meet task expectations.
Reiterate rules often and reinforce students for following rules.

28. Speak with the student to explain: (a) what the student is doing wrong (e.g., easily becoming angry or upset, etc.) and (b) what the student should be doing (e.g., following rules, considering others, controlling impulsive behavior, etc.).

29. Reinforce the student for demonstrating consistent and appropriate behavior: (a) give the student a tangible reward (e.g., classroom privileges, line leading, passing out materials, five minutes free time, etc.) or (b) give the student an intangible reward (e.g., praise, handshake, smile, etc.).

1. Reduce stimuli which would contribute to unrelated or inappropriate behavior (e.g., testing situations, peers, physical activities, etc.).

2. Structure the environment in such a way that time does not permit opportunities for the student to demonstrate inappropriate behavior.

3. Modify or adjust situations that cause the student to demonstrate unrelated or inappropriate behavior (e.g., keep the student from becoming overstimulated in activities).

4. Make the necessary adjustments in the environment to prevent the student from experiencing stress, frustration, anger, etc., as much as possible.

5. Reduce distracting stimuli (e.g., place the student in the front row, provide a carrel or quiet place away from distractions, etc.). This is used as a means of reducing distracting stimuli and not as a form of punishment.

6. Try various groupings in order to determine the situation in which the student demonstrates appropriate behavior.

7. Maintain a consistent routine.

8. Model socially acceptable behavior for the student (e.g., pat on the back, handshake, etc.).

9. Make certain that reinforcement is not inadvertently given for inappropriate comments or behaviors.

10. Prevent the student from becoming overstimulated by an activity (i.e., monitor or supervise student behavior to limit overstimulation in physical activities, games, parties, etc.).

11. Assign a peer to work with the student in order to model appropriate behavior.

12. Reduce the emphasis on competition. Repeated failure may result in unpredictable behavior.

13. Make the student aware of activities or events well in advance in order that he/she may prepare for them.

14. Discuss concerns with other professionals to determine if further investigation is warranted (e.g., abuse or neglect).

15. Explain that concerns or worries, while legitimate, are not unusual for students (e.g., everyone worries about tests, grades, etc.).

16. Provide the student with opportunities for social and academic success.

17. Separate the student from the peer(s) who may be encouraging or stimulating the inappropriate behavior.

18. Provide praise and recognition of appropriate behavior as often as possible.

19. Provide the student with alternative approaches to testing (e.g., test the student orally, make tests shorter, let the student respond orally, let the student take the test in the resource room, etc.).

20. Avoid discussion of topics sensitive to the student (e.g., divorce, death, unemployment, alcoholism, etc.).

21. Provide as many enjoyable and interesting activities as possible.

22. Provide a consistent routine for the student in order to enhance stability.

23. Allow flexibility in meeting academic demands when the student demonstrates sudden or dramatic mood changes (e.g., allow more time, modify assignments, provide help with assignments).

24. Teach the student to recognize sudden or dramatic changes in behavior in order that he/she may deal with it appropriately.

25. Inform the student in advance when a change at school is going to occur (e.g., change in routine, special events, end of one activity and beginning of another, etc.).

26. Give the student adequate time to make adjustments to activity changes, new situations, etc. (e.g., provide the student with several minutes to move from one activity to another).

27. Prevent the occurrence of specific stimuli that cause the student to demonstrate sudden or dramatic changes in behavior (e.g., demanding situations, interruptions, competition, abrupt changes, etc.).

28. Provide the student with a selection of assignments and require the student to choose a minimum number from the total amount (e.g., present the student with ten academic tasks from which six must be finished that day).

29. Provide the student with a schedule of daily events in order that the student will know what is expected of him/her. (See Appendix for Schedule of Daily Events.)

30. Provide the student with a predetermined signal (e.g., quiet sign, hand signal, verbal cue, etc.) when he/she begins to demonstrate an inappropriate behavior.

31. Provide a pleasant/calm atmosphere which will lessen the possibility of sudden or dramatic changes in behavior.

32. Reduce distracting stimuli (e.g., place the student in the front row, provide a carrel or quiet place away from distractions, etc.). This is used as a means of reducing stimuli and not as a form of punishment.

33. Do not criticize. When correcting the student, be honest yet supportive. Never cause the student to feel badly about himself/herself.

34. Treat the student with respect. Talk in an objective manner at all times.

35. Intervene early when there is a problem in order to prevent more serious problems from occurring.

36. Be careful to avoid embarrassing the student by giving him/her orders, demands, etc., in front of others.

37. Teach the student acceptable ways to communicate displeasure, anger, frustration, etc.

38. Encourage the student to use problem-solving skills: (a) identify the problem, (b) identify goals and objectives, (c) develop strategies, (d) develop a plan of action, and (e) carry out the plan.

39. Do not leave a lot of unstructured time for the student.

40. Teach the student to "think" before acting (e.g., ask himself/herself: "What is happening?" "What am I doing?" "What should I do?" "What will be best for me?").

41. Evaluate the appropriateness of the task to determine: (a) if the task is too difficult and (b) if the length of time scheduled to complete the task is appropriate.

42. Communicate with parents (e.g., notes home, phone calls, etc.) in order to share information concerning the student's progress and so that they can reinforce the student at home for demonstrating appropriate behaviors related to situations at school.

43. Write a contract with the student specifying what behavior is expected (e.g., demonstrating appropriate behavior related to the situation) and what reinforcement will be made available when the terms of the contract have been met. (See Appendix for Behavioral Contract.)

44. Remove the student from the group or activity until he/she can demonstrate appropriate behavior and self-control.

45. Reinforce the student for demonstrating appropriate behavior related to the situation based on the length of time the student can be successful.

46. Reinforce those students in the classroom who demonstrate appropriate behavior related to the situation.

47. Establish classroom rules:
1. Work on task.
2. Work quietly.
3. Remain in your seat.
4. Finish task.
5. Meet task expectations.

Reiterate rules often and reinforce students for following rules.

48. Speak with the student to explain: (a) what the student is doing wrong and (b) what the student should be doing.

49. Reinforce the student for demonstrating appropriate behavior: (a) give the student a tangible reward (e.g., classroom privileges, line leading, passing out materials, five minutes free time, etc.) or (b) give the student an intangible reward (e.g., praise, handshake, smile, etc.).

A Reminder: Do not "force" the student to participate in any activity he/she finds unpleasant, embarrassing, etc.

172   Makes sexually-related comments or engages in behavior with sexual overtones

1. Indicate to the student that public displays of sexually-related behavior are inappropriate.

2. Supervise the student closely in order to prevent inappropriate sexually-related behaviors from occurring.

3. Structure the environment so that time does not permit the student to engage in inappropriate behavior (e.g., maintain a full schedule of activities).

4. Seat the student close to the teacher in order to provide more direct supervision.

5. Maintain visibility to and from the student. The teacher should be able to see the student and the student should be able to see the teacher, making eye contact possible at all times.

6. Be mobile in order to be frequently near the student.

7. Do not allow the student to be left alone or unsupervised with other students.

8. Make certain the student understands the natural consequences of inappropriate behavior (e.g., peers will not want to interact with him/her, removal from the group may be necessary, etc.).

9. Model socially acceptable behavior for the student (e.g., pat on the back, appropriate verbal communications, handshake, etc.).

10. Separate the student from the peer(s) who stimulates the inappropriate sexually-related behavior.

11. Make certain the student knows exactly which sexually-related behaviors are unacceptable at school (e.g., words, gestures, comments, touching, exposing, etc.).

12. Intervene early when there is a problem in order to prevent more serious problems from occurring.

13. Do not inadvertently reinforce the student for demonstrating sexually-related behaviors (e.g., attending to the student only when he/she demonstrates sexually-related behaviors, demonstrating shock, etc.).

14. Maintain a professional relationship with students at all times and in all settings, making certain that your behavior does not stimulate sexually-related behaviors.

15. Teach the student acceptable ways to communicate displeasure, anger, frustration, etc.

16. Do not force the student to interact with others.

17. Teach the student to "think" before acting (e.g., ask himself/herself: "What is happening?" "What am I doing?" "What should I do?" "What will be best for me?").

18. Communicate with parents, agencies, or appropriate parties in order to inform them of the problem, determine the cause of the problem, and consider possible solutions to the problem.

19. Establish classroom rules:
1. Work on task.
2. Work quietly.
3. Remain in your seat.
4. Finish task.
5. Meet task expectations.
Reiterate rules often and reinforce students for following rules.

20. Communicate with the parents (e.g., notes home, phone calls, etc.) in order to share information concerning the student's progress and so that they can reinforce the student at home for engaging in appropriate behavior at school.

21. Write a contract with the student specifying what behavior is expected (e.g., communicating with others in an appropriate manner) and what reinforcement will be made available when the terms of the contract have been met. (See Appendix for Behavioral Contract.)

22. Remove the student from the group or activity until he/she can demonstrate appropriate behavior and self-control.

23. Reinforce the student for demonstrating appropriate behavior based on the length of time the student can be successful. Gradually increase the length of time required for reinforcement as the student demonstrates success.

24. Reinforce those students in the classroom who engage in appropriate behavior.

25. Speak with the student to explain: (a) what the student is doing wrong (e.g., making sexual references, touching others, making gestures, etc.) and (b) what the student should be doing (e.g., following rules, working on task, attending to responsibilities, etc.).

26. Reinforce the student for engaging in socially appropriate individual or group behavior: (a) give the student a tangible reward (e.g., classroom privileges, line leading, passing out materials, five minutes free time, etc.) or (b) give the student an intangible reward (e.g., praise, handshake, smile, etc.).

1. Try various groupings in order to determine the situation in which the student is most comfortable.

2. Make the necessary adjustments in the environment to prevent the student from experiencing stress, frustration, anger, etc., as much as possible.

3. Interact frequently with the student to prevent excessive or unnecessary body movements.

4. Maintain visibility to and from the student. The teacher should be able to see the student and the student should be able to see the teacher, making eye contact possible at all times.

5. Facilitate on-task behavior by providing a full schedule of daily events. Prevent lag time when the student is free to engage in excessive and unnecessary body movements. (See Appendix for Schedule of Daily Events.)

6. Reduce stimuli which would contribute to unnecessary or excessive behavior.

7. Interact frequently with the student in order to maintain his/her attention to the activity (e.g., ask the student questions, ask the student's opinion, stand close to the student, seat the student near the teacher's desk, etc.).

8. Give the student additional responsibilities (e.g., chores, errands, etc.) to keep him/her actively involved and give him/her a feeling of success or accomplishment.

9. Modify or eliminate situations at school which cause the student to experience stress or frustration.

10. Maintain supervision at all times and in all parts of the school environment.

11. Prevent the student from becoming overly stimulated by an activity (i.e., monitor or supervise student behavior to limit overexcitement in physical activities, games, parties, etc.).

12. Provide the student with a predetermined signal when he/she exhibits inappropriate behavior.

13. Make certain that reinforcement is not inadvertently given for inappropriate behavior (e.g., attending to the student only when he/she engages in excessive/unnecessary body movements).

14. Separate the student from the peer who stimulates the inappropriate behavior.

15. Provide the student with the most attractive and interesting activities possible.

16. Provide the student with a calm, quiet environment in which to work.

17. Provide the student with a quiet place in the environment to go when he/she becomes upset. This is not meant as punishment, but as a means of helping the student be able to function more successfully in the environment.

18. Provide the student with frequent opportunities to participate, take turns, etc., in order to keep him/her involved in the activity.

19. Avoid discussion of topics sensitive to the student (e.g., divorce, death, unemployment, alcoholism, etc.).

20. Identify a peer to act as a model for the student to imitate staying in his/her seat.

21. Have the student question any directions, explanations, and instructions not understood.

22. Schedule short activities for the student to perform while seated. Gradually increase the length of the activities as the student demonstrates success at staying in his/her seat.

23. Give the student frequent opportunities to leave his/her seat for appropriate reasons (e.g., getting materials, running errands, assisting the teacher, etc.).

24. Seat the student near the teacher.

25. Make certain the student has all necessary materials in order to reduce the need to leave his/her seat.

26. Have the student chart the length of time he/she is able to remain in his/her seat.

27. Work the first few problems of an assignment with the student in order that he/she will know what is expected.

28. Carefully consider the student's age before expecting him/her to sit quietly for a period of time.

29. Intervene early when there is a problem in order to prevent more serious problems from occurring.

30. Make certain the student does not become involved in activities which may be overstimulating.

31. Do not leave a lot of unstructured time for the student.

32. Evaluate the appropriateness of the task to determine: (a) if the task is too difficult and (b) if the length of time required to complete the task is appropriate.

33. Communicate with parents (e.g., notes home, phone calls, etc.) in order to share information concerning the student's progress and so that they can reinforce the student at home for demonstrating physical self-control at school.

34. Remove the student from the group or activity until he/she can demonstrate appropriate behavior and self-control.

35. Write a contract with the student specifying what behavior is expected (e.g., demonstrating physical self-control) and what reinforcement will be made available when the terms of the contract have been met. (See Appendix for Behavioral Contract.)

36. Reinforce the student for demonstrating appropriate behavior based on the length of time the student can be successful. Gradually increase the length of time required for reinforcement as the student demonstrates success.

37. Reinforce those students in the classroom who demonstrate physical self-control.

38. Establish classroom rules:
1. Work on task.
2. Work quietly.
3. Remain in your seat.
4. Finish task.
5. Meet task expectations.

Reiterate rules often and reinforce students for following rules.

39. Speak with the student to explain: (a) what the student is doing wrong (e.g., moving in seat, moving about the room, running, etc.) and (b) what the student should be doing (e.g., practicing self-control, following rules, etc.).

40. Reinforce the student for demonstrating physical self-control: (a) give the student a tangible reward (e.g., classroom privileges, line leading, passing out materials, five minutes free time, etc.) or (b) give the student an intangible reward (e.g., praise, handshake, smile, etc.).

1. Evaluate the visual and auditory stimuli in the classroom in order to determine the level of stimuli the student can respond to appropriately.

2. Reduce visual and auditory stimuli to a level at which the student can successfully function. Gradually allow visual and auditory stimuli to increase as the student demonstrates that he/she can successfully tolerate the increased levels.

3. Seat the student so that he/she experiences the least amount of visual and auditory stimuli.

4. Provide the student with a quiet place in which to work where visual and auditory stimuli are reduced. This is used to reduce distracting stimuli and not as a form of punishment.

5. Place the student away from those peers who create the most visual and auditory stimulation in the classroom.

6. Provide the student with a carrel or divider at his/her desk to reduce visual and auditory stimuli.

7. Make certain that all visual and auditory stimuli in the classroom are reduced as much as possible for all learners.

8. Provide the student with the opportunity to move to a quiet place in the classroom any time that visual and auditory stimuli interfere with his/her ability to function successfully.

9. Provide the student with earphones to wear if auditory stimuli interfere with his/her ability to function. Gradually remove the earphones as the student can more successfully function in the presence of auditory stimuli.

10. Allow the student to close the door or windows in order to reduce visual and auditory stimuli from outside of the classroom.

11. Remove the student from an activity in the classroom if he/she is unable to demonstrate self-control in the presence of visual and auditory stimuli involved with the activity.

12. Require the student to be productive in the presence of visual and auditory stimuli for short periods of time. Gradually increase the length of time the student is required to be productive as he/she becomes more successful.

13. Provide the student with shorter tasks that do not require extended attention in order for the student to be successful. Gradually increase the length of the tasks as the student demonstrates he/she can be successful in the presence of visual and auditory stimuli.

14. Have the student engage in small group activities (e.g., free time, math, reading, etc.) in order to reduce the level of visual and auditory stimuli in the group. Gradually increase group size as the student can function successfully in the presence of visual and auditory stimuli.

15. Teach the student appropriate ways to respond to visual and auditory stimuli in the classroom (e.g., moving to another part of the room, asking others to be quiet, leaving the group, etc.).

16. Model for the student appropriate behavior in the presence of visual and auditory stimuli in the classroom (e.g., continuing to work, asking for quiet, moving to a quieter part of the classroom, etc.).

17. Make the necessary adjustments in the environment in order to prevent the student from experiencing stress, frustration, anger, etc.

18. Provide a consistent routine for the student in order to enhance stability.

19. Allow flexibility in meeting academic demands when the student becomes overexcited (e.g., allow more time, modify assignments, provide help with assignments, etc.).

20. Teach the student to recognize signs of becoming overexcited in order that he/she may deal with it appropriately.

21. Make certain the student does not become involved in overstimulating activities.

22. Provide a pleasant/calm atmosphere which will lessen the possibility of the student becoming overexcited.

23. Post classroom rules in various locations in the classroom in order to enhance the student's ability to remember the rules.

24. Avoid discussion or prevent stimuli in the environment which remind the student of unpleasant experiences/sensitive topics (e.g., divorce, death, unemployment, alcoholism, etc.).

25. Deliver directions in a supportive rather than a threatening manner (e.g., "Please put materials away so we can go to lunch." rather than "You had better put your materials away or we won't go to lunch!").

26. Intervene early when there is a problem in order to prevent more serious problems from occurring.

27. Provide the student with a predetermined signal when he/she begins to display inappropriate behavior.

28. Teach the student to "think" before acting (e.g., ask himself/herself: "What is happening?" "What am I doing?" "What should I do?" "What will be best for me?").

29. Have the student question any directions, explanations, and instructions not understood.

30. Identify a peer to act as a model for the student to imitate demonstrating self-control in the presence of visual and auditory stimuli in the classroom.

31. Communicate with parents (e.g., notes home, phone calls, etc.) in order to share information concerning the student's progress and so that they can reinforce the student at home for demonstrating self-control in the presence of visual and auditory stimuli in the classroom.

32. Write a contract with the student specifying what behavior is expected (e.g., maintaining self-control in the presence of visual and auditory stimuli in the classroom) and what reinforcement will be made available when the terms of the contract have been met. (See Appendix for Behavioral Contract.)

33. Reinforce the student for demonstrating self-control in the presence of visual and auditory stimuli in the classroom based on the length of time the student can be successful. Gradually increase the length of time required for reinforcement as the student demonstrates success.

34. Reinforce those students in the classroom who demonstrate self-control in the presence of visual and auditory stimuli in the classroom.

35. Establish classroom rules:
1. Work on task.
2. Work quietly.
3. Remain in your seat.
4. Finish task.
5. Meet task expectations.
Reiterate rules often and reinforce students for following rules.

36. Speak to the student to explain: (a) what the student is doing wrong (e.g., becoming easily angered or upset) and (b) what he/she should be doing (e.g., following rules, considering others, controlling impulsive behavior, etc.).

37. Reinforce the student for demonstrating self-control in the presence of visual and auditory stimuli in the classroom: (a) give the student a tangible reward (e.g., classroom privileges, line leading, passing out materials, five minutes free time, etc.) or (b) give the student an intangible reward (e.g., praise, handshake, smile, etc.).

175 Lies, denies, exaggerates, distorts the truth

1. Explain to the student that he/she should be satisfied with personal best effort rather than expecting perfection.

2. Provide the student with many social and academic successes.

3. Provide the student with positive feedback which indicates he/she is successful.

4. Reduce competitiveness in information-sharing in order that the student will not feel compelled to make inaccurate statements about his/her experience.

5. Try various groupings in order to determine the situation in which the student is most comfortable and does not feel compelled to lie, deny, exaggerate the truth, etc.

6. Provide the student with experiences which can be shared if the absence of such experiences has been causing the student to fabricate information.

7. Reduce or remove punishment for accidents, forgetting, and situations with inadequate evidence. Punishment in these situations often causes students to lie.

8. Develop a system of shared responsibility (e.g., instead of trying to determine who is guilty, classmates work together to help clean up, return materials, make repairs, etc.).

9. Teach the student that making inaccurate statements does not prevent consequences (e.g., the student has to redo an assignment even though he/she claims the completed assignment was lost).

10. Take no action in situations where conclusive evidence does not exist.

11. Allow natural consequences to occur when the student lies, denies, exaggerates, etc. (e.g., work not completed must be completed, lying to others will cause them not to believe you, etc.).

12. Help the student learn that telling the truth as soon as possible prevents future problems (e.g., admitting that he/she made a mistake, forgot, etc., means that the necessary steps can be taken to correct the situation instead of waiting until the truth is determined in some other way).

13. Treat the student with respect. Talk in an objective manner at all times.

14. Do not punish the student unless you are absolutely sure he/she lied to you.

15. Help the student to understand that by exaggerating the truth he/she may even come to believe what he/she exaggerates and that exaggerating may become a habit.

16. Teach the student to "think" before acting (e.g., ask himself/herself: "What is happening?" "What am I doing?" "What should I do?" "What will be best for me?").

17. Supervise the student closely in order to monitor the accuracy of statements made.

18. Avoid making accusations which would increase the probability of the student making inaccurate statements in response. If it is known that the student is responsible, an admission of guilt is not necessary to deal with the situation.

19. Avoid putting the student in a situation in which he/she has the opportunity to lie, deny, exaggerate, etc. (e.g., highly competitive activities, situations with limited supervision, etc.).

20. Communicate with parents (e.g., notes home, phone calls, etc.) in order to share information concerning the student's progress and so that they can reinforce the student at home for making accurate statements at school.

21. Write a contract with the student specifying what behavior is expected (e.g., making accurate statements) and what reinforcement will be made available when the terms of the contract have been met. (See Appendix for Behavioral Contract.)

22. Speak with the student to explain: (a) what the student is doing wrong (e.g., lying, denying his/her behavior, etc.) and (b) what the student should be doing (e.g., reporting accurately what has occurred or will occur).

23. Reinforce the student for making accurate statements: (a) give the student a tangible reward (e.g., classroom privileges, line leading, passing out materials, five minutes free time, etc.) or (b) give the student an intangible reward (e.g., praise, handshake, smile, etc.).

1. Give the student a predetermined signal when he/she begins to use an unnatural voice.

2. Avoid topics, situations, etc., which cause the student to speak in an unnatural voice (e.g., death, divorce, unemployment, alcoholism, etc.).

3. Require the student to use a natural voice at all times in the classroom.

4. Make certain that all adults at school and home require the student to speak in a natural voice.

5. Place the student in situations in which he/she is comfortable and is most likely to use a natural voice.

6. Make certain that the student's unnatural voice is not inadvertently reinforced by over-attending to it (i.e., the student may speak in an unnatural voice because of the constant attention given to him/her).

7. Ignore the student's unnatural voice if it occurs infrequently or only in stimulating situations.

8. Do not reinforce the student's inappropriate behavior by laughing when the student talks in an unnatural voice.

9. Teach the student acceptable ways to communicate displeasure, anger, frustration, etc.

10. Do not force the student to interact with others.

11. Make sure you express your feelings in a socially acceptable way.

12. Identify a peer to act as a model for the student to imitate the use of a natural voice when speaking.

13. Evaluate the appropriateness of the task to determine: (a) if the task is too difficult and (b) if the length of time scheduled to complete the task is appropriate.

14. Communicate with parents, agencies, or appropriate parties in order to inform them of the problem, determine the cause of the problem, and consider possible solutions to the problem.

15. Communicate with parents (e.g., notes home, phone calls, etc.) in order to share information concerning the student's progress and so that they can reinforce the student at home for using a natural voice at school.

16. Write a contract with the student specifying what behavior is expected (e.g., using a natural voice) and what reinforcement will be made available when the terms of the contract have been met. (See Appendix for Behavioral Contract.)

17. Reinforce the student for speaking in a natural voice based on the length of time the student can be successful. Gradually increase the length of time required for reinforcement as the student demonstrates success.

18. Reinforce those students in the classroom who use a natural voice when speaking.

19. Speak to the student to explain: (a) what the student is doing wrong (e.g., using an unnatural voice) and (b) what the student should be doing (e.g., using a natural voice).

20. Reinforce the student for speaking in a natural voice: (a) give the student a tangible reward (e.g., classroom privileges, line leading, passing out materials, five minutes free time, etc.) or (b) give the student an intangible reward (e.g., praise, handshake, smile, etc.).

1. Allow the student to speak without being interrupted or hurried.

2. Tape record a spontaneous monologue given by the student. Transcribe the student's speech from the tape and have the student listen to what he/she said. Have the student correct errors and practice speaking in more complete statements or thoughts.

3. Have the student keep a list of times and/or situations in which he/she is nervous, anxious, etc., and has more trouble with speech than usual. Help the student identify ways to feel more successful in those situations.

4. Demonstrate acceptable and unacceptable speech, using complete/incomplete statements and thoughts, and have the student critique each example.

5. When the student has difficulty during a conversation, remind the student that this occasionally happens to everyone and he/she should not become upset.

6. When the student fails to use complete thoughts (e.g., says, "ball," and points) elaborate on what was said (e.g., "So you want to play with the ball?"). This provides a model for more complete statements and thoughts.

7. Have the student role-play various situations in which good speech is important (e.g., during a job interview).

8. Make a list of the attributes that are likely to help a person become a good speaker (e.g., takes his/her time, thinks of what to say before starting, etc.).

9. Reduce the emphasis on competition. Competitive activities may cause the student to hurry and fail to speak in complete statements or thoughts.

10. Have a peer act as a model for speaking in complete statements or thoughts. Assign the students to work together, perform assignments together, etc.

11. Break down the qualities a good speaker possesses (e.g., rate, diction, volume, vocabulary, etc.) and have the student evaluate himself/herself on each characteristic. Set a goal for improvement in only one or two areas at a time.

12. Have the student identify someone he/she thinks is a good speaker and give the reasons.

13. Make a list of the most common incomplete statements or thoughts the student uses. Spend time with the student practicing how to make these statements or thoughts complete.

14. Verbally correct the student for not using complete sentences or thoughts when speaking so he/she can hear the correct version of what should be said.

15. Have the student practice descriptive statements or thoughts he/she can use when speaking.

16. Be certain to act as a model for the student to imitate speaking in complete statements or thoughts (e.g., speak clearly, slowly, concisely, and in complete sentences, statements, and thoughts).

17. Prepare simple oral reading passages in written form in which phrases are separated by large spaces (indicating "pause"). Have the student practice reading the passages aloud.

18. Have the student practice techniques for relaxing (e.g., deep breathing, tensing and relaxing muscles, etc.) which the student can employ when he/she starts to become dysfluent.

19. If the student is speaking too rapidly, remind the student to slow down and take time. Be sure to give your undivided attention so he/she will not feel a need to hurry or compete with others for attention.

20. Do not require the student to speak in front of other students if he/she is uncomfortable doing so. Have the student speak to the teacher or another student privately if he/she would be more comfortable.

21. Have the student read simple passages and tape record them. Then have him/her listen and underline words or phrases that were omitted, added, substituted, or rearranged.

22. Teach the student acceptable ways to communicate displeasure, anger, frustration, etc.

23. Do not force the student to interact with others.

24. Write a contract with the student specifying what behavior is expected (e.g., using complete statements or thoughts when speaking) and what reinforcement will be made available when the terms of the contract have been met. (See Appendix for Behavioral Contract.)

25. Reinforce those students in the classroom who use complete statements or thoughts when speaking.

26. Reinforce the student for using complete statements or thoughts when speaking: (a) give the student a tangible reward (e.g., classroom privileges, line leading, passing out materials, five minutes free time, etc.) or (b) give the student an intangible reward (e.g., praise, handshake, smile, etc.).

1. Reduce situations which may contribute to nervous behavior (e.g., testing situations, timed activities, competition, etc.).

2. Prevent the student from becoming overly stimulated by an activity.

3. Try various groupings in order to determine the situation in which the student is most comfortable.

4. Provide the student with as many social and academic successes as possible.

5. Make the necessary adjustments in the environment to prevent the student from experiencing stress, frustration, anger, etc.

6. Assign a peer tutor to work directly with the student in order to prevent stress, frustration, anxiety, etc.

7. Interact frequently with the student in order to maintain his/her involvement in class assignments.

8. Allow the student additional time in which to complete class assignments or homework.

9. Remove from the environment any object which may be used by the student to engage in nervous habits (e.g., pencils, pens, rubberbands, paperclips, etc.).

10. Reduce the emphasis on competition and perfection.

11. Reduce stimuli which may cause the student to engage in nervous habits (e.g., noise, movement, etc.).

12. Prevent situations in which peers contribute to the student's nervous behaviors.

13. Provide the student with another activity designed to result in productive behavior (e.g., coloring, cutting, using a calculator, working with a peer, etc.).

14. Structure the environment in order that time does not allow the student the opportunity to engage in nervous habits.

15. Encourage the student to practice self-control activities designed to allow him/her to gain composure before continuing an activity (e.g., placing hands on desk, sitting with feet on the floor, making eye contact with the instructor, etc.).

16. Provide the student with a high-interest activity which he/she prefers.

17. Provide a calm/pleasant atmosphere.

18. Avoid discussion of topics that are sensitive to the student (e.g., divorce, death, unemployment, alcoholism, etc.).

19. Intervene early when the student begins to engage in nervous habits in order to prevent more serious problems from occurring.

20. Provide the student with a predetermined signal when he/she engages in nervous habits.

21. Evaluate the appropriateness of the task to determine: (a) if the task is too difficult and (b) if the length of time scheduled for the task is appropriate.

22. Communicate with the parents (e.g., notes home, phone calls, etc.) in order to share information concerning the student's progress and so that they can reinforce the student at home for demonstrating appropriate behavior at school.

23. Write a contract with the student specifying what behavior is expected (e.g., demonstrating appropriate behavior) and what reinforcement will be made available when the terms of the contract have been met. (See Appendix for Behavioral Contract.)

24. Remove the student from the group or activity when he/she engages in nervous habits.

25. Reinforce the student for demonstrating appropriate behavior (academic or social) based on the length of time he/she can be successful. Gradually increase the length of time required for reinforcement as the student demonstrates success.

26. Establish classroom rules:
1. Work on task.
2. Work quietly.
3. Remain in your seat.
4. Finish task.
5. Meet task expectations.
Reiterate rules often and reinforce students for following rules.

27. Reinforce those students in the classroom who demonstrate appropriate behavior.

28. Speak with the student to explain: (a) what the student is doing wrong (e.g., chewing on pencil, biting nails, twirling objects, etc.) and (b) what the student should be doing (e.g., practicing self-control, working on task, performing responsibilities, etc.).

29. Reinforce the student for demonstrating appropriate behavior: (a) give the student a tangible reward (e.g., classroom privileges, line leading, passing out materials, five minutes free time, etc.) or (b) give the student an intangible reward (e.g., praise, handshake, smile, etc.).

1. Provide time at the beginning of each day to help the student organize the materials that will be used throughout the day.

2. Provide the student with adequate work space (e.g., a large desk or table at which to work).

3. Provide storage space for materials the student is not using at any particular time.

4. Reduce distracting stimuli (e.g., place the student on the front row, provide a carrel or quiet place away from distractions, etc.). Overstimulation may cause the student to misuse others' property.

5. Interact frequently with the student in order to prompt organizational skills and appropriate use of materials.

6. Assign the student organizational responsibilities in the classroom (e.g., equipment, software materials, etc.).

7. Limit the student's use of materials (e.g., provide the student with only those materials necessary at any given time).

8. Act as a model for organization and appropriate use of work materials (e.g., putting materials away before getting other materials out, having a place for all materials, maintaining an organized desk area, following a schedule for the day, etc.).

9. Provide adequate time for the completion of activities. Inadequate time for completion of activities may result in the student's misuse of others' property.

10. Allow natural consequences to occur as the result of the student's inability to appropriately care for and handle others' property (e.g., property not maintained appropriately will be lost or not serviceable).

11. Assess the quality and clarity of directions, explanations, and instructions given to the student concerning the care and handling of others' property.

12. Assist the student in beginning each task in order to reduce impulsive behavior.

13. Provide the student with structure for all academic activities (e.g., specific directions, routine format for tasks, time units, etc.).

14. Give the student a checklist of materials necessary for each activity.

15. Minimize materials needed.

16. Provide an organizer for materials inside the student's desk.

17. Teach the student appropriate care and handling of others' property (e.g., sharpening borrowed pencils, keeping books free of marks and tears, etc.).

18. Make certain that all personal property is labeled with the student's name.

19. Point out to the student that borrowing personal property from others does not reduce his/her responsibility for the property.

20. Teach the student how to conserve rather than waste materials (e.g., amount of glue, tape, etc., to use; putting lids, caps, and tops on such materials as markers, pens, bottles, jars, cans, etc.).

21. Teach the student appropriate ways to deal with anger and frustration rather than destroying others' property (e.g., pencils, pens, workbooks, notebooks, textbooks, etc.).

22. Teach the student to maintain property belonging to others (e.g., keep property with him/her, know where property is at all times, secure property in locker, etc.).

23. Provide the student with an appropriate place to store/secure others' property (e.g., desk, locker, closet, etc.) and require the student to store all property when not in use.

24. Teach the student that the failure to care for others' property will result in the loss of freedom to use others' property.

25. Provide reminders (e.g., a list of property or materials) to help the student maintain and care for school property.

26. Limit the student's freedom to take property from school if he/she is unable to remember to return the items.

27. Limit the student's opportunities to use others' property if the student is unable to care for his/her own personal property.

28. Reduce the number of materials the student is responsible for. Increase the number as the student demonstrates appropriate care of property.

29. Teach the student safety rules in the care and handling of others' property and materials (e.g., pencils, scissors, compass; biology, industrial arts and home economics materials; etc.).

30. Require that lost or damaged property be replaced by the student. If the student cannot replace the property, restitution can be made by working at school.

31. Make certain the student is not inadvertently reinforced for losing or damaging property by providing him/her with new materials. Provide the student with used or damaged materials, copies of the materials, etc., rather than new materials.

32. Teach the student rules for the care and handling of others' property (e.g., always ask to use others' property, treat the property with care, inform the teacher if the property becomes damaged, return the property in the same or better condition, etc.).

33. Do not permit peers to allow the student to use their property if he/she is not able to care for it properly.

34. Remove others' property from the student if he/she is unable to appropriately care for and handle the property.

35. Maintain mobility throughout the classroom in order to supervise the student's care and handling of others' property.

36. Remove the student from the group or activity until he/she can demonstrate appropriate behavior and self-control.

37. Structure the environment to reduce free or unplanned time which is likely to contribute to the student's inappropriate behavior.

38. Maintain visibility to and from the student. The teacher should be able to see the student and the student should be able to see the teacher, making eye contact possible at all times.

39. Make the necessary adjustments in the environment to prevent the student from experiencing stress, frustration, anger, etc., as much as possible.

40. Prevent the student from becoming overstimulated by an activity.

41. Make the student responsible for specific materials (e.g., tape recorder, overhead projector, microscope, etc.) in the school environment in order to enhance a sense of responsibility and obligation to use the materials with care.

42. Teach the student to respect others and their belongings by respecting the student's belongings.

43. Make certain the student is always under adult supervision.

44. Make certain the student is aware of local and federal laws regarding the destruction of others' property.

45. Require the student to replace damaged items when he/she destroys others' property.

46. Teach the student to "think" before acting (e.g., ask himself/herself: "What is happening?" "What am I doing?" "What should I do?" "What will be best for me?").

47. Have the student question any directions, explanations, and instructions not understood.

48. Talk to the student about ways of handling situations successfully without conflict (e.g., walk away from a situation, change to another activity, ask for help, etc.).

49. Identify a peer to act as a model for the student to imitate appropriate care and handling of others' property.

50. Evaluate the appropriateness of the task to determine: (a) if the task is too difficult, and (b) if the length of time scheduled to complete the task is appropriate.

51. Communicate with parents (e.g., notes home, phone calls, etc.) in order to share information concerning the student's progress and so that they can reinforce the student at home for demonstrating appropriate care and handling of others' property at school.

52. Write a contract with the student specifying what behavior is expected (e.g., putting property away, returning property, etc.) and what reinforcement will be made available when the terms of the contract have been met. (See Appendix for Behavioral Contract.)

53. Reinforce the student for demonstrating appropriate care and handling of others' property based on the length of time the student can be successful. Gradually increase the length of time required for reinforcement as the student demonstrates success.

54. Reinforce those students in the classroom who demonstrate appropriate care and handling of others' property.

55. Establish classroom rules:
1. Work on task.
2. Work quietly.
3. Remain in your seat.
4. Finish task.
5. Meet task expectations.
Reiterate rules often and reinforce students for following rules.

56. Speak to the student to explain: (a) what the student is doing wrong (e.g., defacing property, destroying property, etc.) and (b) what the student should be doing (e.g., putting property away, returning property, etc.).

57. Reinforce the student for demonstrating appropriate care and handling of others' property: (a) give the student a tangible reward (e.g., classroom privileges, line leading, passing out materials, five minutes free time, etc.) or (b) give the student an intangible reward (e.g., praise, handshake, smile, etc.).

1. Have the student work near a peer in order to follow changes in an established routine.

2. Provide the student with a schedule of revised daily events which identifies the activities for the day and the times when they will occur. (See Appendix for Schedule of Daily Events.)

3. Revisions in the schedule for the day's events should be attached to the student's desk and/or carried with the student throughout the day.

4. Post the revised routine throughout the classroom (e.g., on the student's desk, chalkboard, bulletin board, etc.).

5. Attempt to limit the number of times that changes must occur in the student's routine.

6. Discuss any necessary changes in the student's routine well in advance of the occurrence of the changes.

7. Teach the student to tell time in order to enhance his/her ability to accept changes in an established routine.

8. Have the student rely on a predetermined signal (e.g., lights turned off and on, hand signal, etc.) in order to enhance his/her ability to accept change in an established routine.

9. Have the student use a timer to remind him/her of changes in an established routine.

10. Reduce distracting stimuli which might cause the student to be unable to accept changes in an established routine (e.g., movement, noise, peers, etc.).

11. Model acceptance of changes in an established routine.

12. Have the student rely on environmental cues to remind the student when to change activities in his/her revised routine (e.g., other students changing activities, bells, lights, buses arriving, etc.).

13. Have a peer remind the student of changes in routine.

14. Remind the student when it is time to change activities.

15. Have a peer accompany the student to other locations in the building when change in an established routine has occurred.

16. Allow the student an appropriate amount of time to accept changes in an established routine.

17. Explain changes in routine to the student personally.

18. Provide activities similar to those canceled in the student's routine (e.g., if an art activity is canceled due to the art teacher's absence, provide an art activity in the classroom for the student).

19. Provide the student with highly desirable activities to perform when changes in his/her routine are necessary.

20. If change in the student's routine proves too difficult, have the student remain with the established routine (e.g., if an assembly is too overstimulating for the student, have the student continue to work in his/her established routine).

21. Initially limit the number/degree of changes in the student's established routine. Gradually increase the number/degree of changes in the routine as the student demonstrates success.

22. In order to help the student accept change in an established routine, implement environmental changes within the classroom in order to provide the student with experience in change (e.g., change in seating, instructional delivery, task format, etc.).

23. Prepare a substitute teacher information packet that includes information pertaining to the classroom (e.g., student roster, class schedule, class rules, behavior management techniques, class helpers, etc.).

24. Make certain the student understands that classroom rules and consequences are in effect when a substitute teacher is in the classroom.

25. Indicate the names of several teachers and where they can be found in case the substitute teacher should need their assistance.

26. Inform the substitute teacher of the classroom rules and the consequences if the rules are not followed by the student.

27. Have the student work on practice work (e.g., work that has already been taught to the student and that the student knows how to do) when a substitute teacher is in the classroom in order to reduce frustration and feelings of failure.

28. Make certain that the substitute teacher is familiar with the behavioral support system used in the classroom (e.g., rules, point system, reinforcers, etc.).

29. Provide the substitute teacher with detailed information on the activities and assignments.

30. Assign the student specific activities to perform on any day when a substitute teacher may be responsible for the classroom (e.g., assistant to the substitute teacher, errand runner, line leader, class monitor, etc.).

31. Make certain the substitute teacher follows all procedures indicated by the classroom teacher (e.g., academic activities, behavioral support system, etc.).

32. Assign a peer to work with the student to act as a model for appropriate behavior and provide information necessary for success when changes are made in an established routine.

33. If an aide works in the classroom, have the aide monitor the student's behavior, provide reinforcement, deliver instructions, etc., when a substitute teacher is in the classroom.

34. Provide a quiet place for the student to work.

35. Inform the students in advance when it will be necessary for a substitute teacher to be in the classroom, and establish expectations for behavior and academic performance.

36. Let the student know in advance when changes in his/her schedule will occur (e.g., going to P.E. at a different time, going on a field trip, etc.).

37. Teach the student acceptable ways to communicate displeasure, anger, frustration, etc.

38. Have the student question any directions, explanations, and instructions not understood concerning the change in an established routine.

39. Identify a peer to act as a model for the student to imitate appropriate acceptance of changes in an established routine.

40. Evaluate the appropriateness of the change in routine in order to determine if the change is too difficult and if the length of time scheduled is appropriate.

41. Communicate with parents (e.g., notes home, phone calls, etc.) in order to share information concerning the student's progress and so that they can reinforce the student at home for accepting changes in an established routine at school.

42. Write a contract with the student specifying what behavior is expected (e.g., accepting a change in routine) and what reinforcement will be made available when the terms of the contract have been met. (See Appendix for Behavioral Contract.)

43. Reinforce those students in the classroom who accept changes in an established routine.

44. Reinforce the student for accepting changes in an established routine based on the number of times the student can be successful. Gradually increase the number of times required for reinforcement as the student demonstrates success.

45. Establish classroom rules:
  1. Work on task.
  2. Work quietly.
  3. Remain in your seat.
  4. Finish task.
  5. Meet task expectations.
Reiterate rules often and reinforce students for following rules.

46. Speak to the student to explain: (a) what the student is doing wrong (e.g., having a tantrum, refusing to accept the change, etc.) and (b) what the student should be doing (e.g., accepting the change in routine).

47. Reinforce the student for accepting changes in an established routine: (a) give the student a tangible reward (e.g., classroom privileges, line leading, passing out materials, five minutes free time, etc.) or (b) give the student an intangible reward (e.g., praise, handshake, smile, etc.).

181 Reacts physically in response to excitement disappointment, surprise, happiness, fear, etc.

1. Make the necessary adjustments in the environment to prevent the student from experiencing stress, frustration, anger, etc., as much as possible.

2. Maintain visibility to and from the student. The teacher should be able to see the student and the student should be able to see the teacher, making eye contact possible at all times.

3. Facilitate on-task behavior by providing a full schedule of activities. Prevent lag time from occurring when the student would be more likely to engage in involuntary physical behavior.

4. Seat the student close to the teacher.

5. Reduce stimuli that contributes to unnecessary or excessive behavior.

6. Interact frequently with the student in order to direct his/her attention to the activity (e.g., ask the student questions, ask the student's opinion, stand close to the student, seat the student near the teacher's desk, etc.).

7. Maintain supervision at all times and in all parts of the school environment.

8. Prevent the student from becoming overly stimulated by an activity (e.g., monitor or supervise student behavior to limit overexcitement in physical activities, games, parties, etc.).

9. Expose the student to increased stimuli in the environment on a gradual basis after success has been demonstrated.

10. Teach the student appropriate ways to react to personal or school experiences (e.g., calling attention to the problem, practicing problem solving, moving away from the situation if it is threatening, etc.).

11. Provide the student with as many social and academic successes as possible.

12. Present the task in the most attractive and interesting manner possible.

13. Identify individuals the student may contact with his/her worries or concerns (e.g., guidance counselor, school nurse, social worker, school psychologist, etc.).

14. Prevent frustrating or anxiety-producing situations from occurring (e.g., give the student tasks only on his/her ability level, give the student only the number of tasks that can be tolerated in one sitting, reduce social interactions which stimulate the student to demonstrate involuntary physical reactions, etc.).

15. Be mobile in order to be frequently near the student.

16. Structure the environment in such a way that the student does not have time to dwell on problems that are either real or imagined.

17. Teach the student problem-solving skills: (a) identify the problem, (b) identify goals and objectives, (c) develop strategies, (d) develop a plan of action, and (e) carry out the plan.

18. Provide an environment which is calm, consistent, and structured.

19. Provide the student with a predetermined signal if he/she begins to exhibit the inappropriate behavior.

20. Make certain that positive reinforcement is not inadvertently given for inappropriate behavior (e.g., responding to the student when errors are made, responding to the student when he/she feigns a need for help, etc.).

21. Encourage the student to practice self-control activities designed to allow the student to compose himself/herself before continuing an activity (e.g., placing hands on desk, sitting with feet flat on the floor, making eye contact with the instructor, etc.).

22. Provide the student with a quiet place to work when involuntary physical reactions occur. This is not meant as punishment but as a means of helping the student be more successful in the environment.

23. Intervene early when there is a problem in order to prevent more serious problems from occurring.

24. Make certain the student does not become involved in overstimulating activities.

25. Teach the student acceptable ways to communicate displeasure, anger, frustration, etc.

26. Do not force the student to interact with others.

27. Make sure you express your feelings in a socially acceptable way.

28. Encourage the student to use problem-solving skills: (a) identify the problem, (b) identify goals and objectives, (c) develop strategies, (d) develop a plan of action, and (e) carry out the plan.

29. Make certain the student is allowed to voice an opinion in a situation in order to avoid becoming angry or upset.

30. Talk to the student about ways of handling situations successfully without conflict (e.g., walk away from a situation, change to another activity, ask for help, etc.).

31. Try various groupings in order to determine the situation in which the student is most comfortable.

32. Evaluate the appropriateness of the task to determine: (a) if the task is too difficult and (b) if the length of time scheduled to complete the task is appropriate.

33. Communicate with the parents (e.g., notes home, phone calls, etc.) in order to share information concerning the student's progress and so that they can reinforce the student at home for demonstrating physical self-control at school.

34. Remove the student from the group or activity until he/she can demonstrate appropriate behavior and self-control.

35. Write a contract with the student specifying what behavior is expected (e.g., demonstrating physical self-control) and what reinforcement will be made available when the terms of the contract have been met. (See Appendix for Behavioral Contract.)

36. Reinforce the student for demonstrating physical self-control based on the length of time the student can be successful. Gradually increase the amount of time required for reinforcement as the student demonstrates success.

37. Reinforce those students in the classroom who demonstrate physical self-control.

38. Establish classroom rules:
1. Work on task.
2. Work quietly.
3. Remain in your seat.
4. Finish task.
5. Meet task expectations.

Reiterate rules often and reinforce students for following rules.

39. Speak with the student to explain: (a) what the student is doing wrong (e.g., shaking, flapping hands, etc.) and (b) what the student should be doing (e.g., practicing self-control).

40. Reinforce the student for demonstrating physical self-control: (a) give the student a tangible reward (e.g., classroom privileges, line leading, passing out materials, five minutes free time, etc.) or (b) give the student an intangible reward (e.g., praise, handshake, smile, etc.).

182 Engages in inappropriate behaviors related to bodily functions

1. Discuss appropriate social behavior with the student and make certain he/she understands which behaviors are appropriate for public places and which are not.

2. Provide adequate supervision throughout the school environment in order to prevent the student from talking about bodily functions, masturbating, etc.

3. Make certain that the student is not inadvertently reinforced for engaging in inappropriate behavior related to bodily functions (e.g., deal with the problem privately; avoid reacting in a shocked, disgusted, angry manner; etc.).

4. Make certain that natural consequences follow the student's inappropriate behavior related to bodily functions (e.g., others will not want to interact with the student, require the student to clean up urine or feces, etc.).

5. Do not leave the student unsupervised.

6. Remove the student from the group or activity until he/she demonstrates appropriate behavior.

7. Remove the student from the peer or situation which stimulates him/her to engage in inappropriate behavior related to bodily functions.

8. Inform other school personnel in order to make them aware of the problem.

9. Make certain the student knows how to use restroom facilities appropriately.

10. Provide the student with accurate information regarding bodily functions in order to answer questions and clear up misunderstandings.

11. Teach the student alternative ways to deal with anger (e.g., talk with the teacher, move away from the situation, talk to other school personnel, etc.).

12. Share concerns with administration and seek referral to an agency for investigation of possible abuse and neglect.

13. Provide the student with a full schedule of daily events in order to increase active involvement in the environment. (See Appendix for Schedule of Daily Events.)

14. Provide the student with a quiet place to work in order to reduce overstimulation. This is to be used to reduce stimulation and not as a form of punishment.

15. Maintain visibility to and from the student. The teacher should be able to see the student and the student should be able to see the teacher, making eye contact possible at all times.

16. Do not criticize when correcting the student, be honest yet supportive. Never cause the student to feel badly about himself/herself.

17. Maintain trust and confidentiality with the student at all times.

18. Identify a peer to act as a model for the student to imitate appropriate social behavior.

19. Evaluate the appropriateness of the task to determine: (a) if the task is too difficult and (b) if the length of time scheduled to complete the task is appropriate.

20. Communicate with parents, agencies, or appropriate parties in order to inform them of the problem, determine the cause of the problem, and consider possible solutions to the problem.

21. Communicate with parents (e.g., notes home, phone calls, etc.) in order to share information concerning the student's progress and so that they can reinforce the student at home for demonstrating appropriate social behavior at school.

22. Write a contract with the student specifying what behavior is expected (e.g., talking about topics which are appropriate for social situations) and what reinforcement will be made available when the terms of the contract have been met. (See Appendix for Behavioral Contract.)

23. Reinforce the student for demonstrating appropriate social behavior based on the length of time the student can be successful. Gradually increase the length of time required for reinforcement as the student demonstrates success.

24. Reinforce those students in the classroom who demonstrate appropriate social behavior.

25. Speak to the student to explain: (a) what the student is doing wrong (e.g., urinating on floor, masturbating, etc.) and (b) what the student should be doing (e.g., demonstrating appropriate social behavior).

26. Reinforce the student for demonstrating appropriate behavior related to bodily functions: (a) give the student a tangible reward (e.g., classroom privileges, line leading, passing out materials, five minutes free time, etc.) or (b) give the student an intangible reward (e.g., praise, handshake, smile, etc.).

183 Becomes pale, may throw up, or passes out when anxious or frightened

1. Determine that the physical symptom is not the result of a medical problem, neglect, abuse, or drug use.

2. Discuss concerns with other professionals to determine if further investigation is warranted.

3. Take the time to listen so that the student realizes your concern and interest in him/her is genuine.

4. Identify individuals the student may contact if his/her symptoms persist (e.g., guidance counselor, school nurse, social worker, school psychologist, parents, etc.).

5. Provide the student with as many social and academic successes as possible.

6. Prevent frustrating or anxiety-producing situations from occurring (e.g., give the student tasks only on his/her ability level, give the student only those number of tasks which can be tolerated in one sitting, reduce social interactions which stimulate the student to become angry or upset, etc.).

7. Provide the student with success-oriented tasks. The expectation is that success will result in more positive attitudes and perceptions toward self and environment.

8. Provide the student with positive feedback which indicates that he/she is successful, competent, important, valuable, etc.

9. Teach the student problem-solving skills: (a) identify the problem, (b) identify goals and objectives, (c) develop strategies, (d) develop a plan of action, and (e) carry out the plan.

10. Determine which activities the student most enjoys and include those activities as much as possible in the daily routine.

11. Provide the student with opportunities to rest if necessary.

12. Have the parents reinforce the student at home for a balanced program of nutrition, rest, and exercise.

13. Reinforce the student for eating a nutritional lunch at school.

14. Arrange alternative lunches for the student at school (e.g., bring lunch from home, eat off campus, suggest another entree from the cafeteria, etc.).

15. Reduce the emphasis on competition. High levels of competition or repeated failure may result in physical symptoms such as paleness, throwing up, etc.

16. Emphasize individual success or progress rather than comparing performance to other students.

17. Communicate with the parents (e.g., notes home, phone calls, etc.) in order to share information concerning the student's progress and so that they can reinforce the student at home for dealing with problems in appropriate ways at school.

18. Encourage the student to identify problems which result in paleness, throwing up, etc., and act on those problems to resolve their influence.

19. Encourage the student to take responsibility for assignments and obligations in an ongoing fashion rather than waiting until the night before or the day the assignment is due.

20. Help the student recognize problems that are within his/her ability to deal with and not to worry needlessly about situations over which the student has no control.

21. Explain, if appropriate, that some concerns or worries, while legitimate, are not unusual for students (e.g., everyone worries about tests, grades, etc.).

22. Offer to provide extra academic help for the student when he/she experiences a problem that interferes with his/her academic performance.

23. Do not force the student to do something that he/she is not completely comfortable doing.

24. Be careful to avoid embarrassing the student by giving him/her orders, demands, etc., in front of others.

25. Maintain trust and confidentiality with the student at all times.

26. Allow the student to attempt something new in private before doing so in front of others.

27. Go with the student or have someone else accompany the student to an activity the student may be trying to avoid. If something unpleasant is causing the student to pretend to be sick, do all you can to change the situation.

28. Teach the student acceptable ways to communicate displeasure, anger, frustration, etc.

29. Do not force the student to interact with others.

30. Make sure you express your feelings in a socially acceptable way.

1. Evaluate the appropriateness of the expectations for taking part in activities based on the student's ability to perform the task.

2. Make certain the student has adequate time in which to perform activities.

3. Be certain the student makes appropriate use of the time provided for activities.

4. If necessary, provide the student with a private place in which to change clothing for physical education.

5. To the extent necessary, provide assistance to the student for changing his/her clothing for physical education.

6. Make certain that the physical education clothing the student is expected to wear is appropriate.

7. If the student is reluctant to change clothing for physical education in the presence of others, allow the student to change clothing in private. Gradually increase the number of peers in whose presence the student changes clothing as he/she becomes more comfortable.

8. If necessary, provide additional time for the student to change for physical education. Gradually reduce the additional time provided as the student demonstrates success.

9. Make certain the student has the necessary clothing for physical education.

10. Have the student engage in activities which require minimal participation. Gradually increase the student's participation as he/she becomes more comfortable.

11. Prevent peers from making the student uncomfortable when he/she takes part in activities (e.g., prevent other students from making fun, teasing, etc.).

12. Provide a pleasant/calm atmosphere.

13. When requiring the student to engage in an activity in which he/she is uncomfortable, pair the student with a peer/friend in order to reduce his/her discomfort.

14. Evaluate the necessity of requiring the student to participate in activities in which he/she is uncomfortable.

15. Provide the student with alternatives to activities which make him/her uncomfortable (e.g., allow the student to write a poem instead of reciting it in front of a group).

16. Allow the student to be an observer of activities without requiring him/her to be an active participant.

17. Allow the student to perform functions of activities which require little participation (e.g., scorekeeper, note taker, etc.).

18. Ask the student to identify the circumstances under which he/she would be willing to participate in activities (i.e., the student may be able to suggest acceptable conditions under which he/she would be comfortable participating in activities).

19. Provide a schedule whereby the student gradually increases the length of time spent at school each day, in the classroom, in a particular class or activity, etc.

20. Communicate with parents, agencies, or appropriate parties in order to inform them of the problem, determine the cause of the problem, and consider possible solutions to the problem.

21. If the student is extremely uncomfortable at school, allow a parent, relative, or friend to stay with the student all day if necessary. Gradually reduce the length of time the person remains with the student as the student becomes more comfortable.

22. Do not criticize. When correcting the student, be honest yet supportive. Never cause the student to feel badly about himself/herself.

23. Intervene early when there is a problem in order to prevent more serious problems from occurring.

24. Allow the student to attempt something new in private before doing so in front of others.

25. Teach the student acceptable ways to communicate displeasure, anger, frustration, etc.

26. Do not force the student to interact with others.

27. Have the student question any directions, explanations, and instructions he/she does not understand.

28. Identify a peer to act as a model for the student to imitate taking part in activities.

29. Communicate with parents (e.g., notes home, phone calls, etc.) in order to share information concerning the student's progress and so that they can reinforce the student at home for taking part in activities at school.

30. Write a contract with the student specifying what behavior is expected (e.g., changing clothing for physical education) and what reinforcement will be made available when the terms of the contract have been met.

31. Reinforce the student for taking part in activities based on the length of time he/she can do so comfortably. Gradually increase the number of times required for reinforcement as the student demonstrates success.

32. Reinforce those students in the classroom who take part in activities.

33. Speak to the student to explain: (a) what he/she is doing wrong (e.g., avoiding activities) and (b) what he/she should be doing (e.g., taking part in activities).

34. Reinforce the student for taking part in activities: (a) give the student a tangible reward (e.g., classroom privileges, line leading, passing out materials, five minutes free time, etc.) or (b) give the student an intangible reward (e.g., praise, handshake, smile, etc.).

A Reminder: Do not "force" the student to participate in any activity which makes him/her uncomfortable.

185   Does not change behavior from one situation to another

1. Prevent the student from becoming over-stimulated by an activity. Supervise student behavior in order to limit overexcitement in physical activities, games, parties, etc.

2. Have the student time activities in order to monitor personal behavior and accept time limits.

3. Convince the student that work not completed in one sitting can be completed later. Provide the student with ample time to complete earlier assignments in order to guarantee closure.

4. Provide the student with more than enough time to finish an activity and decrease the amount of time as the student demonstrates success.

5. Structure time limits in order that the student knows exactly the amount of time there is to work and when he/she must be finished.

6. Allow a transition period between activities in order that the student can make adjustments in his/her behavior.

7. Employ a signal technique (e.g., turning the lights off and on) to warn that the end of an activity is near.

8. Establish definite time limits and provide the student with this information before the activity begins.

9. Assign the student shorter activities and gradually increase the length of the activities as the student demonstrates success.

10. Maintain consistency in daily routine.

11. Maintain consistency of expectations and keep expectations within the ability level of the student.

12. Establish rules that are to be followed in various parts of the school building (e.g., lunchroom, music room, art room, gymnasium, library, playground, etc.).

13. Allow the student to finish the activity unless it will be disruptive to the schedule.

14. Provide the student with a list of materials needed for each activity (e.g., pencil, paper, textbook, workbook, etc.).

15. Present instructions/directions prior to handing out necessary materials.

16. Collect the student's materials (e.g., pencil, paper, textbook, workbook, etc.) when it is time to change from one situation to another.

17. Provide the student with clearly stated expectations for all situations.

18. Prevent the student from becoming so stimulated by an event or activity that the student cannot control his/her behavior.

19. Identify the expectations of different environments and help the student develop the skills to be successful in those environments.

20. In conjunction with other school personnel, develop as much consistency across the various environments as possible (e.g., rules, criteria for success, behavioral expectations, consequences, etc.).

21. Reduce the student's involvement in activities which prove too stimulating for him/her.

22. Have the student engage in relaxing transitional activities designed to reduce the effects of stimulating activities (e.g., put head on desk, listen to the teacher read a story, put head-phones on and listen to relaxing music, etc.).

23. Provide the student with more than enough time to adapt or modify his/her behavior to different situations (e.g., have the student stop recess activities five minutes prior to coming into the building).

24. Communicate clearly to the student when it is time to begin an activity.

25. Schedule activities so the student has more than enough time to finish the activity if he/she works consistently.

26. Communicate clearly to the student when it is time to stop an activity.

27. Provide the student with a schedule of daily events in order that he/she will know which activity comes next and can prepare for it. (See Appendix for Schedule of Daily Events.)

28. Reduce the emphasis on competition (e.g., academic or social). Fear of failure may cause the student to fail to adapt or modify his/her behavior to different situations.

29. Have the student begin an activity in a private place (e.g., carrel, "office," quiet study area, etc.) in order to reduce the difficulty in adapting or modifying his/her behavior to different situations.

30. Allow the student the option of performing the activity at another time (e.g., earlier in the day, later in the day, another day, etc.).

31. Do not allow the student to begin a new activity until he/she has gained self-control.

32. Evaluate the appropriateness of the situation in relation to the student's ability to successfully adapt or modify his/her behavior.

33. Let the student know in advance when changes in his/her schedule will occur (e.g., a change from class time to recess, when reading class will begin, etc.).

34. Explain to the student that he/she should be satisfied with personal best effort rather than insisting on perfection.

35. Assign a peer to work with the student to provide an appropriate model.

36. Communicate with parents (e.g., notes home, phone calls, etc.) in order to share information concerning the student's progress and so that they can reinforce the student at home for demonstrating acceptable behavior at school.

37. Have the student question any directions, explanations, and instructions not understood.

38. Evaluate the appropriateness of the task to determine: (a) if the task is too difficult and (b) if the length of time scheduled to complete the task is appropriate.

39. Write a contract with the student specifying what behavior is expected (e.g., putting materials away and getting ready for another activity) and what reinforcement will be made available when the terms of the contract have been met. (See Appendix for Behavioral Contract.)

40. Reinforce the student for demonstrating acceptable behavior based on the length of time the student can be successful. Gradually increase the length of time required for reinforcement as the student demonstrates success.

41. Reinforce those students in the classroom who change their behavior from one situation to another without difficulty.

42. Establish classroom rules:
   1. Work on task.
   2. Work quietly.
   3. Remain in your seat.
   4. Finish task.
   5. Meet task expectations.
Reiterate rules often and reinforce students for following rules.

43. Speak to the student to explain: (a) what the student is doing wrong (e.g., failing to stop one activity and begin another) and (b) what the student should be doing (e.g., changing from one activity to another).

44. Reinforce the student for changing his/her behavior from one situation to another without difficulty: (a) give the student a tangible reward (e.g., classroom privileges, line leading, passing out materials, five minutes free time, etc.) or (b) give the student an intangible reward (e.g., praise, handshake, smile, etc.).

A Reminder: Do not "force" the student to participate in any activity which makes him/her uncomfortable.

1. Identify a peer to act as a model for the student to imitate appropriate fastening of articles of clothing.

2. Have the student question any directions, explanations, and instructions not understood.

3. Provide the student with instruction on fastening articles of clothing.

4. Provide the student with time to practice fastening his/her articles of clothing. (The clothing needs to be on the student during practice.)

5. Provide the student with adequate time to fasten articles of clothing.

6. Place visual reminders to fasten articles of clothing inside of restrooms and on the classroom door (e.g., pictures of zipping, buttoning, and snapping).

7. Reinforce the student for gradually improving his/her ability to fasten articles of clothing over time rather than expecting total mastery immediately.

8. Provide the student with a checklist of articles of clothing to fasten (e.g., shirt, pants, shoes, coat, etc.). Have the student complete the checklist routinely throughout the day.

9. Place a full-length mirror in the classroom for the student to make certain that all of his/her articles of clothing are fastened.

10. Teach the student how to fasten articles of clothing when buttons are missing, zippers are broken, etc. (e.g., sewing a button back in place, using a safety pin, etc.).

11. Guide the student's hands through the activities of zipping, buttoning, and snapping his/her own articles of clothing.

12. Have the student practice fastening articles of clothing with over-sized zippers, buttons, and snaps. Gradually reduce the size of the fasteners over time as the student experiences success.

13. Provide the student with verbal reminders to fasten his/her articles of clothing.

14. Reinforce the student at regular intervals throughout the day for having articles of clothing fastened.

15. If the student is incapable of fastening articles of clothing, they should be fastened for the student.

16. Be careful to avoid embarrassing the student by asking him/her to fasten articles of clothing in front of peers.

17. Evaluate the appropriateness of the task to determine: (a) if the task is too difficult and (b) if the length of time scheduled to complete the task is appropriate.

18. Communicate with parents (e.g., notes home, phone calls, etc.) in order to share information concerning the student's progress and so that they can reinforce the student at home for fastening articles of clothing at school.

19. Write a contract with the student specifying what behavior is expected (e.g., fastening his/her articles of clothing) and what reinforcement will be made available when the terms of the contract have been met. (See Appendix for Behavioral Contract.)

20. Reinforce those students in the classroom who fasten their articles of clothing.

21. Speak to the student to explain: (a) what the student is doing wrong (e.g., not fastening articles of clothing) and (b) what the student should be doing (e.g., fastening his/her articles of clothing).

22. Reinforce the student for fastening his/her articles of clothing: (a) give the student a tangible reward (e.g., classroom privileges, line leading, passing out materials, five minutes free time, etc.) or (b) give the student an intangible reward (e.g., praise, handshake, smile, etc.).

187 Does not change clothing for physical education

1. Evaluate the appropriateness of the expectations for changing clothing for physical education based on the student's ability to perform the task.

2. If necessary, provide the student with a private place in which to change clothing for physical education.

3. Make certain the student has adequate time in which to change clothing for physical education.

4. To the extent necessary, provide assistance to the student for changing clothing for physical education.

5. Have the student engage in physical education activities which require minimal clothing changes.

6. Determine those peers with whom changing clothing for physical education would prove less threatening for the student, and place the student with those peers when he/she changes clothing for physical education.

7. Make certain that the physical education clothing the student is expected to wear is appropriate.

8. If the student is reluctant to change clothing for physical education in the presence of others, allow the student to change in private. Gradually increase the number of peers in whose presence the student changes clothing for physical education.

9. Be certain the student makes appropriate use of the time provided to change clothing for physical education.

10. If necessary, provide additional time for the student to change clothing for physical education. Gradually reduce the additional time provided as the student demonstrates success.

11. Make certain the student has the necessary clothing for physical education.

12. Make certain the physical education clothing fits the student.

13. Prevent peers from making the student uncomfortable when he/she changes clothing for physical education (i.e., prevent other students from making fun, teasing, etc.).

14. Evaluate the appropriateness of physical education activities in order to determine if the activities are threatening to the student and cause him/her to be reluctant to change clothing for participation in the activities.

15. Do not criticize. When correcting the student, be honest yet supportive. Never cause the student to feel badly about himself/herself.

16. Avoid embarrassing the student by forcing him/her to change clothing for physical education in front of others.

17. Have the student question any directions, explanations, and instructions not understood.

18. Identify a peer to act as a model for the student to imitate appropriate changing of clothing for physical education.

19. Communicate with parents (e.g., notes home, phone calls, etc.) in order to share information concerning the student's progress and so that they can reinforce the student at home for changing clothing for physical education at school.

20. Write a contract with the student specifying what behavior is expected (e.g., changing clothing for physical education) and what reinforcement will be made available when the terms of the contract have been met. (See Appendix for Behavioral Contract.)

21. Reinforce the student for changing clothing for physical education based on the number of times the student can be successful. Gradually increase the number of times required for reinforcement as the student demonstrates success.

22. Reinforce those students in the classroom who change clothing for physical education.

23. Speak to the student to explain: (a) what the student is doing wrong (e.g., failing to change clothing for physical education) and (b) what the student should be doing (e.g., changing clothing for physical education).

24. Reinforce the student for changing clothing for physical education: (a) give the student a tangible reward (e.g., classroom privileges, line leading, passing out materials, five minutes free time, etc.) or (b) give the student an intangible reward (e.g., praise, handshake, smile, etc.).

188 Does not demonstrate appropriate mealtime behaviors

1. Provide the student with a list of clearly defined mealtime behavioral expectations (e.g., rules for the cafeteria serving line, sitting at tables, remaining seated, using utensils, disposing of trash, etc.).

2. Assess the appropriateness of the student eating with a group of peers. If necessary, have the student eat with one peer and gradually increase the size of the group as the student experiences success.

3. Instruct the student in the appropriate use of eating utensils in both simulation and actual eating situations.

4. Instruct the student in appropriate mealtime conversation (e.g., topics to discuss, asking conversational questions, speaking quietly, etc.).

5. Instruct the student in appropriate mealtime etiquette (e.g., speaking with an empty mouth, chewing with mouth closed, chewing quietly, etc.).

6. Instruct the student in selecting an appropriate amount of food, eating an appropriate amount of food, and taking appropriate-sized bites.

7. Instruct the student in the appropriate clean-up activities upon completion of eating (e.g., disposing of trash, putting trays and tableware in appropriate locations, washing hands, etc.).

8. Instruct the student in the appropriate use of napkins (e.g., keep on lap, wipe mouth, clean up spills, etc.).

9. Instruct the student in appropriate line behavior (e.g., waiting quietly, refraining from making physical contact, moving with the line, etc.).

10. Instruct the student in appropriate behavior when finishing a meal early (e.g., making conversation, remaining seated, excusing himself/herself, etc.).

11. Instruct the student in appropriate ways to get seconds or additional food (e.g., asking for seconds, going through the cafeteria line a second time, purchasing additional food, etc.).

12. Instruct the student in appropriate ways to clean up spills (e.g., ask for assistance, use paper towels and napkins, etc.).

13. Teach the student appropriate ways to respond to food he/she does not want (e.g., sample everything at least once, leave the food on the plate, offer extra portions to others, etc.).

14. Teach the student appropriate ways to drink liquids (e.g., opening milk cartons and juice containers, using a straw, pouring into a glass, drinking from a glass, etc.).

15. Remove the student from eating with peers if he/she cannot demonstrate appropriate mealtime behaviors.

16. Make certain the student sits appropriately while eating (e.g., sits close to the table, sits upright, leans forward, etc.).

17. Instruct the student in appropriate ways to clean clothing when accidents occur during mealtime (e.g., immediately go to the restroom, use paper towels and napkins, etc.).

18. Intervene early when there is a problem in order to prevent more serious problems from occurring.

19. Establish manners that should be followed both at home and at school (e.g., using a napkin to wipe your face and hands, chewing with your mouth closed, etc.).

20. Teach the student how to pass things at the eating table (e.g., the left hand passes to the right hand, pass to the person on your right, etc.).

21. Have the student question any directions, explanations, or instructions not understood.

22. Identify a peer to act as a model for the student to imitate appropriate mealtime behaviors.

23. Evaluate the appropriateness of the task to determine: (a) if the task is too easy, (b) if the task is too difficult, and (c) if the length of time scheduled to complete the task is appropriate.

24. Communicate with parents (e.g., notes home, phone calls, etc.) in order to share information concerning the student's progress and so that they can reinforce the student at home for demonstrating appropriate mealtime behaviors at school.

25. Write a contract with the student specifying what behavior is expected (e.g., disposing of his/her food in the trash can) and what reinforcement will be made available when the terms of the contract have been met.

26. Reinforce the student for demonstrating appropriate mealtime behaviors based on the length of time the student can be successful. Gradually increase the length of time required for reinforcement as the student demonstrates success.

27. Reinforce those students who demonstrate appropriate mealtime behaviors.

28. Speak to the student to explain: (a) what the student is doing wrong (e.g., eating with his/her fingers) and (b) what he/she should be doing (e.g., using a fork).

29. Reinforce the student for demonstrating appropriate mealtime behaviors: (a) give the student an intangible reward (e.g., classroom privileges, line leading, passing out materials, five minutes free time, etc.) or (b) give the student an intangible reward (e.g., praise, handshake, smile, etc.).

1. Reinforce the student for engaging in appropriate behavior: (a) give the student a tangible reward (e.g., classroom privileges, line leading, passing out materials, five minutes free time, etc.) or (b) give the student an intangible reward (e.g., praise, handshake, smile, etc.).

2. Speak with the student to explain: (a) what the student is doing wrong (e.g., taking action before thinking about consequences) and (b) what the student should be doing (e.g., considering consequences, thinking about the correct response, considering other persons, etc.).

3. Establish classroom rules:
1. Work on task.
2. Remain in your seat.
3. Finish task.
4. Meet task expectations.
5. Raise your hand.
Reiterate rules often and reinforce students for following rules.

4. Reinforce those students in the classroom who engage in appropriate behavior.

5. Reinforce the student for demonstrating appropriate behavior based on the length of time the student can be successful. Gradually increase the length of time required for reinforcement as the student demonstrates success.

6. Remove the student from the group or activity until he/she can demonstrate appropriate behavior and self-control.

7. Write a contract with the student specifying what behavior is expected (e.g., acting in a deliberate and responsible manner) and what reinforcement will be made available when the terms of the contract have been met. (See Appendix for Behavioral Contract.)

8. Communicate with parents (e.g., notes home, phone calls, etc.) in order to share information concerning the student's progress and so that they can reinforce the student at home for engaging in appropriate behavior at school.

9. Evaluate the appropriateness of the task to determine: (a) if the task is too difficult and (b) if the length of time scheduled to complete the task is appropriate.

10. Make certain that consequences are delivered consistently for behavior demonstrated (e.g., appropriate behavior results in positive consequences and inappropriate behavior results in negative consequences).

11. Provide the student with many social and academic successes.

12. Structure the environment in such a way as to limit the opportunities for inappropriate behavior (e.g., keep the student engaged in activities, have the student seated near the teacher, maintain visibility to and from the student, etc.).

13. Prevent the student from becoming overstimulated by an activity (e.g., monitor or supervise student behavior to limit overexcitement in physical activities, games, parties, etc.).

14. Provide the student with natural consequences for inappropriate behavior (e.g., for disturbing others during group activities, the student would have to leave the activity).

15. Provide the student with a clearly identified list of consequences for inappropriate behavior.

16. Teach the student problem-solving skills: (1) identify the problem, (2) identify goals and objectives, (3) develop strategies, (4) develop a plan of action, and (5) carry out the plan.

17. Provide a learning experience which emphasizes the cause-and-effect relationship between behavior and the inevitability of some form of consequence (e.g., both negative and positive behaviors and consequences).

18. Point out consequences of other students' behaviors as they occur (e.g., take the opportunity to point out that consequences occur for all behavior and for all persons).

19. Supervise the student closely in situations in which he/she is likely to act impulsively (e.g., maintain close physical proximity, maintain eye contact, communicate frequently with the student, etc.).

20. Prevent peers from engaging in those behaviors that would cause the student to fail to consider or regard consequences of behavior (e.g., keep other students from upsetting the student).

21. Make the consequences of a behavior obvious by identifying the consequence as it occurs and discussing alternative behavior which would have prevented the particular consequence.

22. Avoid placing the student in competitive situations. Failure may prove so frustrating that it causes the student to ignore consequences of his/her behavior.

23. Allow the student more decision-making opportunities relative to class activities and assignments.

24. Present tasks in the most attractive and interesting manner possible.

25. Give the student responsibilities in the classroom (e.g., teacher assistant, peer tutor, group leader, etc.).

26. Evaluate the appropriateness of the task in relation to the student's ability to perform the task successfully.

27. Show an interest in the student (e.g., acknowledge the student, ask the student's opinion, spend time working one-on-one with the student, etc.).

28. Do not criticize when correcting the student; be honest yet supportive. Never cause the student to feel badly about himself/herself.

29. Treat the student with respect. Talk in an objective manner at all times.

30. Be careful to avoid embarrassing the student by giving him/her orders, demands, etc., in front of others.

31. Make certain that your comments take the form of constructive criticism rather than criticism that can be perceived as personal, threatening, etc. (e.g., instead of saying, "You always make the same mistake." say, "A better way to do that might be . . . ").

32. Make certain the student is allowed to voice an opinion in a situation.

A Reminder: Make certain the student understands that it is his/her behavior which determines consequences and not the teacher who makes the consequence necessary.

190   Does not demonstrate the ability to follow a routine

1. Reinforce the student for demonstrating the ability to follow a routine: (a) give the student a tangible reward (e.g., classroom privileges, line leading, passing out materials, five minutes free time, etc.) or (b) give the student an intangible reward (e.g., praise, handshake, smile, etc.).

2. Speak to the student to explain: (a) what the student is doing wrong (e.g., failing to come to class on time, failing to follow the schedule of activities, etc.) and (b) what the student should be doing (e.g., coming to class on time, following the schedule of activities, etc.).

3. Establish classroom rules:
1. Work on task.
2. Remain in your seat.
3. Finish task.
4. Meet task expectations.
5. Raise your hand.
Reiterate rules often and reinforce students for following rules.

4. Reinforce those students in the classroom who demonstrate the ability to follow a routine.

5. Reinforce the student for demonstrating the ability to follow a routine based on the length of time the student can be successful. Gradually increase the length of time required as the student demonstrates success.

6. Write a contract with the student specifying what behavior is expected (e.g., following the schedule of activities) and what reinforcement will be made available when the terms of the contract have been met. (See Appendix for Behavioral Contract.)

7. Communicate with parents (e.g., notes home, phone calls, etc.) in order to share information concerning the student's progress and so that they can reinforce the student at home for demonstrating the ability to follow a routine at school.

8. Evaluate the appropriateness of the task to determine: (a) if the task is too difficult and (b) if the length of time scheduled to complete the task is appropriate.

9. Identify a peer to act as a model for the student to imitate the ability to follow a routine.

10. Have the student question any directions, explanations, and instructions not understood.

11. Have the student work near a peer in order to follow the same routine that the peer follows.

12. Make certain that the student's routine is consistent each day.

13. Provide the student with a schedule of daily events which identifies the daily activities and the times when they occur.

14. Schedules of daily events should be attached to the student's desk and/or carried by the student at all times.

15. Post the class routine throughout the classroom (e.g., on the student's desk, the chalkboard, the bulletin board, etc.).

16. Limit the interruptions in the student's routine by persons or events in the school (e.g., testing; special services; delays; cancellations of classes or activities such as art, music, or P.E.; etc.).

17. Provide the student with a limited routine to follow. Gradually increase the activities in the routine as the student demonstrates success.

18. Discuss any necessary changes in the student's routine well in advance of the occurrence of changes.

19. Make certain the student is able to tell time in order to enhance the ability to follow a routine.

20. Teach the student to tell time in order to enhance the ability to follow a routine.

21. Have the student rely on a predetermined signal in order to enhance the ability to follow a routine (e.g., bells, lights, etc.).

22. Have the student use a timer to indicate when to change activities in his/her routine.

23. Determine an expected length of time for each individual activity in order to help the student follow a routine (i.e., make certain the student can finish an activity in an established length of time in order to help him/her stay within the time restrictions of the routine).

24. Reduce distracting stimuli which might cause the student to be unable to follow a routine (e.g., peers, physical activity, etc.).

25. Monitor the student's performance in activities or tasks to make certain the student begins, works on, and completes assignments in order to be ready to move to the next activity in his/her routine.

26. Provide the student with additional activities in which to engage when he/she finishes an activity early, in order to maintain a routine.

27. Maintain flexibility in following a routine when changes in the routine are required.

28. Discuss the student's routine with him/her at the beginning of each day and make certain that the student knows the expectations.

29. Have a peer remind the student when to change activities according to his/her routine.

30. Have the student rely on environmental events to remind him/her when to change activities according to the routine (e.g., other students changing activities, bells, etc.).

31. Remind the student when it is time to change activities in order to enhance his/her ability to follow a routine.

32. Make certain that the activities in the student's routine are on his/her ability level.

33. Make certain that the teacher is a model for following a routine.

34. Have a peer accompany the student to other locations in the building which are part of the student's routine.

35. Allow the student to contribute to the development of his/her routine in order to enhance the ability to follow the routine (e.g., have the student determine the order of activities).

36. Provide the student with an alternative routine to follow if he/she encounters difficulty in following a regular routine.

37. Be consistent when expecting the student to follow a routine. Do not allow the student to get out of following a routine one time and expect him/her to follow a routine the next time.

38. Do not leave a lot of unstructured time for the student.

1. Reinforce the student for appropriate care of personal property: (a) give the student a tangible reward (e.g., classroom privileges, line leading, passing out materials, five minutes free time, etc.) or (b) give the student an intangible reward (e.g., praise, handshake, smile, etc.).

2. Speak to the student to explain: (a) what the student is doing wrong (e.g., failing to maintain organization or use materials appropriately) and (b) what the student should be doing (e.g., keeping inside of desk organized, organizing materials on top of desk, using materials as instructed, etc.).

3. Establish classroom rules:
1. Work on task.
2. Remain in your seat.
3. Finish task.
4. Meet task expectations.
5. Raise your hand.

Reiterate rules often and reinforce students for following rules.

4. Reinforce the student for appropriate care of personal property based on the length of time the student can be successful. Gradually increase the length of time required for reinforcement as the student demonstrates success.

5. Write a contract with the student specifying what behavior is expected (e.g., organization and appropriate use of materials) and what reinforcement will be made available when the terms of the contract have been met. (See Appendix for Behavioral Contract.)

6. Communicate with parents (e.g., notes home, phone calls, etc.) in order to share information concerning the student's progress and so that they can reinforce the student at home for organization and appropriate use of materials at school.

7. Provide time at the beginning of each day for the student to organize his/her materials.

8. Provide the student with additional work space (e.g., a larger desk or table at which to work).

9. Assign a peer to work directly with the student to serve as a model for appropriate use and organization of materials.

10. Provide time at various points throughout the day for the student to organize his/her materials (e.g., before school, recess, or lunch; at the end of the day).

11. Evaluate the appropriateness of the task to determine: (a) if the task is too difficult and (b) if the length of time scheduled to complete the task is appropriate.

12. Provide storage space for materials the student is not using at any particular time.

13. Reduce distracting stimuli (e.g., place the student in the front row, provide a carrel or quiet place away from distractions, etc.). This is used as a means of reducing distracting stimuli and not as a form of punishment.

14. Interact frequently with the student in order to encourage organizational skills or appropriate use of materials.

15. Assign the student organizational responsibilities in the classroom (e.g., equipment, software materials, etc.).

16. Limit the student's use of materials (i.e., provide the student with only those materials necessary at any given time).

17. Act as a model for organization and appropriate use of work materials (e.g., putting materials away before getting more materials out, having a place for all materials, maintaining an organized desk area, following a schedule for the day, etc.).

18. Provide adequate time for the completion of activities.

19. Provide adequate transition time between activities for the student to organize himself/herself.

20. Establish a routine to be followed for organization and appropriate use of work (e.g., provide the routine for the student in written form or verbally reiterate often).

21. Supervise the student while he/she is performing schoolwork in order to monitor appropriate care of materials.

22. Allow natural consequences to occur as the result of the student's inability to organize or use materials appropriately (e.g., materials not maintained appropriately will be lost or not serviceable).

23. Assess the quality and clarity of directions, explanations, and instructions given to the student.

24. Assist the student in beginning each task in order to reduce impulsive behavior.

25. Provide the student with structure for all academic activities (e.g., specified directions, routine format for tasks, time units, etc.).

26. Give the student a checklist of materials necessary for each activity.

27. Minimize materials needed.

28. Provide an organizer for materials inside the student's desk.

29. Provide the student with an organizational checklist (e.g., routine activities and steps to follow).

30. Teach the student appropriate care of personal property (e.g., sharpening pencils, keeping books free of marks and tears, etc.).

31. Teach the student how to conserve rather than waste materials (e.g., amount of glue, paper, tape, etc., to use; putting lids, caps, and tops on such materials as markers, pens, bottles, jars, and cans; etc.).

32. Make certain that all personal property is labeled with the student's name.

33. Point out to the student that loaning personal property to other students does not reduce his/her responsibility for the property.

34. Teach the student appropriate ways to deal with anger and frustration rather than destroying personal property and school materials (e.g., pencils, pens, workbooks, notebooks, textbooks, etc.).

35. Teach the student to maintain care of personal property and school materials (e.g., keep property with him/her, know where property is at all times, secure property in locker, leave valuable property at home, etc.).

36. Provide the student with an appropriate place to store/secure personal property (e.g., desk, locker, closet, etc.) and require that the student store all property when not in use.

37. Teach the student that failure to care for personal property will result in the loss of freedom to maintain property (i.e., if the student cannot care for property the teacher(s) will hold all property).

38. Provide reminders (e.g., list of property or materials) to help the student maintain and care for personal property.

39. Limit the student's freedom to take property from school if he/she is unable to remember to return the items.

40. Provide the student with verbal reminders of personal property or materials needed for each activity.

41. Limit the student's opportunity to use school materials if he/she is unable to care for personal property.

42. Make certain that failure to have necessary materials results in loss of opportunity to participate in activities or a failing grade for that day's activity.

43. Reduce the number of materials for which the student is responsible. Increase the number as the student demonstrates appropriate care of property.

44. Teach the student safety rules in the handling of personal property and materials (e.g., pencils, scissors, compass; science, industrial arts, and home economics materials; etc.).

45. Teach the student the appropriate use of personal property and materials (e.g., scissors, pencils, compass; science, industrial arts, and home economic materials; etc.).

46. Require that lost or damaged property be replaced by the student. If the student cannot replace the property, restitution can be made by working at school.

47. Make certain that the student is not inadvertently reinforced for losing or damaging property. Provide the student with used or damaged materials, copies of materials, etc., rather than new materials.

48. Carefully consider the student's age and experience when expecting him/her to care for personal property.

49. Allow natural consequences to occur due to the student's inability to care for personal property (e.g., having to write with a crayon because the student lost his/her pencil, using free time to make up homework that was not turned in, etc.).

50. Be consistent when expecting the student to care for personal property. Do not allow the student to get out of caring for personal property one time and expect him/her to care for personal property the next time.

51. Make a list of written directions you want the student to follow (e.g., put away pencils and paper, hang up coat, put bookbag on the back of your chair, etc.).

52. Have the student do those things that need to be done when it is discussed instead of later (e.g., put the lunchbox up now instead of later so that it will not be missing at lunchtime, etc.).

53. Assist the student in performing responsibilities. Gradually require the student to independently assume more responsibility as he/she demonstrates success.

54. Require the student to care for personal property even though he/she "forgot" to do so at the established time.

55. Do not expect the student to pick up toys, games, materials, etc., that others failed to put away. Encourage everyone to pick up toys, games, materials, etc.

56. Do not put out additional toys, games, materials, etc., for the student if he/she is not able to care for the items he/she is using.

57. Provide shelving, containers, organizers, etc., for the student's personal possessions. Label the storage areas and require the student to keep possessions organized.

58. Limit the use of those things which the student is careless in using.

59. Set aside time each day for everyone in the room to care for personal property.

192 Steals or forcibly takes things from students, teachers, the school building, etc.

A Reminder: The problem is not whether the student is willing to admit guilt. The problem here is that the student takes things that belong to others.

1. Teach the student the concept of borrowing by requiring the return of those things the student has been taking from others.

2. Identify those things the student has been taking from others and provide the student with those items as reinforcers for appropriate behavior.

3. Reduce the opportunity to steal by restricting students from bringing unnecessary items to school.

4. Maintain visibility to and from the student. The teacher should be able to see the student and the student should be able to see the teacher, making eye contact possible at all times.

5. Supervise the student in order to monitor behavior.

6. Encourage all students to monitor their own belongings.

7. Make certain the student has necessary school-related items (e.g., pencil, ruler, paper, etc.).

8. Use a permanent marker to label all property brought to school by students and teachers.

9. Secure all school items of value (e.g., cassette tapes, lab materials, industrial arts and home economic supplies, etc.).

10. Make certain the student understands the natural consequences of inappropriate behavior (e.g., the student must make restitution for taking things which belong to others).

11. Communicate with the student's family to establish procedures whereby the student may earn those things he/she would otherwise take.

12. Teach the student to share (e.g., schedule activities daily which require sharing).

13. Help the student build or create a prized possession to satisfy his/her need for ownership (e.g., this can be done in art, home economics, industrial arts, etc.).

14. Deal with the taking of belongings privately rather than publicly.

15. Provide multiples of the items which are being taken in order to have enough for all or most students to use (e.g., pencils, erasers, rulers, etc.).

16. Do not criticize when correcting the student; be honest yet supportive. Never cause the student to feel badly about himself/herself.

17. Intervene early when there is a problem in order to prevent more serious problems from occurring.

18. Teach the student to respect others and their belongings by respecting the student's belongings.

19. Make certain the student is aware of local and federal laws regarding stealing.

20. Treat the student with respect. Talk in an objective manner at all times.

21. Teach the student to "think" before acting (e.g., ask himself/herself: "What is happening?" "What am I doing?" "What should I do?" "What will be best for me?").

22. Structure the environment so that time does not permit inappropriate behavior.

23. Communicate with the parents (e.g., notes home, phone calls, etc.) in order to share information concerning the student's progress and so that they can reinforce the student at home for appropriate use or consideration of others' belongings at school.

24. Write a contract with the student specifying what behavior is expected (e.g., not taking things which belong to others) and what reinforcement will be made available when the terms of the contract have been met. (See Appendix for Behavioral Contract.)

25. Remove the student from the group or activity until he/she can demonstrate appropriate behavior and self-control.

26. Reinforce the student for demonstrating appropriate behavior based on the length of time the student can be successful. Gradually increase the length of time required for reinforcement as the student demonstrates success.

27. Establish classroom rules:
   1. Work on task.
   2. Work quietly.
   3. Remain in your seat.
   4. Finish task.
   5. Meet task expectations.
   6. Raise your hand.
Reiterate rules often and reinforce students for following rules.

28. Reinforce those students in the classroom who demonstrate appropriate behavior in reference to others' belongings.

29. Speak with the student to explain: (a) what the student is doing wrong (e.g., taking things which belong to others) and (b) what the student should be doing (e.g., asking to use things, borrowing, sharing, returning things, etc.).

30. Reinforce the student for demonstrating appropriate behavior: (a) give the student a tangible reward (e.g., classroom privileges, line leading, passing out materials, five minutes free time, etc.) or (b) give the student an intangible reward (e.g., praise, handshake, smile, etc.).

Please note: Do not rely on or encourage students in the classroom to be informants. Do not use peer pressure in the classroom to solve incidents of stealing.

1. Identify a peer to act as a model for the student to imitate appropriate ways to sit in his/her seat.

2. Have the student question any directions, explanations, and instructions not understood.

3. Have desks and/or chairs that can be fastened to the floor or which are designed to prevent tipping.

4. Provide the student with a specific description of appropriate in-seat behavior (e.g., facing forward, feet on floor, back straight, etc.).

5. Implement logical consequences for students who fail to sit appropriately in their seats (e.g., the student will have to sit on the floor, stand next to his/her desk to work, sit in a chair without a desk, etc.).

6. Maintain consistency of expectations for having the student sit appropriately in his/her seat.

7. Make certain the student is aware of the natural consequences that may occur from sitting inappropriately in his/her seat (e.g., injury, damaging property, hurting others, etc.).

8. Place the student in a carrel in order to reduce distracting stimuli which may cause the student to sit inappropriately in his/her seat.

9. Seat the student next to a peer who sits appropriately in his/her seat.

10. Deliver a predetermined signal (e.g., give a hand signal, ring a bell, etc.) when the student begins to sit inappropriately in his/her seat.

11. Model for the student appropriate ways in which to sit in a chair or at a desk.

12. Provide activities which are interesting to the student in order to keep the student on task and sitting appropriately in his/her seat.

13. Seat the student near the teacher.

14. Seat the student away from peers in order to reduce the likelihood that the student will sit inappropriately in his/her seat.

15. Evaluate the necessity of having the student to sit facing forward, feet on floor, back straight, etc.

16. Make certain that the chair or desk the student is assigned to use is appropriate and/or comfortable for him/her (e.g., the desk is not too high, the chair is not too big, etc.).

17. Remove any materials with which the student makes noises while seated.

18. Use natural consequences when the student touches others as they walk by (e.g., move the student to another location in the room, have others walk away from the student, etc.).

19. Intervene early when there is a problem in order to prevent more serious problems from occurring.

20. Teach the student to "think" before acting (e.g., ask himself/herself: "What is happening?" "What am I doing?" "What should I do?" "What will be best for me?").

21. Evaluate the appropriateness of the task to determine: (a) if the task is too easy difficult, and (b) if the length of time scheduled to complete the task is appropriate.

22. Communicate with parents (e.g., notes home, phone calls, etc.) in order to share information concerning the student's progress and so that they can reinforce the student at home for sitting appropriately in his/her seat at school.

23. Write a contract with the student specifying what behavior is expected (e.g., sitting appropriately in his/her seat) and what reinforcement will be made available when the terms of the contract have been met. (See Appendix for Behavioral Contract.)

24. Reinforce the student for sitting appropriately in his/her seat based on the length of time the student can be successful. Gradually increase the length of time required for reinforcement as the student demonstrates success.

25. Reinforce those students in the classroom who sit appropriately in their seats.

26. Establish classroom rules:
1. Work on task.
2. Work quietly.
3. Remain in your seat.
4. Finish task.
5. Meet task expectations.
6. Raise your hand.
Reiterate rules often and reinforce students for following rules.

27. Speak to the student to explain: (a) what the student is doing wrong (e.g., tipping chair) and (b) what the student should be doing (e.g., sitting appropriately in his/her chair).

28. Reinforce the student for sitting appropriately in his/her seat: (a) give the student a tangible reward (e.g., classroom privileges, line leading, passing out materials, five minutes free time, etc.) or (b) give the student an intangible reward (e.g., praise, handshake, smile, etc.).

194 Does not follow directives from teachers or other school personnel

1. Structure the environment in such a way that the student remains active and involved in appropriate behavior.

2. Maintain visibility to and from the student. The teacher should be able to see the student and the student should be able to see the teacher, making eye contact possible at all times.

3. Give the student preferred responsibilities.

4. Present the tasks in the most interesting and attractive manner possible.

5. Maintain maximum supervision of the student and gradually decrease supervision as the student becomes successful at following directives.

6. Have the student maintain a chart representing the amount of time spent following teacher directives or rules, with reinforcement given for increasing appropriate behavior.

7. Be mobile in order to frequently be near the student.

8. Provide the student with many social and academic successes.

9. Provide the student with positive feedback that indicates he/she is successful.

10. Post rules in various places, including on the student's desk.

11. Make certain the student receives the information necessary to perform activities (e.g., written information, verbal directions, reminders, etc.).

12. Teach the student direction-following skills: (a) listen carefully, (b) ask questions, (c) use environmental cues, (d) rely on examples, (e) wait until all directions are given before beginning, etc.

13. Maintain the most positive, professional relationship with the student (i.e., an adversary relationship is likely to result in failure to follow directions).

14. Be a consistent authority figure (e.g., be consistent in relationship with student).

15. Provide the student with optional courses of action in order to prevent total refusal to obey directives from teachers and other school personnel.

16. Intervene early to prevent the student's behavior from leading to contagion for other students.

17. Deliver directions in a step-by-step sequence.

18. Have a peer act as a model for following teacher directives.

19. Interact with the student frequently to determine if directives are being followed.

20. Maintain consistency in rules, routine, and general expectations of conduct and procedure.

21. Allow natural consequences to occur as a result of not following directives from teachers and other school personnel (e.g., assignments are performed incorrectly, accidents will occur, detention will be assigned, etc.).

22. Limit the student's opportunity to engage in activities in which he/she will not follow directives from teachers and other school personnel (e.g., recess, industrial arts activities, field trips, etc.).

23. Do not allow the student to be unsupervised anywhere in the school environment.

24. Along with a directive, provide an incentive statement (e.g., "When you finish your math, you may go outside." "You may have free time after you finish your work.").

25. In order to determine if the student heard a direction, have the student repeat it.

26. Deliver directions in a supportive rather than a threatening manner (e.g., "Please finish your work." rather than "You had better finish your work or else!").

27. Teach the student to respect others and their belongings by respecting the student's belongings.

28. Teach the student to "think" before acting (e.g., ask himself/herself: "What is happening?" "What am I doing?" "What should I do?" "What will be best for me?").

29. Make certain the student is allowed to voice an opinion in a situation in order to avoid becoming angry or upset.

30. Evaluate the appropriateness of the task to determine: (a) if the task is too difficult or (b) if the length of time scheduled to complete the task is appropriate.

31. Communicate with parents (e.g., notes home, phone calls, etc.) in order to share information concerning the student's progress and so that they can reinforce the student at home for following directives from teachers and other school personnel.

32. Write a contract with the student specifying what behavior is expected (e.g., following teacher directives) and what reinforcement will be made available when the terms of the contract have been met. (See Appendix for Behavioral Contract.)

33. Remove the student from the group or activity until he/she can demonstrate appropriate behavior and self-control.

34. Reinforce the student for following the directives of teachers and other school personnel based on the length of time the student can be successful. Gradually increase the amount of time required for reinforcement as the student demonstrates success.

35. Reinforce those students in the classroom who follow directives from teachers and other school personnel.

36. Establish classroom rules:
1. Work on task.
2. Work quietly.
3. Remain in your seat.
4. Finish task.
5. Meet task expectations.
6. Raise your hand.

Reiterate rules often and reinforce students for following rules.

37. Speak with the student to explain: (a) what the student is doing wrong (e.g., failing to follow directions or observe rules) and (b) what the student should be doing (e.g., following established guidelines or expectations).

38. Reinforce the student for following directives from teachers or other school personnel: (a) give the student a tangible reward (e.g., classroom privileges, line leading, passing out materials, five minutes free time, etc.) or (b) give the student an intangible reward (e.g., praise, handshake, smile, etc.).

195 Brings inappropriate or illegal materials to school

1. Communicate with parents, agencies, or appropriate parties in order to inform them of the problem, determine the cause of the problem, and consider possible solutions to the problem.

2. Provide a drug information program for the individual student, the class, or the student body.

3. Provide an orientation to penalties for possession or use of alcohol and drugs at school.

4. Involve the student in extracurricular activities to help him/her develop appropriate interests.

5. Identify individuals the student may contact with his/her concerns (e.g., guidance counselor, school nurse, social worker, school psychologist, etc.).

6. Share concerns with the administration and seek referral to an agency for investigation of alcohol or drug abuse.

7. Encourage the student to become involved in athletic activities.

8. Assign the student activities which would require interactions with a respected role model (e.g., older student, high school student, college student, community leader, someone held in esteem, etc.).

9. Provide the student with intelligent, accurate information concerning drugs and alcohol rather than sensationalized, scare-tactic information.

10. Provide many opportunities for social and academic success.

11. Encourage the student to excel in a particular area of interest (e.g., provide information for the student, provide personal and professional support, sponsor the student, etc.).

12. Maintain frequent contact with the student during school hours (e.g., follow up on details of earlier communications, maintain a direction for conversation, etc.).

13. Maintain anecdotal records of the student's behavior to check patterns or changes in behavior.

14. When natural consequences with peers occur (e.g., criticism, loss of friendship, etc.) as the result of the use of drugs or alcohol at school, bring the consequences to the attention of the student.

15. Encourage the student's parents to be positive and helpful with the student as opposed to being negative and threatening.

16. Act as a resource for parents by providing information on agencies, counseling programs, etc.

17. Teach the student to be satisfied with his/her own personal best effort rather than perfection.

18. Reduce the emphasis on competition and help the student realize that success is individually defined.

19. Be willing to take the time to listen, share, and talk with the student.

20. Increase your own professional knowledge of laws and treatment concerning drug or alcohol use and abuse.

21. Teach the student alternative ways to deal with demands, challenges, and pressures of the school-age experience (e.g., deal with problems when they arise, practice self-control at all times, share problems or concerns with others, etc.).

22. Maintain adequate supervision at all times and in all areas of the school (e.g., hallways, bathrooms, between classes, before and after school, school grounds, etc.).

23. Provide appropriate reading material (e.g., magazines, novels, etc.) at school which is of interest to the student so that he/she will not bring inappropriate reading material to school.

24. Lead and direct the student. Do not lecture and make demands.

25. Make certain the student is aware of local and federal laws regarding inappropriate or illegal materials in the school.

26. Communicate with parents (e.g., notes home, phone calls, etc.) in order to share information concerning the student's progress and so that they can reinforce the student at home for demonstrating appropriate behavior at school.

27. Write a contract with the student specifying what behavior is expected (e.g., not bringing alcohol to school) and what reinforcement will be made available when the terms of the contract have been met. (See Appendix for Behavioral Contract.)

28. Remove the student from the group or activity until he/she can demonstrate appropriate behavior and self-control.

29. Reinforce the student for demonstrating appropriate behavior based on the length of time the student can be successful. Gradually increase the length of time required for reinforcement as the student demonstrates success.

30. Reinforce those students in the classroom who demonstrate appropriate behavior.

31. Establish classroom rules:
1. Work on task.
2. Work quietly.
3. Remain in your seat.
4. Finish task.
5. Meet task expectations.
6. Raise your hand.
Reiterate rules often and reinforce students for following rules.

32. Speak with the student to explain: (a) what the student is doing wrong (e.g., bringing inappropriate or illegal materials to school) and (b) what the student should be doing (e.g., following an established code of conduct, following rules, taking care of responsibilities, etc.).

33. Reinforce the student for demonstrating appropriate behavior: (a) give the student a tangible reward (e.g., classroom privileges, line leading, passing out materials, five minutes free time, etc.) or (b) give the student an intangible reward (e.g., praise, handshake, smile, etc.).

196 Responds inappropriately to redirection in academic and social situations

1. Allow natural consequences to occur when the student fails to respond appropriately to redirection in academic and social situations (e.g., make highly reinforcing activities contingent upon responding appropriately to redirection in academic and social situations).

2. Remove the student from the activity if he/she fails to respond appropriately to redirection in academic and social situations.

3. Make certain that attention is not inadvertently given to the student for failing to respond appropriately to redirection in academic and social situations (e.g., remove attention from the student when he/she fails to respond appropriately to redirection in academic and social situations in those instances when attention is reinforcing the inappropriate behavior).

4. Provide adequate time for the student to respond appropriately to redirection in academic and social situations.

5. Make certain that redirection in academic and social situations is delivered in the most positive manner.

6. Deliver redirection to the student as privately as possible.

7. Deliver instructions in a clear and concise manner.

8. Assist the student in responding appropriately to redirection in academic situations (e.g., help the student correct one or two items in order to get started).

9. Develop subsequent tasks based on errors the student makes rather than requiring an immediate correction of work done incorrectly.

10. Make certain the student understands that natural consequences may occur as a result of failing to appropriately respond to redirection in a social situation (e.g., peers will not include him/her in activities, peers will not want to share materials with him/her, etc.).

11. Make certain that the student's failure to respond to redirection in social situations results in loss of opportunity to engage in that activity for some period of time (e.g., one day).

12. Make certain the student understands the assignment or activity by having him/her rephrase the directions.

13. Make certain the student understands the communication regarding redirection by having the student rephrase the direction.

14. Determine the reasons for errors made by the student.

15. Evaluate the demands made on the student in academic and social situations in order to make certain that all expectations are within the student's ability level.

16. In order to reduce the need for redirection in academic and social situations, require the student to check all work for errors prior to handing in assignments.

17. When redirection is delivered to the student in academic and social situations, make certain that an explanation as to why the redirection has been made is also given (e.g., "You need to return to your seat because we are ready to begin a new activity.").

18. Make certain that the activity is not so overstimulating as to result in the student's inability to respond appropriately to redirection in academic and social situations.

19. Be consistent in expectations when redirecting the student in academic and social situations (e.g., require the student to immediately correct errors after work has been checked, require the student to return to his/her seat within three minutes, etc.).

20. Monitor the student's behavior in order to provide redirection before the student's errors or inappropriate behavior cause an inability to respond appropriately.

21. Base expectations for student response to redirection in academic and social situations on the student's ability level (e.g., one student may be expected to return to his/her seat immediately upon redirection while another student may be given three minutes to respond appropriately).

22. Avoid those circumstances in which the student demonstrates difficulty in responding appropriately to redirection in academic and social situations (e.g., highly competitive situations, situations in which the student is embarrassed by his/her errors, etc.).

23. Make certain that redirection does not become a pervasive aspect of everything the student does by allowing redirection to become a necessary part of every academic and social situation in which the student engages.

24. Make certain the student understands that redirection is designed to help him/her succeed rather than as a form of punishment (e.g., use statements such as, "This sentence would be much easier to read if it were written with correct capitalization and punctuation. Please write it again, and I'll check it for you.").

25. Make certain that communications with the student regarding redirection are appropriate to the student's ability to respond (e.g., match the form in which redirection is delivered to the student's most likely successful response, such as "Would you please go to your seat." rather than "You need to go to your seat immediately.").

26. Do not criticize when correcting the student; be honest yet supportive. Never cause the student to feel badly about himself/herself.

27. Have the student question any directions, explanations, and instructions not understood.

28. Identify a peer to act as a model for the student to imitate appropriate response to redirection in academic and social situations.

29. Write a contract with the student specifying what behavior is expected (e.g., returning to seat when told to do so) and what reinforcement will be made available when the terms of the contract have been met. (See Appendix for Behavioral Contract.)

30. Evaluate the appropriateness of the task to determine: (a) if the task is too difficult and (b) if the length of time scheduled to complete the task is appropriate.

31. Communicate with parents (e.g., notes home, phone calls, etc.) in order to share information concerning the student's progress and so that they can reinforce the student at home for responding appropriately to redirection in academic and social situations at school.

32. Reinforce the student for responding appropriately to redirection within a given period of time based on the number of times the student can be successful. Gradually increase the number of times required for reinforcement as the student demonstrates success.

33. Reinforce those students in the classroom who respond appropriately to redirection in academic and social situations.

34. Establish classroom rules:
1. Work on task.
2. Work quietly.
3. Remain in your seat.
4. Finish task.
5. Correct errors.
6. Meet task expectations.
7. Raise your hand.
Reiterate rules often and reinforce students for following rules.

35. Speak to the student to explain: (a) what the student is doing wrong (e.g., not correcting errors on an assignment, failing to return to seat when told to do so, etc.) and (b) what the student should be doing (e.g., correcting errors on an assignment, returning to seat when told to do so, etc.).

36. Reinforce the student for responding appropriately to redirection in academic and social situations: (a) give the student a tangible reward (e.g., classroom privileges, line leading, passing out materials, five minutes free time, etc.) or (b) give the student an intangible reward (e.g., praise, handshake, smile, etc.).

1. Maintain maximum supervision of the student and gradually decrease supervision as the student is able to follow school rules.

2. Have the student maintain a chart representing the amount of time spent following school rules, with reinforcement given for increasing acceptable behavior.

3. Practice mobility to be frequently near the student.

4. Provide the student with many social and academic successes.

5. Provide the student with positive feedback that indicates he/she is successful.

6. Post school rules in various places, including on the student's desk, in the hallways, etc.

7. Be a consistent authority figure (e.g., be consistent in relationship with students).

8. Provide the student with optional courses of action in order to prevent total refusal to obey school rules (e.g., may return to the classroom).

9. Intervene early to prevent the student's behavior from leading to contagion of other students.

10. Require the student to verbalize the school rules at designated times throughout the day (e.g., before school, during recess, at lunch, at the end of the day, etc.).

11. Have a peer act as a model for following school rules.

12. Interact with the student frequently to determine if school rules are being followed.

13. Make certain that all educators maintain consistent enforcement of school rules.

14. Have the student question any school rules not understood.

15. Provide the student with a list of school rules and/or behavior expectations to carry with him/her at all times in the school environment.

16. Help the student identify specific school rules he/she has difficulty following and make these rules into goals for behavior improvement.

17. Separate the student from the peer(s) who stimulates his/her inappropriate behavior.

18. Make certain that rules and behavior expectations are consistent throughout the school and classroom.

19. Model for the student those behaviors he/she is expected to display in the school environment.

20. Have a peer accompany the student in nonacademic settings.

21. Make certain that behavioral demands are appropriate for the student's ability level (e.g., staying in line, waiting a turn, moving with a group, sitting at a table with a group, moving about the building alone, etc.).

22. Make certain the student is actively involved in the environment (i.e., give the student responsibilities, activities, and errands to run in order to provide purposeful behavior).

23. Reinforce the student for moving from one place to another in an appropriate length of time.

24. Have the student carry a point card at all times so that he/she can be reinforced anywhere in the school environment for following rules.

25. Inform other personnel of any behavior problem that the student may have in order that supervision and assistance may be provided.

26. Be consistent in applying consequences for behavior (e.g., appropriate behavior receives positive consequences while inappropriate behavior receives negative consequences).

27. Reinforce the student for going directly from one location to another.

28. Reinforce the student for remaining in assigned areas (e.g., play areas, student lounge, recreational area, etc.).

29. Use related consequences for the student's inappropriate behavior (e.g., running in the halls results in having to walk with an adult, throwing food in the cafeteria results in having to sit next to an adult when eating, disruption in the library requires additional adult supervision, etc.).

30. Along with a directive, provide an incentive statement (e.g., "When you finish your math, you may go outside to play." "You may have free time after you finish your work.").

31. Intervene early when there is a problem in order to prevent more serious problems from occurring.

32. Before beginning a new activity, make sure the student knows the rules.

33. Teach the student to "think" before acting (e.g., ask himself/herself: "What is happening?" "What am I doing?" "What should I do?" "What will be best for me?").

34. Maintain visibility to and from the student. The teacher should be able to see the student and the student should be able to see the teacher, making eye contact possible at all times.

35. Structure the environment in such a way that the student remains active and involved.

36. Have the student question any directions, explanations, and instructions not understood.

37. Evaluate the appropriateness of the task to determine: (a) if the task is too difficult and (b) if the length of time scheduled to complete the task is appropriate.

38. Communicate with parents (e.g., notes home, phone calls, etc.) in order to share information concerning the student's progress and so that they can reinforce the student at home for following school rules.

39. Write a contract with the student specifying what behavior is expected (e.g., walking in the halls) and what reinforcement will be made available when the terms of the contract have been met. (See Appendix for Behavioral Contract.)

40. Reinforce the student for following school rules based on the length of time the student can be successful. Gradually increase the length of time required for reinforcement as the student demonstrates success.

41. Reinforce those students in the classroom who follow school rules.

42. Establish school rules:
1. Walk in halls.
2. Arrive for class on time.
3. Respect the privacy of others.
4. Talk quietly in the halls.
Reiterate rules often and reinforce students for following rules.

43. Speak to the student to explain: (a) what the student is doing wrong (e.g., failing to follow school rules) and (b) what the student should be doing (e.g., following school rules).

44. Reinforce the student for following school rules: (a) give the student a tangible reward (e.g., classroom privileges, line leading, passing out materials, five minutes free time, etc.) or (b) give the student an intangible reward (e.g., praise, handshake, smile, etc.).

198   Demonstrates inappropriate behavior on the school grounds before and after school

1. Provide the student with a list of school ground rules.

2. Separate the student from the peer(s) who stimulates his/her inappropriate behavior on the school grounds before and after school.

3. Have a peer accompany the student when he/she is on the school grounds before and after school.

4. Make certain the behavioral demands are appropriate for the student's ability level (e.g., interacting with peers, entering the building when appropriate, leaving the building when appropriate, using school equipment with care, etc.).

5. Make certain the student is actively involved on the school grounds before and after school (e.g., team activities, responsibilities before and after school, etc.).

6. Have the student carry a point card at all times so that he/she can be reinforced on the school grounds before and after school.

7. Inform school personnel of any behavior problems the student may have in order that supervision and assistance may be provided on the school grounds before and after school.

8. Be consistent in applying consequences for behavior (e.g., appropriate behavior receives positive consequences while inappropriate behavior receives negative consequences).

9. Reinforce the student for remaining in assigned areas (e.g., play areas, student lounge, recreational areas, etc.).

10. Provide organized activities for the student to participate in on the school grounds before and after school (e.g., kickball, dodge ball, softball, four square, tether ball, jump rope, foot races, etc.).

11. Allow the student to enter the building early or remain in the building after school to work on assignments or special projects, assist teachers, assist the custodian, etc.

12. Reinforce the student for arriving on the school grounds shortly before school begins (e.g., 5 minutes) and leaving the school grounds shortly after school.

13. Change the student's bus assignment in order that the student does not arrive early and does not stay late after school.

14. Have an older peer meet the student before school begins and remain with the student after school until the student leaves the school grounds.

15. Identify a specified area of the school grounds to be used as a "time-out" area when the student demonstrates inappropriate behavior on the school grounds before and after school.

16. Have the student be responsible for a younger peer on the school grounds before and after school.

17. Have the student be responsible for organizing and supervising activities and distributing or collecting materials on the school grounds before and after school.

18. Give the student a specific job to perform on the school grounds before and after school (e.g., crosswalk patrol, bus monitor, raising and lowering the flag, picking up litter on the school grounds, etc.).

19. Intervene early when there is a problem in order to prevent a more serious problem from occurring.

20. Teach the student to "think" before acting (e.g., ask himself/herself: "What is happening?" "What am I doing?" "What should I do?" "What will be best for me?" etc.).

21. Have the student question any school ground rules not understood.

22. Establish school ground rules:
1. Remain in assigned areas.
2. Share school equipment.
3. Use appropriate language.
4. Use school property with care.
Reiterate rules often and reinforce students for following rules.

23. Identify a peer to act as a model for the student to imitate appropriate behavior on the school grounds before and after school.

24. Communicate with parents (e.g., notes home, phone calls, etc.) in order to share information concerning the student's progress and so that they can reinforce the student at home for demonstrating appropriate behavior on the school grounds before and after school.

25. Write a contract with the student specifying what behavior is expected (e.g., playing, sharing school equipment, visiting, etc.) and what reinforcement will be made available when the terms of the contract have been met. (See Appendix for Behavioral Contract.)

26. Reinforce the student for demonstrating appropriate behavior on the school grounds before and after school based on the length of time the student can be successful. Gradually increase the length of time required for reinforcement as the student demonstrates success.

27. Reinforce those students who demonstrate appropriate behavior on the school grounds before and after school.

28. Speak to the student to explain: (a) what the student is doing wrong (e.g., fighting with peers) and (b) what the student should be doing (e.g., playing appropriately, sharing school equipment with peers, visiting, etc.).

29. Reinforce the student for demonstrating appropriate behavior on the school grounds before and after school: (a) give the student a tangible reward (e.g., classroom privileges, line leading, passing out materials, five minutes free time, etc.) or (b) give the student an intangible reward (e.g., praise, handshake, smile, etc.).

1. Structure the environment in such a way that the student remains active and involved while demonstrating acceptable behavior.

2. Maintain visibility to and from the student. The teacher should be able to see the student and the student should be able to see the teacher, making eye contact possible at all times.

3. Give the student preferred responsibilities.

4. Present tasks in the most interesting and attractive manner possible.

5. Have the student maintain a chart representing the amount of time spent following classroom rules, with reinforcement for increasing acceptable behavior.

6. Practice mobility to be frequently near the student.

7. Provide the student with many social and academic successes.

8. Provide the student with positive feedback that indicates he/she is successful.

9. Post rules in various places, including on the student's desk.

10. Make certain the student receives the information necessary to perform activities (e.g., written information, verbal directions, reminders, etc.).

11. Teach the student direction-following skills.

12. Maintain a positive and professional relationship with the student (e.g., an adversary relationship is likely to result in failure to follow directions).

13. Be a consistent authority figure (e.g., be consistent in relationships with students).

14. Provide the student with optional courses of action in order to prevent total refusal to obey teacher directives.

15. Intervene early to prevent the student's behavior from leading to contagion of other students.

16. Have the student question any directions, explanations, and instructions not understood.

17. Require the student to verbalize the classroom rules at designated times throughout the day (e.g., before school, during recess, at lunch, at the end of the day, etc.).

18. Deliver directions in a step-by-step sequence.

19. Have a peer act as a model for following the rules of the classroom.

20. Interact with the student frequently to determine if directives are being followed.

21. Maintain consistency in rules, routine, and general expectations of conduct and procedure.

22. Provide the student with a list of rules and/or behavior expectations.

23. Help the student identify specific rules he/she has difficulty following and make these areas goals for behavior improvement.

24. Separate the student from the peer(s) who stimulates his/her inappropriate behavior.

25. Make certain that rules and behavior expectations are consistent throughout the school and classrooms.

26. Along with a directive, provide an incentive statement (e.g., "When you finish your math, you may go outside to play." "You may have free time after you finish your work.").

27. Intervene early when there is a problem in order to prevent more serious problems from occurring.

28. Before beginning a new activity, make sure the student knows the classroom rules.

29. Teach the student to "think" before acting (e.g., ask himself/herself: "What is happening?" "What am I doing?" "What should I do?" "What will be best for me?").

30. Evaluate the appropriateness of the assigned task to determine: (a) if the task is too difficult, and (b) if the length of time scheduled to complete the task is appropriate.

31. Communicate with parents (e.g., notes home, phone calls, etc.) in order to share information concerning the student's progress and so that they can reinforce the student at home for following the rules of the classroom.

32. Write a contract with the student specifying what behavior is expected (e.g., following classroom rules) and what reinforcement will be made available when the terms of the contract have been met. (See Appendix for Behavioral Contract.)

33. Remove the student from the group or activity until he/she can demonstrate acceptable behavior and self-control.

34. Reinforce the student for following the rules of the classroom based on the length of time the student can be successful. Gradually increase the length of time required for reinforcement as the student demonstrates success.

35. Reinforce those students who follow the rules of the classroom.

36. Establish classroom rules:
1. Work on task.
2. Work quietly.
3. Remain in your seat.
4. Finish task.
5. Meet task expectations.
6. Raise your hand.
Reiterate rules often and reinforce students for following rules.

37. Speak with the student to explain: (a) what the student is doing wrong (e.g., failing to follow classroom rules) and (b) what the student should be doing (e.g., following the rules of the classroom).

38. Reinforce the student for following the rules of the classroom: (a) give the student a tangible reward (e.g., classroom privileges, line leading, passing out materials, five minutes free time, etc.) or (b) give the student an intangible reward (e.g., praise, handshake, smile, etc.).

200 Does not wait appropriately for an instructor to arrive

1. Identify a peer to act as a model for the student to imitate appropriate behavior (e.g., staying in seat or assigned area, remaining quiet, working on assigned task, etc.) when an instructor is detained.

2. Have the student question any directions, explanations, and instructions not understood.

3. Assign a peer to supervise the student when an instructor is detained.

4. Provide a list of possible activities for the students to engage in when an instructor is detained (e.g., color, write a letter to a friend, work on assigned tasks, organize work area, look at a magazine, etc.).

5. Along with a directive, provide an incentive statement (e.g., "If you wait quietly, you can have 5 minutes free time.").

6. Deliver directions in a supportive rather than a threatening manner (e.g., "Please wait quietly." rather than "You had better wait quietly or else!").

7. Make sure the student knows when it is acceptable to get others' attention (e.g., in an emergency).

8. Communicate with parents (e.g., notes home, phone calls, etc.) in order to share information concerning the student's progress and so that they can reinforce the student at home for waiting appropriately for an instructor to arrive at school.

9. Write a contract with the student specifying what behavior is expected (e.g., stay in seat or assigned area, remain quiet, and work on assigned task) and what reinforcement will be made available when the terms of the contract have been met. (See Appendix for Behavioral Contract.)

10. Reinforce the student for waiting appropriately for an instructor to arrive based on the length of time the student can be successful. Gradually increase the length of time required for reinforcement as the student demonstrates success.

11. Reinforce those students in the classroom who stay in their seats or assigned area, remain quiet, and work on assigned tasks.

12. Establish classroom rules:
    1. Work on task.
    2. Remain in your seat.
    3. Finish task.
    4. Meet task expectations.
    5. Raise your hand.
Reiterate rules often and reinforce students for following rules.

13. Speak to the student to explain: (a) what the student is doing wrong (e.g., leaving seat, talking, making noises, etc.) and (b) what the student should be doing (e.g., sitting in seat or assigned area, remaining quiet, etc.).

14. Reinforce the student for waiting appropriately for an instructor to arrive: (a) give the student a tangible reward (e.g., classroom privileges, line leading, passing out materials, five minutes free time, etc.) or (b) give the student an intangible reward (e.g., praise, handshake, smile, etc.).

201 Does not wait appropriately for assistance or attention from an instructor

1. Identify a peer to act as a model for the student to imitate appropriate behavior (e.g., remaining quietly seated or in an assigned area) when waiting for assistance or attention from an instructor.

2. Have the student question any directions, explanations, and instructions not understood.

3. Tell the student that you will assist him/her as soon as possible (e.g., "Stephen, I'll be with you shortly.") in order to increase the probability that the student will wait appropriately for assistance.

4. Identify a peer to whom the student may go for assistance.

5. Attempt to provide assistance immediately. Gradually increase the length of time the student must wait for assistance when you are helping another student, instructing a small group activity, etc.

6. Encourage the student to go on to the next problem, go on to another part of the assignment, begin a new assignment, etc., when waiting for assistance or attention from an instructor.

7. Establish alternative activities for the student to perform when waiting for assistance or attention from an instructor (e.g., check work already completed, color, look at a magazine, organize work area, begin another task, etc.).

8. Position yourself in order that visibility to and from the student may be maintained until assistance can be provided.

9. Maintain verbal communication with the student until assistance can be provided (e.g., "Thank you for waiting quietly. I'll be there shortly.").

10. Along with a directive, provide an incentive statement (e.g., "If you wait quietly, you may have 5 minutes of free time.").

11. Deliver directions in a supportive rather than a threatening manner (e.g., "Please wait quietly." rather than "You had better wait quietly or else!").

12. Make sure the student knows when it is acceptable to interrupt others (e.g., in an emergency).

13. Evaluate the appropriateness of the task to determine: (a) if the task is too difficult and (b) if the length of time scheduled to complete the task is appropriate.

14. Communicate with parents (e.g., notes home, phone calls, etc.) in order to share information concerning the student's progress and so that they can reinforce the student at home for waiting appropriately for assistance or attention from an instructor at school.

15. Write a contract with the student specifying what behavior is expected (e.g., remaining quietly seated or in an assigned area) and what reinforcement will be made available when the terms of the contract have been met. (See Appendix for Behavioral Contract.)

16. Reinforce the student for waiting appropriately for assistance or attention from an instructor based on the length of time the student can be successful. Gradually increase the length of time required for reinforcement as the student demonstrates success.

17. Reinforce those students in the classroom who remain quietly seated in an assigned area.

18. Establish classroom rules:
1. Work on task.
2. Remain in your seat.
3. Finish task.
4. Meet task expectations.
5. Raise your hand.
Reiterate rules often and reinforce students for following rules.

19. Speak to the student to explain: (a) what the student is doing wrong (e.g., leaving his/her seat, talking to other students, etc.) and (b) what the student should be doing (e.g., remaining quietly seated or in an assigned area).

20. Reinforce the student for waiting appropriately for assistance or attention from an instructor: (a) give the student a tangible reward (e.g., classroom privileges, line leading, passing out materials, five minutes free time, etc.) or (b) give the student an intangible reward (e.g., praise, handshake, smile, etc.).

202 Does not demonstrate appropriate use of school-related materials

1. Provide time at the beginning of each day to help the student organize his/her school-related materials.

2. Provide time at various points throughout the day to help the student organize school-related materials (e.g., before school, during recess, during lunch, at the end of the day, etc.).

3. Provide the student with adequate work space (e.g., larger desk or table at which to work).

4. Provide storage space for school-related materials the student is not using at any particular time.

5. Reduce distracting stimuli (e.g., place the student on the front row, provide a carrel or quiet place away from distractions, etc.). This is used as a means of reducing distracting stimuli and not as a form of punishment.

6. Interact frequently with the student in order to prompt organizational skills and appropriate use of school-related materials.

7. Assign the student organizational responsibilities in the classroom (e.g., equipment, software materials, etc.).

8. Limit the student's use of school-related materials (e.g., provide the student with only those school-related materials necessary at any given time).

9. Act as a model for organization and appropriate use of school-related materials (e.g., putting materials away before getting other materials out, having a place for all materials, maintaining an organized desk area, following a schedule for the day, etc.).

10. Provide adequate transition time between activities for the student to organize himself/herself.

11. Establish a routine to be followed for organization and appropriate use of school-related materials.

12. Provide adequate time for the completion of activities.

13. Require the student to organize his/her work area at regular intervals. (It is recommended that this be done at least three times per day or more often if necessary.)

14. Supervise the student while he/she is performing schoolwork in order to monitor quality.

15. Allow natural consequences to occur as the result of the student's inability to organize or use school-related materials appropriately (e.g., materials not maintained appropriately will be lost or not serviceable).

16. Assess the quality and clarity of directions, explanations, and instructions given to the student.

17. Assist the student in beginning each task in order to reduce impulsive behavior.

18. Provide the student with structure for all academic activities (e.g., specific directions, routine format for tasks, time units, etc.).

19. Give the student a checklist of school-related materials necessary for each activity.

20. Minimize school-related materials necessary for each activity.

21. Provide an organizer inside the student's desk for school-related materials.

22. Provide the student with an organizational checklist (e.g., routine activities and steps to follow).

23. Teach the student appropriate care of school-related materials (e.g., sharpening pencils, keeping books free of marks and tears, etc.).

24. Make certain that all of the student's school-related materials are labeled with his/her name.

25. Point out to the student that loaning his/her school-related materials to other students does not reduce personal responsibility for the materials.

26. Teach the student to conserve rather than waste school-related materials (e.g., amount of glue, paper, tape, etc., to use; putting lids, caps, and tops on materials such as markers, pens, bottles, jars, cans, etc.).

27. Teach the student appropriate ways to deal with anger and frustration rather than destroying school-related materials.

28. Teach the student to maintain school-related materials (e.g., keep materials with him/her, know where materials are at all times, secure materials in his/her locker, etc.).

29. Provide the student with an appropriate place to store/secure materials (e.g., desk, locker, closet, etc.) and require him/her to store all materials when not in use.

30. Explain to the student that failure to care for school-related materials will result in the loss of freedom to maintain materials.

31. Provide reminders (e.g., a list of school-related materials) to help the student maintain and care for school-related materials.

32. Limit the student's freedom to take school-related materials from school if he/she is unable to return such items.

33. Provide the student with verbal reminders of school-related materials needed for each activity.

34. Limit the student's opportunity to use school-related materials if the student is unable to care for personal property.

35. Make certain that failure to have necessary school-related materials results in loss of opportunity to participate in activities or a failing grade for that day's activity.

36. Reduce the number of school-related materials for which the student is responsible. Increase the number as the student demonstrates appropriate care of materials.

37. Teach the student safety rules in the handling of school-related materials (e.g., pencils, scissors, compass; biology, industrial arts, and home economics materials; etc.).

38. Teach the student appropriate use of school-related materials (e.g., scissors, pencils, compass, rulers; biology, industrial arts, and home economics materials; etc.).

39. Do not give the student additional materials if he/she is not able to take care of what he/she has.

40. Have the student earn the things he/she needs (e.g., pencils, paper, etc.). If the student has earned something, he/she may be more willing to take care of it.

41. Have the student question any directions, explanations, and instructions not understood.

42. Identify a peer to act as a model for the student to imitate appropriate use of school-related materials.

43. Evaluate the appropriateness of the task to determine: (a) if the task is too difficult and (b) if the length of time scheduled to complete the task is appropriate.

44. Communicate with parents (e.g., notes home, phone calls, etc.) in order to share information concerning the student's progress and so that they can reinforce the student at home for using school-related materials appropriately at school.

45. Write a contract with the student specifying what behavior is expected (e.g., appropriate use of school-related materials) and what reinforcement will be made available when the terms of the contract have been met. (See Appendix for Behavioral Contract.)

46. Reinforce those students in the classroom who use school-related materials appropriately.

47. Reinforce the student for using school-related materials appropriately based on the length of time the student can be successful. Gradually increase the length of time required for reinforcement as the student demonstrates success.

48. Establish classroom rules:
1. Work on task.
2. Remain in your seat.
3. Finish task.
4. Meet task expectations.
5. Raise your hand.

Reiterate rules often and reinforce students for following rules.

49. Speak to the student to explain: (a) what the student is doing wrong (e.g., failing to use school-related materials appropriately) and (b) what the student should be doing (e.g., using school-related materials as directed).

50. Reinforce the student for demonstrating appropriate use of school-related materials: (a) give the student a tangible reward (e.g., classroom privileges, line leading, passing out materials, five minutes free time, etc.) or (b) give the student an intangible reward (e.g., praise, handshake, smile, etc.).

203 Does not demonstrate appropriate care and handling of others' property

1. Provide time at the beginning of each day to help the student organize the materials that will be used throughout the day.

2. Provide time at various points throughout the day to help the student organize materials that will be used throughout the day (e.g., before school, during recess or lunch, at the end of the day, etc.).

3. Provide the student with adequate work space (e.g., a large desk or table at which to work).

4. Provide storage space for materials the student is not using at any particular time.

5. Reduce distracting stimuli (e.g., place the student on the front row, provide a carrel or quiet place away from distractions, etc.). Overstimulation may cause the student to misuse others' property.

6. Interact frequently with the student in order to prompt organizational skills and appropriate use of materials.

7. Assign the student organizational responsibilities in the classroom (e.g., equipment, software materials, etc.).

8. Limit the student's use of materials (e.g., provide the student with only those materials necessary at any given time).

9. Act as a model for organization and appropriate use of work materials (e.g., putting materials away before getting other materials out, having a place for all materials, maintaining an organized desk area, following a schedule for the day, etc.).

10. Provide adequate transition time between activities for the student to organize himself/herself.

11. Provide the student with an organizational checklist (e.g., routine activities and materials needed).

12. Provide adequate time for the completion of activities. Inadequate time for completion of activities may result in the student's misuse of others' property.

13. Require the student to organize his/her work area at regular intervals.

14. Allow natural consequences to occur as the result of the student's inability to appropriately care for and handle others' property (e.g., property not maintained appropriately will be lost or not serviceable).

15. Assess the quality and clarity of directions, explanations, and instructions given to the student for use in the care and handling of others' property.

16. Assist the student in beginning each task in order to reduce impulsive behavior.

17. Provide the student with structure for all academic activities (e.g., specific directions, routine format for tasks, time units, etc.).

18. Give the student a checklist of materials necessary for each activity.

19. Minimize materials needed.

20. Provide an organizer for materials inside the student's desk.

21. Establish a routine to be followed for organization and appropriate use of work materials.

22. Teach the student appropriate care and handling of others' property (e.g., sharpening pencils, keeping books free of marks and tears, etc.).

23. Make certain that all personal property is labeled with the students' names.

24. Point out to the student that borrowing personal property from others does not reduce his/her responsibility for the property.

25. Teach the student how to conserve rather than waste materials (e.g., amount of glue, paper, tape, etc., to use; putting lids, caps, and tops on materials such as markers, pens, bottles, jars, cans, etc.).

26. Teach the student appropriate ways to deal with anger and frustration rather than destroying property belonging to others (e.g., pencils, pens, workbooks, notebooks, textbooks, etc.).

27. Teach the student to maintain property belonging to others (e.g., keep property with him/her, know where property is at all times, secure property in lockers, etc.).

28. Provide the student with an appropriate place to store/secure others' property (e.g., desk, locker, closet, etc.) and require the student to store all property when not in use.

29. Teach the student that the failure to care for others' property will result in the loss of freedom to use others' property.

30. Provide reminders (e.g., a list of property or materials) to help the student maintain and care for school property.

31. Limit the student's freedom to take property from school if he/she is unable to remember to return such items.

32. Limit the student's opportunity to use others' property if the student is unable to care for personal property.

33. Reduce the number of materials the student is responsible to care for or handle. Increase the number as the student demonstrates appropriate care of property.

34. Teach the student safety rules in the care and handling of others' property and materials (e.g., pencils, scissors, compass; biology, industrial arts, and home economics materials; etc.).

35. Require that lost or damaged property be replaced by the student. If the student cannot replace the property, restitution can be made by working at school.

36. Make certain the student is not inadvertently reinforced for losing or damaging property by providing him/her with new materials. Provide the student with used or damaged materials, copies of the materials, etc., rather than new materials.

37. Teach the student rules for the care and handling of others' property (e.g., always ask to use others' property, treat the property with care, inform the teacher if the property becomes damaged, return the property in the same or better condition than when it was borrowed, etc.).

38. Do not permit peers to allow the student to use their property if he/she is not able to care for it properly.

39. Remove others' property from the student if he/she is unable to appropriately care for and handle the property.

40. Maintain mobility throughout the classroom in order to supervise the student's care and handling of others' property.

41. Permit the student to use only the amount of property that he/she can care for and handle appropriately. Gradually increase the amount of property as the student demonstrates success.

42. Have the student earn things he/she wants (e.g., pen, pencil, paper, etc.). If the student has earned something, he/she may be more willing to take care of it.

43. Have the student question any directions, explanations, and instructions not understood.

44. Identify a peer to act as a model for the student to imitate appropriate care and handling of others' property.

45. Evaluate the appropriateness of the task to determine: (a) if the task is too difficult and (b) if the length of time scheduled to complete the task is appropriate.

46. Reinforce those students in the classroom who demonstrate appropriate care and handling of others' property.

47. Reinforce the student for demonstrating appropriate care and handling of others' property based on the length of time the student can be successful. Gradually increase the length of time required for reinforcement as the student demonstrates success.

48. Communicate with parents (e.g., notes home, phone calls, etc.) in order to share information concerning the student's progress and so that they can reinforce the student at home for demonstrating appropriate care and handling of others' property at school.

49. Write a contract with the student specifying what behavior is expected (e.g., putting property away, returning property, etc.) and what reinforcement will be made available when the terms of the contract have been met. (See Appendix for Behavioral Contract.)

50. Speak to the student to explain: (a) what the student is doing wrong (e.g., losing property, destroying property, etc.) and (b) what the student should be doing (e.g., putting property away, returning property, etc.).

51. Reinforce the student for demonstrating appropriate care and handling of others' property: (a) give the student a tangible reward (e.g., classroom privileges, line leading, passing out materials, five minutes free time, etc.) or (b) give the student an intangible reward (e.g., praise, handshake, smile, etc.).

1. Evaluate the appropriateness of requiring the student to raise his/her hand. The student may not be capable or developmentally ready for hand raising. Have the student use other appropriate means of gaining attention.

2. Establish rules specifically for hand raising (e.g., raise hand for permission to talk, do not leave seat, etc.).

3. Allow natural consequences to occur as a result of the student raising or failing to raise his/her hand (e.g., students who raise their hands will have their needs met, those students who fail to raise their hands will not have their needs met until they raise their hands, etc.).

4. Provide the student with verbal reminders to raise his/her hand (e.g., at the beginning of the day, at the beginning of the activity, when the student forgets, etc.).

5. Have a peer model appropriate hand raising for new students, students who do not raise their hands, etc.

6. Post hand-raising rules in the classroom.

7. Make certain that the student is not inadvertently reinforced for failing to raise his/her hand. The student may be getting the teacher's attention by talking out.

8. Acknowledge the student immediately upon raising his/her hand (e.g., let the student know when you see his/her hand, call upon the student, go to the student, etc.).

9. Be certain to let the student know that you will be with him/her as soon as possible when it is necessary to be detained (e.g., when working with another student, speaking with another teacher, instructing a small group, etc.).

10. Do not grant the student's request until his/her hand is raised.

11. Make certain that expectations for hand raising are consistently applied.

12. Provide the student with alternative, appropriate attention-seeking methods (e.g., display "help" sign on desk).

13. Maintain mobility throughout the classroom in order to "catch" the student displaying appropriate attention-seeking behavior (e.g., hand raising).

14. Make certain the student knows when it is acceptable to interrupt others (e.g., in an emergency).

15. Before beginning an activity make certain the student knows the rules (e.g., wait quietly until the teacher is able to help, work quietly at your desk, etc.).

16. Have the student raise his/her hand to question any directions, explanations, and instructions not understood.

17. Identify a peer to act as a model for the student to imitate raising his/her hand when appropriate.

18. Communicate with parents (e.g., notes home, phone calls, etc.) in order to share information concerning the student's progress and so that they can reinforce the student at home for raising his/her hand when appropriate at school.

19. Write a contract with the student specifying what behavior is expected (e.g., raising his/her hand for teacher assistance) and what reinforcement will be made available when the terms of the contract have been met. (See Appendix for Behavioral Contract.)

20. Establish classroom rules:
1. Work on task.
2. Remain in your seat.
3. Finish task.
4. Meet task expectations.
5. Raise your hand.
Reiterate rules often and reinforce students for following rules.

21. Reinforce the student for raising his/her hand when appropriate based on the number of times the student can be successful. Gradually increase the number of times required for reinforcement as the student demonstrates success.

22. Reinforce those students in the classroom who raise their hands when appropriate.

23. Speak to the student to explain: (a) what the student is doing wrong (e.g., talking out, engaging in a behavior without raising his/her hand to get permission, etc.) and (b) what the student should be doing (e.g., raising his/her hand for permission to speak, move about the room, etc.).

24. Reinforce the student for raising his/her hand when appropriate: (a) give the student a tangible reward (e.g., classroom privileges, line leading, passing out materials, five minutes free time, etc.) or (b) give the student an intangible reward (e.g., praise, handshake, smile, etc.).

1. Evaluate the appropriateness of the expectations for the student to go to and from school by himself/herself.

2. Assign a peer to accompany the student when going to and from school in order to monitor and encourage appropriate behavior.

3. Accompany the student when going to and from school in order to teach the student appropriate behavior (e.g., using sidewalks, crossing at crosswalks, taking the most direct route, boarding the bus, sitting quietly, remaining seated, leaving the bus, etc.).

4. Assign the student responsibilities to perform when going to and from school (e.g., act as the bus driver's assistant to monitor behavior, accompany a younger peer to and from school, pick up trash on the way to and from school, etc.).

5. Encourage the student to report problems that occur while going to and from school (e.g., being bullied, approached by strangers, teased by other students, etc.).

6. Allow natural consequences to occur if the student fails to demonstrate appropriate behavior when going to and from school (e.g., parents will have to provide transportation and/or supervision).

7. Make certain the student is seated near the bus driver in order to prevent inappropriate behavior when riding the bus to and from school.

8. Develop a behavioral contract with the bus driver and the student for appropriate behavior on the bus while riding to and from school.

9. Have "block parents" monitor the student's behavior when going to and from school.

10. Before the student leaves the school, make certain that he/she knows the rules about walking to and from school (e.g., walk on the sidewalk, walk nicely with friends, etc.).

11. Establish rules for appropriate behavior when going to and from school:
1. Sit quietly on the bus.
2. Remain seated on the bus.
3. Use a quiet voice while on the bus.
4. Take the most direct route when walking to and from school.
5. Use sidewalks.
6. Follow crossing rules at crosswalks.
7. Refrain from fighting on the way to and from school.

Reiterate rules often and reinforce students for following rules.

12. Have the student question any directions, explanations, and instructions not understood.

13. Identify a peer to act as a model for the student to imitate appropriate behavior going to and from school.

14. Communicate with parents (e.g., notes home, phone calls, etc.) in order to share information concerning the student's progress and so that they can reinforce the student at home for demonstrating appropriate behavior when going to and from school.

15. Write a contract with the student specifying what behavior is expected (e.g., sitting quietly on the bus) and what reinforcement will be made available when the terms of the contract have been met. (See Appendix for Behavioral Contract.)

16. Reinforce the student for demonstrating appropriate behavior going to and from school based on the number of times the student can be successful. Gradually increase the number of times required for reinforcement as the student demonstrates success.

17. Reinforce those students in the classroom who demonstrate appropriate behavior going to and from school.

18. Speak to the student to explain: (a) what the student is doing wrong (e.g., fighting on the bus, taking an indirect route to and from school, etc.) and (b) what the student should be doing (e.g., sitting quietly on the bus, taking the most direct route to and from school, etc.).

19. Reinforce the student for demonstrating appropriate behavior going to and from school: (a) give the student a tangible reward (e.g., classroom privileges, line leading, passing out materials, five minutes free time, etc.) or (b) give the student an intangible reward (e.g., praise, handshake, smile, etc.).

206 Does not take notes during class when necessary

1. Teach the student note-taking skills (e.g., copy main ideas from the board, identify main ideas from lectures, condense statements into a few key words, etc.).

2. Provide a standard format for direction or explanation note-taking (e.g., have paper and pencil or pen ready, listen for the steps in directions or explanations, write a shortened form of directions or explanations, ask to have any steps repeated when necessary, etc.).

3. Provide a standard format for lecture note-taking (e.g., have paper and pencil or pen ready, listen for main ideas of important information, write a shortened form of main ideas or important information, ask to have any main ideas or important information repeated when necessary, etc.).

4. While delivering instructions, directions, lectures, etc., point out to the student that information should be written in the form of notes.

5. Have the student practice legible manuscript or cursive handwriting during simulated and actual note-taking activities.

6. Have the student keep notes organized in a folder for each subject or activity.

7. Check the student's notes before he/she begins an assignment in order to determine if they are correct and adequate for the assignment.

8. Provide the student with an outline or questions to be completed during teacher delivery of instructions, directions, lectures, etc.

9. Provide the student with samples of notes taken from actual instructions, directions, lectures, etc., given in the classroom in order that he/she may learn which information is necessary for note-taking.

10. Make certain the student is in the best location in the classroom to receive information for note-taking (e.g., near the board, teacher, or other source of information).

11. Make certain you can easily provide supervision of the student's note-taking.

12. Make certain to maintain visibility to and from the student when delivering instructions, directions, lectures, etc., in order to enhance the likelihood of successful note-taking.

13. Make certain that instructions, directions, lectures, etc., are presented clearly and loudly enough for the student to hear.

14. Match the rate of delivery of instructions, directions, lectures, etc., to the student's ability to take notes.

15. Provide the student with both verbal and written instructions.

16. Provide instructions, directions, lectures, etc., in sequential steps in order to enhance student note-taking.

17. Provide delivery of information in short segments for the student to take notes. Gradually increase the length of delivery as the student experiences success in note-taking.

18. Make certain that the vocabulary used in delivering instructions, directions, lectures, etc., is appropriate for the student's ability level.

19. Place the student next to a peer in order that the student can copy notes taken by the peer.

20. Make certain the student has all necessary materials for note-taking (e.g., paper, pencil, pen, etc.).

21. Make certain the student uses any necessary aids in order to facilitate note-taking (e.g., eyeglasses, hearing aid, etc.).

22. Make certain the student has adequate surface space on which to write when taking notes (e.g., uncluttered desk top).

23. Present the information in the most interesting manner possible.

24. Reduce distracting stimuli that would interfere with the student's note-taking (e.g., other students talking, outdoor activities, movement in the classroom, hallway noise, etc.).

25. As an alternative to note-taking have the student tape record instructions, directions, lectures, etc.

26. Summarize the main points of instructions, directions, lectures, etc., for the student.

27. Let the student know that directions will only be given once and that you will not remind him/her to follow the directions.

28. Set aside time each day to review the student's notes and help him/her get the notes in order.

29. Have the student question any directions, explanations, and instructions he/she does not understand.

30. Identify a peer to act as a model for the student to imitate appropriate note-taking during class when necessary.

31. Evaluate the appropriateness of note-taking to determine: (a) if the task is too difficult and (b) if the length of time scheduled to complete the task is appropriate.

32. Communicate with parents (e.g., notes home, phone calls, etc.) in order to share information concerning the student's progress and so that they can reinforce the student at home for taking notes during class when necessary.

33. Write a contract with the student specifying what behavior is expected (e.g., taking notes) and what reinforcement will be made available when the terms of the contract have been met. (See Appendix for Behavioral Contract.)

34. Reinforce the student for taking notes during class when necessary based on the length of time the student can be successful. Gradually increase the length of time required for reinforcement as the student demonstrates success.

35. Reinforce those students in the classroom who takes notes during class when necessary.

36. Establish classroom rules:
1. Take notes when necessary.
2. Work on task.
3. Remain in your seat.
4. Finish task.
5. Meet task expectations.
6. Raise your hand.

Reiterate rules often and reinforce students for following rules.

37. Speak to the student to explain: (a) what the student is doing wrong (e.g., failing to take notes) and (b) what the student should be doing (e.g., taking notes).

38. Reinforce the student for taking notes during class when necessary: (a) give the student a tangible reward (e.g., classroom privileges, line leading, passing out materials, five minutes free time, etc.) or (b) give the student an intangible reward (e.g., praise, handshake, smile, etc.).

207 Is under the influence of drugs or alcohol while at school

1. Communicate with parents, agencies, or appropriate parties in order to inform them of the problem, determine the cause of the problem, and consider possible solutions to the problem.

2. Provide a drug information program for the individual, the class, and the building.

3. Provide an orientation to penalties for the use of alcohol and drugs at school.

4. Involve the student in extracurricular activities as a redirection of interest.

5. Identify individuals the student may contact with his/her concerns (e.g., guidance counselor, school nurse, social worker, school psychologist, etc.).

6. Share concerns with the administration and seek referral to an agency for investigation of alcohol or drug abuse.

7. Encourage the student to become involved in athletic activities.

8. Assign the student activities which would require interactions with a respected role model (e.g., older student, high school student, college student, community leader, someone held in high esteem, etc.).

9. Provide the student with intelligent, accurate information concerning drugs and alcohol rather than sensationalized, scare-tactic information.

10. Provide many opportunities for social and academic success.

11. Encourage the student to excel in a particular area of interest (e.g., provide information for him/her, provide personal and professional support, sponsor the student, etc.).

12. Provide the student with personal recognition during school hours (e.g., follow up on details of earlier communications, maintain a direction for conversation, etc.).

13. Lead and direct the student. Do not lecture and make demands.

14. Maintain anecdotal records of the student's behavior to check patterns or changes in behavior.

15. When natural consequences from peers occur as the result of the use of drugs or alcohol at school (e.g., criticism, loss of friendship, etc.), bring the consequences to the attention of the student.

16. Encourage the student's parents to be positive and helpful with the student as opposed to being negative and threatening.

17. Act as a resource for parents by providing information on agencies, counseling programs, etc.

18. Teach the student to be satisfied with personal best effort rather than demanding perfection. Reduce the emphasis on competition and help the student realize that success is individually defined.

19. Be willing to take the time to listen, share, and talk with the student.

20. Listen to the student talk about his/her problems privately.

21. Increase your own professional knowledge of laws and treatment concerning drug and alcohol use and abuse.

22. Teach the student alternative ways to deal with demands, challenges, and pressures of the school-age experience (e.g., deal with problems when they arise, practice self-control at all times, share problems or concerns with others, etc.).

23. Maintain adequate supervision at all times and in all areas of the school (e.g., hallways, bathrooms, between classes, before and after school, etc.).

24. Intervene early when there is a problem in order to prevent more serious problems from occurring.

25. Teach the student to "think" before acting (e.g., ask himself/herself: "What is happening?" "What am I doing?" "What should I do?" "What will be best for me?").

26. Communicate with parents (e.g., notes home, phone calls, etc.) in order to share information concerning the student's progress and so that they can reinforce the student at home for demonstrating appropriate behavior at school.

27. Write a contract with the student specifying what behavior is expected (e.g., demonstrating appropriate behavior) and what reinforcement will be made available when the terms of the contract have been met. (See Appendix for Behavioral Contract.)

28. Remove the student from the group or activity until he/she can demonstrate appropriate behavior and self-control.

29. Reinforce the student for demonstrating appropriate behavior based on the length of time the student can be successful. Gradually increase the length of time required for reinforcement as the student demonstrates success.

30. Reinforce those students in the classroom who demonstrate appropriate behavior.

31. Establish classroom rules:
1. Work on task.
2. Remain in your seat.
3. Finish task.
4. Meet task expectations.
5. Raise your hand.
Reiterate rules often and reinforce students for following rules.

32. Speak with the student to explain: (a) what the student is doing wrong (e.g., using drugs or alcohol) and (b) what the student should be doing (e.g., following an established code of conduct, following rules, taking care of responsibilities, etc.).

33. Reinforce the student for demonstrating appropriate behavior: (a) give the student a tangible reward (e.g., classroom privileges, line leading, passing out materials, five minutes free time, etc.) or (b) give the student an intangible reward (e.g., praise, handshake, smile, etc.).

1. Reinforce the student for waiting to be called on before speaking: (a) give the student a tangible reward (e.g., classroom privileges, line leading, passing out materials, five minutes free time, etc.) or (b) give the student an intangible reward (e.g., praise, handshake, smile, etc.).

2. Speak with the student to explain: (a) what the student is doing wrong (e.g., blurting out answers) and (b) what the student should be doing (e.g., waiting until it is appropriate to speak, waiting to be called on before speaking, etc.).

3. Establish classroom rules:
1. Work on task.
2. Remain in your seat.
3. Finish task.
4. Meet task expectations.
5. Raise your hand.
Reiterate rules often and reinforce students for following rules.

4. Reinforce those students in the classroom who wait to be called on before speaking.

5. Reinforce the student for waiting to be called on before speaking based on the number of times the student can be successful. Gradually increase the number of times required for reinforcement as the student demonstrates success.

6. Remove the student from the group or activity until he/she can demonstrate appropriate behavior and self-control.

7. Write a contract with the student specifying what behavior is expected (e.g., waiting to be called on before speaking) and what reinforcement will be made available when the terms of the contract have been met. (See Appendix for Behavioral Contract.)

8. Evaluate the appropriateness of the task to determine: (a) if the task is too difficult and (b) if the length of time scheduled to complete the task is appropriate.

9. Communicate with parents (e.g., notes home, phone calls, etc.) in order to share information concerning the student's appropriate behavior and so that they can reinforce the student at home for waiting to be called on before speaking.

10. Make certain that reinforcement is not inadvertently given for inappropriate behavior (e.g., blurting out answers without being called on).

11. Give adequate opportunities to respond (i.e., enthusiastic students need many opportunities to contribute).

12. Have the student be the leader of a small group activity if he/she possesses mastery of a skill or has an interest in that area.

13. Provide the student with a predetermined signal if he/she begins to blurt out answers without being called on.

14. Structure the environment in such a way as to limit opportunities for inappropriate behaviors (e.g., keep the student engaged in activities, have the student seated near the teacher, etc.).

15. Give the student responsibilities in the classroom (e.g., running errands, opportunities to help the teacher, etc.).

16. Reduce activities which might threaten the student (e.g., reduce peer pressure, academic failure, teasing, etc.).

17. Provide the student with many social and academic successes.

18. Make the necessary adjustments in the environment to prevent the student from experiencing stress, frustration or anger (e.g., reduce peer pressure, academic failure, teasing, etc.).

19. Maintain visibility to and from the student. The teacher should be able to see the student and the student should be able to see the teacher, making eye contact possible at all times.

20. Interact frequently with the student to reduce the need to blurt out answers without being called on.

21. Assess the appropriateness of the social situation in relation to the student's ability to function successfully.

22. Try various groupings in order to determine the situation in which the student is most comfortable.

23. Reinforce the student for raising his/her hand in order to be recognized.

24. Call on the student when he/she is most likely to be able to respond correctly.

25. Have the student work in small groups in which there are frequent opportunities to speak. Gradually increase the size of the group as the student learns to wait longer for a turn to speak.

26. Make certain that the student's feelings are considered when it is necessary to deal with inappropriate comments (i.e., handle comments in such a way as to not diminish the student's enthusiasm for participation).

27. Encourage the student to model the behavior of peers who are successful.

28. Help the student improve concentration skills (e.g., listening to the speaker, taking notes, preparing comments in advance, making comments in the appropriate context, etc.).

29. Have the student question any directions, explanations, and instructions not understood.

30. Deliver directions, explanations, and instructions in a clear and concise manner in order to reduce the student's need to ask questions.

31. Have the student practice waiting for short periods of time for a turn to speak. Gradually increase the length of time required for reinforcement as the student demonstrates success.

32. Explain to the student the reasons why blurting out answers without being called on is inappropriate (e.g., is impolite, hurts others' feelings, etc.).

33. Attempt to provide equal attention to all students in the classroom.

34. Make the student aware of the number of times he/she blurts out answers without being called on.

35. Do not criticize when correcting the student; be honest yet supportive. Never cause the student to feel badly about himself/herself.

36. Make certain the student does not become overstimulated by an activity.

37. Treat the student with respect. Talk in an objective manner at all times.

38. Provide the student with a predetermined signal when he/she begins to display inappropriate manners.

1. Reinforce the student for demonstrating appropriate behavior: (a) give the student a tangible reward (e.g., classroom privileges, line leading, passing out materials, five minutes free time, etc.) or (b) give the student an intangible reward (e.g., praise, handshake, smile, etc.).

2. Speak to the student to explain: (a) what the student is doing wrong (e.g., interrupting other students who are trying to work, listen, etc.) and (b) what the student should be doing (e.g., waiting for a turn to speak, working quietly, etc.).

3. Establish classroom rules:
1. Work on task.
2. Remain in your seat.
3. Finish task.
4. Meet task expectations.
5. Raise your hand.
Reiterate rules often and reinforce students for following rules.

4. Reinforce those students in the classroom who wait their turn to speak, work quietly, etc.

5. Reinforce the student for demonstrating appropriate behavior (e.g., waiting for a turn to speak, working quietly, etc.) based on the length of time the student can be successful. Gradually increase the length of time required for reinforcement as the student demonstrates success.

6. Write a contract with the student specifying what behavior is expected (e.g., waiting for a turn to speak, working quietly, etc.) and what reinforcement will be made available when the terms of the contract have been met. (See Appendix for Behavioral Contract.)

7. Communicate with parents (e.g., notes home, phone calls, etc.) in order to share information concerning the student's appropriate behavior and so that they can reinforce the student at home for not bothering other students at school.

8. Identify a peer to act as a model for the student to imitate appropriate behavior.

9. Have the student question any directions, explanations, and instructions not understood.

10. Reinforce those students in the classroom who demonstrate on-task behavior.

11. Reduce distracting stimuli (e.g., place the student on the front row, provide a carrel or "office" away from distractions, etc.). This is used as a means of reducing distracting stimuli and not as a form of punishment.

12. Interact frequently with the student in order to maintain his/her involvement in the activity (e.g., ask the student questions, ask the student's opinion, stand close to the student, seat the student near the teacher's desk, etc.).

13. Maintain visibility to and from the student. The teacher should be able to see the student and the student should be able to see the teacher, making eye contact possible at all times.

14. Assess the degree of task difficulty in relation to the student's ability to perform the task successfully.

15. Provide a full schedule of activities. Prevent lag time from occurring when the student can bother other students.

16. Remove the student from the group or activity until he/she can demonstrate appropriate behavior and self-control.

17. Teach the student appropriate ways to communicate needs to others (e.g., waiting a turn, raising his/her hand, etc.).

18. Provide the student with enjoyable activities to perform when he/she completes a task early.

19. Seat the student near the teacher.

20. Provide the student with frequent opportunities to participate, share, etc.

21. Provide students with frequent opportunities to interact with one another (e.g., before and after school, between activities, etc.).

22. Seat the student away from those students he/she is most likely to bother.

23. Do not criticize when correcting the student; be honest yet supportive. Never cause the student to feel badly about himself/herself.

24. Talk to the student before beginning an activity and remind him/her of the importance of listening to others.

25. Treat the student with respect. Talk in an objective manner at all times.

26. Provide the student with a predetermined signal when he/she begins to display inappropriate manners.

27. Make sure the student knows when it is acceptable to interrupt others (e.g., in an emergency).

1. Reinforce the student for working quietly: (a) give the student a tangible reward (e.g., classroom privileges, line leading, passing out materials, five minutes free time, etc.) or (b) give the student an intangible reward (e.g., praise, handshake, smile, etc.).

2. Speak with the student to explain: (a) what the student is doing wrong (e.g., talking to others during quiet activity periods) and (b) what the student should be doing (e.g., waiting until it is appropriate to speak, working quietly, etc.).

3. Establish classroom rules:
1. Work on task.
2. Remain in your seat.
3. Finish task.
4. Meet task expectations.
5. Raise your hand.
Reiterate rules often and reinforce students for following rules.

4. Reinforce those students in the classroom who work quietly.

5. Reinforce the student for working quietly based on the length of time the student can be successful. Gradually increase the length of time required for reinforcement as the student demonstrates success.

6. Remove the student from the group or activity until he/she can demonstrate appropriate behavior and self-control.

7. Write a contract with the student specifying what behavior is expected (e.g., working quietly) and what reinforcement will be made available when the terms of the contract have been met. (See Appendix for Behavioral Contract.)

8. Communicate with parents (e.g., notes home, phone calls, etc.) in order to share information concerning the student's appropriate behavior and so that they can reinforce the student at home for working quietly at school.

9. Have the student be the leader of a small group activity if he/she possesses mastery of skills or an interest in that area.

10. Evaluate the appropriateness of the task to determine: (a) if the task is too difficult and (b) if the length of time scheduled to complete the task is appropriate.

11. Make certain that reinforcement is not inadvertently given for inappropriate behavior (e.g., making inappropriate comments, talking to others during quiet activity periods, etc.).

12. Give the student adequate opportunities to speak in the classroom, talk to other students, etc. (i.e., enthusiastic students need many opportunities to contribute).

13. Provide the student with a predetermined signal if he/she begins to talk to other students during quiet activity periods.

14. Explain to the student that he/she may be trying too hard to fit in and should relax and wait until more appropriate times to interact.

15. Structure the environment in such a way as to limit opportunities for talking to other students during quiet activity periods (e.g., keep the student engaged in activities, have the student seated near the teacher, etc.).

16. Give the student responsibilities in the classroom (e.g., running errands, opportunities to help the teacher, etc.).

17. Reduce activities which might threaten the student (e.g., announcing test score ranges or test scores aloud, making students read aloud in class, emphasizing the success of a particular student or students, etc.).

18. Provide the student with many social and academic successes.

19. Make the necessary adjustments in the environment to prevent the student from experiencing stress, frustration or anger (e.g., reduce peer pressure, academic failure, teasing, etc.).

20. Interact frequently with the student to reduce the need to talk to other students.

21. Maintain visibility to and from the student. The teacher should be able to see the student and the student should be able to see the teacher, making eye contact possible at all times.

22. Assess the appropriateness of the social situation in relation to the student's ability to function successfully.

23. Try various groupings in order to determine the situation in which the student is most comfortable.

24. Reinforce the student for raising his/her hand in order to be recognized.

25. Call on the student when he/she is most likely to be able to respond correctly.

26. Teach the student to recognize appropriate times to talk to other students (e.g., between activities, during breaks, at recess, etc.).

27. Have the student work in small groups in which there are frequent opportunities to speak. Gradually increase the size of the group as the student learns to wait longer for a turn to speak.

28. Make certain that the student's feelings are considered when it is necessary to deal with his/her talking to other students (i.e., handle comments in such a way as to not diminish the student's enthusiasm for participation).

29. Encourage the student to model the behavior of peers who are successful.

30. Help the student improve concentration skills (e.g., listening to the speaker, taking notes, preparing comments in advance, making comments in the appropriate context, etc.).

31. Have the student question any directions, explanations, and instructions not understood in order that he/she does not have to ask other students for information.

32. Deliver directions, explanations, and instructions in a clear and concise manner in order to reduce the student's need to ask other students for information.

33. Provide the student with a predetermined signal when he/she begins to display inappropriate behavior.

34. After telling the student why he/she should not be talking, explain the reason.

35. Do not leave a lot of unstructured time for the student.

1. Reinforce the student for staying in his/her seat: (a) give the student a tangible reward (e.g., classroom privileges, line leading, passing out materials, five minutes free time, etc.) or (b) give the student an intangible reward (e.g., praise, handshake, smile, etc.).

2. Speak with the student to explain: (a) what the student is doing wrong (e.g., leaving seat without permission, etc.) and (b) what the student should be doing (e.g., remaining in his/her seat, asking permission to leave seat, etc.).

3. Establish classroom rules:
1. Work on task.
2. Remain in your seat.
3. Finish task.
4. Meet task expectations.
Reiterate rules often and reinforce students for following rules.

4. Reinforce those students in the classroom who stay in their seats, ask permission to leave their seats, etc.

5. Reinforce the student for staying in his/her seat based on the length of time the student can be successful. Gradually increase the length of time required for reinforcement as the student demonstrates success.

6. Remove the student from the group or activity until the student can stay in his/her seat.

7. Write a contract with the student specifying what behavior is expected (e.g., staying in his/ her seat) and what reinforcement will be made available when the terms of the contract have been met. (See Appendix for Behavioral Contract.)

8. Communicate with parents (e.g., notes home, phone calls, etc.) in order to share information concerning the student's appropriate behavior and so that they can reinforce the student at home for staying in his/her seat at school.

9. Evaluate the appropriateness of the task to determine: (a) if the task is too difficult and (b) if the length of time scheduled to complete the task is appropriate.

10. Try various groupings in order to determine the situation in which the student is most comfortable.

11. Make the necessary adjustments in the environment to prevent the student from experiencing stress, frustration, anger, etc., as much as possible.

12. Interact frequently with the student to prevent the student from leaving his/her seat.

13. Maintain visibility to and from the student. The teacher should be able to see the student and the student should be able to see the teacher, making eye contact possible at all times.

14. Facilitate on-task behavior by providing a full schedule of daily events. Prevent lag time when the student is free to leave his/her seat. (See Appendix for Schedule of Daily Events.)

15. Reduce stimuli which would contribute to the student leaving his/her seat.

16. Interact frequently with the student in order to maintain his/her attention to the activity (e.g., ask the student questions, ask the student's opinion, stand close to the student, seat the student near the teacher's desk, etc.).

17. Give the student additional responsibilities (e.g., chores, errands, etc.) to keep him/her actively involved and provide a feeling of success or accomplishment.

18. Modify or eliminate situations at school which cause the student to experience stress or frustration.

19. Maintain supervision at all times and in all parts of the school environment.

20. Separate the student from the peer who stimulates the inappropriate behavior.

21. Prevent the student from becoming over-stimulated by an activity (i.e., monitor or supervise student behavior to limit overexcitement in physical activities, games, parties, etc.).

22. Provide the student with a predetermined signal when the student begins to leave his/her seat.

23. Make certain that reinforcement is not inadvertently given for inappropriate behavior (e.g., attending to the student only when the student leaves his/her seat).

24. Provide the student with the most attractive and interesting activities possible.

25. Provide the student with a calm, quiet environment in which to work.

26. Provide the student with a quiet place in the environment where he/she may go when becoming upset. This is not meant as punishment but as a means of helping the student to be able to function more successfully.

27. Provide the student with frequent opportunities to participate, take a turn, etc., in order to keep him/her involved in an activity.

28. Avoid discussions of topics sensitive to the student (e.g., divorce, death, unemployment, alcoholism, etc.).

29. Identify a peer to act as a model for the student to imitate staying in his/her seat.

30. Have the student question any directions, explanations, and instructions not understood.

31. Schedule short activities for the student to perform while seated. Gradually increase the length of the activities as the student demonstrates success at staying in his/her seat.

32. Give the student frequent opportunities to leave his/her seat for appropriate reasons (e.g., getting materials, running errands, assisting the teacher, etc.).

33. Seat the student near the teacher.

34. Make certain the student has all necessary materials in order to reduce the need to leave his/her seat.

35. Have the student chart the length of time he/she is able to remain seated.

36. Work the first few problems of an assignment with the student in order that he/she will know what is expected.

37. Make sure the student knows when it is acceptable to leave his/her seat (e.g., in an emergency).

212   Does not come to an activity at the specified time

1.   Reinforce the student for coming to an activity at the specified time: (a) give the student a tangible reward (e.g., classroom privileges, line leading, passing out materials, five minutes free time, etc.) or (b) give the student an intangible reward (e.g., praise, handshake, smile, etc.).

2.   Speak to the student to explain: (a) what the student is doing wrong (e.g., coming late/early to an activity) and (b) what the student should be doing (e.g., coming to an activity at the specified time).

3.   Establish classroom rules:
   1. Come to class on time.
   2. Work on task.
   3. Remain in your seat.
   4. Finish task.
   5. Meet task expectations.
Reiterate rules often and reinforce students for following rules.

4.   Give the student a specific responsibility to be performed at the beginning of each activity in order to encourage the student to be on time.

5.   Reinforce the student for coming to an activity within a given period of time. Gradually reduce the length of time the student has to come to an activity as the student becomes more successful in being punctual.

6.   Write a contract with the student specifying what behavior is expected (e.g., coming to class on time) and what reinforcement will be made available when the terms of the contract have been met. (See Appendix for Behavioral Contract.)

7.   Communicate with parents (e.g., notes home, phone calls, etc.) in order to share information concerning the student's progress and so that they can reinforce the student at home for coming to activities at the specified time at school.

8.   Evaluate the appropriateness of the task to determine: (a) if the task is too difficult and (b) if the length of time scheduled to complete the task is appropriate.

9.   Identify a peer to act as a model for the student to imitate arriving at an activity at the specified time.

10.   Provide the student with a schedule of daily events in order that he/she will know which activities to attend and their times.

11.   Make certain that the student's daily schedule follows an established routine.

12.   Limit the number of interruptions in the student's schedule.

13.   Make certain the student has adequate time to get to an activity.

14.   Make certain that the student knows how to get from one activity to another.

15.   Use a timer to help the student get to activities at specified times.

16.   Reinforce those students in the classroom who come to an activity at the specified time.

17.   Provide the student with verbal cues when it is time to change activities (e.g., "It is time for the red group to have reading." "Now it is time for the red group to put away materials and move to the next activity." etc.).

18.   Determine why the student is not arriving at activities at the specified times.

19.   Ask the student why he/she is not arriving at activities at the specified times. The student may have the most accurate perception as to why he/she is not arriving at activities at the specified times.

20.   Have a peer accompany the student to activities.

21.   Help the student understand that it is permissible to leave work unfinished and return to it at a later time.

22. Determine if there are aspects of activities that the student dislikes. Remove, reduce, or modify the unpleasant aspects of activities in order to encourage the student to be on time for and participate in activities.

23. Make the student responsible for time missed (i.e., if the student misses five minutes of an activity, he/she must make up the time during recess, lunch, or other desired activities).

24. Make certain that the student is successful in school-related activities. The student will be more likely to be on time for activities in which he/she experiences success.

25. Give the student a schedule of classes that must be signed by every instructor in order to document his/her promptness.

26. Make certain that other students do not make it unpleasant for the student to attend activities.

27. Make certain the student has all necessary materials for activities.

28. Record or chart promptness with the student.

29. Begin activities with a task that is highly reinforcing to the student.

30. Give the student a preferred responsibility to be performed at the beginning of each activity.

31. Assess appropriateness of the degree of difficulty of tasks in comparison with the student's ability.

32. Provide the student with as many high-interest activities as possible.

33. Provide the student with many social and academic successes.

34. Provide the student with academic activities in the most attractive manner possible.

35. Make the student a leader of the activity or group.

36. Collect anecdotal information on the student's tardy behavior. If a trend can be determined, remove the student from the situation and/or help the student to be prompt.

37. Have the student document his/her attendance at the end of each activity.

38. Make certain the student is appropriately placed according to ability level in those classes in which the student is enrolled.

39. Reduce the emphasis on competition. Repeated failure may cause the student to avoid being on time for activities which are competitive.

40. Along with a directive, provide an incentive statement (e.g., "When you come to your reading group, you may pass out the books." "Please come to your reading group early to help arrange the chairs." etc.).

41. Deliver directions in a supportive rather than a threatening manner (e.g., "Please come to your reading group now." rather than "You had better come to your reading group or else!" etc.).

42. Give the student a special responsibility before the group meets (e.g., sharpening pencils, arranging chairs, passing out books, etc.).

43. Use a timer to help the student know how much time he/she has to follow through with directions.

44. Treat the student with respect. Talk in an objective manner at all times.

45. Be careful to avoid embarrassing the student by giving him/her orders, demands, etc., in front of others.

46. Carefully consider if there is something the student is trying to avoid by not coming to an activity at the specified time. If it is something unpleasant that is causing the student to not want to participate, do all you can to change the situation.

213 Demonstrates inappropriate behavior when moving with a group

1. Reinforce the student for waiting appropriately in line (e.g., standing against the wall, talking quietly, standing near others without making physical contact, etc.).

2. Reinforce the student for walking at the same pace as other students when moving with a group.

3. Have the student walk with arms crossed, arms against his/her side, hands in pockets, etc., if touching others is a problem.

4. Form a second line or group for those students who move at a slower pace.

5. Separate the student from the peer(s) who stimulates his/her inappropriate behavior when moving with a group.

6. Have the student walk alone, behind the group, beside the teacher, etc., when he/she displays inappropriate behavior when moving with a group.

7. Provide the student with a demonstration of the appropriate way to move with a group.

8. Have the student act as a line leader, line monitor, etc., when moving with a group.

9. Have the students walk in pairs when moving as a group.

10. Stop the line frequently in order to assure student success when moving with a group.

11. Provide the student with rules for moving appropriately with a group:
   1. Walk in the halls.
   2. Go directly from one area to another.
   3. Talk quietly in the halls.
   4. Walk on the right side of the hall.
   5. Use the appropriate stairway.
Reiterate rules often and reinforce the student for following rules.

12. Intervene early when there is a problem in order to prevent future problems from occurring.

13. Before leaving the classroom, remind the student of the rules for walking in a group (e.g., walk behind the person in front of you, keep hands to yourself, walk quietly, etc.).

14. Have the student question any directions, explanations, and instructions not understood.

15. Identify a peer to act as a model for the student to imitate appropriate movement with a group.

16. Evaluate the appropriateness of the expectation of moving with a group to determine: (a) if the task is too difficult and (b) if the length of time scheduled to complete the task is appropriate.

17. Communicate with parents (e.g., notes home, phone calls, etc.) in order to share information concerning the student's progress and so that they can reinforce the student at home for moving appropriately with a group at school.

18. Write a contract with the student specifying what behavior is expected (e.g., walking in the halls) and what reinforcement will be made available when the terms of the contract have been met. (See Appendix for Behavioral Contract.)

19. Reinforce the student for moving appropriately with a group based on the length of time the student can be successful. Gradually increase the length of time required for reinforcement as the student demonstrates success.

20. Reinforce those students who demonstrate appropriate behavior when moving with a group.

21. Speak to the student to explain: (a) what the student is doing wrong (e.g., running, pushing peers, etc.) and (b) what the student should be doing (e.g., walking without touching peers).

22. Reinforce the student for demonstrating appropriate behavior when moving with a group: (a) give the student a tangible reward (e.g., classroom privileges, line leading, passing out materials, etc.) or (b) give the student an intangible reward (e.g., praise, handshake, smile, etc.).

214 Behaves more appropriately alone or in small groups than with the whole class or in a large group activities

1. DO NOT FORCE the student to participate in group situations.

2. Assign a peer to sit/work directly with the student (e.g., in different settings such as art, music, or P.E.; or different activities such as tutoring, group projects, running errands in the building, recess, etc.).

3. Reward or encourage other students for participation in group situations.

4. Give the student the responsibility of helping a peer in group situations.

5. Give the student responsibilities in group situations in order that others might view him/her in a positive light.

6. Call on the student when he/she is most likely to be able to respond successfully (e.g., when discussing a topic in which the student is interested, when you are certain the student knows the answer, etc.).

7. Try various groupings in order to determine the situation in which the student is most comfortable.

8. Have peers invite the student to participate in school or extracurricular activities.

9. Have the student lead a small group activity when he/she possesses mastery or an interest in the activity.

10. Allow the student to be present during group activities without requiring active participation. Require more involvement over time as the student becomes more active in group situations.

11. Reduce the emphasis on competition. Fear of failure may cause the student to be reluctant to participate in group situations.

12. Have the student work with one or two other group members. Gradually increase group size as the student becomes more comfortable.

13. Demonstrate respect for the student's opinions, responses, suggestions, etc.

14. Give the student the opportunity to pick a topic or activity for the group to work on together.

15. Give the student the opportunity to choose a group activity and the group members (e.g., along with the teacher decide what the activity will be, decide what individual group members will do, etc.).

16. Assign the student a role to perform in the group activity which he/she can perform successfully (e.g., secretary, researcher, group behavior monitor, etc.).

17. Make certain the student is productive and accurate in performing individual assignments before placing him/her in group activities.

18. Go over group rules and expectations at the beginning of each group activity.

19. Make certain that the student can follow classroom rules and expectations independently before placing him/her in a group activity.

20. Help the student learn to be satisfied with his/her own best effort rather than some arbitrary measure of success. Success is measured individually according to ability level and progress of any kind is a measure of success.

21. Make certain the student understands instructions/directions for the group activity (e.g., give instructions in a variety of ways, make certain that the student understands his/her role, go over the rules for group behavior before the activity begins, etc.).

22. Make certain the student has all needed materials in order to perform his/her role in the group (e.g., paper, pencil, art supplies, reference materials, etc.).

23. Group the student with peers who will be appropriate role models and are likely to facilitate his/her academic and behavioral success.

24. Group the student with group members who are least likely to be threatening to the student (e.g., younger students, students just learning a skill he/she has mastered, etc.).

25. Make certain the student has enough room to work successfully (e.g., distance from other students, room for all materials, etc.).

26. Make certain the student is actively involved in the group situation (e.g., call on the student frequently, assign the student a responsibility such as teacher assistant, have him/her be group leader, etc.).

27. Remove the student from the group if his/her behavior is inappropriate.

28. Make certain the academic and social demands of the group situation are within the student's ability level.

29. Evaluate the appropriateness of the task to determine: (a) if the task is too difficult and (b) if the length of time scheduled to complete the task is appropriate.

30. Help the student get to know group members before requiring group participation (e.g., introduce the students to one another, allow the students unstructured free time together, etc.).

31. Reduce distracting stimuli which would interfere with the student's success in a group activity (e.g., provide enough room to move without physical contract, keep noise level to a minimum, keep movement in the environment to a minimum, etc.).

32. Schedule group activities as part of the student's daily routine. Group activities should occur on a regularly scheduled basis so that the student will be prepared and know what to expect.

33. Schedule activities in order that your time can be spent uninterrupted with the group.

34. Place the student in group activities he/she prefers and include less desirable activities over time.

35. Provide the student with alternative ways to perform a group assignment and allow him/her to choose the most desirable (e.g., a written paragraph assignment may be accomplished by writing a note to a friend, writing about a recent experience, describing a favorite pastime, etc.).

36. Allow the student to participate in one group activity he/she prefers. Require the student to participate in more group activities as the student experiences success.

37. Schedule group activities when the student is most likely to be successful (e.g., before recess rather than immediately after recess, after the first individual assignment of the day has been completed in order to establish productive behavior, etc.).

38. Program alternative individual activities if the student is unlikely to be successful (e.g., if the schedule has been changed, if a holiday or special event has stimulated the student and made successful group interaction unlikely, etc.).

39. Allow the student to join the group after the activity has begun if he/she is unable to participate appropriately at the beginning of the group activity.

40. Position the student's desk or work area in such a way that he/she works near other students but is not visually distracted by them (e.g., turn the student's desk away from other students).

41. Allow the student to leave a group activity and return to independent work when he/she can no longer be successful in the group activity (e.g., as an alternative to disrupting the group, fighting, etc.).

42. Teach the student to "think" before acting (e.g., ask himself/herself: "What is happening?" "What am I doing?" "What should I do?" "What will be best for me?").

43. Communicate with parents (e.g., notes home, phone calls, etc.) in order to share information concerning the student's progress and so that they can reinforce the student at home for participating in group situations at school.

44. Write a contract with the student specifying what behavior is expected (e.g., working appropriately with peers) and what reinforcement will be made available when the terms of the contract have been met. (See Appendix for Behavioral Contract.)

45. Reinforce other students in the classroom for working appropriately in a group situation.

46. Establish classroom rules:
1. Work on task.
2. Remain in your seat.
3. Finish task.
4. Meet task expectations.
5. Raise your hand.
Reiterate rules often and reinforce students for following rules.

47. Speak with the student to explain: (a) what the student is doing wrong (e.g., failing to take part) and (b) what the student should be doing (e.g., talking, taking turns, playing, sharing, etc.).

48. Reinforce the student for working in a group situation: (a) give the student a tangible reward (e.g., classroom privileges, line leading, passing out materials, five minutes free time, etc.) or (b) give the student an intangible reward (e.g., praise, handshake, smile, etc.).

215 Demonstrates inappropriate behavior in a small academic group setting

1. DO NOT FORCE the student to participate in a small academic group setting.

2. Assign a peer to sit/work directly with the student (e.g., in different settings such as art, music, P.E.; or different activities such as tutoring, group projects, running errands in the building, recess, etc.).

3. Ask the student questions that cannot be answered "yes" or "no."

4. Call on the student when he/she is most likely to be able to respond successfully (e.g., when discussing something in which the student is interested, when you are certain the student knows the answer, etc.).

5. Try various groupings in order to determine the situation in which the student is most comfortable.

6. Have peers invite the student to participate in school or extracurricular activities.

7. Request that the student be the leader of a small group activity if he/she possesses mastery or an interest in the activity.

8. Allow the student to be present during small group activities without requiring active participation. Require more involvement over time as the student demonstrates success.

9. Have the student work with one or two other group members and gradually increase the group size as the student becomes more comfortable.

10. Demonstrate respect for the student's opinions, responses, suggestions, etc.

11. Give the student the opportunity to pick a topic or activity for the group to work on together.

12. Go over group rules/expectations at the beginning of each group activity.

13. Give the student the opportunity to choose a group activity and the group members (e.g., along with the teacher decide what the activity will be, what individual group members will do, etc.).

14. Assign the student a role to perform in the group activity that he/she can perform successfully (e.g., secretary, researcher, group behavior monitor, etc.).

15. Make certain the student is productive and accurate in performing individual assignments before placing him/her in small group activities.

16. Make certain that the student can follow classroom rules/expectations independently before placing him/her in small group activities.

17. Reduce the emphasis on competition. Fear of failure may cause the student to refuse to work in small group activities.

18. Help the student learn to be satisfied with personal best effort rather than some arbitrary measure of success. Success is measured individually according to ability level, and progress of any kind is a measure of success.

19. Place the student with peers who will be appropriate role models and are likely to facilitate his/her academic and behavioral success.

20. Place the student with group members who are least likely to be threatening to the student (e.g., younger students, students just learning a skill he/she has mastered, etc.).

21. Make certain that the student understands instructions/directions for the group activity (e.g., give instructions in a variety of ways, make certain that the student understands his/her role, go over the rules for group behavior before the activity begins, etc.).

22. Remove the student from the group if he/she behaves inappropriately.

23. Make certain that the student has all needed materials in order to perform his/her role in the group (e.g., paper, pencil, art supplies, reference materials, etc.).

24. Make certain that the student has enough room to work successfully (e.g., distance from other students, room for all materials, etc.).

25. Make certain the student is actively involved in the group (e.g., call on the student frequently, assign the student a responsibility such as teacher assistant, have the student be group leader, etc.).

26. Make certain the academic and social demands of the group situation are within the student's ability level.

27. Help the student get to know group members before requiring group participation (e.g., introduce the students to one another, allow the students unstructured free time together, etc.).

28. Reduce distracting stimuli which could interfere with the student's success in a group activity (e.g., provide enough room to move without physical contact, keep noise level to a minimum, keep movement in the environment to a minimum, etc.).

29. Schedule activities in order that your time can be spent uninterrupted with the group.

30. Schedule small group activities as part of the student's daily routine (e.g., small group activities should occur on a regularly scheduled basis so the student will be prepared and know what to expect).

31. Place the student in group activities he/she prefers and include less desirable activities over time.

32. Provide the student with alternative ways to perform a group assignment and allow him/her to choose the most desirable (e.g., a written paragraph assignment may be accomplished by writing a note to a friend, writing about a recent experience, describing a favorite pastime, etc.).

33. Allow the student to participate in one group activity he/she prefers. Require the student to participate in more small group activities as the student experiences success.

34. Schedule small group activities when the student is most likely to be successful (e.g., before recess rather than immediately after recess, after the first individual assignment of the day has been completed in order to establish productive behavior, etc.).

35. Program alternative individual activities if the student is unlikely to be successful (e.g., if the schedule has been changed; if holidays or special events have stimulated the student, making successful group interactions unlikely; etc.).

36. Allow the student to join the group after the activity has begun if he/she is unable to participate appropriately at the beginning of the activity.

37. Position the student's desk or work area in such a way that he/she works near other students but is not visually distracted by them (e.g., turn the student's desk away from other students).

38. Allow the student to leave a small group activity and return to independent work when the student can no longer be successful in the group activity (e.g., as an alternative to disrupting the group, fighting, etc.).

39. Teach the student to "think" before acting (e.g., ask himself/herself: "What is happening?" "What am I doing?" "What should I do?" "What will be best for me?").

40. Have the student question any directions, explanations, and instructions not understood.

41. Evaluate the appropriateness of the task to determine: (a) if the task is too difficult and (b) if the length of time scheduled to complete the task is appropriate.

42. Communicate with parents (e.g., notes home, phone calls, etc.) in order to share information concerning the student's progress and so that they can reinforce the student at home for demonstrating appropriate behavior in small academic group settings at school.

43. Write a contract with the student specifying what behavior is expected (e.g., working appropriately with peers) and what reinforcement will be made available when the terms of the contract have been met. (See Appendix for Behavioral Contract.)

44. Reinforce the student for demonstrating appropriate behavior in a small academic group setting based on the length of time the student can be successful. Gradually increase the length of time required for reinforcement as the student demonstrates success.

45. Reinforce those students in the classroom who demonstrate appropriate behavior in a small academic group setting.

46. Speak to the student to explain: (a) what the student is doing wrong (e.g., failing to take part) and (b) what the student should be doing (e.g., talking, taking turns, sharing, etc.).

47. Establish classroom rules:
1. Work on task.
2. Remain in your seat.
3. Finish task.
4. Meet task expectations.
5. Raise your hand.

Reiterate rules often and reinforce students for following rules.

48. Reinforce the student for demonstrating appropriate behavior in a small academic group setting: (a) give the student a tangible reward (e.g., classroom privileges, line leading, passing out materials, five minutes free time, etc.) or (b) give the student an intangible reward (e.g., praise, handshake, smile, etc.).

216 Demonstrates inappropriate behavior in the presence of a substitute teacher

1. Prepare a substitute teacher information packet that includes all information pertaining to the classroom (e.g., student roster, class schedule, class rules, behavior management techniques, class helpers, etc.).

2. Make certain the student understands that classroom rules and behavioral consequences are in effect when a substitute teacher is in the classroom.

3. Inform the substitute teacher of all privileges the students have both in and outside of the classroom.

4. Indicate various activities that the student may engage in after completing his/her work for the day.

5. Indicate the names of several teachers and where they can be found in case the substitute teacher should need their assistance.

6. Inform the substitute teacher of the classroom rules and the consequences if the rules are not followed by the student.

7. Express the need for the substitute teacher to maintain consistency of discipline while both in and outside of the classroom.

8. Indicate where all needed materials are located in order to maintain structure in the classroom.

9. Have the student work on practice work (e.g., work that has already been taught to the student and that he/she knows how to do) in order to reduce frustration and feelings of failure.

10. Set aside ten minutes at the beginning of the day for the substitute teacher to develop rapport with the students (e.g., introduce himself/herself to the class, learn the students' names, talk about things the students enjoy doing, etc.).

11. Indicate to the student that the substitute teacher is in charge of the classroom at all times.

12. Schedule a fun educational activity (e.g., computer games) during the day in order to provide incentive for the student to stay on task and behave appropriately.

13. Assign a "special job" for the student to perform when there is a substitute teacher in the classroom (e.g., substitute teacher's assistant, line leader, class monitor, etc.). Inform the substitute teacher of this "special job."

14. Have the substitute teacher present instructions/directions in a variety of ways (e.g., orally, written, etc.).

15. Make an attempt to use a substitute teacher who has skills necessary to deal with problem behavior and special-needs students.

16. Make certain that the substitute teacher is familiar with the behavioral support system used in the classroom (e.g., rules, point system, reinforcers, etc.).

17. If possible, communicate directly with the substitute teacher in order to share information which will contribute to the student's success.

18. Identify a student(s) to act as an assistant to the substitute teacher during the day's activities (e.g., the student(s) provides accurate information about the schedule of activities, behavioral support system, etc.).

19. Provide the substitute teacher with detailed information on the activities and assignments.

20. Make certain the substitute teacher follows all procedures indicated by the classroom teacher (e.g., academic activities, behavioral support system, etc.).

21. Have the substitute teacher provide a written review of the day as feedback for the classroom teacher (e.g., activities completed, student behavior, absences, incidents concerning individual students, etc.).

22. Have the student self-record his/her own behavior when a substitute teacher is in the classroom.

23. Assign a peer to work with the student to act as a model for appropriate behavior and provide information necessary for success.

24. If an aide works in the classroom, have the aide monitor the student's behavior, provide reinforcement, deliver instructions, etc.

25. If there is an aide in the classroom, have the aide work with the student on a one-to-one basis throughout the day.

26. Provide the student with an individualized schedule of daily events. The schedule should be attached to the student's desk or carried with him/her at all times.

27. Instruct the substitute teacher to interact with the student frequently in order to provide reinforcement, deliver instructions, provide encouragement, etc.

28. Have the substitute teacher maintain visibility to and from the student. The substitute teacher should be able to see the student and the student should be able to see the substitute teacher, making eye contact possible at all times.

29. Provide the student with as many high-interest activities as possible.

30. Provide a quiet place for the student to work.

31. Make the student aware of the natural consequences concerning inappropriate behavior in the presence of a substitute teacher (e.g., removal from the classroom, loss of privileges, etc.).

32. Have a peer deliver instructions to the student.

33. Begin the day or class with an activity which is of high interest to the student.

34. Present activities in the most attractive and interesting manner possible.

35. Do not schedule highly stimulating activities when a substitute teacher is in the classroom.

36. Structure the environment in order to reduce the opportunity for inappropriate behavior (e.g., reduce periods of inactivity by having the student actively involved at all times).

37. Provide the substitute teacher with a seating chart and indicate the student(s) who needs additional supervision.

38. Indicate, for the substitute teacher, those peers who might be likely to stimulate the student's inappropriate behavior. (It may be necessary to keep the students separated.)

39. Have the substitute teacher check the student's completed assignments in order to make certain that work is not carelessly performed.

40. Write a contract with the student or entire class for reinforcement based on appropriate behavior when a substitute teacher is present.

41. Have the substitute teacher maintain mobility in order to be frequently near the student.

42. Make certain the student receives the necessary information to perform activities (e.g., written information, verbal directions, reminders, etc.).

43. Make certain the substitute teacher is consistent with the program established by the classroom teacher (e.g., schedule, delivering instructions, task requirements, reinforcement, negative consequences, etc.).

44. Provide the student with a clearly identified list of consequences for inappropriate behavior in the presence of a substitute teacher.

45. Have the substitute teacher help the student begin assignments, check his/her work, provide immediate feedback, etc.

46. Have the student maintain a record of his/her academic performance while the substitute teacher is in the classroom.

47. Inform the students in advance when it will be necessary for a substitute teacher to be in the classroom, and establish expectations for behavior and academic performance.

48. Provide the substitute teacher with instructions for action to be taken if the student becomes abusive or threatening.

49. Teach the student to "think" before acting (e.g., ask himself/herself: "What is happening?" "What am I doing?" "What should I do?" "What will be best for me?").

50. Make certain the student is allowed to voice an opinion in a situation in order to hear the student's side of the story.

51. Have the student question any directions, explanations, and instructions not understood.

52. Evaluate the appropriateness of the task to determine: (a) if the task is too difficult and (b) if the length of time scheduled to complete the task is appropriate.

53. Communicate with parents (e.g., notes home, phone calls, etc.) in order to share information concerning the student's progress and so that they can reinforce the student at home for demonstrating appropriate behavior in the presence of a substitute teacher.

54. Write a contract with the student specifying what behavior is expected (e.g., following the substitute teacher's directions) and what reinforcement will be made available when the terms of the contract have been met. (See Appendix for Behavioral Contract.)

55. Reinforce those students in the classroom who demonstrate appropriate behavior in the presence of a substitute teacher.

56. Establish classroom rules:
1. Work on task.
2. Remain in your seat.
3. Finish task.
4. Meet task expectations.
5. Raise your hand.
Reiterate rules often and reinforce students for following rules.

57. Speak to the student to explain: (a) what the student is doing wrong (e.g., not following the substitute teacher's directions, not following classroom rules, etc.) and (b) what the student should be doing (e.g., following the substitute teacher's directions, following classroom rules, etc.).

58. Reinforce the student for demonstrating appropriate behavior in the presence of a substitute teacher: (a) give the student a tangible reward (e.g., classroom privileges, line leading, passing out materials, five minutes free time, etc.) or (b) give the student an intangible reward (e.g., praise, handshake, smile, etc.).

217 Demonstrates inappropriate behavior in a large academic group setting

1. Assign a peer to sit/work directly with the student in large academic group settings.

2. DO NOT FORCE the student to participate in the group.

3. Reward or encourage others for participation in the group.

4. Give the student the responsibility of helping another student in the group.

5. Give the student responsibilities in the group in order that others might view him/her in a more positive light.

6. Ask the student questions that cannot be answered "yes" or "no."

7. Call on the student when he/she is most likely to be able to respond successfully (e.g., when discussing something in which the student is interested, when you are certain the student knows the answer, etc.).

8. Try various groupings in order to determine the situation in which the student is most comfortable.

9. Ask the student to be the leader of a large group activity if he/she possesses mastery or an interest in the activity.

10. Allow the student to be present during large group activities without requiring active participation. Require more involvement over time as the student demonstrates success.

11. Reduce the emphasis on competition. Fear of failure may cause the student to avoid participating in large academic group settings.

12. Have the student work with one or two other group members and gradually increase group size as the student becomes more comfortable.

13. Demonstrate respect for the student's opinions, responses, suggestions, etc.

14. Give the student the opportunity to pick a topic or activity for the group to work on together.

15. Give the student the opportunity to choose a group activity and choose the group members who will participate (e.g., along with the teacher decide what the activity will be, what individual group members will do, etc.).

16. Assign the student a role to perform in the group activity which he/she can perform successfully (e.g., secretary, researcher, group behavior monitor, etc.).

17. Make certain the student is productive and accurate in performing individual assignments before placing him/her in large group activities.

18. Go over group rules/expectations at the beginning of each group activity.

19. Make certain the student can follow classroom rules/expectations independently before placing him/her in a large group activity.

20. Help the student learn to be satisfied with his/her own best effort rather than some arbitrary measure of success. Success is measured individually according to ability level, and progress of any kind is a measure of success.

21. Place the student with peers who will be appropriate role models and are likely to facilitate his/her academic and behavioral success.

22. Place the student with group members who are least likely to be threatening to him/her (e.g., younger students, students just learning a skill he/she has mastered, etc.).

23. Make certain the student has all needed materials in order to perform his/her role in the group (e.g., paper, pencil, art supplies, reference materials, etc.).

24. Make certain the student understands instructions/directions for the group activity (e.g., give instructions in a variety of ways, make certain that the student understands his/her role, go over the rules for group behavior before the activity begins, etc.).

25. Make certain the student has enough room to work successfully (e.g., distance from other students, room for all materials, etc.).

26. Make certain the student is actively involved in the group (e.g., call on the student frequently, assign the student a responsibility such as teacher assistant, have him/her be group leader, etc.).

27. Remove the student from the group if he/she behaves inappropriately.

28. Make certain the academic and social demands of the group situation are within the student's ability level.

29. Help the student become acquainted with group members before requiring group participation (e.g., introduce the students to one another, allow the students unstructured free time together, etc.).

30. Reduce distracting stimuli which could interfere with the student's success in a group activity (e.g., provide enough room to move without physical contact, keep noise level to a minimum, keep movement in the environment to a minimum, etc.).

31. Schedule activities in order that your time can be spent uninterrupted with the group.

32. Schedule large group activities as part of the student's daily routine (e.g., large group activities should occur on a regularly scheduled basis so that the student will be prepared and know what to expect).

33. Provide the student with alternative ways to perform a group assignment and allow him/her to choose the most desirable (e.g., a written paragraph assignment may be accomplished by writing a note to a friend, writing about a recent experience, describing a favorite pastime, etc.).

34. Place the student in group activities he/she prefers and include less desirable activities over time.

35. Have the student participate in at least one group activity per day. Require the student to participate in more group activities as he/she experiences success.

36. Schedule large group activities when the student is most likely to be successful (e.g., before recess rather than immediately after recess, after the first individual assignment of the day has been completed in order to establish productive behavior, etc.).

37. Program alternative individual activities if the student is unlikely to be successful (e.g., if the schedule has been changed; if a holiday or special event has stimulated the student, making successful group interaction unlikely; etc.).

38. Allow the student to join the group after the activity has begun if he/she is unable to participate appropriately at the beginning of the group activity.

39. Position the student's desk or work area in such a way that he/she works near other students but is not visually distracted by them (e.g., turn the student's desk away from other students, seat the student in the front row, etc.).

40. Allow the student to leave a group activity and return to independent work when he/she can no longer be successful in the group activity (e.g., as an alternative to disrupting the group, fighting, etc.).

41. Arrange the student's seating in order that you can interact with him/her frequently (e.g., near the front of the room, on the perimeter of the group, etc.).

42. Assign a peer to sit next to the student to provide assistance.

43. Have the student maintain a list of classroom rules at his/her desk (e.g., attached to the surface of the desk, inside the desk, etc.).

44. Use a "time-out" area to allow the student to gain self-control if problem behaviors occur during a large academic group activity.

45. Provide a carrel or other quiet study area for the student to use if he/she cannot be successful at his/her seat.

46. Use removal from the group as a natural consequence for inappropriate behavior.

47. Present academic tasks in the most attractive and interesting manner possible.

48. Integrate the student into a large academic group activity only after he/she has had success with one other student, a small group, etc.

49. Integrate the student into a large academic group activity gradually (e.g., short periods of time with the group lead to longer periods of time).

50. Provide the student with the opportunity to work with a peer tutor, volunteer, etc., for enrichment or support of content presented in the large academic group activity.

51. Provide structure in order that the large academic group activity does not become overstimulating for the student.

52. Publicly praise the student for appropriate behavior and privately redirect inappropriate behavior.

53. Write group contracts which encourage students to work together for group success.

54. Find related group activities the student can perform successfully (e.g., acting as teacher assistant, giving directions, handing out materials, collecting materials, etc.).

55. Schedule daily activities so that highly desirable activities follow large academic group activities and are contingent upon appropriate behavior in the large academic group activity.

56. Have the student question any directions, explanations, and instructions not understood.

57. Teach the student to "think" before acting (e.g., ask himself/herself: "What is happening?" "What am I doing?" "What should I do?" "What will be best for me?").

58. Make certain that your comments take the form of constructive criticism rather than criticism that can be perceived as personal, threatening, etc. (e.g., instead of saying, "You always make the same mistake." say, "A better way to do that might be . . .").

59. Evaluate the appropriateness of the task to determine: (a) if the task is too difficult and (b) if the length of time scheduled to complete the task is appropriate.

60. Communicate with parents (e.g., notes home, phone calls, etc.) in order to share information concerning the student's progress and so that they can reinforce the student at home for working appropriately in a large academic group setting at school.

61. Write a contract with the student specifying what behavior is expected (e.g., working appropriately with peers) and what reinforcement will be made available when the terms of the contract have been met. (See Appendix for Behavioral Contract.)

62. Reinforce the student for demonstrating appropriate behavior in a large academic group setting based on the length of time he/she can be successful. Gradually increase the length of time required for reinforcement as the student demonstrates success.

63. Reinforce those students in the classroom who demonstrate appropriate behavior in a large academic group setting.

64. Establish classroom rules:
1. Work on task.
2. Remain in your seat.
3. Finish task.
4. Meet task expectations.
5. Raise your hand.
Reiterate rules often and reinforce students for following rules.

65. Speak to the student to explain: (a) what the student is doing wrong (e.g., talking out of turn, failing to take part, etc.) and (b) what the student should be doing (e.g., talking when appropriate, taking turns, sharing, etc.).

66. Reinforce the student for demonstrating appropriate behavior in a large academic group setting: (a) give the student a tangible reward (e.g., classroom privileges, line leading, passing out materials, five minutes free time, etc.) or (b) give the student an intangible reward (e.g., praise, handshake, smile, etc.).

1.   Reinforce the student for working in a group situation: (a) give the student a tangible reward (e.g., classroom privileges, line leading, passing out materials, five minutes free time, etc.) or (b) give the student an intangible reward (e.g., praise, handshake, smile, etc.).

2.   Speak with the student to explain: (a) what the student is doing wrong (e.g., failing to take part) and (b) what the student should be doing (e.g., talking, taking turns, playing, sharing, etc.).

3.   Establish classroom rules:
1. Work on task.
2. Remain in your seat.
3. Finish task.
4. Meet task expectations.
5. Raise your hand.
Reiterate rules often and reinforce students for following rules.

4.   Reinforce other students in the classroom for working appropriately in a group situation.

5.   Write a contract with the student specifying what behavior is expected (e.g., working appropriately with peers) and what reinforcement will be made available when the terms of the contract have been met. (See Appendix for Behavioral Contract.)

6.   Communicate with parents (e.g., notes home, phone calls, etc.) in order to share information concerning the student's progress and so that they can reinforce the student at home for participating in group situations at school.

7.   DO NOT FORCE the student to participate in group situations until he/she can be successful.

8.   Assign a peer to sit/work directly with the student (e.g., in different settings such as art, music, P.E., on the bus; or different activities such as tutoring, group projects, running errands in the building, recess, etc.).

9.   Reward or encourage other students for participation in group situations.

10.   Give the student the responsibility of helping a peer in group situations.

11.   Give the student responsibilities in group situations in order that others might view the student in a positive light.

12.   Call on the student when he/she is most likely to be able to respond successfully (e.g., when discussing a topic in which the student is interested, when the teacher is certain the student knows the answer, etc.).

13.   Try various groupings in order to determine the situation in which the student is most comfortable.

14.   Have peers invite the student to participate in school or extracurricular activities.

15.   Have the student lead a small group activity when he/she possesses mastery or an interest in the activity.

16.   Allow the student to be present during group activities without requiring active participation. Require more involvement over time as the student becomes more active in group situations.

17.   Reduce the emphasis on competition. Fear of failure may cause the student to be reluctant to participate in group situations.

18.   Have the student work with one or two other group members. Gradually increase group size as the student becomes more comfortable.

19.   Demonstrate respect for the student's opinions, responses, suggestions, etc.

20.   Give the student the opportunity to pick a topic or activity for the group to work on together.

21.   Give the student the opportunity to choose a group activity and the group members (e.g., along with the teacher decide what the activity will be, decide what individual group members will do, etc.).

22. Assign the student a role to perform in the group activity which he/she can perform successfully (e.g., secretary, researcher, group behavior monitor, etc.).

23. Make certain the student is productive and accurate in performing individual assignments before placing him/her in a group activity.

24. Go over group rules and expectations at the beginning of each group activity.

25. Make certain that the student can follow classroom rules and expectations independently before placing him/her in a group activity.

26. Help the student learn to be satisfied with his/her own best effort rather than some arbitrary measure of success. Success is measured individually according to ability level, and progress of any kind is a measure of success.

27. Group the student with peers who will be appropriate role models and are likely to facilitate the student's academic and behavioral successes.

28. Group the student with group members who are least likely to be threatening (e.g., younger students, students just learning a skill he/she has mastered, etc.).

29. Make certain the student understands instructions/directions for the group activity (e.g., give instructions in a variety of ways, make certain that the student understands his/her role, go over the rules for group behavior before the activity begins, etc.).

30. Make certain the student has all needed materials in order to perform his/her role in the group (e.g., paper, pencil, art supplies, reference materials, etc.).

31. Make certain the student has enough room to work successfully (e.g., distance from other students, room for all materials, etc.).

32. Make certain the student is actively involved in the group situation (e.g., call on the student frequently, assign the student a responsibility such as teacher assistant, have him/her be the group leader, etc.).

33. Remove the student from the group if his/her behavior is inappropriate.

34. Make certain the academic and social demands of the group situation are within the student's ability level.

35. Evaluate the appropriateness of the assigned task to determine: (a) if the task is too difficult and (b) if the length of time scheduled is appropriate.

36. Help the student get to know group members before requiring group participation (e.g., introduce the students to one another, allow the students unstructured free time together, etc.).

37. Reduce distracting stimuli which could interfere with the student's success in a group activity (e.g., provide enough room to move without physical contact, keep noise level at a minimum, keep movement in the environment to a minimum, etc.).

38. Schedule group activities in order that the teacher's time can be spent uninterrupted with the group.

39. Schedule group activities as part of the student's daily routine (i.e., group activities should occur on a regularly scheduled basis so the student will be prepared and know what to expect).

40. Place the student in those group activities he/she prefers. Gradually require the student to participate in less desirable activities.

41. Provide the student with alternative ways to perform a group assignment and allow the student to choose the most desirable (e.g., a written paragraph assignment may be accomplished by writing a note to a friend, writing about a recent experience, describing a favorite pastime, etc.).

42. Allow the student to participate in one group activity he/she prefers. Require the student to participate in more group activities as he/she experiences success.

43. Schedule group activities when the student is most likely to be successful (e.g., before recess rather than immediately after recess, after the first individual assignment of the day has been completed in order to establish productive behavior, etc.).

44. Program alternative individual activities if the student is unlikely to be successful (e.g., if the schedule has been changed, if holidays or special events have stimulated the student and make successful group interaction unlikely, etc.).

45. Allow the student to join the group after the activity has begun if he/she is unable to participate appropriately at the beginning of the group activity.

46. Position the student's desk or work area in such a way that he/she works near other students but is not visually distracted by them (e.g., turn the student's desk away from other students, etc.).

47. Allow the student to leave a group activity and return to independent work when he/she can no longer be successful in the group activity (e.g., as an alternative to disrupting the group, fighting, etc.).

48. Carefully consider the student's age and experience before expecting him/her to get along in a group.

49. Intervene early when there is a problem in order to prevent more serious problems from occurring.

50. Do not force the student to interact with people with whom he/she is not completely comfortable.

51. Teach the student acceptable ways to communicate displeasure, anger, frustration, etc.

52. Teach the student to "think" before acting (e.g., ask himself/herself: "What is happening?" "What am I doing?" "What should I do?" "What will be best for me?").

53. Encourage the student to use problem-solving skills: (a) identify the problem, (b) identify goals and objectives, (c) develop strategies, (d) develop a plan for action, (e) carry out the plan.

54. Make certain the student is allowed to voice an opinion in a situation in order to avoid becoming angry or upset.

55. Talk to the student about ways of handling situations successfully without conflict (e.g., walk away from the situation, change to another activity, ask for help, etc.).

219 Does not demonstrate appropriate behavior in group games

1. Reinforce the student for demonstrating appropriate behavior in group games: (a) give the student a tangible reward (e.g., classroom privileges, line leading, passing out materials, five minutes free time, etc.) or (b) give the student an intangible reward (e.g., praise, handshake, smile, etc.).

2. Speak to the student to explain: (a) what the student is doing wrong (e.g., failing to follow rules, cheating, etc.) and (b) what the student should be doing (e.g., following rules, playing fairly, etc.).

3. Establish classroom rules:
1. Work on task.
2. Remain in your seat.
3. Finish task.
4. Meet task expectations.
5. Raise your hand.
Reiterate rules often and reinforce students for following rules.

4. Reinforce those students in the classroom who demonstrate appropriate behavior in group games.

5. Reinforce the student for demonstrating appropriate behavior in group games based on the length of time the student can be successful. Gradually increase the length of time required for reinforcement as the student demonstrates success.

6. Write a contract with the student specifying what behavior is expected (e.g., following rules) and what reinforcement will be made available when the terms of the contract have been met. (See Appendix for Behavioral Contract.)

7. Communicate with parents (e.g., notes home, phone calls, etc.) in order to share information concerning the student's progress and so that they can reinforce the student at home for demonstrating appropriate behavior in group games at school.

8. Evaluate the appropriateness of the group game to determine if the game is too difficult and if the length of time scheduled to complete the game is appropriate.

9. Identify a peer to act as a model for the student to imitate appropriate behavior in group games.

10. Have the student question any directions, explanations, and instructions not understood.

11. Evaluate the expectations for participation in group games in order to determine if the student can be successful in the interaction for the expected length of time.

12. Allow the student to choose a group of peers with whom he/she feels comfortable to play group games.

13. Have the student engage in a game activity with one peer and gradually increase the size of the group as the student demonstrates success.

14. Determine the peers with whom the student would most prefer to interact in group games and attempt to facilitate the interaction.

15. Assign outgoing, nonthreatening peers to interact with the student in group games.

16. Structure the environment so that the student has many opportunities to interact with peers in group games.

17. Assign the student to interact with younger peers in group games.

18. Assign the student to group games in which he/she is likely to interact successfully with peers.

19. Conduct a sociometric activity with the class in order to determine those peers who would most prefer to interact with the student in group games.

20. Make certain that the student demonstrates appropriate behavior in nonacademic situations prior to placing him/her with peers for group games.

21. Make certain the student understands that interacting with peers in group games is contingent upon appropriate behavior

22. Have the student practice appropriate interactions with the teacher(s) in group games.

23. Teach the student appropriate ways to interact with peers in group games (e.g., suggest activities, share materials, problem solve, take turns, follow game rules, etc.).

24. Supervise group games closely in order that the peers with whom the student interacts do not stimulate inappropriate behavior.

25. Make certain that group games are not so stimulating as to make successful interactions with peers difficult.

26. Assign older peers with desirable social skills to interact with the student in group games.

27. Involve the student in extracurricular activities in order to encourage interaction with peers in group games.

28. Reduce the emphasis on competition. Failure may stimulate inappropriate behavior in group games.

29. Teach the student problem-solving skills in order that he/she can better deal with problems that may occur in interactions with peers in group games (e.g., talking, walking away, calling upon an arbitrator, compromising, etc.).

30. Find the peer with whom the student is most likely to be able to successfully interact in group games (e.g., a student with similar interests, background, classes, behavior patterns, nonacademic schedule, etc.).

31. Select group games designed to enhance appropriate interaction of the student and peers.

32. Structure the group games according to the needs/abilities of the student (e.g., establish rules, limit the stimulation of the activities, limit the length of the game, consider the time of day, etc.).

33. Limit opportunities for interaction in group games on those occasions when the student is not likely to be successful (e.g., if the student has experienced academic or social failure prior to the scheduled group game).

34. Through interviews with other students and observations, determine those characteristics of the student which interfere with successful interactions during group games in order to determine skills or behaviors the student needs to develop for successful interactions.

35. Make certain beforehand that the student is able to successfully engage in the group game (e.g., the student understands the rules, the student is familiar with the game, the student will be compatible with the other students playing the game, etc.).

36. Make certain the student understands that failing to interact appropriately with peers during group games may result in termination of the game and/or loss of future opportunities to engage in group games.

37. Have the student interact with peers for short periods of time in order to enhance success. Gradually increase the length of time as the student demonstrates success.

38. Have the student study, practice, simulate, etc., the rules for group games before participating.

39. Establish a set of standard behavior rules for group games (e.g., follow rules of the game, take turns, make positive comments, work as a team member, be a good sport, etc.).

40. Remove the student from group games if he/she is unable to demonstrate appropriate behavior.

41. Allow the student to choose the group game which he/she will play with peers.

42. Play the game with the student before he/she engages in the game with peers in order to model appropriate behavior, determine the student's ability to play the game, determine the student's ability to follow behavior rules, etc.

43. Have the student engage in group games of short duration. Gradually increase the duration of group games as the student demonstrates success.

44. Teach the student necessary skills to successfully participate in particular games (e.g., volleyball, basketball, football, baseball, etc.).

45. Carefully consider the student's age and experience before expecting him/her to get along with others when playing group games.

46. Make certain the student sees the relationship between his/her behavior and the consequences which may follow (e.g., failing to get along when playing a group game will result in others not wanting to play with him/her).

47. Intervene early when there is a problem in order to prevent more serious problems from occurring.

48. Do not force the student to play games with someone with whom he/she is not completely comfortable.

49. Find a peer to play with the student who will be a good influence (e.g., someone younger, older, of the same sex, of the opposite sex, etc.).

50. Teach the student acceptable ways to communicate displeasure, anger, frustration, etc.

51. Teach the student to "think" before acting (e.g., ask himself/herself: "What is happening?" "What am I doing?" "What should I do?" "What will be best for me?").

52. Encourage the student to use problem-solving skills: (a) identify the problem, (b) identify goals and objectives, (c) develop strategies, (d) develop a plan for action, and (e) carry out the plan.

53. Make certain the student is allowed to voice an opinion in a situation in order to avoid becoming angry or upset.

54. Talk to the student about ways of handling situations successfully without conflict (e.g., walk away from a situation, change to another activity, ask for help, etc.).

IV. References

Algozzine, B., Christenson, S., & Ysseldyke, J.E.(1982). Probabilities associated with the referral to placement process. *Teacher Education and Special Education, 5* (3), 19-23

Algozzine, B., Ysseldyke, J.E., & Christenson, S.(1983). An analysis of the incidence of special class placement: The masses are burgeoning. *Journal of Special Education, 17,* 141-147

Canter, A. (1987). Pre-referral intervention programs key to quality services. *Communique, 16* (4), 16.

Chalfant, J.C., Pysh, M.V., & Moultrie, R. (1979). Teacher assistance teams: A model for within-building problem solving. *Learning Disability Quarterly, 2* (3), 85-96.

Christenson, S., Ysseldyke, J.E., Wang, J.J., & Algozzine, B. (1983). Teacher attribution for problems that result in referral for psycho-educational evaluation. *Journal of Educational Research, 76,* 174-180

Graden, J.L., Casey, A., Christenson, S.L. (1985). Implementing a prereferral intervention system: Part I. the model. *Exceptional Children, 51* (5), 377-384.

Graden, J.L., Casey, A., Bonstrom, O. (1985). Implementing a prereferral intervention system: Part II. the data. *Exceptional Children, 51* (6), 487-496.

Lilly, M.S., & Givens-Ogle, L.B. (1981). Teacher consultation: Past, present, and future. *Behavioral Disorders, 6,* 73-77.

Reynolds, M.C., Wang, M.C., & Walberg, H.J. (1987). The necessary restructuring of special and regular education. *Exceptional Children, 53,* 391-398.

Stainback, W., Stainback, S., Courtnage, L., & Jaben, T. (1985). Facilitating mainstreaming by modifying the mainstream. *Exceptional Children, 52,* 144-152.

Thurlow, M.L., & Ysseldyke, J.E. (1982). Instructional planning: Information collected by school psychologists vs. information considered useful by teachers. *Journal of School Psychology, 20,* 3-10.

Ysseldyke, J.E., Thurlow, M., Graden, J., Wesson, C., Algozzine, B., & Deno, S. (1983). Generalizations from five years of research on assessment and decision making: The University of Minnesota Institute. *Exceptional Education Quarterly, 4* (1). 75-93.

V. Appendix

Preventing Behavior Problems 475

Typical Methods of Modifying Academic Tasks 476

Reinforcer Survey 477

Reinforcer Menu 478

Rules for School Environments 479

Point Record 480

Point Card 481

Sample Contract 482

Contract 483

Group Contract 484

Schedule of Daily Events 485

Schedule of Daily Events Sample 486

Parent Communication Form 487

Student Conference Report 488

A List of Reinforcers Identified by Elementary-Aged Students 489

A List of Reinforcers Identified by Secondary-Aged Students 490

Mapping Form 491

Note-Taking 492

The Outline Form 493

Double-Column Form 494

Double Column Form Sample 495

Assignment Form 496

Assignment Sheet 497

2-Week Project Outline 498

Studying for a Test 499

Flash Card Study Aid 500

Flash Card Study Aid Sample 501

Preventing Behavior Problems

- **Determine reinforcer preferences**

- **Determine academic ability levels**

- **Determine social interaction skills**

- **Determine ability to remain on task**

- **Determine group behavior**

- **Monitor and limit contemporary determinants of inappropriate behavior such as having to wait, task length, task difficulty, peer involvement, etc.**

- **Base seating arrangements on behavior**

- **Base group involvement on behavior**

- **Maintain teacher mobility in classroom**

- **Maintain teacher/student contact: visual, verbal, and physical**

- **Use criteria for expectations based on observed behavior and performance**

- **Use shaping, fading, and imitation procedures to gradually change behavior**

- **Maintain variety in reinforcers**

- **Use the *Premack Principle* in arranging schedule (i.e., a more desirable behavior can be used to reinforce the completion of a less desirable behavior)**

- **Use curriculum as reinforcement**

- **Use rules, point cards, and schedules of daily events as discriminative stimuli**

- **Use contracting to individualize, specify expected behavior, and identify reinforcers**

- **Arrange seating so all students have visibility to and from the teacher and teacher can scan the entire class**

- **Maintain a full schedule of activities**

- **Use language that is positive and firm, not demeaning, insulting, or harassing**

- **Intervene early when any form of conflict occurs**

- **Do not ignore behavior as an excuse for not intervening**

- **Use time-out to help the student resolve problem behavior**

- **Use removal to prevent contagion, destruction of property, and danger to others**

- **Communicate and coordinate with other teachers**

- **Communicate with home to prevent students playing one adult against another**

Typical Methods of Modifying Academic Tasks

- Reduce the number of problems on a page (e.g., five problems to a page; the student may be required to do four pages of work throughout the day if necessary).

- Use a highlight marker to identify key words, phrases, or sentences for the student to read.

- Remove pages from workbooks or reading material and present these to the student one at a time rather than allowing the student to become anxious with workbooks or texts.

- Outline reading material for the student at his/her reading level, emphasizing main ideas.

- Tape record material for the student to listen to as he/she reads along.

- Read tests/quizzes aloud for the student.

- Tape record tests/quizzes for the student.

- Make a bright construction paper border for the student to place around reading material in order to maintain his/her attention to the task.

- Make a reading window from construction paper which the student places over sentences or paragraphs in order to maintain attention.

- Provide manipulative objects for the student to use in solving math problems.

- Rearrange problems on a page (e.g., if crowded, create more space between the problems).

- Use graph paper for math problems, handwriting, etc.

- Rewrite directions at a more appropriate reading level.

- Tape record directions.

- Have peers deliver directions or explanations.

- Allow more time to take tests or quizzes.

Reinforcer Survey

Name: _____ Age: _____

Date: _____

1. The things I like to do after school are _____
   _____

2. If I had ten dollars I would _____
   _____

3. My favorite TV programs are _____
   _____

4. My favorite game at school is _____
   _____

5. My best friends are _____
   _____

6. My favorite time of day is _____
   _____

7. My favorite toys are _____
   _____

8. My favorite record is _____
   _____

9. My favorite subject at school is _____
   _____

10. I like to read books about _____
    _____

11. The places I like to go in town are _____
    _____

12. My favorite foods are _____
    _____

13. My favorite inside activities are _____
    _____

14. My favorite outside activities are _____
    _____

15. My hobbies are _____
    _____

16. My favorite animals are _____
    _____

17. The three things I like to do most are _____
    _____

The Reinforcer Survey may be given to one student or a group of students. If the students cannot read, the survey is read to them. If they cannot write their answers, the answers are given verbally.

Reinforcer Menu

REINFORCER MENU

Reinforcer	Points Needed
Working with Clay	30
Peer Tutoring	25
Using Colored Markers	30
Using Colored Chalk	30
Feeding Pets	20
Delivering Messages	15
Carrying Wastebasket	20
Operating Projector	30
Playing a Board Game	35
Leading the Class Line	25
Passing out Materials	20
Using a Typewriter	25

CLASS REINFORCER MENU

Reinforcer	Points Needed
See a Film	30
Class Visitor	25
Write and Mail Letters	30
Field Trip	30
Lunch Outdoors	20
Pop Popcorn	35
Take Class Pictures	30
Tape Songs	15
Put on a Play	25
Have Adults in for Lunch	30

The Reinforcer Menu is compiled from information gathered by having a student or students respond to the Reinforcer Survey.

Rules For School Environments

GENERAL SOCIAL RULES. . . .

- **BE QUIET**
- **REMAIN IN YOUR SEAT**
- **WORK ON ASSIGNED TASK**
- **RAISE YOUR HAND**

HALLWAY RULES. . . .

- **WALK IN THE HALL**
- **WALK IN A LINE**
- **WALK ON THE RIGHT**
- **WALK QUIETLY**

CAFETERIA RULES. . . .

- **BE QUIET IN THE CAFETERIA LINE**
- **WALK TO YOUR TABLE**
- **TALK QUIETLY**
- **REMAIN SEATED**

OUTDOOR RULES. . . .

- **TAKE PART IN SOME ACTIVITY**
- **TAKE TURNS**
- **BE FRIENDLY**
- **LINE UP WHEN IT IS TIME**

ACADEMIC RULES. . . .

- **FINISH ONE TASK**
- **MEET YOUR CRITERIA**
  TO EARN 5 POINTS

These rules, except for perhaps the outdoor rules, are applicable to all grade levels and have been used in public schools for general behavioral expectations.

Point Record

ACADEMIC POINTS

Monday

| 1 | 2 | 3 | 4 | 5 | 6 | 7 | 8 | 9 | 10 | 11 | 12 | 13 | 14 |

Tuesday

| 1 | 2 | 3 | 4 | 5 | 6 | 7 | 8 | 9 | 10 | 11 | 12 | 13 | 14 |

Wednesday

| 1 | 2 | 3 | 4 | 5 | 6 | 7 | 8 | 9 | 10 | 11 | 12 | 13 | 14 |

Thursday

| 1 | 2 | 3 | 4 | 5 | 6 | 7 | 8 | 9 | 10 | 11 | 12 | 13 | 14 |

Friday

| 1 | 2 | 3 | 4 | 5 | 6 | 7 | 8 | 9 | 10 | 11 | 12 | 13 | 14 |

SOCIAL POINTS

Monday

Tuesday

Wednesday

Thursday

Friday

The Point Record form provides for Academic Points, top section, for each task completed with criteria met; and Social Points, bottom section, for demonstrating appropriate behavior in and around the classroom. The Point Record is kept with the student at all times, wherever he/she may be, in order that points may be given for following any school rules.

Point Card

TIME	DAYS OF WEEK				
	M	T	W	T	F
8:00 - 8:50					
9:00 - 9:50					
10:00 - 10:50					
11:00 : 11:30					
11:30 - 12:20					
12:30 - 1:20					
1:30 - 2:20					
1:30 - 2:20					
2:30 - 3:20					

Name: _____

This is a Point Card for secondary level students and may be used in special education classes or in regular classes. Teachers assign points, give checks, or sign initials for appropriate behavior demonstrated by the student while in the classroom. These points are relative to rules of the classroom, expected behavior, a contract developed with the student, etc. The card is a 3 x 5 inch index card which is easily kept in a shirt pocket and is small enough to reduce embarrassment for some students who would prefer to keep their behavioral support program more confidential.

CONTRACT

I, _Eric Johnson_ ,

HEREBY DECLARE THAT I WILL _finish my math_ _assignments on time._

THIS JOB WILL BE CONSIDERED SUCCESSFUL _when I_ _finish 3 assignments in a row on time._

NAME _____

FOR THE SUCCESSFUL COMPLETION OF THE ABOVE JOB
YOU MAY _use the computer for 15 minutes._

DATE SIGNED _12/10_

DATE COMPLETED _____

_____ _Ms. Cummins_ _____
(SIGNED)

The Contract is one of the most individualized and personalized approaches of intervening to improve behavior. This component contributes to the personal aspect of the individual reinforcement system due to the private manner in which teacher, student, and parents may work together for behavior improvement. The Contract should specify:

1. Who is working toward the goals
2. What is expected (i.e., social behaviors or academic productivity and quality)
3. The amount of appropriate behavior that is expected
4. The kind of reinforcement that is being earned
5. The amount of the reinforcement
6. When the reinforcement will be made available

CONTRACT

I, _____ ,

HEREBY DECLARE THAT I WILL _____

_____

_____

THIS JOB WILL BE CONSIDERED SUCCESSFUL _____

_____

NAME _____

FOR THE SUCCESSFUL COMPLETION OF THE ABOVE JOB

YOU MAY _____

_____

DATE SIGNED _____

DATE COMPLETED _____

_____
(SIGNED)

GROUP CONTRACT

WE, _____ ,

HEREBY DECLARE THAT WE WILL _____

_____

_____

THIS JOB WILL BE CONSIDERED SUCCESSFUL _____

_____

NAMES _____

FOR THE SUCCESSFUL COMPLETION OF THE ABOVE JOB

WE MAY _____

_____

DATE SIGNED _____

DATE COMPLETED _____

_____

_____
(SIGNED)

Schedule of Daily Events

SCHEDULE OF DAILY EVENTS

NAME: _____

	#1	#2	#3	#4	#5	#6	#7	#8	#9	#10
Monday										
Tuesday										
Wednesday										
Thursday										
Friday										

SCHEDULE OF DAILY EVENTS

NAME: _____

	#1	#2	#3	#4	#5	#6	#7	#8	#9	#10
Tuesday										

Each individual student's Schedule of Daily Events is developed for him/her and attached to his/her desk for a week at a time or for one day at a time. This schedule identifies each activity/task the student is assigned for the day, and the schedule is filled in by the teacher one day at a time. Students tend to know what they are to do next when the schedule is provided, and teachers can expect fewer interruptions for directions when students refer to their schedules.

Schedule of Daily Events Sample

SCHEDULE OF DAILY EVENTS

NAME: _____

	#1	#2	#3	#4	#5	#6	#7	#8	#9	#10
Monday	Reading	Art (Clay)	Math	Art (Paint)	Science	Creative Writing	Social Studies	Listening	Music	P.E.
Tuesday										
Wednesday										
Thursday										
Friday										

Parent Communication Form

Teacher: _____ Date: _____

Parent(s): _____ Student: _____

Grade or Level: _____ Type of Class: _____

Other School Personnel: _____

———————··•··———————

TYPE OF COMMUNICATION: Letter _____ Note _____ Telephone _____

Parent Visit to School _____ Teacher Visit to Home _____

Out-of-School Location _____ Other _____

———————··•··———————

Initiation of Communication: School Scheduled Meeting_____

Teacher Initiation _____ Parent Initiation _____ Other _____

———————··•··———————

Nature of Communication: Information Sharing_____

Progress Update _____ Problem Identification _____ Other_____

———————··•··———————

Communication Summary (Copies of Written Communications Should Be Attached):_____

_____

_____

_____

_____

———————··•··———————

Expectations for Further Communication:_____

_____

_____

———————··•··———————

Signatures of Participants (If Communication Made in Person):_____

_____

_____

_____

The Parent Communication Form is a record of communication made with parents in person, by telephone, or by notes or letters.

Student Conference Report

Student's Name: _____

School Personnel Involved and Titles: _____

_____

Date: _____ Grade Level of Student: _____

————·····———

Initiation of Conference: Regularly Scheduled Conference _____

Teacher Initiation _____ Other Personnel Initiation _____

Student Initiation _____ Parent Initiation _____

————·····———

Nature of Communication: Information Sharing _____

Progress Update _____ Problem Identification _____

Other _____

————·····———

Conference Summary (Copies of Written Communications Should Be Attached): _____

_____

_____

_____

_____

_____

_____

_____

————·····———

Expectations Based on Conference: _____

_____

_____

————·····———

Signatures of Conference Participants: _____

_____

_____

_____

————·····———

The Student Conference Report is used for recording conferences held with the student to identify problems, concerns, progress, etc.

A List of Reinforcers Identified by Elementary-Aged Students

1. Listen to the radio
2. Free time
3. Watch favorite program on TV
4. Talk to best friend
5. Listen to favorite tapes
6. Read a book
7. Candy, especially chocolate
8. Play sports - baseball, kickball, soccer, hockey
9. Ride a bike
10. Do something fun with best friend
11. Go to the zoo
12. Build a model plane or car
13. Go to the arcade and play video games
14. Camping trip
15. Play with pets
16. Go to a fast-food restaurant
17. Pop popcorn
18. Go to a movie
19. Play in the gym
20. Play outside
21. Help clean up classroom
22. Play with puppets
23. Play with dolls and a doll house
24. Ice cream
25. Cookies
26. Go shopping at a grocery store
27. Tacos
28. Hamburgers and french fries
29. Pizza
30. Money
31. Making buttons
32. Parties
33. Teacher's helper
34. Field trips
35. Eat lunch outside on a nice day
36. Recess
37. Student-of-the-month
38. Honor roll
39. Buy sodas
40. Work on puzzles
41. Write on the chalkboard
42. Gumball machine
43. Race cars
44. Use colored markers
45. Roller skating
46. Puppet show
47. Water slide
48. Stickers
49. Pencils
50. Use the computer
51. Fly model airplanes
52. Visit the principal

A List of Reinforcers Identified by Secondary-Aged Students

1. Free time

   - Doing nothing

   - Reading magazines (from home or library)

   - Reading newspapers

   - Writing a letter (to a rock star, favorite author, politician, probation officer, friend)

   - Peer tutoring (your class or another one)

   - Listen to records (from class, library, home)

   - Visit library

   - Work on a hobby

   - See a film

   - Draw - Paint - Create

2. Acting as teacher assistant (any length of time)

3. Acting as principal assistant (any length of time)

4. Have class outside

5. Field trip

6. Go to a movie

7. Have a soda

8. Have an afternoon for a sport activity (some students play and some watch)

9. Play a game (Bingo, cards, board games)

10. Use a camera (take pictures and have them developed)

11. Play Trivia games

12. Time off from school

13. Coach's assistant (any length of time)

14. Picnic lunch

15. Run errands

16. Extra time in high interest areas (shop, art, P.E.)

17. Do clerical work in building (use copy machine, run office errands)

18. Library assistant (any length of time)

19. Custodian's assistant (any length of time)

20. Watch TV

21. Earn a model

22. Typing

23. Attend a sports event

24. Food or treat coupons

25. Iron-on decals

Mapping Form

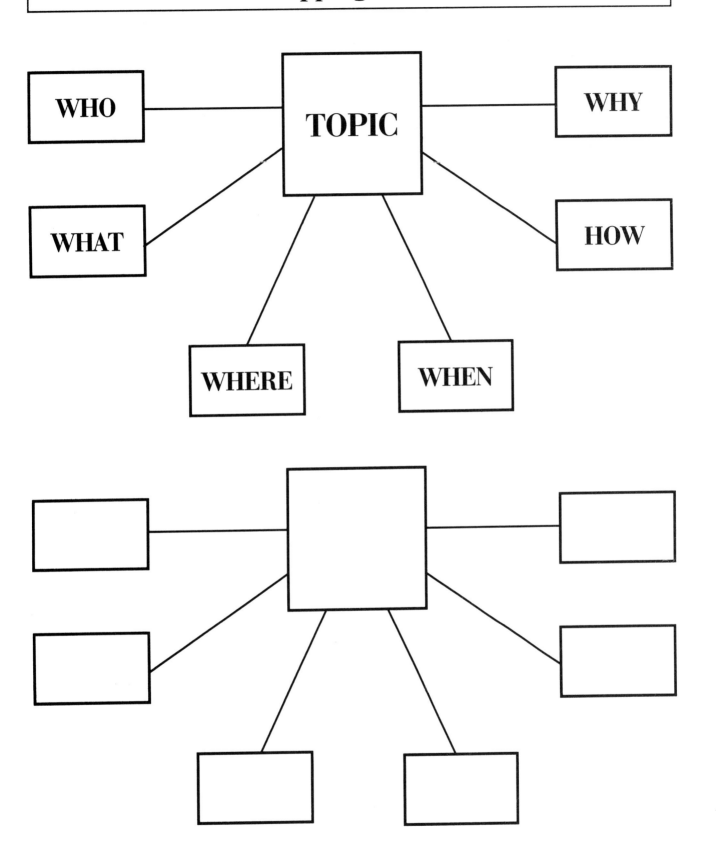

Note Taking

1. For note taking from lecture or written material, follow:

    •   Outline Form
      (e.g., Who, What, Where, When, How, Why)

    • Mapping Form
      (e.g., Who, What, Where, When, How, Why)

    • Double-Column Form
      (e.g., Who, What, Where, When, How, Why)

2. For note taking from directions, follow:

    • Assignment Form
      (e.g., What, How, Materials, When)

    • Assignment Sheet

    • 2-Week Project Outline

❖ (See Appendix for the above forms.)

Outline Form

SUBJECT: _____

Topic: _____

General   **Specific**

Who:

What:

Where:

When:

How:

Why:

Vocabulary:

Double-Column Form

Who	
What	
Where	
When	
How	
Why	

Double-Column Form Sample

SECTION 2: The Santa Fe Trail

Who used this trail?	- settlers
What was the Santa Fe Trail?	-the Santa Fe Trail was a trade route
Where did the trail go?	-the trail went from Independence, Missouri, to Santa Fe, New Mexico
When did the trail begin?	-in the 1820's
How did settlers travel?	-traveled in prairie schooners (covered wagons)
Why was it used?	-settlers used the trail to move west and for trading purposes

Assignment Form

Subject: _____

	General	Specific
What:		
How:		
Materials:		
When:		

Subject: _____

	General	Specific
What:		
How:		
Materials:		
When:		

Assignment Sheet

ASSIGNMENT SHEET

DATE _____

SUBJECT	ASSIGNMENT	DUE DATE	TEACHER SIGNATURE
Math			
Reading			
Science			
Social Studies			
Spelling			
Other			

_____ Comments:

PARENT SIGNATURE

ASSIGNMENT SHEET

DATE _____

SUBJECT	ASSIGNMENT	DUE DATE	TEACHER SIGNATURE
Math			
History			
Science			
English			
Fine Arts/ Practical Arts			
Other			

_____ Comments:

PARENT SIGNATURE

2-Week Project Outline

DAY 1   **Determine exactly what the assignment is**
- **Identify due date**

DAY 2-4   **Project Preparation**
- **READ ASSIGNED MATERIALS**
- **RESEARCH RELATED MATERIALS**
- **GATHER NECESSARY MATERIALS**

DAY 5   **Summarize reading material by answering:**
- **Who, What, Where, When, How, Why**

DAY 6   **Preliminary project construction**
- **Make sketches, determine scale, make revisions**

DAY 7-11   **Project construction**
- **Lay out all materials**
- **Prepare materials to scale**
- **Draw/color**
- **Cut**
- **Glue**
- **Paint**

DAY 12   **Touch up work**
- **Label, check that all items are secure, etc.**

DAY 13   **Write paragraph from summary (Day 5)**

DAY 14   **Turn in!**